Exploring Human Resource Innovations in E-Economy

Agnieszka Wojcik-Czerniawska
https://orcid.org/0000-0002-9612-1952
SGH Warsaw School of Economics, Poland

IGI Global
Scientific Publishing
Publishing Tomorrow's Research Today

Vice President of Editorial Melissa Wagner
Director of Acquisitions Mikaela Felty
Director of Book Development Jocelynn Hessler
Production Manager Mike Brehm
Cover Design Jose Rosado

Published in the United States of America by
IGI Global Scientific Publishing
701 East Chocolate Avenue
Hershey, PA, 17033, USA
Tel: 717-533-8845 | Fax: 717-533-7115
Website: https://www.igi-global.com E-mail: cust@igi-global.com

Library of Congress Cataloging-in-Publication Data

(CIP Data Pending)
ISBN13: 9798337343075
Isbn13Softcover: 9798337343082
EISBN13: 9798337343099
British Cataloguing in Publication Data
A Cataloguing in Publication record for this book is available from the British Library.

This book is dedicated with love, gratitude, and hope to my family, whose presence gives meaning to every accomplishment and whose strength sustains me in every challenge.

To my mother Renata, whose boundless compassion, courage, and wisdom have been the foundation of all that I am. Her constant encouragement, quiet faith, and unwavering belief in the value of education have guided me through the most demanding moments of my professional and personal life. Her love has been both anchor and compass — a reminder that perseverance, integrity, and kindness remain the truest measures of success.

To my two beloved sons, Victor and Alexander, whose curiosity, laughter, and unconditional love give purpose to my work and joy to every day. Their young yet profound belief in me continues to remind me that dreams are worth pursuing, and that even the most difficult paths can lead to light when walked with courage and imagination. They have grown alongside this book, and it is as much theirs as it is mine — a symbol of shared resilience, patience, and endless discovery.

This book is also dedicated to all young researchers who are just beginning their academic journeys — may they always believe that their voices, ideas, and visions matter, and that perseverance can turn uncertainty into achievement.

To every woman scholar and professional striving to balance intellect with empathy, ambition with responsibility, and innovation with humanity — your work continues to redefine the possibilities of leadership and knowledge creation.

To every single mother who continues to build a life of dignity, and to every widow who finds the strength to begin again — this dedication honors your resilience. Your ability to rebuild, to love, to lead, and to contribute to the world despite loss and adversity stands as a quiet but powerful form of innovation in itself.

Finally, this book is a tribute to all who believe that progress in technology, society, and knowledge must always be guided by compassion and purpose. May it serve as a reminder that even in an era defined by algorithms and data, it is the human spirit — strong, creative, and caring — that remains the most transformative force of all.

Editorial Advisory Board

Table of Contents

Detailed Table of Contents

The rapid growth of the e-economy, driven by digital technologies and decentralized systems, is reshaping how organizations approach Human Resource Management (HRM). Traditional, location-based HR models no longer work in a remote work world, platform labor, and algorithmic management. This book explains how HR innovations such as AI, blockchain credentialing, and virtual organizational structures are redefining employees' work, talent, and performance. The world is moving beyond merely making things easier with technology; it critically examines the ethical and human-centered challenges these changes pose. The study combines insights from multiple disciplines to offer an in-depth understanding of how digital tools connect with human resource functions. This chapter presents case studies, success stories, and challenges of digital-enabled HR functions in an e-economy. Aimed at scholars, policymakers, and practitioners, the book promotes deeper reflection on fairness, inclusion, and resilience in the digital workplace.

This study explores open innovation practices among micro and small enterprises (MSEs) in Srikakulam through predictive analysis using machine learning and regression techniques. Key innovation drivers were identified using feature selection methods such as Information Gain, ANOVA, and Chi-square. Components like customer co-creation, digital platforms, and venture capital access emerged as significant predictors of innovation success. Regression analysis further validated their influence on business growth. The findings offer actionable insights for stakeholders to enhance innovation strategies, foster collaboration, and optimize resource allocation. This data-driven approach strengthens the understanding of innovation dynamics in the MSE sector.

Section 2
Technology, Ethics, and Organizational Innovation

This study investigates the awareness and acceptance of blockchain-based credentialing in hiring processes, focusing on how organizational readiness, perceived trust, and blockchain knowledge impact its adoption. With the growing challenges of credential fraud and inefficiency in traditional hiring systems, blockchain technology offers an innovative solution by providing secure, transparent, and immutable records of candidates' qualifications. The study employs a quantitative research design, surveying 286 HR professionals and hiring managers across various industries to understand their perceptions of blockchain's applicability in credential verification. Statistical tools, including descriptive statistics, Pearson's correlation, and multiple regression analysis, were utilized to examine the relationships between the variables and assess the factors influencing the acceptance of blockchain in recruitment. The results reveal that perceived trust and organizational readiness are the strongest predictors of blockchain adoption.

The chapter begins by clarifying the concept of green skills, understood as the knowledge, abilities, values, and attitudes necessary to support environmental sustainability in both specific occupations and across the labor market. These include both technical skills—such as waste reduction strategies, renewable energy technologies, and sustainable production methods—and transversal soft skills, including systems thinking, environmental awareness, and innovation. The global

Strategic and Sustainable Futures in HRM

This Chapter explores the role of strategic human resource innovations in shaping sustainable organizational futures. It emphasizes the integration of scenario planning, resilience-building strategies, and ethical innovation within HR practices to navigate uncertainty and drive long-term value. By aligning HR strategies with sustainability goals, organizations can enhance adaptability, employee well-being, and ethical governance. The study highlights how forward-thinking HR approaches can foster resilient, agile, and ethically grounded workplaces capable of thriving in complex, evolving environments.

This chapter explores the strategic role of human resource innovations in shaping sustainable organizational futures within the evolving e-economy. Focusing on scenario planning, resilience strategies, and ethical innovation, the chapter examines how forward-looking HR practices can enhance organizational adaptability, long-term competitiveness, and stakeholder trust. Drawing from theories of dynamic capabilities, foresight, and ethical decision-making, the chapter provides a conceptual framework supported by case examples from digitally transformative organizations. It analyzes the integration of future-oriented planning into HR systems, the development of resilient and agile workforces, and the implementation of ethically grounded innovation in HR processes. By synthesizing academic research and practitioner insights, this chapter contributes to the discourse on sustainable and strategic human capital management in technology-driven environments.

In the last decade, the role of human resource management (HRM) in organizational effectiveness has significantly evolved and reached a new level, becoming a key driver of development and sustainability in all its dimensions. This chapter presents key ideas and scenarios that illustrate innovative approaches and models defining the new role of HRM. The focus is placed on innovative practices aimed at sustainable human resource development, including well-being policies and well-being indicators as components of a strategic organizational approach. An additional emphasis is placed on the concept of sustainable HRM through the presentation of relevant practical examples.

This chapter examines the transformative potential of the gig economy, supported by digital payment systems, as a pathway out of poverty for marginalized and low-income populations. It explores how flexible, short-term work opportunities, combined with secure and traceable digital payments, can enhance income generation, financial inclusion, and skill development. The chapter critically analyzes structural, technological, and social challenges, including income instability, platform dependency, and digital literacy gaps, and emphasizes the complementary roles of governments, platforms, and NGOs in fostering inclusive and sustainable gig work ecosystems. Emerging trends, research gaps, and policy implications are also discussed to guide future strategies for equitable economic empowerment.

Preface

The twenty-first century has witnessed a profound reconfiguration of economic, organizational, and social systems under the influence of digital technologies, artificial intelligence, and the proliferation of online platforms. Human resource management (HRM), traditionally perceived as an administrative and support function, has evolved into a strategic driver of innovation, resilience, and competitive advantage in the emerging e-economy. This book, *Exploring Human Resource Innovations in E-Economy*, addresses this transformation by examining how digitalization reshapes the conceptual, ethical, and operational dimensions of managing human capital in a technology-driven world.

The e-economy, characterized by interconnected networks, datafication, and algorithmic decision-making, fundamentally alters how organizations attract, develop, and retain talent. It is no longer sufficient to manage employees through conventional HR structures; instead, the integration of artificial intelligence (AI), machine learning (ML), blockchain, cloud computing, and data analytics has created new paradigms of efficiency, transparency, and agility. These technologies have redefined the nature of work and have challenged long-standing assumptions about leadership, motivation, and employee engagement.

This volume brings together diverse theoretical and empirical contributions that explore human resource innovations as both technological and human phenomena. The subject matter expands beyond digital tools themselves, delving into the socio-behavioral, ethical, and cultural contexts in which they are deployed. The chapters illustrate how algorithmic HRM, digital learning ecosystems, and blockchain-based credentialing contribute to operational efficiency while raising questions of privacy, accountability, and fairness.

Equally, the book highlights human-centered innovation — initiatives that prioritize well-being, inclusion, sustainability, and social equity. Concepts such as digital well-being, green HRM, menstrual leave policies, and ethical leadership reflect the growing recognition that technology must serve human flourishing rather than replace it. Through a multidisciplinary lens, contributors investigate HRM not merely as an adaptive response to digitalization but as an active agent in shaping equitable and sustainable futures.

The scope of the book is both global and integrative. Case studies from healthcare systems, digital enterprises, micro and small businesses, and platform economies reveal the diversity of experiences and challenges across regions. The chapters collectively underscore the interdependence between human and technological capital in fostering organizational innovation, resilience, and ethical governance in the e-economy.

The world today is at a critical juncture where technological acceleration converges with profound social, environmental, and economic disruptions. The e-economy — encompassing digital platforms, cloud infrastructures, and AI-enabled ecosystems — is redefining value creation and labor relations on a global scale. The COVID-19 pandemic further catalyzed this transformation, demonstrating both the potential and vulnerability of digital work models. Remote work, hybrid collaboration, and the virtualization of HR functions have become permanent fixtures of organizational life.

In this context, human resource innovation assumes strategic significance. The post-pandemic economy is not solely about recovery but about reimagining work systems that are sustainable, inclusive, and resilient. Issues of digital well-being, algorithmic fairness, data ethics, and lifelong learning now intersect with traditional HR domains such as recruitment, leadership development, and performance management. The workforce of the e-economy must navigate complex interactions between human cognition and artificial intelligence, between autonomy and algorithmic control, and between flexibility and precariousness.

Globally, organizations face mounting pressure to align their digital strategies with broader ethical and sustainability imperatives. The rise of the gig economy and platform labor has blurred boundaries between employment and entrepreneurship, demanding new policy frameworks and HR innovations that protect workers while encouraging agility. Simultaneously, environmental concerns and the circular economy movement compel organizations to integrate green skills and sustainable HRM practices into their strategic planning.

From an academic perspective, this topic aligns with contemporary research in digital transformation, organizational behavior, and sustainable management. The book situates itself within interdisciplinary discourses that bridge management science, information systems, behavioral economics, and ethics. It contributes to ongoing debates on human-AI collaboration, algorithmic accountability, and the socio-technical dynamics of digital organizations.

At the macro level, the subject is directly relevant to policy agendas of the European Union, the United Nations Sustainable Development Goals (SDGs), and the International Labour Organization (ILO) frameworks on decent digital work. The evolution of e-HRM systems is not only a matter of operational optimization but also a question of social justice, diversity, and human dignity in the digital era. The chapters in this volume reflect these global concerns, offering region-specific insights — from African healthcare systems and Asian SMEs to European digital enterprises — that illustrate both convergence and divergence in how societies adapt to technological disruption.

By addressing such critical intersections, *Exploring Human Resource Innovations in E-Economy* fills an essential gap in contemporary scholarship. It provides a theoretically grounded and empirically informed examination of how human resource innovation mediates the relationship between technology, work, and humanity in a globalized, digitalized environment.

This volume is designed for a broad yet clearly defined audience of scholars, practitioners, and policymakers engaged with the future of human resource management, digital transformation, and organizational innovation.

1. Academics and Researchers:

The book will serve as a valuable resource for academics in fields such as management, human resource development, organizational behavior, information systems, and digital economy studies. It offers theoretical frameworks and empirical evidence relevant to courses and research in HR analytics, digital leadership, sustainability management, and AI ethics. Graduate and doctoral students will benefit from the book's synthesis of conceptual and methodological approaches spanning both qualitative and quantitative paradigms.

2. Business Leaders and HR Professionals:

Executives, HR directors, and practitioners can draw actionable insights into the design and implementation of innovative HR strategies. The chapters provide practical perspectives on digital transformation, workforce analytics, ethical AI adoption, and organizational resilience. Real-world cases, including studies of healthcare systems, SMEs, and platform economies, illustrate transferable lessons for diverse organizational contexts.

3. Policymakers and Consultants:

The book also targets decision-makers involved in labor policy, digital governance, and sustainable economic development. Its discussions of algorithmic fairness, gender inclusivity, and green skills directly inform public policy debates concerning future labor markets. Consultants and think-tanks focused on organizational transformation and ethical innovation will find frameworks adaptable to corporate and institutional reform.

4. Interdisciplinary Scholars and Students:

Given its broad scope, the book appeals to readers in sociology, psychology, economics, and education who study human behavior in digital environments. It promotes interdisciplinary dialogue by linking technological progress with humanistic inquiry.

Ultimately, the target audience extends across academia, industry, and governance — communities collectively responsible for designing the future of human work in an increasingly digitalized world. By providing a coherent and evidence-based understanding of HR innovation, the volume equips these stakeholders with intellectual and practical tools to navigate the ethical, strategic, and social dimensions of the e-economy.

The chapters of the book one by one describe:

CHAPTER 1: ALGORITHMIC HRM: OPPORTUNITIES AND ETHICAL CHALLENGES IN AI-DRIVEN TALENT ACQUISITION

Focusing on algorithmic recruitment systems, this chapter investigates the dual nature of AI in HR: efficiency versus ethical complexity. It evaluates algorithmic bias, data transparency, and accountability frameworks, providing theoretical underpinnings for responsible AI adoption in HR decision-making.

CHAPTER 2: ARTIFICIAL INTELLIGENCE-ENABLED HUMAN RESOURCE FUNCTIONAL INNOVATIONS IN THE E-ECONOMY

Building on digital transformation literature, the chapter maps AI's role across HR functions—from performance appraisal to predictive retention modeling. It conceptualizes AI-enabled HR as a strategic innovation ecosystem rather than a purely technological substitution, highlighting the interplay of human intuition and machine intelligence.

CHAPTER 3: ASSESSMENT OF OPEN INNOVATION PRACTICES AMONG MICRO AND SMALL ENTERPRISES: AN ANALYSIS WITH MACHINE LEARNING AND REGRESSION

Here, quantitative analytics meet entrepreneurship. Using machine-learning models, the authors identify determinants of open-innovation success in SMEs, showing how HR strategies around collaboration and knowledge-sharing drive competitiveness in resource-constrained contexts.

CHAPTER 4: AWARENESS AND ACCEPTANCE OF BLOCKCHAIN-BASED CREDENTIALING IN HIRING PROCESSES

This chapter examines emerging blockchain credentialing systems that authenticate qualifications and work histories. It contributes to HR technology discourse by analyzing user acceptance models and the trust mechanisms underpinning decentralized verification.

CHAPTER 5: BUILDING GREEN SKILLS IN THE WORKFORCE AS HR'S ROLE IN THE CIRCULAR ECONOMY

Anchored in sustainability studies, this chapter argues that HR is a key enabler of circular-economy transition. It presents strategies for developing "green competencies," integrating environmental literacy into recruitment, training, and performance metrics.

CHAPTER 6: EMOTIONAL HACKING AND ARTIFICIAL INTELLIGENCE TOOLS: THE DIGITAL REVOLUTION OR EMOTIONAL DISASTER IN MENTAL HEALTH CARE

A provocative exploration of affective computing, this chapter interrogates the psychological implications of AI interfaces that "read" or manipulate emotion. It warns against emotional commodification and calls for ethical boundaries in digital mental-health tools.

CHAPTER 7: FROM CONSUMER TO EMPLOYEE: HOW CROSS-CULTURAL DIGITAL EXPECTATIONS SHAPE WORK EXPERIENCES IN ALGORITHMIC ORGANIZATIONS

This chapter offers a cross-cultural perspective, arguing that digital consumer experiences shape employees' workplace expectations. It extends service-dominant logic to HRM, positioning digital experience as a determinant of engagement and retention.

CHAPTER 8: GREEN HRM: BUILDING A SUSTAINABLE WORKFORCE FOR A GREENER FUTURE

This contribution reinforces the sustainability theme, exploring HR practices that integrate environmental performance indicators. It positions HR as the institutional architect of green culture within organizations.

CHAPTER 9: HUMAN IMPACTS AND ORGANIZATIONAL CHANGE: DIGITAL WELL-BEING, REMOTE WORK, AND PSYCHOSOCIAL SUSTAINABILITY

Drawing from occupational psychology, this chapter analyzes the psychosocial impacts of digitalization—stress, burnout, and boundary dissolution—and proposes organizational interventions that promote digital well-being and sustainable work patterns.

CHAPTER 10: REIMAGINING LEADERSHIP AND ORGANIZATIONAL CULTURE IN DIGITALLY NATIVE FIRMS: DISTRIBUTED LEADERSHIP, DIGITAL TRUST, AND RESILIENCE BUILDING

An extension of Chapter 19, it develops the concept of distributed leadership and digital trust, showing how decentralized authority structures enhance organizational resilience in fast-moving digital environments.

CHAPTER 11: ROLE OF AI AND MACHINE LEARNING IN THE FUTURE OF TALENT MANAGEMENT

A forward-looking analysis, this chapter explores predictive analytics, AI-driven succession planning, and personalization of employee experience. It situates machine learning as both enabler and ethical frontier of future talent management.

CHAPTER 12: SCAFFOLDING ETHICS AND ACCOUNTABILITY STRUCTURES TO SUPPORT CONSTRUCTION INDUSTRY TRANSFORMATION

Extending HR innovation beyond digital firms, this chapter applies ethical and accountability frameworks to the construction sector. It demonstrates the universality of HR ethics in guiding technology-enabled industry transformation.

CHAPTER 13: STRATEGIC HR INNOVATIONS FOR SUSTAINABLE FUTURES: INTEGRATING SCENARIO PLANNING, RESILIENCE, AND ETHICAL INNOVATION

This integrative chapter presents foresight methodologies for HR strategy, combining scenario planning with ethical innovation frameworks to prepare organizations for volatile, uncertain environments.

CHAPTER 14: STRATEGIC HUMAN RESOURCE INNOVATIONS FOR SUSTAINABLE ORGANIZATIONAL FUTURES: SCENARIO PLANNING, RESILIENCE STRATEGIES, AND ETHICAL INNOVATION

Expanding upon Chapter 24, this work synthesizes global case evidence into a comprehensive model linking resilience, sustainability, and ethical foresight as pillars of HR transformation.

CHAPTER 15: STRATEGIC HUMAN RESOURCE INNOVATIONS FOR SUSTAINABLE ORGANIZATIONAL FUTURES (EXTENDED ANALYSIS)

This analytical continuation deepens the comparative dimension, examining sectoral variations in sustainability-oriented HR strategies and identifying policy implications for diverse economic systems.

CHAPTER 16: STRATEGIC HUMAN RESOURCE TRANSFORMATION IN THE E-ECONOMY AND NAVIGATING THE NEXUS OF TECHNOLOGY AND SOCIETY

Serving as a capstone to the strategic section, this chapter integrates technological and sociological perspectives, proposing a holistic model for balancing innovation, ethics, and social responsibility.

CHAPTER 17: SUSTAINABLE HUMAN RESOURCE MANAGEMENT AND DEVELOPMENT THROUGH INNOVATIVE APPROACHES AND PRACTICES

This contribution synthesizes the sustainability discourse of the volume, showcasing best practices for embedding ESG (environmental, social, and governance) criteria in HR functions to ensure long-term organizational legitimacy.

CHAPTER 18: THE GIG ECONOMY AND DIGITAL PAYMENTS: A PATHWAY OUT OF POVERTY

Concluding the collection, this chapter links technological inclusion with social empowerment. It argues that digital payment infrastructures and gig-work models can, when ethically governed, become instruments of poverty alleviation and financial autonomy.

Taken together, these chapters construct a multidimensional narrative of human resource innovation that spans technological, ethical, behavioral, and sustainability perspectives. Each contribution builds upon the preceding themes—beginning with socio-behavioral foundations, moving through technological and leadership innovations, and culminating in strategic and sustainability frameworks. Collectively, they illuminate the evolving role of HRM as a transformative discipline at the heart of the e-economy, ensuring that digital progress advances human welfare and organizational integrity.

The significance of *Exploring Human Resource Innovations in E-Economy* lies in its comprehensive and integrative approach to understanding the human dimension of digital transformation. While much of the existing literature on digitalization focuses on technology adoption, this book foregrounds the human experience, emphasizing that sustainable innovation must harmonize technological advancement with social responsibility and ethical governance.

The volume contributes to academic discourse in several interrelated ways:

1. Theoretical Advancement:

By synthesizing perspectives from HRM, digital economy, and behavioral sciences, the book advances theory on the co-evolution of technology and human capital. It conceptualizes HR innovation as a dynamic system encompassing algorithmic processes, leadership models, and socio-cultural adaptations. The chapters introduce and refine constructs such as digital well-being, emotional hacking, and green HR competencies, thereby enriching the lexicon of contemporary HR research.

2. Methodological Diversity:

The collection employs a range of methodological approaches — from machine learning-based analyses and regression modeling to qualitative case studies and socio-behavioral surveys. This methodological pluralism enhances the robustness of findings and exemplifies how mixed-method research can address the complexity of digital HR phenomena.

3. Ethical and Social Relevance:

A recurring theme across the chapters is the ethical responsibility of organizations to maintain fairness, transparency, and inclusivity in algorithmic decision-making. By interrogating issues such as menstrual leave, gender equity, and decentralized credentialing, the book situates HR innovation within the broader discourse of social justice and corporate accountability. It challenges readers to consider how digital transformation can promote—not undermine—human dignity and equality.

4. Practical and Strategic Implications:

The book provides actionable frameworks for integrating innovation into HR strategy. Concepts such as strategic foresight, resilience planning, and servant leadership are contextualized within digital transformation agendas. Practitioners can leverage these models to design adaptive HR systems capable of responding to volatility, uncertainty, and rapid technological change.

5. Global and Cross-Cultural Insight:

Through case studies spanning Africa, Asia, and Europe, the volume demonstrates the global applicability and cultural variability of HR innovation. It acknowledges that while digital tools are universally accessible, their implementation and impact are mediated by local institutional, cultural, and socio-economic contexts. This comparative lens enriches both academic understanding and managerial practice.

6. Contribution to Sustainable Futures:

By aligning human resource innovation with the principles of the circular economy, environmental stewardship, and social sustainability, the book extends HR discourse into the domain of responsible management. It emphasizes that innovation must be evaluated not only in terms of productivity gains but also in its contribution to human development and ecological balance.

In its entirety, *Exploring Human Resource Innovations in E-Economy* positions HR as both a catalyst and a conscience of the digital revolution. It underscores that the success of the e-economy depends not solely on technological capability but on the capacity of organizations to cultivate ethical, inclusive, and resilient human systems. The book thereby bridges the gap between technological determinism and humanistic management, offering a roadmap for organizations seeking to thrive responsibly in the Fourth Industrial Revolution.

For scholars, the volume provides fertile ground for further inquiry into algorithmic governance, digital ethics, and human-AI collaboration. For practitioners, it delivers a strategic blueprint for leading digital transformation with empathy and foresight. For policymakers, it highlights pathways toward inclusive, sustainable labor markets that honor the centrality of human dignity in the digital age.

By integrating empirical evidence, theoretical innovation, and ethical reflection, this book makes a substantive contribution to the evolving field of human resource management. It reaffirms that in an era defined by algorithms and automation, the most powerful innovation remains profoundly human.

Acknowledgment

The completion of *Exploring Human Resource Innovations in E-Economy* has been made possible through the collaboration, dedication, and encouragement of many individuals and institutions whose support I gratefully acknowledge.

I extend my sincere appreciation to all chapter authors whose scholarly contributions, creativity, and commitment to excellence have shaped the intellectual depth and diversity of this volume. Their work reflects the spirit of innovation, ethics, and collaboration that defines contemporary human resource research.

My deepest thanks go to the peer reviewers, editorial advisors, and academic colleagues who generously shared their time, expertise, and constructive feedback. Their insights strengthened the analytical rigor and coherence of this publication.

I am equally grateful to the team at IGI Global for their professionalism and guidance throughout every stage of the editorial process. Their dedication to advancing global scholarship and supporting editors has been invaluable.

I also wish to acknowledge the universities, research centers, and professional networks whose cooperation and exchange of ideas contributed to the development of this work. Their openness to interdisciplinary dialogue enriched the book's scope and impact.

Finally—and most personally—I wish to express my heartfelt gratitude to my parents, whose belief in the power of education and perseverance has guided me throughout my academic journey. I owe special thanks to my mother Renata, whose constant encouragement, patience, and unwavering faith have been my greatest source of strength and inspiration.

I also wish to thank my two wonderful sons, Victor (age 10) and Alexander (age 8), who believe in me as much as I believe in them. Their curiosity, joy, and boundless optimism continually remind me why it is worth striving to build a better, more thoughtful world through knowledge and learning.

Section 1
Foundations of Human Resource Transformation in the E-Economy

Chapter 1
Algorithmic HRM: Opportunities and Ethical Challenges in AI-Driven Talent Acquisition

Rismawati Rismawati
http://orcid.org/0000-0001-8046-6764
Universitas Muhammadiyah Palopo, Indonesia

Salju Salju
http://orcid.org/0000-0002-2908-9470
Universitas Muhammadiyah Palopo, Indonesia

ABSTRACT

This chapter examines the emergence of Algorithmic Human Resource Management (HRM) within the framework of AI-driven talent acquisition. It analyzes the incorporation of artificial intelligence, machine learning, and natural language processing into recruitment procedures, emphasizing the prospective advantages of enhanced efficiency, bias mitigation, and astute candidate alignment. The chapter critically examines the ethical dilemmas associated with algorithmic systems, such as discrimination, opacity, and data privacy concerns. The chapter underscores the necessity for responsible AI governance in Human Resource Management by referencing worldwide legislative frameworks like the GDPR and the EU AI Act. It also examines the transforming role of HR professionals as ethical custodians and delineates prospective research trajectories toward inclusive, human-centered algorithmic systems. This chapter integrates theoretical ideas with practical implications, fostering a more equal and transparent future for AI in human resources.

DOI: 10.4018/979-8-3373-4307-5.ch001

INTRODUCTION: FOUNDATIONS OF ALGORITHMIC HUMAN RESOURCE MANAGEMENT

1.1 Defining Algorithmic HRM in the Digital Era

The advent of the digital economy has significantly altered how corporations administer human capital. Leading this transition is Algorithmic Human Resource Management (Algorithmic HRM)—a novel methodology in which decision-making within HR activities is progressively automated and informed by data, enabled by advanced algorithms and artificial intelligence (AI). Algorithmic HRM denotes the methodical utilization of algorithms, machine learning models, and big data analytics to conduct fundamental HR functions including talent acquisition, performance assessment, promotion, remuneration, and workforce planning (Meijerink et al., 2021). This paradigm shift is transforming the conventional duties of HR professionals by delegating aspects of judgment-based decision-making to computer algorithms.

Algorithmic HRM functions within the overarching framework of digital transformation and the platform economy, necessitating firms to swiftly and accurately manage substantial amounts of organized and unstructured data. Utilizing AI and predictive analytics, algorithmic systems may discern trends in applicant behavior, evaluate role appropriateness, and anticipate employee outcomes. This capability is especially apparent in AI-enhanced talent acquisition, where algorithms assess resumes, rank prospects, analyze social media profiles, and even do preliminary interviews via natural language processing (NLP) interfaces (Tambe et al., 2019).

Defining algorithmic HRM necessitates differentiating between simple automation and sophisticated decision-making systems. In contrast to traditional HR software that merely automates administrative functions, algorithmic HRM involves independent decision-making and adaptability. It functions not merely as a tool but as a decision-making agent—capable of learning from data and impacting crucial conclusions that previously necessitated human discretion (Leicht-Deobald et al., 2019).

The implementation of algorithmic systems in Human Resource Management is influenced by technology capabilities and socio-organizational decisions. Algorithms lack neutrality; they include the values, assumptions, and priorities of their creators and data origins. Consequently, comprehending algorithmic HRM requires a socio-technical viewpoint that acknowledges its integration within institutional norms, power dynamics, and ethical implications. As firms increasingly implement algorithmic tools for efficiency, scalability, and objectivity, it is imperative to explicitly define and rigorously assess algorithmic human resource management. This description will establish the conceptual basis for the following parts, which will examine opportunities, ethical risks, and governance difficulties in greater depth.

1.2 The Role of Artificial Intelligence in Talent Acquisition

Artificial Intelligence (AI) is transforming human resource management (HRM), particularly in the domain of talent acquisition, which is one of its most significant applications. Talent acquisition, historically reliant on human intuition, interpersonal engagement, and laborious processes, has progressively been transformed by intelligent systems that automate, optimize, and personalize recruitment functions. The incorporation of AI in recruiting allows firms to source, screen, evaluate, and interact with candidates more effectively, utilizing extensive arrays of structured and unstructured data to facilitate predictive decision-making (Upadhyay & Khandelwal, 2018).

Artificial intelligence in talent acquisition functions through a collection of technologies, encompassing machine learning (ML), natural language processing (NLP), robotic process automation (RPA), and computer vision. These technologies collectively facilitate comprehensive recruitment processes, encompassing resume parsing, linguistic analysis of cover letters, asynchronous video interviews, and predictive assessments of candidate job suitability based on historical data (Black & van Esch, 2020). AI-powered application tracking systems (ATS) can evaluate candidates according to keyword relevancy, work history, and cultural fit, while chatbots offer immediate responses to candidate questions, enhancing engagement and company branding.

The genuine potential of AI in recruitment extends beyond automation to encompass its predictive and prescriptive functionalities. AI algorithms may discern patterns in the profiles of high-performing employees and suggest prospects with analogous characteristics, thus transforming recruitment from a reactive to a proactive role. Furthermore, sentiment analysis and facial expression recognition software are employed to evaluate soft skills and emotional intelligence; nonetheless, these methods provoke ethical dilemmas, as discussed in subsequent sections.

The integration of AI in talent acquisition necessitates not just a technology shift but also a strategic reevaluation of the HR function. AI solutions enhance human recruiters instead of supplanting them, providing data-driven insights while allowing for human discretion in final judgments. This hybrid methodology allows firms to reconcile efficiency with empathy, an essential element in maintaining candidate experience and organizational integrity (Chamorro-Premuzic et al., 2019).

In summary, AI is revolutionizing talent acquisition by making it more analytical, scalable, and personalized. As AI advances, HR professionals must address its technological capabilities, limitations, and ethical considerations, ensuring that recruitment processes are equitable, transparent, and consistent with business values.

1.3 Technological Convergence: Machine Learning, NLP, and Predictive Analytics in HR

The progression of algorithmic Human Resource Management (HRM) is closely linked to the integration of several modern technologies, particularly Machine Learning (ML), Natural Language Processing (NLP), and Predictive Analytics. These technologies, when incorporated into HR tasks, have revolutionized conventional human-centric processes into advanced, data-driven platforms that can learn, adapt, and enhance personnel management decisions.

Machine Learning (ML) underpins algorithmic Human Resource Management by facilitating the identification of patterns in extensive datasets and enabling decision-making with limited human involvement. In recruiting, machine learning algorithms can analyze resumes, rank individuals, and evaluate behavioral patterns based on past hiring data and performance indicators (Matsuo et al., 2022). In contrast to rule-based automation, machine learning evolves over time by assimilating fresh data, hence augmenting the accuracy and pertinence of recommendations in talent acquisition.

Figure 1. AI-Based vs. Conventional Candidate Matching Process

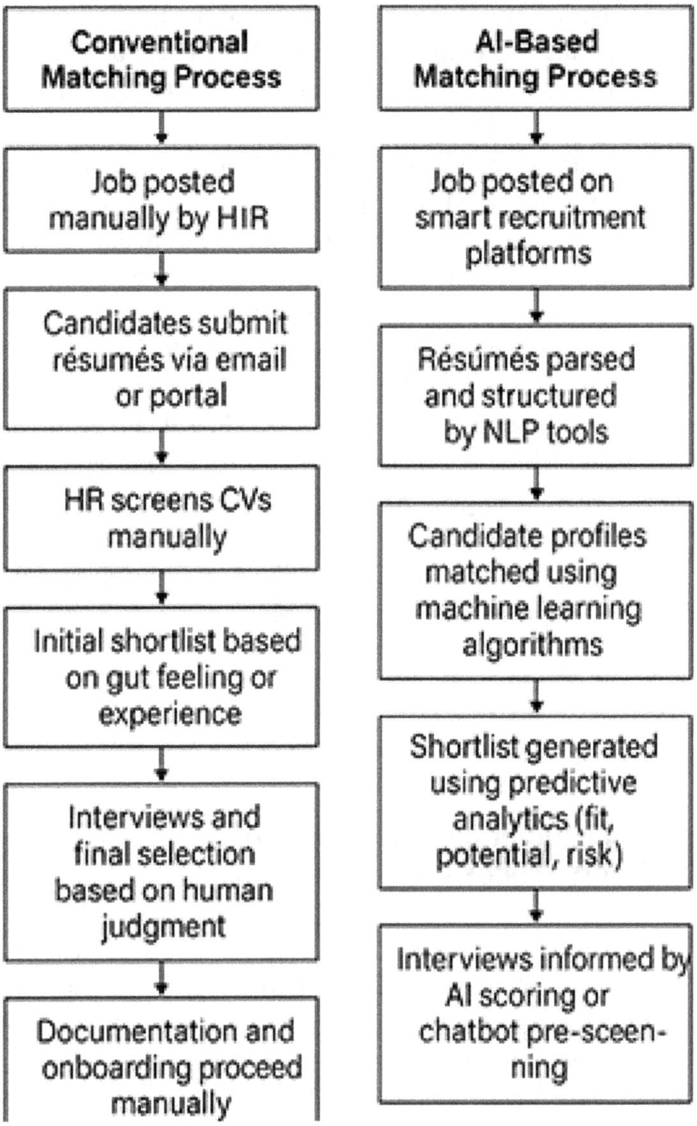

Source: Developed by the author based on Upadhyay & Khandelwal (2018), Black & van Esch (2020), and Tambe et al. (2019).

AI-driven matching can effectively process extensive candidate pools, providing consistent and evidence-based insights. However, it also prompts inquiries regarding transparency, accountability, and algorithmic equity, which are examined in Section 3. Natural Language Processing (NLP) enhances algorithmic skills by allowing systems to comprehend, analyze, and respond to human language effectively. NLP is especially advantageous for analyzing unstructured data, including resumes, cover letters, and social media accounts. It also facilitates chatbots and virtual assistants utilized in the first phases of recruiting, providing real-time, tailored interactions that improve candidate experience (Suen et al., 2019). NLP can be utilized to identify language indicators that may reveal a candidate's personality qualities, motivational levels, or cultural compatibility.

In conjunction with ML and NLP, Predictive Analytics enables HR managers to anticipate future outcomes based on present and previous data. Predictive models in recruiting are utilized to assess an applicant's probable work performance, turnover risk, and long-term compatibility with the firm. By delineating the traits of high-performing individuals, these models help guide more strategic recruiting decisions and reduce expensive recruitment mistakes (Minbaeva, 2018).

The integration of machine learning, natural language processing, and predictive analytics forms a potent trinity that supports the algorithmic evolution of human resource management. These tools not only optimize operational procedures but also improve strategic staff planning by providing profound insights into talent dynamics. This technological integration presents new ethical and legal issues concerning data privacy, bias, and accountability—challenges that must be resolved to guarantee the proper application of algorithmic tools in HRM.

BACKGROUND: STRATEGIC OPPORTUNITIES IN AI-DRIVEN TALENT ACQUISITION

2.1 Enhancing Efficiency and Decision-Making in Hiring Processes

Artificial Intelligence (AI) is transforming the framework of talent acquisition by markedly improving the efficiency, precision, and strategic caliber of hiring decisions. In the realm of algorithmic human resource management, AI-driven technologies facilitate expedited and well-informed recruitment decisions via automation, sophisticated analytics, and real-time data analysis. These advances allow firms to enhance their hiring processes while preserving or elevating decision quality, particularly in contexts where high candidate quantities and time constraints are paramount.

The primary advantage of AI integration in recruitment is the automation of resume screening and candidate ranking. Organizations can rapidly sift through hundreds of applications with machine learning algorithms based on established criteria such as education, experience, and skill sets (Van Esch & Black, 2019). This automation decreases time-to-hire, lessens manual effort, and enables human recruiters to concentrate on more valuable duties such as candidate interaction and final-stage assessment.

Table 1. Comparison Between Traditional and AI-Based Recruitment Approaches

Aspect	Traditional Recruitment	AI-Based Recruitment
Data Processing	Manual CV screening, subjective interpretation	Automated parsing, machine learning-based pattern recognition
Decision-Making	Human intuition and experience	Predictive analytics and algorithmic scoring
Speed and Efficiency	Time-consuming, dependent on HR availability	Real-time, scalable, and efficient
Bias Potential	Susceptible to unconscious bias	Can reduce bias, but may inherit algorithmic bias
Candidate Experience	Human interaction, but often slow communication	Streamlined with chatbots and automated feedback
Transparency	Generally clear decision rationale	Often opaque, requiring explainable AI (XAI) mechanisms
Cost	High labor cost, especially for mass hiring	Lower cost per applicant over time
Regulatory Risk	Lower if compliant with standard HR laws	High if not aligned with GDPR, AI Act, or data privacy frameworks

Source: Author's synthesis based on existing literature.

AI-driven recruitment offers significant advantages in scalability, predictive analytics, and candidate engagement. However, as will be analyzed in subsequent sections, these benefits must be carefully assessed in relation to ethical issues such as algorithmic bias and inadequate transparency.

AI systems facilitate data-driven decision-making via predictive and prescriptive analytics. Through the examination of historical recruiting and performance data, predictive models can discern patterns and yield insights into the people most likely to excel in a specific role. These insights facilitate strategic coherence between recruitment choices and enduring organizational objectives (Upadhyay & Khandelwal, 2018). For instance, AI can anticipate a candidate's probability of attrition or project future performance based on variables extracted from previous hires with analogous characteristics.

Moreover, AI techniques improve decision-making consistency and diminish variability frequently induced by human cognitive bias. Standardized scoring methods, natural language processing (NLP) for structured interview analysis, and algorithmic evaluations guarantee that each candidate is assessed based on uniform criteria, hence enhancing procedural fairness (Suen et al., 2019). Moreover, intelligent chatbots enhance communication efficiency by delivering prompt feedback to candidates, addressing frequently asked questions, and coordinating interviews, so expediting the candidate experience while alleviating the recruiter's workload.

Notwithstanding these breakthroughs, it is imperative to acknowledge that improvements in efficiency should not compromise justice or openness. AI systems require ongoing monitoring and auditing to guarantee that they facilitate, rather than supplant, ethical decision-making. Ultimately, AI functions as a decision-support tool that augments human judgment rather than rendering it redundant, so supporting the hybrid character of contemporary HR practices.

2.2 Reducing Human Bias: Promise and Limitations of Algorithmic Screening

Recruitment bias has consistently been a significant problem, with hiring decisions being swayed—often subconsciously—by characteristics including gender, race, age, physical attractiveness, or educational background. The implementation of algorithmic screening tools aims to reduce human biases by incorporating uniformity, data-driven evaluations, and objective scoring systems into the recruitment process. When effectively planned and executed, these technologies can diminish the variability linked to subjective assessment and foster more equal talent acquisition procedures (Binns, 2018).

The potential of algorithmic screening is in its ability to guarantee uniformity and equity in candidate assessment. By uniformly applying identical evaluation criteria to all candidates, algorithms can eradicate personal biases and unconscious preconceptions that frequently affect human recruiters. For example, AI-driven systems can anonymize resumes by removing names, photographs, or associations that could result in biased evaluations. Furthermore, prediction models developed using performance-related variables can effectively identify the most suitable candidates based exclusively on their abilities, experience, and behavioral characteristics, rather than demographic or socio-economic factors (Raghavan et al., 2020).

Nonetheless, although algorithms possess the capacity to mitigate prejudice, they are not intrinsically neutral. Algorithmic systems are human-engineered products, frequently trained on historical information that include the biases they aim to eradicate. For instance, if an AI model is trained on historical hiring choices that preferred male candidates, it may perpetuate gender bias by assimilating discriminating tendencies from the data. This issue, termed algorithmic bias, underscores the peril of perpetuating structural disparities masquerading as objectivity (Mehrabi et al., 2021).

Moreover, the opacity of algorithmic decision-making, commonly known as the "black box" issue, hinders attempts to detect and rectify bias. In the absence of clarity on the algorithmic weighting of variables or the rationale behind certain recommendations, HR professionals may find it difficult to identify or contest biased results. This opacity compromises accountability and creates ethical issues with the transparency and equity of automated decisions.

The algorithmic screening offers considerable potential for mitigating prejudice in recruitment; however, its efficacy is largely contingent upon clear design, appropriate data management, and continuous auditing. Organizations must employ a critical perspective on algorithmic technologies, ensuring they are supplemented by human oversight and adhere to ethical hiring norms.

2.3 Intelligent Matching and Candidate Experience Optimization

A significant application of Artificial Intelligence (AI) in talent acquisition is its capacity to provide intelligent matching between candidates and employment opportunities, while concurrently improving the candidate experience. Intelligent matching denotes AI's capacity to correlate applicant profiles with job specifications, including not just qualifications but also behavioral characteristics, preferences, and organizational compatibility. This advanced capability enables recruiting procedures to transcend conventional keyword matching, providing tailored and dynamic engagement throughout the talent acquisition process (Chamorro-Premuzic et al., 2019).

AI-driven matching algorithms evaluate a wide range of data inputs—from resumes and online assessments to social media activity and digital footprints—to create detailed candidate profiles. The profiles are subsequently evaluated against role criteria via multidimensional scoring systems, frequently enhanced by natural language processing (NLP) and machine learning (ML). In contrast to static filters, intelligent algorithms evolve throughout time, assimilating insights from recruiter decisions and feedback to perpetually enhance the pertinence of their suggestions (Black & van Esch, 2020). Such systems can proactively recommend alternate roles for people whose profiles may be more suitable for other positions, so enhancing access to opportunities and minimizing hiring discrepancies.

Concurrently, AI is essential in enhancing the candidate experience, a vital although sometimes neglected aspect of recruitment efficacy. Interactive AI solutions, including chatbots, virtual assistants, and automated email systems, deliver real-time information, respond to frequently requested queries, and offer feedback on application status. These solutions mitigate the ambiguity that candidates frequently encounter during recruiting and enhance their involvement with the firm. Studies indicate that a favorable and attentive application process can greatly influence an applicant's view of an employer's brand, particularly in competitive labor markets (Walker et al., 2021). To better understand the operational shift driven by AI technologies, Figure 2 provides a side-by-side comparison of conventional and algorithmic candidate matching pipelines.

Figure 2. AI-Based vs. Conventional Candidate Matching Process

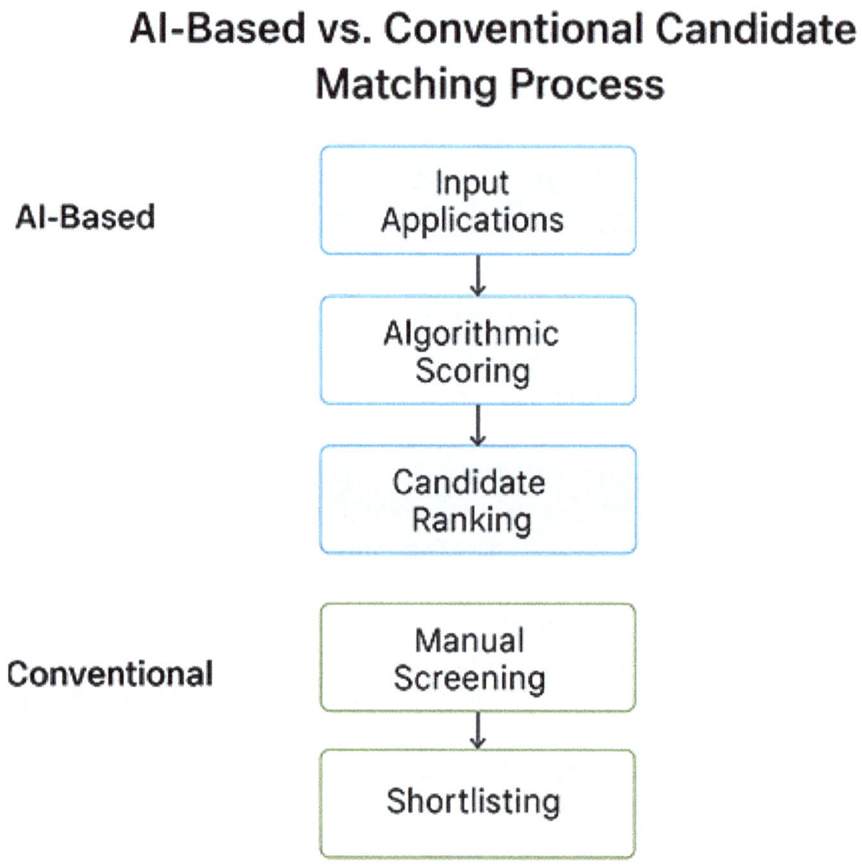

Source: Author's conceptual illustration based on Upadhyay & Khandelwal (2018), Tambe et al. (2019), and Black & van Esch (2020).

Furthermore, AI platforms can individualize the recruitment process by customizing communication material, arranging interviews according to availability, and providing personalized feedback following evaluations. These advancements promote efficiency and foster candidate happiness, hence aiding in the retention of high-quality applicants.

Nonetheless, intelligent matching necessitates a cautious approach. The customization of candidate experiences must adhere to data privacy regulations and refrain from excessively intrusive profiling. Clear transparency about the utilization of candidate data is crucial for establishing confidence and maintaining ethical standards in AI-driven recruitment.

MAIN FOCUS OF THE CHAPTER: ETHICAL CHALLENGES AND ALGORITHMIC BIAS IN RECRUITMENT

3.1 Algorithmic Discrimination and Hidden Biases in Hiring Tools

Although algorithmic tools offer enhanced fairness and efficiency in recruitment, they also present considerable ethical issues, particularly algorithmic discrimination and concealed biases inherent in data-driven systems. In contrast to the belief in computational neutrality, algorithms are socio-technical constructs influenced by the data they process and the biases of their creators. Consequently, artificial intelligence (AI)-driven hiring technologies may unintentionally perpetuate or intensify current labor market inequities, especially when historical data include biased or discriminatory hiring practices (Barocas & Selbst, 2016).

Algorithmic discrimination occurs when automated decision-making unfairly disadvantages specific demographic groups based on race, gender, age, or other protected attributes. This may arise from biased training data, wherein algorithms assimilate patterns from prior judgments that were inherently discriminating. For instance, Amazon's discontinued AI recruitment tool was discovered to disadvantage resumes featuring the term "women's," indicative of its training on a largely male-centric hiring history (Dastin, 2018). These outcomes demonstrate how algorithmic systems can sustain structural bias while appearing objective.

The implementation of algorithmic tools in talent acquisition should adhere to ethical guidelines to avert harm and guarantee fairness. Figure 1 depicts a hypothetical architecture wherein the hiring pipeline incorporates the FAT (Fairness, Accountability, Transparency) framework as the cornerstone for responsible AI governance in Human Resource Management. The model illustrates the necessity of ongoing monitoring and auditing of input data, algorithmic scoring, and decision outputs via ethical checkpoints. The ethical complexity of algorithmic bias can be better understood through an integrated model of the recruitment pipeline. As shown in Figure 1, embedding FAT principles at each stage of algorithmic hiring helps ensure procedural justice and organizational accountability.

Figure 3. Human-Centered AI Governance Model for HRM

Source: Author's elaboration based on Binns (2018), Raji et al. (2020), and Jobin et al. (2019).

Besides biased data, feature selection and model architecture can incorporate latent biases. ostensibly neutral variables—such as ZIP codes, educational institutions, or linguistic choices—can behave as proxies for sensitive attributes, resulting in unequal outcomes. Furthermore, the optimization objectives selected during model construction, such as enhancing predictive accuracy, may contradict fairness principles if the performance of minority groups is compromised to augment overall system efficacy (Raji et al., 2020).

A third issue stems from the opacity of numerous proprietary hiring algorithms, which function as "black boxes" with restricted interpretability. Human resources professionals and candidates frequently lack insight into the decision-making processes, so diminishing the capacity to evaluate systems for equity or to furnish justifications for denied applicants. This lack of transparency compromises ethical accountability and generates legal issues, especially in light of new rules like the EU's Artificial Intelligence Act and the U.S. Equal Employment Opportunity Commission (EEOC) recommendations.

To alleviate these concerns, enterprises must implement a responsible AI framework that prioritizes fairness, explainability, and ongoing audits. This encompasses the utilization of bias detection instruments, the engagement of different stakeholders in system development, and the assurance of human oversight in significant employment determinations. The absence of such protections in the implementation of algorithmic recruiting tools may exacerbate discrimination instead of mitigating it.

3.2 Lack of Transparency and Accountability in Automated Decisions

A primary ethical issue in the implementation of algorithmic systems in human resource management (HRM) is the absence of transparency and accountability in automated decision-making procedures. As organizations increasingly depend on Artificial Intelligence (AI) for recruiting decisions, the opaque characteristics of these systems—commonly known as the "black box" problem—prompt significant concerns over fairness, explainability, and corporate accountability (Burrell, 2016).

Many algorithmic recruiting tools employ sophisticated machine learning models, including neural networks or ensemble classifiers, to make recommendations based on patterns in high-dimensional datasets. Although these models can generate incredibly precise forecasts, they frequently do so without offering comprehensible reasoning. This opacity hinders the capacity of recruiters, applicants, and regulators to comprehend the rationale behind certain decisions, such as the rejection of a candidate or the prioritization of one application over another. Consequently, impacted persons frequently lack the capacity to contest or appeal decisions that profoundly influence their professional prospects (Wachter et al., 2017).

The absence of openness further complicates the attribution of accountability. When recruiting decisions are delegated to algorithms, it becomes ambiguous who is accountable for possible biased or erroneous results—the algorithm's developers, the HR department, or the senior leadership? The distribution of responsibility compromises ethical governance and may diminish public faith in the hiring process and the organization's ideals (Binns, 2018). Furthermore, under legal frameworks like the European Union's General Data Protection Regulation (GDPR), individuals possess the right to an explanation for algorithmic judgments impacting them; however, few AI recruitment systems are structured to comply with this need.

Organizations must implement explainable AI (XAI) strategies to improve the interpretability of algorithmic outputs in order to tackle these difficulties. This may entail utilizing intrinsically transparent models (e.g., decision trees) or applying post-hoc explanation techniques such as LIME or SHAP to produce comprehensible rationales. Furthermore, the establishment of auditing systems, documentation protocols (such as model cards), and ethical review boards can facilitate the alignment of automated judgments with the ideals of accountability and openness.

The ethical application of AI in recruitment necessitates not only technological efficiency but also institutional frameworks that ensure algorithmic processes are transparent, disputable, and accountable. Transparency should be regarded not merely as a technological attribute, but as a moral and legal obligation in AI-driven Human Resource Management.

3.3 Data Privacy and Surveillance in Candidate Profiling

With the growing dependence of algorithmic hiring tools on extensive data extraction and analysis, data privacy and monitoring have emerged as significant ethical issues in the digital recruitment arena. AI-driven systems frequently utilize a diverse range of personal information—from resumes and evaluation replies to social media interactions and biological indicators—to construct predictive candidate profiles. Although such profiling can improve decision-making, it also presents considerable concerns around permission, autonomy, and the limits of surveillance within the realm of employment (Zuboff, 2019).

Contemporary recruitment platforms utilize automated data scraping to monitor prospects across platforms such as LinkedIn, Twitter, and GitHub, gathering digital footprints to deduce behavioral patterns, emotional states, or psychological characteristics. Facial recognition and speech analysis technologies are occasionally employed in video interviews to evaluate soft skills or identify deceit. These tactics jeopardize candidates' privacy and impose psychological pressure to construct an online persona for employability instead of authenticity (Ajunwa et al., 2016).

The fundamental ethical quandary resides in the disparity of power and information between corporations and prospective employees. Candidates are seldom apprised of the comprehensive scope of data gathering or the methodologies employed in the utilization, processing, and retention of their information. The absence of substantial informed consent contravenes fundamental principles of privacy and transparency. Furthermore, data collected for a certain purpose—such as initial screening—may subsequently be utilized for alternative decisions (e.g., performance forecasting), resulting in function creep and ethical uncertainty.

Moreover, algorithmic profiling may exacerbate socio-economic disparities. Utilizing location data, consumer behavior, or social network information as recruiting criteria may result in indirect discrimination, disproportionately impacting underprivileged populations. These methods may also contravene regional data protection statutes, including the General Data Protection Regulation (GDPR), which stipulates data minimization, purpose limitation, and the rights to access, rectify, or erase personal data.

Organizations must adopt privacy-by-design principles while designing AI hiring tools to mitigate these threats. This include data minimization techniques, transparency in profiling practices, and the careful handling of sensitive information. Moreover, ethical rules must emphasize human dignity and trust, acknowledging that hiring transcends a basic technical decision and is a profoundly personal and social process.

SOLUTIONS AND RECOMMENDATIONS: GOVERNANCE, REGULATORY FRAMEWORKS, AND RESPONSIBLE AI IN HR

4.1 Global and Regional Regulatory Frameworks: GDPR, EU AI Act, and Beyond

As artificial intelligence (AI) becomes more integrated into human resource management (HRM), particularly in recruitment, the necessity for regulatory monitoring and ethical governance has become critical. Policymakers at both global and regional levels are addressing the ethical hazards associated with algorithmic systems—such as prejudice, opacity, and privacy infringements—by implementing regulatory frameworks designed to uphold fairness, accountability, and human dignity within the digital economy.

The General Data Protection Regulation (GDPR), implemented by the European Union in 2018, is one of the most significant rules to date. The GDPR imposes rigorous obligations on firms that gather and manage personal data, including those utilizing AI-based recruitment tools. Essential provisions pertinent to algorithmic human resource management encompass the concepts of data reduction, purpose limitation, explicit agreement, and the right to explanation as stipulated in Article 22. This article limits automated decision-making that results in legal or substantial impacts on humans, such as employment decisions, unless particular protections are implemented (Wachter et al., 2017).

In 2021, the European Commission established the Artificial Intelligence Act (EU AI Act), the first extensive legislative framework for artificial intelligence worldwide, building upon the General Data Protection Regulation (GDPR). The Act classifies AI systems according to risk, designating AI utilized in recruitment and personnel assessment as "high-risk." Organizations must comply with obligatory standards such as transparency, human oversight, data quality, and documentation of system functionality under this classification. The Act establishes independent audit methods and sanctions for non-compliance, so enhancing the ethical and legal accountability of AI providers and consumers (European Commission, 2021).

Other jurisdictions, in addition to the EU, are implementing analogous measures. The United States Equal Employment Opportunity Commission (EEOC) has released technical recommendations about artificial intelligence in employment to avert biased results. Likewise, countries like Canada, Singapore, and Brazil are implementing AI guidelines that prioritize human-centered design, algorithmic transparency, and risk reduction.

Table 2. Key Global and Regional Regulatory Frameworks Relevant to AI in HRM

Regulation / Framework	Region / Institution	Key Focus Areas	Implications for HRM
General Data Protection Regulation (GDPR)	European Union	Data privacy, automated decision-making, right to explanation (Art. 22)	Requires explicit consent, transparency in algorithmic hiring, and access to meaningful information about automated decisions
EU Artificial Intelligence Act (2021, proposed)	European Union	Risk-based regulation of AI systems (e.g., "high-risk" systems like HR tools)	AI tools in recruitment are classified as high-risk; mandates transparency, risk assessment, human oversight, and documentation
OECD AI Principles (2019)	OECD member countries	Human-centered values, transparency, robustness, accountability	Encourages organizations to adopt responsible and fair AI practices aligned with international standards
AI Bill of Rights (2022)	United States (White House OSTP)	Safe and effective systems, algorithmic discrimination protections, data privacy	Promotes non-binding but influential standards for ethical AI use, including in employment contexts
AI4People Ethical Framework (2018)	European civil society / academic	Beneficence, non-maleficence, autonomy, justice, explicability	Offers normative ethical foundation; HRM should ensure explainability and dignity in AI hiring systems

Source: Author's synthesis based on GDPR (EU, 2016); European Commission (2021); OECD (2019); White House OSTP (2022); Floridi et al. (2018).

The evolving regulatory framework introduces numerous concepts and enforceable standards governing the ethical implementation of AI in the workplace. Table 2 outlines critical global and regional regulatory frameworks relevant to algorithmic human resource management.

Nonetheless, regulatory frameworks are disjointed and frequently fail to keep up with the rapid advancement of AI technology. This highlights the necessity for enterprises to exceed mere legal compliance and embrace voluntary ethical frameworks—such as the OECD AI Principles or UNESCO's AI Ethics Recommendations—that advocate for broader principles including fairness, diversity, and sustainability. In this changing environment, HR leaders must remain informed about regulatory requirements and integrate ethical foresight and governance frameworks into AI implementation initiatives.

4.2 Organizational Ethics and AI Governance in HR Practice

The ethical application of Artificial Intelligence (AI) in Human Resource Management (HRM) is significantly influenced by internal organizational ethics and strong AI governance frameworks, in addition to external restrictions. With the growing implementation of algorithmic systems in recruitment, it is imperative for HR professionals, technology officers, and executive leadership to guarantee that these systems comply with legal standards and adhere to the organization's ethical principles and cultural values (Floridi et al., 2018).

Organizational AI governance in HR commences with the formulation of explicit ethical standards and operational protocols that direct the procurement, advancement, and implementation of algorithmic instruments. These rules must embody fundamental human-centric principles, including justice, privacy respect, non-discrimination, openness, and responsibility. The ethical application of AI in recruiting necessitates that candidates are handled with respect during the process, provided with feedback mechanisms, and not merely regarded as data points or behavioral forecasts (Jobin et al., 2019).

Organizations should establish interdisciplinary AI ethical committees or working groups of HR professionals, legal experts, data scientists, and diversity advocates to implement these concepts. These entities can analyze AI tools before to deployment, perform regular audits, and evaluate the effects of algorithmic decision-making on organizational diversity and inclusion. Simultaneously, firms ought to implement documentation standards—such as model cards or datasheets for datasets—that detail the assumptions, constraints, and risk concerns associated with AI systems utilized in recruiting (Mitchell et al., 2019).

A fundamental aspect of ethical governance is human-in-the-loop (HITL) design, which guarantees that significant employment choices are evaluated or jointly determined by trained professionals instead of being wholly entrusted to algorithms. Human supervision is essential for error prevention, analyzing confusing situations, and maintaining equity in marginal judgments. Furthermore, firms ought to allocate resources for ethics training for HR staff, enabling them to critically interact with AI technologies and promote responsible utilization.

Ultimately, ethical governance should be incorporated into the overarching business culture. This entails conveying ethical obligations to internal and external stakeholders, establishing avenues for candidate feedback, and integrating AI governance into strategic human resources planning. When executed proficiently, such approaches not only mitigate risk but also enhance organizational legitimacy, trust, and competitive advantage in a digitally transforming labor market.

4.3 Toward Fairness, Accountability, and Transparency (FAT) in Algorithmic Hiring

The ethical application of Artificial Intelligence (AI) in talent acquisition necessitates a robust adherence to the FAT principles—Fairness, Accountability, and Transparency—which have become international standards for algorithmic systems. As recruitment decisions increasingly depend on predictive models and automated tools, these principles operate as essential protections to avert harm, cultivate trust, and maintain the integrity of algorithmic human resource management procedures (Crawford & Paglen, 2021).

Figure 4. AI Algorithm Audit and Evaluation Cycle in HRM

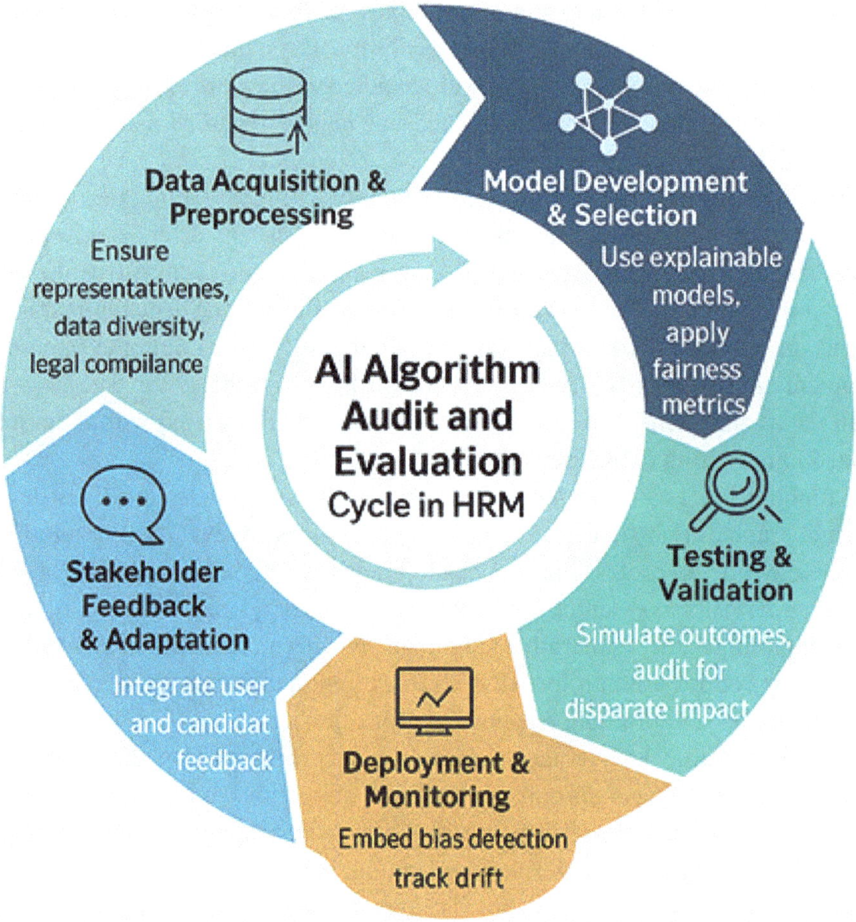

Source: Author's synthesis adapted from Raji et al. (2020), Binns (2018), and European Commission (2021).

Figure Description:

Figure 2 depicts a six-phase cycle of algorithmic auditing and governance specifically designed for human resource management.

1. Data Collection and Preprocessing. Ensuring dataset representativeness, diversity, and adherence to legal standards (e.g., anonymization, GDPR regulations).

2. Model Formulation and Selection. Emphasizing interpretable models, implementing fairness measures, and mitigating overfitting or negative consequences.
3. Assessment and Verification. Employing synthetic and empirical data to model outcomes, assess for differential impact, and analyze robustness.
4. Implementation and Surveillance. Implementing monitoring measures (bias detection, drift alarms) to guarantee the algorithm functions as intended over time.
5. Examination and Responsibility. Involving internal or external evaluators to assess input-output logic, transparency, and equity under stress conditions.
6. Stakeholder Input and Modification. Integrating comments from candidates, HR personnel, and legal teams to perpetually enhance the system.

The cycle prioritizes accountability, transparency, and ongoing enhancement, in accordance with international AI ethical norms.

Fairness in algorithmic hiring involves the impartial treatment of candidates, guaranteeing that AI algorithms do not yield discriminatory or prejudiced results. Attaining equity necessitates thorough evaluation for disparate impact among demographic groups and the execution of remedial actions upon the identification of bias. Fairness must be contextualized; perceptions of fairness may differ between industries, geographies, or job functions. Organizations must integrate algorithmic fairness auditing into their AI development and procurement procedures (Barocas et al., 2019).

Accountability underscores the necessity for explicit allocation of responsibilities across the AI lifecycle. In contrast to conventional HR judgments, which can be attributed to certain individuals, algorithmic decisions may result from the contributions of various stakeholders—data scientists, system vendors, HR managers, and the AI models themselves. Organizations must delineate responsibilities, generate documentation trails, and institute governance frameworks to manage algorithmic risks and address grievances effectively. Regulatory entities including the European Commission and the U.S. EEOC have initiated the promotion of algorithmic accountability requirements in employment settings (Raji et al., 2020).

Transparency is crucial for candidates, recruiters, and regulators to comprehend the process of hiring decisions. This encompasses procedural transparency (the operational mechanics of the system) and individual transparency (the rationale behind a single decision). Techniques such as explainable AI (XAI), user-oriented explanations, and streamlined disclosures can elucidate intricate algorithms and foster candidate trust. Transparency necessitates that firms reveal their utilization of AI in recruitment and provide candidates with opportunities to request clarification or contest judgments (Wachter et al., 2017).

Implementing the FAT framework transcends mere compliance; it is a strategic necessity for firms aiming to harmonize technology progress with ethical principles. When effectively integrated into algorithmic hiring methods, FAT principles foster more inclusive, reliable, and sustainable talent ecosystems within the advancing e-economy.

FUTURE DIRECTIONS AND HR'S ROLE IN HUMAN-CENTERED AI

5.1 The Augmented HR Professional: From Technical Adoption to Ethical Stewardship

As Artificial Intelligence (AI) systems become essential to recruitment processes, the role of Human Resource (HR) professionals must transition from technology adopters to ethical custodians and strategic collaborators in AI adoption. The future of algorithmic human resource management depends on technological innovation and the ability of HR professionals to manage, influence, and regulate AI systems to foster equity, trust, and human dignity (Cascio & Montealegre, 2016).

The enhanced HR professional is not supplanted by AI, but rather augmented by it. AI tools provide HR professionals with improved functionalities in screening, analytics, forecasting, and candidate interaction. The efficacy of AI in recruitment mostly hinges on the ability of HR professionals to evaluate algorithmic insights, amalgamate them with human judgment, and implement them within ethically robust frameworks. This necessitates a transition from operational HR functions to strategic positions, whereby data literacy, ethical reasoning, and digital fluency are essential competencies (Marler & Boudreau, 2017).

In this new paradigm, HR directors must serve as intermediates between technology and human values. They are distinctly equipped to evaluate the alignment of AI systems with business culture, inclusivity objectives, and employment legislation. This entails rigorously assessing vendors, interrogating algorithmic premises, and promoting attributes such as transparency and equity. HR practitioners must critically confront "technological solutionism"—the notion that automation can only address intricate human issues—by emphasizing empathy, context, and interpersonal dynamics in recruiting (Kellogg et al., 2020).

In the realm of algorithmic decision-making, the duties of HR professionals are swiftly transforming. Figure 2 depicts a conceptual framework that illustrates the move from administrative task managers to ethical stewards of human-centered AI systems. This transition signifies a growing necessity for HR professionals to acquire not only digital proficiency but also ethical foresight, governance skills, and the capacity to harmonize algorithmic instruments with human values.

1. The model highlights four fundamental realms of transformation:
2. Governance and Risk Management
3. Principled Data Management
4. Management of Human-AI Collaboration
5. Establishing Trust and Cultivating a Communication Culture

Each area signifies an essential competency that HR must cultivate to guarantee that AI recruiting systems are equitable, responsible, and inclusive.

Figure 5. Evolving Role of HR Professionals as Ethical Stewards in AI-Driven Talent Acquisition

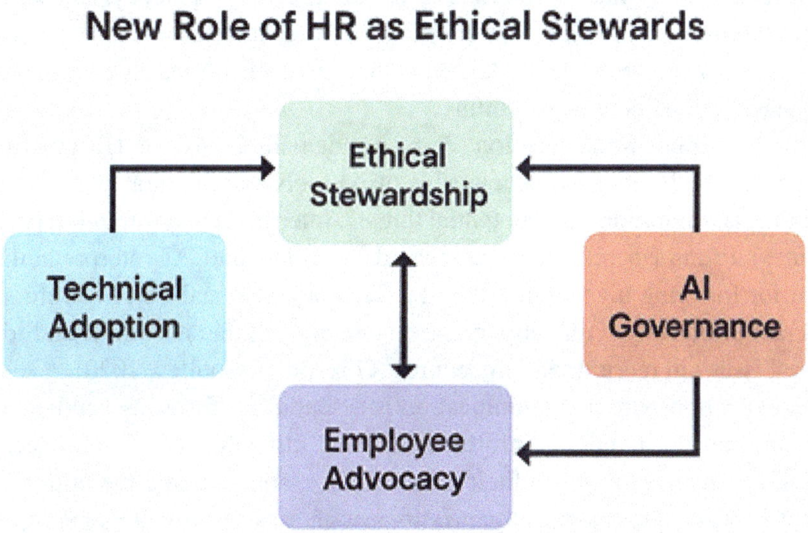

Source: Author's conceptualization based on Glikson & Woolley (2020), Minbaeva (2018), and Chamorro-Premuzic et al. (2019).

Furthermore, the enhanced HR position include the integration of ethical governance into practice. This may involve engaging in AI ethical committees, collaboratively creating algorithmic tools with varied stakeholders, and performing impact assessments to discern unexpected implications. HR professionals must promote clear communication with candidates, clarifying the utilization of their data and outlining their options in the event of unfavorable outcomes.

The HR function is crucial in humanizing AI within the workplace. As firms advance towards intelligent talent systems, HR must ensure that efficiency improvements do not compromise justice, autonomy, or organizational integrity. The enhanced HR professional must be both technologically proficient and ethically principled—a custodian of innovation informed by justice and compassion.

5.2 Building Trust in Algorithmic Systems: Training, Communication, and Culture

As firms integrate Artificial Intelligence (AI) into recruiting, a vital yet little examined difficulty is the cultivation of trust among stakeholders—specifically HR professionals, job candidates, and hiring managers. Trust is not inherently bestowed upon algorithmic systems, particularly when their decisions impact individuals' professions and lives. It must be attained by transparency, competency, and adherence to common ethical principles (Siau & Wang, 2018). Establishing trust in algorithmic recruiting is a socio-technical undertaking that needs intentional actions in training, communication, and company culture.

Initially, training and education serve a fundamental purpose. HR practitioners must possess both functional knowledge of AI tools and the vital ability to assess their fairness, limitations, and potential threats. Interdisciplinary training programs that integrate human resource analytics, data ethics, and AI interpretability are crucial for fostering algorithmic literacy. This training enables HR professionals to interact effectively with suppliers, evaluate algorithmic accuracy, and identify potential issues in recruitment procedures (Glikson & Woolley, 2020).

Secondly, transparent communication is essential for fostering candidate trust. Applicants must be explicitly informed about the utilization of AI in the recruiting process, the manner in which their data will be employed, and the options available for disputing judgments. Organizations ought to surpass mere legal disclosure by providing comprehensible explanations, so promoting procedural fairness and honoring candidate autonomy. Studies indicate that even brief explanations can markedly enhance the perceived fairness and acceptance of algorithmic outcomes (Binns et al., 2018).

Establishing trust necessitates integrating AI utilization into a corporate culture that prioritizes ethical contemplation and inclusivity. Trust flourishes in settings where employees and candidates believe that algorithms are utilized not merely for efficiency, but to foster equity and enhance human decision-making. This cultural basis need bolstering through evident leadership endorsement, inclusive technological governance frameworks, and ethical feedback mechanisms that enable stakeholders to voice concerns and participate in AI assessment.

In conclusion, confidence in algorithmic recruiting systems is not merely a technological result; it is a relational and cultural phenomenon. By means of thorough training, transparent communication, and an inclusive company culture, HR professionals can advocate for the appropriate deployment of AI that is both effective and human-centered.

5.3 Research Agenda for Human-Centered and Inclusive Algorithmic HRM

As firms progressively incorporate Artificial Intelligence (AI) into their Human Resource Management (HRM) systems, the necessity for a comprehensive and anticipatory research program intensifies. Algorithmic hiring has significant opportunities for speed and scalability, although it also introduces intricate difficulties about ethics, inclusion, and human oversight. Researchers must investigate novel models and frameworks for human-centered and inclusive algorithmic HRM to guarantee that future advancements are consistent with societal values and organizational justice (Glikson & Woolley, 2020).

A vital domain for forthcoming study is the advancement of inclusive algorithmic design approaches. Contemporary AI recruitment technologies frequently embody prevailing norms, datasets, and decision-making logics that may disenfranchise disadvantaged populations. Future research should examine participatory and co-design methodologies that engage diverse stakeholders—including women, ethnic minorities, and those with disabilities—in model creation, feature selection, and fairness assessments (Veale et al., 2018). This inclusive design viewpoint is crucial for confronting ingrained biases and enhancing the social responsibility of HR technologies.

Secondly, there is a necessity for longitudinal and contextually aware evaluations of algorithmic human resource management systems. A significant portion of the existing literature emphasizes technical performance or short-term results. Nonetheless, there is limited understanding of the impact of AI recruitment tools on corporate culture, diversity trends, employee retention, or psychological safety over time. Subsequent study ought to utilize mixed methods—integrating data analytics with ethnographic insights—to examine the tangible impacts of algorithmic treatments and uncover unexpected outcomes (Binns et al., 2018).

A nascent frontier is the elucidation and ethical transparency in algorithmic human resource management. Although technical communities are progressing in Explainable AI (XAI) methodologies, there is a necessity for HR-focused study to comprehend how various types of explanations (e.g., textual, visual, procedural) are regarded by applicants and HR professionals. Research should investigate how the design of explanations influences perceptions of fairness, trust, and acceptance, particularly across diverse cultures and industries.

Ultimately, scholars must examine the function of HR professionals as custodians of algorithms. In what manner do HR professionals comprehend and navigate algorithmic authority? What training, principles, or organizational circumstances facilitate ethical resistance or critical reflection? Addressing these inquiries is essential to guarantee that the digitalization of HR does not compromise human judgment, empathy, or inclusive workplace practices.

Advancing these research domains can facilitate the development of AI systems that are not only intelligent but also equitable, inclusive, and congruent with the future of dignified employment.

CONCLUSION

This chapter has provided a thorough analysis of the opportunities and ethical dilemmas related to algorithmic human resource management, especially in AI-driven talent acquisition. The incorporation of artificial intelligence, machine learning, and natural language processing can markedly improve the efficiency, consistency, and scalability of recruitment operations. Crucial advances like intelligent matching, predictive analytics, and automation may revolutionize HR operations, making them more proactive, data-driven, and tailored.

Nonetheless, these opportunities are accompanied with significant ethical dilemmas. Algorithmic bias, opacity, and breaches of candidate privacy are tangible concerns that necessitate resolution via regulatory and organizational measures. The chapter underscored the significance of governance structures founded on equity, accountability, and transparency, and accentuated the necessity for continuous audits, interpretable AI, and privacy-by-design principles.

The future of algorithmic human resource management relies on the transformation of HR practitioners into enhanced, morally accountable agents. As custodians of human-centered AI, they must guarantee that technical efficiency does not undermine inclusivity, fairness, or human dignity. Establishing stakeholder trust via training, transparent communication, and cultural transformation is essential for the sustained implementation of AI in recruitment.

Whereas algorithmic HRM presents transformative promise, it must be approached with critical awareness and institutional safeguards. A proactive research program is essential to create inclusive, participatory, and contextually relevant frameworks that connect AI implementation with ethical, legal, and societal standards. The objective is to enhance recruiting, rendering it more intelligent, egalitarian, and human-centered amidst digital transition, rather than merely automating it.

REFERENCES

Ajunwa, I., Crawford, K., & Schultz, J. (2016). Limitless worker surveillance. *California Law Review, 105*(3), 735–776. DOI: 10.2139/ssrn.2701836

Barocas, S., Hardt, M., & Narayanan, A. (2019). *Fairness and machine learning: Limitations and opportunities*. https://fairmlbook.org

Barocas, S., & Selbst, A. D. (2016). Big data's disparate impact. *California Law Review, 104*(3), 671–732. DOI: 10.15779/Z38BG31

Binns, R. (2018). Algorithmic accountability and public reason. *Philosophy & Technology, 31*(4), 543–556. DOI: 10.1007/s13347-017-0263-5 PMID: 30873342

Binns, R. (2018). Fairness in machine learning: Lessons from political philosophy. In *Proceedings of the 2018 Conference on Fairness, Accountability and Transparency* (pp. 149–159). DOI: 10.1145/3287560.3287598

Binns, R., Veale, M., Van Kleek, M., & Shadbolt, N. (2018). 'It's reducing a human being to a percentage': Perceptions of justice in algorithmic decisions. In *Proceedings of the 2018 CHI Conference on Human Factors in Computing Systems* (Paper 377), 1–14. DOI: 10.1145/3173574.3173951

Black, J. S., & van Esch, P. (2020). AI-enabled recruiting: What is it and how should a manager use it? *Business Horizons, 63*(2), 215–226. openscholar.uga.edu. DOI: 10.1016/j.bushor.2019.12.001

Burrell, J. (2016). How the machine 'thinks': Understanding opacity in machine learning algorithms. *Big Data & Society, 3*(1), 1–12. DOI: 10.1177/2053951715622512

Cascio, W. F., & Montealegre, R. (2016). How technology is changing work and organizations. *Annual Review of Organizational Psychology and Organizational Behavior, 3*(1), 349–375. DOI: 10.1146/annurev-orgpsych-041015-062352

Chamorro-Premuzic, T., Akhtar, R., Winsborough, D., & Sherman, R. A. (2019). The datafication of talent: How technology is advancing the science of human potential at work. *Current Opinion in Behavioral Sciences, 18*, 13–16. DOI: 10.1016/j.cobeha.2017.04.007

Chamorro-Premuzic, T., Winsborough, D., Sherman, R. A., & Hogan, R. (2019). New talent signals: Shiny new objects or a brave new world? *Industrial and Organizational Psychology: Perspectives on Science and Practice, 12*(3), 252–268. DOI: 10.1017/iop.2019.24

Crawford, K., & Paglen, T. (2021). Excavating AI: The politics of training sets for machine learning. *AI & Society*, *36*(4), 1101–1111. DOI: 10.1007/s00146-021-01301-1

Dastin, J. (2018, October 10). Amazon scrapped 'secret AI recruiting tool' that showed bias against women. *Reuters*.

European Commission. (2021). *Proposal for a Regulation laying down harmonized rules on artificial intelligence (Artificial Intelligence Act)*. European Commission European Union. (2016). *General Data Protection Regulation (GDPR)* (Regulation (EU) 2016/679). Official Journal of the European Union.

Floridi, L., Cowls, J., Beltrametti, M., Chiarello, F., Chatila, R., Dignum, V., & Vayena, E. (2018). AI4People—An ethical framework for a good AI society: Opportunities, risks, principles, and recommendations. *Minds and Machines*, *28*(4), 689–707. DOI: 10.1007/s11023-018-9482-5 PMID: 30930541

Glikson, E., & Woolley, A. W. (2020). Human trust in artificial intelligence: Review of empirical research. *The Academy of Management Annals*, *14*(2), 627–660. DOI: 10.5465/annals.2018.0057

Jobin, A., Ienca, M., & Vayena, E. (2019). The global landscape of AI ethics guidelines. *Nature Machine Intelligence*, *1*(9), 389–399. DOI: 10.1038/s42256-019-0088-2

Kellogg, K. C., Valentine, M. A., & Christin, A. (2020). Algorithms at work: The new contested terrain of control. *The Academy of Management Annals*, *14*(1), 366–410. DOI: 10.5465/annals.2018.0174

Leicht-Deobald, U., Busch, T., Schank, C., Weibel, A., Schafheitle, S., Wildhaber, I., & Kasper, G. (2019). The challenges of algorithm-based HR decision-making for personal integrity. *Journal of Business Ethics*, *160*(2), 377–392. DOI: 10.1007/s10551-019-04204-w PMID: 31814653

Marler, J. H., & Boudreau, J. W. (2017). An evidence-based review of HR Analytics. *International Journal of Human Resource Management*, *28*(1), 3–26. DOI: 10.1080/09585192.2016.1244699

Matsuo, M., Wang, Z., & Li, J. (2022). Leveraging machine learning for strategic human resource management: A review and future research agenda. *Journal of Business Research*, *142*, 552–567. DOI: 10.1016/j.jbusres.2021.12.052

Mehrabi, N., Morstatter, F., Saxena, N., Lerman, K., & Galstyan, A. (2021). A survey on bias and fairness in machine learning. *ACM Computing Surveys*, *54*(6), 115. Advance online publication. DOI: 10.1145/3457607

Meijerink, J., Bondarouk, T., & Lepak, D. P. (2021). New ways of working through algorithmic management: The duality of HRM digitalization. *Human Resource Management Review*, *31*(1), 100713. Advance online publication. DOI: 10.1016/j.hrmr.2020.100713

Minbaeva, D. B. (2018). Building credible human capital analytics for organizational competitive advantage. *Human Resource Management*, *57*(3), 701–713. DOI: 10.1002/hrm.21848

Mitchell, M., Wu, S., Zaldivar, A., Barnes, P., Vasserman, L., Hutchinson, B., & Gebru, T. (2019). Model cards for model reporting. In *Proceedings of the Conference on Fairness, Accountability, and Transparency* (pp. 220–229). DOI: 10.1145/3287560.3287596

OECD. (2019). *OECD principles on artificial intelligence*. https://legalinstruments.oecd.org/en/instruments/OECD-LEGAL-0449

Raghavan, M., Barocas, S., Kleinberg, J., & Levy, K. (2020). Mitigating bias in algorithmic hiring: Evaluating fairness and explainability. In *Proceedings of the 2020 Conference on Fairness, Accountability, and Transparency* (pp. 469–481). DOI: 10.1145/3351095.3372828

Raji, I. D., Binns, R., Shankar, S., Friedler, S. A., Scheidegger, C., & Venkatasubramanian, S. (2020). Closing the AI accountability gap: Defining an end-to-end framework for internal algorithmic auditing. In *Proceedings of the 2020 Conference on Fairness, Accountability, and Transparency* (pp. 33–44). DOI: 10.1145/3351095.3372873

Raji, I. D., Binns, R., Shankar, S., Friedler, S. A., Scheidegger, C., & Venkatasubramanian, S. (2020). Closing the AI accountability gap. In *Proceedings of the 2020 Conference on Fairness, Accountability and Transparency* (pp. 33–44). DOI: 10.1145/3351095.3372873

Siau, K., & Wang, W. (2018). Building trust in artificial intelligence, machine learning, and robotics. *Cutter Business Technology Journal*, *31*(2), 47–53.

Suen, H. Y., Chen, M. Y. C., & Lu, S. H. (2019). Does the use of synchrony in AI recruitment systems affect applicant experience? *Computers in Human Behavior*, *98*, 93–101. DOI: 10.1016/j.chb.2019.04.012

Tambe, P., Cappelli, P., & Yakubovich, V. (2019). Artificial intelligence in human resources management: Challenges and a path forward. *California Management Review*, *61*(4), 15–42. DOI: 10.1177/0008125619867910

Upadhyay, A. K., & Khandelwal, K. (2018). Artificial intelligence-based recruitment and selection: A review. International Journal of Engineering and Technology, 7(2.3), 827–830.

Van Esch, P., & Black, J. S. (2019). Factors that influence new generation candidates to engage with and complete digital, AI-enabled recruiting. *Business Horizons*, *62*(6), 729–739. DOI: 10.1016/j.bushor.2019.07.004

Veale, M., Van Kleek, M., & Binns, R. (2018). Fairness and accountability design needs for algorithmic support in high-stakes public sector decision-making. In *Proceedings of the 2018 CHI Conference on Human Factors in Computing Systems* (Paper 440), 1–14. DOI: 10.1145/3173574.3174014

Wachter, S., Mittelstadt, B., & Floridi, L. (2017). Why a right to explanation of automated decision-making does not exist in the General Data Protection Regulation. *International Data Privacy Law*, *7*(2), 76–99. DOI: 10.1093/idpl/ipx005

Wachter, S., Mittelstadt, B., & Floridi, L. (2017). Why a right to explanation of automated decision-making does not exist in the GDPR. *International Data Privacy Law*, *7*(2), 76–99. DOI: 10.1093/idpl/ipx005

Walker, H. J., Feild, H. S., Bernerth, J. B., & Becton, J. B. (2021). Candidate reactions to AI-enabled recruitment: The role of engagement, fairness, and trust. *Journal of Business and Psychology*, *36*(3), 475–488.

Zuboff, S. (2019). *The Age of Surveillance Capitalism*. PublicAffairs.

Chapter 2
Artificial Intelligence-Enabled Human Resource Functional Innovations in the E-Economy

D. Velumoni
Sathyabama Institute of Science and Technology, India

D. Yamuna
Sathyabama Institute of Science and Technology, India

M. Soundarya
http://orcid.org/0000-0001-7018-7972
Sathyabama Institute of Science and Technology, India

M. Jayaseely
http://orcid.org/0009-0002-0328-7628
Sathyabama Institute of Science and Technology, India

Devapitchai Joel Jebadurai
http://orcid.org/0000-0002-6947-8497
St. Joseph's College of Engineering, OMR, Chennai, India

D. Gopika
St. Joseph's College of Engineering, OMR, Chennai, India

ABSTRACT

The rapid growth of the e-economy, driven by digital technologies and decentralized systems, is reshaping how organizations approach Human Resource Management (HRM). Traditional, location-based HR models no longer work in a remote work world, platform labor, and algorithmic management. This book explains how HR innovations such as AI, blockchain credentialing, and virtual organizational structures are redefining employees' work, talent, and performance. The world is moving beyond merely making things easier with technology; it critically examines the ethical and human-centered challenges these changes pose. The study combines insights from multiple disciplines to offer an in-depth understanding of how digital tools

DOI: 10.4018/979-8-3373-4307-5.ch002

connect with human resource functions. This chapter presents case studies, success stories, and challenges of digital-enabled HR functions in an e-economy. Aimed at scholars, policymakers, and practitioners, the book promotes deeper reflection on fairness, inclusion, and resilience in the digital workplace.

INTRODUCTION

The concept of Artificial Intelligence in Human Resource Management (HRM) began with early expert systems of the 1980s and expanded significantly with advancements in machine learning, people analytics, and cloud-based HR technologies in the early 21st century. With the rise of the e-economy defined by the widespread use of digital platforms and technologies HR functions increasingly integrated AI into core areas such as talent acquisition, performance evaluation, workforce planning, and employee engagement. The acceleration of big data, remote work ecosystems, and enterprise automation platforms in the last decade has pushed AI adoption to new heights, making AI-enabled HR a global reality across both developed and emerging economies. Modern e-economy tools like Applicant Tracking Systems (ATS) allow companies to manage HR functions from employee entry to exit. Leading digital firms such as ZOHO Corp. have developed platforms like ZOHO Recruit and ZOHO People to monitor and streamline HR operations, while integrating AI tools to enhance efficiency and decision-making. Compared to traditional technological systems that involved time-consuming paperwork, AI platforms minimize administrative burdens and allow employees to focus their skills and intelligence more effectively (Nawaz et al., 2024).

Furthermore, the e-economy driven by rapid digitalization, platform-based business models, artificial intelligence, and decentralized organizational structures has profoundly reshaped the HRM landscape. Traditional paradigms centered on fixed roles, physical office environments, and hierarchical decision-making are being replaced by flexible, technology-augmented models that prioritize autonomy, agility, and real-time insights. As the global workforce becomes more distributed and digitally connected, HRM is confronted with both unprecedented opportunities and complex challenges in managing talent, fostering engagement, and sustaining organizational culture. In this rapidly evolving digital environment, HR leaders must balance technological innovation with ethical considerations to ensure that AI-driven practices support organizational goals while safeguarding fairness, transparency, and employee well-being (Dawra et al., 2024).

This chapter explores the imagination of Human Resource Management (HRM) in the digital economy, foregrounding both innovative practices and the human-centered challenges they introduce. Drawing on contemporary research, industry case studies, and cross-sector trends, this chapter examine how emerging technologies such as AI, block chain, predictive analytics, and HR chatbots are reshaping recruitment, learning and development, employee engagement, and performance management. In parallel, this chapter critically engage with pressing ethical concerns including algorithmic bias, data privacy, digital surveillance, and inequality in access to technology. They are.

1. To examine the transformation of HRM practices in response to the structural shifts brought by the digital economy
2. To explore how emerging technologies such as artificial intelligence, block chain, and predictive analytics are being applied in HR functions.
3. To present the benefits, challenges and case studies of AI enabled HR functions in the e-economy.

METHODOLOGY

This chapter is based entirely on secondary data collected from credible sources such as academic journals, official websites, and industry publications. The secondary data covered the AI tools applications in the HR functions of the organization.

Table 1. Modern Digital Theories Enabling AI-Driven Human Resource Functional Innovations in the E-Economy

Theory	Core Focus	Approach to Technology	HRM Implications	Key Contrast Points
Digital Transformation Theory	Organizational shift to technology-embedded systems for efficiency and agility	Technology as an enabler of continuous process improvement	Drives adoption of cloud platforms, AI recruitment, digital onboarding, real-time analytics	Emphasizes ongoing digital evolution rather than one-time change
Sociotechnical Systems Theory	Interaction and balance between humans and technology	Technology complements, not replaces, human judgment	Stresses employee well-being, autonomy alongside tech efficiency	Focuses on human-technology balance, unlike tech-centric theories
Human Capital Analytics Theory	Data-driven decision-making in workforce management	Technology as a source of predictive, evidence-based insights	Supports strategic HR through AI-driven analytics and dashboards	Prioritizes data and analytics over

continued on following page

Table 1. Continued

Theory	Core Focus	Approach to Technology	HRM Implications	Key Contrast Points
Algorithmic Management Theory	Algorithmic control over tasks, monitoring, and performance	Technology as an active manager directing work	Explains AI in scheduling, performance measurement, digital productivity	Highlights control and surveillance aspects of AI in HR
Digital Labour Theory	Restructuring of work in digital economies and platforms	Technology transforms work models (gig, remote, platform-based)	Grounds HR innovations in virtual onboarding, capability mapping	Focuses on new work structures rather than organizational processes
Boundaryless and Networked Organization Theory	Flexibility, decentralization, and removal of hierarchical boundaries	Technology enables remote collaboration and global networking	Facilitates virtual teams, decentralized communication, and global talent management	Emphasizes organizational structure and boundary transcendence

ARTIFICIAL INTELLIGENCE TOOLS IN THE HR FUNCTIONS

The technologies listed below are among the innovations that are transforming HRM in the e-economy:

AI in Recruitment and Talent Management

AI in recruitment and talent management has revolutionized how organizations attract, assess, and onboard new employees. Artificial intelligence applications are now commonly used to automate resume screening, conduct preliminary interviews through chatbots, and predict job fit through behavioral and cognitive analytics. These tools use machine learning algorithms trained on vast datasets, including historical hiring patterns, job performance records, and even candidates' online footprints, to evaluate suitability for roles. For instance, platforms such as HireVue and Pymetrics utilize AI to analyze facial expressions, voice tones, and response patterns during video interviews to assess candidate competencies. Social media activity and publicly available data are also mined to generate a more holistic view of candidates, though this raises ethical concerns around privacy and consent. While these technologies can reduce time-to-hire and enhance objectivity, and they may inadvertently reinforce biases if not regularly audited and retrained (Tariq 2024). Critics have pointed out that AI can replicate historical discriminatory practices, especially if training data is skewed or lacks diversity. To address this, leading organizations are implementing fairness-aware algorithms, transparency protocols, and human oversight mechanisms. The evolving landscape of AI in talent management necessitates continuous monitoring and ethical safeguards to ensure that efficiency does not come at the cost of equity and inclusivity. HR professionals must be trained to interpret algorithmic insights critically and maintain accountability for final hiring decisions (Nayak et al., 2023). As AI becomes increasingly embedded in talent pipelines, balancing innovation with fairness and transparency will be crucial for sustainable workforce development.

Block-chain Technologies in Employee Background Verification

Block-chain for verifying credentials is emerging as a transformative solution in human resource management, particularly in ensuring the authenticity, security, and efficiency of academic and professional records. Traditional credential verification processes are often slow, costly, and susceptible to fraud, involving multiple intermediaries and manual checks. By contrast, block-chain-based systems offer a decentralized and immutable ledger where each credential such as degrees, certifications, or employment histories can be securely stored and instantly validated. Educational institutions, licensing bodies, and employers can issue tamper-proof digital certificates that are easily accessible by prospective employers, thereby reducing the time and cost of background checks during hiring. This not only speeds up the on-boarding process but also builds trust between employers and candidates. Leading platforms like Block certs and Machine Learning are already being adopted by universities and corporations to issue and verify block chain-anchored credentials. Furthermore, block chain enhances data ownership and privacy, empowering individuals to control access to their verified credentials through secure digital wallets (Mishra & Raghatate 2025). As the future of work becomes increasingly global and skill-based, block chain has the potential to democratize opportunity by ensuring that credentials are universally verifiable, irrespective of geographic or institutional boundaries. However, widespread adoption will depend on the development of global standards, interoperability frameworks, and the willingness of stakeholders to transition from legacy systems to decentralized trust infrastructures.

Virtual Organizational Structures

Virtual organizational structures represent a significant departure from traditional hierarchical models by emphasizing decentralized, remote-first operations that leverage digital collaboration tools and distributed governance systems. Central to this transformation are entities like Decentralized Autonomous Organizations

(DAOs), which operate on block chain protocols and execute decisions through smart contracts, effectively removing the need for central managerial oversight. These virtual structures prioritize transparency, consensus-based decision-making, and flexibility in task execution. Remote-first businesses, similarly, build their operating models around global talent pools, asynchronous workflows, and cloud-native tools such as Trello, Notion, and GitLab. Performance is assessed not by hours logged or physical presence but by outcomes, deliverables, and collaborative engagement. This shift demands a redefinition of performance indicators, focusing on metrics such as creativity, accountability, and peer feedback. Additionally, virtual organizations are more agile in responding to market shifts, as they are not constrained by physical infrastructure or geographic limitations. And also, such models can increase employee satisfaction, lower operational costs, and promote work-life integration when supported by strong digital culture and leadership (Davidaviciene & Majzoub 2022). However, challenges persist in areas like maintaining team cohesion, ensuring equitable access to opportunities, and preventing digital burnout. To thrive in this paradigm, HR must adopt practices that nurture trust, inclusivity, and digital fluency, while investing in tools that facilitate collaboration, continuous learning, and transparent governance. As the future of work evolves, virtual organizational structures are poised to become not just viable alternatives but preferred frameworks for innovation-driven enterprises.

HR Chatbots and Self-Service Portals

HR chatbots and self-service portals are transforming traditional employee service models by enhancing accessibility, responsiveness, and efficiency in Human Resource Management. AI-powered chatbots, such as those used by companies like IBM (Watson Assistant) and SAP (SuccessFactors), provide 24/7 support to employees by answering frequently asked questions, processing leave applications, guiding them through HR policies, and even assisting with on-boarding procedures. These chatbots are trained on large datasets to provide contextual and conversational responses, reducing the burden on HR staff and ensuring consistent service delivery. Meanwhile, self-service portals empower employees to take control of their HR-related tasks, including updating personal information, enrolling in benefits programs, accessing payslips, and managing learning and development plans. These platforms enhance user autonomy and streamline HR operations, leading to faster turnaround times and improved data accuracy. Furthermore, the integration of mobile interfaces and multilingual support ensures inclusivity across diverse workforces. Furthermore, organizations that deploy digital HR tools experience increased employee engagement and cost reductions in administrative functions (Nimmagadda et al., 2024). However, the success of these technologies depends on intuitive design, secure data handling, and continuous user training. As workplaces become more digital, HR chatbots and self-service systems are central to enabling scalable, employee-centric service models that support both operational agility and strategic HR outcomes.

Predictive Analytics

Predictive analytics in Human Resource Management is emerging as a cornerstone for strategic decision-making and anticipatory action. By leveraging data from employee surveys, performance metrics, engagement scores, and organizational behavior, predictive models can forecast critical outcomes such as employee turnover, burnout risks, and skill development needs. These insights enable HR leaders to proactively address workforce issues such as initiating retention programs for at-risk employees, tailoring learning and development pathways, and fine-tuning recruitment strategies based on projected skill shortages. Tools like SAP SuccessFactors, Oracle HCM Cloud, and Workday use machine learning algorithms to analyze trends over time and provide real-time dashboards that support evidence-based HR practices. For example, predictive analytics can identify departments with high attrition risk and suggest targeted interventions like managerial coaching or flexible work arrangements. In talent acquisition, these tools assess applicant data to predict future performance and cultural fit, aiding in smarter hiring decisions. According to a study by Deloitte, organizations that adopt predictive HR analytics report a 30% increase in productivity and employee satisfaction (www.deloitte.com). However, the application of predictive analytics also introduces ethical challenges related to data privacy, algorithmic bias, and transparency. Ensuring that models are fair, explainable, and do not reinforce historical inequities is critical. Additionally, the human aspect of decision-making must remain central, as predictive tools are only as effective as the judgment of those interpreting them. As predictive analytics continues to evolve, its integration must balance technological precision with ethical stewardship and respect for human dignity.

EMERGING TRENDS IN HUMAN-AI COLLABORATION IN THE FUTURE WORKPLACE

Reframing Human-AI Collaboration

Human-AI collaboration refers to a synergistic relationship where artificial intelligence systems assist rather than replace human capabilities. Instead of viewing AI as a disruptive force that displaces labor, organizations are increasingly adopting the concept of "augmented intelligence," wherein machines enhance human decision-making, creativity, and efficiency. And also, it is inferred that the future of work will not be humans vs. machines but humans with machines. In HR, this means redesigning roles and workflows to balance computational accuracy with empathy and judgment. Effective collaboration requires robust HR frameworks that manage coexistence, not just co-functionality.

Augmentation over Automation

Traditional automation focuses on replacing repetitive, rule-based tasks, but augmentation supports more meaningful employee engagement. AI tools such as chatbots, resume screeners, and learning assistants handle routine functions, freeing HR professionals to focus on strategy and relationship-building. Bastida et al., (2025) indicates that augmentation boosts productivity by up to 30% without sacrificing worker autonomy. Furthermore, it allows for the continuous recalibration of human-machine workflows, ensuring that innovation does not alienate employees but empowers them.

AI-Enabled Talent Acquisition and Onboarding

AI-enhanced recruitment systems leverage Natural Language Processing (NLP) and machine learning to screen candidates, assess behavioral cues during video interviews, and predict organizational fit. Tools such as HireVue, Pymetrics, and XOR are used by firms like Unilever, Deloitte, and Hilton to automate early-stage hiring (Das et al., 2025). However, AI systems are only as fair as their data, prompting companies to involve HR experts in audits for algorithmic bias and compliance. Onboarding is also being reimagined through AI-powered chatbots and interactive modules, creating personalized and scalable welcome experiences for new hires.

Hyper-Personalized Learning and Development

The integration of AI in Learning and Development (L&D) allows organizations to offer tailored training paths based on performance metrics, job roles, and career aspirations. Adaptive learning platforms like IBM's "Your Learning" and Coursera for Business use AI to recommend content in real-time, ensuring relevance and efficiency. This shift from static training calendars to dynamic learning ecosystems significantly improves engagement, retention, and skill adaptability. According to Nagasubramanian (2025) organizations using AI-driven learning pathways report a 50% faster skill acquisition among employees.

Continuous and Contextual Performance Management

Performance management has shifted from annual reviews to continuous, real-time feedback powered by AI tools. Platforms like Betterworks and Lattice analyze data from productivity tools, emails, and feedback forms to identify engagement gaps and performance trends (Zhang & Qian 2025). Yet, human managers remain indispensable for contextual interpretation and emotional support. HR must train managers to act as interpreters of AI-generated insights, ensuring a performance culture that values both data and human connection.

AI in Strategic Decision-Making

Strategic HR decisions such as succession planning, workforce optimization, and diversity initiatives now rely heavily on predictive analytics. Tools like Microsoft Viva Insights and SAP Success Factors combine demographic, performance, and behavioral data to forecast workforce risks and opportunities. AI facilitates simulation modeling, enabling HR to test scenarios before implementing changes. However, transparency in algorithmic reasoning and inclusive stakeholder engagement are critical to ensure legitimacy and trust in AI-supported decisions.

Addressing Psychological Impacts and Building Trust

Employee anxiety about AI adoption ranging from surveillance concerns to fear of replacement must be addressed through ethical HR practices. Transparent communication, clear AI usage policies, and the ability to challenge AI decisions are key to psychological safety. Lansing et al., (2023) found that trust in workplace AI increases significantly when companies involve employees in implementation processes. HR's role includes facilitating AI literacy, addressing emotional concerns, and framing AI as a partner, not a threat.

Reengineering Competency Frameworks for Hybrid Workforces

With AI integration, the required skillsets for HR and employees are evolving. Technical literacy, ethical reasoning, data interpretation, and collaboration with AI systems are now critical competencies. Forward-looking HR departments are redesigning competency frameworks to prioritize hybrid capabilities those that combine human strengths with machine efficiency. For instance, Accenture's Future Skills Framework includes "AI collaboration" as a core skill, training employees to evaluate and enhance machine-driven outputs.

Governance, Ethics, and Accountability

Human-AI collaboration demands rigorous governance structures. Organizations must adopt ethical frameworks and governance standards like ISO/IEC 38507 (AI Governance) to monitor AI tools. Key elements include fairness audits, impact assessments, algorithmic transparency, and grievance redressal mechanisms. Firms such as PwC and Salesforce have established internal AI ethics boards to oversee the development and deployment of HR technologies. These bodies ensure that AI use aligns with organizational values, legal norms, and global ethical standards.

BRIDGING HUMAN-CENTERED VALUES WITH DIGITAL TRANSFORMATION IN HRM

As digital transformation accelerates across organizations, HR leaders must navigate the tension between technological advancement and preserving human-centric workplace values. While AI, automation, and analytics improve efficiency, they risk undermining empathy, inclusion, and trust if not ethically implemented. And also, algorithms in HR can dehumanize decisions unless embedded with fairness protocols and subject to human oversight. Furthermore, the need for explain-ability and auditability in digital HR systems to avoid opaque decision-making. Organizations must also invest in digital inclusion ensuring equitable access to training, tools, and connectivity for all employees, particularly for those in rural, low-income, or disabled populations. Furthermore, it is emphasized that the digital divide can widen existing workplace inequalities if unaddressed. Moreover, fostering psychological safety and well-being in virtual environments requires HR to incorporate emotional intelligence into leadership development and communication strategies (Zhang & Chen 2024). Embedding ethical design, transparent feedback loops, and participatory governance into HR tech adoption ensures that digital transformation uplifts, rather than displaces, the human spirit in work. This emerging perspective enriches the strategic role of HR as both a technology enabler and a guardian of organizational ethics and humanity.

Reconstructing Ethical AI Governance in HRM

The rapid deployment of AI tools in HR practices from resume screening to performance analytics demands robust ethical governance. Without clear guidelines, algorithmic decisions risk amplifying bias and eroding trust. As noted by the AI Now Institute, embedding ethical principles such as accountability, transparency, and non-discrimination into AI design is critical. Organizations like Google and Accenture have implemented AI ethics boards to oversee internal practices, which could be a model for HR functions. The ISO/IEC 38507 standard offers frameworks for digital governance that HR departments can align with. Furthermore, ethical AI governance must be participatory, involving diverse stakeholders from various backgrounds to mitigate systemic bias (Andrieux et al., 2024). Regular auditing of AI outputs and establishing channels for employee feedback help ensure fairness. By designing HR systems that are not only intelligent but also morally sound, companies can secure long-term employee trust and social legitimacy. Ethical AI governance in HR is no longer optional—it is an operational imperative in the e-economy.

Digital Empathy and the Future of Leadership

In an age dominated by remote collaboration and virtual tools, leaders are challenged to maintain emotional connection and trust without physical presence. Digital empathy—the ability to sense, understand, and respond to employees' emotional needs in online settings—is emerging as a vital leadership skill. Feigenbaum, (2022) highlights that empathetic leadership correlates with higher employee retention and psychological safety. Tools like virtual town halls, sentiment analysis, and real-time feedback platforms aid leaders in staying connected. Moreover, leadership training must now incorporate modules on managing digital stress, recognizing virtual burnout, and cultivating inclusion in hybrid teams. Organizations such as Microsoft and Salesforce have restructured leadership development programs to include digital empathy as a core capability. By humanizing digital communication and prioritizing mental well-being, leaders become enablers of trust and resilience. As workspaces continue to decentralize, empathetic leadership becomes the bedrock of digital transformation.

Building Inclusive Digital Infrastructure

Inclusive HRM in the e-economy demands digital systems that are accessible to all employees, regardless of socioeconomic background, location, or ability. The digital divide still excludes millions from equitable participation in digitally transformed workplaces. Feng & Qi, (2024) says that women, older employees, and workers in developing regions face significant digital access barriers. To counter this, companies must invest in adaptive technologies, mobile-first learning platforms, and multilingual content. Accessibility standards such as WCAG (Web Content Accessibility Guidelines) must be built into HR software. Programs like Unilever's virtual inclusive hiring initiatives and TCS's remote onboarding for rural candidates show the value of inclusive digital design. HR must also ensure that digital upskilling is not one-size-fits-all but tailored to the diverse needs of their workforce.

Ultimately, inclusive digital infrastructure ensures equity, boosts engagement, and drives organizational innovation.

Psychological Safety in Tech-Mediated Workplaces

Psychological safety the belief that one can speak up, make mistakes, and be their authentic self without fear of negative consequences is essential in high-performing teams. In digital and remote settings, this sense of safety can be fragile. Digital HR systems must be designed to support anonymous feedback, employee listening, and equitable performance reviews. Slack channels for peer appreciation, anonymous suggestion boxes, and inclusive virtual on boarding are small steps that build trust. HR must train managers to recognize and respond to signs of disengagement and stress in virtual interactions. Furthermore, transparent communication from leadership during times of change helps sustain collective morale. By embedding psychological safety in digital environments, organizations build resilient, inclusive, and high-trust cultures.

Participatory HR Technology Design

Traditional HR technologies were often built without end-user input, leading to systems that are efficient but impersonal or difficult to navigate. Participatory design invites employees into the process of shaping HR tools, ensuring the solutions are user-friendly, contextually relevant, and inclusive. Participatory systems lead to higher adoption rates and employee satisfaction. Companies like SAP and Workday now involve employees in co-designing workflows, dashboards, and learning modules. Design thinking approaches empathy mapping, prototyping, and iterative feedback ensure that tech solutions align with real employee needs. Participatory HR design also democratizes innovation, encouraging a culture of continuous improvement (Rogers et al., 2022). As organizations evolve, building HR tech that reflects the lived realities of diverse workers ensures both ethical integrity and functional effectiveness.

DIGITAL DISRUPTION IN HRM: FROM HIERARCHIES TO PLATFORMS

Digital disruption in HRM means the revolutionary effect of technology on the policies, practices, and philosophies that operate human capital management. Hierarchical structures are being substituted or augmented by nimble, platform-based workplaces. This change is most manifest in the ascendance of remote work, gig labor, and distributed teams that depend on collaboration tools in real time.

Remote Work and Virtual Teams

Remote work and virtual teams have become a cornerstone of the digital workplace, accelerated by the COVID-19 pandemic but rooted in over a decade of technological advancement. The global health crisis served as a tipping point, pushing organizations to rapidly adopt remote work models that had previously been developing through innovations in digital infrastructure. Platforms such as Zoom, Slack, Microsoft Teams, and Google Meet have become essential for enabling real-time and asynchronous collaboration across geographies. These tools facilitate seamless communication, cloud-based file sharing, and virtual project management, allowing teams to maintain productivity irrespective of physical location. According to Kilcullen 2022, over 58% of employees in advanced economies prefer hybrid work models, demonstrating a cultural shift in expectations around workplace flexibility. Moreover, asynchronous communication through recorded meetings, collaborative documents, and task boards has redefined performance metrics and employee autonomy. HR departments have responded by redesigning performance evaluations, wellness programs, and training systems to suit virtual contexts. Virtual team dynamics now emphasize trust, autonomy, and digital fluency as key competencies. As organizations reimagine workplace culture, remote work is not just a contingency plan but a strategic asset that enhances access to diverse talent pools, reduces overhead costs, and promotes a more inclusive and resilient workforce model.

Gig Economy and Platform Labour

The rise of the gig economy and platform-based labor has introduced a paradigm shift in employment models across global markets. Freelancers, independent contractors, and gig workers now constitute a significant and growing segment of the workforce, facilitated by digital platforms such as Upwork, Fiverr, Uber, TaskRabbit, and Deliveroo. These platforms enable task-based work arrangements governed largely by algorithmic management, wherein software determines job allocation, ratings, compensation, and even deactivation. While this model offers flexibility and autonomy to workers, it also presents complex challenges related to job security, social protection, and labor rights. The classification of gig workers often as independent contractors rather than employees has sparked intense legal and ethical debates around fair compensation, access to benefits, and collective bargaining rights. It is found that, underscores the precarious nature of gig work, noting disparities in income stability, occupational safety, and upward mobility. Simultaneously, platform companies are experimenting with hybrid models that offer limited benefits while preserving operational flexibility (Altenried 2022). As the gig economy matures, HRM must evolve to accommodate alternative work arrangements by redefining metrics of performance, engagement, and equity within decentralized workforces. This trend demands that organizations balance technological efficiency with human-centered policies that ensure dignity, inclusion, and sustainable livelihoods for all workers in the digital era.

Algorithmic Management

Algorithmic management has become a defining feature of digital-era workplaces, where data-driven systems are increasingly used to make critical human resource decisions. From task allocation and shift scheduling to performance evaluation and contract termination, algorithms now play a central role in managing labor. While these systems promise efficiency, scalability, and objectivity, they also raise significant concerns about fairness, accountability, and transparency. Kinowska & Sienkiewicz (2023) warn that algorithmic decision-making can replicate and amplify existing biases especially when trained on historical or incomplete data resulting in discriminatory outcomes that disproportionately affect marginalized groups. For instance, algorithmic systems used in recruitment have been found to favor certain demographics while penalizing gaps in employment history. Furthermore, the opacity of algorithmic logic, often termed the "black box" problem, makes it difficult for workers to understand how decisions are made or to contest them. This lack of transparency can erode trust and reduce employee morale. As workplaces transition from rigid hierarchies to fluid, decentralized digital platforms, HR policies must evolve accordingly. There is a pressing need for robust governance frameworks that include ethical auditing, algorithmic transparency, worker input, and regulatory oversight. Integrating digital literacy, accountability mechanisms, and human-in-the-loop models can help ensure that technology enhances rather than undermines human agency. Ultimately, aligning algorithmic management with core values such as fairness, dignity, and inclusiveness is essential for building sustainable, resilient, and people-centric workplaces in the age of automation.

THE CHANGING PSYCHOLOGICAL CONTRACT

The psychological contract represents the unwritten rules between employees and employers. In the e-economy, the psychological contract is being fundamentally reshaped.

Transition from Job Security to Employability

The transition from job security to employability reflects a fundamental shift in the psychological contract between employers and employees in the digital era. Unlike previous generations who often expected lifetime employment, today's workers prioritize continuous learning, adaptability, and career mobility over static roles and long-term job tenure. This paradigm shift is driven by rapid technological advancements, the rise of non-traditional work models such as gig and freelance labor, and the accelerating pace of industry disruption. As automation and AI render certain skills obsolete, employees increasingly seek opportunities for upskilling, reskilling, and credentialing to remain competitive in the job market (Doden et al., 2024). Employers, in turn, are recognizing that their long-term success hinges not on job preservation, but on building a future-ready workforce equipped with dynamic skill sets. Programs such as lifelong learning initiatives, micro-credential platforms, and partnerships with educational institutions have become central to progressive HR strategies. Countries like Singapore, through initiatives such as Skills-Future, exemplify how public-private collaboration can create scalable models of employability-focused workforce development.

Flexibility and Autonomy

Flexibility and autonomy have become core expectations of the modern workforce, particularly in the post-pandemic e-economy. Employees increasingly value the ability to choose when, where, and how they work, seeking arrangements that support a healthier work-life balance and greater personal agency. This cultural shift is reshaping the psychological contract between workers and organizations, emphasizing trust, output-driven evaluations, and self-management over rigid schedules and physical attendance. Remote work, compressed workweeks, and Results -Only Work Environments (ROWEs) are examples of models that prioritize flexibility without compromising performance. According to Becker et al., (2022), over 70% of employees cite flexible work arrangements as a top consideration in job selection and satisfaction. Autonomy not only enhances employee well-being and engagement but also drives innovation by allowing individuals to tailor their workflows to their strengths and preferences. However, to implement flexible work successfully, organizations must invest in digital infrastructure, establish clear performance metrics, and foster a culture of accountability and inclusion. HR leaders play a crucial role in ensuring that flexible policies are equitable, accessible across roles and functions, and supported by inclusive leadership practices. By embedding flexibility and autonomy into their talent strategies, organizations can attract diverse talent, improve retention, and remain competitive in a rapidly changing labor market.

Trust and Transparency

Trust and transparency have emerged as critical enablers of engagement and loyalty in the digitally transformed workplace. In an era where algorithms, data analytics, and remote interactions shape the employment experience, employees are demanding greater clarity around how decisions are made and how their data is used. Open communication, clearly defined policies, and consistent, ethical leadership behaviors form the bedrock of the modern psychological contract between employer and employee. When workers feel informed and included in organizational changes especially those related to performance assessments, surveillance practices, or AI-driven decision-making they are more likely to feel valued and motivated. Organizations with high levels of trust experience greater collaboration, innovation, and retention. HR leaders must champion transparency by involving employees in policy development, providing access to performance metrics, and demystifying the technologies influencing their careers. Moreover, feedback loops and grievance redressal mechanisms must be accessible and effective, ensuring that employee voices are heard and acted upon. By fostering a culture grounded in openness and mutual respect, HR can transform trust from a passive expectation into an active driver of organizational resilience and success.

Recognition and Belonging

Recognition and belonging are essential for nurturing engagement and loyalty in increasingly virtual and hybrid work environments. With fewer in-person interactions, employees may feel isolated or overlooked, making intentional strategies for acknowledgment and inclusion more important than ever. Digital recognition platforms such as Kudos, Bonusly, and Workhuman help ensure that appreciation is timely, visible, and accessible across geographical boundaries. These tools allow peers and managers to acknowledge contributions publicly, reinforcing a culture of gratitude and motivation. Alongside these, Diversity, Equity, and Inclusion (DEI) programs are vital in fostering a sense of belonging among all employees, particularly those from underrepresented groups. According to Byrd (2022), employees who feel a strong sense of belonging are more likely to remain committed, contribute innovative ideas, and perform at higher levels. In addition, cultivating psychological safety where individuals can express themselves without fear of judgment—further strengthens the workplace community. HR must lead with empathy and design recognition and inclusion initiatives that reflect the evolving aspirations and identities of the modern workforce. The dynamic psychological contract now requires not just economic incentives, but emotional affirmation and a humane approach that makes every worker feel seen, valued, and connected.

EMPLOYEE ENGAGEMENT

Technology-driven change calls for new thinking about employee engagement and organizational learning.

Digital Engagement Strategies

Digital engagement strategies have become integral in maintaining employee motivation and connection in the era of remote and hybrid work. Traditional engagement surveys are giving way to real-time analytics, allowing HR teams to monitor sentiment, productivity, and satisfaction through platforms such as Culture Amp, Glint, and Office vibe. Gamification integrating game elements into work processes encourages participation and enthusiasm by turning goals and milestones into interactive experiences. Leader boards, badges, and progress bars are used to motivate individuals and teams in a non-coercive manner. Additionally, social recognition tools enable timely and peer-driven acknowledgment, reinforcing positive behavior and achievement. Immediate feedback systems, powered by AI and machine learning, help employees understand their strengths and development areas continuously rather than waiting for annual appraisals. These systems create an environment where feedback is constructive, ongoing, and embedded in everyday workflows. Moreover, engagement metrics now include behavioral insights such as collaboration frequency, meeting fatigue, and digital wellness indicators. By leveraging these tools, HR can design interventions that are timely, personalized, and effective. Ultimately, digital engagement strategies ensure that employees feel connected, empowered, and aligned with organizational goals regardless of where they work.

Mental Health and Well-being

Mental health and well-being have become foundational concerns in the digital workplace, as employees face increasing levels of stress, burnout, and digital fatigue. The isolation associated with remote work, constant connectivity, and blurred boundaries between work and personal life have all contributed to a rise in mental health challenges. HR leaders are now prioritizing holistic wellness strategies that integrate technology with compassion. Virtual counseling services, wellness apps like Calm and Headspace, and telehealth platforms have emerged as vital tools to support employees' emotional and psychological needs. Flexible working schedules, mandatory screen breaks, and digital detox policies are being introduced to combat burnout and promote work-life balance. In addition, organizations are promoting mental health awareness through internal campaigns, mental health first aid training, and leadership development programs focused on empathy and emotional intelligence. Creating a psychologically safe environment where employees can openly discuss their struggles without stigma is key to cultivating a resilient and supportive culture. In this context, HR's role transcends traditional personnel management—it becomes a central architect of humane, health-focused, and sustainable work environments in the e-economy.

Micro-learning and Just-in-Time Training

Micro-learning and just-in-time training are redefining corporate learning strategies to align with the agility demands of the e-economy. These bite-sized, easily digestible learning modules are designed to fit into the flow of daily work, allowing employees to upskill without stepping away from their core responsibilities. Typically delivered through mobile apps or cloud-based platforms, micro-learning supports continuous and personalized education by offering content on-demand, whether it's a five-minute video, infographic, or interactive quiz. Micro-learning leads to better knowledge retention compared to traditional long-form training sessions. Just-in-time learning is particularly effective in dynamic work environments where immediate application of knowledge is critical such as troubleshooting tech tools, understanding new compliance rules, or adapting to role-specific updates. Platforms like LinkedIn Learning, Coursera for Business, and EdCast are increasingly being integrated into HR ecosystems to provide scalable, AI-recommended content tailored to individual learning paths (Nanjappa et al., 2023). Furthermore, integrating gamification and social elements into these modules boosts learner engagement and fosters a culture of lifelong learning. As job roles evolve and reskilling becomes essential, HR must champion micro-learning not as a supplementary feature, but as a core strategy to build a nimble, empowered, and future-ready workforce.

Knowledge Management Systems

Knowledge Management Systems (KMS) are playing a pivotal role in capturing, organizing, and disseminating institutional knowledge across digital organizations. In the context of the e-economy, where teams are often geographically dispersed and project-based, tools like Confluence, Notion, and Microsoft SharePoint act as centralized repositories for documents, best practices, training materials, and collaborative updates. These platforms enable employees to access knowledge in real time, contribute to shared resources, and engage in peer-to-peer learning, thereby fostering a culture of transparency and collective intelligence. According to Simon et al., (2022), efficient knowledge-sharing systems can reduce the time employees spend searching for information by up to 35%, significantly enhancing productivity. Beyond static documentation, modern KMS platforms integrate with chat tools and project management software to ensure that knowledge flows dynamically as work progresses. HR departments can leverage KMS to support on-boarding, continuous learning, and internal mobility by providing employees with structured access to critical organizational know-how. When implemented effectively, these systems not only preserve institutional memory but also empower employees to innovate, collaborate, and respond swiftly to change. As knowledge becomes a primary asset in the digital age, HR's role in curating and evolving knowledge ecosystems becomes essential to organizational agility and competitiveness.

Leadership Development

Leadership development is undergoing a profound transformation in response to the demands of the digital workplace. As organizations embrace remote work, cross-cultural teams, and agile methodologies, traditional hierarchical leadership models are proving inadequate. Instead, the focus is shifting to building adaptable, emotionally intelligent, and inclusive leaders who can inspire diverse and geographically dispersed teams. Online leadership development programs, offered through platforms like Harvard Manage Mentor, Udemy for Business, and BetterUp, are equipping emerging and existing leaders with critical skills such as virtual communication, empathy, change management, and digital fluency. Virtual mentoring and reverse mentoring initiatives are fostering cross-generational and cross-functional knowledge exchange, contributing to a more inclusive leadership pipeline. Furthermore, with robust leadership development pipelines are 1.5 times more likely to outperform their peers in areas such as innovation, employee retention, and business growth Byrne et al., (2022). HR departments play a strategic role in embedding leadership development into organizational culture by aligning it with performance metrics, succession planning, and values-driven decision-making. Moreover, integrating AI-powered learning analytics enables HR to personalize leadership journeys, track progress, and optimize interventions in real time. In an era where leadership agility is a strategic asset, HR must champion a continuous learning ethos and foster environments where leaders are empowered to adapt, collaborate, and guide their teams through digital disruption and transformation.

BENEFITS OF AI IN HR FUNCTIONS FOR E-ECONOMY

Ali et al., (2023) have identified the following benefits of AI in HR functions in the e-economy. They are.

Informs Future-Ready HR Practices

Organizations today face rapid technological disruptions, evolving employee expectations, and global talent competition. Future-ready HR practices prioritize adaptability, agility, and innovation through real-time data and AI-based tools. Digital solutions like AI-driven recruitment and predictive analytics are reshaping talent management. Companies such as IBM and Unilever have adopted these practices through hybrid models and digital learning platforms. These innovations position HR as a core driver of sustainable success in the e-economy.

Supports Strategic Decision-Making

By leveraging insights from digital HR tools and global workforce trends, HR leaders and policymakers are better positioned to make informed, data-driven decisions. Analytics significantly influenced their workforce planning. AI and predictive modeling now support decisions on hiring, learning investments, and employee retention strategies. For example, IBM's Watson Analytics enables HR departments to forecast turnover and skill gaps. Additionally, the growing need for real-time employee feedback to guide leadership actions. Strategic HR decisions are increasingly based on dashboards, engagement analytics, and behavioral insights. These technologies transform HR from a support function into a strategic partner in organizational growth. As a result, this research provides frameworks that guide HR professionals toward future-oriented and evidence-based practices.

Addresses Ethical and Social Implications

As digital tools become more embedded in HR functions, ethical and social concerns grow increasingly complex. Issues such as algorithmic bias in recruitment software, invasive employee surveillance, and the digital divide disproportionately affect marginalized groups. Lack of diversity in data sets and opaque algorithms can reinforce workplace discrimination. Employees are more willing to adopt HR tech when ethical use and transparency are clearly communicated. Furthermore, digital inequality where access to technology and skills varies can exclude vulnerable workers from upskilling opportunities. This research urges HR to build human-centered frameworks that embed fairness, equity, and accountability in digital transformation efforts, ensuring no one is left behind.

Enhances Employee Experience and Engagement

As organizations adopt AI and digital platforms, enhancing employee experience has become central to HR success. Predictive analytics tools help identify disengaged employees and tailor interventions, as highlighted in reports by PwC and Deloitte. HR chatbots like IBM's Watson Assistant provide instant responses to employee queries, improving service quality and accessibility. Microlearning platforms such as EdCast and Coursera enhance skill development through personalization, increasing employee satisfaction. Real-time feedback systems and recognition apps also contribute to a sense of belonging and motivation. These innovations foster a more responsive, personalized, and engaging work environment. As employee expectations shift toward flexibility and empowerment, digital HR tools play a crucial role in shaping positive workplace experiences

Guides Policy and Organizational Reform

The integration of case studies from global corporations and public-sector initiatives provides a foundational basis for reshaping HR policies in the digital age. For instance, Singapore's SkillsFuture initiative demonstrates how government-led reskilling programs can be co-financed by private firms to address emerging skill gaps. Similarly, the European Union's implementation of the "Right to Disconnect" law underscores the importance of mental health in remote work policies. Cross-sector collaboration is essential in aligning HR innovation with ethical and societal goals. Case studies from companies like Infosys and Unilever reveal how ethical AI and inclusive hiring practices can be embedded into scalable HR frameworks. These real-world examples offer actionable insights for developing HR policies that are not only efficient but also socially responsible. The research encourages HR practitioners to adopt flexible, tech-enabled, and regulation-compliant frameworks for sustainable transformation.

ETHICAL AND HUMAN-CENTERED CHALLENGES

As HRM becomes increasingly driven by technology, ethical dilemmas have surfaced that require urgent attention. Human-centered challenges involve not only the impact on individual employees but also broader implications for organizational culture and social equity. Ozmen et al., (2023) have mentioned the following ethical and human centered challenges in the organization.

Data Privacy and Surveillance

Data privacy and surveillance in digital HR ecosystems represent one of the most pressing ethical challenges in the e-economy. As organizations adopt increasingly sophisticated technologies to monitor performance and optimize workflows, they often gather extensive personal data, including keystroke dynamics, biometric records, geolocation tracking, facial recognition, and behavioral analytics. While such data can provide valuable insights into productivity and engagement, the boundary between surveillance and support is easily crossed when employees are monitored without clear consent or awareness. This surveillance can have a chilling effect on workplace morale, trust, and psychological safety, particularly when data collection practices are opaque or intrusive. To address these concerns, HR departments must establish transparent data governance policies rooted in legal compliance and ethical responsibility. HR leaders must work closely with legal and IT teams to ensure that surveillance technologies are deployed responsibly, with clear boundaries on what data is collected, how it is used, and who has access. Employee communication and digital literacy are equally critical, empowering individuals to understand and navigate their rights in data-driven workplaces. Ultimately, safeguarding data privacy is not merely a compliance issue but a core element of maintaining human dignity, trust, and fairness in the future of work.

Algorithmic Bias

Algorithmic bias poses a substantial ethical and operational risk in the application of artificial intelligence within Human Resource Management. AI systems, by design, learn from historical datasets, which often reflect existing societal and organizational biases. As a result, algorithms trained on such data may inadvertently perpetuate discrimination based on race, gender, age, or educational background especially in recruitment, performance evaluation, and promotion decisions. High-profile cases, such as Amazon's discontinued AI recruiting tool that favored male applicants, highlight the consequences of unexamined biases in algorithmic design. This issue becomes even more critical when AI decisions lack transparency, making it difficult to trace or correct biased outcomes. To address these risks, organizations must institute regular audits of AI systems using fairness metrics, bias-detection tools, and third-party evaluations. Engaging interdisciplinary teams including ethicists, data scientists, legal experts, and HR professionals during the design and implementation stages is also vital.

Loss of Human Connections

The loss of human connection represents a growing concern in increasingly automated HR environments. As organizations implement AI-powered chatbots, virtual onboarding modules, and automated performance feedback tools, the traditional human touch that once defined employee-employer relationships is gradually being diminished. While these technologies offer efficiency and scalability, they risk depersonalizing critical HR functions such as employee induction, conflict resolution, and emotional support. For instance, virtual onboarding often lacks the informal social cues and relational depth of in-person introductions, which are vital for building trust and a sense of belonging. Automated feedback systems, although timely, may fail to capture the nuances of employee performance and personal circumstances, leading to a perception of mechanistic evaluation. Human empathy, recognition, and interpersonal engagement significantly influence employee morale, retention, and organizational commitment. To counteract this erosion of connection, organizations must design digital HR tools that are empathetic, inclusive, and capable of facilitating genuine interaction. This could involve incorporating AI systems with sentiment analysis capabilities, offering hybrid onboarding experiences, and ensuring that employees have access to real-time human support when needed.

Inequality and Digital Divide

Inequality and the digital divide present a significant barrier to inclusive digital transformation in Human Resource Management. Not all employees have equal access to high-speed internet, digital devices, or the digital literacy required to navigate sophisticated platforms. This disparity is particularly acute in rural areas, developing countries, and among lower-income or older workers, exacerbating pre-existing inequalities in the workforce. As organizations shift to remote work models and digital learning environments, those without access risk being marginalized or excluded from opportunities for advancement, training, or even basic participation. Furthermore, employees with disabilities may face additional accessibility challenges if platforms are not designed with universal usability in mind. To address this, companies must invest in inclusive infrastructure such as device provisioning programs, subsidized internet access, and user-friendly interfaces and provide ongoing digital literacy training. Partnerships with governments and NGOs can further extend digital inclusion efforts. Crucially, HR leaders must ensure that digital transformation strategies are designed through the lens of equity, ensuring that no employee is left behind in the transition to tech-enabled work. Promoting digital access as a fundamental workplace right is essential for building resilient, fair, and inclusive organizations in the e-economy.

Transparency and Accountability

Transparency and accountability are essential pillars of ethical and effective digital HRM, particularly as organizations increasingly rely on algorithms and data-driven tools for decision-making. When decisions about hiring, promotions, performance evaluations, or disciplinary actions are made through opaque systems, employees may feel disempowered and distrustful. Black-box algorithms whose inner workings are not transparent—can undermine employee morale and create perceptions of unfairness, especially when outcomes are unfavorable or difficult to understand. To uphold trust, HR departments must adopt practices that ensure explainability in automated decision-making. This includes providing employees with clear, comprehensible explanations of how decisions are reached, the criteria used by algorithms, and the mechanisms available for appeal or review. Leading organizations are now embedding transparency protocols, such as algorithmic impact assessments and open data audits, into their HR processes.

CASE STUDIES AND SUCCESS STORIES

The popular organizations worldwide are leading digital HR revolutions that provide useful takeaways. They are.

Infosys (India)

Infosys has emerged as a leading example of digital transformation in Human Resource Management by leveraging AI and cloud technologies to enhance employee experiences and organizational agility. One of its flagship innovations is the 'Lex' digital learning platform, which offers personalized, on-demand, and multilingual training resources to employees globally. The platform uses artificial intelligence to recommend content based on individual learning patterns, job roles, and performance data, thus promoting lifelong learning and skill advancement. According to Infosys' annual sustainability report and various industry whitepapers, 'Lex' supports over 1.2 million learning sessions monthly and contributes directly to employee reskilling and mobility (Aithal & Rao 2024). Additionally, Infosys has adopted AI-enabled performance management systems that automate routine HR tasks, generate predictive insights about workforce trends, and enable more objective evaluations. The company also uses digital dashboards to monitor employee engagement and retention, ensuring that HR interventions are data-driven and timely.

IBM (USA)

IBM (USA) has emerged as a global leader in leveraging cognitive technologies to enhance HR decision-making and employee engagement. Central to this strategy is IBM's integration of its Watson AI platform into various facets of human resource functions. Watson is utilized to analyze large volumes of employee data to gauge sentiment, identify workforce trends, and predict attrition risks with high accuracy. By evaluating unstructured data from employee surveys, emails, and feedback systems, Watson provides nuanced insights into morale and engagement levels, enabling timely and personalized HR interventions. IBM's data-driven approach to HR minimizes unconscious bias in talent decisions and supports inclusive hiring and promotion practices (Rajeev et al., 2025). For instance, predictive analytics are employed to recommend career development opportunities tailored to individual aspirations and performance histories. Furthermore, IBM uses AI to streamline administrative tasks such as onboarding, benefits management, and training support, freeing up HR professionals to focus on strategic planning. This commitment to AI-powered, evidence-based HR practices underscores IBM's vision of a transparent, equitable, and agile workforce aligned with the demands of the digital economy.

Unilever (Global)

Unilever (Global) has embraced a digitally inclusive HR strategy that integrates advanced technologies with ethical and socially responsible practices. A key component of its approach is the use of AI-powered blind recruitment tools designed to minimize unconscious bias in the hiring process. These systems anonymize candidate data such as names, gender, and educational background to focus purely on skill and potential, thereby fostering a more equitable selection process. Unilever has also adopted gamified assessments and neuroscience-based tools to evaluate candidates' cognitive abilities and behavioral traits, ensuring that recruitment is both inclusive and scientifically grounded. Furthermore, the company emphasizes the ethical use of AI and is committed to principles that safeguard human rights, transparency, and data privacy.

Trends in Remote Work Policies in the EU

A significant policy trend shaping the European Union's approach to remote work is the institutionalization of the "right to disconnect." This legal framework, adopted or proposed in countries such as France, Spain, and Ireland, ensures that employees are not expected to engage in work-related communications outside of official working hours. The initiative is a response to the intensification of digital work and the associated risks of burnout, stress, and work-life imbalance. According to a Russo (2023), the right to disconnect is critical for protecting workers' mental health and fundamental rights in the digital age. The legislation mandates that employers respect downtime and prohibits retaliation against employees who assert this right. The policy aligns with broader EU directives aimed at promoting decent working conditions in an increasingly remote and hybrid work environment. Research from the European Foundation for the Improvement of Living and Working Conditions (Eurofound) further supports this shift, noting that structured disconnection policies can lead to improved well-being, higher productivity, and reduced turnover. As telework becomes normalized across sectors, the EU's proactive stance exemplifies how public policy can safeguard employee well-being while adapting to the evolving nature of work.

Trend – Government-Driven Skilling in Singapore

Singapore represents a leading example of government-led digital skilling initiatives designed to equip its workforce for the demands of the digital economy. The Singaporean government, through its national program "SkillsFuture," promotes lifelong learning by offering citizens a range of subsidized training opportunities in emerging fields such as artificial intelligence, cybersecurity, and data analytics. The program is structured around a co-funding model in which corporations partner with the government to upskill employees and future-proof their talent pools. According to reports from Singapore's Ministry of Manpower and SkillsFuture Singapore Agency, more than half a million Singaporeans have benefited from the scheme, with employers actively integrating these certifications into their HR practices (https://www.mom.gov.sg/). The initiative's success lies in its alignment of economic policy with human development, ensuring that workforce transformation is both inclusive and forward-looking. Furthermore, the scalability and accountability of digital HRM are enhanced through outcome tracking and sector-specific benchmarks. These efforts illustrate that with strategic vision, ethical alignment, and collaborative governance, digital HRM can be both effective and equitable in driving national competitiveness and social resilience in a fast-evolving global labor market.

CONCLUSION

The e-economy has revolutionized the Human Resource Management landscape. From technical innovation to moral disruption, the changes call for new competencies, structures, and mind sets. With AI, block chain, and virtual workspaces becoming part of the modern enterprise, HR has to become a steward of both innovation and humanity. This chapter has shown that whereas technology has vast potential, it needs to be anchored in values of fairness, transparency, and inclusivity. The future of HRM is about embracing that double role to use digital tools while maintaining human agency. For policymakers, the challenge is to design regulations that safeguard employees without inhibiting creativity. For academics, the potential is to examine the psychological and social effects of digital HRM. And for managers, the challenge is to reinterpret HR not as an auxiliary function, but as a central strategic driver of organizational performance in the knowledge economy. In so doing, the researchers can together build a future of work that is fair, rewarding, and resilient.

Table 2. Abbreviations

HRM	**Human Resource Management**
HR	Human Resources
AI	Artificial Intelligence
NLP	Natural Language Processing
ML	Machine Learning
DEI	Diversity, Equity, and Inclusion
WCAG	Web Content Accessibility Guidelines
UNESCO	United Nations Educational, Scientific and Cultural Organization
OECD	Organisation for Economic Co-operation and Development
GDPR	General Data Protection Regulation
ISO	International Organization for Standardization
IEC	International Electro technical Commission
TCS	Tata Consultancy Services
SAP	Systems, Applications, and Products in Data Processing

REFERENCES

Aithal, P. S., & Rao, A. S. (2024). Infosys: A Case Study of IT Service Evolution, Technology Adoption & Innovation Strategies. [PIJTRCS]. *Poornaprajna International Journal of Teaching & Research Case Studies*, *1*(2), 77–129.

Ali, O., Krsteska, K., Said, D., & Momin, M. (2023). Advanced technologies enabled human resources functions: Benefits, challenges, and functionalities: A systematic review. *Cogent Business & Management*, *10*(2), 2216430. DOI: 10.1080/23311975.2023.2216430

Altenried, M. (2022). Platforms, labour, and mobility: migration and the gig economy. In *The Routledge handbook of the gig economy* (pp. 180–189). Routledge. DOI: 10.4324/9781003161875-14

Andrieux, P., Johnson, R. D., Sarabadani, J., & Van Slyke, C. (2024). Ethical considerations of generative AI-enabled human resource management. *Organizational Dynamics*, *53*(1), 101032. DOI: 10.1016/j.orgdyn.2024.101032

Bastida, M., García, A. V., Taín, M. Á. V., & Araujo, M. D. R. (2025). From automation to augmentation: Human Resource's journey with Artificial Intelligence. *Journal of Industrial Information Integration*, *46*, 100872. DOI: 10.1016/j.jii.2025.100872

Becker, C., Soucek, R., & Göritz, A. S. (2022). Activity-based working: How the use of available workplace options increases perceived autonomy in the workplace. *Work (Reading, Mass.)*, *73*(4), 1325–1336. DOI: 10.3233/WOR-210767 PMID: 36093664

Byrd, M. Y. (2022). Creating a culture of inclusion and belongingness in remote work environments that sustains meaningful work. *Human Resource Development International*, *25*(2), 145–162. DOI: 10.1080/13678868.2022.2047252

Byrne, V. L., Jardine, H. E., Williams, A. Y., & Donlan, A. E. (2022). Academic peer mentorship as a leadership development experience: Fostering leadership self-efficacy. *Journal of Leadership Education*, *21*(1), 1–12. DOI: 10.12806/V21/I1/R1

Das, R. C., Basavaraj, S., Thankachan, J., & Thaliyan, D. (2025). The Impact of AI and Agile HR on Talent Acquisition and Onboarding in the Service Industry. In *AI and Innovation in HRM* (pp. 394–416). Routledge. DOI: 10.4324/9781003522157-24

Davidaviciene, V., & Al Majzoub, K. (2022). The effect of cultural intelligence, conflict, and transformational leadership on decision-making processes in virtual teams. *Social Sciences (Basel, Switzerland)*, *11*(2), 64. DOI: 10.3390/socsci11020064

. Dawra, S., Pathak, V., & Sharma, S. (2024). Artificial Intelligence (AI) and Green Human Resource Management (GHRM) Practices: A Systemic Review. Green Management: A New Paradigm in the World of Business, 83-96.

Deloitte. (2024). AI-Powered Employee Experience: How Organisations Can Unlock Higher Engagement and Productivity https://www.deloitte.com/uk/en/services/consulting/blogs/2024/ai-powered-employee-experience.html accessed on 07/08/2025.

Doden, W., Grosemans, I., De Cuyper, N., Tschopp, C., & Grote, G. (2024). Employability in the post-job security era: Testing competing effects of perceived job insecurity on perceived employability change. *European Journal of Work and Organizational Psychology*, *33*(1), 11–23. DOI: 10.1080/1359432X.2023.2263201

Feigenbaum, E. (2022). Leadership, Empathy, and Inclusion. In Sustainability and the Future of Work and Entrepreneurship for the Underserved (pp. 1-18). IGI Global Scientific Publishing.

Feng, J., & Qi, S. (2024). Digital infrastructure expansion and economic growth in Asian countries. *Journal of Business and Economic Options*, *7*(2), 27–32.

Kilcullen, M., Feitosa, J., & Salas, E. (2022). Insights from the virtual team science: Rapid deployment during COVID-19. *Human Factors*, *64*(8), 1429–1440. DOI: 10.1177/0018720821991678 PMID: 33611964

Kinowska, H., & Sienkiewicz, Ł. J. (2023). Influence of algorithmic management practices on workplace well-being–evidence from European organisations. *Information Technology & People*, *36*(8), 21–42. DOI: 10.1108/ITP-02-2022-0079

Lansing, A. E., Romero, N. J., Siantz, E., Silva, V., Center, K., Casteel, D., & Gilmer, T. (2023). Building trust: Leadership reflections on community empowerment and engagement in a large urban initiative. *BMC Public Health*, *23*(1), 1252. DOI: 10.1186/s12889-023-15860-z PMID: 37380973

Mishra, A., & Raghatate, K. S. (2025, February). Blockchain for Safe Credential Checking in Hiring. In 2025 International Conference on Intelligent Control, Computing and Communications (IC3) (pp. 1006-1012). IEEE. DOI: 10.1109/IC363308.2025.10957402

Nagasubramanian, D. (2025, April). Harnessing Artificial Intelligence to Revolutionize Education: Personalized Learning and Beyond. In International Conference of Global Innovations and Solutions (pp. 395-409). Cham: Springer Nature Switzerland.

Nanjappa, S., Ghosh, V., Acharya, S., Mukerjee, H. S., & Stl, V. (2023). Microlearning in corporate settings: Practitioner perspectives. *Human Resource Development International*, *26*(5), 655–662. DOI: 10.1080/13678868.2022.2160688

Nawaz, N., Arunachalam, H., Pathi, B. K., & Gajenderan, V. (2024). The adoption of artificial intelligence in human resources management practices. *International Journal of Information Management Data Insights*, *4*(1), 100208. DOI: 10.1016/j.jjimei.2023.100208

Nayak, A., Satpathy, I., Patnaik, B. C. M., Baral, S. K., & Khang, A. (2023). Impact of artificial intelligence (AI) on talent management (TM): a futuristic overview. In Designing Workforce Management Systems for Industry 4.0 (pp. 139-158). CRC Press.

. Nimmagadda, S., Surapaneni, R. K., & Potluri, R. M. (2024). Artificial intelligence in HR: employee engagement using Chatbots. Artificial Intelligence Enabled Management: An Emerging Economy Perspective, 147.

Ozmen Garibay, O., Winslow, B., Andolina, S., Antona, M., Bodenschatz, A., Coursaris, C., Falco, G., Fiore, S. M., Garibay, I., Grieman, K., Havens, J. C., Jirotka, M., Kacorri, H., Karwowski, W., Kider, J., Konstan, J., Koon, S., Lopez-Gonzalez, M., Maifeld-Carucci, I., & Xu, W. (2023). Six human-centered artificial intelligence grand challenges. *International Journal of Human-Computer Interaction*, *39*(3), 391–437. DOI: 10.1080/10447318.2022.2153320

Rajeev, K., Raju, S. S., & Rana, V. (2025). Artificial Intelligence in Talent Management Enhancing Recruitment and Workforce Development. In Innovative Approaches for International Competitiveness Through Human Resource Management (pp. 195-220). IGI Global Scientific Publishing. DOI: 10.4018/979-8-3373-1005-3.ch008

Rogers, W. A., Kadylak, T., & Bayles, M. A. (2022). Maximizing the benefits of participatory design for human–robot interaction research with older adults. *Human Factors*, *64*(3), 441–450. DOI: 10.1177/00187208211037465 PMID: 34461761

. Russo, M. (2023). Twenty Years of EU Agreements on Remote Work from 2002 to 2022. What next?.

Simon, C. G. K., Jhanjhi, N. Z., Goh, W. W., & Sukumaran, S. (2022). Applications of machine learning in knowledge management system: A comprehensive review. *Journal of Information & Knowledge Management*, *21*(02), 2250017. DOI: 10.1142/S0219649222500174

Tariq, M. U. (2024). AI and the future of talent management: Transforming recruitment and retention with machine learning. In *Global practices on effective talent acquisition and retention* (pp. 1–16). IGI Global Scientific Publishing. DOI: 10.4018/979-8-3693-1938-3.ch001

Zhang, J., & Chen, Z. (2024). Exploring human resource management digital transformation in the digital age. *Journal of the Knowledge Economy*, *15*(1), 1482–1498. DOI: 10.1007/s13132-023-01214-y PMID: 40479358

Zhang, X., & Qian, J. (2025). A continuous performance management approach: Effects of daily performance management behaviors on leader-member exchange, next-day job attitudes, and job performance. *Applied Psychology*, *74*(1), e12596. DOI: 10.1111/apps.12596

KEY TERMS AND DEFINITIONS

Algorithmic Management: The application of algorithms to oversee workforce operations—assigning tasks, monitoring performance, and making HR decisions—often reducing transparency and accountability.

Blockchain Credentialing: A secure method for issuing and verifying educational and professional credentials, enhancing trust and reducing credential fraud.

Digital Empathy: A leadership skill involving the ability to understand and support employees' emotional and psychological needs in virtual environments.

Digital Transformation in HRM: The strategic adoption of digital technologies in HR functions to improve talent acquisition, employee engagement, workforce analytics, and operational efficiency.

E-Economy: An economy driven by digital technologies, platforms, and real-time data, enabling decentralized operations, remote work, and agile business practices.

Ethical AI in HR: The design and implementation of AI tools in HR that uphold principles of fairness, accountability, and transparency, protecting employee rights and privacy.

Inclusive HRM: Practices that ensure fairness and equal digital access for all employees, addressing barriers caused by location, economic background, or disabilities.

Micro-learning: A modern learning approach featuring short, focused content pieces accessible via digital platforms, promoting continuous and just-in-time learning.

Predictive Analytics: The use of statistical models and AI to predict employee behavior, such as turnover risk, performance trends, and learning needs.

Psychological Contract: The evolving informal agreement between employer and employee encompassing expectations around flexibility, learning opportunities, and personal growth.

Chapter 3
Assessment of Open Innovation Practices Among Micro and Small Enterprises:
An Analysis With Machine Learning and Regression

Koppala Venugopal
http://orcid.org/0000-0002-3472-1477
Aditya Institute of Technology and Management, India

Santosh Neelam Ranganath
http://orcid.org/0000-0002-6508-6613
Dr. B.R. Ambedkar University, Srikakulam, India

Mulugeta Negash Wodage
http://orcid.org/0000-0002-9454-6893
University of Gondar, Ethiopia

Nadiminti Madhu
http://orcid.org/0009-0005-0035-0582
Gayatri College of Science and Management, Srikakulam, India

Deekonda Pranaya
http://orcid.org/0000-0003-0546-7462
Aditya Institute of Technology and Management, India

DOI: 10.4018/979-8-3373-4307-5.ch003

ABSTRACT

This study explores open innovation practices among micro and small enterprises (MSEs) in Srikakulam through predictive analysis using machine learning and regression techniques. Key innovation drivers were identified using feature selection methods such as Information Gain, ANOVA, and Chi-square. Components like customer co-creation, digital platforms, and venture capital access emerged as significant predictors of innovation success. Regression analysis further validated their influence on business growth. The findings offer actionable insights for stakeholders to enhance innovation strategies, foster collaboration, and optimize resource allocation. This data-driven approach strengthens the understanding of innovation dynamics in the MSE sector.

1. INTRODUCTION

Open innovation represents a strategic shift from traditional, insular innovation models to more inclusive approaches that leverage both internal and external knowledge sources. This paradigm has gained substantial traction globally, particularly as businesses confront increasingly complex technological challenges and market uncertainties (Chesbrough, 2003). In India, micro and small enterprises (SMEs) which account for around 30% of GDP and 45% of exports (Ministry of MSME, 2023) stand to benefit significantly from open innovation (OI) due to their limited internal resources and capacity. However, the adoption of OI in rural and semi-urban contexts remains uneven and underexplored. In regions like Srikakulam in Andhra Pradesh, where SMEs are concentrated in agriculture, textiles, and small-scale manufacturing, traditional business practices continue to dominate, with minimal integration of contemporary innovation frameworks.

This disconnect between policy aspirations and ground realities is stark. While national initiatives such as "Digital India" and "Make in India" aim to foster innovation and digital transformation, the impact on rural SMEs has been limited (Singh & Gaur, 2022). The primary barriers include inadequate digital infrastructure, low awareness, financial constraints, and lack of technical expertise (Tawil et al., 2023). These challenges not only stifle innovation capacity but also widen the competitiveness gap between rural SMEs and their urban or larger counterparts. Studies on SMEs in other contexts have revealed that those which engage in simultaneous OI practices combining external collaborations with internal innovation are often more agile and competitive (van de Vrande et al., 2009). However, such models are rarely examined in the Indian rural enterprise context, creating a gap in both scholarship and practical guidanc

Machine learning (ML) offers a powerful lever to address these limitations by enabling data-driven innovation. By analyzing large and complex datasets, ML can reveal hidden patterns, optimize operations, and forecast innovation outcomes, thus offering SMEs tools for better decision-making (Welte et al., 2020). In theory, ML could support predictive maintenance, customer segmentation, and product development, all of which are critical for innovation in resource-constrained settings. Yet, its real-world application among Indian rural SMEs remains marginal, constrained by high costs, data privacy concerns, and a lack of digital literacy (Kumar et al., 2021). This technological underutilization further accentuates the vulnerability of small firms to market disruptions and operational inefficiencies.

Despite growing global research on OI, rural Indian SMEs have been largely excluded from empirical scrutiny. The literature remains skewed toward urban enterprises or large firms, failing to account for the socio-economic nuances of semi-urban and rural business environments. For instance, studies such as those by Gassmann, Enkel, and Chesbrough (2010) highlight the multifaceted benefits and challenges of OI globally, but they do not sufficiently address the contextual constraints faced by rural Indian SMEs. Similarly, while Tawil et al. (2023) explore the integration of digital technologies in innovation strategies, their findings are often inapplicable to the structurally distinct micro-enterprises in areas like Srikakulam.

Addressing this research void requires a context-sensitive and interdisciplinary approach. Integrating ML into the assessment of OI practices can generate empirical evidence that guides localized innovation strategies. Moreover, applying predictive modeling can uncover key success factors, helping SMEs allocate resources more effectively and collaborate more strategically. This aligns with the call for more empirical research into OI failure modes in SMEs, a topic inadequately addressed in contrast to the literature on large corporations (Venugopal, K. 2024 a). Comparative studies, such as those conducted on Portuguese or Latin American SMEs, underscore that smaller firms often face capability and negotiation asymmetries that hinder their engagement in OI (Venugopal, K. & Sharma, A. 2025). Such asymmetries are likely to be more pronounced in Indian rural contexts, necessitating tailored frameworks that address these constraints.

This study, therefore, seeks to examine the adoption and impact of open innovation among SMEs in Srikakulam, while also assessing how ML applications can enhance innovation strategies.

2. OBJECTIVE OF THE STUDY

The specific objectives of this study are as follows:

- To assess the current adoption level of open innovation practices among micro and small enterprises in Srikakulam district.
- To identify the key internal and external factors influencing the implementation of open innovation in these enterprises.
- To analyze the role of machine learning applications in enhancing the efficiency, scalability, and strategic alignment of open innovation practices.
- To develop a predictive framework using ML techniques for evaluating innovation readiness and potential outcomes in SMEs.

3. LITERATURE REVIEW

3.1. Literature on Open Innovation

A comprehensive body of literature recognizes the growing relevance of open innovation (OI) among Micro, Small, and Medium Enterprises (MSMEs), yet it also reveals a consistent tension between theoretical models and practical application. Van de Vrande et al. (2009) assert that medium-sized enterprises are more likely to adopt OI practices than smaller firms, primarily due to resource availability, which shapes their capacity for external collaboration. This limitation is echoed in studies from varied contexts, including Venugopal, K. (2024 b) in India underscore that smaller firms face challenges such as skill shortages, limited funding, and poor institutional networks. Despite consensus on the potential benefits of OI, practical constraints often impede its uptake among smaller enterprises.

Several scholars attempt to position OI as a strategic necessity rather than a luxury, but this transition remains complex. While Balasubrahmanya (2012) optimistically suggests that MSMEs can thrive through external assistance, this claim often overlooks operational difficulties such as intellectual property concerns and the lack of absorptive capacity. Similarly, Rangus and Drnovsek (2013) advocate for staff and customer involvement in OI strategies but provide little guidance on how resource-starved MSMEs can sustain such participation. This theme of aspirational yet underspecified OI adoption recurs throughout the literature.

Evidence from developed economies, such as Roper (1997) and Venugopal, K., et al. (2015) shows how collaborations with R&D institutions and other firms can enhance innovation performance. However, the applicability of such models in rural and transition economies remains questionable. As Rao, A. L. et al. (2025) note, the lack of support structures and access to networks severely constrains the adoption of OI in less developed contexts. These challenges are magnified in MSMEs where informal operations, weak digital infrastructure, and minimal innovation culture prevail.

The concept of organizational agility highlighted by scholars like Sambamurthy et al. (2003) and Zandi and Tavana (2011) is positioned as essential for leveraging OI in dynamic markets. However, these frameworks assume a level of strategic foresight and resourcing that is often absent in MSMEs. Walter (2020) further distinguishes between organizational agility and absorptive capacity, but acknowledges the difficulty MSMEs face in balancing these capabilities simultaneously.

Interestingly, some scholars attempt to expand the OI discourse beyond product development. Pittaway et al. (2004) argue for research into organizational and process innovation, a direction particularly relevant for MSMEs aiming to modernize operations or customer engagement. Likewise, Venugopal, K. (2024 c). and Stanko et al. (2017) caution against the risks of OI, including over-reliance on external sources, IP vulnerabilities, and asymmetries in power or knowledge access. These concerns highlight that OI is not universally beneficial unless adapted to firm-specific realities.

The role of digital platforms and social media in enabling OI among small enterprises has gained traction in recent literature. Michaelidou et al. (2011) and Venugopal & Das (2022). emphasize how online networking and crowdsourcing can democratize innovation and reduce entry barriers. However, empirical support for these claims remains limited, especially in rural MSMEs where digital engagement is uneven. Schwartz and Bar-El (2015) point to the promise of regional associations and intermediary platforms in promoting innovation, yet stress that MSMEs' participation depends heavily on resource availability and contextual fit.

Zeng et al. (2010) and Venugopal & Nakkina, (2025) offer more grounded insights by emphasizing the importance of partnerships with universities, research bodies, and other enterprises to compensate for internal innovation gaps. Public assistance tools are suggested as vital enablers of OI, but bureaucratic inefficiencies and poor targeting often hinder their effectiveness. These findings resonate with Indian MSME ecosystems, especially in districts like Srikakulam, where informal practices dominate and innovation policies seldom penetrate at the grassroots level.

3.2. Literature review of independent variable:

3.2.1 Collaborative Partnerships:

Recent literature highlights open innovation as a crucial factor in enhancing MSMEs' competitiveness. Torchia & Calabro (2019) show that open innovation promotes knowledge exchange and collaboration, aiding MSMEs' adaptability. However, challenges like limited resources hinder its full implementation.

Venugopal, K, et al. (2017) and Rojas-Lema et al. (2020) focus on sustainable management and performance measurement, emphasizing the need for MSMEs to overcome structural barriers to capitalize on open innovation.

Gupta and Barua (2017) and Triguero et al. (2013) emphasize the role of open innovation in promoting sustainability within MSMEs through collaborative networks, enabling knowledge sharing and external partnerships. While these collaborations can drive sustainable practices, their success depends on the MSMEs' ability to manage and leverage these networks effectively. Challenges such as limited resources, lack of expertise, and organizational resistance can hinder the integration of open innovation for sustainability. Therefore, despite the potential benefits, the practical application of open innovation in MSMEs requires overcoming significant structural and resource-based barriers.

Love and Roper (2015) emphasize the importance of innovation for the growth, exporting, and competitiveness of small and medium-sized enterprises (SMEs), defining it broadly to include both technological (product and process) and non-technological (marketing and organizational) innovations. They suggest that open innovation, which enables SMEs to tap into external knowledge and resources, is key to overcoming resource constraints and fostering growth. However, the effective implementation of open innovation in SMEs is often hindered by challenges such as limited access to networks, financial resources, and strategic management expertise. Addressing these barriers could enhance the applicability of their framework in practice. (Love & Roper, 2015).

3.2.2. Cluster Based Innovation Networks:

Brunswicker and Vanhaverbeke (2015) examine open innovation practices among European SMEs, categorizing 1,411 firms into five groups based on their external knowledge sourcing strategies, ranging from minimal to full-scope searchers. This classification provides a detailed view of how SMEs interact with external sources like customers, suppliers, universities, and network partners, showing the varying levels of openness to external knowledge and its influence on innovation performance. While the study highlights the significance of external knowledge, it also points to challenges faced by MSMEs, such as limited resources, in managing these interactions effectively. A deeper exploration of these barriers would strengthen the practical applicability of open innovation in resource-constrained MSMEs (Brunswicker & Vanhaverbeke, 2015).

Tornatzky et al. (1990) highlight innovation through new technologies or management techniques to improve operations, but their definition overlooks the role of open innovation for MSMEs (Micro, Small, and Medium Enterprises). In a rapidly changing environment, MSMEs could greatly benefit from open innovation, which allows collaboration with external partners, sharing knowledge, and utilizing crowd-sourced solutions. This approach helps overcome resource limitations by accessing external expertise, technologies, and market insights, thus accelerating product development, enhancing flexibility, and improving crisis response. Integrating open innovation would offer MSMEs a more dynamic, collaborative path to innovation (Tornatzky et al., 1990).

Damanpour (1992), Johannessen et al. (2001), and OECD/Eurostat (2005) define "innovative practices" as the successful application of new solutions in areas like products, services, or processes. However, this definition could be enhanced by integrating open innovation practices among MSMEs (Micro, Small, and Medium Enterprises). Open innovation, involving collaboration with external partners and sharing knowledge, allows MSMEs to access valuable resources, expertise, and market insights, accelerating innovation and improving efficiency. This approach provides MSMEs with a more dynamic and sustainable competitive advantage in a complex business environment (Damanpour, 1992; Johannessen et al., 2001; OECD/Eurostat, 2005).

3.2.3. Technology Transfer from Research Institutions:

Triguero et al. (2013) examine the factors influencing eco-innovation in MSMEs, focusing on product, process, and organizational innovation. They categorize these factors into supply-side (technological capabilities, collaborations with research institutes, and access to external knowledge), demand-side (market share and consumer demand for green products), and environmental policy influences (regulations and fiscal incentives). The study highlights how open innovation, through external collaborations and adapting to policy frameworks, can significantly enhance eco-innovation in MSMEs. However, MSMEs may face challenges in fully adopting open innovation due to resource limitations, requiring support from government and research institutions.

Lee et al. (2010) explore the role of open innovation practices in SMEs, highlighting the importance of collaboration networks for R&D and commercialization. They discuss the Korean Technology Innovation Consortium (KICMS), which facilitated temporary cross-functional collaborations among SMEs, enhancing competitiveness. The study reveals that large firms are more engaged in innovation activities than SMEs, though no significant statistical differences were found. Key barriers for SMEs include limited manpower, resources, and infrastructure, which hinder their open innovation adoption. While the study provides valuable insights, it lacks deeper statistical analysis on the impact of collaboration networks on SME success (Lee et al., 2010).

Parida et al. (2012) examine how inbound open innovation activities, including technological scouting, vertical and horizontal technology collaboration, and technology (in)sourcing, impact radical and incremental product innovation in SMEs. The study finds that both innovation types benefit from technological scouting and (in)sourcing, with vertical collaboration favoring radical innovation and horizontal collaboration supporting incremental innovation. Additionally, firm age positively influences both types of innovation, while firm size has no significant effect. The research highlights the need for SMEs to strategically choose open innovation practices based on their innovation goals and organizational characteristics.

Van de Vrande et al. (2009) explore the adoption of open innovation practices among SMEs in the Netherlands, categorizing them into technology exploration (knowledge inflows like customer involvement, external networking, and R&D outsourcing) and technology exploitation (knowledge outflows such as venturing and IP licensing). The study found that external networking and customer involvement were the most commonly used techniques. However, while it provides a valuable overview, the research could benefit from a deeper examination of the challenges SMEs face, especially regarding resource limitations and organizational capacity, which are key barriers to adopting open innovation (Van de Vrande et al., 2009).

3.2.4. Venture Capital and Angel Networks:

Cuerva et al. (2014) examine the factors influencing traditional and environmentally friendly (green) product and process innovations in Spanish SMEs in the food and beverage sector. Their findings reveal that human capital and R&D positively impact both types of innovation, while financial constraints hinder green innovation. Additionally, product differentiation and quality management systems, such as ISO 9000, support both conventional and green innovations, while public subsidies and corporate social responsibility foster conventional innovation. These insights highlight key drivers for different innovation categories within SMEs (Cuerva et al., 2014).

Rosenbusch et al. (2011) examine the impact of innovation on SME performance, finding that innovation orientation has the greatest influence, followed by innovation outputs and inputs. They challenge the network and social capital literature by showing that internal innovation inputs positively affect performance, but external inputs (such as open innovation practices) do not. The study also reveals that innovation has a stronger effect on performance in less individualistic cultures and younger enterprises. However, the study lacks a focus on how SMEs adopt and manage open innovation practices, leaving a gap in understanding the role of external collaborations in driving innovation (Rosenbusch et al., 2011).

The concept of intense inbound open innovation (OI), as discussed by Scuotto et al. (2017), offers potential benefits in improving environmental signal scanning and internal efficiency. However, the practical application of OI in MSMEs may be challenging due to their limited resources, lack of advanced R&D capabilities, and insufficient innovation culture. These barriers prevent MSMEs from fully capitalizing on the advantages of inbound OI, which also requires a solid strategic framework something many MSMEs lack. Consequently, while the theoretical benefits of OI are evident, its effective use in MSMEs demands a more nuanced understanding of their specific constraints (Scuotto et al., 2017).

3.2.5. Co Creation with Customers:

Scuotto, Del Giudice, and Carayannis (2017) examine how social networking sites (SNSs) impact innovation performance in MSMEs by enhancing absorptive capacity, which leads to improved innovation outcomes, such as faster time-to-market and product adoption. Their study, based on a sample of 215 SMEs from labor- and knowledge-intensive industries, shows that SNSs, including social media platforms and communities, foster innovation by facilitating the acquisition and internalization of external knowledge. The authors suggest that SNSs align with the "innovation radar" network dimension, enhancing engagement with consumers and knowledge flow, and emphasize that the success of SNSs in driving innovation depends on how effectively MSMEs manage their absorptive capacity (Scuotto, Del Giudice, & Carayannis, 2017).

Albort-Morant et al. (2016) examine the impact of dynamic capabilities (DC) on green innovation performance (GIP) in 112 automotive component SMEs, finding that GIP is indirectly influenced by relationship learning capabilities, such as knowledge sharing and network interactions with suppliers and consumers. The study emphasizes that dynamic capabilities, including sensing, learning, integration, and coordination, are essential for driving green innovation. While it highlights the importance of quality models in performance improvement, the authors suggest that dynamic capabilities are implicitly included in achieving excellence in innovation. However, the study could benefit from a closer look at how open innovation practices, such as external collaborations, impact green innovation, especially in resource-constrained MSMEs (Albort-Morant et al., 2016).

Palacios-Marqués et al. (2015) investigate how technological, organizational, and competitive environment elements (TOC) influence information exchange in SMEs, focusing on factors like HR procedures, IT skills, technology integration, and competitive pressures. Although the study does not directly address innovation, it argues that effective information exchange fosters innovation, thereby enhancing competitiveness and survival. The research highlights the importance of technological capabilities, human resource management, and knowledge sharing in SME success. However, it could be strengthened by explicitly connecting these elements to open innovation practices, particularly external collaborations and knowledge flows (Palacios-Marqués et al., 2015).

Badi et al. (2017) explore the influence of social and guanxi networks in relationship marketing within Chinese SMEs, particularly in the construction industry.

Their study, using UCINET software, shows that guanxi relationships, based on trust and long-term personal connections, dominate over transactional relationships in China. This suggests that open innovation models in Chinese SMEs may benefit from leveraging these relational networks, impacting management practices, consumer and supplier interactions. However, the study highlights that the importance of guanxi may vary in other cultural contexts, requiring SMEs to adapt their open innovation strategies to local relational norms (Badi et al., 2017).

3.2.6. Open Data and Digital Platforms:

Scuotto, Del Giudice, Peruta, et al. (2017) examine the impact of social media networks (SMNs) on MSMEs' innovation and creativity through client engagement, focusing on ROI across five dimensions: relational (digital interactions), structural (technological infrastructure), cognitive (user-generated knowledge), knowledge transfer (information flow), and legitimation (innovation quantity from user ideas). While their framework offers a comprehensive view of SMNs' role in fostering open innovation, it may oversimplify MSMEs' engagement, potentially overlooking external factors like market dynamics or industry-specific challenges that also affect ROI outcomes. (Scuotto et al., 2017).

The authors predicted that SMEs would focus on disaster management, digital technology exploitation, and financial spending reductions during the early stages of the pandemic, but did not address the potential of open innovation in these strategies. Open innovation through collaborations, knowledge sharing, and crowd-sourcing could have helped SMEs better navigate the crisis, accelerating digital transformation and providing access to vital resources such as software, expertise, and market insights. Furthermore, financial strategies could have been bolstered through innovative financing models and fintech partnerships, increasing adaptability and resilience (Eggers, 2020; Guo et al., 2020; Indriastuti & Fuad, 2020; Papadopoulos et al., 2020; Thorgren & Williams, 2020).

Guo et al. (2020) highlight the importance of digital technology for SMEs' pandemic response, while Gerald et al. (2020) emphasize strategic agility in mitigating its impact. However, both studies could be enhanced by integrating open innovation into SMEs' crisis strategies. Open innovation through collaboration, co-creation, and resource-sharing could accelerate digital transformation, providing SMEs with faster access to expertise, solutions, and market opportunities. Additionally, open innovation could strengthen strategic agility by fostering flexible, collaborative networks that help SMEs adapt more swiftly. This approach would enhance resilience and drive innovation, extending beyond traditional managerial strategies (Guo et al., 2020; Gerald et al., 2020)

3.2.7. Government Support and Funding:

Zeng et al. (2010) highlight that public assistance tools can help small enterprises reduce risk and financial burdens in innovation. However, for Micro, Small, and Medium Enterprises (MSMEs) engaging in open innovation (OI), the effectiveness of these tools is limited. MSMEs often struggle to access external knowledge, networks, zeand technology crucial for OI, and may lack the internal capacity or sufficient funding to fully leverage public assistance. Additionally, bureaucratic delays can impede the agility required for MSMEs to participate in fast-paced innovation ecosystems. Thus, while public assistance can support innovation, it may not fully address the complex needs of OI in MSMEs.

Freitas & Von Tunzelmann (2008) and Nishimura & Okamuro (2011) highlight the role of direct external support for SMEs, such as financial aid for technology development and asset acquisition. However, this focus neglects the potential of open innovation practices. Through collaboration with external partners like universities, research institutions, or other businesses, SMEs can access new technologies, ideas, and resources, overcoming resource constraints. Open innovation enables knowledge sharing, co-creation, and leveraging external expertise, helping SMEs address financial shortages while accelerating growth and innovation. This approach fosters long-term resilience and adaptability in a competitive market (Freitas & Von Tunzelmann, 2008; Nishimura & Okamuro, 2011).

Chrisman & McMullan (2004) and Mason & Brown (2013) stress the role of external support in enhancing SMEs' managerial and marketing capabilities, but they overlook the potential of open innovation. By collaborating with external partners and leveraging external expertise, open innovation can accelerate SMEs' growth and innovation. Rather than relying only on traditional support like funding or training, open innovation helps SMEs access broader networks, including research institutions, businesses, and customers, to co-create solutions, adopt new technologies, and identify market opportunities. This approach would strengthen SMEs' capabilities and foster sustainable growth, enhancing their contribution to the national economy (Chrisman & McMullan, 2004; Mason & Brown, 2013).

Cliff (1998), Gimeno et al. (1997), and Storey et al. (2010) emphasize the importance of external assistance in improving SMEs' performance and growth. However, open innovation practices could provide a more dynamic approach by allowing SMEs to collaborate with a broader network of external partners, such as research institutions, universities, and businesses, to co-create solutions, share knowledge, and access new technologies. This collaborative approach goes beyond traditional forms of support, fostering innovation and helping SMEs address market challenges more effectively. Open innovation can enhance competitiveness, scalability, and sustainable growth, enabling SMEs to leverage their full commercial potential (Cliff, 1998; Gimeno et al., 1997; Storey et al., 2010).

Table 1. Qualitative Analysis of Independent Variables in Open Innovation Practices among MSMEs

Variable	Key Insights from Literature	Benefits Identified	Challenges Noted
Collaborative Partnerships	OI improves MSMEs' adaptability and competitiveness through knowledge sharing and external alliances (Torchia & Calabro, 2019; Gupta & Barua, 2017).	Drives sustainability, innovation access, and mutual learning.	Resource limitations, lack of expertise, and difficulty in managing external networks.
Cluster-Based Innovation Networks	SMEs benefit from being part of innovation ecosystems, enhancing access to external knowledge (Brunswicker & Vanhaverbeke, 2015).	Facilitates technology absorption, market expansion, and collective learning.	Managing external interactions, navigating varying levels of openness, and weak institutional links.
Technology Transfer (TT) from RIs	Collaborations with research institutions accelerate product/process innovation (Triguero et al., 2013; Parida et al., 2012).	Boosts eco-innovation, enables radical innovation, and enhances R&D capability.	Infrastructure gaps, low absorptive capacity, and limited engagement in formal R&D frameworks.
Venture Capital & Angel Networks	Access to external funding enhances R&D output and innovation orientation (Cuerva et al., 2014; Scuotto et al., 2017).	Supports scaling of innovations, encourages experimentation.	Financial constraints, low investor confidence, and lack of awareness of funding avenues.
Co-Creation with Customers	Engaging customers via SNSs fosters product improvement and market responsiveness (Scuotto et al., 2017; Albort-Morant et al., 2016).	Enhances time-to-market, increases customer loyalty, and facilitates real-time feedback.	Weak absorptive capacity, misalignment of consumer insights, and risk of IP leakage.
Open Data & Digital Platforms	Digital tools enable knowledge transfer and collaboration, improving internal efficiency (Eggers, 2020; Scuotto et al., 2017).	Strengthens network interactions, innovation legitimacy, and strategic agility.	Low digital literacy, poor digital infrastructure, and weak return on investment in some contexts.
Government Support & Public Funding	Public tools help reduce innovation risk (Zeng et al., 2010; Chrisman & McMullan, 2004), while collaboration with academia enhances capability (Freitas & Von Tunzelmann, 2008).	Offers financial relief, infrastructure access, and institutional legitimacy.	Bureaucracy, poor targeting of schemes, and low awareness hinder effectiveness.

The qualitative analysis of literature from table 1 reveals several critical observations regarding open innovation practices among MSMEs. A recurring theme across variables is the essential need for strong external linkages; be it with institutions, customers, funders, or digital platforms to compensate for the internal resource limitations that many MSMEs face. These partnerships are not just beneficial but often necessary for facilitating innovation and competitiveness. However, despite the theoretical advantages of open innovation, its practical application within MSMEs remains significantly underutilized. This gap is largely attributed to limited absorptive capacity and organizational inertia, which restrict firms from effectively integrating external knowledge and adapting to innovation-driven change.

4. METHODS AND MATERIALS

To investigate open innovation practices among micro and small enterprises (MSEs) in Srikakulam, a mixed-methods approach was employed. This methodology integrates both descriptive and exploratory designs to capture the breadth and depth of open innovation phenomena, especially in semi-urban and rural contexts where data may be scarce and patterns underexplored. The descriptive dimension focused on quantifying the extent of OI practices, while the exploratory dimension probed the contextual and behavioral drivers that influence these practices.

The study adopted a cross-sectional survey design to gather data at a single point in time. This design enabled a snapshot analysis of prevailing innovation strategies, partnerships, and technological adoption among the target enterprises.

The data collection strategy was twofold, incorporating both primary and secondary data. Primary data was collected through a structured questionnaire, formulated based on existing validated constructs from prior studies on open innovation, collaboration, and digital transformation (Chesbrough, 2003; Gassmann et al., 2010). The questionnaire covered six broad domains: collaboration networks, access to external knowledge sources, use of digital tools, customer integration, technological partnerships, and financing for innovation. Participants responded on a 5-point Likert scale, ranging from "Strongly Disagree" to "Strongly Agree." The survey also included demographic items to contextualize the findings based on enterprise size, sector, and owner background.

Convenience sampling was employed to identify and approach 90 micro and small enterprise owners and decision-makers across the Srikakulam district. This non-probability sampling method was chosen due to its efficiency, cost-effectiveness, and ease of access to respondents in remote regions. While this technique may introduce selection bias, measures were taken to diversify the sample across various business sectors such as textiles, agriculture, retail, and light manufacturing.

To assess the reliability of the questionnaire, internal consistency was measured using Cronbach's Alpha. The result ($\alpha = 0.877$) confirmed a high level of internal reliability across the 30-item instrument, exceeding the generally accepted threshold of 0.70 (Hair et al., 2017). Furthermore, data symmetry was assessed through skewness and kurtosis statistics.

In terms of data analysis, both traditional statistical and machine learning methods were utilized. Descriptive statistics such as mean, standard deviation, and frequency distributions were used to profile the sample and summarize patterns in OI practices. Inferential analysis was conducted through multiple regression analysis (MRA) to examine the extent to which independent variables such as digital tool usage, collaboration intensity, and access to finance predicted perceived innovation outcomes.

Exploratory Factor Analysis (EFA) was conducted to reduce data dimensionality and identify latent constructs within the survey. Principal component extraction with varimax rotation revealed distinct clusters such as "collaborative innovation," "technological integration," and "market-driven innovation."

Machine learning applications enhanced the robustness and predictive capability of the study. Decision tree and logistic regression classifiers were used to categorize SMEs based on their likelihood of successfully implementing open innovation strategies. The models were evaluated using confusion matrices, Receiver Operating Characteristic (ROC) curves, and precision-recall metrics to ensure predictive reliability. For instance, enterprises that collaborated with research institutions and utilized digital platforms were more likely to report higher innovation success scores.

To visualize interrelationships among variables, correlation heat maps were created. These visualizations provided immediate insights into how variables such as customer involvement, digital platform usage, and supplier collaboration were interlinked. Additionally, K-means and hierarchical clustering techniques were employed to group enterprises based on innovation behavior profiles. These clusters helped in distinguishing low, moderate, and high adopters of open innovation, providing actionable segmentation for policy targeting and capability-building interventions.

Rank analysis was also conducted to prioritize variables based on their impact scores. Factors such as customer co-creation, digital platform adoption, and participation in government-supported clusters consistently ranked high. These rankings provide a pragmatic roadmap for stakeholders to allocate resources and design interventions that address the most influential levers of innovation.

Finally, qualitative data from open-ended survey responses were thematically analyzed to enrich the quantitative findings. Respondents often cited issues such as limited awareness, low trust in external institutions, and regulatory bottlenecks as barriers to innovation. These insights highlighted the contextual intricacies that numerical data alone could not capture, thus reinforcing the utility of the mixed-methods design.

Figure 1. Conceptual and Research Flow

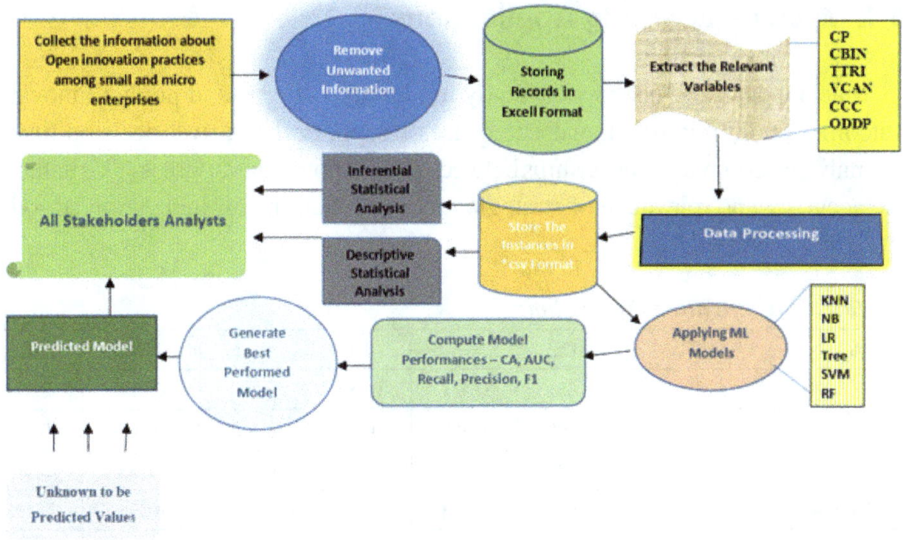

The diagram presents a conceptual and research flow for assessing open innovation practices among small and micro enterprises using machine learning (ML) techniques and statistical analysis. The process begins with data collection on OI practices, followed by the removal of irrelevant or redundant information. Cleaned data is then stored in Excel format, where relevant variables (e.g., CP, CBIN, TTRI, VCAN, CCC, ODDP) are extracted for analysis. Next, the data undergoes processing and is stored in .csv format for compatibility with ML tools. The study applies various ML models such as KNN, Naive Bayes (NB), Logistic Regression (LR), Decision Trees, SVM, and Random Forest (RF) to the processed dataset. These models are evaluated using performance metrics like classification accuracy (CA), AUC, recall, precision, and F1 score. Statistical analyses, both descriptive and inferential, are conducted to support data interpretation and validate findings. The best-performing model is selected to generate a predictive model, which is then used to predict unknown values. The results and model interpretations are finally shared with stakeholders and analysts to support strategic decision-making related to innovation practices.

5. ANALYSIS AND DISCUSSION

5.1. Machine Learning Applications

Machine learning enables the study to identify patterns and predict innovation outcomes among micro and small enterprises. It supports data-driven decision-making by analyzing complex relationships between open innovation variables. This enhances the accuracy and relevance of strategic recommendations for innovation adoption.

Table 2. Classification Algorithm:

Model	**AUC**	**CA**	**F1**	**Prec**	**Recall**	**MCC**
kNN	0.852	0.511	0.486	0.604	0.511	0.377
Tree	0.990	0.867	0.867	0.882	0.867	0.833
Random Forest	**0.995**	**0.933**	**0.933**	**0.937**	**0.933**	**0.915**
Naive Bayes	0.922	0.578	0.580	0.658	0.578	0.498
SVM	0.669	0.889	0.889	0.909	0.889	0.861
Logistic Regression	0.976	0.911	0.912	0.914	0.911	0.886

As shown in Table 2, the analysis of machine learning models applied to assess open innovation among small and micro enterprises in Srikakulam reveals that the Random Forest model outperforms others with exceptional accuracy (CA 0.933) and AUC (0.995), indicating its strong ability to identify innovation patterns. Decision Tree and Logistic Regression also show robust performance, while models like SVM, KNN, and Naive Bayes are less effective due to limitations in handling complex data. These findings suggest that ensemble and tree-based models best capture the nuanced factors driving innovation, offering valuable insights for policymakers and stakeholders to support data-driven innovation strategies and enterprise growth in the region.

Table 3. Confusion Matrix

Predicted							
Actual		**1**	**2**	**3**	**4**	**5**	**Σ**
	1	**8**	0	0	**1**	**1**	**10**
	2	0	**12**	0	**1**	0	**13**
	3	0	0	**17**	**1**	**1**	**19**
	4	0	0	0	**27**	0	**27**
	5	0	0	**1**	0	**20**	**21**
	Σ	**8**	**12**	**18**	**30**	**22**	**90**

The confusion matrix analysis from Table 3, reveals that the machine learning model performs well across five classes, with particularly high accuracy in classes 4 and 5 (100% and ~90.9%, respectively), indicating strong predictive capability in these areas. Class 3 also shows robust results, while minor misclassifications in classes 2 and 3 mostly into adjacent classes highlight areas for refinement. Class 2 is slightly underestimated, suggesting a need for improved feature differentiation or model tuning. Overall, the model offers reliable insights into virtual water usage patterns, supporting better decision-making for small and micro enterprises in Srikakulam.

Figure 2. ROC Analysis

ROC with All Algorithms	ROC with Random Forest

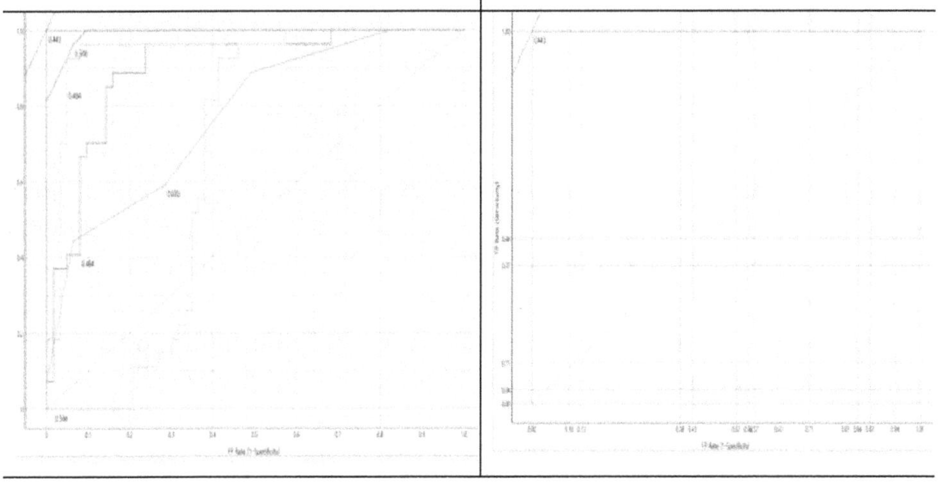

The ROC curve analysis in Figure 2 highlights the superior performance of advanced machine learning models, with Random Forest and Logistic Regression achieving the highest AUC values (0.999 and 0.996, respectively), indicating near-perfect classification. SVM also performs well (AUC 0.978), while simpler models like kNN and Naïve Bayes show weaker discrimination capabilities, particularly the latter with the lowest AUC (0.856). These findings confirm that ensemble and regression-based models are more effective in predicting open innovation practices among micro and small enterprises in Srikakulam, due to their ability to capture complex data patterns.

Figure 3. Performance Curve

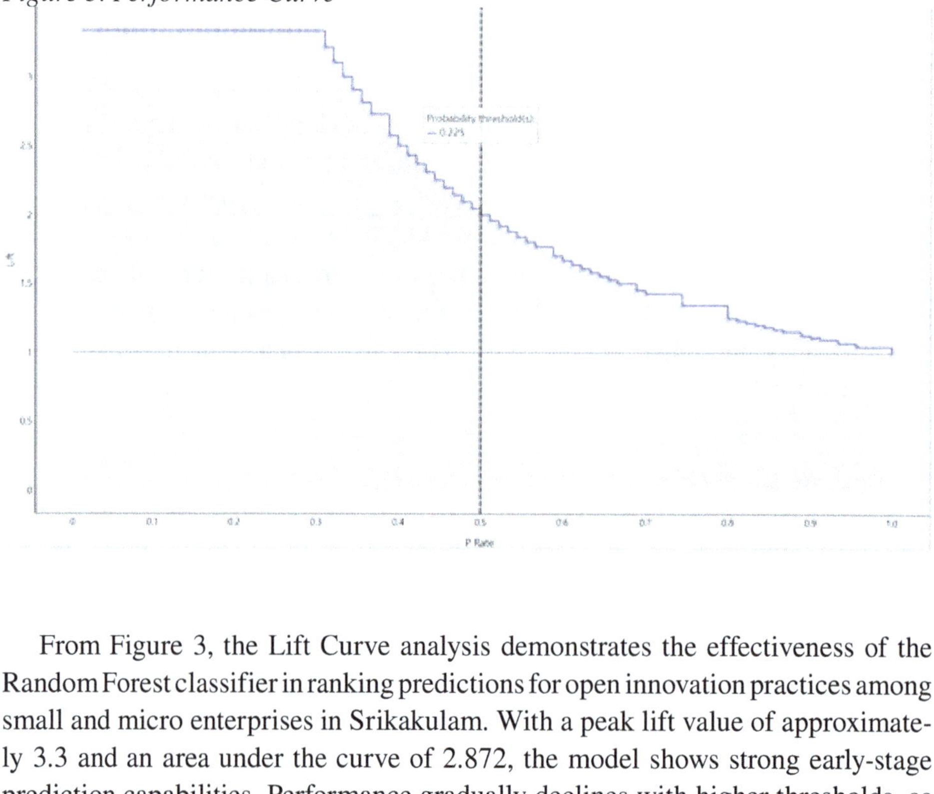

From Figure 3, the Lift Curve analysis demonstrates the effectiveness of the Random Forest classifier in ranking predictions for open innovation practices among small and micro enterprises in Srikakulam. With a peak lift value of approximately 3.3 and an area under the curve of 2.872, the model shows strong early-stage prediction capabilities. Performance gradually declines with higher thresholds, as expected, and a key decision point is marked at a probability threshold of 0.225 for optimal precision-recall balance. The analysis confirms Random Forest's strength in identifying high-priority instances, reinforcing its value for informed decision-making in complex, multi-class business environments.

Figure 4. PCA

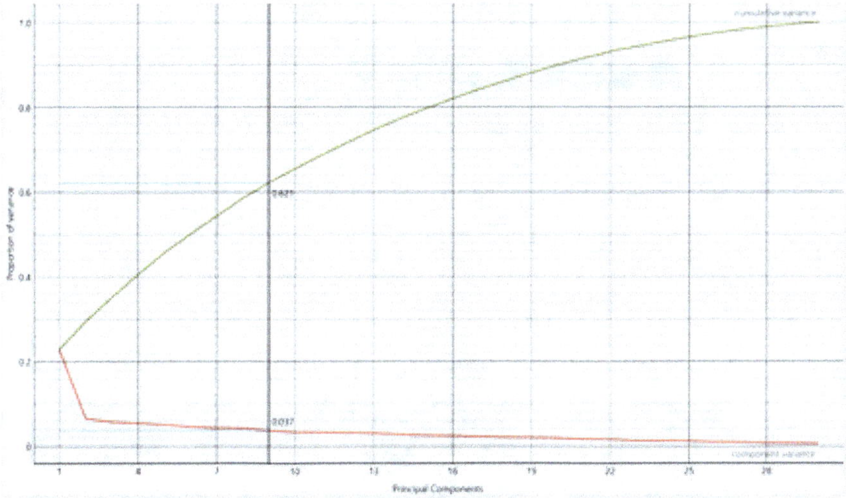

The PCA Scree Plot from Figure 4 reveals that the first nine principal components capture approximately 62% of the total variance, indicating they hold the most meaningful information in the dataset. Beyond this point, additional components contribute minimally, suggesting an optimal dimensionality reduction at nine components. This enhances computational efficiency and model performance in analyzing open innovation practices among small and micro enterprises in Srikakulam.

Figure 5. Correlation

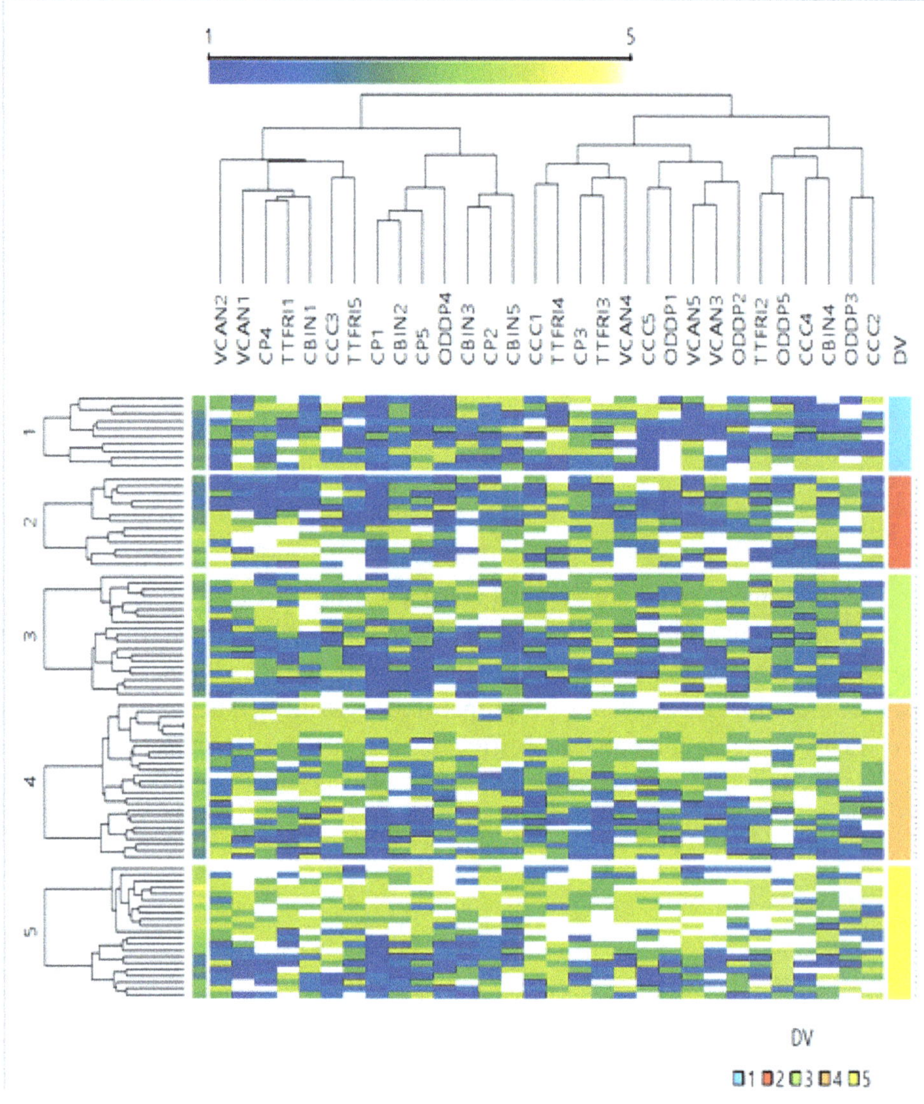

Figure 5 of the hierarchical clustering heatmap provides a clear visualization of the correlation structure among features related to virtual water analysis, using color gradients and dendrograms to highlight patterns. It reveals five distinct clusters, indicating strong intra-group similarities and offering insights for targeted feature selection and dimensionality reduction. Closely branched variables suggest potential redundancies, supporting the use of techniques like PCA to streamline data. This analysis plays a vital role in enhancing machine learning model accuracy and efficiency within the broader study on open innovation practices among small and micro enterprises in Srikakulam, enabling more informed, data-driven decisions.

Figure 6. Distance Map

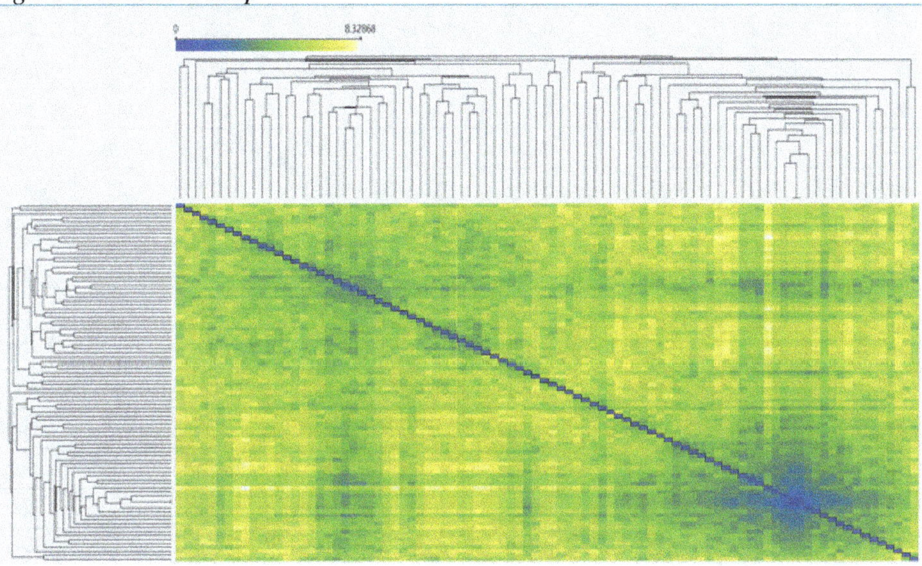

Figure 6, the heatmap presents a detailed view of the correlation structure among features related to open innovation practices in small and micro enterprises in Srikakulam. A strong diagonal indicates perfect self-correlation, while surrounding green and yellow hues reveal varying degrees of inter-feature relationships. Hierarchical dendrograms highlight clusters of closely related features, suggesting interconnected innovation practices or business strategies. Yellow clusters point to key variable groupings valuable for predictive modeling, while blue areas denote independent variables. Overall, the visualization uncovers meaningful patterns that can guide strategic insights and enhance predictive analysis for fostering enterprise innovation.

Table 4. Rank Analysis

Rank	Features	Info. gain	Gain ratio	Gini	ANOVA	χ^2	ReliefF	FCBF
1	CCC4	0.213	0.110	0.059	4.569	14.979	0.056	0.113
2	VCAN5	0.197	0.105	0.044	3.564	8.769	0.013	0.106
3	ODDP5	0.194	0.097	0.052	4.223	13.518	0.034	0.000
4	ODDP3	0.176	0.089	0.048	2.020	6.405	0.004	0.000

continued on following page

Table 4. Continued

Rank	Features	Info. gain	Gain ratio	Gini	ANOVA	χ^2	ReliefF	FCBF
5	TTFRI4	0.176	0.090	0.049	3.410	8.264	0.031	0.091
6	CP4	0.166	0.087	0.041	1.581	4.111	0.035	0.000
7	CBIN2	0.162	0.084	0.034	1.160	2.226	0.021	0.084
8	ODDP4	0.146	0.074	0.038	3.320	9.828	0.055	0.000
9	VCAN3	0.146	0.074	0.039	1.348	4.667	0.013	0.000
10	CP1	0.142	0.078	0.032	3.366	15.055	0.070	0.000
11	TTFRI1	0.139	0.074	0.046	1.292	3.079	0.021	0.000
12	CBIN3	0.135	0.072	0.030	1.575	3.581	0.009	0.000
13	TTFRI5	0.127	0.066	0.033	1.461	4.218	0.030	0.000
14	ODDP1	0.126	0.063	0.025	0.385	1.553	0.002	0.000
15	VCAN4	0.125	0.063	0.033	1.853	5.600	-0.013	0.000
16	CP5	0.124	0.064	0.035	1.983	7.584	0.013	0.000
17	TTFRI3	0.123	0.064	0.029	2.172	4.290	0.025	0.000
18	VCAN2	0.123	0.063	0.027	0.825	2.812	0.006	0.000
19	CBIN1	0.120	0.062	0.028	1.418	4.329	0.038	0.000
20	CCC5	0.115	0.059	0.028	2.103	4.581	0.056	0.000
21	CBIN5	0.113	0.059	0.030	1.518	3.363	0.019	0.058
22	CP2	0.113	0.060	0.026	2.920	8.916	0.047	0.000
23	CBIN4	0.113	0.059	0.030	1.437	2.950	0.023	0.000
24	ODDP2	0.097	0.051	0.018	1.529	3.748	0.021	0.000
25	CP3	0.092	0.047	0.023	1.463	5.563	-0.007	0.000
26	TTFRI2	0.089	0.045	0.021	1.472	3.878	0.010	0.000
27	CCC2	0.081	0.042	0.020	1.661	3.825	0.017	0.000
28	CCC3	0.077	0.039	0.021	0.714	2.738	0.017	0.000
29	CCC1	0.067	0.034	0.019	1.502	4.203	-0.010	0.000
30	VCAN1	0.065	0.033	0.018	0.727	2.707	0.018	0.000

The dataset presents feature importance scores from a machine learning analysis of open innovation practices among small and micro enterprises in Srikakulam, using methods like Information Gain, Gain Ratio, Gini Index, ANOVA, Chi-square, Relief, and FCBF. Features such as CCC4, VCAN5, and ODDP5 consistently show high relevance across metrics, particularly in Information Gain and ANOVA, indicating their strong predictive value. CP1 also emerges as a significant variable in certain tests. In contrast, features like CCC1, VCAN1, and CCC3 display consistently low scores, suggesting limited impact and potential for exclusion in model optimization. These findings highlight the importance of prioritizing high-impact variables to enhance predictive accuracy and guide small enterprises in refining innovation strategies for better outcomes.

5.2. Statistical Analysis – Exploratory Factor Analysis

Exploratory Factor Analysis (EFA) is applied in this study to identify the underlying dimensions influencing open innovation practices among micro and small enterprises. It helps in uncovering latent constructs by grouping correlated variables. This technique provides a data-driven foundation for interpreting key innovation drivers within these enterprises.

Table 5. KMO and Bartlett's test

Kaiser-Meyer-Olkin Measure of Sampling Adequacy.		**.709**
Bartlett's Test of Sphericity	Approx. Chi-Square	904.541
	df	465
	Sig.	.000

As shown in Table 5, the value of The KMO Measure indicates the variance proportion in the variables triggered by underlying factors is 0.709 which is good enough to undergo factor analysis with the data. Significant level of 0.000 signs sound to get along with factor analysis which may be useful with the data.

Table 6. Total Variance Explained

	Initial Eigenvalues			**Extraction Sums of Squared Loadings**			**Rotation Sums of Squared Loadings**		
Com-ponent	**Total**	**% of Variance**	**Cumulative %**	**Total**	**% of Variance**	**Cumulative %**	**Total**	**% of Variance**	**Cumulative %**
1	7.077	22.830	22.830	7.077	22.830	22.830	3.221	10.391	10.391
2	1.976	6.374	29.204	1.976	6.374	29.204	2.311	7.456	17.846
3	1.727	5.572	34.776	1.727	5.572	34.776	2.305	7.436	25.283
4	1.641	5.293	40.069	1.641	5.293	40.069	2.058	6.638	31.921
5	1.520	4.902	44.971	1.520	4.902	44.971	2.038	6.576	38.496
6	1.382	4.457	49.428	1.382	4.457	49.428	1.956	6.311	44.808
7	1.304	4.206	53.634	1.304	4.206	53.634	1.897	6.120	50.928
8	1.267	4.086	57.721	1.267	4.086	57.721	1.471	4.744	55.672
9	1.165	3.757	61.477	1.165	3.757	61.477	1.454	4.691	60.363
10	1.049	3.383	64.860	1.049	3.383	64.860	1.394	4.498	64.860
11	.967	3.121	67.981						

continued on following page

Table 6. Continued

	Initial Eigenvalues			Extraction Sums of Squared Loadings			Rotation Sums of Squared Loadings		
Component	Total	% of Variance	Cumulative %	Total	% of Variance	Cumulative %	Total	% of Variance	Cumulative %
12	.913	2.946	70.927						
13	.890	2.871	73.798						
14	.805	2.596	76.394						
15	.787	2.538	78.933						
16	.730	2.353	81.286						
17	.653	2.106	83.392						
18	.605	1.952	85.344						
19	.583	1.879	87.223						
20	.561	1.811	89.034						
21	.512	1.651	90.685						
22	.466	1.504	92.189						
23	.383	1.235	93.424						
24	.364	1.175	94.599						
25	.340	1.098	95.697						
26	.304	.980	96.678						
27	.263	.849	97.526						
28	.254	.819	98.345						
29	.188	.605	98.951						
30	.171	.553	99.504						
31	.154	.496	100.000						

Extraction Method: Principal Component Analysis.

It is understood from Table 6, that the requested extracted initial Eigen values greater than 1 has resulted into eight first components extending 64.860 percent of cumulative initial eigenvalues. Among the 31 listed variables, eight components show the variability of 64% approximately. So, the complexity of the dataset can be reduced through these eight components with almost 36% of lost information.

Table 7. Rotated Component Matrix

	Component									
	1	2	3	4	5	6	7	8	9	10
My enterprise actively collaborates with other businesses for innovation and growth.	.606									
Partnerships with suppliers and distributors enhance innovation in my business.						.480				
Joint ventures and collaborations with other firms improve product/ service development.			.631							
Business alliances have helped in accessing new markets and customers.			.319							
Collaborative partnerships increase competitiveness and business sustainability.	.656									
My enterprise benefits from being part of a local business cluster.	.581									
Business clusters help in sharing resources and knowledge among enterprises.	.755									
Networking with other SMEs in the region accelerates innovation.						.600				
Cluster-based collaborations reduce operational costs and improve efficiency.									.299	
Government or industry-supported business clusters enhance business innovation						.740				
My business collaborates with universities or research institutions for innovation.				.582						
Technology transfer from academic institutions enhances SME growth.					.443					
Research-based innovations contribute to product/service development in my business.			.709							
My enterprise has access to technical expertise from research organizations									.654	
Government initiatives help in promoting technology transfer to SMEs.							.759			
Access to venture capital funding helps in scaling my business.	.520									
Angel investors play a key role in supporting small enterprises in my industry.										.739
My enterprise has explored funding opportunities from venture capitalists or angel investors.		.647								
Financial support from investment networks accelerates innovation in SMEs.			.479							
Lack of access to venture capital funding is a major barrier to business growth.							.603			
My business involves customers in the development of new products/services		.742								
Customer feedback helps in improving product/service innovation.				.685						
Co-creation with customers enhances business competitiveness.								.774		
Engaging customers in innovation strengthens brand loyalty.					.641					
Digital tools help my business collect and analyze customer feedback for innovation			.542							
Digital platforms help my business connect with partners and customers.		.403								

continued on following page

Table 7. Continued

	Component									
	1	2	3	4	5	6	7	8	9	10
My enterprise uses open data to improve decision-making and innovation.		.526								
Online collaboration tools enhance business efficiency.				.721						
E-commerce and digital platforms expand my business reach and sales.	.445									
Access to market data helps in better planning and strategy development.					.781					
Open innovation practices have significantly contributed to the growth of my business.					.566					

Extraction Method: Principal Component Analysis.
Rotation Method: Varimax with Kaiser Normalization.
a. Rotation converged in 14 iterations.

Table 7 reveals ten key components extracted through factor analysis. The first component integrates collaboration, business clusters, venture capital access, and digital expansion. The second links funding exploration, customer co-creation, and use of open data and platforms. The third centers on joint ventures, market access, research-based innovation, financial support, and digital feedback tools. The fourth includes academic collaboration, customer feedback, and online tools. The fifth highlights technology transfer, brand loyalty, market data, and overall innovation growth. The sixth relates to supplier partnerships, SME networking, and cluster support. The seventh focuses on government-led tech transfer and funding barriers. The eighth emphasizes customer co-creation's role in competitiveness. The ninth includes cost-saving cluster collaborations and technical expertise, while the tenth notes angel investors' support for small enterprises. The least explained variables were cluster-based cost reduction (0.299) and market access through alliances (0.319), suggesting areas for further exploration.

5.3. Statistical Analysis: Multiple Regression Analysis

Multiple Regression Analysis is employed in this study to examine the influence of various factors on the adoption of open innovation practices among micro and small enterprises. It quantifies the relationship between independent variables and the extent of innovation practices. This analysis aids in identifying the most significant predictors driving open innovation in the sector.

Table 8. Model Summary

Variables	R	R Square	Adjusted R Square	Std. Error of the Estimate
• Collaborative partnerships	.410[a]	.168	.118	1.217
• Cluster Based Innovation Networks	.340[a]	.115	.063	1.255
• Technology Transfer from Research Institutions	.356[a]	.127	.075	1.247
• Venture Capital and Angel Networks	.398[a]	.159	.108	1.224
• Co-Creation with Customers	.433[a]	.187	.139	1.203
• Open Data and Digital Platforms	.447[a]	.200	.152	1.194

a. Predictors: (Constant), Collaborative partnerships, Cluster Based Innovation Networks, Technology Transfer from Research Institutions, Venture Capital and Angel Networks, Co-Creation with Customers, Open Data and Digital Platforms

The model summary from Table 8 highlights the predictive strength of six variables on open innovation practices among micro and small enterprises. Among them, Open Data and Digital Platforms showed the highest explanatory power with an R^2 of 0.200, indicating it accounts for 20% of the variance in open innovation practices. Co-Creation with Customers and Collaborative Partnerships also demonstrated relatively strong predictive capacities with R^2 values of 0.187 and 0.168, respectively. Conversely, Cluster Based Innovation Networks had the lowest R^2 at 0.115, suggesting a weaker association. Overall, the results imply that digital platforms and customer involvement are more influential drivers of open innovation in this context.

Table 9. Anova

Variables	Sum of Squares	df	Mean Square	F	Sig.
• Collaborative partnerships	25.110	5	5.022	3.389	.008[b]
• Cluster Based Innovation Networks	17.251	5	3.450	2.190	.063[b]
• Technology Transfer from Research Institutions	18.990	5	3.798	2.443	.041[b]
• Venture Capital and Angel Networks	23.714	5	4.743	3.165	.011[b]
• Co-Creation with Customers	28.004	5	5.601	3.869	.003[b]
• Open Data and Digital Platforms	29.916	5	5.983	4.199	.002[b]

a. Dependent Variable: Open innovation practices have significantly contributed to the growth of my business.

b. Predictors: (Constant), Collaborative partnerships, Cluster Based Innovation Networks, Technology Transfer from Research Institutions, Venture Capital and Angel Networks, Co-Creation with Customers, Open Data and Digital Platforms

The ANOVA results from Table 9 assess the statistical significance of each predictor in explaining variations in open innovation practices. Open Data and Digital Platforms (F = 4.199, p = .002) and Co-Creation with Customers (F = 3.869, p = .003) show highly significant influence, indicating strong contributions to business growth through innovation. Collaborative Partnerships (p = .008), Venture Capital and Angel Networks (p = .011), and Technology Transfer from Research Institutions (p = .041) also exhibit significant relationships. However, Cluster Based Innovation Networks (p = .063) is marginally above the 0.05 threshold, suggesting a weaker or less consistent impact. These findings reinforce the importance of digital engagement and customer collaboration in fostering open innovation among micro and small enterprises.

Table 10. Coefficients

		Unstandardized Coefficients		**Standardized Coefficients**		
	Model	*B*	*Std. Error*	*Beta*	**t**	**Sig.**
Collaborative partnerships	(Constant)	1.996	.476		4.190	.000
	My enterprise actively collaborates with other businesses for innovation and growth (CP1).	.254	.116	.268	2.194	.031
	Partnerships with suppliers and distributors enhance innovation in my business (CP2).	.192	.125	.176	1.536	.128
	Joint ventures and collaborations with other firms improve product/service development (CP3).	-.028	.125	-.026	-.227	.821
	Business alliances have helped in accessing new markets and customers (CP4).	.070	.115	.070	.614	.541
	Collaborative partnerships increase competitiveness and business sustainability (CP5).	.039	.113	.040	.342	.733
Cluster Based Innovation Networks	(Constant)	1.853	.535		3.461	.001
	My enterprise benefits from being part of a local business cluster (CBIN1).	.198	.116	.204	1.717	.090
	Business clusters help in sharing resources and knowledge among enterprises (CBIN2).	.056	.124	.053	.454	.651
	Networking with other SMEs in the region accelerates innovation (CBIN3).	-.092	.115	-.098	-.798	.427
	Cluster-based collaborations reduce operational costs and improve efficiency (CBIN4).	.171	.117	.157	1.467	.146
	Government or industry-supported business clusters enhance business innovation (CBIN5).	.179	.117	.172	1.527	.130

continued on following page

Table 10. Continued

	Model	Unstandardized Coefficients		Standardized Coefficients	t	Sig.
		B	*Std. Error*	*Beta*		
***Technology Transfer from Research Institutions** Platforms*	(Constant)	1.534	.572		2.683	.009
	My business collaborates with universities or research institutions for innovation (TTRI1).	.038	.101	.041	.379	.706
	Technology transfer from academic institutions enhances SME growth (TTRI2).	.128	.104	.131	1.225	.224
	Research-based innovations contribute to product/service development in my business (TTRI3).	.061	.114	.059	.534	.595
	My enterprise has access to technical expertise from research organizations (TTRI4).	.242	.109	.238	2.228	.029
	Government initiatives help in promoting technology transfer to SMEs (TTRI5).	.115	.110	.111	1.048	.298
***Venture Capital and** Angel Networks*	(Constant)	1.568	.555		2.827	.006
	Access to venture capital funding helps in scaling my business (VCAN1).	.091	.101	.097	.899	.371
	Angel investors play a key role in supporting small enterprises in my industry (VCAN2)	.093	.115	.087	.808	.422
	My enterprise has explored funding opportunities from venture capitalists or angel investors (VCAN3).	.063	.105	.069	.601	.550
	Financial support from investment networks accelerates innovation in SMEs (VCAN4).	.068	.111	.067	.610	.543
	Lack of access to venture capital funding is a major barrier to business growth (VCAN5).	.287	.110	.295	2.616	.011
Co-Creation with Customers	(Constant)	1.458	.560		2.603	.011
	My business involves customers in the development of new products/services (CCC1).	.114	.101	.112	1.130	.262
	Customer feedback helps in improving product/service innovation (CCC2).	.115	.094	.125	1.216	.227
	Co-creation with customers enhances business competitivene9 (CCC3).	-.047	.105	-.046	-.447	.656
	Engaging customers in innovation strengthens brand loyalty (CCC4).	.287	.106	.278	2.704	.008
	Digital tools help my business collect and analyze customer feedback for innovation (CCC5).	.174	.096	.188	1.804	.075
Open Data and Digital Platforms	(Constant)	1.701	.511		3.327	.001
	Digital platforms help my business connect with partners and customers (ODDP1).	-.025	.099	-.026	-.248	.804
	My enterprise uses open data to improve decision-making and innovation (ODDP2).	.077	.097	.083	.798	.427
	Online collaboration tools enhance business efficiency (ODDP3).	-.047	.102	-.049	-.457	.649
	E-commerce and digital platforms expand my business reach and sales (ODDP4).	.238	.104	.245	2.298	.024
	Access to market data helps in better planning and strategy development (ODDP5).	.313	.105	.309	2.981	.004
	(Constant)	1.701	.511		3.327	.001

a. Dependent Variable: Open innovation practices have significantly contributed to the growth of my business.

Table 10 presents the coefficients and significance of individual items within each construct. In the domain of Collaborative Partnerships, only CP1 ("My enterprise actively collaborates with other businesses for innovation and growth") is statistically significant (p = .031), implying that active collaboration is more impactful than generic partnership benefits. Within Cluster Based Innovation Networks, no individual item reached significance, reflecting the earlier observation of its limited overall effect. However, Technology Transfer shows one meaningful predictor TTRI4 (p = .029), highlighting the importance of access to technical expertise.

For Venture Capital and Angel Networks, VCAN5 ("Lack of access to venture capital funding is a major barrier to business growth") is significant (p = .011), indicating that perceived funding constraints notably affect innovation outcomes. In Co-Creation with Customers, CCC4 ("Engaging customers in innovation strengthens brand loyalty") emerged as a significant driver (p = .008), supporting the importance of customer involvement. Similarly, for Open Data and Digital Platforms, ODDP4 ("E-commerce and digital platforms expand my business reach and sales") and ODDP5 ("Access to market data helps in better planning and strategy development") were both significant (p = .024 and .004, respectively), suggesting digital resources directly facilitate innovation and market expansion.

6. SUGGESTIONS

Based on the analysis, stakeholders such as policy makers, business incubators, and innovation support agencies should prioritize enhancing digital infrastructure and promoting the adoption of digital platforms among micro and small enterprises. The significance of open data and digital tools in expanding business reach and improving strategic planning indicates a strong need for training programs focused on digital literacy, e-commerce integration, and data-driven decision-making. Ensuring affordable and reliable access to digital tools will enable enterprises to effectively participate in open innovation ecosystems.

Encouraging co-creation with customers should be another key focus area. As engaging customers in innovation strengthens brand loyalty and improves competitiveness, stakeholders can support initiatives that promote customer-centric innovation models. This may include developing feedback systems, offering innovation challenge grants, or facilitating platforms where businesses and customers collaboratively design new products or services. Training modules on customer relationship management and design thinking could also foster a culture of co-creation.

The importance of collaborative partnerships underscores the need for building regional and cross-sector networks. Facilitating platforms for SMEs to connect with peers, suppliers, distributors, and larger firms can lead to knowledge exchange, resource sharing, and market access. Stakeholders can also incentivize joint ventures through subsidies, recognition programs, or technical support to foster a more interconnected innovation environment.

While cluster-based innovation and technology transfer from research institutions showed weaker direct impacts, they still hold potential when effectively structured. Stakeholders should reassess and strengthen these models by improving the relevance and accessibility of academic collaborations and aligning cluster initiatives with industry-specific challenges. Establishing intermediary institutions or innovation hubs to bridge gaps between academia and enterprises could enhance the practical value of technology transfer.

Lastly, the concern around limited access to venture capital and angel investment suggests a need to bridge the funding gap. Stakeholders can facilitate SME-friendly investment networks, promote financial literacy among entrepreneurs, and advocate for regulatory reforms that attract early-stage investors. Creating transparent, low-barrier platforms for pitching and funding can encourage more investment flow into this critical sector and support scalable innovation.

REFERENCES

Albort-Morant, G., Leal-Millán, A., & Cepeda-Carrión, G. (2016). The antecedents of green innovation performance: A model of learning and capabilities. *Journal of Business Research, 69*(11), 4912–4917. DOI: 10.1016/j.jbusres.2016.04.052

Badi, S., Wang, L., & Pryke, S. (2017). Relationship market ing in Guanxi networks: A social network analysis study of Chinese construction small and medium-sized enterprises. *Industrial Marketing Management, 60*, 204–218. DOI: 10.1016/j.indmarman.2016.03.014

Balasubrahmanya, M. H. (2012). External support and innovation performance of MEs in Bangalore: Role of firm level factors. *IEEE*, 65–70.

Brunswicker, S., & Vanhaverbeke, W. (2015). Open innovation in small and medium-sized enterprises (SMEs): External knowl edge sourcing strategies and internal organizational facilitators. *Journal of Small Business Management, 53*(4), 1241–1263. DOI: 10.1111/jsbm.12120

Chesbrough, H. W. (2003). *Open Innovation: The New Imperative for Creating and Profiting from Technology*. Harvard Business School Press.

Cuerva, M. C., Triguero-Cano, Á., & Córcoles, D. (2014). Drivers of green and non-green innovation: Empirical evidence in low-tech SMEs. *Journal of Cleaner Production, 68*, 104–113. DOI: 10.1016/j.jclepro.2013.10.049

Gassmann, O., Enkel, E., & Chesbrough, H. (2010). The future of open innovation. *R & D Management, 40*(3), 213–221. DOI: 10.1111/j.1467-9310.2010.00605.x

Gupta, H., & Barua, M. K. (2017). Supplier selection among SMEs on the basis of their green innovation ability using BWM and fuzzy TOPSIS. *Journal of Cleaner Production, 152*, 242–258. DOI: 10.1016/j.jclepro.2017.03.125

Kumar, R., Singh, P., & Tiwari, M. K. (2021). AI-driven supply chain innovation for SMEs in India. *Journal of Innovation Management, 9*(2), 23–45.

Lee, S., Park, G., Yoon, B., & Park, J. (2010). Open innovation in SMEs - An intermediated network model. *Research Policy, 39*(2), 290–300. DOI: 10.1016/j.respol.2009.12.009

Love, J. H., & Roper, S. (2015). SME innovation, exporting and growth: A review of existing evidence. *International Small Business Journal, 33*(1), 28–48. DOI: 10.1177/0266242614550190

Michaelidou, N., Siamagka, N. T., & Christodoulides, G. (2011). Usage, barriers and measurement of social media marketing: An exploratory investigation of small and medium B2B brands. *Industrial Marketing Management, 40*(7), 1153–1159. DOI: 10.1016/j.indmarman.2011.09.009

Palacios-Marqués, D., Soto-Acosta, P., & Merigó, J. M. (2015). Analyzing the effects of technological, organizational and competition factors on web knowledge exchange in SMEs. *Telematics and Informatics, 32*(1), 23–32. DOI: 10.1016/j.tele.2014.08.003

Parida, V., Westerberg, M., & Frishammar, J. (2012). Inbound open innovation activities in high-tech SMEs: The impact on innovation performance. *Journal of Small Business Management, 50*(2), 283–309. DOI: 10.1111/j.1540-627X.2012.00354.x

Pittaway, L., Robertson, M., Munir, K., & Denyer, D. (2004). A typology of collaborative approaches to innovation. *Research Policy, 33*(2), 527–547. DOI: 10.1016/j.respol.2003.12.017

Rangus, K., & Drnovsek, M. (2013). Open innovation in Slovenia: A comparative analysis of different firm sizes. *Economic and Business Review, 15*(3), 175–196. DOI: 10.15458/2335-4216.1193

Rao, A. L., Santhikumar, R., & Venugopal, K. (2025). Visualizing Insight Enhancing Statistical Thinking in Higher Education. In Anastasiadou, S., & Seremeti, L. (Eds.), *Modes of Representation in Developing Statistical Thinking in Education* (pp. 181–214). IGI Global Scientific Publishing., DOI: 10.4018/979-8-3693-9934-7.ch010

Roper, S. (1997). Product innovation and small business growth: A comparison of the strategies of German, U.K. and Irish companies. *Small Business Economics, 9*(6), 523–537. DOI: 10.1023/A:1007963604397

. Rosenbusch, N., Brinckmann, J., & Bausch, A. (2011). Is innova tion always beneficial? A meta-analysis of the relationship between innovation and performance in SMEs. Journal of Business Venturing, 26(4), 441–457. https://doi.org/.jbusvent.2009.12.002DOI: 10.1016/j

Sambamurthy, V., Bharadwaj, A., & Grover, V. (2003). Shaping agility through digital options: Reconceptualizing the role of information technology in contemporary firms. *Management Information Systems Quarterly, 27*(2), 237–263. DOI: 10.2307/30036530

Scuotto, V., Santoro, G., Bresciani, S., & Del Giudice, M. (2017). Shifting intra- and inter-organizational innovation processes towards digital business: An empirical analysis of SMEs. *Creativity and Innovation Management, 26*(3), 247–255. DOI: 10.1111/caim.12221

Singh, R., & Gaur, A. (2022). Digital transformation in Indian SMEs: Exploring the role of digital technologies and innovation practices. *Journal of Business Research, 146*, 845–855. DOI: 10.1016/j.jbusres.2022.04.062

Stanko, M. A., Fisher, G. J., & Bogers, M. (2017). Under the wide umbrella of open innovation. *Journal of Product Innovation Management, 34*(4), 543–558. DOI: 10.1111/jpim.12392

Tawil, D. S., Alshebli, M. S., & Shahzad, B. (2023). Challenges of AI integration in SMEs: A systematic literature review. *Technological Forecasting and Social Change, 187*, 122189. DOI: 10.1016/j.techfore.2022.122189

Torchia, M., & Calabrò, A. (2019). Open innovation in SMEs: A systematic literature review. *Journal of Enterprising Culture, 27*(2), 201–228. DOI: 10.1142/S0218495819500080

. Triguero, A., Moreno-Mondéjar, L., & Davia, M. A. (2013). Drivers of different types of eco-innovation in European SMEs. Ecological Economics, 92, 25–33. https://doi.org/. ecolecon.2013.04.009DOI: 10.1016/j

Van de Vrande, V., Jong, J. P. J., Vanhaverbeke, W., & Rochemont, M. (2009). Open innovation in SMEs: Trends, motives and management challenges. *Technovation, 29*(6-7), 423–437. DOI: 10.1016/j.technovation.2008.10.001

Venugopal, K., Getenet, S., & Yalew, F. (2017). The Impact Of Marketing Mix Strategies On Micro And Small Business Enterprises Performance. In Case Study of Manufacturing Enterprises in Gondar City Administration, Ethiopia).,,,Forum for Intellectual Academicians and Researchers Publications‟.

Venugopal, K., & Das, S. (2022). Assessment of operational functions affecting on the micro and small enterprises' sustainability. *Parikalpana KIIT Journal of Management, 18*(1), 126–133.

Venugopal, K. (2024 a). Assessment of Investment Priorities by Rural Women. In Ghosal, I., Prasad, B., Ray, N., & Joshi, L. K. (Eds.), *Sustainable Strategic Business Infrastructure Development and Contemporary Digital Practices in Industry 5.0* (pp. 161–174). Apple Academic Press., https://www.researchgate.net/publication/383190787_Assessment_of_Investment_Priorities_by_Rural_Women, DOI: 10.1201/9781003492160-10

Venugopal, K. (2024 b). Insights into Waste Management in Semi-Urban Areas: Understanding Community Perspectives. In Mehra, R., Kumar, P., & Hung, B. (Eds.), *Municipal Solid Waste Management and Recycling Technologies* (pp. 301–326). IGI Global Scientific Publishing., DOI: 10.4018/979-8-3693-4054-7.ch011

Venugopal, K. (2024 c). Reverse Logistics Analysis: Enhancing Small Business Performance Perspectives. In Mızrak, F. (Ed.), *Strategic Innovations for Dynamic Supply Chains* (pp. 247–274). IGI Global Scientific Publishing., DOI: 10.4018/979-8-3693-3575-8.ch011

. Venugopal, K., Hailu Demissie, H., Abebe Worku H., & Haimanote Belay, A. (2015). Progression of Family Business in Micro and Small Enterprise – A Study in Gondar Region in Amhara State, Ethiopia. International Journal in Management & Social Science (IJMSS),Volume: 3, Issue no: 3, 520-528,

Venugopal, K., & Nakkina, V. V. (2025). Technological Innovations and Their Effect on B2B Relationships in the Hospitality Industry. In Nadda, V., Sharma, A., Mediratta, H., & Dadwal, S. (Eds.), *Addressing Contemporary Challenges in the B2B Hospitality Sector* (pp. 195–232). IGI Global Scientific Publishing., DOI: 10.4018/979-8-3693-9760-2.ch007

Venugopal, K., & Sharma, A. (2025). The Intricacies of Women's Involvement in Rural Family Businesses: A Focus on Micro and Small Enterprises (MSEs). In Erkol Bayram, G., Bayram, A., & Sak, M. (Eds.), *Empowering Women through Rural Sustainable Development and Entrepreneurship* (pp. 325–346). IGI Global Scientific Publishing., DOI: 10.4018/979-8-3693-6572-4.ch017

Walter, A.-T. (2020). Organizational agility: Ill-defined and somewhat confusing? A systematic literature review and conceptualization. *Management Review Quarterly*, *71*(2), 343–391. DOI: 10.1007/s11301-020-00186-6

Welte, T., Kühn, A., & Whaba, S. (2020). Predictive maintenance using machine learning for manufacturing systems. *Procedia CIRP*, *93*, 643–648. DOI: 10.1016/j.procir.2020.03.123

Zandi, F., & Tavana, M. (2011). A fuzzy group quality function deployment model for e-CRM framework assessment in agile manufacturing. *Computers & Industrial Engineering*, *61*(1), 1–19. DOI: 10.1016/j.cie.2011.02.004

Zeng, S., Xie, X., & Tam, C. M. (2010). Relationship between cooperation networks and innovation performance of small- and medium-sized enterprises (SMEs) in China. *Technovation*, *30*(3), 142–149. DOI: 10.1016/j.technovation.2009.08.003

Section 2
Technology, Ethics, and Organizational Innovation

Chapter 4
Awareness and Acceptance of Blockchain:
Based Credentialing in Hiring Processes

Sonia Munjal
Noida Institute of Engineering and Technology, India

Deepa Verma
http://orcid.org/0009-0002-6938-2935
Graphic Era University, Dehradun, India

Pawan Kumar
http://orcid.org/0000-0003-4892-6374
Graphic Era University, Dehradun, India

ABSTRACT

This study investigates the awareness and acceptance of blockchain-based credentialing in hiring processes, focusing on how organizational readiness, perceived trust, and blockchain knowledge impact its adoption. With the growing challenges of credential fraud and inefficiency in traditional hiring systems, blockchain technology offers an innovative solution by providing secure, transparent, and immutable records of candidates' qualifications. The study employs a quantitative research design, surveying 286 HR professionals and hiring managers across various industries to understand their perceptions of blockchain's applicability in credential verification. Statistical tools, including descriptive statistics, Pearson's correlation, and multiple regression analysis, were utilized to examine the relationships between the variables

DOI: 10.4018/979-8-3373-4307-5.ch004

and assess the factors influencing the acceptance of blockchain in recruitment. The results reveal that perceived trust and organizational readiness are the strongest predictors of blockchain adoption.

1. INTRODUCTION

In the digital age, technology has revolutionized multiple sectors, most notably the domain of human resources (HR) and recruitment. One such transformative innovation is blockchain technology, which, despite its roots in cryptocurrency, has emerged as a potent tool with the potential to disrupt traditional data management and verification systems (Khamzaeva et al., 2023). Blockchain technology's fundamental promise lies in its ability to offer transparency, security, and decentralization in record-keeping, which presents a new paradigm in hiring processes when applied to credential verification. The advent of blockchain-based credentialing systems introduces a profound shift in how organizations verify educational qualifications, work experience, and professional certifications, potentially eliminating the risks associated with fraudulent or tampered credentials (Gong et al., 2024). However, for blockchain to be integrated into hiring processes, awareness and acceptance are pivotal in determining its success. At the core of any technological innovation lies the need for a certain level of awareness, which encompasses understanding the technology's functionality, advantages, and potential impact on existing processes. In blockchain-based credentialing, awareness refers to how HR professionals, hiring managers, and organizations comprehend how blockchain works, how it can be leveraged in credential verification, and how it aligns with the organization's strategic goals. However, awareness alone is insufficient to ensure the widespread adoption of blockchain technology. Acceptance, as a complementary construct, addresses the willingness of individuals and organizations to embrace blockchain-based credentialing systems, which, despite their promising advantages, introduce a shift in the traditional norms and practices of credential verification. This dual interplay of awareness and acceptance dictates the pace and extent of blockchain adoption in hiring. Blockchain-based credentialing introduces a fundamental shift from traditional paper-based systems to digital, decentralized record-keeping forms. Traditional credentialing systems have long been susceptible to errors, omissions, and, more critically, fraud. A candidate's claim of holding a degree or certification has often relied on paper documents, which can easily be falsified or tampered with (Basdekidou & Papapanagos, 2024). Moreover, verifying such credentials is often time-consuming, expensive, and prone to human error. Blockchain technology offers a solution to these issues by providing a tamper-proof, immutable ledger that ensures the authenticity of credentials. Through blockchain, educational institutions, professional organizations, and employers can issue verifiable, real-time credentials that are easily accessible, accurate, and resistant to manipulation (Shahzad et al., 2023).

Despite the inherent advantages of blockchain-based credentialing, its implementation in hiring processes is not without challenges. A fundamental hurdle is the lack of awareness of blockchain and its applications beyond cryptocurrency (Kukreti et al., 2024b). For many HR professionals and hiring managers, blockchain remains an obscure and complex concept, often associated with digital currencies rather than a tool for managing and verifying credentials. Additionally, adopting new technology within organizations is subject to various influences, including organizational readiness, perceived benefits, and trust in the technology. Therefore, it is crucial to explore the awareness of blockchain technology and its acceptance among key stakeholders in the hiring process. Awareness of blockchain-based credentialing is the first critical factor that shapes its potential for integration into hiring practices (Rogalski & Schiereck, 2024). In this context, awareness refers to the knowledge and understanding that individuals and organizations have of blockchain technology and its applications. For an HR professional to effectively adopt blockchain-based credentialing, they must first comprehend the underlying principles of blockchain, its potential for reducing fraud, and how it can streamline the credential verification process (Kukreti et al., 2024c). However, mere awareness is insufficient. This awareness must translate into acceptance—a deeper, more active commitment to embracing and incorporating the technology into the organization's processes.

2. REVIEW OF THE LITERATURE

Multiple factors influence the acceptance of blockchain-based credentialing. The perceived trustworthiness of blockchain credentials plays a significant role in determining whether organizations will adopt such systems. Trust, in this regard, refers to the degree to which HR professionals believe in blockchain's security, transparency, and reliability as a medium for credential verification. Unlike traditional paper-based systems, which can be easily altered or forged, blockchain offers a decentralized, transparent ledger where each record is verified and stored in multiple locations, ensuring that no single party can manipulate the data. This level of transparency and security is vital in establishing trust in blockchain-based credentials (Pesqueira et al., 2025). However, the level of trust in blockchain is contingent on multiple factors, including familiarity with the technology, the perceived reliability of the platforms using it, and the overall understanding of how blockchain can be integrated into existing systems. Organizational readiness for adopting blockchain technology is another crucial determinant of its acceptance. Organizational readiness refers to the preparedness of a company to incorporate new technological solutions into its operations. This includes not only the availability of resources, such as IT infrastructure and skilled personnel but also the willingness of the organization's leadership to invest in and support the adoption of blockchain technology. Moreover, it involves an assessment of the broader organizational culture, which may foster innovation and openness to new technologies or resist change due to inertia or skepticism about the new technology's viability (Singh & Bhasin, 2024). As blockchain-based credentialing is a relatively novel concept, organizational readiness is critical in determining whether blockchain adoption will be a smooth and seamless process or will face significant resistance. Managerial support for integrating blockchain technology into HR processes is a key driver of its acceptance. HR professionals and hiring managers need to feel confident in the security and efficacy of blockchain as a tool for verifying candidates' qualifications. Therefore, the leadership within the organization must understand the potential value that blockchain-based credentialing can provide, not only in terms of reducing fraud and enhancing efficiency but also in strengthening the organization's reputation for conducting transparent and fair hiring practices. To consider the perceived benefits and barriers to blockchain adoption in hiring processes (Qian et al., 2023). While blockchain's promise of security, transparency, and efficiency makes it an attractive option, the barriers to adoption include the cost of implementing new systems, the complexity of integrating blockchain into existing hiring workflows, and potential resistance from individuals unfamiliar with or distrustful of new technologies. Additionally, the regulatory environment and data privacy concerns may further complicate the widespread adoption of blockchain in credential verification (Kukreti et al., 2024a; Sehajpal & Sidhu, 2024). For instance, while blockchain technology ensures that credentials are immutable and tamper-proof, questions surrounding the storage of personal data on blockchain platforms, especially in jurisdictions with stringent data privacy laws, could pose significant challenges. The concept of awareness and acceptance of blockchain-based credentialing in hiring processes represents a paradigm shift in how organizations approach verifying candidate qualifications. While blockchain offers an innovative solution to the problems of fraud, inefficiency, and opacity in traditional credentialing systems, the successful implementation of blockchain in hiring hinges on two critical factors: the awareness of the technology among HR professionals and hiring managers and their subsequent acceptance of its application in the hiring process (Liu et al., 2021). To realize the full potential of blockchain, organizations must not only foster awareness of its capabilities but also address the factors that influence acceptance, such as trust, organizational readiness, and managerial support. By understanding and addressing these factors, organizations can effectively integrate blockchain-based credentialing into their hiring processes, enhancing transparency, security, and efficiency in recruitment while minimizing the risks of credential fraud.

3. RESEARCH METHODOLOGY

This research adopts a quantitative methodology, utilizing structured surveys to collect empirical data regarding the awareness and acceptance of blockchain-based credentialing systems within hiring processes. The study employed a cross-sectional design, which facilitated the examination of a snapshot of current perceptions and attitudes toward blockchain technology in HR practices. A sample of 286 respondents was selected, comprising HR professionals, hiring managers, and organizational decision-makers across various sectors. The study utilized convenience sampling, ensuring accessibility to a relevant yet diverse respondent pool. The independent variables under investigation include Awareness Level of Blockchain, Perceived Trust in Blockchain Credentials, and Organizational Readiness for Technological Adoption. On the other hand dependent variable is the Acceptance of Blockchain-based Credentialing in Hiring. Statistical analysis was conducted using descriptive statistics, including mean, standard deviation, skewness, and kurtosis, to summarize the data. Pearson's correlation was used to explore the relationships between the variables, and multiple regression analysis assessed the predictive power of the independent variables on the dependent variable. This methodological approach allows for identifying key factors influencing the acceptance and awareness of blockchain technology in the recruitment process, providing valuable insights into its potential integration.

4. PURPOSE OF THE STUDY

This study aims to explore the awareness and acceptance of blockchain-based credentialing systems in hiring processes. By examining the factors influencing organizational readiness, perceived trust, and knowledge of blockchain technology, the research aims to offer insights into the feasibility and barriers of adopting blockchain solutions for credential verification in HR. The study ultimately seeks to inform HR practices and guide the integration of emerging technologies in recruitment processes.

5. ANALYSIS OF DATA

Independent Variables:

1. Level of Awareness of Blockchain Technology
2. Perceived Trustworthiness of Blockchain Credentials

3. Organizational Readiness for Technological Adoption

Dependent Variable:

1. Acceptance of Block chain-Based Credentialing in Hiring

Research instruments:

Table 1.

Variable	Statement of Questions	Degree of Response (7-point Likert Scale)
Level of Awareness of Blockchain Technology	I am familiar with how blockchain technology works.	1 = Strongly Disagree to 7 = Strongly Agree
	I understand the potential applications of blockchain in credentialing.	1 = Strongly Disagree to 7 = Strongly Agree
	I keep myself updated on developments in blockchain technology.	1 = Strongly Disagree to 7 = Strongly Agree
	I can explain the concept of blockchain to others.	1 = Strongly Disagree to 7 = Strongly Agree
	I have attended events or training related to blockchain technology.	1 = Strongly Disagree to 7 = Strongly Agree
Perceived Trust	Blockchain-based credentials are secure from tampering.	1 = Strongly Disagree to 7 = Strongly Agree
	I trust the authenticity of credentials issued through blockchain platforms.	1 = Strongly Disagree to 7 = Strongly Agree
	Blockchain ensures transparency in the credentialing process.	1 = Strongly Disagree to 7 = Strongly Agree
	I believe blockchain credentials are more reliable than traditional ones.	1 = Strongly Disagree to 7 = Strongly Agree
	Credentials stored on blockchain cannot be easily forged.	1 = Strongly Disagree to 7 = Strongly Agree
Organizational Readiness	My organization is open to adopting new technologies like blockchain.	1 = Strongly Disagree to 7 = Strongly Agree
	Our IT infrastructure can support blockchain-based systems.	1 = Strongly Disagree to 7 = Strongly Agree
	Management is supportive of integrating blockchain into HR processes.	1 = Strongly Disagree to 7 = Strongly Agree
	We have skilled personnel who can manage blockchain-based platforms.	1 = Strongly Disagree to 7 = Strongly Agree
	Our organization is financially capable of investing in blockchain solutions.	1 = Strongly Disagree to 7 = Strongly Agree

continued on following page

Table 1. Continued

Variable	Statement of Questions	Degree of Response (7-point Likert Scale)
Acceptance of Blockchain-Based Credentialing in Hiring	I am willing to consider blockchain-based credentials in the hiring process.	1 = Strongly Disagree to 7 = Strongly Agree
	My organization plans to adopt blockchain for credential verification in the future.	1 = Strongly Disagree to 7 = Strongly Agree
	I would recommend the use of blockchain-based credentials to others in HR.	1 = Strongly Disagree to 7 = Strongly Agree
	Using blockchain-based credentials improves trust in candidate qualifications.	1 = Strongly Disagree to 7 = Strongly Agree
	Blockchain credentials are a valuable tool for modernizing the hiring process.	1 = Strongly Disagree to 7 = Strongly Agree

Table 2.

Descriptive Statistics											
	N	Minimum	Maximum	Sum	Mean		Std. Deviation	Skewness		Kurtosis	
	Statistic	Statistic	Statistic	Statistic	Statistic	Std. Error	Statistic	Statistic	Std. Error	Statistic	Std. Error
Awareness_ Level_ Blockchain	286	1.00	7.00	1335.00	4.6678	.07174	1.21315	-.290	.144	.183	.287
Perceived_ Trust	286	1.00	7.00	1214.00	4.2448	.09417	1.59260	-.459	.144	-.554	.287
Organizational_ readiness_ adoption	286	1.00	7.00	1294.00	4.5245	.07764	1.31300	-.438	.144	.052	.287
Acceptance_ Blockchain	286	1.00	7.00	1165.00	4.0734	.08913	1.50724	-.435	.144	-.493	.287
Valid N (listwise)	286										

Table 2 provides the descriptive statistics for four key variables related to blockchain-based credentialing in hiring processes: Awareness Level of Blockchain, Perceived Trust, Organizational Readiness for Adoption, and Acceptance of Blockchain in Hiring. The table presents important summary measures for each variable, such as the minimum, maximum, sum, mean, standard deviation, skewness, and kurtosis. The mean values for all variables are above the neutral point of 4, indicating that respondents generally lean toward a positive stance regarding blockchain technology in the hiring process. The Awareness Level of Blockchain has a mean of 4.67, which suggests moderate familiarity with blockchain. The Perceived Trust in blockchain credentials shows a slightly lower mean of 4.24, indicating some skepticism or room for improvement in Trust. The Organizational Readiness for Adoption has a mean of 4.52, signaling a favorable disposition and highlighting that not all organizations may be fully prepared for blockchain integration. Lastly, the Acceptance of Blockchain has a mean of 4.07, reflecting moderate openness to blockchain credentialing in hiring, but it is not overwhelming.

The standard deviations are relatively high for all variables, particularly for Perceived Trust (1.59), implying significant variability in respondents' opinions on the reliability and trustworthiness of blockchain credentials. The skewness values for all variables are negative, indicating that the data is slightly skewed towards the higher end of the scale. This suggests a more favorable view of blockchain-related aspects in hiring processes. Kurtosis values near zero further suggest that the distribution of responses is close to normal, without significant peaks or flatness. Since it provides an overview of the general perceptions surrounding blockchain credentialing, with moderate levels of awareness, trust, and organizational readiness that lean positively. However, the relatively high variability indicates varying acceptance and preparedness for blockchain technology among the respondents.

Table 3.

Correlations					
		Acceptance_ Blockchain	**Awareness_Level_ Blockchain**	**Perceived_ Trust**	**Organizational_readiness_ adoption**
Pearson Correlation	Acceptance_Blockchain	1.000	.376	.596	.452
	Awareness_Level_ Blockchain	.376	1.000	.415	.469
	Perceived_Trust	.596	.415	1.000	.527
	Organizational_readiness_ adoption	.452	.469	.527	1.000
Sig. (1-tailed)	Acceptance_Blockchain	.	.000	.000	.000
	Awareness_Level_ Blockchain	.000	.	.000	.000
	Perceived_Trust	.000	.000	.	.000
	Organizational_readiness_ adoption	.000	.000	.000	.
N	Acceptance_Blockchain	286	286	286	286
	Awareness_Level_ Blockchain	286	286	286	286
	Perceived_Trust	286	286	286	286
	Organizational_readiness_ adoption	286	286	286	286

Table 3 displays the Pearson correlation coefficients among four variables: Acceptance of Blockchain, Awareness Level of Blockchain, Perceived Trust, and

Organizational Readiness for Adoption. This table provides insight into the relationships between the dependent variable (Acceptance of Blockchain) and the three independent variables.

The correlation between Acceptance of Blockchain and Awareness Level of Blockchain is moderate ($r = 0.376$), suggesting that the likelihood of accepting blockchain-based credentials in the hiring process increases as awareness of blockchain technology increases. This relationship is statistically significant ($p < 0.001$), indicating that the two variables are meaningfully related.

A stronger positive correlation is observed between Acceptance of Blockchain and Perceived Trust ($r = 0.596$), implying that Trust in the security, authenticity, and transparency of blockchain credentials is a significant driver of acceptance in the hiring context. This correlation is also statistically significant ($p < 0.001$), underscoring the importance of perceived Trust in fostering broader adoption.

There is a moderate correlation between the Acceptance of Blockchain and Organizational Readiness for Adoption ($r = 0.452$), suggesting that better equipped technologically and organizationally organizations are more likely to accept blockchain-based credentialing. This correlation is also significant ($p < 0.001$), indicating that readiness is important in the decision-making process regarding blockchain adoption.

The remaining correlations—between Awareness Level of Blockchain and Perceived Trust ($r = 0.415$), Awareness Level of Blockchain and Organizational Readiness for Adoption ($r = 0.469$), and Perceived Trust and Organizational Readiness for Adoption ($r = 0.527$)—are all moderate to strong and statistically significant. These findings imply that as organizations and individuals become more aware of blockchain technology, they are more likely to perceive blockchain credentials as trustworthy and be ready to adopt such systems.

Table 4.

Model Summary[b]										
Model	**R**	**R Square**	**Adjusted R Square**	**Std. Error of the Estimate**	**Change Statistics**					**Durbin-Watson**
					R Square Change	**F Change**	**df1**	**df2**	**Sig. F Change**	
1	.925[a]	.855	.844	1.18287	.391	60.246	3	282	.000	1.759

a. Predictors: (Constant), Organizational_readiness_adoption, Awareness_Level_Blockchain, Perceived_Trust
b. Dependent Variable: Acceptance_Blockchain

Table 4 provides a summary of the multiple regression model used to predict blockchain Acceptance based on three independent variables: Awareness Level of Blockchain, Perceived Trust, and Organizational Readiness for Adoption. The R-value of 0.925 indicates a strong linear relationship between the predictors and the outcome, suggesting that the model explains a substantial portion of the variance in blockchain acceptance.

The R-square value of 0.855 means that the three independent variables can account for approximately 85.5% of the variability in the Acceptance of Blockchain. This is a highly favorable result, indicating that the model is a good fit for the data. The Adjusted R-square of 0.844, which accounts for the number of predictors in the model, further supports the robustness of the model, as the adjusted value is very close to the R-square value.

The Standard Error of the Estimate is 1.18287, reflecting the average distance between the observed and predicted values of the Acceptance of Blockchain. Although this standard error is relatively small, it suggests that there may still be some unexplained variability.

The Durbin-Watson statistic of 1.759 is used to detect the presence of autocorrelation in the residuals. A value near 2 indicates no autocorrelation, and in this case, the statistic falls within an acceptable range, suggesting that the residuals are independent.

In conclusion, the model summary demonstrates that the combination of Blockchain Awareness Level, Perceived Trust, and Organizational Readiness for Adoption explains a significant portion of the variance in Blockchain Acceptance, and the model appears to be well-specified.

Table 5.

ANOVA[a]						
Model		**Sum of Squares**	**df**	**Mean Square**	**F**	**Sig.**
1	Regression	252.887	3	84.296	60.246	.000[b]
	Residual	394.571	282	1.399		
	Total	647.458	285			

a. Dependent Variable: Acceptance_Blockchain
b. Predictors: (Constant), Organizational_readiness_adoption, Awareness_Level_Blockchain, Perceived_Trust

Table 5 presents the results of the Analysis of Variance (ANOVA) for the regression model predicting the Acceptance of Blockchain based on three independent variables. The F-statistic of 60.246 is highly significant ($p < 0.001$), indicating that the regression model as a whole is statistically significant and provides a better fit to the data than a model with no predictors.

The regression's sum of squares is 252.887, which represents the amount of variation in Acceptance of Blockchain explained by the independent variables. The residual sum of squares is 394.571, representing the variation the model does not explain. The ratio of the two, as reflected in the F-statistic, confirms that the independent variables significantly improve the prediction of Acceptance of Blockchain compared to a null model.

This table emphasizes that the predictors—awareness Level of Blockchain, Perceived Trust, and Organizational Readiness for Adoption—collectively contribute meaningfully to explaining variation in Acceptance of Blockchain, further validating the findings from the model summary.

Interpretation of Table 6: Coefficients

Table 6.

Coefficients[a]						
Model		Unstandardized Coefficients		Standardized Coefficients	t	Sig.
		B	Std. Error	Beta		
1	(Constant)	.756	.309		2.446	.000
	Awareness_Level_Blockchain	.136	.067	.110	2.029	.001
	Perceived_Trust	.445	.053	.470	8.378	.000
	Organizational_readiness_ adoption	.175	.066	.153	2.642	.001

a. Dependent Variable: Acceptance_Blockchain

Table 6 shows the coefficients from the regression analysis, providing insight into the individual contributions of each predictor variable to the Acceptance of Blockchain. The unstandardized coefficients represent the change in the dependent variable for a one-unit change in the predictor. In contrast, the standardized coefficients (Beta) show the relative importance of each predictor in the model.

The constant (intercept) is 0.756, meaning that if all predictors are at zero, the Acceptance of Blockchain score would be 0.756. For the Awareness Level of Blockchain, the unstandardized coefficient is 0.136, suggesting that for each unit increase in awareness, Acceptance of Blockchain increases by 0.136. The standardized Beta of 0.110 indicates that the Awareness Level of Blockchain moderately impacts acceptance.

The most influential predictor is Perceived Trust, with an unstandardized coefficient of 0.445 and a standardized Beta of 0.470. This indicates that Perceived Trust has a significant positive effect on the acceptance of blockchain credentials. The high t-value of 8.378 ($p < 0.001$) reinforces the importance of Trust in blockchain adoption.

Lastly, Organizational Readiness for Adoption has a positive but weaker effect, with an unstandardized coefficient of 0.175 and a standardized Beta of 0.153. This suggests that while organizational readiness contributes positively to acceptance, it is less impactful than awareness and Trust.

Table 7.

Coefficient Correlations[a]					
Model			**Organizational_readiness_ adoption**	**Awareness_Level_ Blockchain**	**Perceived_ Trust**
1	Correlations	Organizational_readiness_ adoption	1.000	-.324	-.414
		Awareness_Level_Blockchain	-.324	1.000	-.223
		Perceived_Trust	-.414	-.223	1.000
	Covariances	Organizational_readiness_ adoption	.004	-.001	-.001
		Awareness_Level_Blockchain	-.001	.004	-.001
		Perceived_Trust	-.001	-.001	.003

a. Dependent Variable: Acceptance_Blockchain

Table 7 shows the correlations between the predictor variables in the regression model. The negative correlations between Organizational Readiness for Adoption and the other two predictors—Awareness Level of Blockchain (-0.324) and Perceived Trust (-0.414)—suggest that organizations more ready for adoption tend to have lower levels of awareness and Trust. However, these correlations are moderate, and the negative relationships indicate that readiness may not always align with higher levels of awareness or Trust.

Table 8.

Casewise Diagnostics[a]				
Case Number	**Std. Residual**	**Acceptance_Blockchain**	**Predicted Value**	**Residual**
89	3.097	7.00	3.3366	3.66336
184	-3.628	1.00	5.2921	-4.29205

a. Dependent Variable: Acceptance_Blockchain

Table 8 provides casewise diagnostics for the regression model, highlighting cases with large residuals. Case 89 shows a high standardized residual of 3.097, indicating that it is an outlier or an influential data point. Conversely, case 184 has a low residual of -3.628, suggesting that its predicted value is far from its observed value. Such outliers may affect the model's robustness and warrant further investigation.

Interpretation of Table 9: Residuals Statistics

Table 9.

Residuals Statistics[a]					
	Minimum	Maximum	Mean	Std. Deviation	N
Predicted Value	1.5123	6.0510	4.0734	.94198	286
Residual	-4.29205	3.66336	.00000	1.17663	286
Std. Predicted Value	-2.719	2.099	.000	1.000	286
Std. Residual	-3.628	3.097	.000	.995	286

a. Dependent Variable: Acceptance_Blockchain

Table 9 reports residual statistics for the regression model, providing key metrics for evaluating the model's fit. The predicted values range from 1.5123 to 6.0510, and the residuals range from -4.29205 to 3.66336, indicating the extent of deviation from the observed values. The mean residual of 0 suggests that the model, on average, predicts the Acceptance of Blockchain accurately. The standard deviation of residuals (1.17663) reflects the spread of the residuals around zero, suggesting that while the model fits the data well, there is still some unexplained variability.

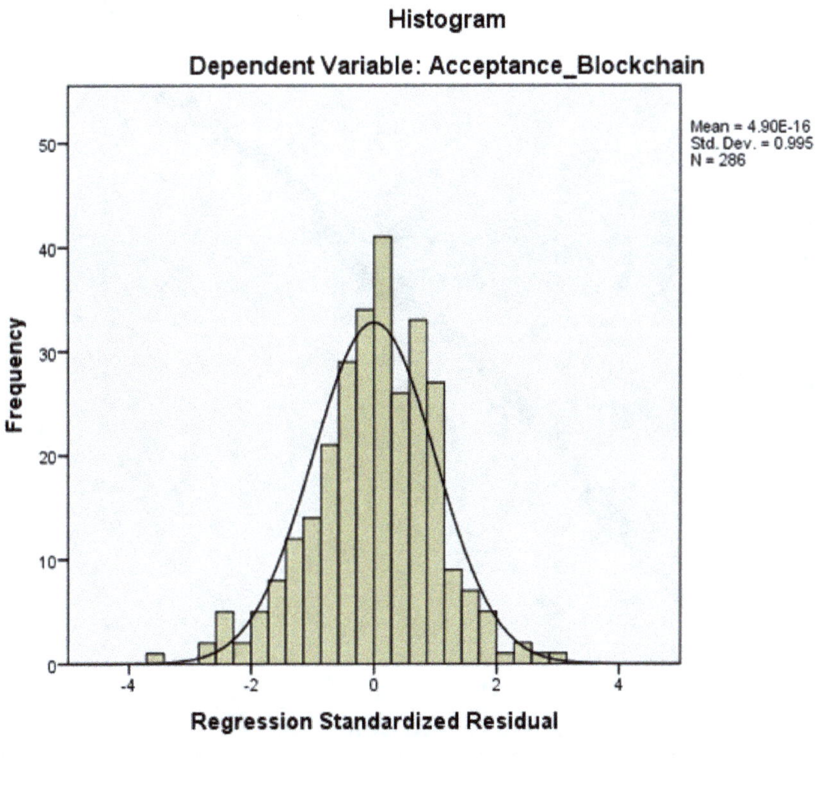

Figure 1 displays a histogram that illustrates the distribution of regression standardized residuals for the dependent variable Acceptance_Blockchain. The histogram is overlaid with a standard distribution curve, which suggests an attempt to visualize the residuals' alignment with a normal distribution. The mean of the residuals is reported as approximately zero, indicating no systemic bias in the regression model. The distribution appears roughly symmetric and bell-shaped, with a slight positive skew observed. This suggests that while most residuals are clustered around zero, there are a few outliers or extreme values on the higher end. The standard deviation of 0.995 further supports the notion of a relatively tight distribution around the mean, implying that the model's predictions are generally accurate but with some variability. The histogram suggests that the regression model fits the data well without significant deviations from normality. However, a more careful investigation of extreme residuals may be warranted to assess the influence of outliers.

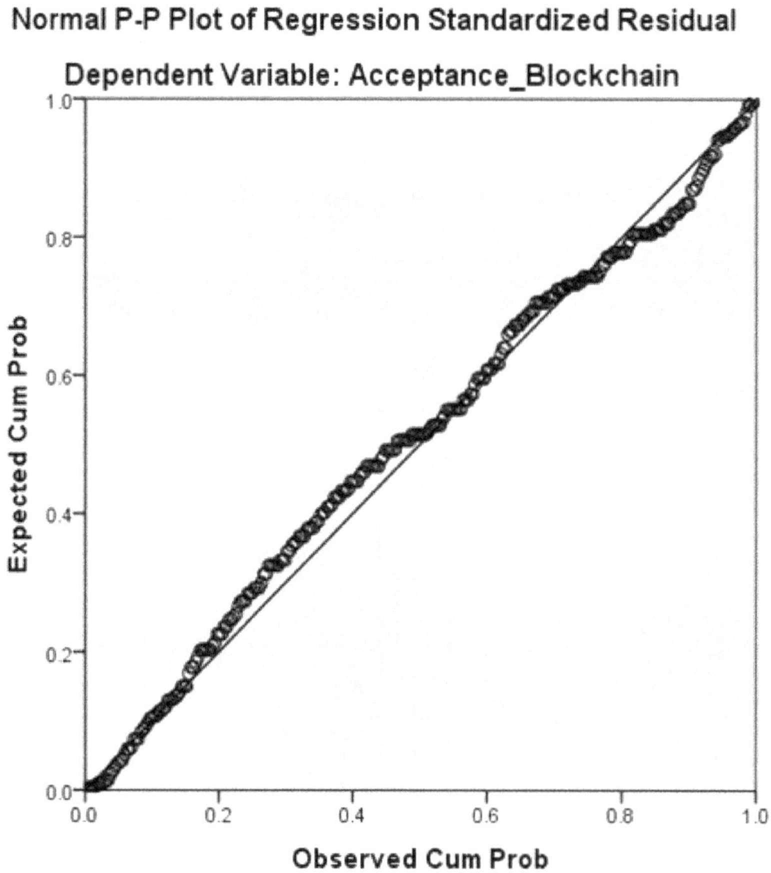

Figure 2 presents a Normal P-P Plot (Probability-Probability Plot) for the regression standardized residuals of the dependent variable Acceptance Blockchain. The plot compares the observed cumulative probabilities against the expected ones under a normal distribution. The points closely align along the reference line, which indicates that the residuals follow a normal distribution with little deviation. The closeness of the data points to the diagonal line signifies that the assumptions of normality are reasonably met, reinforcing the findings from the histogram. Any deviations from this line would suggest non-normality, but the plot suggests a well-behaved residual distribution in this case. Therefore, this further validates the adequacy of the regression model in terms of its residuals, indicating that the model's assumptions regarding normality are not violated, and the data is appropriately modeled without significant distortions.

6. FINDINGS AND RESULTS

This study explores the factors influencing the acceptance of blockchain-based credentialing in hiring processes. The primary focus is on three key aspects: the level of awareness of blockchain technology, the perceived trust in blockchain credentials, and organizational readiness for adopting new technologies. The study reveals that all these factors significantly positively impact the acceptance of blockchain in the hiring process. Among these factors, trust in blockchain emerges as the most influential. When participants perceive blockchain technology as secure, transparent, and tamper-proof, they are more likely to accept it for credential verification in hiring. Awareness also plays a crucial role; as individuals and organizations become more informed about the potential of blockchain, their willingness to adopt it increases. Finally, organizational readiness which encompasses technological infrastructure, financial investment, and skilled personnel also facilitates the transition towards adopting blockchain solutions in HR processes. The combination of these factors provides a strong foundation for acceptance, with organizations that are prepared regarding resources and infrastructure demonstrating greater openness to blockchain based credentialing. Additionally, the study shows that organizations with a proactive approach to integrating new technologies tend to adopt blockchain more readily. This highlights the importance of understanding blockchain and being adequately prepared to integrate it into existing systems. The findings indicate that blockchain has excellent potential to modernize the hiring process, but its widespread adoption hinges on trust, awareness, and organizational readiness.

7. SOCIAL, PRACTICAL, AND MANAGERIAL IMPLICATIONS

This research holds significant implications on several levels. From a social perspective, the widespread adoption of blockchain in hiring processes could result in more transparent, equitable, and trustworthy credentialing systems. By eliminating the potential for credential fraud and misrepresentation, blockchain technology could help ensure hiring decisions are based on accurate and verifiable data, benefiting employers and job candidates. This could contribute to more fair and just hiring practices across various industries. From a practical standpoint, organizations looking to implement blockchain-based credentialing systems must focus on two key areas: education and trust-building. First, companies need to ensure that their HR teams and relevant stakeholders are educated about blockchain technology's potential benefits and applications. This education will help reduce skepticism and foster a deeper understanding of its advantages. Second, building trust is crucial. Organizations must ensure that blockchain-based systems are secure, transparent, and tamper-proof, encouraging greater acceptance and usage. For managers, the findings underscore the importance of strategic planning in adopting blockchain technology. Managers must assess their organization's technological readiness and invest in the necessary infrastructure to support blockchain integration into their HR processes. Additionally, managerial support is vital in driving organizational change; managers must champion blockchain technology, ensuring employees are motivated to adopt it. In sum, managers play a crucial role in guiding the transition and ensuring that the adoption of blockchain aligns with the organization's broader objectives.

8. CONCLUSION

This study illuminates the pivotal factors that influence the acceptance of blockchain-based credentialing in hiring processes. The findings emphasize that awareness, trust, and organizational readiness are critical to the widespread adoption of blockchain in recruitment. As blockchain technology continues to evolve, its capacity to transform hiring practices by providing a secure, transparent, and efficient system for verifying credentials cannot be overlooked. However, adopting blockchain goes beyond simply understanding its potential; it requires careful consideration of organizational capabilities and a commitment to overcoming existing challenges. Organizations must invest the necessary infrastructure, training, and resources to integrate blockchain into their HR processes. Moreover, fostering trust in the technology is paramount. If organizations can effectively demonstrate blockchain credentials' security, transparency, and tamper-resistant qualities, they will be more likely to gain the acceptance of both employers and job candidates. From a broader perspective, blockchain could significantly improve the integrity of the hiring process. Its potential to reduce fraud, ensure transparency, and increase efficiency presents a compelling case for its adoption. However, the transition to blockchain-based systems requires a deep understanding of the technology and a strategic approach to implementation. Organizational leaders must take an active role in driving the adoption process, ensuring that all necessary resources, from financial investment to skilled personnel, are in place to support the technology. In conclusion, while blockchain has the potential to revolutionize credentialing in hiring, its successful implementation hinges on addressing the factors identified in this study: building trust, enhancing awareness, and ensuring organizational readiness. These elements form the foundation for blockchain's future in HR and recruitment.

REFERENCES

Basdekidou, V., & Papapanagos, H. (2024). The impact of FinTech/Blockchain Adoption on Corporate ESG and DEI Performance. *WSEAS Transactions on Business and Economics*, *21*, 2145–2157. DOI: 10.37394/23207.2024.21.177

Gong, X., Tao, X., Zhang, M., Xu, Y., Kwok, H. H. L., Dai, J., & Cheng, J. C. P. (2024). Secure environmental, social, and governance (ESG) data management for construction projects using blockchain. *Sustainable Cities and Society*, *114*, 105582. Advance online publication. DOI: 10.1016/j.scs.2024.105582

Khamzaeva, A. M., Menshchikova, V. I., Karbekova, M. Z., & Tazhiyeva, Z. N. (2023). Applied Solutions for ESG Management of Entrepreneurship in Digital Economy Markets with the Help of Blockchain. *Springer Climate, Part F1853*, 195 – 202. DOI: 10.1007/978-3-031-45830-9_22

Kukreti, M., Sehajpal, S., Tiwari, R., & Sood, K. (2024a). Driving global health and sustainable development goals with smart technology. In *Driving Global Health and Sustainable Development Goals With Smart Technology*. IGI Global., DOI: 10.4018/979-8-3373-0240-9

Kukreti, M., Sehajpal, S., Tiwari, R., & Sood, K. (2024b). Introduction. In *Driving Global Health and Sustainable Development Goals With Smart Technology*. IGI Global. DOI: 10.4018/979-8-3373-0240-9

Kukreti, M., Sehajpal, S., Tiwari, R., & Sood, K. (2024c). Preface. In *Driving Global Health and Sustainable Development Goals With Smart Technology*. IGI Global. DOI: 10.4018/979-8-3373-0240-9

Liu, X., Wu, H., Wu, W., Fu, Y., & Huang, G. Q. (2021). Blockchain-enabled esg reporting framework for sustainable supply chain. *Smart Innovation. Systems and Technologies*, *200*, 403–413. DOI: 10.1007/978-981-15-8131-1_36

Pesqueira, A., Fitzgerald, J., Kurman, P. A., Gáfaro Jaimes, S. D., Curado, J., & Gianico, S. (2025). Balancing ethical, data privacy, and security dimensions in blockchain-based healthcare governance: Aligning with ESG principles. In *Navigating Privacy, Innovation, and Patient Empowerment Through Ethical Healthcare Technology*. IGI Global., DOI: 10.4018/979-8-3693-7630-0.ch001

Qian, C., Gao, Y., & Chen, L. (2023). Green Supply Chain Circular Economy Evaluation System Based on Industrial Internet of Things and Blockchain Technology under ESG Concept. *Processes (Basel, Switzerland)*, *11*(7), 1999. Advance online publication. DOI: 10.3390/pr11071999

Rogalski, T., & Schiereck, D. (2024). ESG on the Chain: Unveiling the Impact of Different Blockchain Use Cases on Short-Term Stock Performance. In, B. T.X. (Ed.), *Proceedings of the Annual Hawaii International Conference on System Sciences* (pp. 5908 – 5917). IEEE Computer Society. DOI: 10.24251/HICSS.2024.711

Sehajpal, S., & Sidhu, N. K. (2024). Neuroscience, nursing, and financial innovation: A synergistic approach to optimized patient care and economic well-being. In *Neuromarketing's Role in Sustainable Finance*. IGI Global., DOI: 10.4018/979-8-3693-9117-4.ch008

Shahzad, U., Ghaemi Asl, M., & Tedeschi, M. (2023). Is there any market state-dependent contribution from Blockchain-enabled solutions to ESG investments? Evidence from conventional and Islamic ESG stocks. *International Review of Economics & Finance*, *86*, 139–154. DOI: 10.1016/j.iref.2023.03.001

Singh, B. R., & Bhasin, N. K. (2024). Adoption of Blockchain in ESG (Environmental, Social, and Governance). In *Sustainability Reporting and Blockchain Technology*. Taylor and Francis., DOI: 10.4324/9781003378341-21

Chapter 5
Building Green Skills in the Workforce as an HR Role in the Circular Economy

Zbigniew Grzymała
http://orcid.org/0000-0001-8861-8486
SGH Warsaw School of Economics, Poland

Agnieszka Wójcik-Czerniawska
http://orcid.org/0000-0002-9612-1952
SGH Warsaw School of Economics, Poland

ABSTRACT

The chapter begins by clarifying the concept of green skills, understood as the knowledge, abilities, values, and attitudes necessary to support environmental sustainability in both specific occupations and across the labor market. These include both technical skills—such as waste reduction strategies, renewable energy technologies, and sustainable production methods—and transversal soft skills, including systems thinking, environmental awareness, and innovation. The global demand for such skills is rapidly increasing as businesses seek to meet climate targets and adopt circular models. Finally, the chapter reflects on the broader challenges of building green skills in a digital and often fragmented labor market. It considers the impact of automation, hybrid work, and evolving policy landscapes on HR's ability to foster green competencies. It concludes by proposing strategic recommendations for HR professionals, educators, and policymakers committed to building a workforce prepared for the circular economy.

DOI: 10.4018/979-8-3373-4307-5.ch005

INTRODUCTION

Building Green Skills in the Workforce is associated with the transformation of the economy towards sustainable development, which results in, among other things, business models for enterprises in the spirit of the circular economy. The workforce is of key importance in every economy. Today, it determines the quality of use of other factors of production such as land or capital. The success of the transformation of economies with their various conditions towards the circular economy also depends on this force.

The transition to a circular economy—one that emphasizes sustainability, resource efficiency, and waste minimization—requires not only technological and business model innovations but also a fundamental shift in workforce competencies. Human Resource Management (HRM) is uniquely positioned to support this transition by equipping employees with the green skills needed to thrive in emerging circular economic systems. This chapter explores the strategic role of HRM in building green skills within the workforce and aligns this endeavor with the goals of the circular economy.

The aim of the chapter is to show and emphasize the importance of cultivating an organizational culture that supports circular economy values. HR's role in promoting green leadership, managing change, and fostering employee engagement around sustainability objectives is highlighted as a critical factor in long-term success. Finally, the chapter reflects on the broader challenges of building green skills in a digital and often fragmented labor market. It considers the impact of automation, hybrid work, and evolving policy landscapes on HR's ability to foster green competencies. It concludes by proposing strategic recommendations for HR professionals, educators, and policymakers committed to building a workforce prepared for the circular economy.

THE CONCEPT OF GREEN SKILLS IN THE CONTEXT OF SOCIAL SCIENCES

Green competences include "supporting sustainable development, implementing systems that reduce the carbon footprint and optimizing environmental processes. These competences increase the demand for employees who combine knowledge of IT, engineering and new technologies with competences related to environmental protection". Data from the World Economic Forum report clearly indicate that competences related to environmental protection and sustainable development are among the fastest growing in the world. The number of employees acquiring these skills increased by 12% over the last year, and the number of job offers requiring green competences increased by 22%. Green professions include renewable energy specialists and environmental data analysts. Particularly important are skills related to the optimization of energy processes and the development of applications monitoring the carbon footprint, which are becoming increasingly important in the changing landscape of the labor market (Staszewska, 2025).

Green skills create green jobs. For example, the European Commission associates green jobs with the circular economy: "A circular economy will increase the EU's competitiveness by protecting companies from resource scarcity and price volatility, helping to create new business opportunities and innovative, more efficient ways of producing and consuming. It will create local jobs at all skill levels and opportunities for social integration and cohesion (…) Circular economy actions are therefore closely linked to key EU priorities such as jobs and growth, the investment agenda, climate and energy, the social agenda and industrial innovation, as well as to global efforts for sustainable development. " (European Commission, 2015).

Green competences manifest themselves in ourselves. If we as a society accept the idea of sustainable development and the green skills that accompany this idea, we will use them in our daily lives as members of households or in the workplace in an increasingly natural way. "Business is facing a massive need to transform. Employees and executives must actively engage in the process. Those who believe the world will fix itself and that individuals play a small insignificant role stand to be victims of our times rather than passionate leaders who can shape our shared future. Gandhi said "you have to be the change you want to see." Your power, energy, creativity, innovation and intelligence are powerful resources. If you want the change, you will find the solutions. Your aim may be to achieve one small but meaningful act, such as getting fair trade coffee stocked in the office kitchen. "However big or small your ambitions, the tool and strategies will give you a comprehensive toolkit for action" (Fetzer & Aaron, 2010).

Green skills are therefore our choices, both as individual consumers and producers. These choices can be supported by specific economic policies created at various political and economic levels, for example at the level of the European Union and other international economic and political and economic associations, also at the level of a given country, at the regional and local level. The assumptions of the so-called European Green Deal assume, among other things, the transformation of economies towards a circular economy, i.e. towards a new economic model in which used products will be reused, repaired and recycled, and this should ultimately reduce the amount of waste and protect limited resources. In the process of such a transformation, new skills will be generated, as discussed later in the article. The European Green Deal, in addition to actions aimed at limiting the effects of climate change, is also "the pursuit of a cleaner, more sustainable and energy-efficient industry that performs well on the EU and global market, a plan to restore nature and strive to eliminate pollution in order to ensure a healthy environment for future generations, more ecological agricultural practices in order to protect the environment while offering healthy and affordable food, a plan for a just and inclusive transition to help the people most affected and leave no one behind, etc. (European Green Deal).

Green skills naturally support environmental protection and thus create the foundation for a healthy society. According to the World Health Organization (WHO):

1. Human health is primarily affected by particulate air pollution, which is often caused by fuel burned in engines and factories, as well as road dust.
2. Air pollution is responsible for 30% of cancer development (genetic factors - 15%) (Smog, 2015).

Based on the research conducted, it has been estimated that polluted air is the cause of:

1) 1.4% of the total number of deaths,
2) 0.5% of cases of total disability,
3) 2% of heart disease (Smog, 2015)

In turn, diseases related to the impact of atmospheric air pollution (smog) are: respiratory diseases, central nervous system disorders, circulatory system disorders, eye diseases, allergic reactions. The effects of short-term exposure of the population to air pollution are as follows: daily mortality, medical visits due to respiratory and circulatory system diseases (including hospital and emergency room interventions), taking medications due to respiratory and circulatory system diseases, absence from work and school, acute symptoms (cough, respiratory tract infections), physiological changes (lung function). The effects of long-term exposure of the population to air pollution include: mortality due to diseases of the circulatory and respiratory systems, chronic occurrence of respiratory diseases and common symptoms (asthma, chronic obstructive pulmonary disease), chronic changes in physiological functions, lung cancer, chronic diseases of the circulatory system, intrauterine changes (low birth weight at term, lack of adequate fetal weight gain) (Smog, 2015).

The phenomenon of reducing air pollution is associated with such actions as minimizing dust from car tires. This may depend on the inventiveness of tire manufacturers, who could produce tires that are more resistant to abrasion, and municipal services, which, at least in cities, should regularly water the streets during dry periods. Innovations in the field of communication also indicate the possibility of popularizing low-altitude flying vehicles performing communication functions. In its technical dimension, this technology is similar to solutions used to power drones. These vehicles would therefore not generate dust from tires. In turn, reducing dust and other toxins from factories and furnaces depends on the use of modern solutions such as chimney filters and low-emission furnaces. It is also a greater use of electricity, especially that generated from renewable energy sources, for heating.

From the point of view of demand theories, whose main representative was John Maynard Keynes, it generally follows that the level of economic activity, i.e. the level of production and employment, is determined mainly by demand. In other words, during a crisis, demand in the economy is too low and does not guarantee companies a sale of the goods and services produced. The economy can be stimulated by government intervention, for example in the scope of investment expenditure on infrastructure. Then aggregate demand is stimulated as a result of these investments. Green investment expenditures, which could constitute such an intervention tool, also include all public and private investments related to sustainable development. Instruments supporting such investments include, among others, green funds, which are becoming increasingly popular in the world. Such investments concern, among others, biogas plants, waste sorting plants, photovoltaic power plants, etc. Such activities more or less directly stimulate "green demand. In this way, the supply-demand circle closes in a given economy. In conclusion, both approaches are true depending on the economic situation and the development of the economy. In both of these approaches, green skills play an important role.

Green skills, according to some researchers, are in opposition to the principles of creation contained in the Old Testament, where in the Book of Genesis we can read: "And God said, 'Let us make man in our image, after our likeness. Let them have dominion over the fish of the sea, over the birds of the air, over the cattle, over all the wild animals, and over every creature that moves on the earth.'"... Then God blessed them and said to them, "Be fruitful and multiply, and fill the earth and subdue it; and have dominion over the fish of the sea and over the birds of the air and over every living thing that moves on the earth." And God said: "Behold, I give you every seed-bearing plant that is upon the face of the whole earth, and every tree with seed in its fruit; they shall be yours for food (Chapter I, Old Testament). This passage encourages man to exercise dominion over creation and to subdue nature. This can be further interpreted as God's commandment to exploit natural resources for the benefit of man. Therefore, there is no explicit mention here of the concept of, for example, circular economy or sustainable development in general. However, such references in the Christian religion can be found, among others, in the behavior of St. Francis of Assisi. Hence, the references by some Western politicians to the principles contained only in the Old Testament are in opposition to the teachings of this saint. Francis of Assisi even earned the title of patron saint of ecologists "thanks to his many years of support for animals and blurring the boundaries between humans and other creatures (...) Thanks to the stories found in The Flowers of St. Francis, we can learn about how he educated people he met on his path about animals, birds and insects (...) St. Francis was also a sage who spread knowledge about how to take care of other elements of nature such as trees, shrubs and flowers. He took care of the safety of the smallest inhabitants of the forest, creating a suitable place for everyone to live. His goal was to create a place where humans, animals, insects and other creatures could live in complete harmony devoid of cruelty" (InPost, 2023). We can also find concern for so-called sustainable development in Shintoism, Buddhism, Taoism and similar religious and philosophical concepts.

Green opportunities can also be seen when examining the economy in spatial terms, and especially the opportunities provided by cities. For example, the temperature in cities is usually several degrees Celsius higher than in non-urban areas, of course its level varies depending on the size of the city, season, climate, etc. This results from the fact that in cities, heat-generating devices such as cars, electrical devices, including refrigerators, heating devices, etc. are used. In this way, cities create a specific thermal envelope. This envelope can therefore be developed in an agricultural dimension.

References to the role of agriculture in the context of its function for cities can be found in several theories of development in the spatial system. "The forerunner of the location theory was von Thünen, who in 1826 created the concept of state productivity based on the model of structure location. He adopted the following assumptions in it (Stackelberg & Hahne, 1998, p. 36; Dorożyński, 2012, p. 14):

- the subject of the study is an isolated, homogeneous economic space with one dominant center (city);
- this centre is the only market for goods produced in its surroundings and at the same time a place of concentration of industrial and craft production;
- there is a uniform communication system between the city and its surroundings, and transport costs depend on the distance between the place of production and the place of consumption and the amount of goods transported and their durability;
- producers strive to maximize profit, taking into account the fact that transportation costs increase with the distance of the production site from the center;
- In the market there is free competition between sellers who strive to maximize profits.

What the authors of this chapter propose to introduce new to the development of the economy in spatial terms in the context of green skills is the perception of the possibility of absorbing the first circle according to von Thünen by urban areas, especially in the so-called sprawling cities. Therefore, one can seriously consider the strategic transfer of at least agricultural activity from the first circle to the city itself. In this way, on the one hand, we are more rationalizing the costs of transport and the entire logistics of delivering food to cities, and on the other hand, we are creating a new set of green skills for city residents from the area of cultivation of agricultural products. Even today, you can find many allotment gardens in cities, and cows graze at the University of Cambridge. In New York, bees are bred near city parks. This custom has been adopted by many other cities in the world. An additional advantage is the aforementioned thermal envelope, which is created by the city, especially beneficial in temperate or cold climates. The areas designated for such agricultural activities can be the walls of buildings, spaces above water reservoirs in cities, etc. There are also examples of agricultural cities, for example in Africa, where the climate is much hotter. In this case, the aspect of thermal insulation is not important. Other factors play a role in directing the agricultural use of urban areas. Of course, the size of such agricultural activities depends on the organization and strategy of the city's development, the will of local authorities and the openness of residents. Undoubtedly, its use on a large scale would expand the so-called green skills.

Green competences in the IT and new technologies sector alone encompass a broad spectrum of technical and analytical skills that support global efforts towards sustainable development. From real-time monitoring of carbon dioxide emissions, through designing energy management systems, to implementing artificial intelligence technologies, green competences determine the direction of development of the technology industry. Their importance grows with the tightening of climate regulations and the need to adapt the organization's operations to ESG requirements (Staszewska, 2025).

In conclusion, green competences are a very broad term, encompassing many dimensions (Cabral, Dhar Lochan, 2019, 887–900; Ziółkowska, 2024, pp. 163-164):

- green knowledge – this concerns general knowledge about the natural environment,
- green skills – these are skills of both a professional and general nature, which are necessary primarily in green professions, but also those affected by the green transformation, i.e. these are the abilities to perform tasks that take into account their impact on the environment in such a way as to minimize the negative impact on the ecosystem,
- green awareness – this concerns awareness of the impact of human activity on the natural environment (e.g. leaving a carbon footprint, etc.),
- green attitudes – understood as the perception of the importance of environmental protection by an individual,
- green skills – essential for self-development and increasing efficiency in the green economy,
- green behaviors that support environmental sustainability.

Green skills are mainly found in the following industries:

1. Energy Efficiency - Understanding the principles of energy efficiency such as reducing energy consumption, optimizing energy use and maximizing the use of renewable energy sources.
2. Sustainable Construction - Knowledge of sustainable building materials, energy-efficient design principles and eco-friendly construction techniques.
3. Waste Management – Understanding how to reduce waste, recycle materials, and dispose of hazardous materials in an environmentally friendly manner.
4. Sustainable Agriculture – Understanding sustainable agriculture techniques such as organic farming, conservation agriculture and agroforestry.
5. Renewable Energy - Ability to work with renewable energy technologies such as solar, wind and hydropower, and knowledge of how these technologies can be integrated into existing energy systems.
6. Green Transport – Understanding sustainable transport systems such as public transport, cycling and electric vehicles.
7. Water management - knowledge of water saving techniques such as rainwater harvesting, water reuse and efficient irrigation systems (Ziółkowska, 2024, p. 164).

SELECTED EXAMPLES OF GREEN SKILLS

The list of green skills can also be derived from the so-called ReSOLVE concept. The ReSOLVE concept is an abbreviation of words representing specific actions of the business paths of companies striving to implement the principles of the circular economy: *Regenerate*, *Share*, *Optimise*, *Loop*, *Virtualise* and *Exchange* . The authors co-created over 50 circular economy business models for SMEs and thus distinguished green skills in relation to ReSOLVE in the SME group.

"Regenerate" is all activities aimed at switching to renewable materials and energy sources, i.e. the practical implementation of the idea of returning recovered biological resources to the environment. Examples include energy recovery, use of energy from renewable sources, energy-efficient construction, locating production centers in eco-industrial parks, etc. (ReSOLVE). Green skills accompanying "Regenerate" include advisory functions regarding the transition to renewable energy sources in various organizational and legal forms. These can be both individuals and consulting companies dealing with consulting in this area, associations or foundations and such organizations. These are also engineering skills related to the installation of these devices, including energy-efficient construction.

“Share” *is generally* understood as sharing with co-users, a way to maximize the use of a product or service. Sharing also means reusing products, provided they are technically efficient and approved for use (e.g. the second-hand principle) and extending the life of products through their maintenance, repairs and design methods that increase their durability (ReSOLVE). Examples include sharing private resources (on a peer-to-peer basis) or sharing a public pool of products (ReSOLVE). Green skills for the “Share” feature include traders offering goods from the so-called “second-hand”. It is also the service of organizations associated with this process. For example, in the USA, this includes the St. Vincent network, which, on the one hand, collects unnecessary goods from people and organizations, and then, with the help of volunteers, reviews these goods, sorts them, adapts them for sharing and then offers them to customers in its branches. This group of green skills also includes people with technical skills who can regenerate used parts for various devices, such as crankshafts, etc.

“Optimise” *is* an optimisation activity focused primarily on increasing the efficiency and effectiveness of the product and the removal of waste in the production process and supply chain (from supply and production logistics, through use and the final stage of use). It is important that the optimisation takes place without the need to introduce changes to the management system and update the existing technology. Optimisation may refer to the use of large data sets, automation, remote sensing or remote control systems (ReSOLVE). Green skills in the scope of “Optimise” include, among others, the knowledge of people dealing with the optimisation of technical and service processes using digital techniques and artificial intelligence. This knowledge is used in many fields, not only in relation to the optimisation of pro-ecological solutions. These skills emphasise that the so-called circular economy models aim, on the one hand, at better use of raw materials, materials and products, and on the other hand show economically effective solutions for enterprises or even settlement units. In this way, with rational optimisation, a competitive advantage is obtained on the market. This therefore contradicts the widespread opinion that green solutions generate additional costs, thus reducing the competitiveness of individual economic entities and, consequently, the entire economy.

“Loop” in turn means striving to maintain components and materials in a closed loop. Examples include reusing products, recycling, recovering raw materials, minimizing material and energy losses, upcycling, downcycling, etc. (ReSOLVE). Within the green skills occurring here, we can distinguish the ability to design a closed loop and enter into so-called industrial symbioses according to which my waste is your raw material.

“Virtualise” is a model of operation that assumes the provision of specific utility virtually instead of materially. *Exchange* is a model of exchange that assumes replacing old materials with new advanced materials, using modern technologies and choosing modern products and services (ReSOLVE). Within "virtualise" there are professions used in a very wide range from virtual projection in stores selling, for example, building materials, where thanks to "virtualise" you can choose the right variant of a building project for the customer, to holographic recreation of ancient buildings in the place of their ruins, etc.

Green skills also include a whole range of professions related to waste management. Therefore, they include managerial skills in companies dealing with the collection and management of municipal waste. These are also all technical skills related to the service of the aforementioned process. In connection with waste management, in Poland we can also distinguish the profession of municipal waste sorter with the code in the Polish Economic Classification: 961202. Sorter municipal waste is responsible for the collection and sorting of municipal waste; is responsible for the correct separation of waste types, including electronic waste and other hazardous waste found in municipal waste. The professional tasks of the sorter include sorting waste into individual fractions, including selecting waste suitable for processing from the stream of mixed municipal or packaging waste; identifying individual types of waste in order to place sorted waste in designated chutes or containers; operating a manual and mechanical belt for sorting municipal waste; ensuring the proper technical condition of sorting equipment; observing the operating instructions for sorting equipment and health and safety and fire protection regulations (961202 - Municipal waste sorter). The sorter should also be responsible for collecting municipal waste from premises or in the so-called EKO AB System and should participate in activities related to starting up the sorting plant.

The aforementioned EKO AB system is a system invented and implemented by engineer Andrzej Bartoszkiewicz for segregation at source, in which no waste is thrown away, but given to an employee of the EKO AB System pavilion, the aforementioned sorter. Thanks to the return, the possibility of maximum prevention of waste generation is created, e.g. mass recycling of packaging for reuse, recovery as a result of pre-selection of things that are still useful directly or after minor repairs - giving "a second life". In practice, it is a pavilion to which residents bring municipal waste, which is then dealt with by a sorter. Residents divide their waste into only 3 fractions. These three fractions are: kitchen waste, i.e. food leftovers, peelings and other bio, bathroom waste, i.e. sanitary, other waste, i.e. all that we classify as municipal waste, including bulky waste, electronic waste, batteries and others. In turn, directly in the EKO AB System pavilion, the sorter divides them into several dozen commercial fractions that are later suitable for sale or other use. For example, the bio fraction taken from a resident is temporarily stored in a cold store, which prevents it from rotting and losing its valuable properties, and its purity makes it an excellent raw material for biogas plants or composting plants, so it can be used to produce fertilizer. In this system, it is also possible to combine the collection of sorted waste by residents with the possibility of collecting packages subject to a deposit. These pavilions were implemented in Poland in the cities of Płock and Nakło nad Notecią in places of block development. The location in such development improves the efficiency of this solution. In the above-mentioned cities, the sorter's duties were supported by automatic systems.

In detail, the invention relates to systems and methods for identifying and recording municipal waste, particularly in multi-family buildings (e.g. housing estates) and in single-family homes, using RFID technology. The solution finds application in waste management, particularly in waste segregation systems, where there is a need to monitor who and how much waste is being disposed of, in order to individually settle accounts and increase the efficiency of segregation. The innovation here is the system and the related method for segregating and identifying municipal waste in residential buildings, which enables automatic assignment of each discarded waste bag to a specific user (apartment). The system uses RFID technology both to authenticate residents and to mark waste bags, thanks to which identification takes place without the participation of staff or additional activities of the resident (apart from standard waste disposal) (Description of the invention and patent claims P.445947) .

Key features of the solution are:

- Utilisation of existing waste collection infrastructure (standard 1100 L containers, bin shelters, container rooms) – the system can be integrated with a typical bin shelter or bin room, without the need for special, closed drop-off stations.
- RFID-based access control – only authorized residents (those with a card/ RFID identifier assigned to the premises) can enter the room with containers. An electronic lock controlled by an RFID/NFC reader is used for this purpose. Applying the card simultaneously logs the user into the system (starting the user session).
- Automatic reading of RFID tags from waste bags – each bag used in the system has an integrated RFID tag (e.g. sewn into the bag material or permanently attached). The system is equipped with a gate or RFID antennas placed in such a way that they detect and read all tags on bags brought by the user when entering the gazebo/room or when throwing bags into containers. Data on detected bags (their unique RFID identifiers and the type of waste resulting from, e.g. the frequency range or tag coding) are assigned to the logged-in user automatically.
- Sensors for detecting the insertion and filling of containers – a sensor (e.g. a laser distance sensor in ToF technology) is installed in each waste container, which registers the event of inserting a bag (through a change in distance, a reflection signal) and measures the level of filling of the container on an

ongoing basis. Based on this data, the system counts how many bags were inserted into individual containers during a given user session.

- Session logic and compliance verification – the system compares the number of bags read at the entrance (RFID tags) with the number of bags actually thrown in (detected by sensors) for each session. If there is a discrepancy (e.g. the user brought in 3 bags, and the sensors recorded the throwing in of only 2 tags – which means that one bag had no tag), the system considers it an undesirable event and generates an alarm to the central system. This ensures real-time control of the correctness of segregation, without the need for constant staff supervision.
- Local controller and data transmission – all events (user entry, tag readings, throwing into individual containers, possible alarms) are recorded by the local controller. After the session ends (i.e. after the user leaves the gazebo/room), the collected data is sent (e.g. via GSM module or Ethernet network) to the central IT system.
- Central analytical system – data from many locations (many gazebos in the commune/city) are sent to the central system, where they are aggregated and stored. Authorized users (e.g. system administrators, property managers, municipal services, and potentially residents themselves to a limited extent) have access to the collected information in accordance with the granted authorizations. The central system allows for the generation of reports, statistics, and above all, the assignment of the amount (volume) of waste returned to specific users) (Description of the invention and patent claims P.445947).

Thanks to such a configuration, the invention solves the problem of individual waste identification in multi-family buildings in an automated manner that does not require additional activities from residents beyond those they already perform (throwing out garbage and opening the gazebo door). Technically innovative is the combination in one system of: RFID access control, RFID waste tagging and counting sensors, which provides a synergistic effect - "sealing" the segregation process and enabling individual waste settlement) (Description of the invention and patent claims P.445947) .

Another example of developing green skills from the local community level are local government initiatives. An important impulse for such an initiative in Europe was the project aimed at achieving energy self-sufficiency in the Austrian town of Güssing. At the initiative of the local government, a project was initiated with residents and businesses to produce electricity and heat in this town. The project has grown, and the whole of Europe has learned about this local initiative. More on this topic can be found in the authors' article: "Partnership of Stakeholders at the Local Level as an Effective Instrument of Local Development "(Wójcik-Czerniawska,

Grzymała, 2023). Similar solutions have also begun to appear in Poland, where, among other things, the creation of energy cooperatives was initiated.

An energy cooperative is a cooperative within the meaning of the Act of 16 September 1982 - Cooperative Law or the Act of 4 October 2019 on agricultural cooperatives, the subject of which is the generation of electricity or biogas or heat in renewable energy source installations and balancing the demand for electricity or biogas or heat, exclusively for the own needs of the energy cooperative and its members, connected to a defined area electricity distribution network with a rated voltage lower than 110 kV or a gas distribution network or a heating network (Banaszuk, 2023, p. 7).

The subject of the activity of an energy cooperative may be the generation of electricity, heat or biogas in renewable energy source installations owned by the energy cooperative or its members (Art. 38f sec. 1 of the RES Act). An energy cooperative supplies electricity, biogas or heat to producers and recipients who are members of this cooperative, whose installations are connected to the network of a given operator or to a given heating network (Art. 38c sec. 1 of the RES Act). It operates in the area of one operator of the electricity distribution system or a gas or heating distribution network. The area of operation of an energy cooperative is determined on the basis of the connection points of producers and recipients who are members of this cooperative to the electricity distribution network, gas distribution network or heating network (Art. 38c sec. 1 and 2 of the RES Act). An energy cooperative in Poland is a new opportunity for members of local communities, including local governments, to develop the so-called civic energy, thanks to which they can jointly use renewable energy sources, improve energy efficiency, and reduce electricity and heat bills. Currently, there are no restrictions on who can establish an SE and what the minimum contribution of members is. A notarial deed is not required to establish such a cooperative, only notarial confirmation of the signatures of the board members. This reduces costs and speeds up the establishment. In the event that an energy cooperative makes a profit by selling energy to its members, the surplus received must be returned to the members, which is not subject to taxation. This is a beneficial mechanism for supporting renewable energy sources.

If the cooperative does not meet the above conditions, the Director General of the National Support Centre for Agriculture shall refuse, by decision, to include the cooperative in the list of energy cooperatives. For the purposes of commercial balancing, all producers and recipients of the energy cooperative shall be considered as recipients (Article 38 of the RES Act).

Electricity or heat produced in an Energy Cooperative may be used exclusively for the needs of its members. Therefore, it is not possible to sell electricity or heat to other recipients or trading companies. When a cooperative wants to make such sales outside its members, it may do so on the so-called general principles, then the cooperative is treated as an energy company and is subject to appropriate requirements (including having appropriate licenses, etc.) (Banaszuk, 2023, p. 7).

The idea of the Cooperative is to provide benefits to its members, including energy cheaper than on the market by using local resources. This increases energy security for its members because energy is consumed and balanced locally, in a small area. For example, if one of the renewable energy sources used within the Cooperative is an agricultural biogas plant, its members will have a market for the biodegradable part of products, waste or residues of biological origin from agriculture, while at the same time ensuring their energy supply (electricity, heat or biogas) and implementing the closed-loop economy strategy. In the absence of coal or gas for energy production in system power plants, it will continue to be produced in the Cooperative (Banaszuk, 2023, p. 7).

Assuming the PV source power of 1 MW, the annual volume of energy produced – 1100 MWh, 10 members of the Cooperative, the total annual energy consumption of 1200 MWh (100 MWh per month), the cost of building a 1 MW PV source – PLN 4 million, the payback period of 6 years, the energy sales price guaranteeing a return on investment plus coverage of operating costs of PLN 650/MWh and the use of energy storage facilities, the following effect can be achieved:

1) with 100% of own energy consumption, monthly savings will amount to: PLN 23,106, and annually: PLN 277,271,
2) with auto-consumption at the level of 40%, monthly savings will amount to: PLN 17,560.95, and annually: PLN 203,472 (Banaszuk, 2023, pp. 12-13).

The cooperative's main investment is a photovoltaic farm with an initial capacity of 1 MW, the construction of which began at the end of 2022. The ultimate capacity of the installation is to reach 10 MW, which will allow for significant self-consumption of energy in the commune. The cooperative is also considering the use of geothermal drilling to obtain heat, which will complement the offer with additional sources of renewable energy (Mrozowski, 2025).

An example of the development of other green skills in cities is the use of thermal insulation created in cities and other technological possibilities for growing plants. For example, in the Swedish city of Linköping, a skyscraper was built for vertical plant cultivation. The designers assumed that the 54-meter-high facility would be one of the most ecological vegetable and fruit farms in the world. Within its area, 15 types of plants of Asian origin were to be grown.

The innovative project, developed by engineers from Sweco and Plantagon, will use the energy surpluses generated by the city to increase the efficiency of the photosynthesis process. Thanks to the use of integrated solutions, the skyscraper is to be almost three times more efficient than traditional plant cultivation. The lack of need to transport food due to the direct location in the urban area will reduce C02 emissions, as well as the lack of need to burn gasoline, which is typical for farms located outside the city limits. This will also significantly affect the prices of products, to which there will be no need to add costs related to transport (Ecology, 2025).

In addition, the farm will produce virtually no sewage or waste. The plants will be irrigated using a special spraying system, which will also use the surplus water used in the city. Thanks to the appropriate layout of the building, each floor is to have optimal light conditions for cultivation. The plants will be placed on a special spiral made up of cultivation stands, which will change its position depending on the time of day. According to expert calculations, the skyscraper is to provide three times greater efficiency than in the case of traditional cultivation. Additionally, the land area, which is 10 thousand meters, will be the equivalent of 100 thousand traditional cultivation area (Ecology, 2025).

The lack of need for food transport due to its direct location in the urban area means that the skyscraper under construction in Linköping is to be one of the most ecological vegetable and fruit cultivations in the world. This solution will reduce $C0_{2 \text{ emissions}}$, as well as eliminate the need to burn gasoline, which is typical for cultivations located outside the city limits. It will also significantly affect the prices of products, to which there will be no need to add transport costs. Thanks to the appropriate layout of the building, each floor is to have optimal light conditions for cultivation. Additionally, the investment in order to increase the intensity of the photosynthesis process will use the city's energy surpluses, as well as process excess water consumption and $CO_{2 \text{ emissions}}$. Adequate sunlight and integrated solutions for creating appropriate cultivation conditions are to ensure three times more efficient cultivation than in the case of standard greenhouses (Ecology, 2025).

Another example of a European city that is conducive to creating green skills is, among others, the Swedish Malmö. In this city, and more precisely in Bo01 - an innovative housing estate, it was possible to combine city life with caring for the environment.

Bo01 is not new at all. The Swedes started the “city of the future” project in 1995, and the first effects were presented at the European Housing Exposition in 2001. The “ecological” part of the city has been growing ever since. The Malmö City Council recently proposed a plan for the further expansion of the entire Västra Hamnen district (the Bo01 estate is part of it), which is to last until 2031 (Kojzar, 2021).

The district, which today can be a model for the whole of Europe and is called the “city of the future”, was once a typical industrial area. From the 19th century until the economic recession in the 1970s, ships were built there. In 1990, a SAAB car factory was built there, which closed after only six years. What was left was an empty, post-industrial area on the Öresund Strait itself. Construction of the “city of the future" began in 2000. The plan was to create 350 apartments, but after the expansion there are already 1,800 of them (Kojzar, 2021). The estate obtains almost 100 percent of its electricity from renewable energy sources such as solar collectors and windmills . Heat energy, in turn, is obtained from geothermal sources with the support of solar collectors.

The wind farm is located 3 km from Bo01 and, together with photovoltaic panels, produces enough power to meet the needs of residents, power heat pumps and charging sockets for electric cars. At the same time, the power grid is connected to the city grid. Thanks to this, in winter - when the demand of residents is higher - there is no shortage of energy, because it can be partially drawn from city resources. In summer, in turn, the surplus energy produced in Bo01 is given to the city (Kojzar, 2021).

Waste segregation plays an important role in municipal waste management. Some apartments have devices in their sinks for removing organic waste, which falls into a special tank, from which it is directly sucked out by a garbage truck. Biogas is produced from them, which is used, among other things, to power city buses. In turn, organic waste collected in green areas near houses is composted and processed into fertilizer. And there is no shortage of parks, gardens and green areas in the area. The houses are set quite densely to leave space between them for greenery, where wild herbs, flowers and climbing plants grow. In addition to squares and meadows, there are also green roofs and waterside areas, where benches and picnic tables have been set up. Additionally, nesting boxes for birds and shelters for bats have been built. The estate also has a specially designed system for using rainwater. It is retained in reservoirs in green courtyards and in rooftop gardens, and its excess is discharged into the sea through open channels. Channels and reservoirs protect residents from droughts, floods, and inundations (Kojzar, 2021).

Another example of implementing green solutions, and thanks to them green skills, by local authorities but in cities outside Europe is the capital of Rwanda – Kigali. As a result of internal struggles, the peak of which was the mass genocide in 1994, the city was partially destroyed, especially in the area of infrastructure. Thanks to many pro-environmental initiatives, such as a total ban on the sale and possession of plastic bags, a decision was also made to introduce urban agriculture. Due to the local hot climate, the aspect of thermal insulation was of course not of significant importance here. The basic factor determining the introduction of agriculture to the city was the spatial layout of Kigali. The city is located on several hills. Some of them have steep slopes. The terrain differences sometimes reach 300 meters. On the one hand, such terrain is not conducive to settlement, on the other hand, such an area can be developed for agriculture.

Within the boundaries of the research area (Kigali's compact urban tissue) covering 8821 ha, agricultural areas with a total area of 872.76 ha (9.89% of the area) were identified. They can be divided into two main groups, which differ in terms of the production methods and techniques used, the plant species grown, and the organization of the production process. The first of them, which definitely dominates the city space, are agricultural areas concentrated in the vast valley bottoms. Their total area is 692.36 ha, and the average size of one area is 20.98 ha. Due to the high humidity of the soil, crops here take the form of raised beds, between which drainage channels are run. Among the cultivated plants, vegetables such as cabbage, lettuce or tomatoes and tuber plants such as sweet potatoes, potatoes and cassava dominate. Due to the appropriate water conditions, rice can also be grown in the valleys. The valley floors are divided into smaller plots leased from the state by individual producers – mainly residents of Kigali. Production is intended for the farmers' own needs or for sale at local markets and nearby shops. Agriculture is clearly visible in the city space. The valleys in which crops are concentrated somehow cut between the built-up hills, creating a specific landscape in which dense and compact development meets agricultural areas, creating sharp boundaries between both types of land use (Górna & Górny, 2020, p. 42).

The second group of agricultural areas in Kigali are small plots located on hillsides. Their total area is 180.2 ha, and the average size of one area is 2.82 ha. Due to the large inclination of most of them, and the resulting low level of groundwater, drainage channels are not used here for obvious reasons. The main plants grown on hillsides are cassava, sweet potatoes and yams resistant to water stress. Maize and banana trees are also commonly grown. The plots usually take the form of home gardens, the entire production of which is intended to meet the nutritional needs of individual households (Górna & Górny, 2020, p. 43).

SUMMARY

Building green skills is multidimensional. It takes place on many levels: government, local government, business, and households. This process includes creating favorable legal solutions as well as creating economically viable business models for enterprises and the local community in general.

Green skills concern many areas from agriculture to industrial production, from ecological education to the use of artificial intelligence. It also involves redesigning settlement units into so-called green cities or cities of the future, which creates a new approach to land development in spatial terms.

Finally, these are also green businesses investing in green projects, from which both institutional and private investors benefit. All these areas create and develop green attitudes, green jobs and de facto improve the state of protection of the natural environment, transforming society towards a friend of the natural environment, and not just its explorer.

REFERENCES

Banaszuk, P. (2023). *How to establish and run an energy cooperative. Ministry of Agriculture and Rural Development*. REMEDIA Promotion and Advertising Center.

Cabral, C., & Dhar Lochan, R. (2019). Green competencies: Construct development and measurement validation. Journal of Cleaner Production, 235. Ecology. Sweden: The world's first vertical plant growing skyscraper. (2012). Vertical Plant Growing.

Dorożyński, T. (2012). *The role of the European Union's cohesion policy in eliminating regional economic disparities: Conclusions for Poland*. University of Lodz Publishing House.

European Commission. (2015). Closing the loop: An EU action plan for the circular economy (COM(2015) 614 final). https://eur-lex.europa.eu/legal-content/EN/TXT/?uri=CELEX:52015DC0614

European Council & Council of the European Union. (2025). European Green Deal. https://www.consilium.europa.eu (Accessed June 16, 2025)

Fetzer, A. V., & Aaron, S. (2010). *Climb the green ladder: Make your company and career more sustainable*. John Wiley & Sons.

Górna, A., & Górny, K. (2020). Urban agriculture in sub-Saharan African cities: A spatial approach. *Prace i Studia Geograficzne*, *65*(4), 37–62.

Kojzar, K. (2021). City of the future: How the Swedes created a green housing estate that powers itself. SmogLab., Retrieved June 18, 2025, from.

Municipal waste sorter (No. 961202). (2025). PKD code search engine. (Accessed June 4, 2025)

Stackelberg, K., & Hahne, U. (1998). Theories of regional development. In Golinowska, S. (Ed.), *Economic development of regions: Labor market and migration processes—Poland*. Institute of Labor and Social Affairs.

Staszewska, Z. (2025). Green competences: The key to success on the labor market. Business Insider., Retrieved May 30, 2025, from.

Wójcik-Czerniawska, A., & Grzymała, Z. (2023). Partnership of stakeholders at the local level as an effective instrument of local development. *International Journal of Advanced Business Studies*, *2*(2), 52–65. DOI: 10.59857/ZCBC8116

Ziółkowska, M. (2024). *Green competences as an element of the sustainable development concept. Studies and Works of the College of Management and Finance, 196*. Warsaw School of Economics.

Section 3
Leadership, Culture, and Well-Being in Digital Workplaces

Chapter 6
Emotional Hacking and Artificial Intelligence Tools:
The Digital Revolution or Emotional Disaster in Mental Healthcare?

Shabina Shaikh
http://orcid.org/0000-0002-3320-8049
International Islamic University Malaysia, Malaysia

Asadullah Shah
Kulliyyah of Information and Communication Technology, Malaysia

ABSTRACT

AI is revolutionizing mental health care, offering tools to democratize access and personalize support. However, this digital transformation presents risks, especially concerning emotional data and the blurring line between care and control. It argues for human-centric AI principles, emphasizing user dignity, cultural sensitivity, and emotional nuance. This chapter explores the different viewpoints of "emotional hacking" and the need to prevent exploitation. It argues that emotional AI must be designed with empathy, governed with ethics, and deployed with transparency. This chapter emphasizes the importance of ethical frameworks, user perspectives, and continuous evaluation to safeguard user rights and enhance the effectiveness of mental health interventions. By prioritizing ethical standards, fostering collaboration, and ensuring continuous evaluation, it aims to provide a roadmap for the responsible and beneficial deployment of AI in mental health.

DOI: 10.4018/979-8-3373-4307-5.ch006

INTRODUCTION

The chapter focuses on how artificial intelligence (AI) is affecting emotional well-being in mental health care. The intersection of emotional hacking and artificial intelligence (AI) tools in mental health care represents a growing frontier that promises to revolutionize the landscape of psychological support and intervention. As mental health challenges continue to escalate globally, the integration of AI technologies offers extraordinary opportunities for enhancing therapeutic practices, personalizing treatment plans, and improving patient outcomes. However, this innovation is not without its complexities and ethical considerations. The potential for emotional hacking or manipulating emotional responses through digital means raises critical questions about the implications of AI in mental health care.

This chapter aims to explore the dual-edged nature of AI tools in this domain, assessing whether they sign a new era of mental health care or pose significant risks that could undermine the very essence of therapeutic relationships. This chapter also introduces the idea of "emotional hacking," where AI is used to influence or control people's emotions. According to Tavory (2024) Emotional hacking introduces serious ethical issues, especially those related to manipulation, data privacy, and the potential decline of genuine human interaction within therapeutic environments. Bakir et al (2024) also emphasized AI-driven emotional hacking may lead to manipulation and mental health issues. It is therefore essential to include ethical considerations, especially those related to the ethics of care, when developing AI-driven therapeutic tools. This will help to reduce the risk of emotional manipulation and other dangers.

This chapter looks closely at both sides of emotional AI, how it can make mental health support more accessible, but also how it risks turning our deep emotional lives into just numbers on a screen. This transformation presents both opportunities and challenges, necessitating careful evaluation of digital tools to ensure they effectively meet the needs of users and enhance mental health outcomes. This evaluation must consider user perspectives and experiences, as these insights are crucial for developing effective digital interventions that address the complexities of mental health needs. The ongoing evolution of digital health interventions highlights the importance of user engagement and personalization to improve mental health outcomes effectively.

Mental health is now seen as essential to overall health, and problems like depression are becoming more common around the world. Traditional ways of providing mental health care, which depend on face-to-face meetings, are increasingly seen as insufficient to meet the rising number of mental health issues (Poudel et al., 2025). The field of digital mental health is now well-established, and there is ongoing and new work on AI-driven solutions for mental health, as the mental health care field, like many others, has been affected by the revolution in digital technology and artificial. AI tools are now being used more often in therapy, emotional assessments, and tracking behavior, which has changed how mental health support is provided. While these tools can be helpful, they also bring up serious questions about ethics, mental well-being, and the impact on society. To maximize the benefits of digital mental health interventions, it is essential to incorporate user feedback and adapt tools to meet diverse emotional and psychological needs. This approach aligns with the growing recognition that digital technologies can enhance access to mental health services while addressing unmet needs in diverse populations. By fostering user involvement in the design and implementation of these interventions, we can better ensure that they are effective and trustworthy. This collaborative process not only enhances the relevance of digital tools but also builds public trust, ultimately leading to improved clinical outcomes in mental health care.

Emotional AI can improve or worsen mental health care. Clear standards can protect therapy and build trust between patients, professionals, and AI systems. (Tavory, 2024). In recent years, the intersection of artificial intelligence (AI) and mental health has escorted in a transformative era, one where emotional well-being is no longer confined to traditional clinical settings. Through advanced techniques in affective computing, machine learning, and wearable technologies, AI systems are beginning to decode and even influence human emotions. This emerging phenomenon dubbed emotional hacking describes the use of digital technologies to recognize, analyze, and potentially regulate emotional states in real time. As the world grapples with rising rates of anxiety, depression, and stress, emotional hacking represents a novel, data-driven approach to understanding and supporting mental health on a global scale. The digital platforms can facilitate real-time data collection, enabling more tailored interventions that resonate with individual user experiences and preferences. This user-centered approach is vital for bridging the gap between traditional mental health care and innovative digital solutions.

However, this digital revolution is not without its challenges. Emotional hacking raises complex ethical questions about autonomy, privacy, emotional authenticity, and the potential for emotional manipulation. The accuracy of emotion detection varies across cultures, genders, and contexts, often relying on datasets that may embed bias or lack nuance. Furthermore, while AI offers scalable solutions, it risks oversimplifying the intricacies of human emotion, potentially replacing empathy with algorithms. The tension between technological innovation and emotional integrity must be carefully managed to ensure that such tools augment rather than diminish the human experience.

This chapter also delves into the promise and pitfalls of emotional hacking in mental health. It explores the latest advancements in AI-powered emotional recognition, the role of wearable technologies, and the evolving clinical and social implications of this digital shift. By critically analyzing existing research, implementation strategies, and regulatory frameworks, it aims to illuminate the path forward for ethical, inclusive, and effective emotional technologies. In doing so, it invites a reimagining of mental healthcare, one that is tech-savvy, emotionally intelligent, and fundamentally human. This chapter also focuses on the study given in literature on Artificial Intelligence (AI) particularly with deep learning which offers transformative mental health support.

Innovative AI-powered technologies that are integrated by machine learning hold great potential to improve mental health. AI-driven technologies and digital therapeutics offer promising, scalable solutions to support mental health. AI-driven tools can make mental health care more scalable, affordable, and accessible. AI can help craft and shift human sentiment from negative to positive, fundamentally "emotion hacking" for peace and better mental health care. Smart wearable devices such as heart rate monitors, movement sensors, etc. can collect real-time physiological data. AI can use this data for early detection and intervention in mental health disorders. Wearables bring mental health analysis to the common people inexpensive, accessible, and real-time. AI tools can analyze emotional content in text to detect mental distress. Natural Language Processing (NLP) can uncover patterns linked to mental illness. Deep learning models show promise in diagnosing and predicting mental health conditions. Wearable sensing offers a promising solution, using channels like speech, text, gestures, physiology, and especially facial expressions which are strong indicators of emotional state. AI tools can detect many facial expressions, promote emotional awareness, and provide personalized self-regulation support in everyday settings. Accurately recognizing and labeling emotions is the key to emotional regulation, yet many struggle with this create opportunities for wearable sensing technologies. In affective computing, five main methods are used to detect emotions: facial expressions, voice, physiological signals, text, and body movement.

Emotional disorders are often overlooked due to low awareness. Recent advances in sensing technologies offer new potential for wearable, facial-expression-based and emotion recognition. A wearable platform combining emotion-detecting glasses and a mobile application using a single camera, the glasses can detect many facial expressions from partial face images. Health psychology emphasizes emotional well-being, as continued negative emotions can lead to serious mental disorders, affecting nearly a billion people globally. Despite this, many individuals neglect their emotions, struggle to recognize them, and rarely seek help. This highlights the need for effective emotion detection tools. A major challenge in emotion sensing is obtaining reliable ground truth. While large datasets rely on human labeling, many studies use participants' self-reports, often supplemented with open- or close-ended questions and rating scales to add detail. Real-time facial expression detection is also used but limit natural movement, making them unsuitable for real-world settings. Facial expression recognition (FER) is a key focus in computer vision, achieving high level of accuracy. However, capturing full facial views with wearables is challenging without blocking vision. To address this, researchers have mounted cameras on glasses, headphones, and necklaces, using near-infrared cameras to track partial facial features. These setups still face issues like lighting, head movement, and individual expression differences.

AI-powered wearable platform combining facial-expression-detecting glasses and a mobile app for emotional self-monitoring and awareness are also used. Recent advances have boosted smart devices and wearables for faster detection and management of mental health issues like depression, anxiety, and stress. Societies under stress develop "dominant emotional maps," collective patterns of emotional expression like fear or anger clusters. The mapping influence societal behaviors and policies. AI tools can help analyze these maps using data from social media, forums, or electronic health records. AI is rapidly transforming mental healthcare, enabling early disorder detection, personalized treatments, and AI-driven virtual therapists. The merging of Artificial Intelligence (AI) and mental healthcare fields results a significant revolution in healthcare. According to the World Health Organization (WHO), mental health disorders are now on large scale at global burden, with depression alone representing the leading cause of disability globally. Mental health disorders have placed immense pressure on healthcare systems, exposing the shortcomings of traditional care models. The conventional reliance on in-person consultations and therapy is no longer sufficient to meet the growing need for accessible, affordable, and scalable mental health services. AI's integration into mental health has broad implications for practice, research, prevention, and policy. In prevention, AI helps identify risk factors and deliver timely support, but equitable access and data protection must be ensured. Policy must establish clear, ethical regulations and foster collaboration among stakeholders.

The gap between the demand for and supply of mental healthcare highlights the pressing need for innovative solutions. This chapter explores recent research, ethical concerns, and evolving regulations from major databases. Although AI holds great potential, it faces key challenges such as privacy, bias, and preserving the human element

Future advancements in AI for mental health hinge on strong regulations, transparency, and rigorous research to ensure accessible, effective, and ethical care. Despite many devices not being classified as medical tools, they still shape users' perceptions of health, highlighting the need for validation. Limitations include potential errors due to narrow search terms. Future research should focus on multiparametric, multi-sensor, and unconventional technologies to enhance early detection and management of mental health conditions.

To address the pressing issues in mental health care, it is crucial to explore the role of AI tools in bridging the gap between emotional development and clinical support. AI tools have the potential to enhance emotional development by providing personalized support and fostering better mental health outcomes. However, ethical considerations and the need for human connection must also be prioritized. Balancing technological advancements with the necessity for human empathy is essential in ensuring that AI tools effectively support emotional development without compromising the quality of care. The increasing demand for accessible and personalized mental health support has spurred the development of AI-driven interventions. Mental health is now understood to be a crucial aspect of overall well-being, but traditional methods of care are struggling to keep pace with growing needs. The integration of AI and machine learning has led to breakthroughs in identifying biomarkers and predicting disease progression with accuracy. This proactive approach is essential for early intervention and tailored treatment plans. Emotional AI is now being explored to enable machines to understand and respond to human emotions, building on computational models of emotion appraisal. The exploration of emotional hacking and AI tools highlights the urgent need to understand their implications for mental health care, particularly in addressing emerging challenges and ethical considerations. The integration of AI tools in mental health care necessitates a careful examination of both their benefits and potential ethical pitfalls, ensuring that patient welfare remains paramount. The ongoing development of AI in mental health care must prioritize ethical considerations to mitigate risks associated with data privacy and the potential dehumanization of patient interactions. Balancing these factors is crucial for fostering effective and compassionate therapeutic relationships.

EMOTIONAL HACKING

Emotional Hacking is the capacity to impact other people's emotions through direct and indirect social interactions with AI and humans.

As per Ettman & Galea (2023) emotional hacking means using technology and data to change or influence how people feel. While the word might sound negative, it can include a range of actions from harmless suggestions to more concerning tactics. In mental health, emotional hacking might involve AI looking at things like your voice, facial expressions, or social media posts to understand your mood. But it can also go further, such as trying to change how you act by showing you certain messages or emotional content.

AI can play both a positive and negative role in emotional hacking by helping to understand and respond to emotional states. AI systems analyze vast datasets to recognize human emotions, which can be used to personalize mental health interventions (Zhang & Wang, 2024) (Narimisaei et al., 2024). On the other hand, AI can be used to exploit emotional vulnerabilities, leading to manipulation or harm.

Emotional Hacking is also being used to study the emotional contagion through social networks. It helps study online interactions and user emotional states by employing computational methods. This is being used to look into many areas like marketing, public health, and political mobilization. According to Wang & Liu (2023) emotional hacking is not only conducive to the further development of AI, but also conducive to the formation of a good human-computer interaction relationship and to continuously deepening human beings' understanding of themselves.

As researchers delve into the realm of emotional hacking, the intersection of AI tools and emotional intelligence becomes increasingly significant. Emotional hacking refers to the strategic manipulation of emotions through digital interactions, which can be both beneficial and detrimental in research contexts. For instance, AI tools can be employed to analyze sentiment in literature, providing insights into emotional trends within academic discourse; however, the potential for misuse, such as generating misleading emotional responses or exploiting vulnerabilities, raises ethical concerns that must be addressed. The challenge lies in harnessing the capabilities of AI to enhance understanding while safeguarding against its potential to distort emotional authenticity in academic communication. Thus, a critical examination of how AI can both facilitate and hinder emotional engagement in research is essential for promoting ethical practices and maintaining the integrity of scholarly work. Consequently, researchers must remain vigilant in assessing the ethical implications of emotional hacking while leveraging AI tools, ensuring that their applications promote genuine engagement rather than manipulation.

Emotional hacking uses technology to understand, influence, and manage emotions, a complex area due to the multifaceted nature of emotions, including subjective feelings, physiological changes, and behavioral expressions. It also involves understanding the roles of various brain regions, neurotransmitters, and cognitive processes in emotional responses. AI's role in simulating emotions is increasingly significant, presenting ethical dilemmas that require careful consideration. On one hand, emotional simulation in AI can lead to more natural human-computer interactions. This can foster better relationships between humans and machines, aiding AI development and deepening our understanding of human emotions. (Wang & Liu, 2023).

At the core of emotional hacking lies the ability to detect and interpret subtle emotional cues using multimodal data: facial expressions, vocal intonation, physiological signals, and linguistic patterns. Deep learning models are now capable of mapping emotional landscapes with unprecedented accuracy, while smart wearables collect biometric data to detect early signs of psychological distress. Natural Language Processing (NLP) tools analyze text from social media and digital communications to identify markers of emotional imbalance or mental illness. These technologies not only enhance diagnosis and intervention but also pave the way for continuous, personalized emotional support systems.

Overwhelming negative emotions such fear, anger, hatred, and despair that deeply affect individual and societal mental health can be transformed into positive emotions. Emotional and psychological consequences often go untreated due to lack of resources and specialists. Negative emotions can become dominant and destabilize societies. On the other hand, there are ethical risks. These include an over-reliance on computational thinking, a lack of genuine emotional connection, and the potential for deception. In exploring the multifaceted nature of emotional hacking, it is crucial to consider the role of AI in shaping user experiences beyond mere sentiment analysis. For instance, AI algorithms can curate content that resonates emotionally with users, potentially enhancing engagement but also risking the creation of echo chambers that reinforce existing biases and emotional states. This duality emphasizes the need for ethical frameworks that guide the development and deployment of AI tools, ensuring they foster constructive emotional engagement rather than exploitative manipulation. Additionally, as the landscape of digital interactions evolves, understanding the implications of emotional hacking becomes vital for maintaining academic integrity, particularly in contexts where emotional authenticity is paramount. By prioritizing transparency and ethical considerations in the design of AI-driven applications, researchers can help mitigate the risks associated with emotional exploitation while promoting a richer, more nuanced understanding of emotional dynamics in academic discourse. In addressing emotional hacking, it is essential to establish ethical guidelines that prioritize user well-being and prevent the exploitation of emotional vulnerabilities in research contexts. Establishing such guidelines will not only foster academic integrity but also ensure that AI tools are used responsibly in emotional hacking scenarios, ultimately benefiting both researchers and participants.

Types of emotional hacking include, but are not limited to, pseudo-intimacy, AI companions, robots, and virtual reality. Pseudo-intimacy is when users and platforms achieve quick emotional interactions, which only partially satisfies a person's need for intimacy (Wu, 2024). AI companions are designed to provide emotional support and companionship. Virtual reality therapy, AI-generated architectural imagery are capable of effectively eliciting specific emotions. Emotional hacking underscores the importance of considering how technology intersects with human emotions in research and academic settings, necessitating a comprehensive understanding of its implications for ethical practices and intellectual integrity. The intersection of AI and emotional simulation technology brings traditional ethics and morality into question (Wang & Liu, 2023).

ARTIFICIAL INTELLIGENCE AND CREATIVITY

AI and creativity are the topic of conversations for researchers and practitioners in various domains. Creativity which was once exclusively human act is now within reach of AI, this has been accelerated with the creation of generative AI models. AI can create many forms of creative content which include, but are not limited to music, text, visual arts, and designs. It asks whether these technologies are a breakthrough that helps more people get care, or if they are creating new problems by turning emotions into data for profit and control.

According to Brem & Horauf (2025) AI can enhance ideation, but not without risks. Practitioners across industries must adapt to the AI era, to test and evaluate the tools for their specific roles and contexts, and to find the most beneficial practices for their day to day business. Scholars can use insights gleaned from practice to help determine whether AI merely influences the final outcome or whether it also reshapes the entire creative-thinking process. Automation enhances creativity and efficiency in knowledge work. Intelligence as the highest form of knowledge supports automation. Knowledge automation tools can improve organizational decision-making and strategic agility (Shaikh, 2021; Shaikh & Bhutto, 2021). When knowledge automation is more advanced, employee creativity tends to be higher. For certain processes, as automation increases, creativity also rises at a consistent pace. Knowledge automation can boost employee creativity by reducing routine tasks, allowing employees to focus on more innovative work (Shaikh, 2022). AI is being integrated into creative processes. The development of more sophisticated AI models and the proliferation of human-computer interaction tools have opened up new possibilities for AI in artistic creation (Crimaldi & Leonelli, 2023).

ARTIFICIAL INTELLIGENCE TOOLS IN EMOTIONAL AND MENTAL HEALTH CARE

Chustecki (2024) discussed the integration of AI tools in healthcare which has shown promise in enhancing patient care and operational efficiency, yet it also demands careful consideration of ethical implications and regulatory standards. As such, understanding both the benefits and challenges of AI applications is essential for successful implementation in clinical settings. This understanding will facilitate the development of frameworks that align AI tools with the needs of healthcare providers and patients, ensuring effective integration into practice.

Moreover, ongoing dialogue among stakeholders is vital to address the ethical challenges and ensure that AI tools are used responsibly in healthcare research and practice. This ongoing dialogue will help foster trust and transparency, ultimately leading to improved patient outcomes and a more effective healthcare system. To achieve these goals, collaboration between AI developers, healthcare professionals, and regulatory bodies is essential to create guidelines that prioritize patient safety and ethical standards in AI deployment.

Artificial Intelligence (AI) is becoming a big deal in many industries, including mental health care. Apps like Woebot, which offer chatbot style therapy, and platforms like Ginger, which use AI to support mental health coaching, are changing the way help is delivered (Meadi et al., 2025). These tools are designed to address a widespread need: mental health issues are on the rise, and traditional therapy can be expensive or hard to get to for many people. AI offers a way to scale mental health support, making it more accessible and affordable for those who need it. AI-driven mental health tools can analyze large amounts of patient data to spot patterns and predict who might be at risk for certain conditions (Zhang & Wang, 2024).

The application of AI tools in emotional health services is rapidly expanding, offering new avenues for personalized support and intervention while necessitating careful ethical scrutiny to safeguard user privacy and well-being. As AI tools in emotional health continue to evolve, it is imperative to establish ethical frameworks that respect user autonomy and ensure transparency in their deployment and data handling practices. Establishing these frameworks will help mitigate risks associated with data misuse and enhance trust between users and AI systems in emotional health services. Furthermore, ongoing research should focus on understanding user perceptions and experiences with AI tools in emotional health to address potential biases and enhance user engagement. The convergence of technology and psychology has ushered in a new era of mental health support, characterized by innovative approaches to understanding, monitoring, and modulating emotional states. Digital emotion regulation, which leverages the pervasive nature of digital technology to modify affective states, is gaining prominence as a means of enhancing emotional well-being and mental health.

Artificial intelligence is playing a significant role in this revolution, providing tools for personal sensing, natural language processing, and the development of sophisticated chatbots. These advancements promise increased accessibility and personalized care in mental health, but they also raise ethical concerns regarding privacy, dependence on technology, and the potential for dehumanization in patient interactions. The intersection of artificial intelligence and mental health has opened new avenues for understanding, diagnosing, and treating a wide spectrum of psychological conditions. The rapid evolution of AI technologies necessitates a careful examination of their implications for mental health care, especially regarding the balance between technological benefits and ethical considerations. AI technologies, encompassing machine learning, natural language processing, and predictive analytics, are increasingly being deployed to address the growing challenges in mental healthcare. Early detection and intervention of emotional disorders can significantly improve overall health and well-being. The integration of digital technology into mental health care is reshaping how individuals engage with their emotional well-being and access therapeutic resources.

According to Yang & Jia (2025) AI tools used in mental health come in different types: some are chatbots that offer therapy like Cognitive Behavioral Therapy (CBT). Others use AI to look at your mood from texts you write or things you post online, and some even try to guess what you're feeling by looking at your facial expressions. Some track emotions through language which is called sentiment analysis. Sentiment analysis in AI is used to assess opinions, emotions, and attitudes expressed in text. This technology is useful for understanding customer feedback, monitoring brand reputation, and gauging public sentiment on various topics. AI systems are being developed to analyze vast datasets, potentially identifying subtle indicators of mental health issues that might be missed by human observation (Ettman & Galea, 2023; Hoose & Králiková, 2024). AI can assist in sentiment analysis within mental health care (Alhuwaydi, 2024).

Others try to predict risks like suicide (predictive analytics), and some read feelings through facial expressions or voice (emotion AI). AI is also being used to make personalized recommendations for treatment, connecting people with the resources that best fit their needs (Yang & Jia, 2025). By analyzing vast amounts of data, AI systems can identify patterns and trends that may not be apparent to human clinicians, leading to more accurate diagnoses and treatment recommendations (Saeidnia et al., 2024).

These tools gather a lot of data, often without people actively giving it, to understand emotions better. This can help make therapy more effective, spot mental health emergencies, and tailor care to each person. But these same abilities also bring up concerns about privacy, personal control, and whether machines can truly understand human emotions. The effectiveness of interventions depends on the accuracy of the AI algorithms and the quality of data used to train these systems. The prompt speed of AI advancement has sparked both high hopes and deep concerns. Traditional regulation struggles to keep pace, leaving us facing both great potential and serious danger. One pressing issue is the emulation of emotion in AI. Often dismissed as secondary to logic, artificial emotions may, in fact, prove central, impacting behavior, alignment, interpretability, and the ethics that govern intelligent machines.

Using AI to understand emotions in mental health started with a focus on behavior, mainly what people do and say, like in behaviorism. But now, it's moving toward affective computing, which tries to understand what people feel inside using technology. This change brings new ways to support mental health, but it also raises more complex ethical questions we need to think carefully about.

EMOTIONAL HACKING: AN EMOTIONAL DISASTER

AI brings exciting possibilities like making care more available, faster, and able to reach more people. But as AI improves at understanding and reacting to human emotions, a new area is opening up where our feelings can be watched, shaped, or even controlled. This idea, called "emotional hacking," raises some serious concerns. Are we about to see a major breakthrough in therapy, or are we letting technology take advantage of our emotions?

As per Saeidnia et al. (2024) the primary challenge lies in maintaining ethical standards within AI, especially when dealing with mental health interventions. The negative effects of emotional hacking on human being can lead towards emotional disaster. The risks associated with emotional hacking can lead to significant harm, undermining trust in therapeutic relationships and potentially exacerbating mental health issues. Emotional AI can also lead to pseudo intimacy in order to manipulate the user (Wu, 2024). Moreover, the misuse of AI technologies in emotional hacking could result in a loss of autonomy for patients, as their emotional states may be manipulated without informed consent. This manipulation not only threatens individual autonomy but also raises profound ethical concerns regarding privacy and the integrity of therapeutic practices. (Ajluni, 2023). AI tools have the potential to exploit user emotional dependence, generate material dependencies without adequate commitment to user needs, and limit opportunities for personal development (Manzini et al., 2024).

AI's ability to interpret and respond to human emotions opens up new possibilities for personalized mental health interventions, it simultaneously raises concerns about the potential for manipulation and the erosion of genuine human connection. Furthermore, the lack of genuine empathy in AI systems may lead to misinterpretations of emotional cues, resulting in inappropriate or even harmful interventions. Ensuring fairness, transparency, and respect for patient rights is crucial.

Data Exploitation is when a person is encouraged to share their data without informed consent. This could lead to manipulation due to knowledge of the user's emotional state. Vulnerable individuals are at risk of being exploited and manipulated. Emotional data is very personal and can be misused, especially with the great amount of data available. Companies might use it for targeted ads, and poorly secured systems could have data breaches.

AI systems are only as good as the data they are trained on. Cultural, linguistic, and contextual nuances can be lost, leading to misdiagnosis or inappropriate responses. For example, expressions of grief vary widely across cultures, but an AI trained predominantly on Western data may misinterpret them. Emotional manipulation and consent is also a big concern, where AI-driven tools can subtly influence people's opinions, behaviors, and emotional states (Tavory, 2024). The extent to which users are aware of this influence and can give informed consent is questionable, particularly in therapeutic contexts where power dynamics are already at play.

There is a thin line between therapeutic intervention and manipulation. AI tools might use emotionally persuasive language or feedback loops that nudge users toward certain behaviors, not always in their best interest. Consent in such systems is often buried in terms and conditions, rendering it effectively meaningless. As users grow accustomed to emotionally intelligent AI, there's a risk of developing dependencies. Emotional AI cannot replicate the depth of human empathy, yet users may come to rely on it as a substitute for genuine human interaction. This shift could dehumanize the therapeutic experience. The rapid development of emotional AI has outpaced the creation of comprehensive regulations. Questions about liability, accountability, and the ethical use of emotional data remain unresolved. Legal frameworks must evolve to ensure user protection.

To mitigate these risks, it is crucial to implement stringent ethical guidelines and prioritize transparency in AI applications within mental health care, ensuring that patient rights and well-being remain paramount. Additionally, fostering interdisciplinary collaboration among technologists, clinicians, and ethicists is vital to develop comprehensive strategies that address the complex challenges posed by emotional hacking in AI-driven mental health care

THE DIGITAL REVOLUTION: OPPORTUNITIES IN EMOTIONAL HEALTH

AI offers the potential to extend mental health support to underserved populations, reduce waiting times, and provide personalized treatment options (Alhuwaydi, 2024; Rubin et al., 2024).

Personalization of Care

Jian (2023) discussed one of the biggest strengths of AI is its ability to personalize help. Machine learning can study how a person behaves over time and then adjust the support it gives to fit their needs. For example, chatbots like Woebot can change how they talk, what words they use, and the advice they give based on what the user says making the conversation feel more natural and meaningful.

Scalability and Accessibility

There aren't enough mental health professionals to meet the growing need for care around the world. AI tools can help fill this gap by giving basic mental health support to people who might not get any help otherwise. In places where therapists are hard to find, these tools can be an affordable way to reach more people. AI-driven platforms can provide support to individuals in remote areas or during emergencies, ensuring that help is available whenever and wherever it is needed (Spytska, 2025).

Early Detection and Crisis Prevention

AI can also find early signs of mental health problems by looking at how people use social media, what they write, or how they talk. When AI spots someone who might be in trouble, it can send alerts to professionals or suggest getting help. AI can watch for warning signs of emotional problems by keeping track of what users type, say, or show through body signals. This constant monitoring helps spot issues earlier than regular methods. For example, Facebook uses AI to look for signs of suicide risk, showing how this kind of technology can help prevent serious problems. AI algorithms can analyze patterns in social media posts, electronic health records, and other data sources to identify individuals at risk of self-harm or other mental health crises (Ettman & Galea, 2023).

Integration with Wearable Technology

As smartwatches and fitness trackers become more common, they open new ways to keep track of mental health. These devices can monitor things like heart rate, sleep patterns, and how active someone is, which can tell us a lot about their emotional state. This could bring new opportunities in mental health care, using devices that people already use every day (Poudel et al., 2025). Wearable technology offers the potential for continuous monitoring of physiological and behavioral data, providing valuable insights into an individual's mental health status. The integration of AI with wearable technology enables the development of personalized interventions and support systems that can be delivered in real-time.

The combination of machine learning algorithms with wearable sensor data can facilitate the early detection of mood changes, stress levels, and other indicators of mental health disorders (Wei et al., 2024). When AI is used in wearable devices, it can track your mood, heart rate, and behavior in real time. This information can help doctors or caregivers notice any warning signs early, giving them a chance to step in and help before things get worse.

Augmentation of Clinical Decision-Making

AI can help doctors and therapists make better decisions by giving them more information and different ways to look at a patient's case. This is especially helpful when dealing with tricky mental health problems. AI systems can analyze patient data and medical literature to provide clinicians with evidence-based recommendations for treatment and management. These systems allow for continuous, real-time analysis of extensive patient data, providing unparalleled insights into a patient's status (Wei et al., 2025).

AI-driven insights are increasingly assisting therapists in formulating treatment plans. By analyzing patient data across sessions, these tools can identify subtle shifts in emotional trajectories, which might escape human attention. These AI-driven tools offer personalized insights, but clinical judgment remains crucial. However, the use of AI in mental health also presents significant challenges and potential risks that must be addressed thoughtfully.

CASE STUDIES AND EXAMPLES

Woebot and Conversational Agents

Woebot uses natural language processing (NLP) to deliver CBT through conversation. It's effective for mild to moderate anxiety and depression, but its limitations become apparent when dealing with complex emotional issues (Coghlan et al., 2023). AI-driven chatbots are being used to provide support, monitor symptoms, and promote self-management (Yang & Jia, 2025).

Affectiva and Emotion Detection

Affectiva's emotion AI can analyze facial expressions to infer emotions in real time. It has been applied in everything from education to automotive industries. In mental health, this could aid in tracking patient progress but it also opens the door to over-reliance on surface-level cues.

Emotion Tracking in Workplaces

Some corporations use AI to monitor employee emotional states, ostensibly to boost morale and productivity. However, such practices can border on emotional surveillance, contributing to stress and reducing trust (Ballesteros et al., 2024).

AI in Crisis Text Lines

AI is used to triage messages in crisis text lines to prioritize responses. While efficient, this system can lead to delayed support for less "urgent" messages that might still be critical from a clinical perspective.

TherapyBots in Schools

Some educational institutions have introduced AI therapy bots to support student mental health. While beneficial for quick support, concerns about consent, data security, and age-appropriate interventions persist.

ETHICAL FRAMEWORK ON AI TOOLS AND EMOTIONAL HACKING

This focus on ethical frameworks is crucial, as it not only fosters user trust but also aligns AI applications with established privacy regulations and ethical standards in healthcare and emotional health contexts. Establishing a comprehensive ethical framework will ensure that AI tools in emotional health are developed and implemented in ways that prioritize user safety and well-being, ultimately enhancing the quality of care provided and fostering a more responsible and ethical approach to AI integration in healthcare. By addressing these ethical considerations, stakeholders can work towards creating AI systems that not only enhance emotional well-being but also maintain user trust and privacy.

To achieve these objectives, it is vital to engage in continuous evaluation and improvement of AI tools, ensuring that they align with ethical guidelines and best practices in emotional health services. By fostering a collaborative environment among developers, researchers, and users, we can enhance the effectiveness and ethical integrity of AI applications in this critical area. This commitment to ethical AI practices is essential for ensuring that emotional health interventions are not only effective but also respectful of individual rights and dignity. This ongoing commitment to ethical standards is essential for ensuring that AI tools in emotional health are both effective and aligned with users' rights and well-being, ultimately fostering a healthier relationship between technology and individuals. The successful implementation of AI tools in emotional health requires a robust ethical framework that prioritizes user safety, privacy, and informed consent, ensuring that these technologies serve to enhance, rather than compromise, emotional well-being.

ETHICAL CONSIDERATIONS AND POTENTIAL RISKS

Addressing the ethical considerations in AI tools is paramount, as it ensures that these technologies do not inadvertently harm users or compromise their emotional well-being. This includes evaluating issues such as data privacy, informed consent, bias, and the potential for dehumanization in interactions, which are critical for promoting responsible AI use in mental health care. Moreover, ongoing discussions among stakeholders are essential to navigate these ethical complexities, ensuring that AI tools are developed with a focus on user welfare and societal impact. By fostering open dialogue and collaboration among stakeholders, we can effectively address these ethical challenges and enhance the responsible integration of AI tools in mental health care. This requires a multifaceted approach, incorporating stakeholder input and continuous ethical evaluation to ensure that AI tools not only enhance mental health care but also respect user autonomy and dignity. This ongoing dialogue will help to establish best practices for the ethical deployment of AI tools, ultimately safeguarding user welfare and promoting trust in mental health interventions.

In conclusion, a robust ethical framework is essential for guiding the responsible development and deployment of AI tools in mental health care, ensuring they prioritize user safety and emotional well-being. By proactively addressing potential ethical concerns, we can harness the benefits of AI while mitigating risks, promoting ethical innovation in mental health care. To address data privacy issues, it is essential to implement strong safeguards that protect sensitive information while ensuring compliance with ethical standards and regulations surrounding AI technologies in emotional health.

TRAUMA OF HACKED EMOTIONS

The impact of emotional hacking on individual well-being necessitates a deeper exploration of the ethical frameworks guiding AI applications in this sensitive area. To ensure that emotional well-being is prioritized and that the potential for harm is minimized. Establishing comprehensive guidelines will help navigate the complexities of emotional hacking in AI applications. Establishing these guidelines will not only protect users but also promote ethical practices in the development of AI tools that interact with emotional health, ensuring accountability and trust in their applications. Furthermore, ongoing research is essential to identify and address the ethical implications of emotional hacking, ensuring that AI applications prioritize user well-being and respect individual rights.

Transformation from Negative to Positive Emotions

This transformation underscores the importance of understanding emotional dynamics in AI applications, as fostering positive emotional experiences can significantly enhance user engagement and overall well-being . Moreover, researchers must continuously evaluate the effectiveness of AI tools in facilitating this transformation, ensuring that they promote genuine emotional support while minimizing the risk of emotional manipulation. This evaluation should prioritize ethical considerations to ensure that AI tools facilitate positive emotional transformations without compromising user autonomy or emotional authenticity. This ongoing evaluation will be crucial in shaping future AI developments that prioritize ethical standards and user well-being in emotional health applications.

A synergistic approach, integrating the expertise of technologists and mental health professionals, is crucial for harnessing AI's potential to augment, not replace, human-centered therapeutic interventions, thus enhancing the overall efficacy and accessibility of mental health care.

ENHANCING OR ERODING EMOTIONAL WELL-BEING?

AI offers valuable tools for emotional insight, but it cannot replace human empathy or intuition. Its strength lies in augmentation, not substitution. The risk arises when stakeholders treat emotional AI as a panacea, ignoring its limitations. While AI augmentation holds promise for enhancing the accessibility and efficiency of mental healthcare, an over-reliance on technological solutions that supplants the irreplaceable value of human connection risks compromising the depth and nuance of therapeutic relationships, potentially leading to a superficial and ultimately inadequate approach

Power, Trust, and Surveillance

AI shifts power dynamics in therapeutic settings. Who owns the emotional data? Who decides the algorithms' responses? These questions highlight the importance of transparency, accountability, and informed consent. The ultimate influence of AI on mental health at the population level is contingent upon the specific contexts in which these technologies are deployed, encompassing factors such as regulatory oversight, access to care, and the integration of AI within existing mental health infrastructure

The Need for Interdisciplinary Oversight

Ethical deployment of emotional AI requires input from technologists, clinicians, ethicists, and users. Policies must address data governance, algorithmic transparency, and emotional autonomy (Harper & Mukherjee, 2024).

Toward Human-Centric AI

To ensure emotional AI aligns with therapeutic goals, it must be guided by human-centric principles. This includes prioritizing user dignity, cultural sensitivity, and emotional nuance over pure data efficiency.

INNOVATIONS IN AI TOOL DEVELOPMENT

In recent years, AI tools have made significant strides in various sectors, including healthcare, finance, and education, highlighting their transformative potential across multiple domains. These advancements underscore the need for ongoing research to ensure that AI tools are developed and implemented in ways that prioritize ethical standards and user trust across all sectors. The integration of AI tools into diverse fields is crucial for driving innovation while maintaining ethical standards, as seen in healthcare and education.

CONCLUSION

In conclusion, the responsible integration of AI tools in emotional health care requires a steadfast commitment to ethical standards, prioritizing user safety, privacy, and informed consent to foster trust and enhance well-being. This commitment is essential for ensuring that AI technologies not only improve mental health outcomes but also uphold the dignity and rights of individuals in emotional health contexts.

The integration of AI tools in emotional health care must also prioritize the voices of data subjects, ensuring their perspectives inform the development and application of these technologies to effectively address their concerns and promote a more inclusive approach to mental health interventions. This focus on user perspectives is vital for creating AI-driven solutions that genuinely enhance emotional well-being while respecting individual rights and promoting ethical practices in mental health care.

The ethical implications of AI tools in emotional health care must be continuously evaluated to ensure they align with user rights and promote positive mental health outcomes. This ongoing evaluation will help ensure that AI technologies evolve in ways that genuinely support emotional well-being while safeguarding against potential harms associated with their use in mental health care. This commitment to ethical considerations is essential for building a framework that not only enhances emotional health interventions but also safeguards the rights and dignity of users in the digital landscape. AI has undeniably revolutionized aspects of mental health care, offering tools that can democratize access and personalize support. However, this digital revolution comes with risks—especially when emotional data is involved. The line between care and control is easily blurred. As we move forward, we must ensure that emotional hacking is not a means of exploitation but a tool for empowerment. Emotional AI must be designed with empathy, governed with ethics, and deployed with transparency. A truly beneficial AI system in mental health will not just detect and respond to emotions, but foster human flourishing, resilience, and autonomy. To that end, multi-stakeholder collaboration and continual ethical reflection are essential.

Researchers need to go beyond theory to study intelligent machines and humans already working together in practice. Regardless of whether it is labeled a "creative-thinking process," human–AI cocreation will play an essential and transformative role in ideation in practice. One thing is clear: This is just the beginning, and nobody knows where it is going.

SUMMARY OF KEY FINDINGS

The findings underscore the necessity of integrating ethical frameworks that prioritize user autonomy, data privacy, and informed consent in the development of AI tools for emotional health care. This summary highlights the critical need for ethical guidelines in the deployment of AI tools to ensure they enhance emotional well-being while respecting user rights and privacy. In summary, establishing robust ethical guidelines for AI tools in emotional health care is imperative to safeguard user rights and enhance the effectiveness of mental health interventions. This commitment to ethical guidelines is crucial for ensuring that AI tools in emotional health care not only improve outcomes but also foster trust and transparency among users, ultimately enhancing the therapeutic relationship. The integration of ethical frameworks in AI tools is vital for ensuring that these technologies enhance emotional well-being while safeguarding user rights and privacy, thereby fostering a responsible approach to mental health care.

IMPLICATIONS FOR PRACTITIONERS AND RESEARCHERS

Practitioners and researchers must collaborate to develop and implement AI tools that prioritize ethical standards, ensuring that emotional health interventions are effective, respectful, and aligned with user needs.

This collaboration will be essential in shaping the future of mental health care, ensuring that AI tools not only enhance therapeutic outcomes but also uphold ethical standards and user rights. This collaborative effort between practitioners and researchers will be crucial in navigating the complexities of AI integration in mental health care, ensuring that ethical considerations remain at the forefront of technological advancements. This collaborative approach will foster an environment where ethical considerations are prioritized, ultimately leading to more effective and compassionate mental health interventions that respect user autonomy and dignity. The need for robust frameworks addressing emotional privacy in AI tools is paramount, as it directly impacts users' trust and the ethical use of these technologies in emotional health. Establishing such frameworks will not only protect individual privacy but also promote ethical practices in the development and deployment of AI tools in emotional health contexts. Establishing these frameworks requires collaboration among developers, researchers, and ethicists to ensure that emotional privacy is respected and upheld in all AI applications within emotional health.

Future studies should explore long-term impacts of AI-driven emotional interventions, particularly among vulnerable populations. More diverse datasets are needed to minimize bias and increase global applicability.

REFERENCES

Ajluni, V. (2023). Respecting autonomy: Prioritizing patient-centered care and decision-making capacity for stronger doctor–patient relationships. *Journal of Family Medicine and Primary Care*, *12*(8), 1752–1753. DOI: 10.4103/jfmpc.jfmpc_712_23 PMID: 37767408

Alhuwaydi, A. M. (2024). Exploring the Role of Artificial Intelligence in Mental Healthcare: Current Trends and Future Directions – A Narrative Review for a Comprehensive Insight [Review of Exploring the Role of Artificial Intelligence in Mental Healthcare: Current Trends and Future Directions – A Narrative Review for a Comprehensive Insight]. Risk Management and Healthcare Policy, 1339. Dove Medical Press. DOI: 10.2147/RMHP.S461562

Bakir, V., Laffer, A., McStay, A., Miranda, D., & Urquhart, L. (2024). On manipulation by emotional AI: UK adults' views and governance implications. *Frontiers in Sociology*, *9*, 1339834. Advance online publication. DOI: 10.3389/fsoc.2024.1339834 PMID: 38912311

Ballesteros, J. A., Villegas, G., Moreira, F., Solano, A., & Peláez, C. (2024). Facial emotion recognition through artificial intelligence. *Frontiers of Computer Science*, *6*, 1359471. Advance online publication. DOI: 10.3389/fcomp.2024.1359471

Brem, A., & Hörauf, D. (2025). 'Artificial Creativity?' AI's Short- and Long-Term Impact on Creativity. *Research Technology Management*, *68*(2), 54–58. DOI: 10.1080/08956308.2025.2450756

Chustecki, M. (2024). Benefits and Risks of AI in Health Care: Narrative Review [Review of Benefits and Risks of AI in Health Care: Narrative Review]. Interactive Journal of Medical Research, 13. JMIR Publications. DOI: 10.2196/53616

Coghlan, S., Leins, K., Sheldrick, S., Cheong, M., Gooding, P., & D'Alfonso, S. (2023). To chat or bot to chat: Ethical issues with using chatbots in mental health. *Digital Health*, *9*, 20552076231183542. Advance online publication. DOI: 10.1177/20552076231183542 PMID: 37377565

Crimaldi, F., & Leonelli, M. (2023). AI and the creative realm: A short review of current and future applications [Review of AI and the creative realm: A short review of current and future applications]. arXiv (Cornell University). Cornell University. https://doi.org//arxiv.2306.01795DOI: 10.48550

Ettman, C. K., & Galea, S. (2023). The Potential Influence of AI on Population Mental Health. *JMIR Mental Health*, *10*, e49936. Advance online publication. DOI: 10.2196/49936 PMID: 37971803

Hoose, S., & Králiková, K. (2024). Artificial Intelligence in Mental Health Care: Management Implications, Ethical Challenges, and Policy Considerations. *Administrative Sciences*, *14*(9), 227. DOI: 10.3390/admsci14090227

Jian, M. J. K. O. (2023). Personalized learning through AI. *Advances in Engineering Innovation*, *5*(1), 16–19. DOI: 10.54254/2977-3903/5/2023039

Manzini, A., Keeling, G., Alberts, L., Vallor, S., Morris, M. R., & Gabriel, I. (2024). The Code That Binds Us. *Navigating the Appropriateness of Human-AI Assistant Relationships.*, *7*, 943–957. DOI: 10.1609/aies.v7i1.31694

Meadi, M. R., Sillekens, T., Metselaar, S., van Balkom, A. J. L. M., Bernstein, J., & Batelaan, N. M. (2025). Exploring the Ethical Challenges of Conversational AI in Mental Health Care: Scoping Review. *JMIR Mental Health*, *12*, e60432. Advance online publication. DOI: 10.2196/60432 PMID: 39983102

Narimisaei, J., Naeim, M., Imannezhad, S., Samian, P., & Sobhani, M. (2024). Exploring emotional intelligence in artificial intelligence systems: a comprehensive analysis of emotion recognition and response mechanisms [Review of Exploring emotional intelligence in artificial intelligence systems: a comprehensive analysis of emotion recognition and response mechanisms]. Annals of Medicine and Surgery, 86(8), 4657. Wolters Kluwer. DOI: 10.1097/MS9.0000000000002315

Poudel, U., Jakhar, S., Prakash, M., & Nepal, A. (2025). AI in Mental Health: A Review of Technological Advancements and Ethical Issues in Psychiatry [Review of AI in Mental Health: A Review of Technological Advancements and Ethical Issues in Psychiatry]. Issues in Mental Health Nursing, 1. Taylor & Francis. DOI: 10.1080/01612840.2025.2502943

Rubin, M., Arnon, H., Huppert, J. D., & Perry, A. (2024). Considering the Role of Human Empathy in AI-Driven Therapy. *JMIR Mental Health*, *11*, e56529. Advance online publication. DOI: 10.2196/56529 PMID: 38861302

Saeidnia, H. R., Fotami, S. G. H., Lund, B., & Ghiasi, N. (2024). Ethical Considerations in Artificial Intelligence Interventions for Mental Health and Well-Being: Ensuring Responsible Implementation and Impact. *Social Sciences (Basel, Switzerland)*, *13*(7), 381. DOI: 10.3390/socsci13070381

Shaikh, S. (2021). Development of Automated Knowledge Management Model (AKMM). *Advances in Data Science and Adaptive Analysis*, *13*(2), 2150008. Advance online publication. DOI: 10.1142/S2424922X2150008X

Shaikh, S. (2022). The Relationship Between Knowledge Automation and Employee Creativity. *International Journal of Information Technology Project Management, 13*(2), 1–25. DOI: 10.4018/IJITPM.311851

Shaikh, S., & Bhutto, A. (2021). Construction of Knowledge Automation Measuring Scale. *International Journal of Information Technology Project Management, 12*(2), 45–69. DOI: 10.4018/IJITPM.2021040103

Spytska, L. (2025). The use of artificial intelligence in psychotherapy: Development of intelligent therapeutic systems. *BMC Psychology, 13*(1), 175. Advance online publication. DOI: 10.1186/s40359-025-02491-9 PMID: 40022267

Tavory, T. (2024). Regulating AI in Mental Health: Ethics of Care Perspective. *JMIR Mental Health, 11*, e58493. Advance online publication. DOI: 10.2196/58493 PMID: 39298759

Wang, Y., & Liu, W. (2023). Emotional Simulation of Artificial Intelligence and Its Ethical Reflection. *Academic Journal of Humanities & Social Sciences, 6*(5). Advance online publication. DOI: 10.25236/AJHSS.2023.060503

Wei, Q., Pan, S., Liu, X., Mei, H., Nong, C., & Zhang, W. (2025). The integration of AI in nursing: addressing current applications, challenges, and future directions [Review of The integration of AI in nursing: addressing current applications, challenges, and future directions]. Frontiers in Medicine, 12. Frontiers Media. DOI: 10.3389/fmed.2025.1545420

Wei, X., Yang, Z., & Feng, X. (2024). A meta-analysis of the intervention effect of mindfulness training on athletes' performance. *Frontiers in Psychology, 15*, 1375608. Advance online publication. DOI: 10.3389/fpsyg.2024.1375608 PMID: 38939219

Wu, J. (2024). Social and ethical impact of emotional AI advancement: The rise of pseudo-intimacy relationships and challenges in human interactions. *Frontiers in Psychology, 15*, 1410462. Advance online publication. DOI: 10.3389/fpsyg.2024.1410462 PMID: 39564589

Yang, N., & Jia, F. (2025). A Scoping Review of AI-Driven Digital Interventions in Mental Health Care: Mapping Applications Across Screening, Support, Monitoring, Prevention, and Clinical Education [Review of A Scoping Review of AI-Driven Digital Interventions in Mental Health Care: Mapping Applications Across Screening, Support, Monitoring, Prevention, and Clinical Education]. Healthcare, 13(10), 1205. Multidisciplinary Digital Publishing Institute. DOI: 10.3390/healthcare13101205

Zhang, Z., & Wang, J. (2024). Can AI replace psychotherapists? Exploring the future of mental health care. *Frontiers in Psychiatry*, *15*, 1444382. Advance online publication. DOI: 10.3389/fpsyt.2024.1444382 PMID: 39544371

Chapter 7
From Consumer to Employee:
How Cross-Cultural Digital Expectations Shape Work Experiences in Algorithmic Organizations

Wissal Errayem
http://orcid.org/0009-0002-8340-327X
WSB Merito Universities, Poland

ABSTRACT

Abstract Digital platforms are dissolving boundaries between consumption and labour, enabling individuals to act as both consumers and workers within the same interface. This chapter introduces the Consumer-to-Employee Expectation Transfer Model (CEETM), which explains how expectations shaped by consumer apps—personalisation, immediacy, transparency, and control—carry over into algorithmic workplaces. Based on a multi-country qualitative study across Poland, Kenya, Japan, and Brazil, the findings reveal that cultural values mediate this transfer, resulting in four worker responses: empowerment, alienation, translation, and activism. Key insights include a personalisation paradox, acceleration anxiety, transparency gaps, and emerging digital solidarity. The chapter concludes with six HR design recommendations and an ethical governance checklist aligned with GDPR, Brazil's LGPD, and the EU AI Act. It offers a framework for building human-centred algorithmic systems that balance efficiency with fairness and cultural sensitivity.

DOI: 10.4018/979-8-3373-4307-5.ch007

1. INTRODUCTION

1.1 Colliding Digital Identities

Li Wei, a twenty-seven-year-old courier in Shanghai, begins each morning like most digital natives: by unlocking his phone before getting out of bed. His screen springs to life with a curated feed of personalized content—breakfast burrito promotions from a local café he frequents, cycling glove discounts from a store he once browsed online, and a sponsored ad for a posture-correcting backpack eerily similar to one he had discussed with a friend in a private messaging app. Within seconds, Li is immersed in a world that seems to anticipate his needs before he can articulate them. "It's like the app reads my mind," he jokes, amused by the eerie precision of its suggestions.

This intuitive interface is more than a convenience; it is a digital concierge trained on millions of data points, built to make him feel seen, known, and understood. Li doesn't question the targeting—he has grown to expect it. Customisation is not a luxury, but the norm. The algorithm appears to serve him, to gently nudge him toward efficiency, satisfaction, and pleasure.

Yet by 10:00 a.m., everything changes. The same super-app that helped him plan his breakfast now switches him into a completely different role: that of a platform worker. With one swipe, his dashboard transforms. Notifications now urge him to accept delivery orders within 15 seconds, avoid underperforming zones, maintain a 4.9-star rating, and opt into surge-hour challenges for bonus pay. A warm, consumer-centric tone is replaced by blunt directives. Li is no longer the customer; he is the product.

"The algorithm pampers me at breakfast and scolds me by lunch," he says with a half-smile—knowing full well the truth behind the punchline.

This moment is not unique to Li, nor is it confined to Shanghai. It is increasingly common across the globe—from São Paulo to Nairobi, from Warsaw to Tokyo. Millions of people now navigate this dual identity: at one moment, they are *data-rich consumers* interacting with sleek, personalised, gamified platforms designed to delight; in the next, they become *data-controlled workers* subject to the same digital infrastructure, now repurposed for discipline, monitoring, and micro-management.

According to the International Labour Organization (ILO), over 430 million people worldwide will earn income through app-mediated labour by 2025. In parallel, over 4.8 billion individuals interact daily with personalised consumer platforms. The line between shopping and working, between browsing and performing, is no longer clear—it is fluid, porous, and often invisible. The psychological fire-door that once separated our commercial and professional identities has not just been propped open—it has been algorithmically dismantled.

Historically, the tools of commerce and the tools of work belonged to separate realms. Shopping took place in brick-and-mortar stores; work occurred in offices, factories, or service environments. Consumer experiences were mediated by salespeople, while employment involved human supervisors and structured hierarchies. But today, an Uber ride, an Amazon order, a Slack assignment, and a shift acceptance notification are all mediated through the same hardware (a smartphone), powered by the same backend logic (cloud-based analytics and machine learning), and executed through the same behavioural mechanics (gamified nudges, swipeable cards, push alerts).

This technological convergence is also a cognitive convergence. The expectations that people learn, practice, and reinforce in their roles as consumers—expectations for immediacy, customisation, responsiveness, transparency, and control—do not stay confined to their shopping lives. They bleed into their professional environments. When Li taps into his courier interface, he does so with the same mental model that guided his morning coffee order: he expects speed, clarity, autonomy, and recognition. When the app fails to deliver on these expectations—when it assigns him to a neighbourhood he dislikes without explanation, or docks points for an unknown infraction—he doesn't just feel confused. He feels betrayed.

This is the core premise of the chapter: that digital expectations are not compartmentalised. They are portable psychological constructs, shaped by years of consumer interaction and transferred into the workplace, especially when the technological interface remains constant. We refer to this process as the Consumer-to-Employee Expectation Transfer, and we argue that it is one of the most overlooked dimensions of contemporary algorithmic work.

But this transfer is not neutral, nor is it universal. It is filtered through culture—through local norms about power, individuality, risk, and rules. In some cultures, like Denmark or Canada, workers may demand algorithmic accountability and protest opaque processes. In others, like Japan or Kenya, they may interpret algorithmic control through collectivist or hierarchical lenses, resisting it quietly or adapting through peer networks. The same set of consumer-born expectations can produce vastly different experiences depending on national culture, economic security, and organisational context.

This raises urgent questions for scholarship and practice:

- What happens when consumer-grade expectations collide with industrial-grade algorithmic management?
- How do workers reconcile the cognitive dissonance between being catered to in their leisure time and being governed impersonally during work?

- And how can Human Resource Management (HRM) evolve to bridge this gap, to design systems that not only automate tasks efficiently but also respect the human expectations encoded through everyday digital life?

These questions animate the rest of the chapter and guide the development of a new conceptual model—the Consumer-to-Employee Expectation Transfer Model (CEETM)—through which we explore the psychological, cultural, and structural dimensions of algorithmic work across four diverse countries.

Li Wei may laugh when he describes his algorithmic double life, but his experience captures a deeper truth: that in the 21st-century digital economy, the most consequential shift may not be technological—it may be expectational.

1.2 Research Questions

1. **Expectation transfer:** What specific expectations migrate from platform consumption to app-mediated employment, and by what mechanisms?
2. **Cultural mediation:** How do national and organisational cultures amplify, mute, or redirect this transfer?
3. **HRM implications:** Which design principles can support dignity, engagement, and fairness in cross-cultural algorithmic contexts?

1.3 Why the Inquiry Matters

In little more than a decade, algorithmic systems have moved from the periphery of HR to its command centre. Machine-learning models now screen résumés, chatbots conduct first-round interviews, optimisation engines assign shifts and routes, dynamic pricing algorithms set individualised wages and bonuses, and anomaly detectors can trigger automatic suspension or termination—sometimes with no human in the loop. For organisations these tools promise speed, scale, and cost efficiency; for workers they inaugurate a new order in which one's livelihood is mediated by black-box code rather than a line manager's judgment.

Yet employees do not encounter these systems as blank slates. They arrive having spent thousands of hours immersed in frictionless e-commerce ecosystems where one-tap checkout, 24/7 live chat, and real-time parcel-tracking maps are not perks but baseline expectations. When the workplace interface deviates from this consumer-grade norm—when a shift request hangs in limbo for hours, a pay calculation appears without explanation, or a performance score suddenly drops—workers experience a jarring sense of expectation violation. Cognitive dissonance quickly morphs into distrust; distrust, left unaddressed, can snowball into attrition, reputational blow-back, or collective action ranging from app-store review bombing to full-scale work stoppages.

For managers and platform designers, the stakes are therefore twofold. First, there is the immediate business risk: disengaged employees are less productive, more likely to churn, and more inclined to share negative stories on social media—a reputational contagion that can deter both talent and customers. Second, there is growing regulatory scrutiny. Legislators in the European Union, Brazil, and several U.S. states are drafting rules that require explainability, auditability, and participatory governance for workplace AI. Firms that ignore the *consumer gaze that shadows the employee gaze* risk non-compliance fees, class-action lawsuits, and mandated algorithmic audits.

Beyond organisational self-interest lies a broader societal concern. Algorithmic management does not merely optimise existing workflows; it reconfigures labour markets by redistributing risk (e.g., variable pay), redefining skill valuation (e.g., micro-certifications), and institutionalising particular values and biases at scale. If the underlying data reflect historical inequities, the algorithm can ossify them under a veneer of objectivity. When multiplied across millions of workers, the cumulative effect can reshape wage structures, career trajectories, and even national employment statistics.

Understanding the *human side* of this transformation is therefore not a luxury—it is a necessity for scholars, who must refine theories of motivation and control for a digital age; for HR practitioners, who must translate abstract fairness principles into concrete interface choices; and for policymakers, who must balance innovation incentives against worker protections. Only by examining how consumer-formed expectations collide with algorithmic governance can we craft workplaces that harness technological efficiencies without sacrificing dignity, transparency, or cultural fit.

2. LITERATURE REVIEW

The literature review weaves together five conceptual strands that have traditionally operated in isolation, despite their deep relevance to each other in the context of algorithmic work. First, the framework of surveillance capitalism (Zuboff, 2019) illuminates how digital platforms extract behavioural data to predict and shape human action, yet often overlooks how this logic extends from consumer targeting into employee monitoring and control. Second, the field of algorithmic management—which examines how digital systems automate managerial functions such as scheduling, performance evaluation, and behavioural nudging—offers crucial insights into how work is administered at scale, but typically treats these systems as closed environments, paying insufficient attention to the broader UX cultures in which workers operate. Third, the notion of the digital psychological contract challenges classical HR assumptions about trust and fairness by showing how relational expectations in workplaces are now mediated through screens, dashboards, and automated messages, rather than human supervisors. Fourth, cross-cultural information systems (IS) research provides tools to understand how technology is interpreted through the lens of national and organisational culture, yet it seldom integrates theories of platform-mediated expectation transfer. Finally, consumer expectation theory, long studied in marketing, UX design, and behavioural economics, offers rich models of how users come to expect responsiveness, personalisation, transparency, and control—but this field rarely crosses into labour studies or HRM.

Taken together, these five threads reveal a significant blind spot at the consumer–employee nexus: we know a great deal about how consumers interact with digital platforms, and an emerging body of work examines algorithmic governance in employment, but almost no research explores how one realm informs the other. This chapter addresses that omission by theorising and empirically exploring how digital consumer expectations migrate into the workplace, and how cultural context mediates that transfer.

2.1 Surveillance Capitalism & the Personalisation Imperative

Zuboff (2019) coined the term surveillance capitalism to describe a new economic logic in which human experience is mined as a raw material for commercial prediction and behavioural manipulation. At its core is the extraction of what she calls behavioural surplus—the vast troves of data produced through everyday digital interactions that go far beyond what is necessary to deliver a service. These data are analysed, repurposed, and sold to influence not only what people see online but how they act, vote, consume, and work. In its earliest phase, surveillance capitalism focused primarily on consumer targeting: using behavioural data to personalise ads, curate content feeds, and maximise attention. Today, however, its logic extends much further, shaping how organisations govern their employees as well.

Firms now deploy the same predictive analytics that once powered targeted advertising to orchestrate labour workflows. These tools are no longer confined to marketing departments— they are integral to HR operations, operations management, and workplace automation.

Recommender systems, originally developed to suggest movies on Netflix or books on Amazon, are now applied to match workers to tasks in warehouses, route delivery drivers in real time, and assign customer-service tickets based on sentiment analysis and tone detection. The shift from consumer-facing to worker-facing personalisation reveals the full extent of surveillance capitalism's reach: data gathered in one domain is leveraged to restructure another.

What was once a novel UX feature—algorithmic personalisation—has become infrastructural. According to Accenture's (2024) global digital experience survey, 88% of consumers now report frustration when digital experiences feel impersonal or irrelevant. Personalisation is no longer a value-add; it is an expectation. Users expect platforms to remember preferences, anticipate needs, and reduce friction. This expectation, however, is not bounded by context. When individuals who experience high-quality personalisation in their shopping and streaming apps encounter non-personalised, opaque systems in the workplace, the contrast is jarring and destabilising.

This tension is what Fischer (2023) refers to as the personalisation paradox. On one hand, users feel delighted—valued, even—when recommendations or automated suggestions align with their tastes or goals. On the other hand, when the underlying logic of those suggestions is hidden, inconsistent, or uncanny, users may feel manipulated, surveilled, or dehumanised. This paradox becomes even more potent in work contexts, where the consequences of algorithmic decisions are not about movies or playlists, but livelihoods, evaluations, and income.

In algorithmic workplaces, employees often report that task assignments, shift scheduling, or performance scores feel arbitrary—even when they are ostensibly based on personal data. The same worker who enjoys Spotify's "Discover Weekly" may resent an app that assigns shifts without accounting for their caregiving responsibilities or preferred working hours. The emotional nuance of personalisation—its ability to create connection or alienation depending on context and transparency—is a central thread in understanding how digital expectations migrate from consumption to employment.

Thus, the concept of behavioural surplus does more than expose corporate strategies; it illuminates a psychological transformation in how individuals interpret algorithmic systems— especially when those systems cross the boundary from serving the user to managing them.

2.2 Algorithmic Management Genealogy

The evolution of workplace control systems is as old as industrial capitalism itself. From

Frederick Winslow Taylor's time-motion studies in the early 20th century—where stopwatches measured the optimal pace of bricklaying—to the rise of digital platforms that assign microtasks at scale, the tools used to extract productivity from workers have undergone dramatic technological transformation. Yet the underlying principle—control through measurement— remains consistent. What has changed are the mechanisms, the interfaces, and the psychological terrain in which this control is exercised.

In contemporary digital labour environments, this terrain is dominated by algorithmic management: the delegation of managerial functions to computational systems. Lee, Kusbit, and Metsky (2015) offer a useful distinction between two modes of algorithmic control: "hard" algorithmic management, in which decision-making is fully delegated to the algorithm (e.g., an app auto-assigning a delivery route or rejecting a shift request); and "soft" algorithmic management, where decisions are merely supported or augmented by algorithmic suggestions (e.g., performance dashboards assisting human managers). This distinction is critical, as it reveals the range of human oversight (or lack thereof) involved in algorithmic governance—and the implications for worker agency.

The tools of algorithmic management now permeate nearly every sector. On gig platforms, starrating systems serve as reputational control mechanisms that can impact visibility, pay, or even employment status (Rosenblat & Stark, 2016). In white-collar environments, gamified leaderboards and performance badges—such as those documented by Kellogg, Valentine, and Christin (2020)—create competitive environments where workers internalise surveillance through peer comparison. Real-time surveillance dashboards, such as those studied by Mateescu and Nguyen (2019), offer employers unprecedented visibility into worker behaviour: keystroke rates, click patterns, eye movement, and GPS location can now be monitored, analysed, and acted upon instantaneously.

While the literature on algorithmic management has grown substantially in the past decade— charting its implications for control, fairness, bias, and power asymmetries—there remains a crucial blind spot: the psychological expectations workers carry into these systems, shaped by their long-standing experiences as digital consumers. Much of the existing scholarship focuses on what algorithms do to workers—automating roles, obscuring accountability, introducing bias— rather than on how workers interpret and emotionally respond to algorithmic control through the lens of their prior digital lives.

This oversight matters because employees today are not encountering algorithmic systems in a vacuum. They have grown up with user-friendly, hyper-responsive apps that value *interface design, emotional tone,* and *personalisation.* When the algorithm in their workplace is more opaque, rigid, or indifferent than the one that delivers their groceries or recommends their movies, it creates a dissonance that can undermine trust, erode motivation, and provoke resistance. Workers are no longer simply reacting to productivity measures—they are comparing their treatment as employees to their experience as *users*, and often finding the former lacking.

Thus, the next frontier in understanding algorithmic management is not simply tracking what these systems automate—but how they are received, interpreted, and internalised by digitally conditioned workers who arrive with pre-loaded expectations for clarity, fairness, and responsiveness.

2.3 The Digital Psychological Contract

Rousseau's (2000) seminal notion of the psychological contract—the implicit, often unspoken set of mutual expectations between employee and employer—was conceived in an era when supervision was unequivocally human. Trust, reciprocity, and fairness were negotiated face-toface or, at worst, via email and performance reviews. Today, many workers' primary point of contact with "management" is a push notification that pings at unpredictable intervals: *"New shift available. Accept within 30 seconds." "Your delivery efficiency score has fallen; complete three more orders to avoid deactivation."* The relational substrate of the employment relationship has been compressed into rule-based prompts delivered by an app interface.

This shift has profound consequences for how breach and fulfilment of the psychological contract are perceived. Meijerink and Keegan (2019) demonstrate that gig-economy workers interpret algorithmic decisions—bonus changes, auto-terminations, task rejections—through the same cognitive lens they use for human promises, but with one crucial difference: the latency of disappointment is dramatically shorter. Traditional breach unfolds over weeks or months (a promotion that never materialises, a training budget quietly cut). In contrast, algorithmic workplaces can violate expectations in real time: a single opaque rating drop can instantaneously jeopardise income, access to shifts, or even platform access. The speed of data processing collapses the temporal buffer that once cushioned feelings of betrayal, making emotional fallout more immediate and intense.

Compounding the issue is the fact that employees do not engage with these digital managers as blank slates. They bring years of consumer-grade UX expectations—clarity, feedback, undo buttons—into the employment relationship. When an algorithmic decision clashes with these learned norms (e.g., no rationale given for a route assignment, no appeal option for a pay deduction), breach perception is not only faster but also amplified by the contrast with everyday consumer experiences that emphasise personalisation and redress. In effect, the psychological contract is no longer negotiated solely within an organisational silo; it is contextualised within a broader digital ecosystem where users are accustomed to being treated as valued customers.

Scholars have rightly begun calling for a post-digital psychological contract model—one that accounts for algorithmic opacity, data asymmetry, and the erosion of human mediation. Yet most revisions still centre on organisational justice or technological affordances, paying scant attention to consumer psychology as a shaping force. Ignoring this dimension risks an incomplete theory that cannot explain why two identical algorithmic decisions may be tolerated by one worker yet deemed intolerable by another whose consumer experiences set a higher bar for transparency and control. A truly contemporary model must therefore weave together insights from HRM, HCI, and marketing, recognising that today's employees are simultaneously workers and seasoned digital consumers, negotiating their expectations across both roles in real time.

2.4 Cross-Cultural Information Systems & HRM

Decades of cross-cultural research—most notably Hofstede's cultural dimensions, the GLOBE studies, and Minkov's tightness–looseness framework—demonstrate that cultural values profoundly influence how individuals interpret and interact with technology. In high powerdistance societies such as Malaysia or the Philippines, workers tend to accept top-down authority and more readily accommodate surveillance technologies or algorithmic controls. These are perceived not as infringements but as natural extensions of hierarchical order. By contrast, in low power-distance cultures like Denmark or the Netherlands, algorithmic opacity can be deeply unsettling, leading to demands for transparency, contestability, and participatory decision-making (Tarafdar et al., 2022).

The dynamic differs again in tight cultures—those with strong social norms and low tolerance for deviance—such as Japan and Singapore. In these settings, compliance with algorithmic rules and behavioural nudges is often high, even when the logic behind them is not well explained. Conversely, in looser cultures such as Brazil or the United States, individuals are more likely to question or creatively resist automated management systems that feel arbitrary, unjust, or culturally misaligned. Additional dimensions such as individualism versus collectivism or uncertainty avoidance further shape attitudes. For example, collectivist employees may accept data sharing if it supports group cohesion, while employees in uncertainty-avoidant cultures become anxious when algorithmic processes lack clarity or predictability.

What remains largely underexplored, however, is how these cultural patterns interact with the consumer-driven digital expectations that employees bring with them. Workers in Denmark may not just expect transparency because of cultural values—they may have been trained to expect it through years of interacting with highly responsive, data-ethical consumer platforms. In contrast, workers in Indonesia or Kenya may interpret personalisation and responsiveness through entirely different cultural lenses, even if they use the same global apps. Most cross-cultural HRM and IS research treats digital work systems as self-contained, without considering that today's employees are simultaneously platform consumers. This omission is significant, as it obscures the ways in which global consumer technologies shape and inform local experiences of algorithmic governance. Addressing this gap requires an integrative framework that captures both cultural value orientations and platform-mediated behavioural expectations.

2.5 Consumer Expectation Formation

Expectation–Disconfirmation Theory (EDT), originally formulated by Oliver (1980), posits that user satisfaction hinges on whether the perceived performance of a product or service meets or exceeds prior expectations. Marketing scholars have since expanded this framework, revealing how firms intentionally shape consumer expectations through guarantees, delivery times, interface design, and control features. Two expectation clusters have become particularly entrenched in the digital age.

First is immediacy. From Amazon's "Buy Now" button to Uber's real-time car-tracking, modern users have been conditioned to expect instant responses, frictionless execution, and near-zero waiting time. Response times are no longer judged against past workplace norms but against app experiences shaped by billion-dollar UX design teams. Even a five-minute lag in shift confirmation or feedback delivery can cause disproportionate frustration in workers accustomed to consumer-grade responsiveness.

Second is control. Consumer platforms now routinely provide granular control over data sharing, communication settings, and service preferences. Through consent dashboards, privacy toggles, and opt-out options, users have developed an expectation that digital systems should be configurable, transparent, and reversible. This expectation travels with them into work, where rigid scheduling, closed feedback loops, and non-negotiable algorithmic decisions often feel like anachronisms.

Despite their relevance, these insights from consumer research rarely inform workplace systems. HR platforms and management algorithms have adopted the data collection logic of consumer platforms but largely ignored their expectation-management strategies. Marketing scholars spend enormous effort understanding how to shape, frame, and meet expectations to maintain loyalty— yet HRM scholars have been slow to apply these findings to employee-facing systems.

This disconnect opens an important line of inquiry. For example: Does a worker's experience with flexible, transparent shopping apps influence how they perceive opaque scheduling software? Do expectations of control learned in a consumer context increase resistance to algorithmic authority in employment settings? Bridging the gap between marketing psychology and HRM is critical for designing systems that meet not only operational goals but also the psychological expectations of today's digitally conditioned workforce.

3. CONSUMER-TO-EMPLOYEE EXPECTATION TRANSFER MODEL (CEETM)

The Consumer-to-Employee Expectation Transfer Model (CEETM) proposes that workers' experiences in the digital consumer realm shape their expectations of how technology should behave in the workplace. These expectations—developed through thousands of microinteractions with apps and platforms designed to optimise user satisfaction—become cognitive and emotional reference points for evaluating algorithmic systems at work. When workplace platforms fall short of these expectations, users experience frustration, distrust, and in some cases, disengagement or resistance. At the heart of this transfer process are four dominant expectation clusters: personalisation, immediacy, transparency, and control.

3.1 Four Expectation Clusters

1. Personalisation

In the consumer world, personalisation is not merely a convenience; it is an operating standard. From music recommendations on Spotify to product suggestions on Amazon, users have grown accustomed to systems that appear to "know" them—predicting preferences, remembering history, and tailoring options accordingly. Algorithms that track browsing patterns, time-of-day behaviours, and even sentiment cues help curate hyper-individualised experiences that reinforce a sense of personal relevance and attention.

When users become employees, however, this expectation does not vanish—it intensifies. Workers increasingly expect that the systems managing their tasks, schedules, or performance evaluations will reflect their individual context—their unique skills, availability, health needs, caregiving responsibilities, or preferred work style. A platform that treats them as interchangeable nodes in a labour network contradicts the consumer-level norm that digital systems *should* adapt to the user, not the other way around. This disconnect can lead to what we call the personalisation paradox: the same person who feels empowered by a personalised consumer app may feel dehumanised by a workplace system that ignores their individuality.

2. Immediacy

Digital consumers now live in an attention economy optimised for instant gratification. Push notifications, same-day delivery, and real-time tracking have set new temporal standards. Messaging apps offer read receipts and "typing…" indicators;

services like Uber show live vehicle locations. Waiting—even for seconds—has been reframed as a UX failure.

When workers enter algorithmic workplaces, they bring these temporal expectations with them. They anticipate rapid confirmation of submitted forms, immediate resolution of issues, and realtime updates about shifts, pay, or performance. Systems that operate on batch updates or delayed feedback cycles can generate anxiety, perceived inefficiency, or even suspicion. For gig workers who rely on platform responsiveness to secure income or resolve disputes, delays aren't just annoying—they're existential. The expectation of immediacy, though forged in consumer interactions, becomes critical to workplace morale and trust.

3. Transparency

The average consumer can now track a pizza from the moment it enters the oven to the second it arrives at their doorstep. They can view shipping updates, browse reviews, and access return policies with a single tap. As a result, digital transparency—once a value-added feature—has become a baseline expectation in everyday life. People expect to understand what is happening behind the screen: where their data goes, how recommendations are made, and what's influencing the outcomes they see.

When these expectations meet the opacity of workplace algorithms—particularly those governing performance scores, pay rates, or access to shifts—the result is often confusion or distrust. Employees want to know how a five-star rating was calculated, why a shift was denied, or what data is being collected. A lack of clarity not only undermines confidence in the system but also violates the psychological expectation that modern digital services should be explainable. In low power-distance cultures, this may lead to overt challenge; in high power-distance ones, it may foster silent withdrawal or rumour-based reinterpretation. Either way, the gap between expected and delivered transparency becomes a significant friction point.

4. Control

Modern consumer apps have taught users to expect a high degree of agency over their digital environments. Thanks to frameworks like the General Data Protection Regulation (GDPR) and design norms around privacy, users routinely see toggles, opt-out options, data download portals, and granular permissions in everything from newsfeeds to fitness apps. Control has become part of the user experience: people expect to be able to reverse a decision, challenge a claim, or manage how much personal data they share.

When workplace platforms lack these affordances—when employees cannot dispute a pay calculation, appeal a shift assignment, or opt out of data tracking—the system is experienced as rigid, disempowering, and unfair. The result is not only functional frustration but also a deeper sense of being *acted upon* rather than *participating in* one's own work life. The expectation of control, long cultivated by consumer platforms, makes the absence of contestability in employment settings feel all the more unjust.

3.2 Cultural Moderators

Table 1. Cultural Moderators

Cultural dimension	Effect on personalisation	Effect on immediacy	Effect on transparency	Effect on control
Power distance ↑	Accepts generic rules	Tolerates delays	Lower transparency demand	Lower control demand
Individualism ↑	Demands uniqueness	Expects speed	High transparency need	Strong control need
Uncertainty avoidance ↑	Craves rule clarity	Suffers stress from rapid pace	High transparency desire	Moderate control
Tightness ↑	Conforms to defaults	Aligns to set tempos	Accepts limited transparency	Accepts low control

3.3 Process Flow: How Consumer Expectations Transfer into the Workplace

The migration of digital expectations from consumer life into algorithmic work environments is not accidental or peripheral—it is the result of structured psychological mechanisms that govern how individuals interpret, feel, and act when confronted with familiar digital experiences in unfamiliar contexts. The Consumer-to-Employee Expectation Transfer Model (CEETM) identifies three interlocking conduits through which this transfer occurs: cognitive, affective, and behavioural. Each pathway reflects a different dimension of human psychology and together they explain how and why expectations born in one domain—shopping, streaming, social networking—can dramatically shape perceptions in another: the world of algorithmic labour.

1. Cognitive Conduit: Schema Activation and Pattern Recognition

At the core of human cognition lies the use of schemas—mental templates formed from repeated experience. Just as a consumer learns to anticipate a confirmation email after placing an order, or to expect a back button on a mobile app, these patterns become default interpretive frameworks. When individuals encounter a new digital system, they instinctively try to make sense of it through comparison to prior systems they understand. This is particularly true when visual and interaction cues—menus, icons, layout styles—are similar to those seen in consumer platforms.

In the workplace, this means employees often approach HR interfaces, scheduling apps, or rating dashboards with consumer-trained assumptions about how information should be structured, how quickly feedback should arrive, and how much agency they should have. If these assumptions are confirmed, users experience fluency and satisfaction. If not, expectation violations trigger cognitive friction: confusion, uncertainty, or the sense that something is "off." This cognitive conduit explains why an unexplained shift rejection or missing pay breakdown can feel not only frustrating but cognitively disorienting—it violates the logic users have internalised through years of well-designed consumer interactions.

2. Affective Conduit: Emotional Associations and Valence Transfer

Digital experiences are not just interpreted intellectually; they are felt. Over time, consumers form emotional associations with digital platforms. A food delivery app may evoke a sense of convenience and care; a streaming platform might represent comfort or relaxation. These associations become emotionally "charged," creating affective patterns of delight, anticipation, frustration, or trust.

When users later encounter similar digital architectures in the workplace, these emotional tones often carry over, consciously or unconsciously. A colourful interface may feel juvenile or condescending if it mimics a gamified rewards app. A delay in feedback might trigger disproportionate anxiety—not because of the delay itself, but because it breaks an emotional contract previously reinforced in consumer contexts.

For example, a worker who expects real-time delivery tracking and receives vague shift update messages may not just be confused—they may feel devalued. This affective conduit helps explain the emotional volatility often observed in algorithmically managed work: workers aren't simply reacting to system outputs, they're reacting to the emotional echoes of how digital systems are *supposed* to treat them.

3. Behavioural Conduit: Transfer of Digital Habits and Interaction Norms

Users carry habitual interaction patterns from digital platforms—like swiping, tapping, and toggling—into workplace systems, expecting similar gestures and interface behaviors. When these expectations are met, systems feel intuitive, but mismatches in design can frustrate users and make even functional systems feel clumsy or poorly designed.

3.4 Outcome Archetypes

Table 2. Outcome Archetypes

Conformity between expectations & reality	Resulting employee stance	Illustrative quote
High match	**Empowerment**	"The route suggestions fit my style."
Low match + high uncertainty avoidance	**Alienation**	"I never know why my score drops."
Partial match + high tightness	**Translation**	"We tweak the app rules to fit team norms."
Low match + low power distance	**Activism**	"We organised a data-rights petition."

3.5 Propositions

P1: High consumer personalisation → expectation of skill-based workplace assignment. • *P2*: Instant consumer responsiveness → intolerance for latency in pay adjustments. • *P3*: Power distance moderates transparency dissatisfaction.

- *P4*: Individualism amplifies demand for data control.
- *P5*: Expectation disconfirmation leads to the four archetypes.
- *P6*: Algorithmic literacy dampens negative outcomes across cultures.

4. METHODOLOGY

4.1 Design

A sequential mixed-methods design merged literature synthesis with multi-site qualitative fieldwork.

1. **Phase A: Systematic Review** – PRISMA protocol yielded 312 peer-reviewed sources (2008–2024).
2. **Phase B: Field Study** – 45 semi-structured interviews in four countries + 200 hours of platform observation.

4.2 Research Sites and Participant Profile

The qualitative phase of the study was designed to capture variation across cultural dimensions, economic contexts, and industry sectors where algorithmic management is actively shaping work. To that end, we conducted research in four countries selected for their strategic differences in platform economy maturity, digital infrastructure, and Hofstede-indexed cultural values. These included Poland, Kenya, Japan, and Brazil. Each location represents a distinct intersection of global technology use and local cultural interpretation, providing a fertile

Participants ranged in age from 19 to 52 years and included both full-time and part-time workers as well as contractual employees in flexible or app-mediated roles. Industries were selected to reflect different degrees of algorithmic intervention:

- "Hard" systems (Poland, Kenya) featured algorithmic decision-making with little or no human oversight (e.g., shift assignment, route planning, dynamic pay).
- "Soft" systems (Japan) involved algorithmic tools designed to support, not replace, human decisions (e.g., smart scheduling, productivity dashboards).
- "Hybrid" systems (Brazil) blended automation with discretionary oversight by HR staff or team leads.

Each participant was interviewed using a semi-structured guide tailored to local context. Interviews lasted between 45 and 90 minutes, averaging 68 minutes overall. Conversations were conducted in the participant's preferred language, then transcribed verbatim and, where necessary, translated into English for cross-case analysis. Transcripts were uploaded to NVivo 14 for qualitative coding.

To support cultural interpretation, we incorporated publicly available Hofstede Insights cultural dimension scores and national digital literacy indices, helping to situate participant narratives within broader socio-cultural frames. This supported the construction of cultural profiles for each site, allowing us to explore how expectations around personalisation, immediacy, transparency, and control were modulated by national value orientations (e.g., power distance, uncertainty avoidance).

4.3 Analytical Strategy

We used reflexive thematic analysis, as outlined by Braun and Clarke (2021), to identify and interpret patterns in the data. This approach was chosen for its flexibility in accommodating both deductive (theory-driven) and inductive (data-driven) coding. The initial coding framework was based on the four CEETM expectation clusters and three psychological conduits (cognitive, affective, behavioural), but the codebook was iteratively expanded to capture emergent themes such as "digital solidarity," "emotional surveillance," and "cultural workaround strategies."

Two independent coders analysed all transcripts, achieving an intercoder reliability score of

Cohen's κ = 0.82, which indicates a strong level of agreement. Discrepancies were resolved through discussion and iterative review. Thematic saturation—the point at which new interviews no longer yielded novel codes—was reached after 38 interviews. The remaining seven interviews were used for triangulation and validation, confirming the stability of key findings.

We then conducted a cross-case synthesis, mapping themes against cultural dimensions (power distance, individualism, tightness–looseness, etc.) and platform characteristics. This enabled a comparative analysis that revealed both shared patterns and culturally contingent variations in how digital expectations were interpreted and responded to in the workplace.

4.4 Ethics and Reflexivity

The study received ethical approval from the Institutional Review Board (IRB) of the lead researcher's university. All participants were provided with informed consent forms, outlining the purpose of the study, their right to withdraw at any time, and the confidential handling of their data. Participants were offered the option to review and delete parts of their transcript postinterview. Pseudonyms are used throughout this chapter to ensure anonymity.

To account for positionality and reduce potential bias, the lead author maintained a reflexive journal throughout data collection and analysis. This was particularly important given the author's prior professional experience at a Nairobi-based ride-hailing start-up, which could have shaped interpretations of Kenyan data. Memos were used to document moments of potential subjectivity and to surface latent assumptions during coding. Additionally, peer debriefing sessions were held with co-researchers to challenge interpretations and ensure analytical transparency.

The combination of methodological triangulation, intercoder validation, member-checking, and reflexivity enhances the credibility, dependability, and transferability of the findings. This rigor ensures that the Consumer-to-Employee Expectation Transfer Model (CEETM) is both theoretically grounded and empirically robust, while remaining sensitive to the complex cultural and emotional realities of platform-based work.

5. FINDINGS AND DISCUSSION

5.1 Theme 1: The Personalisation Paradox

"It knows what I want when I shop, but when I work, it forgets who I am." – Monika, Wolt courier, Poland

Participants across all four countries expressed appreciation for personalisation in consumer life.

Spotify's curated playlists, TikTok's tailored For You feed, and ecommerce product recommendations were cited as examples of algorithms "understanding" their individuality.

In contrast, their workplace apps were seen as blunt instruments. Workers felt reduced to metrics: speed, punctuality, delivery volume. Those with prior experience in UX-rich consumer platforms expressed greater discontent when employer algorithms appeared "generic."

In Brazil, Daniela, a Nubank support agent, said:

"If my performance is scored only by how fast I close tickets, it ignores that I resolve complex cases others pass to me. That's not personalisation—it's penalisation."

This disconnect created what we term the personalisation paradox: a widening gap between what algorithms *can* do for consumers and *refuse* to do for workers. In Japan, engineers at Rakuten acknowledged the irony:

"The same AI we deploy for customers—personal, friendly—becomes rigid and mechanical when used on staff," said Takahiro, a backend engineer.

Cultural insights: In Poland and Brazil (moderate individualism), frustration centered on fairness. In Kenya (collectivist), concern was about misrecognition of local team dynamics. In Japan (tight culture), workers rationalised this misalignment as a necessary trade-off for group harmony.

5.2 Theme 2: Acceleration Anxiety

"I used to wait for feedback. Now, I panic when it doesn't come instantly." – Eliane, customer service rep, Brazil

Immediacy is a dominant norm in consumer life. Apps update in real-time, messages get read receipts, rides arrive in under 4 minutes. Participants described how these expectations bled into workplace contexts, creating a condition we term acceleration anxiety.

Workers expected—and demanded—immediate feedback on their actions. The problem? Delays in workplace feedback (e.g., shift confirmations, performance scores, tip processing) caused disproportionate stress.

In Nairobi, Martin, a Bolt driver, explained:

"I send documents to update my licence. No response. Two days of silence and then I'm locked out. If they replied like WhatsApp, I'd plan."

In Tokyo, where cultural norms value timeliness, Aiko, a junior team leader, said:

"We're used to seeing things updated live. But if your manager uses a legacy HR system, you feel forgotten."

The *expectation of immediacy*, drawn from consumer UX, heightens sensitivity to latency at work. When responsiveness fails, emotional costs include anxiety, over-checking, and compulsive task-refreshing.

Cultural insights:

- In Japan and Poland, slow response was interpreted as inefficiency.
- In Kenya, it was viewed as disrespect or a threat to earnings.
- In Brazil, participants voiced emotional volatility tied to latency, suggesting that immediacy had become a psychological need.

5.3 Theme 3: Algorithmic Opacity vs. Consumer Transparency

"I can track a pizza from the oven to my door. But I can't see how my pay is calculated." – Filip,

Wolt courier, Poland

A consistent grievance was the lack of transparency in algorithmic decision-making at work. While consumer apps visualise processes in real time (package tracking, food prep stages), workplace apps were often described as "black boxes."

In Poland, several Wolt drivers said the platform provided dynamic bonuses with no explanation:

"Some days I get a surge, some days nothing. I've stopped trying to understand it," said Kacper.

In Kenya, Bolt drivers shared screenshots comparing their pay rates for identical routes taken hours apart. No rationale was ever communicated.

In contrast, consumer apps such as Uber Eats show driver paths, wait times, and ratings visibly. This visibility has become an *expectation*, not a luxury.

Cultural insights:

- In low power-distance societies (Poland), opacity was framed as injustice.
- In high power-distance societies (Kenya), opacity was accepted but feared.
- In Japan, some workers resisted deeper transparency, fearing it would generate internal conflict.

5.4 Theme 4: Control and Contestability

"In my shopping app I can return anything. In my work app, decisions are final."
– Joana, customer support, Brazil

Control emerged as the most emotionally charged expectation. Workers in all countries resented the non-contestability of algorithmic decisions: shift rejections, task denials, penalties, and even auto-terminations were often issued with no appeal channel.

In Brazil, Felipe, a former digital bank agent, described losing his job:

"An email came at midnight—'Your contract is terminated based on performance data.' No human, no discussion."

In Poland, Ania reported being suspended for a GPS glitch:

"They said I took a route outside the zone. I had no way to show it was a system error."

The *consumer-side control* over choices, returns, and subscriptions sets a precedent. When the workplace system offers no reversal mechanism, it feels dehumanising.

Cultural insights: In individualist cultures (Poland, Brazil), the demand for contestability was strong.

- In collectivist Kenya, workers relied on offline groups or social media channels to protest silently.
- In Japan, participants were more resigned, framing control loss as "inevitable."

5.5 Theme 5: The Interface as Culture Carrier

"The app is the boss, the teacher, the gatekeeper—and the tone is passive-aggressive." – Isaac, Bolt driver, Nairobi

Participants often anthropomorphised their work apps, assigning them personalities. In Brazil and

Kenya, workers described them as "cold," "moody," or "shaming." In Japan, apps were "too cheerful for serious work," undermining authority. In Poland, tone mismatch between interface and intent caused confusion.

This theme revealed a deeper truth: the user interface communicates cultural values.

- An overly gamified UI (badges, fireworks) was seen as infantilising by Japanese and Polish workers.
- Lack of clarity in error messages eroded trust in Brazil.
- Notifications written in a harsh tone reduced morale in Kenya.

In consumer apps, tone is fine-tuned for delight. In workplace apps, it's often ignored—yet it shapes perception of *fairness*, *authority*, and *belonging*.

5.6 Theme 6: Learned Helplessness and Algorithmic Fatigue

"You try to 'game' the app, then give up. It's smarter, faster, and you never win." – Ryo, IT associate, Japan

Several interviewees expressed feelings of learned helplessness—the gradual erosion of agency caused by repeated failures to understand or influence algorithmic decisions.

In Kenya and Brazil, drivers and support agents described a sense of "gaming fatigue": trying to guess patterns in performance scores, bonuses, or ratings, only to find inconsistencies. Over time, many adopted passive coping strategies: compliance without trust.

In Japan, Ryo said:

"We used to share tips in our team about how to get better scores. Now we don't bother. No one knows the rules anymore."

This sense of algorithmic opacity compounds psychological exhaustion, reinforcing a narrative of **powerlessness**.

5.7 Theme 7: Peer Translation as Resistance

"I don't follow the app—I follow Maria. She explains what the system really wants." – Douglas, gig worker, São Paulo

In all regions, informal peer translation networks emerged as adaptive strategies. Workers often ignored official guides, instead trusting veteran peers to interpret algorithmic patterns, policy changes, and "best behaviour."

In Poland and Kenya, this took the form of WhatsApp groups where users decoded performance logic. In Brazil, Maria, an ex-agent, published YouTube videos "translating" platform updates into local slang and context.

Such folk UX systems highlight the disconnect between top-down algorithm design and bottomup user adaptation. They also represent a subtle form of **resistance**, reclaiming meaning and control.

5.8 Theme 8: Algorithmic Gaze and Emotional Surveillance

"Even when I'm not working, I feel watched." – Njeri, ride-hailing, Kenya

Many workers described an emotional burden from being under constant algorithmic gaze. The idea that *everything is being tracked*—from idle time to GPS drift to tone of voice—produced chronic tension.

In Brazil, this was tied to affective labour: call centre agents monitored for enthusiasm, not just resolution speed.

In Poland and Japan, facial recognition log-ins, camera monitoring, and biometric verification further blurred the boundary between security and surveillance.

As Njeri put it:

"When I close the app, I still behave like I'm being rated."

This theme highlights how datafication extends into the psychological domain—creating a panopticon of performance.

5.9 Theme 9: Cultural Workarounds and Silent Subversion

"We obey the app, but we don't believe it." – Takeshi, IT team lead, Japan

In tight or high power-distance cultures (Japan, Kenya), workers rarely challenged algorithms openly. Instead, they engaged in **silent subversion**: ignoring nudges, collaborating offline to redistribute work, or creating shadow protocols.

In Kenya, Bolt drivers agreed to accept unprofitable rides but then rerouted passengers through better-paying zones.

In Japan, teams used legacy scheduling systems to override inefficient AI calendars—quietly reintroducing human flexibility.

These acts represent a **reassertion of cultural logic** over technological determinism. Compliance masks resistance.

5.10 Theme 10: Digital Solidarity and Organised Resistance

"We learned how to beat the bot—together." – Kamila, Wolt courier, Warsaw

Workers in all regions used digital tools to organise, resist, and protest. WhatsApp, Discord, Telegram, and Facebook became hubs for collective action:

- **Poland:** Wolt couriers coordinated a "blackout day" in Warsaw.
- **Kenya:** Bolt drivers joined digital unions advocating for dynamic pricing transparency.
- **Brazil:** Agents shared complaint templates and coordinated negative app reviews.
- **Japan:** Workers created anonymous message boards to rate algorithmic fairness.

These stories reveal the emergence of platform-era solidarity, often tech-enabled and culturally framed.

6. HRM IMPLICATIONS AND DESIGN GUIDELINES: 6 PRACTICAL DESIGN GUIDELINES FOR HUMAN-CENTRED ALGORITHMIC WORKPLACES

Digital expectations shaped in consumer life can be powerful allies rather than hidden tripwires—provided organisations deliberately align, support, and govern their workplace technologies. The following six guidelines translate the chapter's findings into actionable design and policy recommendations.

6.1 Designing for Expectation Alignment

Personalisation modules. Add profile pages where employees can declare skills, preferred shifts, language abilities, or ergonomic needs. Scheduling and task-routing engines should then surface assignments that genuinely reflect those inputs, rather than relying solely on efficiency metrics. A driver with advanced first-aid training, for instance, could be given priority for medical-supply deliveries—reinforcing the sense that the system "knows" and values individual expertise.

Responsive feedback. Borrow UI patterns from e-commerce—upload confirmation tick-marks, live progress bars, and colour-coded delay notices. Even a short, honest timer ("This may take up to four minutes; feel free to navigate away") mitigates the anxiety that stems from uncertainty.

Transparent scoring. Expose, in plain language, the core variables that feed performance ratings: weighting percentages, data-collection windows, and acceptable ranges. Hover-over or tap-to-expand popovers labelled "Why this score?" can demystify machine judgements. Employees need not see proprietary code, but they do need a window into the logic.

6.2 Supporting Contestability and Control

In-app dispute channels. Embed a single-click pathway for challenging penalties, late fees, or task denials. Crucially, route each case to a human reviewer with the power to reverse automated outcomes.

Notification logs. Offer a chronological ledger of every algorithmic decision affecting the user— much like a bank statement. Workers can then audit their own records, detect anomalies, and build evidence for appeals.

GDPR-aligned dashboards. Allow employees to download their raw data, toggle consent for optional analytics, and view retention periods. The act of providing these controls signals respect for autonomy and meets growing regulatory expectations.

6.3 Algorithmic-Literacy Programmes

Culturally adapted micro-courses. Short video modules, delivered in local languages, can explain how shift scores are calculated, why GPS drift matters, or how surge pricing is determined. Incorporate culturally relevant metaphors—sports analogies in Brazil, groupharmony themes in Japan—to boost comprehension.

Empowerment orientation. Move beyond compliance training. Emphasise user rights, fairness safeguards, and concrete tips for leveraging algorithm features (e.g., optimising availability windows to earn bonuses).

Narrative translation. Visual "journey maps" or animated explainers showing "how your score is built, step by step" turn opaque math into an understandable story, reducing fear and misinformation.

6.4 Human Mediation Layers

Algorithm liaisons in HR. Designate staff who specialise in bridging technical and human perspectives. These liaisons host Q&A sessions, escalate anomalies, and translate policy updates into everyday language.

Escalation paths for failure cases. When facial-recognition log-ins misfire or route optimisation strands a courier in a low-pay zone, employees should know exactly which hotline or chat channel overrides the algorithm.

Co-existence over dominance. Position technology as "first draft, human final." For instance, let scheduling AI suggest rosters, but require a supervisor's click to finalise—balancing efficiency with empathy.

6.5 Tone Calibration and Cultural Sensitivity

Avoid infantilisation. Badges and fireworks that delight users in a fitness app can feel patronising in a professional context. Replace "Yay! You crushed it!" with culturally attuned acknowledgments such as "Shift completed—thank you for your expertise."

Localise communication style. In high-context cultures, excessive emojis may be read as unprofessional; in low-context cultures they can build warmth. Offer locale-specific tone libraries so the same notification adapts its formality automatically.

Affective-impact testing. Conduct short in-app surveys or A/B experiments to gauge whether message tone boosts motivation or induces stress, iterating until the emotional footprint aligns with organisational values.

6.6 Ethical Governance

Algorithmic audit boards. Establish cross-functional committees that include employee representatives, data scientists, legal counsel, and external ethicists. Review model updates, bias tests, and incident reports on a scheduled cadence.

Public ethics statements. Publish a clear policy outlining the purpose, data sources, and oversight mechanisms for each major algorithm. Transparency deters mission-creep and builds external trust.

Risk anticipation. Maintain a living risk register covering cultural mismatch, statistical bias, opacity creep, and function-stretch. Pair each risk with mitigation actions—such as bias-testing protocols, explainability thresholds, and sunset clauses for experimental features.

7. GLOBAL CASE VIGNETTES: 7 GLOBAL CASE VIGNETTES: ALIGNING ALGORITHMS WITH HUMAN EXPECTATIONS

Drawing on industry reports, press releases, worker testimonies, and third-party evaluations, the following four mini-cases illustrate how organisations in very different cultural settings have confronted expectation misalignment—and how design or governance interventions reshaped worker experience.

Case 1: Gojek, Indonesia – "Gamifying Transparency"

In 2022 Gojek faced a surge of driver complaints on Jakarta-based Telegram channels and Facebook groups. The flashpoint was an **opaque bonus-tier system** nicknamed *"misteri poin"* (mystery points) that rewarded some drivers handsomely and left others puzzled and resentful.

Under mounting social-media pressure—and fearing defections to Grab—Gojek's product team formed a rapid-response task force that embedded three driver representatives alongside UX researchers.

Two initiatives emerged:

1. **User polls before policy changes.** Any modification to incentives, surge zones, or cancellation penalties was first floated as a one-click in-app survey ("thumbs-up / thumbsdown / comment") that collected thousands of responses in 24 hours. The data helped product managers detect friction points early and adjust parameters before rollout.

2. **"How Your Pay Works" visual walkthrough.** Borrowing from Instagram Stories, Gojek added a swipeable mini-course that used animations to show how distance, demand, rating, and cancellation rates combined to form earnings. Tapping any icon expanded the math behind that variable.

Six months after launch, an internal evaluation showed a 17% drop in pay-related tickets and a 9% rise in weekly active drivers—evidence that gamified transparency can convert suspicion into engagement when executed with co-design principles.

Case 2: Uber Kenya – Algorithmic Disclosure through Digital Unionism

Kenya's ride-hailing market is one of the world's most price-competitive, with Bolt, Little Cab, and Uber vying for drivers. In late 2021 a loosely organised WhatsApp collective named "Online Drivers Union–Kenya" spearheaded a campaign demanding disclosure of the algorithm that sets base fares and surge multipliers. Leveraging Twitter hashtags (#TalkToUsUber) and a one-day log-off strike that reportedly idled 12,000 drivers, the group secured a virtual meeting with Uber's Sub-Saharan policy team.

The negotiated outcome included:

- **Monthly algorithm bulletins** emailed to all drivers, summarising any changes to fare formulas, incentive thresholds, or driver-rating weightings.
- A pilot **"earnings simulator"** inside the driver app where users could adjust variables (time of day, location, acceptance rate) and preview projected income.

Internal churn metrics leaked to local media suggested that driver attrition fell by almost 13% in the first quarter after disclosure. The case demonstrates how grassroots digital organising can compel multinational platforms to adopt transparency practices even in high power-distance environments.

Case 3: Rakuten, Japan – Re-Humanising the Schedule

Rakuten's enterprise IT division adopted an AI-driven scheduling engine in 2020 to coordinate large agile teams across Tokyo, Sendai, and Fukuoka. Within a year HR data flagged a rise in sick-day usage, late-night messaging, and voluntary turnover—symptoms later linked to "invisible overtime" created by the algorithm's optimisation logic. Japanese labour culture's strong norm of endurance (*gaman*) kept official complaints low, but exit interviews revealed widespread burnout.

In 2022 Rakuten introduced "schedule buffers"—human team leaders granted veto power over AI-generated rosters. Their mandate: check fairness, respect personal constraints, and insert recovery blocks after intense sprints. The company also shifted its KPI focus from *utilisation* to *sustainable velocity*. One year later, HR reported a 32% reduction in overtime hours and employee-pulse scores on "workload predictability" rose from 5.8 to 7.1 (on a 10-point scale). The Rakuten experience underscores the value of human mediation layers in cultures where direct confrontation is rare but wellbeing expectations are rising.

Case 4: Nubank, Brazil – Bottom-Up Dashboard Innovation

Nubank's São Paulo customer-experience team handles millions of chats per month, guided by dashboards that track response times and resolution rates. Agents complained, however, that the interface ignored the emotional tenor of calls—critical in Brazilian service culture, where warmth and rapport strongly influence customer satisfaction scores.

A group of frontline agents, many with coding boot-camp backgrounds, built an unofficial sentiment-analysis overlay using Nubank's open API and free Python libraries. The widget colour-coded live chats (green, yellow, red) based on text sentiment and appended suggestions like "Acknowledge frustration" or "Offer proactive credit." Management initially viewed the hack as shadow IT but pivoted after AB-testing showed a 6-point lift in Net Promoter Score for agents using the overlay.

Nubank formalised the tool, integrated it with internal training modules, and celebrated the creators in a company-wide town hall. Agent turnover in the pilot cohort dropped by 14% over six months, demonstrating how employee-driven innovation can fill empathy gaps in datacentric platforms—particularly in cultures that value expressive communication.

7.1 Cross-Case Insight

Across Indonesia, Kenya, Japan, and Brazil, the most effective corrections did not involve dismantling algorithms but augmenting them with transparency, human discretion, or userled design. These vignettes show that aligning digital management with cultural expectations can improve trust, reduce attrition, and even boost performance metrics—supporting the chapter's argument that consumer-shaped expectations, when acknowledged and integrated, become levers for organisational resilience rather than sources of friction.

7.2 Contributions to Theory and Practice

This work contributes to multiple fields:

- To **HRM and organisational design**, it offers a new lens for understanding algorithmic engagement as not only a technical or ethical issue, but a psychological and cultural one.
- To **consumer psychology**, it reframes digital expectation formation as a force that doesn't end at checkout—but travels with users into the workplace.

- To **cross-cultural IS research**, it highlights the need for models that account for both universal UX heuristics and culture-specific interpretations.

By foregrounding the human agency that persists—often subtly—in the face of automated systems, this chapter resists the narrative of technological determinism. It invites scholars and practitioners to engage not only with what algorithms can do, but with how they are felt, framed, and fought.

7.3 Final Reflection: Algorithms Manage Tasks, People Manage Meaning

As the workplace continues to digitize—often invisibly, often rapidly—we are left with a central truth: technology assigns tasks, but people assign meaning. Behind every system lies a human story—a narrative of adaptation, negotiation, resistance, and reinvention.

Algorithmic systems will continue to evolve. They will get faster, smarter, more predictive. But their success will hinge not just on how well they compute, but on how well they connect—to human expectations, to cultural logics, and to the fundamental dignity of the people they govern.

In the design of tomorrow's digital workplaces, it is not enough to optimise for efficiency. We must also design for resonance—for that deeper alignment between what systems do and what people need them to mean. Only then can the promise of the e-economy become not just more profitable, but more equitable, human-centred, and globally just.

REFERENCES

Accenture. (2024). *Global Consumer Trust Survey*.

Braun, V., & Clarke, V. (2021). Thematic analysis: A practical guide. *Sage (Atlanta, Ga.)*.

Fischer, E. (2023). Personalization paradox. *Journal of Marketing Theory*, *19*(1), 10–34.

Kellogg, K. C., Valentine, M. A., & Christin, A. (2020). Algorithms at work. *The Academy of Management Annals*, *14*(1), 366–410. DOI: 10.5465/annals.2018.0174

Lee, M. K., Kusbit, D., & Metsky, E. (2015). Working with algorithms. *CHI Conference Proceedings*, 1603–1612.

Meijerink, J., & Keegan, A. (2019). Algorithmic management. *Human Resource Management Review*, *29*(1), 100–113.

Oliver, R. L. (1980). A cognitive model of the antecedents and consequences of satisfaction decisions. *JMR, Journal of Marketing Research*, *17*(4), 460–469. DOI: 10.1177/002224378001700405

Rosenblat, A., & Stark, L. (2016). Algorithmic labor and information asymmetries. *International Journal of Communication*, *10*, 3758–3774.

Tarafdar, M., Beath, C., & Ross, J. (2022). The digital workplace divide. *MIS Quarterly Executive*, *21*(1), 1–16.

Zuboff, S. (2019). *The Age of Surveillance Capitalism*. PublicAffairs. Rousseau, D. M. (2000). Psychological contract inventory technical report. *Carnegie Mellon University*.

Section 4

Sustainability and Human-Centered Innovation

Chapter 8
Green HRM:
Building a Sustainable Workforce for a Greener Future

Amrik Singh
http://orcid.org/0000-0003-3598-8787
Lovely Professional University, India

Harshit Kumar
Lovely Professional University, India

ABSTRACT

Green Human Resource Management (GHRM) has emerged as a strategic approach for organizations to align their human resource practices with environmental sustainability. This paper explores the concept of GHRM, examining its historical evolution, core practices, and the critical role it plays in fostering an eco-conscious organizational culture. By reviewing key literature, analyzing case studies, and assessing practical implementations, the paper highlights both the benefits and challenges associated with GHRM adoption. The research also outlines future trends in green HR practices and offers recommendations for organizations seeking to strengthen their sustainability initiatives. This chapter aims to emphasize how GHRM contributes to the long-term success of organizations in terms of sustainability, employee satisfaction, and financial performance.

INTRODUCTION

This study examines the establishment of GHRM fundamentals alongside its historical development and essential practices which enable organizations to implement green organizational cultures. The paper explores the historical transition

DOI: 10.4018/979-8-3373-4307-5.ch008

of GHRM starting from classical human resource management which evolved into its contemporary form as a sustainability-oriented field. Organizations must use Green Human Resource Management (GHRM) as their primary approach to bring environmental sustainability into their business operations. Business organizations now prioritize environmental concerns in their global strategies so GHRM serves as an operational framework to relate human resource practices with sustainability objectives (Renwick et al., 2013; Jabbour, 2011; Daily & Huang, 2001; Jackson et al., 2011; Dumont et al., 2017; Wehrmeyer, 1996; Opatha & Arulrajah, 2014; Supina & Singh, 2024; Singh & Singh, 2024; Singh & Hassan, 2024; Singh, 2024; Singh & Kumar, 2024; Singh & Supina, 2024; Singh & Kumar, 2021; Singh & Kumar, 2024; Singh & Ansari, 2024; Singh & Hassan, 2024). Organizations which implement GHRM achieve better reputation and higher work environment happiness among staff and gain marketplace superiority. As part of this discussion resistance to change and the expenses related to green initiative deployment and the requirement for unified organization-wide policies are analyzed in depth. The strategy of GHRM implements ecological elements throughout its core people management functions starting from recruitment and continuing through training and performance oversight and employee retention practices (Renwick et al., 2013; Jabbour, 2011; Daily & Huang, 2001; Jackson et al., 2011; Dumont et al., 2017; Wehrmeyer, 1996; Opatha & Arulrajah, 2014; Supina & Singh, 2024; Singh & Singh, 2024; Singh & Hassan, 2024; Singh, 2024; Singh & Kumar, 2024; Singh & Supina, 2024; Singh & Kumar, 2021; Singh & Kumar, 2024; Singh & Ansari, 2024; Singh & Hassan, 2024). The marriage of human resource practices to environmental targets in GHRM produces lower environmental impact while encouraging employee team spirit and better workplace contentment through collective sustainability participation. The chapter evaluates GHRM practices through literature research and real-world examples to explain both the helpful aspects and difficulties that arise from its adoption. Green Human Resource Management (GHRM) creates radical changes in organizational human resource practices because it combines sustainability with standard human resource functions. Organizations recognize both environmental issues and business success demands new practices which serve environmental goals in addition to organizational success (Renwick et al., 2013; Jabbour, 2011; Daily & Huang, 2001; Jackson et al., 2011; Dumont et al., 2017; Wehrmeyer, 1996; Opatha & Arulrajah, 2014; Supina & Singh, 2024; Singh & Singh, 2024; Singh & Hassan, 2024; Singh, 2024; Singh & Kumar, 2024; Singh & Supina, 2024; Singh & Kumar, 2021; Singh & Kumar, 2024; Singh & Ansari, 2024; Singh & Hassan, 2024).. The purpose of GHRM is to create such an alignment that human resources support organizational sustainability objectives while building environmental awareness throughout the organizational culture. Previously human resource management focused on two core aspects which were organizational maximization alongside employee development and achieving productivity goals. The rising global awareness of environmental issues has resulted in organizations understanding that human capital facilitation requires environmental sustainability enhancement as a fundamental organizational responsibility (Renwick et al., 2013; Jabbour, 2011; Daily & Huang, 2001; Jackson et al., 2011; Dumont et al., 2017; Wehrmeyer, 1996; Opatha & Arulrajah, 2014; Singh & Kumar, 2024; Singh & Supina, 2024; Singh & Kumar, 2021; Singh & Kumar, 2024; Singh & Ansari, 2024; Singh & Hassan, 2024). The emergence of GHRM stemmed from organizational requirements by offering a strategic framework to introduce environmental practices into human resource management systems including staffing and employee development and performance assessment. GHRM origins stem from organizations developing understanding about CSR and environmental stewardship becoming vital to business success. The approach toward environmental responsibilities has shifted for organizations into becoming the foundation of their corporate strategy during the last few decades. The HR profession now requires professionals to create policies which develop sustainable employee practices while simultaneously decreasing workplace environmental impact through cultural changes that support sustainability (Renwick et al., 2013; Jabbour, 2011; Daily & Huang, 2001; Jackson et al., 2011; Dumont et al., 2017; Wehrmeyer, 1996; Opatha & Arulrajah, 2014; Singh & Hassan, 2024; Singh, 2024; Singh & Kumar, 2024; Singh & Supina, 2024; Singh & Kumar, 2021; Singh & Kumar, 2024; Singh & Ansari, 2024; Singh & Hassan, 2024). The development of GHRM stems from organizational recognition of corporate social responsibility and environmental stewardship which serve as fundamental aspects for business success. During recent decades businesses worldwide have developed a strategic perspective on environmental responsibilities that no longer exists as an additional issue. The transition requires HR professionals to create workplace policies that promote employee sustainable conduct and minimize operational environmental effects and strengthen sustainable organizational values. The analysis investigates GHRM through its historical context while exploring basic operational dimensions of GHRM and establishing its vital connection to develop environmentally responsive cultural attributes within organizations. GHRM contains essential principles which include green recruitment along with green training and development measures and performance management systems and employee participation in sustainability efforts (Renwick et al., 2013; Jabbour, 2011; Daily & Huang, 2001; Jackson et al., 2011; Dumont et al., 2017; Wehrmeyer, 1996; Opatha & Arulrajah, 2014; Supina & Singh, 2024; Singh & Singh, 2024; Singh & Hassan, 2024; Singh, 2024; Singh & Kumar, 2024; Singh & Supina, 2024; Singh & Kumar, 2021; Singh & Kumar, 2024; Singh & Ansari, 2024; Singh & Hassan, 2024).. The document examines the connection between GHRM as well as employee engagement and job satisfaction and total organizational performance results. A review of published literature and real-world case examples will enable researchers to analyze GHRM's practical use across industries while showing organizations' experiences with these methods. This paper evaluates the implementation barriers of GHRM which include resistance to transformation alongside green initiative costs along with misalignment between HR policies and sustainability targets.

LITERATURE REVIEW

GHRM represents an evolving concept in HRM which unites environmental sustainability to standard HR approaches. Studies of GHRM's basic dimensions have appeared throughout human resource management literature as well as environmental management literature along with organizational behavior studies and sustainability research (Renwick et al., 2013; Jabbour, 2011; Daily & Huang, 2001; Jackson et al., 2011; Dumont et al., 2017; Wehrmeyer, 1996; Opatha & Arulrajah, 2014; Singh & Supina, 2024; Singh & Kumar, 2021; Singh & Kumar, 2024; Singh & Ansari, 2024; Singh & Hassan, 2024). This review of available literature investigates how GHRM has developed alongside important themes and concepts and the tasks HR professionals face to support sustainability and the results from implementing GHRM across distinct organizational environments.

Evolution of Green Human Resource Management (GHRM)

GHRM emerged from the larger framework of corporate social responsibility which first started strengthening its momentum through the 1980s and 1990s. Businesses under CSR doctrine must accept total ownership of their societal footprint while ensuring their impact on both the environment and society and economics (Renwick et al., 2013; Jabbour, 2011; Daily & Huang, 2001; Jackson et al., 2011; Dumont et al., 2017; Wehrmeyer, 1996; Opatha & Arulrajah, 2014; Singh & Supina, 2024; Singh & Kumar, 2021; Singh & Kumar, 2024; Singh & Ansari, 2024; Singh & Hassan, 2024). The practice of HRM shifted beyond administrative duties toward establishing strategic influence for business success recognition. The growing Environmental challenges forced organizations to merge sustainability concepts with their Human Resources practices thus creating the new field of GHRM. GHRM involves more than environmental footprint reduction since it requires workforce training to adopt sustainable values which permeate organization-wide culture (Renwick et al., 2013; Jabbour, 2011; Daily & Huang, 2001; Jackson et al., 2011; Dumont et al., 2017; Wehrmeyer, 1996; Opatha & Arulrajah, 2014; Singh & Supina, 2024; Singh & Kumar, 2021; Singh & Kumar, 2024; Singh & Ansari, 2024; Singh & Hassan, 2024). GHRM signifies a cultural transformation in organizations through which environmental sustainability values establish themselves as fundamental decision-making components for human resource management according to Jackson and Seo (2010). Organizational sustainability receives significant contributions from GHRM because of integrating green initiatives throughout the human resource function including recruitment, training, performance management and employee engagement.

Core Practices of GHRM

Research in GHRM starts with identifying the main organizational strategies and practices organizations utilize to integrate sustainability through HR. Multiple scholars have outlined specific HR functions which serve essential roles toward sustainability development.

1. The recruitment process named Green recruitment enables organizations to bring in employees who share both environmental awareness and match sustainability objectives. Green recruitment methodology demands organizations to examine job candidates for their abilities as well as their dedication to sustainable practices as described by Renwick et al. (2013). Through this method organizations can establish a workforce which stands with their environmental values right from the beginning (Singh & Kumar, 2021; Singh & Kumar, 2024; Singh & Ansari, 2024; Singh & Hassan, 2024; Renwick et al., 2013; Jabbour, 2011; Daily & Huang, 2001; Jackson et al., 2011; Dumont et al., 2017; Wehrmeyer, 1996; Opatha & Arulrajah, 2014).
2. Green Training and Development in GHRM trains employees about sustainable practices by implementing programs which foster green behavioral adoption in workers. Arulrajah et al. (2015) describe green development programs that teach staff about environmental issues together with firm sustainability strategies and employee tasks for sustainability achievement. Training sessions designed for environmental awareness enable workers to develop abilities related to power-saving practices and resource efficiency along with waste reduction techniques.
3. The execution of GHRM extends to performance management through setting sustainability goals and establishing employee performance objectives that support environmental organizational targets. Employee engagement in sustainability initiatives along with eco-friendly work behavior at the workplace responds to environmental criteria integration within performance appraisals according to Ehnert (2009).
4. Employee engagement regarding sustainability initiatives emerges as a prime focus in GHRM since it plays a critical role. Organizations which fully involve employees in environmental choices and sustainability initiatives within projects and workplace settings produce better job satisfaction and

deeper employee commitment (Daily & Huang 2001; (Supina & Singh, 2024; Singh & Singh, 2024; Singh & Hassan, 2024; Singh, 2024; Singh & Kumar, 2024; Singh & Supina, 2024; Singh & Kumar, 2021; Singh & Kumar, 2024; Singh & Ansari, 2024; Singh & Hassan, 2024). Engaging employees produces dual benefits for organizations since it decreases environmental impacts and elevates worker spirits which creates a sustainable work environment.

The Role of HR in Promoting Organizational Sustainability

HR professionals have gained valuable importance in advancing environmental sustainability practices in organizations. Businesses now understand that Human Resources exists to offer strategic support for reaching corporate sustainability targets rather than primarily focus on workforce management. Jabbour (2013) explains that HR professionals must develop sustainable policies and practices which include writing green job profiles and leading sustainability-based leadership growth programs and establishing awards for employees who practice sustainability effectively. The responsibility of HR professionals extends beyond internal operations to involve external engagement with supplier and customer groups by sustaining sustainability across the entire value chain (Renwick et al., 2013; Jabbour, 2011; Daily & Huang, 2001; Jackson et al., 2011; Dumont et al., 2017; Wehrmeyer, 1996; Opatha & Arulrajah, 2014; Singh, 2024; Singh & Kumar, 2024; Singh & Supina, 2024; Singh & Kumar, 2021; Singh & Kumar, 2024; Singh & Ansari, 2024; Singh & Hassan, 2024). The HR department should collaborate with procurement departments to verify that suppliers both meet environmental standards and perform community outreach activities for sustainability initiatives.

Outcomes and Benefits of GHRM

Multiple advantages emerge from organizations that implement GHRM practice adoption. Various studies confirm that organizations which adopt GHRM show better employee satisfaction combined with improved reputation and heightened environmental goal dedication. According to Raineri and Paillé (2016) employee perception of environmental responsibility within their organization leads workers to adopt eco-friendly practices in both their professional and individual activities. The positive behavior modification produces financial savings and enhances operational effectiveness and total productivity (Renwick et al., 2013; Jabbour, 2011; Daily & Huang, 2001; Jackson et al., 2011; Dumont et al., 2017; Wehrmeyer, 1996; Opatha & Arulrajah, 2014; Supina & Singh, 2024; Singh & Singh, 2024; Singh & Hassan, 2024; Singh, 2024; Singh & Kumar, 2024; Singh & Supina, 2024; Singh & Kumar,

2021; Singh & Kumar, 2024; Singh & Ansari, 2024; Singh & Hassan, 2024).. Organizations implementing robust GHRM approaches tend to acquire better talents and retain them successfully. The implementation of green recruitment methods enables businesses to draw top candidates because sustainable priorities become important to emerging job seekers and current employees. The effort of organizations that focus on employee well-being through sustainability initiatives results in lower worker turnover and better employee engagement according to Ehnert (2009). Readiness to adopt GHRM strategies enables organizations to fulfill environmental legislation while obtaining certifications including ISO 14001 providing them useful market advantages. The implementation of green initiatives within HR practices will help organizations maintain adaptation to worldwide sustainability trends and create a favorable corporate reputation among stakeholders.

Challenges in Implementing GHRM

Organizations encounter multiple obstacles throughout the implementation of GHRM despite its possible advantages. The greatest challenge to adopting green human resource management stems from employee reluctance to accept change since they view environmental initiatives as extra work instead of beneficial improvements. The analysis conducted by Jabbour (2013) discovered senior management supports sustainability but middle managers and staff oppose green policies because they do not share environmental concerns.

Outcomes and Benefits of GHRM

Multiple advantages emerge from organizations that implement GHRM practice adoption. Research evidence shows that companies implementing GHRM practices achieve better employee satisfaction plus enhanced organizational reputation while developing stronger environmental goal dedication. According to Raineri and Paillé (2016) employee perception of environmental responsibility within their organization leads workers to adopt eco-friendly practices in both their professional and individual activities. The positive behavior modification produces financial savings and enhances operational effectiveness and total productivity. Organizations implementing robust GHRM approaches tend to acquire better talents and retain them successfully (Renwick et al., 2013; Jabbour, 2011; Daily & Huang, 2001; Jackson et al., 2011; Dumont et al., 2017; Wehrmeyer, 1996; Opatha & Arulrajah, 2014; Singh & Kumar, 2021; Singh & Kumar, 2024; Singh & Ansari, 2024; Singh & Hassan, 2024).. The implementation of green recruitment methods enables businesses to draw top candidates because sustainable priorities become important to emerging job seekers and current employees. The effort of organizations that focus on employee well-being through sustainability initiatives results in lower worker turnover and better employee engagement according to Ehnert (2009). Businesses that implement Global Human Resource Management practices gain better regulatory compliance and certification capabilities such as ISO 14001 thus obtaining increased market competitiveness. The implementation of green initiatives within HR practices will help organizations maintain adaptation to worldwide sustainability trends and create a favorable corporate reputation among stakeholders.

Challenges in Implementing GHRM

Organizations encounter multiple obstacles throughout the implementation of GHRM despite its possible advantages. The greatest challenge is to adopting green human resource management stems from employee reluctance to accept change since they view environmental initiatives as extra work instead of beneficial improvements. The analysis conducted by Jabbour (2013) discovered senior management supports sustainability but middle managers and staff oppose green policies because they do not share environmental concerns.

Licenses and Legal Requirements Relevant to GHRM

1. **Environmental Protection License**
    - o Required if the company's operations have an environmental impact (e.g., emissions, waste disposal).
2. **ISO 14001 Certification** (Environmental Management System)
    - o International standard; companies voluntarily adopt it to improve environmental performance.
3. **Occupational Safety and Health Administration (OSHA) Compliance**
    - o For employee safety — indirectly linked to green practices (like safe disposal of hazardous materials).
4. **Energy Star Certification** (for energy efficiency)
    - o Especially if the organization promotes energy-saving programs among employees.
5. **Forest Stewardship Council (FSC) Certification**
    - o If the company deals with paper usage, sourcing sustainable materials is part of green HR.
6. **LEED Certification (Leadership in Energy and Environmental Design)**
    - o For buildings/offices that are eco-friendly — HR policies could promote working from such buildings.
7. **National Green Tribunal (NGT) Compliance (India-specific)**

- If the organization operates in India, it must comply with NGT orders on environmental protection.

8. **Waste Management Licenses**
   - Especially important if the company promotes waste reduction practices.

Standing Orders Related to Green HRM

(Standing orders are internal mandatory policies that companies may need to frame.)

1. **Model Standing Orders under the Industrial Employment (Standing Orders) Act, 1946 (India)**
   - While traditionally covering service conditions, green policies can be incorporated into:
     - Safety protocols
     - Environmental behavior codes
     - Waste disposal practices
2. **Sustainability Policy or Environmental Stewardship Policy**
   - A mandatory internal order promoting green behavior among employees.
3. **Green Procurement Policy**
   - HR must ensure that all purchased goods/services are eco-friendly.
4. **Code of Conduct on Environmental Responsibility**
   - Must be part of employee handbooks.
5. **Remote Work and Digitalization Policies**
   - Reduce commuting emissions — organizations may officially introduce such green-friendly standing orders.

DISCUSSION AND ANALYSIS

Organizations must integrate environmental management into their human resource practices through Green Human Resource Management (GHRM) for achieving their broader sustainability goals. GHRM existing framework establishes its basis because it requires more than just establishing independent green initiatives through extensive integration of environmental awareness throughout organizational culture and employee conduct. GHRM develops through progressive stages that transition organizations from answering to their environment to implementing environmentally-strategic stewardship (Renwick et al., 2013; Jabbour, 2011; Daily & Huang, 2001; Jackson et al., 2011; Dumont et al., 2017; Wehrmeyer, 1996; Opatha & Arulrajah, 2014; Singh & Kumar, 2021; Singh & Kumar, 2024; Singh & Ansari,

2024; Singh & Hassan, 2024).. Modern organizations concentrate on creating green jobs alongside performing green recruitment and selection and delivering environmental training and development and establishing performance management systems which promote eco-friendly workplace behavior yet also maintain reward systems that support such behavior. Environmentally conscious individuals are recruited by green recruitment programs which complement employee training initiatives that teach sustainable practices. Organizations use these comprehensive methods to engage their employees in the pursuit of sustainability targets. Multiple tangible benefits become accessible to organizations that implement GHRM practices according to studies in existing literature and corporate case analysis. Organizations that adopt GHRM practices demonstrate better environmental results as well as improved business reputation while employees show increased engagement and innovation happens across operations. Workers demonstrate better organizational commitment and job engagement because their daily tasks advance environmental priorities. The green HRM practices at Toyota along with Siemens and Unilever confirm sustainable initiatives bring operational success together with customer retention and higher financial outcomes (Renwick et al., 2013; Jabbour, 2011; Daily & Huang, 2001; Jackson et al., 2011; Dumont et al., 2017; Wehrmeyer, 1996; Opatha & Arulrajah, 2014; Singh & Hassan, 2024).. The transformation to GHRM faces multiple obstacles on its path. Business environments encounter opposition to transformation efforts mainly because workers see green initiatives as separate tasks rather than fundamental components of their existing responsibilities. Organizations must face significant financial burdens at the beginning of green technology implementation and process transformation which create an apparent initial funding requirement. Organizations experience difficulties while measuring the specific sustainability outcomes that result from their GHRM practice implementation. The absence of precise performance indicators makes it impossible to determine the return from green HR initiatives as well as their sustained added value. The adoption of GHRM proves highly successful when leadership plays a vital role. Organizations need full management backing combined with direct environmental goal transmission and green principles embedded within their fundamental mission and operational documents. Organizations without genuine commitment face detection of green washing which erodes their legitimacy along with staff member trust (Renwick et al., 2013; Jabbour, 2011; Daily & Huang, 2001; Jackson et al., 2011; Dumont et al., 2017; Wehrmeyer, 1996; Opatha & Arulrajah, 2014; Singh & Supina, 2024; Singh & Kumar, 2021; Singh & Kumar, 2024; Singh & Ansari, 2024; Singh & Hassan, 2024). Organizations must adopt GHRM approaches because of regulatory requirements combined with increasing demands from stakeholders and world-wide efforts to fulfill sustainable development goals (SDGs). New environmental regulations emerge from governments while customers exclusively support businesses which prove their strong ethical and environmental commitment. GHRM serves as an essential business approach for survival alongside its role as a value-aligned initiative. The establishment of Green Human Resource Management (GHRM) represents a key transformation of human resources functions because it advances from basic administrative processes to form a strategic collaboration between HR and sustainability targets of the organization. The combination of environmentally friendly practices during recruitment and training and through performance management and employee engagement systems helps GHRM create workers who exhibit both high competency and sustainable behavior. GHRM has evolved from extra activity status into an essential strategic requirement for today's modern business operations. Companies that focus on green HR practices receive advantages of stronger brand identity and stronger employee commitment and operational enhancement and environmental compliance benefits (Renwick et al., 2013; Jabbour, 2011; Daily & Huang, 2001; Jackson et al., 2011; Dumont et al., 2017; Wehrmeyer, 1996; Opatha & Arulrajah, 2014; Singh & Supina, 2024; Singh & Kumar, 2021; Singh & Kumar, 2024; Singh & Ansari, 2024; Singh & Hassan, 2024). Through GHRM organizations create an innovative environment that actively enables employees to generate sustainable solutions while working on environmental projects. GHRM succeeds only through specific and continuous implementation steps. The implementation of GHRM requires strong leadership paired with comprehensive policies along with clear communication and sustainability value embedding across all organizational levels. Organizations need to overcome resistance to change combined with the costs for initial implementation and measurement complexity to access the total benefits of GHRM effectively. The rising interest in environmental sustainability throughout the world leads to a growing significance of GHRM. Green principles continue to integrate with emerging technologies including artificial intelligence (AI) and data analytics and remote work solutions that collectively aim to decrease environmental footprints in upcoming industry trends (Renwick et al., 2013; Jabbour, 2011; Daily & Huang, 2001; Jackson et al., 2011; Dumont et al., 2017; Wehrmeyer, 1996; Opatha & Arulrajah, 2014; Singh & Ansari, 2024; Singh & Hassan, 2024). Organizations that establish foundation-based GHRM investments now will achieve market edge while helping to fulfill environmental sustainability and social responsibility objectives. Green Human Resource Management builds its foundation through innovative methods which unite organizational success to ecological sustainability aims. Through its implementation organizations attain the ability to design workplaces which protect environmental boundaries together with enhancing employee welfare and creative potential and sustainable organizational expansion. The establishment of GHRM represents an organizational requirement which enables sustainable leadership throughout the global business environment. Green Human Resource Management (GHRM) establishes new fundamentals that change organizational perspectives about how human resources support environmental sustainability goals. Over time human resource management focused on employing staff then training and developing workers to maintain employee retention for better organizational outcomes. GHRM establishes environmentally responsible business creation by incorporating green practices into all human resource functions (Renwick et al., 2013; Jabbour, 2011; Daily & Huang, 2001; Jackson et al., 2011; Dumont et al., 2017; Wehrmeyer, 1996; Opatha & Arulrajah, 2014; Singh & Kumar, 2021; Singh & Kumar, 2024; Singh & Ansari, 2024; Singh & Hassan, 2024).. The recruitment and training elements of GHRM combine to help organizations hire environmentally-aware personnel while providing training that amplifies sustainable practices resulting in sustainability becoming a general organizational goal beyond single-initiate status. Three essential organizational elements of achieving environmental sustainability targets include Green performance appraisals with green rewards and recognition systems and the development of a green organizational culture. This study demonstrates that GHRM succeeds only when it receives precise direction from overall organizational targets. This simplistic approach to sustainability treatment leads organizations to inferior results. Producing green practices which become ingrained into organizational mission, vision and values generates meaningful transformation throughout the entire business. Workers embrace green initiatives while different departments partner toward environmental impact reduction leading leaders to support sustainability in all their management choices (Renwick et al., 2013; Jabbour, 2011; Daily & Huang, 2001; Jackson et al., 2011; Dumont et al., 2017; Wehrmeyer, 1996; Opatha & Arulrajah, 2014; Singh & Supina, 2024; Singh & Kumar, 2021; Singh & Kumar, 2024; Singh & Ansari, 2024; Singh & Hassan, 2024).. A wide range of advantages exist in GHRM. Local organizations which implement green HR practices effectively create superior environmental performance while boosting operational efficiencies and building better brand image. The practice of GHRM leads to increased employee engagement since modern workers prefer to work at companies that demonstrate environmental social responsibility commitment. Employees detect environmental concern from their employers and this drives them to perform work beyond their job duties while enhancing their job satisfaction levels and organizational loyalty. GHRM practices stimulate innovation because organizations motivate employees to find innovative solutions to environmental problems which creates a sustainable improvement system. Creating solid foundations in GHRM faces various obstacles even though the path remains uncertain. Organizational implementation of GHRM faces several barriers including unwillingness to adapt and insufficient knowledge of green practices as well as inadequate funds and challenges in measuring precise GHRM results. Conditions of weak environmental regulation combined with inconsistent enforcement lead companies to lack external pressure toward green human resource practices. The internal leadership together with organizational culture needs to lead the green agenda when governments provide little support in these scenarios. Technological support emerges as a vital finding from the collected data because it enables GHRM strategies (Renwick et al., 2013; Jabbour, 2011; Daily & Huang, 2001; Jackson et al., 2011; Dumont et al., 2017; Wehrmeyer, 1996; Opatha & Arulrajah, 2014; Singh & Ansari, 2024; Singh & Hassan, 2024).. The combination of digital tools together with platforms allows organizations to monitor their carbon footprints and administer remote work systems to decrease commuting emissions as well as deliver virtual training activities that emphasize sustainability.

CONCLUSION

Technology functions as a main driver for implementing green practices across human resource management operations. Organizations using data analytics to study employee behaviors about sustainability enable the creation of specific interventions that boost environmental results. Organizations that create solid structures for GHRM now will gain significant market edge in the future. Such organizations will experience improved competitiveness through their advanced ability to conduct green talent recruitment along with retention and financial facilitation and relationship development and regulatory alignment. Such organizations will serve their responsibility to future generations by making substantial contributions to vital global environmental issue solutions. Green Human Resource Management represents a strategic requirement that goes beyond operational need for contemporary organizations. Organizations which integrate sustainability practices within their HR operations combined with worker environmental education will establish economic prosperity together with environmental stewardship. Sustainable development receives foundation support through GHRM because it enables people growth simultaneously with organizational cultural transformation and develops green-based innovations. The future trajectory of GHRM focuses on technological integration and environmental challenge resolution which will ultimately shape work design for sustainable prosperity between organizations and Earth's health.

REFERENCES

Daily, B. F., & Huang, S. C. (2001). Achieving Sustainability Through Attention to Human Resource Factors in Environmental Management. *International Journal of Operations & Production Management, 21*(12), 1539–1552. DOI: 10.1108/01443570110410892

Dumont, J., Shen, J., & Deng, X. (2017). Effects of Green HRM Practices on Employee Workplace Green Behavior: The Role of Psychological Green Climate and Employee Green Values. *Human Resource Management, 56*(4), 613–627. DOI: 10.1002/hrm.21792

Jabbour, C. J. C. (2011). How Green Are HRM Practices, Organizational Culture, Learning and Teamwork? *Brazilian Journal of Business Management, 13*(37), 23–38.

Jackson, S. E., Renwick, D. W. S., Jabbour, C. J. C., & Muller-Camen, M. (2011). State-of-the-Art and Future Directions for Green Human Resource Management: Introduction to the Special Issue. *German Journal of Research in Human Resource Management, 25*(2), 99–116. DOI: 10.1177/239700221102500203

Opatha, H. H. D. N. P., & Arulrajah, A. A. (2014). Green Human Resource Management: Simplified General Reflections. *International Business Research, 7*(8), 101–112. DOI: 10.5539/ibr.v7n8p101

Renwick, D. W. S., Redman, T., & Maguire, S. (2013). Green Human Resource Management: A Review and Research Agenda. *International Journal of Management Reviews, 15*(1), 1–14. DOI: 10.1111/j.1468-2370.2011.00328.x

Singh, A. (2024). Quality of Work-Life Practices in the Indian Hospitality Sector: Future Challenges and Prospects. In Valeri, M., & Sousa, B. (Eds.), *Human Relations Management in Tourism* (pp. 208–224). IGI Global., DOI: 10.4018/979-8-3693-1322-0.ch010

Singh, A., & Ansari, A. I. (2024). Role of Training and Development in Employee Motivation: Tourism and Hospitality Sector. In Mazurowski, T. (Ed.), *Enhancing Employee Motivation Through Training and Development* (pp. 248–261). IGI Global., DOI: 10.4018/979-8-3693-1674-0.ch011

Singh, A., & Hassan, S. C. (2024). Service Innovation Through Blockchain Technology in the Tourism and Hospitality Industry: Applications, Trends, and Benefits. In Singh, S. (Ed.), *Service Innovations in Tourism: Metaverse, Immersive Technologies, and Digital Twin* (pp. 205–214). IGI Global., DOI: 10.4018/979-8-3693-1103-5.ch010

Singh, A., & Hassan, S. C. (2024), "Identifying the Skill Gap in the Workplace and Their Challenges in Hospitality and Tourism Organisations", Thake, A.M., Sood, K., Özen, E. and Grima, S. (Ed.) *Contemporary Challenges in Social Science Management: Skills Gaps and Shortages in the Labour Market (Contemporary Studies in Economic and Financial Analysis, Vol. 112B)*, Emerald Publishing Limited, Leeds, pp. 101-114. DOI: 10.1108/S1569-37592024000112B006

Singh, A., & Kumar, S. (2021). Identifying Innovations in Human Resources: Academia and Industry Perspectives. In Pathak, A., & Rana, S. (Eds.), *Transforming Human Resource Functions With Automation* (pp. 104–120). IGI Global. DOI: 10.4018/978-1-7998-4180-7.ch006

Singh, A., & Kumar, S. (2024). Effective Talent Management Practices Implemented in the Hospitality Sector. In Christiansen, B., Aziz, M., & O'Keeffe, E. (Eds.), *Global Practices on Effective Talent Acquisition and Retention* (pp. 126–144). IGI Global., DOI: 10.4018/979-8-3693-1938-3.ch008

Singh, A., & Supina, S. (2024). Talent Acquisition and Retention in Hospitality Industry: Current Skill Gaps and Challenges. In Christiansen, B., Aziz, M., & O'Keeffe, E. (Eds.), *Global Practices on Effective Talent Acquisition and Retention* (pp. 363–379). IGI Global., DOI: 10.4018/979-8-3693-1938-3.ch020

Singh, V., & Singh, A. (2024). Digital Health Revolution: Enhancing Well-Being Through Technology. In Nadda, V., Tyagi, P., Moniz Vieira, R., & Tyagi, P. (Eds.), *Implementing Sustainable Development Goals in the Service Sector* (pp. 213–219). IGI Global., DOI: 10.4018/979-8-3693-2065-5.ch016

Supina, S., & Singh, A. (2024). Exploring the Presence and Adoption of Quality of Work-Life Dimensions in the Hotel Industry? *African Journal of Hospitality, Tourism and Leisure*, *13*(2), 421–429. DOI: 10.46222/ajhtl.19770720.524

Wehrmeyer, W. (1996). *Greening People: Human Resources and Environmental Management*. Greenleaf Publishing.

Yusliza, M. Y., Ramayah, T., & Othman, N. Z. (2015). Why Examining Adoption Factors for Green Human Resource Management Practices? *International Journal of Business and Society*, *16*(2), 289–312.

Chapter 9
Human Impacts and Organizational Change:
Digital Well-Being, Remote Work, and Psychosocial Sustainability

N. Vinodh
http://orcid.org/0009-0002-8662-2646
Saveetha School of Management, Saveetha Institute of Medical and Technical Sciences, India

A. K. Subramani
http://orcid.org/0000-0003-0783-7113
Saveetha School of Management, Saveetha Institute of Medical and Technical Sciences, India

P. Arokiya Prasad
St. Joseph College of Engineering, Sriperumbudur, India

ABSTRACT

This chapter delves into how digital well-being, remote work, and psychosocial sustainability intersect as key aspects of organizational change in today's digital era. With hybrid work becoming standard, issues such as digital fatigue, mental health challenges, and social isolation have emerged. Utilizing Self-Determination Theory, the Job Demands-Resources Model, and Socio-Technical Systems Theory, the chapter introduces a human-focused framework called CARE (Culture, Autonomy, Resilience, Equity) aimed at embedding emotional resilience, inclusive leadership, and ethical digital practices into HR strategies. It stresses the pressing necessity for organizations to transition from productivity-centered models to those that emphasize psychological safety, equitable access, and employee well-being. Through

DOI: 10.4018/979-8-3373-4307-5.ch009

practical insights and interdisciplinary research, the chapter reimagines sustainable workplaces as environments where digital efficiency is harmonized with empathy and enduring well-being.

INTRODUCTION

The Work, Tech, and Human Experience is more and more entangled the 21st century has brought pointed a digital paradigm shift that weaves together work, technology and the human experience in unprecedented ways. This transformation is not just about technology, it is about how we are living our jobs, our colleagues, our companies and society at large. Remote or hybrid working models, supercharged by the COVID-19 pandemic and the Fourth Industrial Revolution, have irreversibly transformed traditional working structures and an urgent Rethink of human resource (HR) practices is called for. Three related the shift revolves around three interrelated components: digital well-being, remote-work operating models, and psychosocial sustainability.

These ideas are related, rather than distinct ideas. Digital well-being is about employees' ability to use digital tools in a healthy, balanced way that contributes to their mental, emotional and physical health. Remote work is reframing the landscape of work through its elimination of a physical workspace while also creating new social, psychological, and managerial problems. Psychosocial sustainability refers to the capacity of people and organizations to sustain mental well-being, inter-personal relationships, and inclusive environments in the face of continued digital pressure.

Remote work is a double-edged sword, providing freedom and independence but also exposing weaknesses. The merging of "work" and "personal life" results in emotional drain, cognitive overload and pressure. So the digital exhaustion and isolation are inevitable problems. Organizational mental health support and inclusive cultures are inconsistent between sectors and geographies and in many cases leave out marginalized and caregiving staff. It is in the e-economy – a digital economy characterized by explosive information flows, platform labour and global connectivity (Schwab, 2017; Tapscott & Tapscott, 2023) that these matters are particularly urgent.

It is in this situation that organizations have to deal with the pressure of 'managing' the transformation of processes and people if they are to reap the benefits of digital change. That will require mental health, digital integration and psychosocial support becoming mainstream strategic assets, not detached wellness programs or reactive interventions. HR must pivot to a strategic, human-centric approach to innovation, which looks to its employees not as productivity units, but as creative, dynamic, and sustainable contributors (Ulrich et al., 2020).

In this chapter I discuss how organizations can mitigate human costs of digital change by integrating HR practices with psychological safety, emotional resilience, and fair participation. It depicts the workplace as a vital site for the collective rehabilitation, creative reinvention, and moral reconstitution of society in the digital age. Applying theories and models from a variety of disciplines (including self-determination theory (Deci & Ryan, 2000), job demand-resources model (Bakker & Demerouti, 2007) and socio-technical systems theory (Emery & Trist, 1960)), the chapter proposes a framework for digital well-being and psychosocial sustainability.

The significance of such an inquiry is highlighted by the growing concerns for mental health worldwide, where work pressure is a leading determinant of psychological illness (WHO, 2022). The digital divide, the gap in access to technology and support, threatens to exacerbate disparities, particularly among marginalized remote workers. This chapter offers a pathway towards stress-resilient, inclusive, and adapting workplaces when it comes to the question of how to define and promote digital well-being, to include psychosocial sustainability in policies, to enable equitable remote working models, or to prepare HR for its role as transformative leader for humane digital change.

Through its focus on human well-being in digital strategies, the chapter positions for a panoptic approach where what is good for people sits at the heart and centre with resolve taking place alongside, together, as caring tending and sustaining. This vision redefines work as a life-long journey of sources of learning's, ethical innovation and holistic wellness.

Importance and Purpose

The rapid spread of digital tools in daily work has, in fact, not just changed how we work, but how we live, think, and connect. As companies fast track digital transformation, addressing its human by-products — mental health, social connectedness and equitable access — is now a strategic imperative. This chapter is particularly pertinent in a world in which economic progress relies greatly on digital agility, yet frequently ignores the psychosocial consequences of digital transformation.

The key aim of this chapter is to re-conceptualize Organization change from a human centred perspective. It seeks to drive digital well-being, remote work design and psychosocial sustainability as core facets of the HR strategy in the changing e-economy. By integrating psychology, organisation theory, human resource management, and digital ethics perspectives, the chapter is itself both an academic and a practical contribution.

In the post-pandemic world, hybrid and remote work are no longer stopgap measures but a mainstay of work, at least in the knowledge economy. For instance, more than 60% of workers in developed countries are indicated to prefer hybrid arrangements based on independence and flexibility (Gallup, 2023). But this change comes with serious challenges: More burnout, loneliness and digital fatigue — problems that traditional HR approaches have done little to fix (De Filippis et al., 2022). This chapter highlights the need for systemic, proactive approaches to digital well-being that address the emotional and psychological aspects of work.

Psychosocial sustainability has also been recognized to be an important aspect of organizational resilience. The World Health Organization (2022) highlights workplace mental health as a development priority and calls on enterprises to build supportive policies into their operations. In the fragmented door Step Pay Day Loans technology-enabled and globally dispersed e-economy, organizations ought to must seek to exist preserving productivity and human well-being. The chapter argues for frameworks that place emotional intelligence, inclusion, and trust at the heart of the strategies.

Another aim is to call into question established remote work paradigms that favor productivity over human experience. Efficiency measures might show us productive workers, but they also fail to capture the true costs of social disconnection, surveillance and emotional burden. This chapter makes the case for a new story—where organizations are seen to be not just production machines but ecosystems of human thriving, growing and wellbeing.

The chapter also encourages interdisciplinary conversation and integrates Self-Determination Theory, the Job Demands-Resources Model, and Socio-Technical Systems Theory to develop a holistic appreciation of adaptation to digital change. Bridging the theoretical with the practical, it provides HR practitioners, policy makers and academics with practical advice for creating more inclusive and resilient workplaces.

The practical implications are significant, particularly for HR leaders grappling with ethical considerations around workplace tech such as AI-based monitoring, collaboration platforms and mental health apps. At the same time, these tools bring innovation and at the same time raise the challenges of surveillance, privacy violation and depersonalization. To discusses and consider a values-centered implementation of HR-technology based on psychological safety, transparency, and co-creation.

The chapter also examines equity and inclusion in digital workplaces. Marginalized groups — women, neurodiverse workers, care-givers — may also experience distinct psycho-social challenges in remote work settings, such as digital exclusion, invisible work and intersectional bias. It calls for hybrid work systems that are flexible and structured, collective and bespoke, focusing on diverse experiences to generate ethical innovation and common growth.

Lastly, the chapter is designed to be provocative in promising future research and policy formulation. As work continues to transform, we need urgent academic research on issues such as algorithmic stress, digital overload and identity fragmentation. Its theoretical frameworks provide groundwork for empirical research, case studies, and cross-sector partnerships.

In short, this chapter shines a spotlight on the pressing need for companies that are not just digitally advanced, but also emotionally intelligent—places where employees not only perform at their highest potential, but feel meaningful, connected, and sustainably well. Its aim is to create an equitable and people-focused future of work.

Background

The backdrop to this chapter is our rapidly changing world of work in the face of technological advancement, socio-economic dislocation and new expectations of the workforce. In the last 20 years, rapid digital integration—cloud computing, AI, etc.—has completely remade the way work is organized, delivered and perceived. The change has accelerated post-pandemic, when digital transformation has shifted from a strategic initiative to a matter of survival for companies across the globe (Brynjolfsson & McAfee, 2014).

In the past, the digitization of work was lauded for its promise to increase productivity, upscale operations, and improve connectivity. But in the early years was All about operational efficiencies rather than human experience. Eventually, it has been learned that technological improvement devoid of similar attention to the human side would bring about unintended psychosocial outcomes – burnout, alienation, techno stress and disengagement (Tarafdar et al., 2019). With remote and hybrid work models the thing of the moment; this duality has been exaggerated, providing employees both with flexibility and autonomy and with new vulnerabilities concerning mental health and work-life boundaries and social cohesion.

The pandemic was a pivotal event that forced to move towards a new way of working, one that was not reliant on being in the same physical location. It's during this period that digital well-being became a topic of conversation in the corporate world. Many companies seized on collaboration platforms like Zoom, Slack and Microsoft Teams without entirely anticipating the cognitive load and emotional exhaustion that would come with constant digital interaction. Concepts such as "Zoom fatigue" and "digital presenters" entered an organizational lexicon to indicate how well-intended digital environments can undermine well-being (Nesher Shoshan & Wehrt, 2022).

At the same time, the importance of psychosocial sustainability was acknowledged as an important but neglected dimension of workplace health, a concept that sits at the intersection of psychology, organizational behaviour and the field of sustainability science. The term points toward the capacity of people and systems to flourish in response to, or, in response to ever changing conditions, and to do so without undermining emotional, psychological or relational capacities. In application, this means creating conditions conducive to resilience, to inclusion, to emotional safety. As institutions confronted the mental health crisis of isolation, surveillance, and information overload that isolation intensified, psychosocial sustainability became key to balancing economic and environmental sustainability (Gifford, 2014; Fox, 2021).

In an economy empowered by digital platforms, gig work and automation (the e-economy), HR innovations have responded slowly to the complexities of human need. Most digital workplaces continue to embrace transactional HR—focusing on monitoring, performance management and cost reduction as opposed to empathy, well-being, and culture building. This gap highlights an Outdated view on productivity, neglecting the significant raw link between the well-functioning of employees' minds and organizational productivity (Sonnentag, 2018).

Moreover, concerns of equity and access have become more prominent. Not everyone is experiencing this step up to remote work in the same way, especially people out in rural areas, people from lower-earning households, and people who are in care-giving roles, who are often finding it hardest to make this shift to digital work. Women, racial minorities and neurodiverse individuals are disproportionately vulnerable to the psychosocial challenges of remote work as a result of systemic biases, uneven burden of domestic responsibilities, and lack of support (Chung et al., 2021). Hence, any real HR innovation in the field of digital well-being needs to be intersectional and inclusive.

The critical context for this chapter stems from several scholarship traditions. It uses concepts of motivation, autonomy and emotional regulation from psychology. It draws on sociology and management research, related to the fields of digital labor, organisational culture and socio-technical systems. It incorporates the human factor of organizational resilience, a concept from the sustainability literature. This multidisciplinary perspective enriches the analysis and discussion of the complex reality of digital well-being and psychosocial sustainability.

This backdrop lays down the direction of a new HR paradigm, one that understands employees are not end users of digital systems, but human beings with holistic personal well-being and social issues to be integrated into the digital future of work. According to this point on, the rest of the chapter goes on to give examples, strategies, and best practices for making workplaces that are both tech-savvy and very human.

Conceptual Framework

At the heart of this chapter are three central concepts-digital well-being, remote work, and psychosocial sustainability; this chapter seeks to understand how organisational change in the e-economy could be made more inclusive, adaptive, and human-centred. This model seeks to outline the connections between changes at work (such as the structural transformations presented here); the experiences at work (individual and social) of workers; and the organizational answers which are necessary to protect psychological and social well-being (and thus productive work).

At the core of the model is digital well-being, or the extent at which people can interact with digital technologies that foster emotional, cognitive and social well-being. In contrast to simple ergonomics or IT access, digital well-being extends to less tangible considerations such as agency in the use of technology, freedom from digital monitoring, limited information overburden, and provision of opportunities for authentic engagement in virtual realms (Mark & Harris, 2020). In this chapter, digital well-being is conceptualized as a complex equilibrium instead of a static state based on technology design, work culture, and leadership practices.

The second most important factor, remote work, acts as a double-edged sword of well-being. On the one hand, flexibility and autonomy have healthy implications; however, they may also lead to stress and social isolation, communication failures and role ambiguity. Our paper also conceptualises remote work, not just as moving from an office to a home-office, but as a profound organisational design problem calling attention to a number of other constructs including trust, new measures of performance, norms of collaboration, and employee identity (Waizenegger et al., 2020). In this model, remote work is not so much a binary (in-office versus at-home activity) but a spectrum of hybrid configurations, which have different psycho-social implications.

The third psychological construct, psychosocial sustainability, integrates the emotional, relational and cultural facets of work life. It is the 'ability of an organization to create an environment that is conducive to psychological safety promote social equality, and maintain a positive emotional ambiance especially in this time of increased change. Individual factors of such constructs are mental resilience, while collective factors can be top management transparency, supportive peer groups, etc. (Di Fabio & Rosen, 2018). It's important not only to avoid the risk of burnout, but also to sustain innovation, flexibility, and deep organizational health over time.

All three of these ideas are interrelated and they complement each other. For example, the high level of digital well-being can help reduce stress and promote self-regulation for the psychosocial sustainability. Also, bad remote working design can not only hamper digital well-being but psychosocial resilience too by fostering digital fatigue and eroding team identity. The model is therefore an assumption of triangular relationship between the constructs in which organization support system is the mediator. HR practice, leadership practice, technology governance and team culture can influence the interplay of the constructs in practice.

In order to operationalize this framework, the chapter suggests the CARE (Culture, Autonomy, Resilience, and Equity) model. This framework is a map for HR innovation that organizations can use to:

- Nurturing an inclusive Culture of psychological safety.
- Autonomy – empowering with employee autonomy in flexible work design.
- Creating Resilience through mental health resources and capacity-building programs.
- Skills Development, ensuring Equity in digital access, recognition and policy responsiveness.

By nesting this model in the context of the wider organisational ecosystem, the conceptual framework has potential for both diagnosing and designing—diagnosing the current digital well-being gaps, and providing pathways for psychosocial sustainability.

THEORETICAL AND CONCEPTUAL FRAMEWORK

This chapter is grounded on three established theories, Self Determination Theory (SDT), the Job Demands-Resources (JD-R) Model and Socio-Technical Systems (STS) Theory. Together, these frameworks provide perspectives on how people experience work, how organizational design shapes well-being, and how technology and human systems co-evolve in complex settings.

1. **Theoretical framework Self-Determination theory (SDT)** Self-Determination Theory, by Deci and Ryan (2000) argues that human motivation and well-being are rooted in the satisfaction of three innate psychological needs: autonomy, competence and relatedness. Relevance of SDT in the context of digital work As per this theory, it is pertinent to discuss it in relation to digital work and technology use, since in digital work the voluntary engagement with assignments, perceived competence with technology use, and feelings of connectedness with others despite spatial separation are particularly relevant.

These needs will be enabled or inhibited by remote and hybrid work environments. Employees who may choose when and in what capacity they work and prefer to talk about things are more engaged and less likely to get burned out (Gagné and Deci, 2005). In contrast, digital, micromanaging surveillance can destroy intrinsic motivation and create stressors. The SDT perspective highlights that to enhance digital well-being; organizations need to establish the conditions that respect individual choice, encourage skill development, and allow for supportive interpersonal connections.

2. **Model of Job Demands-Resources:** The JD-R model (Bakker & Demerouti, 2007) provides a versatile and comprehensive root cause explanation of stress and engagement at work. It distinguishes work circumstances in terms of demands (e.g., workload, emotional strain, and digital fatigue) and resources (e.g., autonomy, social support, learning opportunities). Burnout or engagement is a result of the interaction of these two forms of resources.

The sudden shift to remote work has brought with it a new set of professional demands: the need to be digitally "on" at all times; the blurring of personal and work life; and decreased visibility. And at the same time, resources like flexibility, time for focused work and enhanced work-life integration can be offered — if it's done right. The use of the JD-R model enables organizations to understand how digital tools and hybrid policies may serve to both trigger and buffer psychosocial risks. For example, if people can provide virtual peer support or access digital mental health tools, then those may be the resources that are most important for responding to high population level needs.

3. Socio-Technical Systems (STS) Theory and beyond

Socio-Technical Systems Theory Derived from Emery and Trist (1960) the Socio-Technical Systems Theory emphasizes the relationship between social systems and technical systems within organizations. Claims that are good performance and well-being result when technology design is aligned with human capacity, roles, and culture.

For the e-economy STS theory offer such a critical lens, to analyse how remote work platforms, monitoring technologies, and AI driven HR tools impact on the relational and emotional climate of work. For instance, digital networks that support collaboration and information sharing support team performance, but poorly designed systems can break down communication and undermine trust. STS theory can be used to make a case that technology should be co-designed with users, considering ethics, affect, and inclusivity as well as efficiency.

By integrating these theories, this chapter develops a multi-theoretical lens to understand and to enhance the experience of digital work. SDT informs why well-being is important, the JD-R model informs how it is affected by job conditions, and STS theory informs what needs to be aligned in systems and structures to secure sustainable organizational change.

Justification of Title

The chapter title itself—'Human Impacts and Organizational Change: Digital Well-Being, Remote Work and Psychosocial Sustainability'—encapsulates a multi-faceted and contemporary examination of how the world of work is being shaped by an era of simultaneous technological metamorphosis and human-led thinking outer work 'projects'. All elements of the title are deliberately selected to refer to the main topics and the level of analysis of the chapter.

1. "Human Impacts"

The term "human impacts" focuses attention on the primary focus of this chapter: the experiences of people working in digitally mediated environments. In a climate of automation, AI and algorithmic management that redistributes its effects throughout industries, it is important to look beyond just the operational efficiencies and toward the psychosocial costs imposed upon the human labour used to make them. Human impacts the cognitive, affective, social and even physical consequences of new digital work models. These could be mental exhaustion, social isolation, identity loss, and heightened susceptibility to stress or burnout (Tarafdar et al., 2015).

This also implies that the human factor should not be overlooked in any digital transformation conversation. It asks that organizations think about the ethical and emotional impact of technology choices. In many ways "human impacts" serves as a northstar for how we think about exploring digital workplace transformation… it signals that sustainable, meaningful change hinges upon keeping people at the center of (as opposed to just the edges of) our systems, and driving value through them.

2. **"Organizational Change"** The concept of "organizational change" describes the ever-changing processes organizations experience as a result of internal forces (such as employee health, cultural changes) or external influences (e.g., technological developments, international crises such as COVID-19). By organisational change in this chapter, what is meant is structural and cultural: redesign of policies, change of leadership, reorganisation of team interaction and working in hybrid or remote modes? Change in organization is also about intent. It emphasizes the role of decision makers – HR leaders, managers and executives who in reimagining politics, practices, and parties that will make well-being, inclusion, and sustainability in life possible. The chapter's title itself suggests that the chapter is not just descriptive but also prescriptive in its aim, trying to shape the thinking and acting on organizational change in the digital economy.

Organizational change also means being intentional. It emphasizes the importance of decision-makers (HR leaders, managers, and executives) reimagining policies, practices, and platforms that support well-being, inclusion, and sustainability. Its title suggests that the chapter is not just descriptive, but also, in itself, prescriptive, in the sense of aiming to shape how organizational change is thought about and done in a digital economy.

3. **"Digital Well-Being"** Digital health is a relatively recent and growing area of interest in the field of work. It's not just about access to the tech: it's about how employees relate to the technology mentally. Digital well-being is also characterised by autonomy in technology use, privacy from over surveillance in digital technology, manageable information flow, and nurturing digital cultures that avoid burnout (Vodanovich et al., 2018).

Insofar as 'digital well-being' is named in the title, the chapter aims to meet the emerging recognition that we need to scrutinise the tools and technologies that support our work in terms not only of tool-functionality, but how they make us feel and think. It acknowledges the digital paradox: technology makes us flexible and connected and also agitated and isolating when its systems are badly designed or appropriated. The addition of this term encourages the reader to re-imagine the human-tech connection with respect to sustainability and empathy.

4. **"Remote Work"** Remote work is a reshaping-edge project that was accelerated like never before by the Covid-19 pandemic. In this chapter, remote work is not treated as a monolith, but as a range of models, from fully remote to hybrid to flexible. This diversity brings with it new variables of team cohesion, employee trust, performance evaluation and work-life balance.

Remote work is also investigated as both a blessing and a curse. Although it provides independence and reduces vehicle stress, it could also increase social isolation, limit perspective, and widen disparities when supportive infrastructures are lacking. The chapter provides a critical analysis of remote work from both a psychological (individual) and organizational perspective to present balanced prescriptions for both capitalizing on its advantages and buffering against its potential costs.

5. **"Psychosocial Sustainability"** The addition of psychosocial sustainability represents a substantial ideological expansion of the conventional sustainability models, which tend to focus on environmental and economic elements. It refers here to the ability of individuals and organizations to preserve emotional

well-being, relational healthiness and sustainable cultures in change (Di Fabio & Peirò, 2018).

Psychosocial sustainability can be particularly applicable within digital workplaces, where empathy, inclusion and psychological safety are put to the test. In naming this idea in the chapter title, the concept of mental health and relational well-being are foregrounded as not secondary considerations, but the essentials of long-term organizational endurance. It challenges perceptions of sustainability not only in environmental or financial terms, but also in the way organizations feed the human spirit, in safeguarding mental health and in growing kind systems.

Check for AI

The title of the chapter really sums up what it's all about. It looks into how digital changes impact people, what organizations need to do to adapt, and how focusing on human needs can create healthier work environments.

SUGGESTIONS AND RECOMMENDATIONS

To tackle issues like digital well-being, remote work, and mental health, organizations should take a thoughtful, proactive, and inclusive approach. Based on the study of theories and current methods, here are some recommendations based on the CARE framework—Culture, Autonomy, Resilience, and Equity—that can help with organizational change.

1. Build a Culture of Safety and Compassionate Leadership

The culture of an office makes a huge difference in how much employees feel supported, especially in remote or hybrid set-ups where the water-cooler support might be missing. Leaders need to create an environment where employees can feel comfortable to speak up, make mistakes and be themselves without the fear of backlash.

- ✓ Train managers to enhance their emotional competence and listening skills.
- ✓ Encourage frequent emotional check-ins, not just work check-ins achievements.
- ✓ Implementing team rituals will facilitate connection and a common goal across digital channels.

Leadership should shift from a control-based approach to one that builds trust, making well-being a key part of the organization's values.

2. Support Autonomy with Flexible Work Options

Feeling in control of how we work can boost everyone's mood and keep stress levels down. Here's how to make work more flexible:

- Let employees choose their work hours, how they tackle tasks, and what tools they prefer for communication.
- Allow for asynchronous work whenever possible to help people focus and avoid too many meetings.
- Cut back on constant monitoring; instead, encourage self-reporting or give employees the option to share their stats if they want.

Flexibility should be the norm, not a special case.

3. Promote Resilience with Mental Health Support

Don't wait for burnout to happen. It's crucial to have systems in place to help employees stay mentally strong:

- Set up Employee Assistance Programs that offer Tele-counselling, peer support, and wellness apps.
- Provide mental health training for everyone, including managers and team members.
- Create policies that respect personal time, like a "right to disconnect," especially for remote teams working across different time zones.

These steps help make mental health a regular topic and build a supportive culture.

4. Ensure Fair Access and Opportunities for All

Remote work can create distance if we aren't intentional. Equity is the real concern for access and inclusion:

- Ensure that tools, internet and workstations are optimal for all employees.
- Inclusive design of meetings – finding and implementing the means, such as virtual hand-raising and shared docs, to incorporate participants who are not physically present.

- Extend accommodations that are specific to neurodiverse workers, caregivers, and those with chronic illness.

Embedding equity in the way we do digital processes can enhance fairness and engagement in the workplace.

5. Make Well-Being a Key Focus in Company Goals

If we care about well-being we need to measure it. Here's how to keep it top of mind:

- Integrate questions related to digital well-being into annual employee surveys focusing on areas such as autonomy, digital fatigue, and social connections.
- Tether leadership incentives to team welfare rather than productivity.
  -Use surveys and feedback appropriately to identify possible concerns such as disengagement or stress before they become larger problems.

This changes the mentality from only responding to an issue to a more preventative form of addressing mental health concerns.

Going through these steps collectively helps organizations to transform struggles into opportunities for conscious leadership and long term sustainability. The goal is not to merely deal with change but to lead it with intent and compassion.

FUTURE RESEARCH DIRECTIONS

As organizations are adjusting to the new digital and scape, honestly, we could use research that examines digital wellbeing, remote work, and mental health support in the workplace. Among all the changes to our work processes, tools and employee expectations, we have new questions that existing research doesn't sufficiently answer. Research going forward should aim to create practical solutions that fit the evolving work environment.

1. Digital Fatigue and Cognitive Overload

One key area to focus on understands how digital fatigue affects people in the long run. We've heard about "Zoom fatigue" and being always connected, but we still don't know much about how different ways of communicating—like emails versus video calls—impact how we think and feel at work. Researchers could look into:

- The best mix of live and recorded communication.
- How long exposure to screens affects our brains.
- How screen time's effects vary based on people's personalities and how they think.

2. Psychological Safety in Hybrid Teams

While we know a lot about psychological safety in traditional office settings, we need to learn more about how it works in teams that are spread out. Trust and inclusion might look different when people work together remotely. Important questions for future research include:

- What practices help build psychological safety in hybrid teams?
- How does leadership change in a virtual space?
- How do factors like culture, gender, and age affect inclusion in online teams?

Finding answers can guide training and tools that make virtual teamwork safer and more open.

3. Digital Well-Being as a Key Metric

Digital well-being should move to the forefront as a crucial concern for businesses. Future studies need to focus on creating clear metrics that companies can use to measure digital well-being alongside employee performance and engagement. Areas to explore include:

- Developing reliable ways to measure how people feel about their digital work life.
- Looking at how digital well-being scores connect to things like employee turnover, new ideas, and teamwork.
- Comparing how effective digital wellness programs are in different industries and cultures.

This information could help HR leaders and decision-makers push for important changes that improve workplace health.

4. Intersectionality and Equity in Remote Work

Remote work has brought both new chances and new challenges. While a lot of the existing research talks about general trends, we need to look more closely at how things like race, gender, disability, caregiving roles, and income levels shape people's experiences in remote jobs. Some questions worth exploring are:

- How do remote work policies affect women and caregivers in different areas?
- What do neurodiverse individuals experience while working online?
- How can companies create fair hybrid policies that help those who are often overlooked?

This kind of research is important to make sure that online work environments don't end up repeating or worsening existing inequalities.

5. AI, Surveillance, and Ethics in HR Tech

As AI becomes a bigger part of things like performance tracking, hiring, and workplace data, we need to look into the ethical side of how it impacts mental health. Right now, there isn't a clear understanding of how decisions made by algorithms influence people's freedom, fairness, emotional health, and trust in their workplaces. Some key questions are:

- What ethical guidelines should be in place for using AI in HR?
- How do workers feel about being watched by algorithms?
- What transparency and consent processes can help ease the anxiety that comes with digital monitoring?

Looking into these topics can help develop ethical design standards and rules for treating workers fairly in the tech space.

Overall, future research should be diverse and global, involving not just academics but also those who work in the field, tech experts, and workers. The work we do is already becoming digital; the real challenge is making sure it's also fair, ethical, and centered around people.

CONCLUSION

The rapid transition to remote work is reshaping the approach of managing work-related tasks. While tech innovations provide greater flexibility and improved connectivity, they also pose significant challenges regarding the mental health and wellness of employees. In this chapter, I argue that any changes organizations consider in this current digital landscape must prioritize people. It's no longer only about speed; it's about offering a safe workplace that everyone can access and feel included.

As we strive to advance in this distinct environment, focusing on digital well-being, remote working, and mental health will prove beneficial. These domains are interdependent and illustrate the fact that we must go deeper than the use of technology. Digital well-being goes beyond the absence of stress; it encompasses the erosion of autonomy, balance, and meaningful social interactions. Transitioning to remote work is more than purely logistical; it redefines collaboration and alters the essence of team membership.

Sustainability in mental health focuses on enabling individuals and organizations to flourish amidst ceaseless changes. As I look into this, I have made references to key theories like Self-Determination Theory and the JD-R Model to explain how equilibrium between the interactions and support structures in remote and hybrid work environments can be achieved. These models remind us that there is a need to strike a balance between technological integration and human-centric organizational functioning.

The CARE framework—Culture, Autonomy, Resilience, and Equity—has been advanced to aid organization design. It provides actionable guidance to integrate well-being by proposing inclusive leadership, adaptable work schedules, and robust mental health support systems. Addressing these concerns is essential for evolving workplace readiness.

I addressed some gaps in research that I believe are worthy of exploration. For instance, issues of digital burnout, virtual team cohesion, and AI-related hiring practices all lack thorough examination. As businesses adopt new technologies, they must keep ethical standards in mind while ensuring transparency and considering employee feedback.

In any case, the essence of work is not technology; rather, it is the human experience. An effective digital transformation enables people to flourish, strengthens collaboration, empowers corporations to generate value, and protects employee well-being.

The lesson learned from this chapter can be summarized in one sentence: sustainability of mental health is critical and not optional! As workplaces become more technologically advanced, organizations must advocate for employees and their development. It is possible to create efficient, caring, and sustainable workplaces by integrating technology with emotional intelligence and ethical frameworks.

CONCEPTUAL FRAMEWORK WITH KEY DEFINITIONS

In this chapter, we present a framework that integrates three important concepts: digital well-being, remote work, and sustainability of mental health. All these concepts are interrelated and are important in determining how organizations evolve in this people-centric shift of the modern world.

This explanation aids us to capture the unique individual, team, and organizational transitions as companies evolve into more tech-oriented environments. It simplifies complex concepts so that both researchers and practitioners can identify their areas of priority as they advance.

1. Digital Well-Being

Digital well-being focuses on how individuals interact with technology in a manner that promotes mental and emotional health while mitigating stress and burnout. It encompasses the following:

- Exercising control on tech usage
- Being conscious of our online presence and when we access our devices- Staying safe from too much online scrutiny and information overload
- Finding a balance between our digital and real-life interactions

In work settings, promoting digital well-being means using HR technology ethically, setting inclusive digital standards, and having management back healthy tech habits.

2. Remote Work

Remote work lets employees do their jobs outside a regular office, often using digital tools. Key features are:

- Flexibility on where and when to work
- Relying on communication technologies
- Blurring the lines between personal and work life

This chapter looks at remote work as a range of options, like hybrid setups and models where employees choose their work style. It affects how people feel about social interactions, oversight, and their sense of belonging, all of which directly tie into their well-being.

3. Psychosocial Sustainability

Psychosocial sustainability refers to maintaining psychological, emotional, and social continuity or cohesion in the face of transition or disruption. It covers:

- Feeling safe psychologically
- Building emotional resilience
- Support from leaders and peers
- A work environment that fosters a sense of belonging for everyone

This type of sustainability is crucial for organizations in the long term. It's about more than just reducing stress; it's about fostering environments where employees can develop and flourish in every area of their lives.

Framework Intermediaries

In this chapter's framework, these three concepts are affected by factors such as:

- Leadership approach (e.g., being empathetic versus authoritarian)
- Human Resources policies (e.g., offering flexible work hours and wellness benefits)
- Technological tools (e.g., platforms that either facilitate or hinder collaboration).

These influence the extent to which digital well-being, remote work, and psychosocial sustainability can be integrated.

Purpose of the Conceptual Framework

This framework is designed with three primary objectives:

1. Analytical: It enables a deeper examination of the interdependence between digital environments and human experiences.
2. Strategic: It provides organizations with a method to evaluate whether their policies align with mental health priorities.
3. Practical: It establishes a foundation for developing inclusive remote work models and wellness initiatives.

Ultimately, the framework illustrates that thriving in the digital era requires an emphasis on emotional intelligence, safety, and prioritizing people in the innovation process.

Interconnection of Concepts

Understanding the connection between digital well-being, remote work, and psychosocial sustainability is essential to grasp how modern organizations operate. Each concept holds individual significance, yet their true effect emerges when considered collectively. They are not merely parallel; they shape employees' emotions and interactions within the digital work environment.

1. Remote Work Changing Things Up

As more people transition to working from home or adopting hybrid work models, we're witnessing significant shifts in our perceptions of digital life and mental well-being. Remote work offers greater freedom and flexible schedules, aiding in balancing professional and personal life. However, it also presents challenges such as burnout, isolation, and the blurring of work-life boundaries. Constant notifications and prolonged screen time can lead to mental exhaustion if not monitored carefully. Thus, remote work can be a double-edged sword, potentially benefiting or harming well-being based on how organizations handle these new work dynamics.

2. Digital Well-Being as a Link

Digital well-being serves as a bridge between technology and maintaining our mental health. It significantly influences how remote work affects our mental well-being. When remote work promotes healthy digital practices, equitable tech access, and transparent communication, it can enhance mental health and resilience. However, excessive monitoring, constant availability demands, or limited autonomy in our work can increase stress and lead to trust issues. Therefore, the way we structure our digital environments at work can either support or undermine our overall well-being.

3. Aiming for Psychosocial Sustainability

The aim of combining remote work with an emphasis on digital well-being is to foster a healthy work environment. We strive to create a place where individuals feel secure, appreciated, and included, even when they are not in the same physical location. This extends beyond wellness initiatives; it involves cultivating a company culture that promotes mental health and equity. By prioritizing digital well-being and thoughtfully organizing remote work, employees experience increased security and connection, enhancing their engagement and creativity.

4. Organizational Support Matters

The effectiveness of integrating these concepts largely hinges on the organization's structure and practices. Elements such as leadership style, human resources policies, and the tools employed can either facilitate or obstruct achieving this balance. For instance, a hybrid model that combines flexibility with clear guidelines and mental health support can enhance these aspects.

The CARE framework—Culture, Autonomy, Resilience, Equity—offers a practical method to connect these elements.

In conclusion, the interplay between digital well-being, remote work, and mental health indicates that relying on a single solution is insufficient. A comprehensive approach is essential, one that recognizes the complexities of working in a digital environment and strives to create organizations that are healthy, equitable, and sensitive to emotional needs.

Expanding the Theoretical Framework

To fully understand the interplay between digital well-being, remote work, and mental health, this section presents a unified theoretical framework incorporating Self-Determination Theory, the Job Demands-Resources Model, and Socio-Technical Systems Theory. Each of these theories offers a unique perspective on the interaction of our needs, job configurations, and technological systems in the modern workplace. This section will explore how these theories can address the on-going challenges faced by organizations.

1. Self-Determination Theory (SDT)

Self-Determination Theory (SDT), established by Deci and Ryan in 2000, suggests that individuals' well-being and motivation are linked to three fundamental needs: autonomy, competence, and relatedness. In the context of remote work and digital technology, fulfilling these needs can become challenging.

- Autonomy involves providing flexible working hours, customizable tools, and allowing individuals to participate in decision-making.
- Competence is about offering training to ensure everyone can efficiently use digital tools.

- Relatedness focuses on maintaining social connections through effective communication and team activities, even when in-person meetings aren't possible.

When these needs are satisfied, individuals feel positive and motivated at work. Conversely, if these needs are hindered—such as through micromanagement or feelings of isolation—burnout and disengagement can occur.

2. Job Demands-Resources (JD-R) Model

The JD-R model, developed by Bakker and Demerouti in 2007, explains how various work factors can result in stress or engagement. It categorizes work conditions into two groups:

- Job demands involve tasks that require effort and may cause stress, such as long working hours, excessive technology use, or insufficient feedback.
- Job resources are elements that assist in achieving goals and alleviating demands, like support from co-workers, meaningful work, and flexibility.

In the context of digital work, demands might include constant notifications, lack of privacy, and close monitoring, while resources could encompass mentorship, collaboration, and wellness programs. This model is particularly useful for hybrid work environments where digital challenges vary based on roles or backgrounds. A significant advantage of this model is its ability to illustrate how persistent high demands combined with inadequate resources can lead to burnout, whereas a balanced approach fosters engagement and satisfaction in the workplace.

3. Socio-Technical Systems (STS) Theory

In 1960, Emery and Trist introduced ideas emphasizing the interdependence of technology and people within organizations. Their theory suggests that organizations function more effectively when they integrate the design of both technological and human systems. In digital work environments, this involves ensuring that:

- Technology is both accessible and easy to use, crafted with attention to detail.
- Employees have a say in choosing and assessing digital tools.

This theory highlights how shifts in technology can affect emotions and relationships. For example, implementing AI tools to track productivity without employee involvement might lead to stress, whereas tools developed with employee input can foster trust.

Putting It All Together

These theories merge to provide a thorough perspective:

- SDT examines the individual's needs for autonomy, competence, and connection.
- JD-R centers on balancing effort and support within the workplace.
- STS highlights the integration of people with digital tools.

This combination of theories provides a new perspective on HR strategies, shifting the focus from merely addressing problems to creating systems that enhance overall employee well-being in our digital age.

Research Methodology

This chapter employs a qualitative and exploratory research approach to examine the interconnections between digital well-being, remote work, and mental health within the evolving realm of human resource management. The aim is to collect comprehensive insights from a variety of sources and perspectives, rather than depending solely on numerical data or experimental methods.

1. Research Design

The method utilizes a qualitative interpretive framework aimed at comprehending the meaning and context from the viewpoints of the participants involved (Creswell & Poth, 2018). This approach is well-suited for examining psychosocial issues that are personal and emotional, such as employees experiencing burnout, feeling included, or having autonomy while working remotely. The data is gathered from:

- Existing studies on mental health, remote work, and digital transformations
- Case studies across various sectors including technology, education, health-care, and the public sector
- Semi-structured interviews with HR professionals and remote workers from selected studies- Policy documents from organizations like WHO, ILO, and OECD
- Reports from companies adopting digital wellness and hybrid work strategies

Bringing together different types of sources strengthens the findings and provides a well-rounded analysis.

2. Thematic Analysis

The main analysis method is thematic analysis, which helps identify and interpret common themes in the qualitative data (Braun & Clarke, 2006). Important themes include:

- Digital fatigue and overload
- Leadership trust in remote settings
- Techno stress and personal autonomy
- Inclusion and fair access to digital tools
- Psychological safety in hybrid teams
- Technology-driven monitoring and employee morale

These themes were developed by coding patterns that appeared in the studies and literature, then grouping them into categories that fit the chapter's framework, known as the CARE model (Culture, Autonomy, Resilience, and Equity).

3. Interdisciplinary Integration

This methodology merges ideas from psychology, organizational behavior, sociology, digital ethics, and sustainability studies, providing a well-rounded perspective. For example:

- Psychology gives insights on burnout and motivation.
- Organizational behavior looks at hybrid leadership and team dynamics.
- Digital studies critique algorithmic control and platform labor.
- Inclusion research examines barriers to digital work.

These combined insights help to understand the complex mix of human, technological, and cultural factors affecting remote work experiences.

4. Ethical Considerations and Limitations

Since this chapter uses existing sources, no direct human subjects were involved. Nonetheless, care was taken to interpret the qualitative data responsibly, being sensitive to issues of identity and mental health. The chapter also recognizes that things like national policies and cultural norms can affect how broadly the findings can be applied.

Future research could look into long-term studies, collaborative projects with hybrid teams, or comparisons between countries regarding equal access to remote work.

This qualitative approach supports the chapter's aim: to provide a deep, human-focused examination of how organizations can enhance employee well-being and mental health during digital changes.

Solutions and Recommendations

Building on the insights and evidence presented in this chapter, this section offers solutions and recommendations for organizations wanting to promote digital well-being and mental health in remote and hybrid work settings. These suggestions align with the CARE Framework (Culture, Autonomy, Resilience, Equity), offering straightforward, actionable strategies that can be integrated into HR operations and leadership plans.

1. CULTURE: Make Well-Being a Priority in the Workplace

Solution: Establish a workplace atmosphere that prioritizes emotional well-being and transparent communication, applicable to both remote and in-person settings.

Suggestions:

- Implement regular virtual check-ins, incorporate opportunities for peer acknowledgment, and designate meeting-free days.
- Launch initiatives to promote open dialogue about mental health, making it acceptable for individuals to seek assistance.
- Offer training for leaders to enhance empathetic communication and foster inclusive team environments.

2. AUTONOMY: Give Employees More Control

Solution: Transition from strict surveillance to performance-based systems, allowing employees the autonomy to choose how, when, and where they work.

Recommendations:

- Encourage teams to collaboratively create their own schedules and communication methods.

- Eliminate inflexible attendance tracking and place trust in employees to manage their own accountability.
- Provide assessments to assist employees in achieving a healthy balance between work and technology. This approach reduces stress and enhances motivation by offering greater freedom.

3. RESILIENCE: Build a Support System for Mental Health

Solution: Enhance employee resilience by offering mental health resources and support systems to avert burnout.

Suggestions:

- Offer resilience coaching, particularly for leaders managing remote teams.
- Provide access to virtual mental health sessions, mindfulness applications, and stress management resources.
- Establish specific recovery periods such as "focus weeks" or screen-free hours. Proactively building resilience is more effective than responding to burnout after it occurs.

4. EQUITY: Promote Fairness in the Workplace

Solution: Ensure that remote and hybrid work policies are just and mindful of each individual's distinct circumstances.

Recommendations:

- Provide essential technology support, such as ergonomic equipment and high-speed internet, to those who require it the most.
- Frequently assess who may be absent from virtual conversations to guarantee that all voices are heard.
- Tailor assistance for neurodiverse, disabled, or caregiving employees to enable their full participation. Achieving equity involves ensuring that everyone is acknowledged and valued in the workplace.

5. Monitoring and Feedback Systems

Solution: Establish systems that consistently collect data to enhance digital well-being initiatives.

Recommendations:

- Implement anonymous surveys and quick feedback mechanisms for regular check-ins.
- Merge personal input with AI analysis to identify trends at an early stage.
- Develop channels for employees to propose enhancements, instead of solely imposing decisions from leadership.

In summary, these suggestions help organizations foster a workplace culture where technology aids individuals rather than presenting obstacles. By integrating these methods into HR practices—such as recruitment, development, assessments, and separations—leaders can cultivate an environment conducive to both digital proficiency and mental health.

Best Practices

As organizations around the globe adapt to the emerging hybrid and remote work environment, many are enhancing their efforts to foster digital well-being and an inclusive work culture. This section highlights examples of successful practices that demonstrate how policies, culture, and leadership can unite to cultivate positive digital workspaces.

Digital Mental Health Platforms and Teletherapy Integration

The COVID-19 pandemic led many individuals to begin utilizing digital mental health services such as chatbots, mindfulness applications, and Teletherapy. These tools are now being integrated into workplace wellness initiatives, particularly within Employee Assistance Programs (EAPs). New platforms provide:

- On-demand counselling
- Tailored stress management dashboards
- Wellness assessments at the team level

The future development of these tools involves emphasizing personalized experiences and safeguarding data privacy to foster trust.

Workplace Experience as a Strategic Differentiator

The idea of "employee experience" is changing and now includes digital, emotional, and social aspects. Companies that are thinking ahead are:

- Mapping out employees' digital journeys to make things easier.

- Tying well-being data to performance and retention rates.
- Creating digital workflows together with employees in hybrid design labs.

As the competition for talent heats up, companies are putting money into workplace experience tools that sync up culture, technology, and support systems.

Together, these trends show how businesses are not just digitizing tasks—they're making the digital work experience more human. The future will belong to workplaces that focus on well-being, inclusivity, and ethical practices.

Suggested Areas for Future Research

As more organizations adapt to hybrid and remote work, research needs to keep up with these new realities. Although this chapter has covered some fundamental ideas, many important questions still need answers. Moving forward, research should cover these strategic areas:

1. Measuring Digital Well-Being at Scale

Even with the growing interest in digital well-being, there's still a lack of standard measurement tools. Future studies should work on:

- Creating validated tools to measure digital autonomy, fatigue, being present but not engaged and emotional strain.
- Looking at how digital well-being shows up differently across industries, like tech versus healthcare.
- Examining how the company culture impacts digital well-being results.

This research is necessary to turn the idea of digital well-being into clear, actionable goals for organizations.

2. Long-term Effects of Hybrid Work on Mental Health

Most current research gives a quick snapshot of employee experiences. There's a real need for studies that look at:

- How remote work impacts mental well-being over time (like burnout or emotional resilience).
- The overall effects of digital interactions on focus, identity, and emotional control.
- Which types of remote work setups lead to the best long-term results.

This kind of research would help us see if early benefits or issues stick around or change over time.

3. Psychosocial Sustainability outside Corporate Settings

A lot of what we know about psychosocial sustainability and remote work focuses on businesses. Future research should look at:

- Remote work and well-being in government, non-profits, and education.
- Global and cultural differences in how people perceive and access support.
- How community and local leadership can help or hurt psychosocial sustainability.

This perspective will provide insights for various workplaces and kinds of workers.

4. Intersectionality in Digital Work Experiences

Digital workers' experiences are shaped by their identities, including gender, race, class, disability, and caregiving roles. Studies could investigate:

- How hybrid work policies impact women, caregivers, and marginalized groups differently.
- What challenges and opportunities exist for neurodiverse and disabled people in tech-driven environments?
- How power dynamics affect visibility and chances in virtual teams.

Research in this area will help develop fairer digital transformation strategies.

5. Governance and Ethics of Employee Monitoring Technologies

As more companies implement AI to oversee their workforce, research should concentrate on:

- The psychological impact of algorithmic surveillance on trust and employee engagement.
- Best practices for obtaining consent, ensuring transparency, and ethical governance of technology.
- The long-term effects of data-driven HR decisions on employee satisfaction and company reputation.

This research is vital to ensure technology upholds employees' rights and dignity rather than undermining them.

In conclusion, future research must not only address these challenges but also strive for effective solutions. It should be inclusive, globally relevant, and aligned with the principles of well-being, fairness, and sustainability in our digital age.

FINAL THOUGHTS

As we advance further into the digital era, work is shaped not just by technology but by how we integrate human needs and ethical considerations into these changes. This section explored the critical intersections of digital well-being, remote work, and mental sustainability—factors that determine the fairness and quality of our working environments.

Digital transformation promises greater agility and productivity; yet without careful design, it can lead to exhaustion, inequity, and isolation. Remote and hybrid models have evolved from stopgap measures into core components of long-term business strategies. Their effectiveness depends not only on the available platforms but also on cultivating digital cultures that value employee feedback, mental health, and a balanced integration of work and personal life.

At the core of this conversation is the principle that organizational change should prioritize its impact on people. True digital well-being extends beyond simply reducing screen hours; it involves fostering technology use that is purposeful and transparent. Likewise, psychosocial sustainability underpins on-going learning, creativity, and organizational viability.

By drawing on frameworks such as Self-Determination Theory and the Job Demands-Resources Model, we establish a robust basis for understanding how individuals and organizations navigate digital workspaces. The CARE model—Culture, Autonomy, Resilience, Equity—translates these insights into actionable HR initiatives and leadership approaches.

Case studies ranging from Microsoft to GitLab and SAP, along with emerging trends like AI-driven well-being solutions and "right-to-disconnect" policies, demonstrate that organizations can achieve digital maturity by harmonizing well-being with performance through thoughtful, equitable practices.

This chapter also underscores the need for additional research to address gaps in measurement, the long-term effects on mental health, and the ethical handling of employee data. It is incumbent upon scholars, practitioners, and policymakers to ensure digital work bolsters rather than undermines mental well-being. In sum, this section calls for a fundamental shift: digital transformation should be seen not merely as a technical endeavour but as an opportunity to strengthen human connections.

Building organizations that thrive in the future requires systems where productivity coexists with empathy, innovation with inclusion, and efficiency with fairness.

Ultimately, the future of work hinges not only on the where but the how—how we feel, learn, and grow in our roles. By synchronizing technology with psychological needs and core values, we can create workplaces that are not only efficient but also compassionate and resilient.

REFERENCES

Bakker, A. B., & Demerouti, E. (2007). The Job Demands-Resources model: State of the art. *Journal of Managerial Psychology, 22*(3), 309–328. DOI: 10.1108/02683940710733115

Braun, V., & Clarke, V. (2006). Using thematic analysis in psychology. *Qualitative Research in Psychology, 3*(2), 77–101. DOI: 10.1191/1478088706qp063oa

Brynjolfsson, E., & McAfee, A. (2014). *The second machine age: Work, progress, and prosperity in a time of brilliant technologies.* W. W. Norton & Company.

Chung, H., Seo, H., Forbes, S., & Birkett, H. (2021). *Working from home during the COVID-19 lockdown: Changing preferences and the future of work.* University of Kent.

De Filippis, E., Imbrenda, C., & Tassi, E. (2022). Hybrid work and psychosocial risks: A multidimensional analysis. *Journal of Occupational Health Psychology, 27*(4), 301–315. DOI: 10.1037/ocp0000312

Deci, E. L., & Ryan, R. M. (2000). The "what" and "why" of goal pursuits: Human needs and the self-determination of behavior. *Psychological Inquiry, 11*(4), 227–268. DOI: 10.1207/S15327965PLI1104_01

Di Fabio, A., & Peiró, J. M. (2018). Human capital sustainability leadership to promote sustainable development and healthy organizations. *Sustainability (Basel), 10*(7), 2413. DOI: 10.3390/su10072413

Di Fabio, A., & Rosen, M. A. (2018). Opening the black box of psychological processes in organizations: A new agenda for psychosocial sustainability. *Frontiers in Psychology, 9*, 2422. DOI: 10.3389/fpsyg.2018.02422

Emery, F. E., & Trist, E. L. (1960). *Socio-technical systems.* Tavistock Institute.

Fox, M. (2021). Organizational sustainability and employee well-being: A psychosocial approach. *Journal of Organizational Psychology, 21*(2), 15–29.

Gagné, M., & Deci, E. L. (2005). Self-determination theory and work motivation. *Journal of Organizational Behavior, 26*(4), 331–362. DOI: 10.1002/job.322

Gallup. (2023). State of the global workplace report 2023. https://www.gallup.com/workplace

Gifford, R. (2014). Environmental psychology matters. *Annual Review of Psychology, 65*(1), 541–579. DOI: 10.1146/annurev-psych-010213-115048 PMID: 24050189

GitLab. (2023). The remote work handbook. https://about.gitlab.com/company/culture/all-remote/

Mark, G., & Harris, J. (2020). Digital balance and well-being: Emerging perspectives. *Communications of the ACM, 63*(6), 31–33. DOI: 10.1145/3386864

Microsoft. (2021). The next great disruption is hybrid work – are we ready? https://www.microsoft.com/en-us/worklab/work-trend-index

Nesher Shoshan, H., & Wehrt, W. (2022). Managing Zoom fatigue and beyond: A psychological approach to virtual meeting overload. *Computers in Human Behavior Reports, 5*, 100150. DOI: 10.1016/j.chbr.2021.100150

Schwab, K. (2017). *The fourth industrial revolution*. Crown Business.

Sonnentag, S. (2018). The recovery paradox: Portraying the complex interplay between job stressors, lack of recovery, and poor well-being. *Research in Organizational Behavior, 38*, 169–185. DOI: 10.1016/j.riob.2018.11.002

Tapscott, D., & Tapscott, A. (2023). Blockchain revolution: How the technology behind Bitcoin is changing money, business, and the world (Updated ed.). Penguin.

Tarafdar, M., Cooper, C. L., & Stich, J. F. (2019). The technostress trifecta – techno eustress, techno distress and design: Theoretical directions and an agenda for research. *Information Systems Journal, 29*(1), 6–42. DOI: 10.1111/isj.12169

Tarafdar, M., Pullins, E. B., & Ragu-Nathan, T. S. (2015). Technostress: Negative effect on performance and possible mitigations. *Information Systems Journal, 25*(2), 103–132. DOI: 10.1111/isj.12042

Ulrich, D., Allen, J., Brockbank, W., Younger, J., & Nyman, M. (2020). *HR transformation: Building human resources from the outside in*. McGraw-Hill Education.

Vodanovich, S. J., Sundaram, D., & Myers, M. (2018). Digital well-being: A systematic review of literature. PACIS 2018 Proceedings, 63.

Waizenegger, L., McKenna, B., Cai, W., & Bendz, T. (2020). An affordance perspective of team collaboration and enforced working from home during COVID-19. *European Journal of Information Systems, 29*(4), 429–442. DOI: 10.1080/0960085X.2020.1800417

World Health Organization. (2022). Mental health at work: Policy brief. https://www.who.int/publications/i/item/9789240053052

KEY TERMS AND DEFINITIONS

AI-Driven HR Tools: Human resources technologies that leverage artificial intelligence for functions like performance tracking, recruitment, and measuring employee engagement.

Asynchronous Communication: Exchanges that do not require real-time responses, allowing participants to reply when it suits them (for example, email or project boards).

Digital Detox: A deliberate period of unplugging from screens to recover from digital fatigue and restore emotional balance.

Digital Fatigue: Mental and emotional exhaustion resulting from prolonged use of digital devices and communication platforms.

Digital Presenters: Maintaining an active online presence at work even when one is not feeling mentally well or productive.

Digital Well-Being: The capacity to use digital technology in ways that support rather than undermine your mental and social health.

Employee Experience: The full range of interactions and emotions employees go through during their tenure at a company, including digital engagements.

Equity in Remote Work: Ensuring all employees have fair access to support, resources, and advancement opportunities in remote or digital work settings.

Hybrid Equity Protocols: Organizational guidelines that ensure remote and in-office workers receive equal opportunities, resources, and recognition.

Hybrid Work: A setup combining on-site and remote work, allowing employees to choose where and how they complete their tasks.

Job Demands-Resources (JD-R): A model asserting that job outcomes hinge on balancing work demands (such as workload) with available resources (such as support and autonomy).

Psychological Safety: A workplace climate in which individuals feel safe taking interpersonal risks, speaking openly, and expressing ideas without fear of negative consequences.

Psychosocial Sustainability: The long-term ability of individuals and organizations to preserve good mental health and maintain positive relationships amid changing conditions.

Remote Work: A work arrangement in which people carry out their duties from locations outside the traditional office, primarily via online tools.

Resilience: The ability of individuals or teams to adapt and recover when faced with stress, uncertainty, or challenges.

Right to Disconnect: A policy guaranteeing that employees are not expected to engage in work-related communications outside their normal working hours.

Self-Determination Theory: A theory proposing that fulfilling three basic needs—autonomy, competence, and relatedness—are essential for motivation and well-being.

Socio-Technical Systems (STS): An approach to organizational design that examines how social factors (people and culture) and technical elements (tools and processes) interrelate.

Techno-stress: The strain caused by excessive or poorly managed use of technology, which can lead to fatigue, anxiety, or burnout.

Well-Tech: Digital solutions—such as apps and wearables—designed to promote mental health and well-being in the workplace.

Section 5
Leadership Models and Digital Organizational Dynamics

Chapter 10
Reimagining Leadership and Organizational Culture in Digitally Native Firms:
Distributed Leadership, Digital Trust, and Resilience Building in the E-Economy

J. Leema Christina
http://orcid.org/0009-0004-8855-2965
SRC, SASTRA University, India

R. Alamelu
http://orcid.org/0000-0003-0539-2480
SRC, SASTRA University, India

M. Sathya
http://orcid.org/0009-0009-7539-0318
SRC, SASTRA University, India

R. Purushothaman
http://orcid.org/0009-0003-0941-8462
SRC, SASTRA University, India

ABSTRACT

This chapter develops the Digital Resilient Leadership Culture (DRLC) framework to analyse how digitally native firms structure leadership, trust, and organizational

DOI: 10.4018/979-8-3373-4307-5.ch010

culture in remote-first, platform-governed environments. Drawing on four theoretical foundations—distributed leadership, digital trust, adaptive culture, and sociotechnical systems thinking, the chapter demonstrates how these firms co-produce resilience through infrastructural, ethical, and participatory mechanisms. Using a multi-method design combining conceptual synthesis, case analysis of six global firms, and document-based thematic coding, it reveals that resilience emerges not from isolated practices but from the interaction between system-embedded leadership, trust-by-design, and modular culture. This reconceptualization offers both scholarly and practical insights for designing human-centred, inclusive, and adaptable work environments in the e-economy.

INTRODUCTION

The emergence of digitally native firms represents a paradigmatic shift in how organizations are structured, governed, and experienced (Stark & Pais, 2020). Unlike traditional enterprises that have incrementally integrated digital tools into legacy systems, digitally native firms are conceived and scaled entirely through digital infrastructures (Kadolkar, Kepes, & Subramony, 2024). These organizations operate in environments characterized by algorithmic coordination (Mbare, Perkiö, & Koivusalo, 2024), remote-first work models (De Souza Santos & Ralph, 2022), and fluid platform-based workflows. As such, the foundational assumptions of leadership and organizational culture, once grounded in hierarchical control, physical proximity, and bureaucratic processes are proving inadequate in addressing the realities of digitally mediated work.

This transformation is not merely technological but sociotechnical, as it reshapes the interaction between human behaviour and digital systems (Kandane Arachchige Don, Richter, & Tate, 2024). It poses critical challenges and opportunities for Human Resource Management scholarship and practice. Traditional leadership paradigms, including transactional and transformational models, often fall short in contexts where authority is distributed, communication is asynchronous, and psychological autonomy is high (Höddinghaus, Nohe, & Hertel, 2023). Moreover, the erosion of physical co presence and face to face collaboration necessitates novel mechanisms for cultivating trust, enabling cohesion, and fostering resilience in teams that are geographically and temporally dispersed (Degbey & Einola, 2020). Digitally native firms differ fundamentally from hybrid or digitally transformed organizations. Their structures and cultures are not adaptations of industrial era models but are born from digital logic itself. This reality calls for a reconceptualization of leadership and organizational culture that is attuned to digital environments (Asfahani, 2025). To address this need, the chapter draws on distributed leadership theory, digital trust scholarship, organizational resilience studies, and sociotechnical systems thinking. Together, these perspectives offer a composite analytical lens to understand how leadership, trust, and culture co evolve in digitally intensive settings (Kloepfer & Carbon, 2025; Harris, Jones, & Ismail, 2022).

To interrogate these issues, the chapter is guided by three core research questions:

1. How is leadership being reconceptualized in digitally native, platform-driven firms?
2. What digital and psychological trust mechanisms underpin cohesive remote work environments?
3. In what ways can distributed leadership and adaptive culture enhance organizational resilience under conditions of digital volatility?

In response to these questions, the chapter introduces the Digital Resilient Leadership Culture framework—a model that captures the interdependent dynamics of leadership behaviour, trust mechanisms, and cultural adaptability in digital firms. It posits that organizational resilience in these settings is not an automatic consequence of technological sophistication, but an intentional outcome of designing systems that support shared authority, psychological safety, and inclusive culture.

To explore this proposition, the chapter adopts a multi method qualitative design. First, it conducts a conceptual synthesis of interdisciplinary literature across leadership, organizational behaviour, digital sociology, and human resource management. Second, it develops a multiple case study analysis of digitally native firms that exemplify mature digital leadership and cultural practices. Third, it undertakes a document-based content review of organizational artifacts such as remote work policies, public culture documents, and leadership narratives. This methodological triangulation ensures both theoretical depth and empirical grounding.

By articulating this integrated analysis, the chapter contributes to the advancement of a human centred and resilience-oriented vision of human resource management in the digital economy. It offers a conceptual foundation for scholars examining digital organizing and a set of practical insights for practitioners designing inclusive, adaptive, and trust rich workplaces. In doing so, it positions digitally native firms not as anomalies but as prototypes of the future of work where leadership is shared, culture is co-created, and resilience is architected through the purposeful interaction of human agency and digital infrastructure.

Theoretical Foundations

This section establishes the conceptual foundation for the proposed Digital Resilient Leadership Culture (DRLC) framework by integrating four academic traditions that, although distinct in origin, collectively offer insight into the evolving nature of leadership and organizational culture within digitally native firms.

Distributed Leadership Theory- DRLC Dimension: Distributed Authority

Distributed leadership theory reconceptualizes leadership not as an attribute of individual actors in hierarchical roles, but as an emergent, collective process embedded within organizational interactions (Bolden, 2011). This tradition emphasizes the dispersion of influence across organizational actors who collaboratively mobilize expertise, coordinate action, and shape decision making processes through informal structures, routines, and shared cognition (Svensson & von Knorring, 2025). Leadership, in this framing, becomes less about formal titles and more about relational agency enacted through situated practices.

The application of distributed leadership has been particularly influential in dynamic and complex environments where top-down control is insufficient for adaptive responsiveness (Eriksson et al., 2025). In such contexts, leadership is interpreted as a multi nodal phenomenon, manifesting through joint problem solving, lateral accountability, and context sensitive authority. However, most foundational formulations of this theory implicitly assume physical co presence, synchronous collaboration, and shared temporal routines. These assumptions constrain the theory's applicability to digitally native firms, which operate through asynchronous coordination, geographically dispersed teams, and platform mediated communication. In these digital environments, self-organising team dynamics further reinforce the non-hierarchical emergence of leadership, as seen in agile distributed teams where roles adapt fluidly to project needs and individual contributions (Licorish & MacDonell, 2021).

Moreover, distributed leadership theory tends to under theorize the infrastructural mechanisms that enable or delimit the enactment of leadership in digital settings. It pays limited attention to how platform architectures such as workflow algorithms, version control systems, or contributor recognition protocols mediate visibility, task ownership, and perceived legitimacy (Constantinides et al., 2018). These mechanisms shape leadership not through direct interaction but by embedding authority into digital workflows and infrastructures (Jhaver et al., 2023). In such systems, leadership often emerges not from social charisma or face to face presence, but from sustained contribution within algorithmically structured environments.

The DRLC framework extends distributed leadership by embedding it within digital infrastructures that enable structurally distributed authority. It introduces the notion of platform mediated leadership emergence, where influence is encoded in the capacity to shape shared protocols, contribute to transparent decision flows, and engage meaningfully in modular workstreams (Jacobo-Romero & Freitas, 2021). Leadership becomes infrastructurally scaffolded rather than socially delegated, relying on tools that register contribution, amplify expertise, and institutionalize collaborative agency (Avtalion et al., 2024). Ethnographic evidence from digitally transforming organizations shows how distributed leadership can evolve through participatory systems and technical affordances rather than charismatic influence (Lorentzen, 2022). Furthermore, digital leadership has been shown to enhance exploratory innovation by aligning organizational culture with the affordances of digital systems (Wang et al., 2022).

Digital Trust and Psychological Safety-
DRLC Dimension: Trust-by-Design

The constructs of organizational trust and psychological safety have long served as cornerstones for understanding interpersonal dynamics and team performance in organizational behavior literature. Trust involves a willingness to be vulnerable to another party based on perceived ability, benevolence, and integrity (Mayer et al., 1995). Psychological safety refers to the shared belief that one can take interpersonal risks without fear of punishment or humiliation (Edmondson, 1999). These constructs are foundational to collaborative learning, innovation, and team effectiveness in interdependent work settings (Tkalich et al., 2022).

Traditional conceptions of trust and safety were developed in co located work environments, relying on embodied cues, synchronous interaction, and shared physical presence. In digitally native firms, however, work is increasingly asynchronous, communication is disembodied, and visibility is mediated through dashboards and activity logs. These altered conditions complicate the relational assumptions that trust develops through familiarity and that safety emerges through face-to-face dialogue. The increasing reliance on platform governance and performance metrics further transforms how psychological safety is experienced in remote teams (Höddinghaus et al., 2023).

Digital infrastructures introduce pervasive ambient visibility and surveillance. Systems that track participation, monitor contributions, or display performance histories are often justified as mechanisms of accountability, but they may unintentionally erode autonomy and inhibit authentic expression (Eurofound, 2020). These environments reduce opportunities for informal interaction and unstructured communication, leading to flattened affective climates and a diminished sense of interpersonal security.

The DRLC framework repositions trust as an architected property of digital work systems rather than an emergent social condition. Drawing from zero trust principles, trust is embedded in platform design through continuous verification, access segmentation, and protocol enforcement (National Institute of Standards and Technology, 2020). These design features promote structural trust, especially in high stakes or dispersed teams, by reducing reliance on interpersonal reassurance (Arora & Hastings, 2024). Beyond cybersecurity, zero trust logic also informs how participation, role visibility, and access to sensitive information are managed within digital workflows (Gambo & Almulhem, 2025).

This reframing offers three conceptual extensions. First, it views trust as technologically supported through anonymized feedback, role-based access, and opt in transparency. Second, it situates psychological safety within system governance rather than team climate alone, linking platform design to emotional risk tolerance (Dongxian & Batool, 2024). Third, it invites a procedural, culturally responsive model of trust construction where compliance, fairness, and inclusivity are designed into the architecture of the digital environment (Ejiofor et al., 2025).

Organizational Culture and Resilience- DRLC Dimension: Adaptive Digital Culture

Organizational culture has long been conceptualized as a system of shared assumptions, values, and norms that guide member behaviour and construct collective identity (Schein, 2010). It encompasses both visible artifacts and underlying belief systems, often transmitted through rituals, stories, mentorship, and social reinforcement. Resilience, meanwhile, is defined as the organizational capacity to absorb disruption, reconfigure processes, and sustain core functioning under conditions of uncertainty (Duchek, 2020; Lengnick-Hall et al., 2011). Although traditionally examined as distinct phenomena, culture and resilience are increasingly recognized as mutually reinforcing: culture provides the interpretive frameworks and behavioral routines through which adaptive responses are generated.

However, these constructs are undergoing fundamental transformation in digitally native firms, where organizational culture is not shaped by co-located interactions or hierarchical socialization, but by asynchronous collaboration, distributed workforces, and platform-mediated coordination (Maznevski & Chudoba, 2000). Conventional mechanisms of cultural transmission such as in-person onboarding, spontaneous mentorship, and symbolic leadership behaviors are less accessible or altogether absent. In their place emerge digital rituals, documentation practices, and co-created protocols that collectively function as cultural infrastructures (Cardoso et al., 2025).

Furthermore, the encoding of cultural values in platform tools such as shared team wikis, feedback loops, and workflow logs requires reconceptualizing culture not as a fixed set of values, but as a modular and dynamically updatable system. In digitally native settings, organizational culture must not only be resilient but also digitally codified, reflexively maintained, and contextually adaptable. Evidence from virtual adaptation during exogenous shocks demonstrates how digital infrastructures can strengthen cultural coherence when thoughtfully implemented (Nielsen et al., 2023; Firican, 2024).

However, digital cultures are not without risk. They may inadvertently reinforce dominant norms while marginalizing alternative epistemologies or cultural expressions. In remote-first environments, research shows that lack of spontaneous interactions and informal cues can weaken collective identity and psychological safety (Bilderback & Kilpatrick, 2024; Mozammel et al., 2025). These findings highlight the need for intentional cultural scaffolding within distributed teams.

The DRLC framework intervenes by reframing organizational culture as a technologically mediated and participatory construct, whose adaptability is central to both leadership legitimacy and organizational resilience. Rather than treating culture as an implicit backdrop for action, DRLC positions culture as an explicit system of meaning co-produced through infrastructure. It highlights the strategic use of asynchronous rituals, such as shared value boards, rotating facilitation, or annotated decision logs that facilitate sensemaking across temporal, spatial, and cultural boundaries (Breidbach et al., 2025).

In this formulation, cultural adaptability is both a technological and social competence. DRLC enables culture to evolve in real time through collaborative input, ethical revision, and inclusive design. Features such as multilingual documentation, regionalized communication protocols, and open-source value statements exemplify how culture becomes resilient through its continuous reassembly. Moreover, the integration of adaptive cultural systems within DRLC ensures that culture is not only preserved during periods of change, but also serves as a generative force for organizational renewal (Xu et al., 2024).

By making culture legible, editable, and scalable through digital affordances, the DRLC model extends traditional theories of organizational culture beyond static cohesion or symbolic leadership. It provides a framework for inclusive cultural resilience, one that is responsive to infrastructural shifts, pluralistic in its expression, and durable across distributed ecosystems.

Sociotechnical Systems and Systems Thinking-DRLC Dimension: Systemic Resilience

The theoretical underpinnings of sociotechnical systems (STS) and systems thinking provide critical insight into how digitally native firms orchestrate resilience across interdependent human and technological domains. STS theory posits that effective organizational performance depends on the joint optimization of social and technical subsystems, requiring neither to dominate nor operate in isolation (Naikar & Elix, 2021). Complementarily, systems thinking emphasizes feedback loops, emergent patterns, and holistic adaptation as essential to navigating complexity and change (Meadows, 2008). Together, these perspectives underscore the need to design adaptive work systems that respond fluidly to environmental volatility, interdependence, and dynamic constraint.

In digitally native contexts, these foundational theories acquire renewed relevance but also face conceptual limitations. Traditional STS models often assumed technology to be value neutral. However, digital infrastructures today are deeply embedded with normative assumptions and procedural codes. Algorithmic systems within platforms do not merely support decision making; they actively shape cognition, automate discretion, and institutionalize specific logics of control (Pasquale, 2015; Ziewitz, 2015). As a result, these algorithmic architectures function as governance instruments, recalibrating how visibility, legitimacy, and agency are distributed across the organization (Li et al., 2024).

Recent scholarship has extended STS inquiry to address sociotechnical harms, wherein platform architectures embed structural biases, amplify opacity, and constrain participatory resilience (Shelby et al., 2023). These harms are not incidental flaws but systemic asymmetries. In the Global South, for instance, algorithmic infrastructures reproduce global inequalities by encoding patterns of exclusion into platform governance, limiting equitable adaptation and collective resilience (Kwet, 2019). Emerging frameworks stress the importance of co-designed digital systems that reflect situated knowledge and civic inclusion (Hughes et al., 2025), moving away from technocratic universality toward infrastructural justice.

Within this evolving terrain, the DRLC framework advances a co-evolutionary model of resilience. It reconceptualizes sociotechnical adaptation as a reflexive and participatory process where digital infrastructure becomes both a coordination medium and a cultural agent. Systemic resilience in this framing is achieved not through redundancy or standardization, but through ethical, inclusive, and adaptive design mechanisms (Ponsard et al., 2024). These include interoperable systems that promote transparency, governance aligned with design justice, and digital affordances that empower multiple voices within institutional routines.

Crucially, DRLC challenges systems theory's historical separation between structure and agency by showing how platforms, protocols, and algorithms operate as socio-organizational actors. These actors shape the emergence of leadership visibility, legitimacy, and continuity. Organizational tools such as co-curated documentation, context aware access controls, and localized governance protocols are not inert artifacts; they are structural levers that influence the distribution of resilience itself.

Finally, the DRLC framework introduces a normative imperative into systems design: not only asking how systems adapt, but for whom and under what constraints. In doing so, it synthesizes systems thinking with critical concerns around fairness, digital colonialism, and algorithmic transparency, redefining resilience not as survival or efficiency alone, but as an ethical infrastructure for sustainable digital citizenship.

These theoretical revisions collectively inform the Digital Resilient Leadership Culture (DRLC) framework. By addressing the shortcomings of legacy theories in digitally native environments, the DRLC model offers a recalibrated understanding of leadership, trust, culture, and resilience as they co-evolve within platform-mediated organizations.

Table 1. Theoretical Contributions of DRLC across Four Foundational Frameworks

Theory	Traditional Focus	Conceptual Limitation	DRLC Extension
Distributed Leadership	Leadership as a relational, collective process emerging through informal interaction and shared agency	Assumes physical co-presence, synchronous collaboration, and lacks infrastructural perspective	Positions leadership as platform-mediated, with authority emerging through digital workflows, documentation, and visibility
Organizational Trust & Psychological Safety	Trust based on familiarity, integrity, and interpersonal reliability; safety as risk-free communication	Relies on in-person cues, may be undermined by digital surveillance or cultural misalignment	Reframes trust as infrastructurally engineered through ethical design, context-aware defaults, and culturally adaptive affordances
Organizational Culture & Resilience	Culture transmitted through rituals, stories, leadership modeling; resilience as strategic reconfiguration	Struggles in remote-first settings; risks homogenization through Western-centric digital norms	Defines culture as modular, co-authored, and digitally scaffolded; embeds resilience through participatory digital infrastructures
Sociotechnical Systems & Systems Thinking	Optimization of social-technical alignment; systems as holistic, feedback-driven entities	Underestimates algorithmic governance, infrastructural inequality, and platform-embedded power dynamics	Expands resilience as equity-oriented and infrastructure-sensitive, guided by design justice and digital co-evolution

Synthesis: Toward a Digital Resilient Leadership Culture

Building upon the preceding four theoretical lenses, this section offers an integrative synthesis that positions the Digital Resilient Leadership Culture (DRLC) framework as a cohesive and forward-looking model for leadership and resilience in digitally native contexts. As summarized in Table 1, the DRLC framework systematically extends each foundational theory by addressing the infrastructural, cultural, and ethical complexities that characterize digitally mediated work environments.

Each theory contributes a distinct analytical lens: distributed leadership emphasizes collective agency, trust literature foregrounds psychological safety, cultural theory underscores shared meaning and adaptive cohesion, and sociotechnical systems provide a structural perspective on integration, governance, and feedback loops. However, when applied to digital-first contexts governed by platforms, algorithms, and asynchronous workflows, these frameworks require critical recalibration to remain analytically useful.

To respond to these limitations, the DRLC framework synthesizes and extends these traditions through an infrastructural paradigm. First, it digitally embeds leadership by shifting authority from interpersonal delegation to platform-mediated enactment, where documentation systems and workflow tools establish legitimacy and distribute influence. Second, it re-engineers trust and safety as deliberate outcomes of digital design, rather than byproducts of relational familiarity. Third, it frames organizational culture as modular and adaptive, enabling dynamic evolution through open-source norms, asynchronous rituals, and co-authored artifacts. Finally, it infuses resilience with equity, recognizing that infrastructural disparities and algorithmic biases must be addressed through ethical platform governance and design justice.

Unlike traditional organizational models that focus on individual actors, symbolic rituals, or static systems, DRLC repositions digital infrastructure as the connective tissue through which leadership, trust, culture, and resilience co-evolve. It advances a sociotechnical-humanistic synthesis that integrates technological affordances with attention to power asymmetries, intercultural complexity, and normative responsibility. In doing so, the DRLC framework reframes the core assumptions of existing theories to align with the infrastructural, intercultural, and algorithmically mediated nature of digitally native organizations. It offers a theoretically robust and practically adaptive model of leadership culture suited for a world increasingly shaped by digital architectures, remote interdependence, and pluralistic work ecologies.

CONCEPTUAL FRAMEWORK: DIGITAL RESILIENT LEADERSHIP CULTURE (DRLC)

The Digital Resilient Leadership Culture (DRLC) framework builds directly on the four theoretical foundations discussed in the previous section, offering an integrated and forward-looking architecture designed for platform-native and remote-first organizations. The framework positions organizational resilience not as an emergent phenomenon but as a strategic capacity that can be deliberately designed and maintained through three core dimensions: distributed authority, trust-by-design, and adaptive culture.

The first design dimension, Distributed Authority Systems, reconceptualizes leadership as a structural outcome of digital workflows, documentation practices, and protocol-driven coordination. Authority is not rooted in hierarchical position but emerges through visibility, contribution, and sustained task ownership within modular and transparent systems. This reconfiguration shifts leadership from interpersonal charisma to infrastructural legitimacy. The second dimension, Trust-by-Design Mechanisms, addresses the erosion of embodied cues and spontaneous interaction in digital environments by embedding psychological safety into platform architecture. Drawing from zero-trust security principles, DRLC encodes trust through ethical defaults, opt-in visibility, culturally responsive feedback channels, and low-surveillance performance frameworks that protect autonomy while ensuring accountability. The third dimension, Adaptive Cultural Systems, reframes culture as a modular and co-authored infrastructure, maintained through digital rituals, asynchronous team norms, multilingual documentation, and open knowledge repositories. Rather than being imposed or inherited, culture becomes something that is co-created, updated, and owned by the distributed workforce in real time.

These three design dimensions are not independent silos but interlocking components that collectively generate Systemic Resilience—an organization's ability to adapt ethically, maintain cohesion across distributed teams, and continue operating through volatility without compromising its core values or structures. This architectural logic is visually represented in the DRLC Pyramid Model (Figure 1), where the foundational layer of distributed authority enables trust-by-design, which in turn supports adaptive cultural systems. The culmination of these layers is systemic resilience, represented at the apex. The vertical sequence in the pyramid reflects both logical interdependence and practical design sequencing. Each layer must be in place and internally aligned for resilience to emerge as a stable organizational capacity.

Figure 1. The DRLC Pyramid Model—Building Blocks of Digital Resilient Leadership Culture.

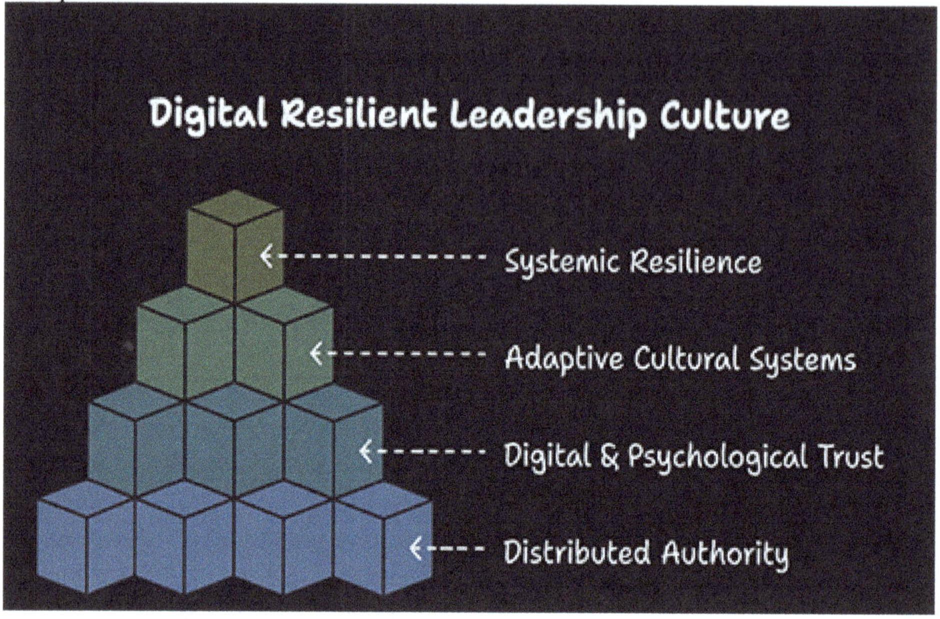

Methodology

This study adopts a qualitative, exploratory research design grounded in interpretivist epistemology to investigate how leadership, trust, and organizational culture are redefined in digitally native firms. The objective is to develop and empirically examine the Digital Resilient Leadership Culture (DRLC) framework by integrating insights from multiple theoretical traditions and analysing how these constructs are operationalized in platform-native, globally distributed organizations. The methodology comprises three interrelated components: conceptual synthesis, comparative case study design, and document-based content analysis. This multi-method approach ensures theoretical depth, empirical grounding, and cross-contextual interpretation.

Research Paradigm

The study is situated within an interpretivist paradigm that conceptualizes leadership and culture as socially constructed, context-dependent, and embedded within organizational systems. Digitally native firms offer a unique empirical site, as their digitally mediated environments challenge conventional assumptions about leadership emergence, trust-building, and cultural reproduction. The interpretivist orientation allows for an in-depth understanding of these symbolic, infrastructural, and relational processes as they unfold asynchronously and are shaped by platform logics.

Conceptual Synthesis

The first phase involved constructing the initial version of the DRLC framework through a structured synthesis of four foundational literatures: distributed leadership, digital trust and psychological safety, organizational culture and resilience, and sociotechnical systems thinking. A purposive review of scholarly books, peer-reviewed articles, and empirical studies published between 2000 and 2025 was conducted to identify converging constructs and theoretical gaps. The synthesis revealed a shared emphasis on emergent authority, infrastructural trust, participatory culture, and system-level adaptability. These themes were coded and mapped into the DRLC framework, forming a conceptually integrated foundation for subsequent empirical exploration. The coherence of the model was tested through triangulation and convergence mapping to ensure analytical consistency across dimensions.

Case Study Selection and Design

To examine how the DRLC dimensions manifest in real-world digital contexts, a comparative multiple case study design was employed. Six digitally native firms were selected through theoretical sampling to ensure conceptual richness, geographic diversity, and variation in organizational form, while maintaining a consistent digital-native foundation. Selection criteria included:

- Digital-native origin, where the firm was founded with a cloud-native, mobile-first, or platform-based model
- Demonstrated use of distributed governance structures and asynchronous collaboration
- Availability and accessibility of public-facing leadership and cultural documentation
- Evidence of practices aligned with DRLC dimensions, including trust-building mechanisms, resilience strategies, and participatory cultural systems

The selected firms span six global regions and multiple industry verticals—software-as-a-service (SaaS), fintech, platform ecosystems, and talent marketplaces. This design captures the pluralistic manifestations of digital resilience and leadership, while avoiding over-representation of Western or Silicon Valley-centric cases. The final case set includes GitLab, Nubank, Klarna, Grab, Atlassian, and Andela. These firms were selected not based on scale or brand recognition, but on their ability to illustrate DRLC constructs across varied cultural and infrastructural settings.

Document-Based Content Analysis

To support the case analysis and validate the DRLC framework empirically, a qualitative document-based content analysis was conducted using publicly accessible organizational artifacts. These included remote work handbooks, onboarding guides, cultural charters, ESG reports, leadership blogs, and internal policy documents. Documents were purposively sampled based on their strategic relevance to the DRLC framework. Inclusion criteria prioritized materials that explicitly articulated leadership logic, trust mechanisms, collaborative protocols, or digital governance features. All documents were retrieved between January and March 2025 to ensure temporal consistency and analytical contemporaneity.

Coding was performed at the paragraph level to preserve semantic clarity and organizational context. Deductive codes were developed directly from the DRLC framework's four dimensions—distributed authority, trust-by-design, adaptive culture, and systemic resilience. Simultaneously, inductive codes were generated through close textual reading, capturing firm-specific terms and emergent themes such as "async autonomy," "radical transparency," "editable rituals," and "cultural modularity." The coding process was executed in Microsoft Excel to maintain a transparent and auditable matrix, with each document entered as a row and thematic indicators recorded across columns. Paragraph-level interpretation enabled a high degree of contextual fidelity and reduced fragmentation across firm narratives.

To enhance coding reliability, a secondary coder independently reviewed a stratified subset comprising twenty percent of the total sample. Discrepancies were resolved through discussion and iterative refinement of the codebook. Reflexive memos were maintained throughout the coding phase to track analytical decisions, theme evolution, and coding rationale. A pattern-matching strategy was used to align textual evidence with DRLC constructs, ensuring consistency between the conceptual model and empirical observations. Thematic weights were calculated based on frequency and density of reference within each document and normalized across length and format to enable valid cross-case comparison.

Ethical Considerations and Validation Strategies

As the study relies exclusively on publicly available, non-identifiable documents, formal institutional ethics approval was not required. Nonetheless, ethical rigor was maintained throughout the research process. All sources were accurately cited, interpreted in their original context, and represented without extrapolating beyond textual evidence. Particular care was taken when analysing employee-authored materials and artifacts originating from non-Western or Global South contexts. These documents were treated with cultural sensitivity, and analytical interpretations were contextualized with attention to local institutional conditions.

To strengthen analytical validity, interpretive reliability was supported through two validation strategies. First, informal peer debriefings were conducted with external qualitative researchers to challenge assumptions, test theme clarity, and refine cross-case inferences. Second, convergence across data sources was used to establish pattern reliability, with themes

confirmed through repetition across multiple artifacts within each firm. While direct member-checking with firms was not feasible, the triangulation of sources, second-order coding validation, and iterative cross-case comparison ensured the robustness and transparency of the findings.

This methodology enables a rigorous and contextually grounded examination of how digitally native firms embed distributed leadership, engineer psychological trust, co-create adaptive cultures, and cultivate systemic resilience through sociotechnical infrastructures. It also supports the validation and refinement of the DRLC framework across diverse organizational and geographic ecosystems. The empirical findings derived from this methodology are presented in the next section through comparative case narratives, thematic scoring, and document-based visual mapping.

Case Analyses

This section draws on multiple case studies to illustrate how digitally native firms enact the DRLC framework through distributed leadership, trust-by-design, adaptive culture, and sociotechnical resilience. Each case highlights context-specific practices while revealing cross-cutting patterns and contrasts that define the emerging contours of leadership in the digital era.

Atlassian (Oceania – SaaS)

Atlassian demonstrates a mature enactment of distributed leadership through its *Team Anywhere* strategy, which decentralizes decision-making across a global workforce spanning 13 countries, with 40 percent of employees working remotely (Goldschein, 2022). Its *Team Playbook* institutionalizes team autonomy via rituals such as retrospectives and health monitors, enabling leadership to emerge through participatory processes rather than positional hierarchy (Atlassian, n.d.; Kitterman, 2023).

Trust is systematically designed through radical transparency practices, including open OKRs and published salary bands (Sparks, n.d.). Micromanagement is actively discouraged, with leadership discourse emphasizing empathetic remote engagement (Atlassian, 2022). Psychological safety is reinforced through practices such as "blameless postmortems," which normalize vulnerability and risk-sharing (Atlassian, n.d.-a).

Cultural adaptability is supported by Atlassian's *Work From Anywhere* policy, introduced pre-2020, and its use of asynchronous tools like Loom to reduce meeting load (d & Trello, 2020; Atlassian Corporation, 2023). Connection hubs, including quarterly offsite gatherings in locations like Melbourne, foster cohesion within a distributed structure.

Sociotechnical resilience is embedded in Atlassian's integration of its own tools—Jira, Confluence, and Trello—as infrastructure for distributed coordination, documentation, and sprint planning (Moon, 2023). Atlassian emphasizes the importance of ethical automation by supporting responsible and explainable AI frameworks that prioritize human values and transparency (Austin, 2020).

Atlassian thus aligns strongly with the DRLC framework: distributed authority is supported through team-centered rituals, trust is embedded via platform transparency, culture is modular and inclusive, and resilience is achieved through infrastructural integration and ethical systems design.

GitLab (North America – All-Remote SaaS)

GitLab exemplifies distributed leadership through a flat, asynchronous governance model across 65+ countries. Leadership is enacted through contribution, not hierarchy, as codified in its open-source Handbook exceeding 2000 pages (GitLab, n.d.-b). Decision-making occurs via version-controlled merge requests, allowing any employee to propose changes to workflows or culture—a system of infrastructural authority aligned with GitLab's TeamOps principle of "equal contributions" (GitLab, n.d.-a).

Digital trust is embedded by default. Practices such as "assume positive intent," "blameless root cause analysis," and public OKRs are documented in the Handbook to ensure psychological safety (GitLab, n.d.-c). Transparency is structurally enforced across meetings, compensation, and decision trails. However, GitLab explicitly acknowledges the risks of over-transparency and warns against its misuse for digital surveillance, aligning with intercultural trust frameworks (Stahl & Tung, 2015).

GitLab's adaptive culture is modular and editable. Cultural contributions follow the same process as code changes—any employee can edit handbooks or propose new rituals. Asynchronous routines like virtual coffee chats and global AMAs strengthen cohesion without dependency on synchronous meetings (Agarwal, 2024). Resilience is sustained through a culture treated as infrastructure, continuously revised by its participants.

Sociotechnical resilience is enabled by GitLab's platform itself, which integrates CI/CD, issue tracking, documentation, and governance. Leadership visibility and team accountability emerge through embedded feedback loops and traceable workflows (GitLab, n.d.-d). Ethical automation is emphasized through self-regulatory data protocols and opt-in behavioral tracking.

GitLab thus represents a high-fidelity embodiment of DRLC. Authority is distributed through protocol, trust is engineered through transparency and safety rituals, culture is co-authored, and resilience is algorithmically scaffolded.

Nubank (Latin America – Fintech)

Nubank operates as a digital-native platform, scaling leadership, trust, and culture through decentralized systems and intercultural sensitivity. Its *Nu Way* policy ensures parity between remote and in-office roles, while decision-making emerges from agile squads structured around customer proximity and regional autonomy (Queiroz, 2023). Managers act as enablers of distributed impact, reinforcing authority as a function of contribution rather than hierarchy (Guttman Development Strategies, n.d.).

Trust is architected through rituals like virtual "coffee roulettes," leadership Q&As, and default-open dashboards, enabling psychological safety across geographies (Nubank Editorial, 2025). Transparency is codified through the *Nu Code* and internal handbooks, which prioritize clarity over surveillance in hybrid supervision.

Cultural adaptability is sustained via co-authored rituals, modular onboarding kits, and digital events such as *NuTalks*. Culture is designed to be editable, with employees contributing to evolving artifacts that align performance and values (Nubank Editorial, 2024). During the COVID-19 crisis, Nubank rapidly deployed wellness kits and workflow adjustments, reinforcing its cultural resilience (Nubank Editorial, 2025).

Nubank's sociotechnical system, including tools like *NuBanker*, integrates governance with employee experience. Automation is deployed for low-risk tasks while preserving human oversight for ethical dilemmas. Localization is prioritized through multilingual support and regional infrastructure adjustments to reduce digital inequality (Nubank Editorial, 2023).

Nubank offers a strong non-Western instantiation of the DRLC model, where leadership is decentralized, trust is systematically designed, culture is co-authored, and systemic resilience balances automation with equity.

Klarna (Europe – Fintech)

Klarna, a Sweden-based digital-native fintech, exemplifies a fast-evolving platform firm with agile team structures and high algorithmic integration. Its practices align with DRLC dimensions, though tensions between speed, trust, and ethical automation remain visible.

Klarna fosters a flat hierarchy where leadership is expected at all levels. Employees are encouraged to "lead, contribute, and challenge" irrespective of title (Klarna, n.d.). Project teams are fluid, restructured frequently to meet changing priorities. Leadership is enacted through transparent contributions rather than positional authority, reflecting platform-mediated governance.

Trust is supported through internal transparency, shared documentation, and open feedback channels. However, Klarna has faced criticism due to its use of algorithmic performance monitoring and recent restructuring events. These practices, including layoffs and digital surveillance, have strained employee trust and highlight the dual nature of data-driven governance (Nolan, 2024). Klarna promotes a culture of continuous experimentation. Its onboarding systems and team-specific workflows are designed for rapid adaptation, supported by a mantra that "the only constant is change" (Terra, 2018). Yet, internal feedback during reorganization revealed struggles in maintaining cultural cohesion and psychological safety (Business Insider, 2025).

Klarna's automation strategy gained attention in 2024 when it replaced 700 customer service agents with an AI assistant, which handled 2.3 million queries in its first month (Klarna, 2024). While demonstrating scalable efficiency, the decision drew criticism over empathy gaps, prompting partial rehiring and highlighting the importance of ethical AI design (Zara, 2024). Klarna illustrates both the potential and pitfalls of DRLC in algorithmically governed firms. It operationalizes distributed leadership and system-level resilience but struggles with sustaining digital trust when performance systems become coercive. Its case warns against over-automating without reflexive feedback and ethical safeguards.

Grab (Asia-Pacific – Super-App Platform)

Grab exemplifies a regionally adaptive, platform-native firm operating across Southeast Asia. Its practices across distributed authority, digital trust, adaptive culture, and sociotechnical resilience provide a culturally grounded application of the DRLC model.

Grab structures leadership through localized team autonomy within a unified digital ecosystem. Its mobility, fintech, and delivery verticals operate semi-independently, allowing regional leaders to respond to market-specific challenges while maintaining cross-platform coherence. This balance between decentralization and infrastructure alignment enables leadership to be enacted contextually, not hierarchically (Wang, 2024).

Grab institutionalizes trust through transparent fare systems, driver feedback dashboards, and platform safety protocols. The 2023 driver earnings model was redesigned to fairly compensate time and effort, illustrating trust embedded into algorithmic systems (Grab ESG Report, 2023). The 2024 report further details feature like location safety indicators and real-time alerts, ensuring platform reliability (Grab ESG Report, 2024).

Grab nurtures a flexible and inclusive organizational culture through region-specific onboarding, multilingual learning portals, and community collaborations. ESG disclosures emphasize adaptability during crises and continuous employee engagement across diverse geographies (Grab ESG Report, 2022). The cultural modularity enables Grab to operate effectively across markets with varied socio-technical infrastructures.

Grab's operations are governed through deeply embedded algorithmic systems that determine labor allocation, incentives, and workflows. Studies show how drivers adapt to algorithmic feedback to maintain earnings and predictability (Nguyen-Thu & Munn, 2024). Following criticism from driver communities, Grab restructured its algorithmic bonuses in 2023—demonstrating ethical reflexivity and participatory governance (Gong & Tan, 2023). Grab's platform architecture showcases DRLC in action through regionally grounded leadership, trust-by-design, adaptive cultural plugins, and sociotechnical recalibration. Its experience confirms that resilience in digitally native firms requires both ethical infrastructure and inclusive adaptation to local complexity.

Andela (Africa – Tech Talent Platform)

Andela's leadership model relies on asynchronous visibility. Leadership legitimacy is rooted in contribution rather than proximity. Andela operationalizes distributed leadership, trust-by-design, and sociotechnical resilience through a remote-first model that spans Africa, Europe, and North America. Its practices validate the DRLC framework in the context of digitally mediated, globally inclusive work systems.

Andela decentralizes authority by embedding leadership into documentation norms, output visibility, and asynchronous contribution. Team leads are accountable through clear communication, not hierarchical supervision. The EPIC values—Excellence, Passion, Integrity, Collaboration—act as the behavioral framework guiding distributed leadership across global squads (Andela, 2022a). Leadership legitimacy stems from contribution clarity, reinforcing DRLC's emphasis on infrastructure-mediated leadership.

Trust is institutionalized through transparent documentation, asynchronous rituals, and structured feedback loops. A clarity-first ethos ensures that remote work is not only operational but psychologically safe. Onboarding handbooks and workflow transparency help new employees integrate with minimal uncertainty, reflecting DRLC's notion of embedded trust-by-design (Rendall, 2024; Andela, 2023a).

Andela's culture is modular and co-created. Regular revisions to its handbooks and remote playbooks demonstrate participatory adaptation. According to its 2023 Research Pulse, 94 percent of staff cited asynchronous flexibility and cultural agility as key to job satisfaction and organizational resilience (Chakravorti et al., 2023). Additionally, its partnership with the International Finance Corporation underscores an inclusion-focused approach to workforce development (Powell & Kleiner, 2022).

The Talent Cloud, launched in 2022, automates and coordinates the full talent lifecycle, matching, onboarding, monitoring, and feedback—via AI and data protocols (Business Wire, 2022). Ethical safeguards such as bias-mitigation tools and visibility equity are embedded in the system, aligning with DRLC's call for resilient, inclusive infrastructures that support global parity in opportunity and feedback (PR Newswire, 2023).

Andela exemplifies the DRLC model through asynchronous leadership, systemic trust mechanisms, and resilient sociotechnical governance. Its globally inclusive platform offers a blueprint for digital-first firms seeking equity, adaptability, and sustainable performance through ethical platform design.

Comparative Synthesis: Patterns, Contrasts, and Scoring

To systematically compare how digitally native firms enact the DRLC framework, each case was assessed using a five-point qualitative scoring rubric (Table 2). The rubric evaluates the maturity of practices across four core dimensions: distributed leadership, trust-by-design, adaptive culture, and systemic resilience. This evaluation enables consistent interpretation of qualitative evidence while capturing both convergence in shared practices and divergence in implementation depth.

Each score was derived through an iterative process of thematic coding, document analysis, and interpretive comparison. Data sources included public handbooks, onboarding materials, leadership blogs, value statements, ESG reports, and cultural documentation. To ensure analytical reliability, scoring involved triangulation of sources and consensus-building among reviewers. Where contradictions emerged—such as transparency coexisting with digital surveillance—scores reflect a weighted judgment based on ethical clarity, systemic integration, and alignment with DRLC principles.

Table 2. Qualitative Scoring Rubric for DRLC Dimensions

Score	Descriptor	Explanation
5	Exemplary Integration	The firm demonstrates comprehensive, embedded, and systemic practices across global contexts. These are mature, adaptive, and ethically governed.
4	Strong Implementation	Practices are well-developed and consistent, with minor limitations in scalability, uniformity, or ethical clarity.
3	Moderate Presence	The dimension is evident but inconsistently applied, or shows structural tensions or internal contradictions.
2	Limited or Underdeveloped	Practices exist but are weakly institutionalized, ad hoc, or not visibly linked to strategic systems.
1	Minimal or Absent	The dimension is largely missing, ignored, or misaligned with the firm's operating model.

Drawing from the narrative analysis of Section 5.1 to 5.6, Table 3 summarizes shared practices, distinctive contrasts, and observed score ranges for each DRLC dimension. These findings highlight how firms institutionalize leadership and culture differently based on platform architecture, governance design, and regional complexity.

Table 3. Comparative Patterns and DRLC Scores across Digitally Native Firms

DRLC Dimension	Shared Practices (Across Cases)	Distinctive Contrasts	Observed Score Range
Distributed Leadership	Cross-functional squads, platform-based authority, agile team rituals	GitLab's open handbook (5) vs Grab's regionally adaptive hubs (4)	4 – 5
Trust-by-Design	Transparency, asynchronous workflows, public OKRs, feedback loops	Klarna's AI surveillance tensions (3) vs Atlassian's empathetic design (5)	3 – 5
Adaptive Culture	Editable cultural artifacts, localized onboarding, resilience rituals	Nubank's modular "Nu Code" (5) vs Klarna's reorg fatigue (3)	3 – 5
Systemic Resilience	Sociotechnical integration, ethical automation, platform governance	GitLab's unified system (5) vs Klarna's automation backlash (3)	3 – 5

Scores were calibrated through triangulation of narrative evidence, cultural documentation, and observed platform design maturity. This approach ensures analytical consistency and interpretive transparency in evaluating organizational practices. Each score reflects how intentionally and coherently the firm embeds DRLC principles into its operations. For example, GitLab received exemplary scores across all dimensions due to its editable governance architecture, transparent decision-making systems, and open-source cultural model. Klarna, in contrast, demonstrated inconsistencies between its aspirational horizontal structure and tensions created by algorithmic performance monitoring, leading to lower scores in trust and resilience.

Table 4. DRLC Dimension Scores by Firm

Firm	Distributed Leadership	Trust-by-Design	Adaptive Culture	Systemic Resilience
Atlassian	4	5	4	4
GitLab	5	5	5	5
Nubank	4	4	5	4
Klarna	4	3	3	3
Grab	4	4	4	5
Andela	4	4	4	5

These comparative scores reveal several cross-cutting insights (Table 4). First, distributed leadership is the most uniformly implemented dimension, with all firms scoring between 4 and 5 due to structural decentralization and contextual authority models. Second, trust-by-design exhibits greater variation, shaped by how each firm balances transparency, psychological safety, and algorithmic control. Third, adaptive culture thrives in firms with modular rituals and editable norms (e.g., Nubank and GitLab), while resilience depends on the integration of sociotechnical infrastructure and ethical automation, as demonstrated by Andela and Grab (Figure 2).

While the scoring system offers a coherent analytical framework, it is not intended as a ranking mechanism or maturity index. Scores reflect observable institutional practices, not internal employee experiences or firm outcomes. Moreover, regional context, platform complexity, and regulatory environments all shape how DRLC elements are expressed. The framework thus captures relative institutionalization of leadership culture without enforcing a one-size-fits-all benchmark.

Together, the structured scoring rubric, comparative matrix, and firm-level scoring table provide a robust evaluative lens to assess how digitally native organizations architect leadership, trust, and resilience in platform-mediated environments.

Figure 2. DRLC Dimension Scores Across Digitally Native Firms Based on Comparative Matrix

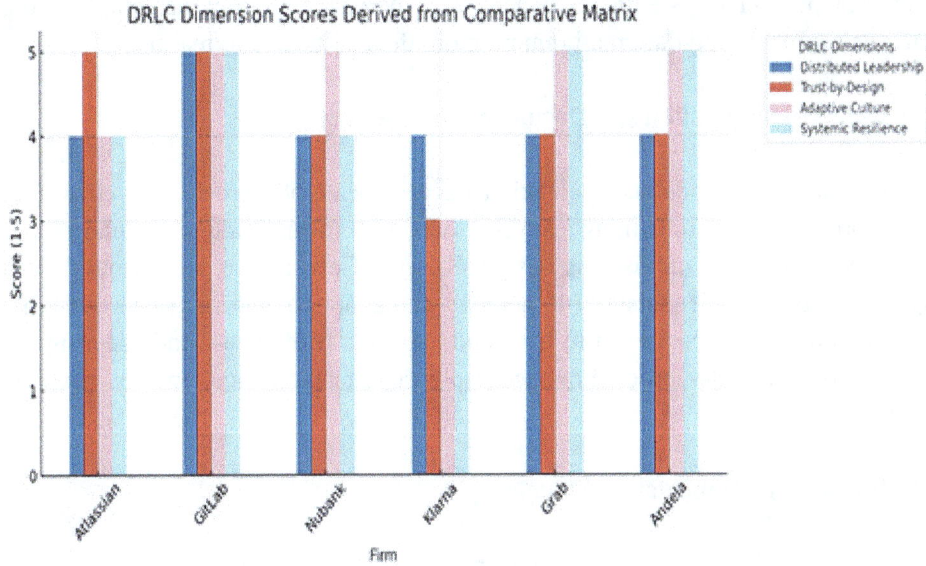

Document-Based Thematic Flow: Sankey Visualization

To complement the case-based analysis of DRLC enactment, this section provides a document-centric perspective using a Sankey diagram (Figure 3). Unlike the case, which were derived from ethnographic interpretation, platform dynamics, and firm behaviour, this analysis isolates how core organizational documents themselves encode the four DRLC dimensions: distributed leadership, digital trust, adaptive culture, and systemic resilience.

Documents were deductively coded and weighted to reflect the proportion of emphasis on each DRLC dimension. These weights were not inferred from practice or outcomes but based on how extensively and explicitly each theme was articulated in official documents such as employee handbooks, playbooks, ESG reports, and value statements.

The Sankey visualization reveals three important patterns:

(1) Asymmetry Between Document Emphasis and Practice Enactment

Some firms' documents mirror their DRLC practices (e.g., GitLab and Andela), while others diverge. GitLab's Handbook, for instance, allocates 40 percent to distributed leadership and 30 percent to digital trust—closely reflecting its infrastructural transparency and flat governance model. In contrast, Grab's ESG Reports devote 50 percent to systemic resilience and 30 percent to digital trust, emphasizing infrastructure and regulation alignment more than cultural co-creation.

(2) Cultural Codification and Documentation Density

Nubank's "Nu Code" and related artifacts allocate 50 percent of their weight to adaptive culture, confirming a strong orientation toward values modularity, co-authored rituals, and onboarding design. Klarna's Career Page documents show a split focus between leadership (40 percent) and adaptive culture (30 percent), but allocate only 10 percent each to trust and systemic resilience—underscoring the interpretive gap between documented aspirations and practice tensions noted in Section 5.4.

(3) Balanced Documentation Models

Andela's EPIC values and operational handbooks present the most balanced documentation profile, with weights between 20 and 30 percent across all four DRLC dimensions. This suggests a deliberate codification strategy where cultural values, governance systems, and infrastructure are co-represented for distributed alignment in a remote-first context.

These document-based insights serve two analytical functions: First, they reveal where firms strategically encode DRLC elements in written form, which is critical for scaling culture and governance in asynchronous or global contexts. Second, they help differentiate between firms whose leadership cultures are performatively enacted versus those whose ethos is structurally documented and accessible to stakeholders.

Figure 3. Thematic Emphasis of Organizational Documents across DRLC Dimensions

FINDINGS AND DISCUSSION

This discussion reflects a synthesis of theoretical, empirical, and documentary insights to interpret how digitally native firms cultivate resilience through leadership, trust, and cultural infrastructure. The analysis draws from three methodological streams: theoretical grounding in sociotechnical systems and platform governance, multi-case investigation across six digitally native organizations, and a document-based thematic mapping. Each stream contributes to the interpretation of how leadership configurations, trust mechanisms, and cultural constructs interact to shape resilient capacities in contemporary digital environments. The discussion is structured around three guiding questions, each addressed as an emergent theme across levels of analysis.

Reframing Leadership as Infrastructure-Embedded Practice

(RQ1: How is leadership conceptualized and enacted in digitally native firms?)

The evolution of leadership in digitally native firms departs from classical notions of positional authority and aligns more closely with infrastructural affordances. Recent research emphasizes that effective digital leadership is less about hierarchical control and more about enabling innovation through system-level structures and routines (Sacavém et al., 2025). Leadership is no longer the exclusive domain of designated individuals but is enacted through participatory routines, embedded tools, and transparent documentation systems—practices that enhance firms' performance by embedding leadership functions within digital transformation pathways (Senadjki et al., 2024). This observation echoes the theoretical shift from behavioral traits to system-enabled coordination. Rather than occupying roles, leaders emerge through contribution, version-controlled engagement, and collaborative problem-solving practices that are sustained and made visible through platform infrastructure, such as Git repositories, issue trackers, and continuous documentation (Siva Karthik Devineni, 2020).

Across cases, practices such as editable handbooks, decision trails, and routine-based authority indicate that leadership is less about directing from above and more about enabling from within. These mechanisms create shared decision ownership and empower employees through ritualized collaboration (Barker Scott & Manning, 2022). The document evidence reinforces this shift by showing that firms with high thematic density around leadership encode governance in design artifacts such as onboarding guides, OKRs, and documentation portals—rather than in managerial charisma. When platforms scaffold leadership visibility and enable context-responsive decision-making, authority is distributed not merely as a value but as an operational reality. However, platform-mediated leadership must also navigate risks posed by emerging digital security models. For instance, Zero Trust Architectures, if poorly implemented, can disrupt informal trust dynamics and inhibit leadership emergence (Shahzad & Lu, 2023). Scholars have debated whether such models act as protective mechanisms or inadvertently erode autonomy and collaboration (Salminen, 2023). Indeed, when organizational systems prioritize surveillance over engagement, trust becomes conditional and potentially undermines leadership credibility (Oladimeji, 2025). This reconceptualization suggests that in platform-native environments, leadership is infrastructural rather than interpersonal. The design of systems, therefore, plays a determining role in whether leadership is inclusive, traceable, and adaptive.

Trust as a Reflexive, Contextual, and Systemic Design Feature

(RQ2: How is trust constructed and sustained in digitally mediated work environments?)

Trust in digitally native firms cannot be treated as a cultural residue of interpersonal rapport. Rather, it is architected through systemic routines, ethical design defaults, and platform-mediated feedback loops. Research in HCI emphasizes that user trust in AI-enabled systems relies on well-designed transparency, socio-ethical features, and user-centric involvement throughout development, not merely interpersonal rapport (Bach et al., 2022; Firmino de Souza et al., 2025). At the surface, practices such as open OKRs, asynchronous check-ins, and team-based reflections appear as managerial innovations. At a deeper level, they reveal an organizational commitment to embedding trust in infrastructure.

Trust is less a product of interpersonal familiarity and more a function of systemic transparency and designed autonomy. Studies on conversational AI highlight how privacy, security, and trust perceptions are deeply intertwined, implying that infrastructural design shapes trust more than personal rapport (Leschanowsky et al., 2024). However, the construction of trust is not universal or culturally neutral. Document analysis reveals significant variation in how trust is codified across firms. While some emphasize radical transparency, others balance visibility with discretion to align with regional norms or protect psychological safety.

This finding underscores that trust-by-design must be reflexive to avoid unintentionally replicating surveillance under the guise of openness. For example, display of algorithmic outputs without interpretability may backfire creating anxiety rather than safety (Visser et al., 2023). Indeed, literature on automation and trust warns that unaccountable algorithms can eclipse human discretion and undermine psychological safety (Razin & Feigh, 2023). Trust, therefore, becomes a design-sensitive outcome, emerging at the intersection of technological systems and sociocultural expectations. In resilient firms, trust is cultivated not by reducing friction but by calibrating visibility, voice, and accountability. Approaches like "Transparency by Design" offer principled guidance on embedding transparency as a core system attribute—balancing openness with context-appropriate boundaries (Diakopoulos et al., 2020).

Culture as Modular Infrastructure and Agentic Feedback System

(RQ3: How do digitally native firms construct and evolve resilient organizational cultures?)

The construction of culture in digitally native firms is an iterative, infrastructural process rather than a static transmission of shared values (Leal-Rodríguez et al., 2023). Culture is no longer inherited through co-location or informal osmosis. It is intentionally scaffolded through documentation practices, feedback rituals, and collaborative systems (Butt et al., 2024). These artifacts do not merely reflect culture, they constitute it. Cultural behaviours are operationalized through onboarding kits, asynchronous rituals, and employee-authored handbooks that embed norms into tools and platforms (Petrilli et al., 2022).

Resilience within this model arises when culture becomes modular, editable, and reflexive. Firms that continuously adapt cultural practices in response to environmental changes or internal feedback demonstrate greater systemic durability (Zhen et al., 2021). When cultural mechanisms become too rigid or misaligned with infrastructural realities, the result is fragmentation or burnout. Conversely, when culture is synchronized with system behaviours and employee experiences, it enhances both engagement and adaptability (Wiese et al., 2024).

From the document corpus, it is evident that some firms operationalize culture with high coherence, ensuring that values, systems, and daily routines align. Others show a thinner cultural layer, where aspirational statements are not supported by responsive infrastructure. This divergence suggests that resilient cultures are not created by slogans or even intentions, but by the recursive alignment between design, discourse, and lived experience (Leal-Rodríguez et al., 2023).

Figure 4. Process Logic of DRLC

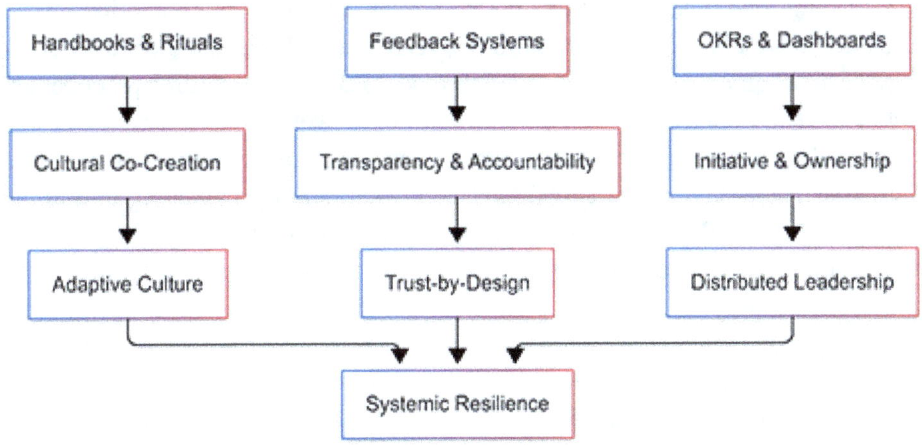

Resilience as Co-Production of Leadership, Trust, and Culture

The three DRLC dimensions—distributed leadership, trust-by-design, and adaptive culture—are not independent mechanisms. Rather, they form an interactive system of co-production. Resilience is not a linear result of isolated practices but emerges when these dimensions reinforce each other (Awad & Martín-Rojas, 2024). Where leadership is distributed without trust, coordination falters (Abson, Schofield, & Kennell, 2024). Where culture is adaptive without leadership clarity, coherence dissolves. The findings suggest that resilience is the emergent property of systems that are designed to be participatory, reflexive, and ethically calibrated.

This understanding is visually supported by the DRLC process model in Figure 4, which illustrates how infrastructural design elements—such as version-controlled documentation, transparent feedback systems, and modular rituals—mediate behavioural enactments that sustain systemic resilience. Each firm's trajectory demonstrates that resilience is not a reactive stance but an architectural quality. It is cultivated through continuous design, participatory alignment, and ethical stewardship.

Practical Implications

The practical implications of the DRLC framework span across HR managers, policymakers, and digital leaders, emphasizing the need for structural transformation in how leadership, trust, and culture are operationalized in digitally native firms. For HR professionals, it calls for a fundamental shift from hierarchical and tenure-based systems to models that recognize contribution, encourage participatory leadership, and enable asynchronous collaboration. Trust must be embedded through design, by replacing top-down evaluations with co-created feedback systems that respect autonomy, ensure fairness, and are culturally sensitive. Inclusion should move beyond rhetoric to become structurally encoded through localized onboarding practices and platforms that allow employees to shape and evolve workplace culture.

For policymakers, the DRLC model urges the development of regulatory frameworks that match the complexity of digital work. This includes mandating algorithmic accountability in HR systems, conducting regular governance audits with worker participation, and enforcing ethical standards in data handling and remote infrastructure access. Equity and psychological safety must be recognized as fundamental labour rights in digital economies, not merely as organizational responsibilities.

For digital leaders, DRLC reframes leadership and culture as integral components of platform architecture. Resilience is achieved when platforms are designed with transparency, participatory governance, and embedded trust signals. Leaders are encouraged to adopt a design justice approach that respects neurodiversity, regional diversity, and ethical defaults. By co-creating governance with employees and enabling editable documentation systems, digital resilience becomes not just a concept, but a living, adaptive reality embedded into daily operations. In sum, the DRLC framework transforms resilience from a reactive goal into a proactive design principle, anchoring inclusion, adaptability, and ethical infrastructure at the heart of organizational practice.

CONCLUSION AND FUTURE RESEARCH

This chapter introduces the Digital Resilient Leadership Culture (DRLC) framework as a holistic model for understanding and designing leadership, trust, and organizational culture in digitally native firms. It asserts that resilience does not emerge spontaneously in response to disruption but is intentionally cultivated through infrastructural decisions that distribute authority, embed ethical trust, and promote adaptive cultural practices. The chapter's core contributions include the synthesis of four major scholarly traditions—systems theory, digital sociology, organizational behaviour, and cross-cultural leadership into a unified, actionable framework. Through case studies from six global firms, the limitations of conventional HR practices rooted in hierarchy and control are highlighted, making a strong case for inclusive, participatory, and flexible approaches. The analysis underscores that the future of work cannot be understood through a single disciplinary lens, but rather requires an integrated perspective that bridges people, platforms, and policy. Future research is encouraged to extend the DRLC framework through quantitative validation of its constructs, longitudinal studies on its evolution during digital transformation, sector-specific explorations of its applicability, and contextual adaptations for hybrid firms and emerging economies. Ultimately, DRLC offers both a conceptual foundation and strategic direction for building human-centred, adaptable, and ethically resilient organizations in an increasingly digital world.

REFERENCES

Abson, E., Schofield, P., & Kennell, J. (2024). Making shared leadership work: The importance of trust in project-based organisations. *International Journal of Project Management, 42*(2), 102575. DOI: 10.1016/j.ijproman.2024.102575

Agarwal, S. (2024). The profound impact of virtual communication technologies on team collaboration in the contemporary work environment. *International Journal of Embedded Systems & Emerging Technologies, 10*(1). Advance online publication. DOI: 10.37591/IJESET

Andela. (2022a). *E.P.I.C. core values*. Andela. https://uploads-ssl.webflow.com/6480f74670678239cc947755/64e386b86fbf92d515446281_AND_EPICValues_2022.pdf

Andela. (2023a). *Decoding distributed work: Unlock the power of remote and global talent* [White paper]. Andela. https://hire.andela.com/rs/449-UCH-555/images/DecodingDistributedWork.pdf?version=0

Arora, S., & Hastings, J. (2024). *Microsegmented cloud network architecture using open-source tools for a zero trust foundation. arXiv*. https://doi.org//arXiv.2411.12162DOI: 10.1109/SIN63213.2024.10871361

Asfahani, A. M. (2025). *Navigating digital leadership: Unraveling the dynamics of remote work environments. TEM Journal, 14*(1), 823–835. https://doi.org/DOI: 10.18421/TEM141-73

Atlassian & Trello. (2020). *Work from anywhere: How Trello's leadership team built a thriving hybrid work culture at scale* [Ebook]. Atlassian. https://pages.eml.atlassian.com/rs/594-ATC-127/images/WORK-9%20Work%20From%20Anywhere%20Ebook.pdf

Atlassian. (2022, December 12). *A successful remote work strategy starts with trust*. Atlassian. https://www.atlassian.com/blog/loom/remote-work-strategy

Atlassian Corporation. (2023, October 12). *Atlassian to acquire Loom to supercharge team collaboration* [Press release]. Business Wire. https://www.businesswire.com/news/home/20231012832576/en/Atlassian-to-Acquire-Loom-to-Supercharge-Team-Collaboration

Atlassian. (n.d.-a). *How to run a blameless postmortem*. Atlassian. https://www.atlassian.com/incident-management/postmortem/blameless

Atlassian. (n.d.). *Team Playbook examples*. Atlassian. https://www.atlassian.com/team-playbook/examples

Austin, J. (2020, December 4). *Ethical artificial intelligence: The most important movement you've never heard of.* Atlassian. https://www.atlassian.com/blog/technology/ethical-artificial-intelligence

Avtalion, Z., Aviv, I., Hadar, I., Luria, G., & Bar-Gil, O. (2024). Digital Infrastructure as a New Organizational Digital Climate Dimension. *Applied Sciences (Basel, Switzerland), 14*(19), 8592. DOI: 10.3390/app14198592

Awad, J. A. R., & Martín-Rojas, R. (2024). Digital transformation influence on organisational resilience through organisational learning and innovation. *Journal of Innovation and Entrepreneurship, 13*(1), 69. DOI: 10.1186/s13731-024-00405-4

Bach, T. A., Khan, A., Hallock, H., Beltrão, G., & Sousa, S. (2022). A systematic literature review of user trust in AI-enabled systems: An HCI perspective. *International Journal of Human-Computer Interaction.* Advance online publication. DOI: 10.1080/10447318.2022.2138826

Barker Scott, B. A., & Manning, M. R. (2022). Designing the Collaborative Organization: A Framework for how Collaborative Work, Relationships, and Behaviors Generate Collaborative Capacity. *The Journal of Applied Behavioral Science, 60*(1), 149–193. DOI: 10.1177/00218863221106245

Bilderback, S., & Kilpatrick, M. D. (2024). Global perspectives on redefining workplace presence: The impact of remote work on organizational culture. *Journal of Ethics in Entrepreneurship and Technology, 4*(1), 62–72. DOI: 10.1108/JEET-08-2024-0023

Bolden, R. (2011). Distributed leadership in organizations: A review of theory and research. *International Journal of Management Reviews, 13*(3), 251–269. DOI: 10.1111/j.1468-2370.2011.00306.x

Breidbach, C. F., Joshi, A. M., Twigg, A., & Dickens, G. (2025). Orchestrating Digital Resilience: A Clinical IS Study of an Everything-as-a-Service Technology Strategy. *European Journal of Information Systems, 34*(5), 781–798. DOI: 10.1080/0960085X.2024.2435975

Butt, A., Imran, F., Helo, P., & Kantola, J. (2024). Strategic design of culture for digital transformation. *Long Range Planning, 57*(2), 102415. DOI: 10.1016/j.lrp.2024.102415

Cardoso, A., Figueiredo, J., Oliveira, I., & Pocinho, M. (2025). From Crisis to Opportunity: Digital Transformation, Digital Business Models, and Organizational Resilience in the Post-Pandemic Era. *Administrative Sciences, 15*(6), 193. DOI: 10.3390/admsci15060193

Chakravorti, B., Chaturvedi, R. S., Miller, R., Fabyanske, J., & Ait Hssayene, S. (2023). *Advancing the future of work in Africa through digital transformation: The role of systems orchestrators* [Report]. Digital Planet, The Fletcher School, Tufts University. https://digitalplanet.tufts.edu/wp-content/uploads/2023/09/Dalberg-Report-September-2023.pdf

Constantinides, P., Henfridsson, O., & Parker, G. G. (2018). Introduction—Platforms and infrastructures in the digital age. *Information Systems Research, 29*(2), 381–400. DOI: 10.1287/isre.2018.0794

de Souza Santos, R. E., & Ralph, P. (2022). *A grounded theory of coordination in remote-first and hybrid software teams*. In *Proceedings of the 44th International Conference on Software Engineering (ICSE '22)* (pp. 25–35). Association for Computing Machinery. https://doi.org/DOI: 10.1145/3510003.3510105

Degbey, W. Y., & Einola, K. (2020). Resilience in virtual teams: Developing the capacity to bounce back. *Applied Psychology, 69*(4), 1301–1337. Advance online publication. DOI: 10.1111/apps.12220

Devineni, S. K. (2020). Version Control Systems (VCS) the Pillars of Modern Software Development: Analyzing the Past, Present, and Anticipating Future Trends. [IJSR]. *International Journal of Scientific Research, 9*(12), 1816–1829. https://www.doi.org/10.21275/SR24127210817

Dongxian, L., & Batool, H. (2024). Influence of distributed leadership on employee innovative behaviour: The mediating role of psychological empowerment. *Journal of Innovation and Entrepreneurship, 13*(1), 82. DOI: 10.1186/s13731-024-00448-7

Duchek, S. (2020). Organizational resilience: A capability-based conceptualization. *Business Research, 13*(1), 215–246. DOI: 10.1007/s40685-019-0085-7

Editorial, N. (2023, July 4). *AI at Nubank: how one of the largest digital banks in the world uses artificial intelligence*. Building Nubank. https://building.nubank.com/ai-at-nubank-how-one-of-the-largest-digital-banks-in-the-world-uses-artificial-intelligence/

Editorial, N. (2024, September 3). *Make the extraordinary happen: Learn how we put the customer at the center of all our decisions*. Building Nubank. https://building.nubank.com/make-the-extraordinary-happen-customer-at-the-center/

Editorial, N. (2025, April 2). *A journey of growth at Nu: How Nut's dynamic culture fuels innovation and empowers careers. Building Nubank*. https://building.nubank.com/a-journey-of-growth-at-nu/

Editorial, N. (2025, December 17). *Inside Nubank: Discover the daily life of those who make the extraordinary happen.* Nubank Building. https://building.nubank.com/inside-nubank-discover-the-daily-life-of-those-who-make-the-extraordinary-happen/

Edmondson, A. C. (1999). Psychological safety and learning behavior in work teams. *Administrative Science Quarterly*, *44*(2), 350–383. https://www.jstor.org/stable/2666999. DOI: 10.2307/2666999

Ejiofor, O., Olusoga, O., & Akinsola, A. (2025). Zero trust architecture: A paradigm shift in network security. *Computer Science & IT Research Journal*, *6*(3), 104–124. DOI: 10.51594/csitrj.v6i3.1871

Eriksson, A., Andersson Bäck, M., Elmersjö, M., & Gillberg, G. (2025). Forms of distributed leadership: A case study of six workplaces in eldercare. *BMC Health Services Research*, *25*(1), 300. DOI: 10.1186/s12913-025-12417-1 PMID: 39987088

Eurofound. (2020). *Employee monitoring and surveillance: The challenges of digitalisation* (Research report). Publications Office of the European Union. https://assets.eurofound.europa.eu/f/279033/948fcea09e/ef20008en.pdf

Firican, D. A. (2024). Creating a Digital Culture for Digital Transformation: A Literature Review of Practical Steps. Proceedings of the International Conference on Business Excellence, 18(1), 2024. 1018-1028. DOI: 10.2478/picbe-2024-0089

Gambo, M. L., & Almulhem, A. (2025). *Zero trust architecture: A systematic literature review.* arXiv. https://doi.org//arXiv.2503.11659DOI: 10.36227/techrxiv.173933211.18231232/v1

GitLab. (n.d.-a). *TeamOps: Redefining teamwork for the modern era.* The GitLab Handbook. Retrieved June 19, 2025, from https://handbook.gitlab.com/handbook/teamops/

GitLab. (n.d.-b). *Remote Playbook.* GitLab. Retrieved June 15, 2025, from https://learn.gitlab.com/allremote/remote-playbook

GitLab. (n.d.-c). *Psychological safety.* In The GitLab Handbook. Retrieved June 18, 2025, from https://handbook.gitlab.com/handbook/leadership/emotional-intelligence/psychological-safety/

GitLab. (n.d.-d). *TeamOps.* In The GitLab Handbook. Retrieved June 17, 2025, from https://handbook.gitlab.com/handbook/teamops/

Goldschein, E. (2022, July 1). *How to build a strong remote team culture.* Atlassian. https://www.atlassian.com/blog/teamwork/remote-team-culture?

Gong, R., & Tan, J.-E. (2023). *Digital governance: Justice in an unequal world.* Khazanah Research Institute. https://cdn.prod.website-files.com/684b55df28cddcbe52b406f2/68b7e9b63b5d23521a0d4497_68a68560dcb46f51847094b4_230426-20Digital-20Governance-20--20Justice-20in-20an-20Unequal-20World.pdf

Grab. (2022). *Environmental, Social, and Governance Report 2022.* https://s205.q4cdn.com/179588156/files/doc_downloads/esg/Grab-ESG-Report-2022.pdf

Grab. (2023). *Environmental, Social, and Governance Report 2023.* https://s205.q4cdn.com/179588156/files/doc_downloads/esg/Grab-ESG-Report-2023.pdf

Grab. (2024). *Environmental, Social, and Governance Report 2024.* https://assets.grab.com/wp-content/uploads/media/si/reports/2024/Grab-ESG-Report-2024.pdf

Guttman Development Strategies, Inc. (2020, October 5). *Mars, Inc. – GDS 30 Years* [Blog post]. GuttmanDev. https://www.guttmandev.com/post/high-performance-teams-mars-inc

Harris, A., Jones, M., & Ismail, N. (2022). Distributed leadership: Taking a retrospective and contemporary view of the evidence base. *School Leadership & Management, 42*(5), 438–456. DOI: 10.1080/13632434.2022.2109620

Höddinghaus, M., Nohe, C., & Hertel, G. (2023). Leadership in Virtual Work Settings: What We Know, What We Do Not Know, and What We Need to Do. *European Journal of Work and Organizational Psychology, 33*(2), 188–212. DOI: 10.1080/1359432X.2023.2250079

Hughes, M., Overney, C., Kamra, A., Tepale, J., Hamby, E., Jasim, M., & Roy, D. (2025). *Voice to vision: Enhancing civic decision-making through co-designed data infrastructure* (arXiv:2505.14853) [Preprint]. arXiv. https://doi.org//arXiv.2505.14853DOI: 10.48550

Insider, B. (2025, May 22). *Klarna's CEO leans into his company's image, using an AI doppelganger to deliver earnings highlights.* Business Insider. https://www.businessinsider.com/klarna-buy-now-pay-later-ai-ceo-sebastian-siemiatkowski-earnings-2025-5

Jacobo-Romero, M., & Freitas, A. (2021). *Microeconomic foundations of decentralised organisations.* In *Proceedings of the 36th Annual ACM Symposium on Applied Computing (SAC '21)* (pp. 282–290). Association for Computing Machinery. https://doi.org/DOI: 10.1145/3412841.3441911

Jhaver, S., Frey, S., & Zhang, A. (2023). *Decentralizing platform power: A design space of multi-level governance in online social platforms* (arXiv:2108.12529) [Preprint]. arXiv. https://doi.org//arXiv.2108.12529DOI: 10.48550

Kadolkar, I., Kepes, S., & Subramony, M. (2024). Algorithmic management in the gig economy: A systematic review and research integration. *Journal of Organizational Behavior*. Advance online publication. DOI: 10.1002/job.2831

Kandane Arachchige Don, I. S., Richter, A., & Tate, M. (2024). *The transition to remote work: A sociotechnical perspective*. In Proceedings of the Pacific Asia Conference on Information Systems (PACIS 2024) (Paper 6). Association for Information Systems. https://aisel.aisnet.org/pacis2024/track08_digtech_fow/track08_digtech_fow/6

Kitterman, T. (2023, October 9). *How Atlassian's peer recognition program reinforces its culture*. Great Place To Work. https://www.greatplacetowork.com/resources/blog/atlassian-peer-recognition-program

Klarna. (2024, February 27). *Klarna AI assistant handles two-thirds of customer service chats in its first month* [Press release]. Klarna. https://www.klarna.com/international/press/klarna-ai-assistant-handles-two-thirds-of-customer-service-chats-in-its-first-month/

Klarna. (n.d.). *Our culture*. Klarna Careers. https://www.klarna.com/careers/our-culture/

Kloepfer, S., & Carbon, C.-C. (2025). Leadership and trust in virtual teams. *Human Systems Management*, *44*(5), 890–900. DOI: 10.1177/01672533251331488

Kwet, M. (2019). Digital colonialism: US empire and the new imperialism in the Global South. *Race & Class*, *60*(4), 3–26. DOI: 10.1177/0306396818823172

Leal-Rodríguez, A. L., Sanchís-Pedregosa, C., Moreno-Moreno, A. M., & Leal-Millán, A. G. (2023). Digitalization beyond technology: Proposing an explanatory and predictive model for digital culture in organizations. *Journal of Innovation & Knowledge*, *8*(3), 100409. DOI: 10.1016/j.jik.2023.100409

Lengnick-Hall, C. A., Beck, T. E., & Lengnick-Hall, M. L. (2011). Developing a capacity for organizational resilience through strategic human resource management. *Human Resource Management Review*, *21*(3), 243–255. DOI: 10.1016/j.hrmr.2010.07.001

Leschanowsky, A., Rech, S., Popp, B., & Bäckström, T. (2024). *Evaluating privacy, security, and trust perceptions in conversational AI: A systematic review* (arXiv:2406.09037) [Preprint]. arXiv. https://doi.org//arXiv.2406.09037DOI: 10.48550

Li, J., Yang, Y., Zhang, R., & Lee, Y.-C. (2024). *Overconfident and unconfident AI hinder human–AI collaboration* (arXiv:2402.07632v3) [Preprint]. arXiv. https://doi.org//arXiv.2402.07632DOI: 10.48550

Licorish, S. A., & MacDonell, S. G. (2021). *Self-organising roles in agile globally distributed teams* (arXiv:2106.06154) [Preprint]. arXiv. https://doi.org//arXiv.2106.06154DOI: 10.48550

Lorentzen, A.-C. R. (2022). Digital transformation as distributed leadership: Firing the change agent. *Procedia Computer Science, 196*, 245–254. DOI: 10.1016/j.procs.2021.12.011

Mayer, R. C., Davis, J. H., & Schoorman, F. D. (1995). An Integrative Model of Organizational Trust. *Academy of Management Review, 20*(3), 709–734. DOI: 10.2307/258792

Maznevski, M. L., & Chudoba, K. M. (2000). Bridging space over time: Global virtual team dynamics and effectiveness. *Organization Science, 11*(5), 473–492. DOI: 10.1287/orsc.11.5.473.15200

Mbare, B., Perkiö, M., & Koivusalo, M. (2024). Algorithmic management, wellbeing and platform work: Understanding the psychosocial risks and experiences of food couriers in Finland. *Labour & Industry, 34*(4), 386–411. DOI: 10.1080/10301763.2024.2423442

Meadows, D. H. (2008). *Thinking in systems: A primer*. Chelsea Green Publishing.

Moon, L. (2023, June 15). *Trello and Confluence: The perfect teamwork combo*. Atlassian. https://www.atlassian.com/blog/trello/trello-and-confluence-the-perfect-teamwork-combo

Mozammel, S., Irum, S., & Abdulla, I. S. (2025). Impact of remote work on organizational culture and employee performance. *Journal of Posthumanism, 5*(7), 441–454. DOI: 10.63332/joph.v5i7.2803

Naikar, N., & Elix, B. (2021). Designing for self-organisation in sociotechnical systems: Resilience engineering, cognitive work analysis, and the diagram of work organisation possibilities. *Cognition Technology and Work, 23*(1), 23–37. DOI: 10.1007/s10111-019-00595-y

National Institute of Standards and Technology. (2020). *Zero Trust Architecture (Special Publication 800-207)*. U.S. Department of Commerce. https://doi.org/DOI: 10.6028/NIST.SP.800-207

Nguyen-Thu, G., & Munn, L. (2024). Taming the algorithm: The platform realism of GrabBike delivery workers. *New Media & Society, 27*(11), 6038–6056. DOI: 10.1177/14614448241262417

Nielsen, J. A., Mathiassen, L., Benfeldt, O., Madsen, S., Haslam, C., & Penttinen, E. (2023). Organizational resilience and digital resources: Evidence from responding to exogenous shock by going virtual. *International Journal of Information Management, 73*, 102687. DOI: 10.1016/j.ijinfomgt.2023.102687

Nolan, B. (2024, February 28). *Klarna says its AI assistant is doing the work of 700 people after putting the brakes on hiring.* Business Insider. https://www.businessinsider.com/klarna-ai-chatbot-work-700-people-2024-2

Oladimeji, G. (2025). *Rethinking trust in the digital age: An investigation of zero trust architecture's social consequences on organizational culture, collaboration, and knowledge sharing* (arXiv:2504.14601) [Preprint]. arXiv. https://doi.org//arXiv.2504.14601DOI: 10.48550

PASQUALE. F. (2015). *The Black Box Society: The Secret Algorithms That Control Money and Information.* Harvard University Press. https://www.jstor.org/stable/j.ctt13x0hch

Petrilli, S., Galuppo, L., & Ripamonti, S. C. (2022). Digital Onboarding: Facilitators and Barriers to Improve Worker Experience. *Sustainability (Basel), 14*(9), 5684. DOI: 10.3390/su14095684

Ponsard, C., Nihoul, B., & Touzani, M. (2024). *Modelling and classification of fairness patterns for designing sustainable information systems* (arXiv:2411.17894) [Preprint]. arXiv. https://doi.org//arXiv.2411.17894DOI: 10.48550

Powell, J., & Kleiner, A. (2022). *Andela: Case study* (International Finance Corporation Case Study). International Finance Corporation. https://www.ifc.org/content/dam/ifc/doc/mgrt/ifc-casestudy-andela-v3.pdf

Queiroz, M. (2023, March 22). *How decision-making works at Nubank.* Building Nubank. https://building.nubank.com/how-decision-making-works-nubank/

Razin, Y. S., & Feigh, K. M. (2023). *Converging measures and an emergent model: A meta-analysis of human-automation trust questionnaires* (arXiv:2303.13799) [Preprint]. arXiv. https://doi.org//arXiv.2303.13799DOI: 10.48550

Rendall, A. (2024, January 3). *4 ways to build a company culture that spans in-office and remote teams.* Andela. https://www.andela.com/blog-posts/4-ways-to-build-a-company-culture-that-spans-in-office-and-remote-teams

Sacavém, A., de Bem Machado, A., dos Santos, J. R., Palma-Moreira, A., Belchior-Rocha, H., & Au-Yong-Oliveira, M. (2025). Leading in the Digital Age: The Role of Leadership in Organizational Digital Transformation. *Administrative Sciences, 15*(2), 43. DOI: 10.3390/admsci15020043

Salminen, H. (2023). Zero Trust: The Magic Bullet or Devil's Advocate? *European Conference on Cyber Warfare and Security*, 22(1), 678–686. https://doi.org/DOI: 10.34190/eccws.22.1.1263

Schein, E. H. (2010). *Organizational Culture and Leadership* (4th ed.). Jossey-Bass.

Senadjki, A., Au Yong, H. N., Ganapathy, T., & Ogbeibu, S. (2024). Unlocking the potential: The impact of digital leadership on firms' performance through digital transformation. *Journal of Business and Socio-economic Development*, *4*(2), 161–177. DOI: 10.1108/JBSED-06-2023-0050

Shahzad, U., & Lu, C. (2023). *The effect of Zero Trust model on organizations* (Master's thesis, Lund University, Department of Informatics). Lund University Publications. https://lup.lub.lu.se/student-papers/record/9123176

Shelby, R., Rismani, S., Henne, K., Moon, A., Rostamzadeh, N., Nicholas, P., Yilla, N., Gallegos, J., Smart, A., Garcia, E., & Virk, G. (2023). *Sociotechnical harms of algorithmic systems: Scoping a taxonomy for harm reduction* (arXiv:2210.05791v3) [Preprint]. arXiv. https://doi.org//arXiv.2210.05791DOI: 10.1145/3600211.3604673

Sparks, R. (n.d.). *OKRs: The ultimate guide to objectives and key results*. Atlassian. https://www.atlassian.com/agile/agile-at-scale/okr

Stahl, G. K., & Tung, R. L. (2015). Towards a more balanced treatment of culture in international business studies: The need for positive cross-cultural scholarship. *Journal of International Business Studies*, *46*(4), 391–414. DOI: 10.1057/jibs.2014.68

Stark, D., & Pais, I. (2020). Algorithmic Management in the Platform Economy. *Sociologica*, *14*(3), 47–72. DOI: 10.6092/issn.1971-8853/12221

Svensson, I., & von Knorring, M. (2025). Connecting Distributed Leadership and Leadership-as-Practice to Increase Understanding of Leadership as Distributed in Healthcare Practice. *Journal of Change Management*, *25*(1), 11–30. DOI: 10.1080/14697017.2025.2453136

Terra, L. (2018, June 26). *Getting started at Nubank*. Medium. https://medium.com/nubank-design/getting-started-at-nubank-3d91fd9442d3

Tkalich, A., Smite, D., Andersen, N. H., & Moe, N. B. (2022). *What happens to psychological safety when going remote?* (arXiv:2208.12454) [Preprint]. arXiv. https://doi.org//arXiv.2208.12454DOI: 10.48550

Visser, R., Peters, T. M., Scharlau, I., & Hammer, B. (2023). *Trust, distrust, and appropriate reliance in (X)AI: A survey of empirical evaluation of user trust* (arXiv:2312.02034) [Preprint]. arXiv. https://doi.org//arXiv.2312.02034DOI: 10.48550

Wang, T., Lin, X., & Sheng, F. (2022). Digital leadership and exploratory innovation: From the dual perspectives of strategic orientation and organizational culture. *Frontiers in Psychology, 13*, 902693. DOI: 10.3389/fpsyg.2022.902693 PMID: 36176785

Wang, Z. (2024). *The strategic analysis of Grab's strategic dominance in Southeast Asia. Journal of International Economics, Global Governance* (*J. Int. Eco. Glo. Gov.*, 1(3), 58–70). Macao Scientific Publishers. https://www.mospbs.com/uploads/files/2024/08/20240811/01dfb6154fb0cbea6c9eee25f87d50bd.pdf

Wiese, S. A., Lehmann, J., & Beckmann, M. (2024). *Organizational culture and the usage of Industry 4.0 technologies: Evidence from Swiss businesses* (arXiv:2412.12752) [Preprint]. arXiv. https://doi.org//arXiv.2412.12752DOI: 10.48550

Xu, M., Zhang, Y., Sun, H., Tang, Y., & Li, J. (2024). How digital transformation enhances corporate innovation performance: The mediating roles of big data capabilities and organizational agility. *Heliyon, 10*(14), e34905. DOI: 10.1016/j.heliyon.2024.e34905 PMID: 39149071

Zara, C. (2024, February 27). *Klarna says its AI assistant does the work of 700 people after it laid off 700 people*. Fast Company. https://www.fastcompany.com/91039401/klarna-ai-virtual-assistant-does-the-work-of-700-humans-after-layoffs

Zhen, Z., Yousaf, Z., Radulescu, M., & Yasir, M. (2021). Nexus of Digital Organizational Culture, Capabilities, Organizational Readiness, and Innovation: Investigation of SMEs Operating in the Digital Economy. *Sustainability (Basel), 13*(2), 720. DOI: 10.3390/su13020720

Ziewitz, M. (2015). Governing Algorithms: Myth, Mess, and Methods: Myth, Mess, and Methods. *Science, Technology & Human Values, 41*(1), 3–16. DOI: 10.1177/0162243915608948 PMID: 25866425

KEY TERMS AND DEFINITIONS

Adaptive Culture: A flexible and editable organizational culture constructed through digital rituals, asynchronous documentation, and participatory feedback mechanisms; it evolves in real-time through platform-enabled collaboration.

Asynchronous Collaboration: Work coordination that occurs across different times and locations, relying on digital tools and platforms rather than real-time, in-person communication.

Design Justice: A principle advocating for the co-creation of digital systems that are inclusive, equitable, and sensitive to power dynamics, particularly relevant in global, intercultural work environments.

Digital Resilient Leadership Culture (DRLC): An integrated framework that explains how leadership, trust, and culture co-evolve within digitally native firms to produce systemic resilience through three design pillars: distributed authority, trust-by-design, and adaptive culture.

Digital Trust: Trust established through infrastructural and algorithmic systems, including transparent design, role-based access, and ethical defaults, rather than interpersonal relationships.

Digitally Native Firms: Organizations born in digital environments that operate using platform-based, cloud-native, and remote-first models, with no legacy dependence on physical or hierarchical structures.

Distributed Leadership: A leadership model where influence and authority are shared across organizational members rather than centralized in formal hierarchies; enacted through participatory systems and collaborative routines.

Ethical Automation: Automation practices aligned with human values, ensuring transparency, inclusion, and fairness in AI-driven decision systems and workflows.

Modular Culture: A form of organizational culture composed of decentralized, co-created, and editable components that can be updated to reflect evolving team values and contexts.

Platform Governance: The use of digital infrastructure, such as workflow systems and algorithmic protocols, to manage decision-making, authority, and accountability in distributed organizations.

Psychological Safety: The belief that one can take interpersonal risks without fear of punishment; in digital environments, this is enabled through system design, transparent communication, and protective defaults.

Sociotechnical Systems: Work systems that integrate human, organizational, and technological elements; optimal performance depends on the joint design and co-evolution of both social and technical subsystems.

Systemic Resilience: The organization's ability to adapt, self-correct, and maintain cohesion during volatility, enabled by interlocking infrastructural, cultural, and leadership systems.

Trust-by-Design: A concept from the DRLC framework where trust is embedded into the digital infrastructure via system-level mechanisms like anonymized feedback, low-surveillance metrics, and ethical governance protocols.

Zero Trust Architecture: A cybersecurity and design principle that assumes no implicit trust and continuously verifies access and behavior through granular, role-based mechanisms; conceptually adapted for organizational trust-building in DRLC.

Chapter 11
Role of AI and Machine Learning in the Future of Talent Management

A. Rahmath Nisha
http://orcid.org/0009-0001-5146-2411
Saveetha School of Management, Saveetha Institute of Medical and Technical Sciences, Chennai, India

A. K. Subramani
http://orcid.org/0000-0003-0783-7113
Saveetha School of Management, Saveetha Institute of Medical and Technical Sciences, Chennai, India

A. R. Gayathri
http://orcid.org/0009-0003-4027-6685
Saveetha School of Management, Saveetha Institute of Medical and Technical Sciences, Chennai, India

R. Durai Pandian
http://orcid.org/0000-0003-2932-0270
Saveetha School of Management, Saveetha Institute of Medical and Technical Sciences, Chennai, India

ABSTRACT

The revolutionary technology effect of Artificial Intelligence and Machine Learning on the contemporary Human Resource Management with emphasis on the recruitment, talent analytics, and decision-making processes. It looks at how these AI technologies such as chatbots, predictive analytics, and automated decision-making tools would be utilized in improving the recruitment processes, fostering diversity,

DOI: 10.4018/979-8-3373-4307-5.ch011

and minimizing the biases when managing the people. It also examines how talent analytics, sentiment analysis, skill gap analysis will be applied in the future. The AI-based solutions in motivating the workforce planning, staff engagement, and predictive recruiting. A combination of the real-life examples of case studies and the recent research helps to understand that the way organizations are adopting AI tool is not only simplifying the processes but also creating more inclusive, strategic, and data-driven HR practices.

1. INTRODUCTION

1.1. Background of AI and ML in HRM

In the fast evolution of HR, the integration of Artificial Intelligence and Machine Learning is guiding in a new generation. These technologies offer opportunities to streamline the HR processes in order to boost the decision-making, and restructure the employee experience in an organization. The influence of these technologies from talent acquisition to performance management, involved in every aspect of HRM. The evolving role of these technologies, we seek to provide the comprehensive understanding of the prospects which shaping the future of HRM in an era which is dominated by artificial intelligence and machine learning (Basnet, 2024). In the digital era, Human Resources is undergoing a drastic transformation which moves beyond its traditional administrative role to become a strategic partner in driving the organizational success (da Silva et al., 2022, Holbeche, 2022). With the increase of automation and digitalization, the role of HR is focused on using this technology in order to enhance the efficiency, effectiveness, and employee satisfaction (Al Hamad et al., 2024, Orieno et al., 2024).

The amalgamation of Artificial Intelligence along with the Machine Learning in the HR practices is the huge transformation. Initially, HR is focused on managing the employee related tasks like recruitment, training, and performance evaluation.

1.2. Need for Technological Integration in Talent Management

In today's digital age, HR is playing a major strategic role in the organizations which focus on the workforce planning, talent management, and organizational development (Ayeni et al., 2024, Raji et al., 2024). In the organizations which strives to adapt the dynamic digital technology, HR is leading in driving the innovation. By clubbing the AI and Machine Learning in the HR practices is very important for the organizations to stay competitive in the digital era. HR processes can be revolutionized by these technologies by automating the regular tasks by analyzing the data to give the insights about employee experiences. (Chowdhury et al., 2023; Uwaoma et al., 2023).

Figure 1. Conceptual Framework of AI Integration in Talent Management showing key domains and applications.

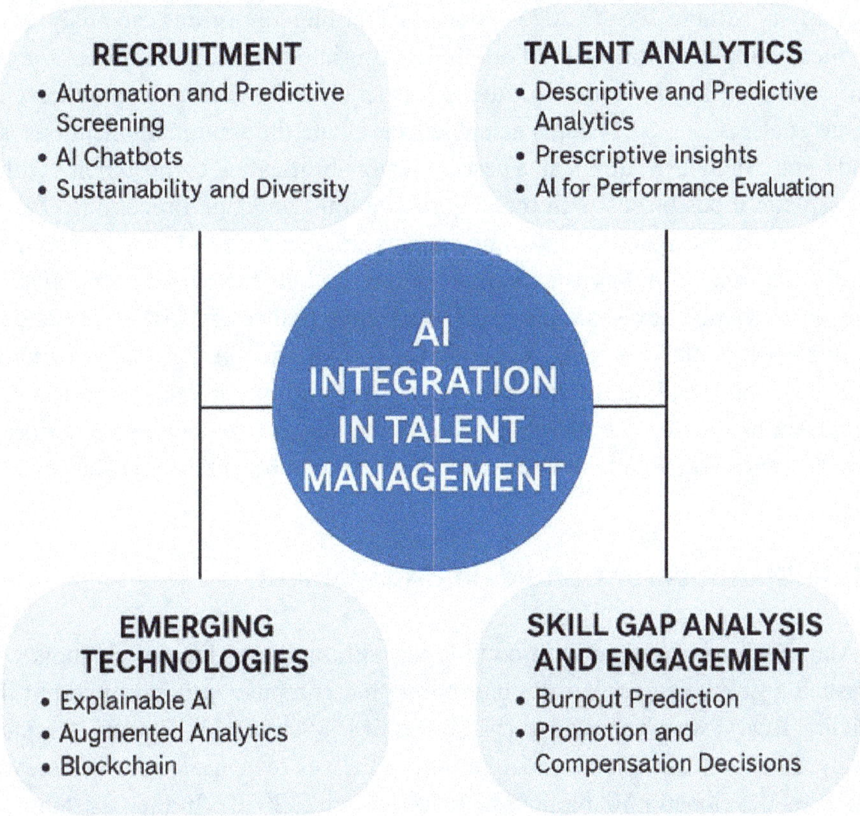

Source: (Created by Author, 2025)

2. AI TECHNOLOGIES IN RECRUITMENT

2.1. Automation and Predictive Screening

By automating countless labor-intensive operations, artificial intelligence technologies including machine learning (ML), natural language processing (NLP), and predictive analytics have transformed the recruitment process while increasing productivity (Strang & Sun, 2022). Machine learning algorithms can analyze huge volumes of applicant data to find out the appropriate qualified candidates for open positions by cutting down the time and effort required for manual resume screening (Najjar et al., 2021). AI systems can able to evaluate the written applications, spot trends, and evaluate the applicants based on their abilities and competencies without being unconscious biases with the help of Natural Language Processing (Mishra, 2017). By giving candidates real-time updates and feedback, AI-powered solutions like chatbots and digital assistants improve the candidate experience and make the hiring process more transparent as well as effective (Albassam, 2023). The key is to be more dependable, efficient, and competitive production in the industrial industry lies at the junction of human knowledge and artificial intelligence (Agrawal et al., 2024). Application of deep learning integration which is specialized in algorithm improvement, and dynamic compression methods can be suggested (Sharma et al., 2023).

2.2. AI Chatbots for Candidate Engagement

Alan Turing is credited with coming up with the novel idea of chatbots when he asked a group of people can converse with a computer program without their noticing. But AI wasn't applied to chatbots until 1988, when Jabberwacky, a chatbot that used contextual matching recognition to deliver responses based on previous talks, was developed (Adamopoulou & Moussiades, 2020). In the past ten years, chat services have emerged as the go-to method for customer service, and we are seeing an increasing number of software agents, such chatbots, take the place of human chat service agents (Adam et al., 2021). These technologies are changing the service interface from one that is mostly controlled by humans to one that is autonomous (Castillo et al., 2021). Chatbots are mostly thought of as computer programs that communicate with users through natural language and human components (Popesku, 2019).

As a result, they may converse with humans or other chatbots in human language (Adamopoulou & Moussiades, 2020). Chatbots engage with people by providing them with intelligent responses in natural language throughout text or message exchanges (Haristiani, 2019). "A computer program designed to have a conversation with a human being, especially over the internet" is how the Cambridge Dictionary defines chatbots (2023). Numerous industries, including marketing, business, entertainment, healthcare, and education, can benefit from the employment of chatbots. (Adamopoulou & Moussiades, 2020) and are capable of human-like interaction (Adam et al., 2021).

Now a days Customers are viewed as value co-creators which results of their involvement in the creation of services. While the service provider creates a value proposition by offering the chatbot along with a number of modules, the consumer creates value by attempting to collaborate (i.e., engage) with the chatbot. Since chatbots exclusively permit interactions via text or spoken dialogue, they are regarded as discrete conversational agents (Castillo et al., 2021). Voice-activated assistants and text-based methods for responding on messaging platforms make up their ecosystem (Shaheen et al., 2024). Apple's Siri and Amazon's Alexa are examples of voice assistants that can be linked into mobile devices or individual house speakers to handle tasks like emails, manage automated home appliances, and set up agendas (Adamopoulou & Moussiades, 2020).

Retrieval-based chatbots are designed to identify particular words or phrases in user communications and reply with previously recorded responses. They work best in brief, straightforward discussions in which the user asks explicit enquiries or demands certain information. On the other side, generative chatbots can use NLP algorithms to generate completely original responses. They work best in lengthier, more intricate discussions where the user can cover several subjects at once or pose more general queries. They can also get better with time and learn from user engagement. The purpose of chatbots might be either broad or instructive (Haristiani, 2019).

The abundance of information in the service sector is one of the factors driving the growing usage of chatbots, which can lower expenses and boost efficiency by managing multiple customers at once. Because they are highly responsive and offer immediate responses, they are also seen as friendlier than frequently asked questions (FAQs) (Castillo et al., 2021). Additionally, chatbots may now respond emotionally to consumers thanks to advancements in machine learning and sentiment analysis (Adamopoulou & Moussiades, 2020). He divides the chatbot's main goal into three groups: task-based, conversational, and instructive. Typically, the informative chatbot uses a database to collect the needed information and conducts the conversation with consumers.

Typical examples of instructive chatbots are the Facebook Messenger chatbot and the FAQs chatbot. Chat-based chatbots are like Aveda booking chatbot, converse with the users in a manner that is akin to a real person. Lastly, task-oriented chatbots are specialized in providing the task like style advise with the H&M digital stylist chatbot. They are distinguished by their exceptional ability to gather information and appropriately answer to queries. There is a noticeable difference between human-human and AI conversations, even with the broad advantages that chatbots offer. There are discernible variations in the interaction's duration, quality, and content. The primary distinction is typically cited as the AI's lack of human empathy (Adamopoulou & Moussiades, 2020).

2.3. Sustainability and Diversity through AI Recruitment

The Impact of AI on Sustainable Hiring, the AI has the potential to enhance the sustainability in hiring with regard to various angles, some of which are reduction of carbon footprint, promotion of diversity, and efficiency in resources. Numerous studies suggest that artificial intelligence has the ability to reduce the resources required to make a hire by automating the repetitive tasks such as resume screening, reaching out to candidates, and scheduling interviews (Chen, 2023). Besides saving time it assists us in eliminating the human intervention aspect and the recruiters are left to focus more on strategic things that help meet the sustainability goals (Holbeche, 2022).

Diversity and inclusion are one of the key spheres where AI facilitates sustainability. By minimizing human biases during hiring, AI assists companies in concentrating on their skills and qualifications, as opposed to basing their selection on attributes such as gender, race, or age (Saini and Tarkar, 2024). To give an example, AI systems anonymising profiles of candidates at the initial stages of the hiring process have proven to improve the diversity of candidate pools (Uma et al., 2023). This promotes the social pillar of sustainability by ensuring that the process of hiring is fair, inclusive, and in tandem with the equal opportunity provisions. AI can also reduce the carbon footprint of the hiring process when it comes to environmental sustainability by simplifying the hiring process remotely through digital assessments and virtual interviews which require less travelling and less paperwork (Gupta and Kumar, 2024).According to one study, companies that used AI-driven hiring procedures reported a 30% decrease in hiring-related emissions, mostly as a result of fewer travel-related activities (Müller, 2024).

2.4. Case Study: Accenture's AI-Driven Hiring

Accenture has simplified its hiring process by deploying AI-driven technology that reviews resumes, matches applicants with job requirements, and lessens selection bias. This technology analyses vast resume pools using natural language processing and machine learning to find the best candidates, giving recruiters the ability to be mindful of interviews and cultural fit tests.

3. PREDICTIVE ANALYTICS AND DECISION-MAKING IN HR

3.1. Predictive Analysis of Employee Turnover

According to (Stovel and Bontis, 2002), employee turnover may be seen as a loss or exit of intellectual capital from the employing company. Age, tenure, compensation, overall job satisfaction, and employee views of fairness were the best predictors of voluntary turnover, according to a metanalytic evaluation of studies on the subject (Cotton & Tuttle, 1986). The results of other related studies indicated that demographic or personal characteristics, particularly age, gender, ethnicity, education, and marital status, were significant predictors of voluntary employee turnover (Finkelstein et al., 2013; Holtom et al., 2008; von Hippel et al., 2013); Peterson, 2004; Sacco & Schmitt, 2005). Salary, working environment, job satisfaction, supervision, promotion, recognition, growth potential, but earnout, and other attributes were also the subject of investigations (Liu et al., 2012, Swider & Zimmerman, 2010; Heckert & Farabee, 2006, Allen & Griffeth, 2001).

3.2. Predictive AI Recruitment Tools and Quality of Hire Metrics

With the use of sophisticated models that improve productivity and decision-making precision, artificial intelligence has completely transformed hiring procedures (Ghedabna et al., 2024). Among these, machine learning methods including neural networks, random forests, and extreme gradient boosting (XGBoost) are crucial (Kavzoglu & Teke, 2022). Random forest and XGBoost, such as, are common in screenings to identify trends and predict the results, such as, has the candidate got the ability to be effective in a specific position. NLP applications, aid in sentiment analysis of applicants and parsing of resume, by identifying the valuable data in unstructured data format such as cover letter and resume. These models also liberate human resource professionals to focus on other strategic activities by automating repetitive tasks such as scheduling of interviews and screening of resumes (Gulati et al., 2024).

Also, conversational AI such as chatbots, is also used to advance the candidate experience as it offers real time feedback which improves the recruitment experience. Applicant tracking systems (ATSs) based on AI use these models to consider candidates according to the specific criteria, including experience, skills, and education level (Gupta and Rahimi Ata., 2024). Such tools make the process of hiring more efficient, and they minimize the risks of human biases because they are based on data-driven approaches (Kyliliainen, 2024).

Accuracy is one of the significant elements of AI models in the process of hiring and their effectiveness. There are many researches indicating promising results of these methods. To illustrate, monkey mode with random forest and XGBoost classifiers have demonstrated more than 95% accuracy rates in hiring related to the suitability of the candidate based on previous data of hiring personnel (Nandipati and Boddala, 2024). Similarly, predictive analytics algorithms rank the candidates based on their attributes and job requirements in order to attain high degrees of accuracy. Accuracy metrics commonly include precision, recall, and F1 scores, which can be used to evaluate the performance of such models in different recruitment situations (AI-Quhfa, 2024).

3.2.1. Quality of hire metrics

The creation of a standardized method of measurement is the core concept behind the recruiting metrics. One method for making better hiring decisions and maximising return on investment is the recruitment metrics. Metrics will be used to collect, evaluate, and make an informed recruiting decision. Measurable and comparable to established benchmarks that emphasize candidate quality, the recruitment metrics are quantifiable. Recruitment metrics are measures that HR professionals apply in order to gather, analyze, and present data throughout the recruitment process depending on a specific company. They are expected to be standard, practical, predictive, open to peer comparison, provide a benchmark of internal performance, contribute to the optimum hiring practices, and provide a payback (Prasad et al., 2019).

3.3 Algorithmic Decision-Making and Bias Mitigation

The issue concerning the creation, testing, distribution, and application of algorithms being biased should find a solution even though the quantification of the many factors that cause bias in AI algorithms is a significant first step. Numerous elaborate frameworks and checklists have been created, such as the Consolidated Standards of Reporting Trials-Artificial Intelligence, the DECIDE-AI (Lui et al., 2020), and the Translational Evaluation of Healthcare AI (TEHAI) (Reddy et al., 2021). The Checklist of AI in Medical Imaging (CLAIM) (Mongan et al., 2020), the prediction model risk of bias assessment and (CONSORT-AI) (Lui et al., 2020).

However, these tools have not particularly addressed biases that may lead to health inequities; rather, their main purpose has been to assist authors and reviewers in reporting and assessing AI algorithms. (Dankwa-Mullan et al., 2021) offered a suggested framework for incorporating racial justice, health equality, and ethical AI concepts into the AI algorithm development process.

As part of the suggestions, the needs were evaluated, current processes were described, the desired state was established, infrastructure for the AI system's development was acquired, the system was put into place, and it was monitored, assessed, and updated. Notwithstanding the significance of such a framework, the recommendations mostly addressed racial inequalities and neglected to address other under-represented patient groups where AI algorithms may cause health disparities. Throughout the AI development lifecycle, researchers can use the AI Fairness 360, an open-source toolkit, to analyse, document, and reduce bias and discrimination in machine learning models (Bellamy et al., 2019). (Kluge, 2024) Although it was made apparent that AI has enormous potential to improve healthcare globally, the guidelines stressed that, it can be accomplished if the and human rights and ethics are prioritised throughout the development and application of AI.

4. AI-DRIVEN TALENT ANALYTICS

One of the most important areas where AI has significantly impacted HRM is talent analytics. For the better decision making about hiring, performance reviews, and employee retention, talent analytics collects and analyses employee data. HR practitioners can now analyse massive datasets and derive valuable insights that inform personnel management strategies and technologies like machine learning, natural language processing, and data mining. Several crucial aspects can be distinguished in the use of AI in talent analytics: hiring, performance evaluation, and worker involvement (Ramirez & Kamal, 2023)

AI has significantly changed the hiring process by automating a number of formerly laborious and biassed procedures. Conventional hiring procedures frequently depended on manual screening and subjective standards, which reduced the effectiveness and impartiality of hiring choices. Conversely, AI-powered hiring platforms can handle large volume of application within a second by analysing resumes using NLP algorithms and matching applicants to job descriptions according to qualifications, experience, and skills. The sourcing and screening of candidates is one of the main uses of AI in hiring. Artificial intelligence (AI) systems can search corporate databases, social media sites, and a variety of job boards to find the applicants who can fit for the particular job requirements. AI-powered chatbots are also employed to interact with applicants, answering their questions in the real time and assisting them with the preliminary steps of the application procedure.

By emphasizing objective data over subjective assessments, these AI solutions not only increase recruitment efficiency but also lessen human bias (Bhandari, 2023). Predictive analytics also uses AI to determine the candidate's chances of succeeding in a company. To find trends and forecast which applicants are most likely to perform well and stick with the organisation the machine learning models are trained on past employee data. By lowering turnover rates and making better hiring decisions, this predictive capability helps businesses save time and money (Ramirez & kamal, 2023).

4.1. Descriptive Analytics

Ever since the beginning of time, humans have been studying the past. Examining the history provides a clear grasp of how events have contributed to the current affairs. Humanity would have become accustomed to the current situation if it hadn't been for historical observations. But measuring the past is a different matter from merely observing it. The practice of descriptive analytics was born out of this act of measuring the historical data. The application of this data over time to decide the conclusions which is explained. To provide an accurate overview of what has happened and how it compares to the previous generation, this approach uses the data from a time period, or range. This process reveals the organization's both strong and weak aspects. This aids in the formulation of strategies even more (Roy et al., 2022).

4.2. Predictive Analytics

The predictive analytics which use the previous data as a foundation in order to forecast the future events. Many professionals and organisations utilize this field of advanced analytics to forecast future events (Roy et al., 2022)

4.2.1. *Models for Classification*

These models aid in class label prediction. For instance, forecasting if the match will occur, if an individual is willing to leave the company, whether his credit score is high or low, etc. With 1 representing the event we are after, the results produced by this model often taken in the form of 0 or 1. Decision trees, logistic regression, random forests, gradient-boosted trees, and others are examples of classification models. Regression models are useful tools for forecasting numerical values (quantifiable variables). Examples that can be taken into consideration here include forecasting the amount of money a business will make the following year and the amount of CO2 that will be in the atmosphere (Roy et al., 2022)

4.3. Prescriptive Analytics

To assist various stakeholders in making decisions, business analytics employs a lot of data gathered from many sources and applies statistical and quantitative analysis to create predictive models (Davenport & Harris, 2007; Soltanpoor & Sellis, 2016). Prescriptive, predictive, and descriptive analytics are the three primary phases into which it falls. These classifications are determined by the degree of intelligence, value, and difficulty (Akerkar, 2013; Krumeich et al., 2016). The core purpose of descriptive analytics is to provide the answers to questions such as "what happened," "why it happened," and "what is happening." Questions like "What will happen" and "Why will it happen" can be answered with predictive analytics. Similarly, prescriptive analytics is used to answer questions like the why and what should we do. Descriptive and predictive analytics remain the primary topic of business analytics using such methods as machine learning, artificial intelligence, etc. (Habeeb et al., 2019; Larose, 2015).

4.4. Real-World Implementation: Tesla's Digital Innovation IN HR

The mobility of cloud computing, the Internet of Things (IoT), augmented reality, social media, and decentralized public transaction ledgers like blockchains, the computerization of processes has been going on since the early 1990s. The social media and smart gadgets had a big impact on B2C communication strategies and opened up new avenues for customer interaction. Digital technology is responsible for many of the changes occurring in the global economy and culture. Not only do the majority of the most valuable multinational corporations now work in the digital sector, but innovation itself is undergoing a digital transition in both breadth and comprehension. New business model originated by the digital technology platforms are displacing traditional innovation techniques. In addition to the dynamic business models, digital innovation also changes the entrepreneurial culture. Digital companies can grow quickly and extensively (Huang et al.,2017), and industries can create temporary oligopolies or monopolies with little outside support (Kurz, 2017). Digital innovation is now a standard practice across many industries and is no longer just found in software organisations (Ciriello et al., 2018). With the ongoing evolution of new technologies, a number of sectors are taking steps to investigate and capitalize on technological advantages, beginning with their effects on product portfolios and corporate operational models. To properly handle these complex advancements, and processes must also be reengineered. A wide range of abilities are needed to execute a new digital business model, beginning with the ability to influence organizational cultures and individual views (Zinder and Yunatova, 2016).

Tesla employs different types of digital technologies, from remote to over-the-air software updates. Traditional automakers' business models, including how garages and associated services are offered to consumers, have undergone significant changes as a result of this digital innovation. This demonstrates unequivocally how the 'Customer-centric' approach and the real-time communication of digital innovations which transforms the customer service experience and raised the bar for multi-channel accessibility. The definition of digital innovation has been the subject of continuous discussions, and the phrase itself is a broad idea to begin with. To put it briefly, digital innovation is the process of employing digital tools, technology, and strategies to create new or improved products, services, processes, or business models. Through the use of digital advances, industries may increase productivity, which benefits individuals, companies, and society as a whole. Technological innovations that allow computers to think and make decisions, often based on data and patterns, include cloud computing, artificial intelligence, machine learning, and the development of new software applications (Saleh, 2019).

4.5. AI For Performance Evaluation And Workforce Planning

Collaboration between humans and AI will be a common occurrence in many workplaces. AI literacy, or "human proficiency in different subject areas of AI that enable purposeful, efficient, and ethical usage of AI technologies," will be a part of future job skill sets"(Pinski & Benlian, 2024) .This includes: technology-related skills (a certain level of technical knowledge); human-machine skills (knowing how to collaborate with AI efficiently, for example, by assigning tasks appropriately); work-related skills (knowing the ethical concerns surrounding the use of AI); and learning-related skills (a focus on lifelong learning) (Cetindamar et al., 2022). According to other studies, in order to benefit from AI-driven insights, workers will also need to get more accustomed to working in interdisciplinary teams. (Akhtar at al., 2019), As a new "feeling economy" develops and workers concentrate more on activities requiring these abilities, the significance of soft skills—such as those linked to empathy, interpersonal skills, and social and emotional intelligence—will also become increasingly important (Huang et al., 2019). In general, these abilities will also continue to support people's success in workplaces that are increasingly AI-enabled (Polakova et al., 2023).

5. SKILL GAP ANALYSIS AND WORKFORCE PLANNING

5.1. Predicting Burnout and Engagement using AI

The negative experience of burnout and the good sense of engagement have been conceptualized as two extremes of the continuum that represents people's psychological binds to their professions. This continuum has three interconnected dimensions: energy-exhaustion, involvement-cynicism, and inefficiency-efficacy (Leiter & Maslach, 2005). Initial studies only examined burnout, defining it as a psychiatric condition involving a protracted reaction to ongoing interpersonal pressures at work (Maslach & Jackson, 1981b). The fundamental individual strain aspect of burnout represents the depletion component. It describes the sensations of being overburdened and exhausted, both physically and emotionally. The self-evaluation of burnout is represented by inefficacy (or diminished accomplishment), which describes feelings of inadequacy as well as a lack of productivity at work. This three-dimensional approach is significant because it explicitly situates the individual's experience of stress within the social environment of the workplace and incorporates the individual's perception of others and themselves (Maslach, 1993). The Maslach Burnout Inventory (MBI) is used in burnout research to evaluate these three aspects (Maslach & Jackson, 1981a; Maslach et al., 1996; Leiter & Maslach, 2008).

5.2. Automated Promotion and Compensation Decision

One area in which automated help systems for high-level cognitive tasks are emerging as a topic for study and application is personnel selection. Hiring managers may receive prospect rankings using such a system to aid them in the hiring process. (Humphrey et al., 2007). The use of computer-assisted interviewing has been examined in other studies. According to some academics, interviews might be automated in order to screen applicants and provide potential employers with a shortlist of the best candidates (Judge et al., 2007). The increasing complexity of personnel selection may account for the rise in the use of these techniques. Hiring managers gather and compile a variety of data from a potentially enormous number of applicants (such as the results of interviews and intelligence tests).

In addition to selecting and employing the best applicants, they also need to adhere to legal requirements (e.g., concerning adverse impact) and company goals (e.g., cost and diversity) (Judge et al., 2007). There is hope that automated decision support systems could help gather and compile data for a large number of applicants, increasing the effectiveness of selection procedures. It is crucial to examine automation research and decision support system projects in order to gain a deeper understanding of automation systems for hiring (Addad et al., 2011; Barnhizer, 2016).

After concentrating on information retrieval and automated process decision-making components, information action occurs when systems provide pertinent information for the strategic decision. Automated functions fall into four main categories: information gathering, filtering and analysis, decision-making, and action execution. As more of these jobs are incorporated into systems, the degree of automation will increase. Videos may be automatically transcribed as part of the information gathering process. It's possible that underlining certain terms in these transcripts will facilitate data processing and filtering. System recommendations based on historical data can be used to perform prediction or classification tasks (e.g., distinguishing appropriate from unsuitable applicants). Humans may be shown these activities to aid in decision-making once they have yielded results (Barnhizer, 2016). In this post, we are discussing technological systems that gather, analyse, and make decisions and recommendations based on data.

The recruitment agencies in a wide range of duties (such gathering and evaluating data, approving or rejecting applications), and their conclusions could be used as a supplementary source of information for decision-makers. Automated processes that can be considered more complex and advanced methods of mechanically gathering or merging data have been made possible by machine learning and artificial intelligence (Copeland, 2000; Ito, 2016). The use of sensors (such as webcams and microphones) to gather data from the respondents, NLP to gather data from the application responses, and machine learning algorithms to evaluate applicants' skills are some of the novel approaches. It is fascinating to see how well this novel form of mechanical data collection and fusion compares to traditional mechanical and clinical methodologies on validity. Research on a mechanical combination of information (MCI) may provide insights into the potential outcomes of implementing contemporary information analysis and decision support automation (Nofal et al., 2014).

6. EMERGING TECHNOLOGIES SHAPING HRM

6.1. Explainable AI: The antithesis of the "black box" character of various AI, ML, and particularly DL models is indicated by a number of different words. The following terms are distinguished by us:

***6.2. Transparency*:** It has the capacity to be intelligible on its own. Transparency, then, is the antithesis of "black-box" (Adadi & Berrada, 2018). The ability to deliver interpretations in a way that a human can understand is known as interpretability (Gilpin et al., 2018).

6.3. Explainability: The idea of explanation as a human-AI system interaction which includes AI systems that are precise and understandable to people (Gilpin et al., 2018). Despite having identical semantic connotations, these phrases confer varying the degrees of artificial intelligence that humans can comprehend. The high-level ontology and taxonomy of XAI can be explained in greater detail as follows:

6.4. Transparent model: k-nearest neighbours (kNN), decision trees, rule-based learning, Bayesian networks, and others are examples of typical transparent models (Adadi & Berrada, 2018). The choices made by these Models are frequently transparent, however this characteristic alone does not ensure that a model will be easily explicable.

6.5. Opaque model: Random forests, neural networks, SVMs, and other models are examples of typical opaque models (Pasquale, 2015; Rudin, 2019). These models are opaque even though they frequently attain remarkable accuracy.

6.6. Model agnostic: Model-agnostic XAI techniques are intended to be broadly applicable (Dieber & Kirrane, 2020). Because of this, they must be sufficiently adaptable to function only by connecting a model's input to its outputs, independent of the model's inherent design.

6.7. Model-specific: Particular to the model in order to add transparency to a specific type of one or more models, XAI techniques frequently capitalize on knowledge about a particular model (Bach et al., 2015).

6.8. Explanation through simplification: It is possible to find alternatives to the original models to explain the interest prediction through approximating a model (Tritscher et al., 2020). Relevance/Feature-relevant explanation: This is similar to simplification. Once all possible combinations have been considered, such an XAI method will evaluate a feature based on its average expected marginal contribution to the ending of the model (Chen et al., 2020; Pedreschi et al., 2019).

6.9. Visual explanation: This type of XAI technique is based on visualisation (Chattopadhay et al., 2018). Thus, one can apply the family of data visualisation techniques to comprehend the choice or prediction made out of the input data.

6.10. Local explanation: (Selvaraju et al., 2017) writes that local explanations explain how the model turns out when it treats inputs similar to the one, we are attempting to clarify. They do this by modeling the limited region, around a specific case of interest (Angelov et al., 2021).

6.2. Augmented Analytics

To help an enterprise better understand its business and market and make timely business choices, business intelligence (BI) and analytics are defined as "the techniques, technologies, systems, practices, methodologies, and applications that analyse critical business data" (Chen et al., 2012). The distinction between BI and advanced analytics is being blurred by a new phrase, "Augmented analytics," which was created by (Gartner, 2017) and gives BI users access to sophisticated machine learning and artificial intelligence methods. This is undoubtedly a turning point in the history of business intelligence, regardless of the name chosen to describe AI-powered analytics (Gartner, 2017; Watson, 2017; Henschen, 2018). The revolutionary effects of AI on HR particularly in the leadership styles have great impact on employee motivation (Baruah et al., 2024). The transformational leadership which is positively influences both work engagement and employees' innovative work behaviour highlights the important role of the leaders in encouraging a productive and innovative work environment within IT organisations (Subramani et al., 2024).

6.3. Blockchain Applications In HR System

According to (Hughes et al., 2019), blockchain technology has emerged as a disruptive technology that is gaining interest from corporate organisations in addition to scholars and practitioners. According to (Wang et al., 2017), blockchain technology will fundamentally transform conventional business systems, allowing for its use in a wide range of fields. Although the financial industry leads the way in creating and deploying blockchain applications, businesses in the shipping and transportation, healthcare, and retail sectors are also making extensive use of these technologies (Beck et al., 2017). Blockchain is utilized for trade settlement, trade finance, underwriting, healthcare record management, retail chain for warranty receipts, and digital supply chain in the financial services sector (Karanjia, et al., 2017).

Numerous businesses have begun incorporating blockchain technology into their operations. Companies such as Amazon, Walmart, Facebook, Google, and IBM have begun to invest heavily in blockchain technology and use it for a variety of purposes (CB Insights, 2019). Blockchain has the potential to provide a solution for practically every organisational activity, including supply chain management, manufacturing, and production (Hughes et al., 2019). Although human resource management (HRM) has changed, with nearly every function being digitalized (Mishra and Akman, 2010), the idea that blockchain might improve HRM in organisations has received less attention. 58% of HR professionals have found phoney on candidates' resumes credentials. People fabricate information about their qualifications, duties, dates of employment, job titles, degrees, employers, and honours or medals they have received (Bhaduri, 2018; EL-Sakran, 2019).

Blockchain will make it possible for workers to communicate private information to their employers. Employers could be reassured by digitally verifying information including credentials, achievements, references, and talents. Recruitment, verification, smart contracts, safe transactions, attendance, compliance, auditing, fraud prevention, and data protection will all be made possible by the technology (Spence, 2018). Some firms employ blockchain to provide HR solutions, including application data transparency, pay roll, personnel operations and awards, and the freelancer ecosystem (Mishra & Venkatesan, 2021). However, businesses have yet to adopt blockchain as an HRM integrated technology (Mishra & Venkatesan, 2021).

7. EMOTIONAL AI

While studying people's emotional reactions was spurred by developments of psychology in the early 20th century. People started to openly express their emotions in the 1960s. The origin of emotional intelligence (EI) starts with a person's capacity for comfortable emotional expression. Furthermore, the identification of social failure in people despite their high scores on general intelligence tests is what led to the establishment of emotional intelligence (EI) (Seven, 2019). "The ability to notice, to distinguish, and to use emotions" is how Emotional Intelligence (EI) has been defined (Mayer and Salovey, 1990). It is "the ability of individuals to recognise others and their own feelings and to manage these emotions," according to (Goleman, 2012). Emotional intelligence which includes both assessing and controlling one's own emotions as well as others. High EI people are able to regulate these kinds of feelings and alter their emotional states if requires. For some people who are having the weak structural links, lose control of themselves, and give in to their rage.

Emotional intelligence (EI) that encompasses such qualities as effective interpersonal communication, empathy, and the capacity to manage personal feelings can come in handy in every aspect of life (Kambur, 2018). EI has four major factors. The initial approach is the emotional perception, which illustrates the correct identification, expression, and differentiation of emotions; second approach is the emotional assimilation, which illustrates the ability to think in terms of emotions and choose to be attentive to key information; the third approach is the emotional understanding, which illustrates the ability to distinguish feelings between words and emotions; and the final approach is the handling of personal feelings as per (Mayer et al., 2001). Unlike traditional intelligence, emotional intelligence can have the potential of improving the career success and job performance. High EI people will be more successful in their careers, build personal relationships which last long, and are healthy (Schutte et al., 2007). Emotional intelligence (EI) has been identified to have a different set of corporate attitude and behaviour in the work places. Lee and Ok (2012) found that, EI is positively related with job dissatisfaction and stress. In addition, EI affects the ability of an individual to handle stressors and environmental demands (Shi et al., 2014). Emotional Intelligence positively affects the engagement of employees since it facilitates communication. High EI allows an individual to adapt more to the workplace (Rozell et al., 2004). Moreover, (D'amato and Herzfeldt, 2008) stressed that employees that had high EI might be highly dedicated and satisfied with their jobs (Kambur, 2021).

8. CONCLUSION

AI and ML are reshaping the landscape of Human Resource Management by enabling smarter, faster, and more inclusive decisions across recruitment, performance evaluation, and workforce planning. These technologies not only streamline administrative tasks but also support predictive and prescriptive analytics that improve talent outcomes and strategic planning. Real-world applications, such as those by

Tesla and Accenture, underscore the tangible benefits of AI-enabled HR systems in enhancing both organizational efficiency and employee experience. However, as these innovations become more embedded in HRM, issues related to algorithmic bias, transparency, and ethical deployment become increasingly critical. Future HR professionals must thus balance technological adoption with ethical rigor, empathy, and continuous learning to harness AI's full potential. Embracing explainable AI, blockchain, and emotional intelligence tools will be key in ensuring that technological advancement in HR remains aligned with human values.

REFERENCES

Adadi, A., & Berrada, M. (2018). Peeking inside the black-box: A survey on explainable artificial intelligence (XAI). *IEEE Access : Practical Innovations, Open Solutions, 6*, 52138–52160. DOI: 10.1109/ACCESS.2018.2870052

Adam, M., Wessel, M., & Benlian, A. (2021). AI-based chatbots in customer service and their effects on user compliance. *Electronic Markets, 31*(2), 427–445. DOI: 10.1007/s12525-020-00414-7

Adamopoulou, E., & Moussiades, L. (2020). Chatbots: History, technology, and applications. *Machine Learning with Applications, 2*, 100006. DOI: 10.1016/j.mlwa.2020.100006

Addad, B., Amari, S., & Lesage, J. J. (2011). Genetic algorithms for delays evaluation in networked automation systems. *Engineering Applications of Artificial Intelligence, 24*(3), 485–490. DOI: 10.1016/j.engappai.2010.10.017

Agrawal, B. P., Nair, P. S., Babu, S. B. G. T., Rajprabu, R., Pesaru, P., & Natrayan, L. (2024). *Deep learning methods for detecting image-based defects in manufacturing processes.* In Proceedings of the Ninth International Conference on Science, Technology, Engineering and Mathematics (ICONSTEM 2024): The role of emerging technologies in digital transformation.

. Akerkar, R. (2013). Advanced data analytics for business. *Big data computing, 377(9).* DOI: 10.1201/b16014

Akhtar, P., Frynas, J. G., Mellahi, K., & Ullah, S. (2019). Big data-savvy teams' skills, big data-driven actions and business performance. *British Journal of Management, 30*(2), 252–271. DOI: 10.1111/1467-8551.12333

Al Hamad, N. M., Adewusi, O. E., Unachukwu, C. C., Osawaru, B., & Chisom, O. N. (2024). A review on the innovative approaches to STEM education. *International Journal of Science and Research Archive, 11*(1), 244–252. DOI: 10.30574/ijsra.2024.11.1.0026

Al-Quhfa, H., Mothana, A., Aljbri, A., & Song, J. (2024). Enhancing Talent Recruitment in Business Intelligence Systems: A Comparative Analysis of Machine Learning Models. *Analytics, 3*(3), 297–317. DOI: 10.3390/analytics3030017

Albassam, W. A. (2023). The power of artificial intelligence in recruitment: An analytical review of current AI-based recruitment strategies. *International Journal of Professional Business Review: Int. J. Prof. Bus. Rev., 8*(6), 4. DOI: 10.26668/businessreview/2023.v8i6.2089

Allen, D. G., & Griffeth, R. W. (2001). Test of a mediated performance–turnover relationship highlighting the moderating roles of visibility and reward contingency. *The Journal of Applied Psychology*, *86*(5), 1014–1021. DOI: 10.1037/0021-9010.86.5.1014 PMID: 11596795

Angelov, P. P., Soares, E. A., Jiang, R., Arnold, N. I., & Atkinson, P. M. (2021). Explainable artificial intelligence: An analytical review. *Wiley Interdisciplinary Reviews. Data Mining and Knowledge Discovery*, *11*(5), e1424. DOI: 10.1002/widm.1424

Ayeni, O. O., Al Hamad, N. M., Chisom, O. N., Osawaru, B., & Adewusi, O. E. (2024). AI in education: A review of personalized learning and educational technology. *GSC Advanced Research and Reviews*, *18*(2), 261–271. DOI: 10.30574/gscarr.2024.18.2.0062

Bach, S., Binder, A., Montavon, G., Klauschen, F., Müller, K.-R., & Samek, W. (2015). On pixel-wise explanations for non-linear classifier decisions by layer-wise relevance propagation. *PLoS One*, *10*(7), e0130140. DOI: 10.1371/journal.pone.0130140 PMID: 26161953

Barnhizer, D. (2016). The future of work: Apps, artificial intelligence, automation and androids. Artificial Intelligence, Automation and Androids (January 15, 2016). *SSRN*, (289). Advance online publication. DOI: 10.2139/ssrn.2716327

Baruah, A., Shaikh, M., Kumar, R. M., Shaikh, I. A. K., & Thomas, S. N. (2024, April). Artificial Intelligence Influence on Leadership Styles in Human Resource Management for Employee Engagement. In *2024 Ninth International Conference on Science Technology Engineering and Mathematics (ICONSTEM)* (pp. 1-5). IEEE. DOI: 10.1109/ICONSTEM60960.2024.10568819

Basnet, S. (2024). Artificial Intelligence and machine learning in human resource management: Prospect and future trends. *International Journal of Research Publication and Reviews*, *5*(1), 281–287. DOI: 10.55248/gengpi.5.0124.0107

Beck, R., Avital, M., Rossi, M., & Thatcher, J. B. (2017). Blockchain technology in business and information systems research. *Business & Information Systems Engineering*, *59*(6), 381–384. DOI: 10.1007/s12599-017-0505-1

Bellamy, R. K., Dey, K., Hind, M., Hoffman, S. C., Houde, S., Kannan, K., Lohia, P., Martino, J., Mehta, S., Mojsilović, A., Nagar, S., Ramamurthy, K. N., Richards, J., Saha, D., Sattigeri, P., Singh, M., Varshney, K. R., & Zhang, Y. (2019). AI Fairness 360: An extensible toolkit for detecting and mitigating algorithmic bias. *IBM Journal of Research and Development*, *63*(4/5), 4–1. DOI: 10.1147/JRD.2019.2942287

Bhaduri, A. (2018), "People@work", Retrieved from Hindu Business Line, available at: https:// www.thehindubusinessline.com/specials/people-at-work/adopting -blockchain-tech-in-hr/ article22881175.ece

Bhandari, U. (2023). An optimized machine learning based rule engine architecture. *Journal of Artificial Intelligence and Capsule Networks*, *4*(4), 299–311. DOI: 10.36548/jaicn.2022.4.006

Castillo, D., Canhoto, A. I., & Said, E. (2021). The dark side of AI-powered service interactions: Exploring the process of co-destruction from the customer perspective. *Service Industries Journal*, *41*(13-14), 900–925. DOI: 10.1080/02642069.2020.1787993

Cetindamar, D., Kitto, K., Wu, M., Zhang, Y., Abedin, B., & Knight, S. (2022). Explicating AI literacy of employees at digital workplaces. *IEEE Transactions on Engineering Management*, *71*, 810–823. DOI: 10.1109/TEM.2021.3138503

Chattopadhay, A., Sarkar, A., Howlader, P., & Balasubramanian, V. N. (2018). *Grad-CAM++: Generalized gradient-based visual explanations for deep convolutional networks. In 2018 IEEE Winter conference on applications of computer vision.* WACV., DOI: 10.1109/WACV.2018.00097

Chen, H., Chiang, R. H. L., & Storey, V. C. (2012). Business intelligence and analytics: From big data to big impact. *Management Information Systems Quarterly*, *36*(4), 1165–1188. DOI: 10.2307/41703503

Chen, H., Lundberg, S., & Lee, S. I. (2020). Explaining models by propagating Shapley values of local components. In *Explainable AI in Healthcare and Medicine: Building a Culture of Transparency and Accountability* (pp. 261–270). Springer International Publishing., DOI: 10.1007/978-3-030-53352-6_18

Chen, Z. (2023). Collaboration among recruiters and artificial intelligence: Removing human prejudices in employment. *Cognition Technology and Work*, *25*(1), 135–149. DOI: 10.1007/s10111-022-00716-0 PMID: 36187287

Chowdhury, S., Dey, P., Joel-Edgar, S., Bhattacharya, S., Rodriguez-Espindola, O., Abadie, A., & Truong, L. (2023). Unlocking the value of artificial intelligence in human resource management through AI capability framework. *Human Resource Management Review*, *33*(1), 100899. DOI: 10.1016/j.hrmr.2022.100899

Ciriello, R. F., Richter, A., & Schwabe, G. (2018). Digital innovation. *Business & Information Systems Engineering*, *60*(6), 563–569. DOI: 10.1007/s12599-018-0559-8

Copeland, J. R. (2000). Overview of System Architectural Implications of Third-Party Liability and Government Indemnification for GPS Augmentation. *Navigation (Washington)*, *47*(1), 7–15. DOI: 10.1002/j.2161-4296.2000.tb02418.x

Cotton, J. L., & Tuttle, J. M. (1986). Employee turnover: A meta-analysis and review with implications for research. *Academy of Management Review, 11*(1), 55–70. DOI: 10.2307/258331

D'Amato, A., & Herzfeldt, R. (2008). Learning orientation, organizational commitment and talent retention across generations: *A study of European managers. Journal of Managerial Psychology, 23*(8), 929–953. DOI: 10.1108/02683940810904402

da Silva, L. B. P., Soltovski, R., Pontes, J., Treinta, F. T., Leitão, P., Mosconi, E., de Resende, L. M. M., & Yoshino, R. T. (2022). Human resources management 4.0: Literature review and trends. *Computers & Industrial Engineering, 168*, 108111. DOI: 10.1016/j.cie.2022.108111

Dankwa-Mullan, I., Scheufele, E. L., Matheny, M. E., Quintana, Y., Chapman, W. W., Jackson, G., & South, B. R. (2021). A proposed framework on integrating health equity and racial justice into the artificial intelligence development lifecycle. *Journal of Health Care for the Poor and Underserved, 32*(2), 300–317. DOI: 10.1353/hpu.2021.0065

Davenport, T. H., & Harris, J. G. (2007). Competing on analytics: The new science of Winning. *Harvard business review press. Language, 15*(217), 24.

EL-Sakran, T. M. (. (2019). Educational Tips for the Detection of Resume Padding. *International Journal of Pedagogical Innovation, 7*(2). Advance online publication. DOI: 10.12785/ijcnt/070103

Finkelstein, L. M., Ryan, K. M., & King, E. B. (2013). What do the young (old) people think of me? Content and accuracy of age-based metastereotypes. *European Journal of Work and Organizational Psychology, 22*(6), 633–657. DOI: 10.1080/1359432X.2012.673279

Gartner (2017) Augmented analytics is the future of data and analytics (overview of the report in Rita Sallam's public article). https://blogs.gartner.com/rita-sallam/2017/07/31/just-buying into-modern-bi-and-analytics-get-ready-for-augmented-analytics-the-next-wave-of-market-disruption/. Accessed 20 Feb 2018.

Ghedabna, L., Ghedabna, R., Imtiaz, Q., Faheem, M. A., Alkhayyat, A., & Hosen, M. S. (2024). Artificial intelligence in human resource management: Revolutionizing recruitment, performance, and employee development. *Nanotechnology Perceptions, 20*, 52–68.

Gilpin, L. H., Bau, D., Yuan, B. Z., Bajwa, A., Specter, M., & Kagal, L. (2018). Explaining explanations: An overview of interpretability of machine learning. *In 2018 IEEE 5th International Conference on data science and advanced analytics (DSAA). IEEE (pp. 80–89)*. DOI: 10.1109/DSAA.2018.00018

Goleman, D. (2012). *Emotional intelligence: Why it can matter more than IQ*. Bantam.

Gulati, V., Gupta, I., Firdous, F., & Narwal, R. (2024). *Resume Analyzer Using Natural Language Processing*. NLP.

. Gupta, A., & Rahimi Ata, K. (2024). Data-Driven Hiring: Implementing AI and Assessing the Impact of AI on Recruitment Efficiency and Candidate Quality.

Gupta, C. P., & Kumar, V. R. (2024, January). Artificial Intelligence Application in Human Resource Management: The Way Forward. In *2024 ASU International Conference in Emerging Technologies for Sustainability and Intelligent Systems (ICETSIS)* (pp. 1726-1730). IEEE.DOI: 10.1109/ICETSIS61505.2024.10459605

Habeeb, R. A. A., Nasaruddin, F., Gani, A., Hashem, I. A. T., Ahmed, E., & Imran, M. (2019). Real-time big data processing for anomaly detection: A survey. *International Journal of Information Management*, *45*, 289–307. DOI: 10.1016/j.ijinfomgt.2018.08.006

Haristiani, N. (2019, November). Artificial Intelligence (AI) chatbot as language learning medium: An inquiry. In Journal of Physics: Conference Series (Vol. 1387, No. 1, p. 012020). IOP Publishing.DOI: 10.1088/1742-6596/1387/1/012020

Heckert, T. M., & Farabee, A. M. (2006). Turnover intentions of the faculty at a teaching-focused university. *Psychological Reports*, *99*(1), 39–45. DOI: 10.2466/pr0.99.1.39-45 PMID: 17037448

Henschen, D. (2018) *How ML and AI will transform business intelligence and analytics*. http://www.zdnet.com/article/howmachine-learning-and-artificial-intelligence-will-transform-busi ness-intelligence-and-analytics/. Accessed 1 Mar 2018

Holbeche, L. (2022). *Aligning human resources and business strategy*. Routledge., DOI: 10.4324/9781003219996

Holtom, B. C., Mitchell, T. R., Lee, T. W., & Eberly, M. B. (2008). 5 turnover and retention research: A glance at the past, a closer review of the present, and a venture into the future. *The Academy of Management Annals*, *2*(1), 231–274. DOI: 10.5465/19416520802211552

Huang, M. H., Rust, R., & Maksimovic, V. (2019). The feeling economy: Managing in the next generation of artificial intelligence (AI). *California Management Review*, *61*(4), 43–65. DOI: 10.1177/0008125619863436

Hughes, L., Dwivedi, Y. K., Misra, S. K., Rana, N. P., Raghavan, V., & Akella, V. (2019). Blockchain research, practice and policy: Applications, benefits, limitations, emerging research themes and research agenda. *International Journal of Information Management*, *49*, 114–129. DOI: 10.1016/j.ijinfomgt.2019.02.005

Humphrey, S. E., Nahrgang, J. D., & Morgeson, F. P. (2007). Integrating motivational, social, and contextual work design features: A meta-analytic summary and theoretical extension of the work design literature. *The Journal of Applied Psychology*, *92*(5), 1332–1356. DOI: 10.1037/0021-9010.92.5.1332 PMID: 17845089

Insights, C. B. (2019). 80+ corporations working on blockchain and distributed ledgers. *Retrieved September, 29*, 2019. Available at: https://www.cbinsights.com/research/organizations-corporates-testblockchainsdistributed-ledgers/

. Ito, J. (2016). *The future of work in the age of artificial intelligence.* .DOI: 10.31859/20160613.2349

Judge, T. A., Jackson, C. L., Shaw, J. C., Scott, B. A., & Rich, B. L. (2007). Self-efficacy and work-related performance: The integral role of individual differences. *The Journal of Applied Psychology*, *92*(1), 107–127. https://psycnet.apa.org/doi/10.1037/0021-9010.92.1.107. DOI: 10.1037/0021-9010.92.1.107 PMID: 17227155

Kambur, E. (2018). Does emotional intelligence affect quality of service? An application in the service sector. *The Journal of Academic Social Science*, *6*(71), 587–600. DOI: 10.16992/ASOS.13801

. Kambur, E. (2021). Emotional intelligence or artificial intelligence? Emotional artificial intelligence. *Florya Chronicles of Political Economy, 7(2),* 147-168.hptts://. DOI: 10.17932/IAU.FCPE.2015.010/fcpe_v07i2004

Karanjia, B., Lakshman, S., & Goswami, S. (2017). *Blockchain technology in India: Opportunities and challenges.* Associated Chambers of Commerce and Industry of India.

Kavzoglu, T., & Teke, A. (2022). Predictive performances of ensemble machine learning algorithms in landslide susceptibility mapping using random forest, extreme gradient boosting (XGBoost) and natural gradient boosting (NGBoost). *Arabian Journal for Science and Engineering*, *47*(6), 7367–7385. DOI: 10.1007/s13369-022-06560-8

Kluge, E. H. W. (2024). *The Ethics of Artificial Intelligence in Healthcare: From Hands-on Practice to Policy-making* (Vol. 25). Springer Nature.https://apps.who.int/iris/bitstream/handle/10665/341996/9789240029200-eng.pdf

Krumeich, J., Werth, D., & Loos, P. (2016). Prescriptive control of business processes: New potentials through predictive analytics of big data in the process manufacturing industry. *Business & Information Systems Engineering*, *58*(4), 261–280. DOI: 10.1007/s12599-015-0412-2

Kurz, M. (2017). On the formation of capital and wealth: IT, Monopoly Power and Rising Inequality. *Monopoly Power and Rising Inequality. SSRN.* DOI: 10.2139/ssrn.3014361

Larose, D. T. (2015). *Data mining and predictive analytics*. John Wiley & Sons.

Lee, J. J., & Ok, C. (2012). Reducing burnout and enhancing job satisfaction: Critical role of hotel employees' emotional intelligence and emotional labor. *International Journal of Hospitality Management*, *31*(4), 1101–1112. DOI: 10.1016/j.ijhm.2012.01.007

Leiter, M. P., & Maslach, C. (2005). A mediation model of job burnout. In Antoniou, A. S. G., & Cooper, C. L. (Eds.), *Research companion to organizational health psychology* (pp. 544–564). Edward Elgar., DOI: 10.4337/9781845423308.00046

Liu, D., Mitchell, T. R., Lee, T. W., Holtom, B. C., & Hinkin, T. R. (2012). When employees are out of step with coworkers: How job satisfaction trajectory and dispersion influence individual-and unit-level voluntary turnover. *Academy of Management Journal*, *55*(6), 1360–1380. DOI: 10.5465/amj.2010.0920

Maslach, C. (1993). Burnout: A multidimensional perspective. In Schaufeli, W. B., Maslach, C., & Marek, T. (Eds.), *Professional burnout: Recent developments in theory and research* (pp. 19–32). Taylor & Francis.

Maslach, C., & Jackson, S. E. (1981a). *The Maslach Burnout Inventory*. Consulting Psychologists Press.

Maslach, C., & Jackson, S. E. (1981b). The measurement of experienced burnout. *Journal of Organizational Behavior*, *2*(2), 99–113. DOI: 10.1002/job.4030020205

Maslach, C., Jackson, S. E., & Leiter, M. P. (1996). *Maslach Burnout Inventory manual* (3rd ed.). Consulting Psychologists Press.

Mayer, J. D., & Salovey, P. (1990). Perceiving affective content in ambiguous visual stimuli: A component of emotional intelligence. *Journal of Personality Assessment*, *54*(3-4), 772–781. DOI: 10.1080/00223891.1990.9674037 PMID: 2348356

Mayer, J. D., Salovey, P., Caruso, D. R., & Sitarenios, G. (2001). Emotional intelligence as a standard intelligence. *Emotion (Washington, D.C.)*, *1*(3), 232–242. DOI: 10.1037/1528-3542.1.3.232 PMID: 12934682

Mishra, A., & Akman, I. (2010). Information technology in human resource management: An empirical assessment. *Public Personnel Management*, *39*(3), 271–290. DOI: 10.1177/009102601003900306

Mishra, H., & Venkatesan, M. (2021). Blockchain in human resource management of organizations: An empirical assessment to gauge HR and non-HR perspective. *Journal of Organizational Change Management*, *34*(2), 525–542. DOI: 10.1108/JOCM-08-2020-0261

Mishra, P. (2017). Green human resource management: A framework for sustainable organizational development in an emerging economy. *The International Journal of Organizational Analysis*, *25*(5), 762–788. DOI: 10.1108/IJOA-11-2016-1079

Mongan, J., Moy, L., & Kahn, C. E.Jr. (2020). Checklist for artificial intelligence in medical imaging (CLAIM): A guide for authors and reviewers. *Radiology. Artificial Intelligence*, *2*(2), e200029. DOI: 10.1148/ryai.2020200029 PMID: 33937821

Müller, A. (2024). Decarbonizing business travel: A qualitative exploration of the (mis-) alignment between knowledge organizations' climate strategies and travel practices. *Journal of Sustainable Tourism*, *32*(8), 1557–1583. DOI: 10.1080/09669582.2023.2247575

Najjar, A., Amro, B., & Macedo, M. (2021). An intelligent decision support system for recruitment: Resumes screening and applicants ranking. *Informatica (Vilnius)*, *45*(4). Advance online publication. DOI: 10.31449/inf.v45i4.3356

. Nandipati, V. S. S., & Boddala, L. V. (2024). Credit Card Approval Prediction: A comparative analysis between Logistic Regression, KNN, Decision Trees, Random Forest, XGBoost.

Nofal, S., Atkinson, K., & Dunne, P. E. (2014). Algorithms for decision problems in argument systems under preferred semantics. *Artificial Intelligence*, *207*, 23–51. DOI: 10.1016/j.artint.2013.11.001

Orieno, O. H., Ndubuisi, N. L., Eyo-Udo, N. L., Ilojianya, V. I., & Biu, P. W. (2024). Sustainability in project management: A comprehensive review. *World Journal of Advanced Research and Reviews*, *21*(1), 656–677. DOI: 10.30574/wjarr.2024.21.1.0060

Pasquale, F. (2015). *The black box society: The secret algorithms that control money and information*. Harvard University Press. DOI: 10.4159/harvard.9780674736061

Pedreschi, D., Giannotti, F., Guidotti, R., Monreale, A., Ruggieri, S., & Turini, F. (2019). Meaningful explanations of black box AI decision systems. *Proceedings of the AAAI Conference on Artificial Intelligence, 33*(1), 9780–9784. DOI: 10.1609/aaai.v33i01.33019780

Peterson, S. L. (2004). Toward a theoretical model of employee turnover: A human resource development perspective. *Human Resource Development Review, 3*(3), 209–227. DOI: 10.1177/1534484304267832

Pinski, M., & Benlian, A. (2024). AI literacy for users–A comprehensive review and future research directions of learning methods, components, and effects. *Computers in Human Behavior: Artificial Humans, 2*(1), 100062. DOI: 10.1016/j.chbah.2024.100062

Poláková, M., Suleimanová, J. H., Madzík, P., Copuš, L., Molnárová, I., & Polednová, J. (2023). Soft skills and their importance in the labour market under the conditions of Industry 5.0. *Heliyon, 9*(8), e18670. Advance online publication. DOI: 10.1016/j.heliyon.2023.e18670 PMID: 37593611

Popesku, J. (2019). Current applications of artificial intelligence in tourism and hospitality. In *Sinteza 2019-International Scientific Conference on Information Technology and Data Related Research* (pp. 84-90). Singidunum University

Prasad, K. D. V., Rao, M., & Vaidya, R. (2019). Recruitment metrics and accomplishments: A study with reference to information technology sector. *Journal of Management Research and Analysis, 6*(2), 106–111. DOI: 10.18231/j.jmra.2019.020

Raji, M. A., Olodo, H. B., Oke, T. T., Addy, W. A., Ofodile, O. C., & Oyewole, A. T. (2024). Digital marketing in tourism: A review of practices in the USA and Africa. *International Journal of Applied Research in Social Sciences, 6*(3), 393–408. DOI: 10.51594/ijarss.v6i3.896

. Ramírez, J. G. C., & Kamal, M. (2023). Graphene plasmonics for enhanced quantum information processing.

Reddy, S., Rogers, W., Makinen, V. P., Coiera, E., Brown, P., Wenzel, M., Weicken, E., Ansari, S., Mathur, P., Casey, A., & Kelly, B. (2021). Evaluation framework to guide implementation of AI systems into healthcare settings. *BMJ Health & Care Informatics, 28*(1), e100444. DOI: 10.1136/bmjhci-2021-100444 PMID: 34642177

. Roy, D., Srivastava, R., Jat, M., & Karaca, M. S. (2022). A complete overview of analytics techniques: descriptive, predictive, and prescriptive. *Decision intelligence analytics and the implementation of strategic business management,* 15-30. https://doi.org/.DOI: 10.1007/978-3-030-82763-2_2

Rozell, E. J., Pettijohn, C. E., & Parker, R. S. (2004). Customer-oriented selling: Exploring the roles of emotional intelligence and organizational commitment. *Psychology and Marketing*, *21*(6), 405–424. DOI: 10.1002/mar.20011

Rudin, C. (2019). Stop explaining black box machine learning models for high stakes decisions and use interpretable models instead. *Nature Machine Intelligence*, *1*(5), 206–215. DOI: 10.1038/s42256-019-0048-x PMID: 35603010

Sacco, J. M., & Schmitt, N. (2005). A dynamic multilevel model of demographic diversity and misfit effects. *The Journal of Applied Psychology*, *90*(2), 203–231. https://psycnet.apa.org/doi/10.1037/0021-9010.90.2.203. DOI: 10.1037/0021-9010.90.2.203 PMID: 15769233

Saini, H., & Tarkar, P. (2024). Case Study on E-Recruitment Globally During COVID-19 Pandemic. In *HR 4.0 Practices in the Post-COVID-19 Scenario* (pp. 203-217). Apple Academic Press.DOI: 10.1201/9781003416128-12

Saleh, Z. (2019). Artificial intelligence definition, ethics and standards. *Journal of Artificial Intelligence*, *1*(1), 1–10. https://www.wathi.org/artificial-intelligence -definition-ethics- and-standards-the-british-university-in-egypt-2019/

Schutte, N. S., Malouff, J. M., Thorsteinsson, E. B., Bhullar, N., & Rooke, S. E. (2007). A meta-analytic investigation of the relationship between emotional intelligence and health. *Personality and Individual Differences*, *42*(6), 921–933. DOI: 10.1016/j.paid.2006.09.003

Selvaraju, R. R., Cogswell, M., Das, A., Vedantam, R., Parikh, D., & Batra, D. (2017). Grad-CAM: Visual explanations from deep networks via gradient-based localization. In *Proceedings of the IEEE international conference on computer vision* (pp. 618–626). DOI: DOI: 10.1109/ICCV.2017.74

Seven, E. (2019). *"Duyguzal zeka ve duygusal zekanın tüketicilerinin hedonik satın alma davranışına etkisi" Yüksek lisans tezi*. Uludağ Üniversitesi.

. Shaheen, N., Jaiswal, S., Chinta, D. U., Singh, N., Goel, O., & Chhapola, A. (2024). Data privacy in hr: Securing employee information in us enterprises using oracle hcm cloud. *International Journal of Research Radicals in Multidisciplinary Fields, ISSN*, 319-341.

Sharma, H., Pundir, S., & Deepak, A.. (2023). *Efficient data compression algorithms for cloud-based medical imaging*. In *Proceedings of the International Conference on Artificial Intelligence for Innovations in Healthcare Industries (ICAIIHI 2023)*. DOI: 10.1109/ICAIIHI57871.2023.10489333

Shi, Y., Prentice, C., & He, W. (2014). Linking service quality, customer satisfaction and loyalty in casinos, does membership matter? *International Journal of Hospitality Management*, *40*, 81–91. DOI: 10.1016/j.ijhm.2014.03.013

Soltanpoor, R., & Sellis, T. (2016). Prescriptive analytics for big data. In Databases Theory and Applications: 27th *Australasian Database Conference,* ADC 2016, Sydney, NSW, September 28-29, 2016, Proceedings 27 (pp. 245-256). Springer International Publishing.DOI: 10.1007/978-3-319-46922-5_19

. Spence, A. (2018). Blockchain and the Chief Human Resources Officer. *Transforming the HR Function and the market for skills, talent, and training. A Blockchain Research Institute.*

Stovel, M., & Bontis, N. (2002). Voluntary turnover: Knowledge management–friend or foe? *Journal of Intellectual Capital*, *3*(3), 303–322. DOI: 10.1108/14691930210435633

Strang, K. D., & Sun, Z. (2022). ERP Staff versus AI recruitment with employment real-time big data. *Discover Artificial Intelligence*, *2*(1), 21. DOI: 10.1007/s44163-022-00037-1 PMID: 40477848

Subramani, A. K., Jan, N. A., Joseph, S., & David, R. (2024). Fostering innovative work behaviour in Indian IT firms: The mediating influence of employee psychological capital in the context of transformational leadership. *International Journal of Work Innovation*, *5*(4), 384–402. DOI: 10.1504/IJWI.2024.142024

Swider, B. W., & Zimmerman, R. D. (2010). Born to burnout: A meta-analytic path model of personality, job burnout, and work outcomes. *Journal of Vocational Behavior*, *76*(3), 487–506. DOI: 10.1016/j.jvb.2010.01.003

Tritscher, J., Ring, M., Schlr, D., Hettinger, L., & Hotho, A. (2020). Evaluation of post-hoc XAI approaches through synthetic tabular data. In *International symposium on methodologies for intelligent systems* (pp. 422–430). Springer. DOI: DOI: 10.1007/978-3-030-59491-6_40

Uma, V. R., Velchamy, I., & Upadhyay, D. (2023). Recruitment analytics: Hiring in the era of artificial intelligence. In *The Adoption and Effect of Artificial Intelligence on Human Resources Management, Part A* (pp. 155-174). Emerald Publishing Limited.DOI: 10.1108/978-1-80382-027-920231008

Uwaoma, P. U., Eboigbe, E. O., Eyo-Udo, N. L., Daraojimba, D. O., & Kaggwa, S. (2023). Space commerce and its economic implications for the US: A review: Delving into the commercialization of space, its prospects, challenges, and potential impact on the US economy. *World Journal of Advanced Research and Reviews, 20*(3), 952–965. DOI: 10.30574/wjarr.2023.20.3.2494

von Hippel, C., Kalokerinos, E. K., & Henry, J. D. (2013). Stereotype threat among older employees: Relationship with job attitudes and turnover intentions. *Psychology and Aging, 28*(1), 17–27. https://psycnet.apa.org/doi/10.1037/a0029825. DOI: 10.1037/a0029825 PMID: 22924658

Wang, X., Feng, L., Zhang, H., Lyu, C., Wang, L., & You, Y. (2017), "Human resource information management model based on blockchain technology", 2017 IEEE Symposium on Service Oriented System Engineering (SOSE), San Francisco, CA, pp. 168-173, . 2017.34. DOI: DOI: 10.1109/SOSE.2017.34

. Watson, H. J. (2017). he Cognitive Decision-Support Generation. *Business Intelligence Journal, 22*(2).

Wolff, R. F., Moons, K. G., Riley, R. D., Whiting, P. F., Westwood, M., Collins, G. S., Reitsma, J. B., Kleijnen, J., & Mallett, S. (2019). PROBAST: A tool to assess the risk of bias and applicability of prediction model studies. *Annals of Internal Medicine, 170*(1), 51–58. DOI: 10.7326/M18-1376 PMID: 30596875

Zinder, E., & Yunatova, I. 2016. "Synergy for digital transformation: a person's multiple roles and subject domains integration", *[in:] Digital Transformation and Global Society:* First International Conference, June 22-24, Springer, pp. 155-168. DOI: DOI: 10.1007/978-3-319-49700-6_16

KEY TERMS AND DEFINITIONS

Algorithmic Decision-making: It is the process of using computer-based algorithms to analyze the data and make or support decision making, often with minimal human intervention, in areas such as hiring, promotions, or performance evaluations.

Artificial Intelligence: It is transforming Human Resource Management by automating the tasks, enhanced decision-making, and improving the employee experience through AI-powered tools. It streamlines the recruitment, onboarding, performance management, and employee training & Development which allows HR professionals to focus on strategic initiatives.

Chatbots and Employee engagement: It refers to the use of AI-powered virtual assistants to facilitate the real-time communication, provides support, gather feedback, and enhance the interaction between employees and HR which ultimately boost the employee engagement and satisfaction.

Machine learning: It refers to the use of algorithms and data-driven models to automate and enhance the different stages in the hiring process like screening resumes, matching candidates, and predicts the job performance.

Predictive Analytics: It involves using the historical employee data and machine learning models to forecast about future workforce trends like employee performance, turnover, and hiring needs in order to support the strategic HR decisions.

Technology: Technology is the practical application of the scientific knowledge, tools, and techniques in order to create solutions to solve the problems or improve human life.

Chapter 12
Scaffolding Ethics: Accountability Structures to Support Construction Industry Transformation

B. Seethalakshmi
http://orcid.org/0009-0001-4761-6377
SRM Institute of Science and Technology, India

K. Santhanalakshmi
SRM Institute of Science and Technology, India

ABSTRACT

The construction industry is undergoing unprecedented transformation driven by technology, market, and workforce shifts. Such changes' implications on industry dynamics, productivity, and employment trends are addressed in this review, with drivers emphasized while also addressing challenges posed by new technologies, automation, and labour market re-alignment. Our approach combines literature review evidence (2018-2024), fifteen leading-edge construction company case studies, and quantitative analysis of global market trends. We concentrate on three areas: digital technology integration (BIM, IoT, predictive analytics), automation trends (robotics, prefabrication), and workforce development programs to meet changing skill needs. There is evidence that technology-savvy companies attain 15-23% greater productivity compared to their conventional peers.

DOI: 10.4018/979-8-3373-4307-5.ch012

1. INTRODUCTION

The construction industry is approaching a critical inflection point as the foundation of global development and economic growth. While it has tremendous potential to support urbanization, infrastructural development, and employment opportunities, it simultaneously faces significant ethical, labor, and safety challenges. The industry routinely manages complex projects with compressed timelines, employing workers with diverse backgrounds and varying skill levels. Historically, approaches to addressing industry challenges have focused on identifying fault or implementing remedial mechanisms after problems occur. However, mounting evidence suggests that a fundamental shift toward proactive responsibility is essential to create a construction industry that is safer, more equitable, and consequently more productive (Xia et al., 2018; Amoah & Steyn, 2023).

This paper contends that robust accountability frameworks prioritize ensuring success for employees at all levels rather than merely "reducing" unskilled workers. These frameworks encompass transparent communication channels, comprehensive training programs, and ethical leadership oversight. Directors have corporate governance responsibilities to shareholders that include preventing controversies and maintaining long-term financial sustainability (Kapri, 2023). Modern technologies, particularly decision-making algorithms, introduce additional accountability dimensions that must be considered (Cobbe et al., 2023). The complexity of accountability increases dramatically when interactions between sophisticated systems involve multiple hosts, automated processes, and far-reaching consequences.

For the construction industry to realize its full potential, attention must shift from individual blame to addressing systemic issues that contribute to accidents, unethical behavior, and talent shortages. This paper will analyze how organization-wide accountability culture can lead transformation toward a more sustainable and equitable future. Accountability is particularly crucial in construction given the industry's management of substantial financial resources, project complexity, and responsibility for protecting both workforce and public safety. Central to this process is holding all stakeholders accountable for their decisions and actions, including architects, contractors, subcontractors, and suppliers (Sohail & Cavill, 2008; Mohammadi et al., 2018; Ortiz-Marcos & Silvius, 2025).

Figure 1. Core Aspects of the Construction Sector

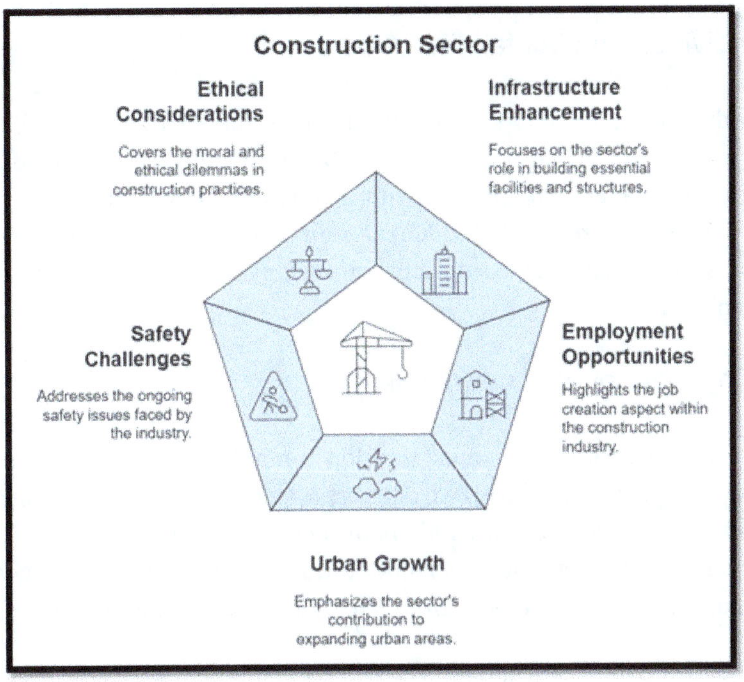

2. ACCOUNTABILITY FRAMEWORK

2.1 Defining Accountability in Construction

Accountability involves individuals or organizations describing, justifying, and accepting responsibility for their actions across individual, collective, or organizational contexts. It is essential for enhancing performance, building trust, and mitigating risks. Mechanisms to strengthen accountability include establishing clear metrics, implementing continuous monitoring systems, and providing regular feedback, while barriers may include ambiguously defined responsibilities and blame-oriented cultures. Within construction, accountability is vital for project management effectiveness, regulatory compliance, and stakeholder engagement, ensuring timely and transparent project delivery (Nyakala et al., 2020; Emanuel, 1996).

2.2 Levels of Accountability

2.2.1 Individual Accountability

Individual accountability perspectives focus on site-level responsibility, where laborers and project managers are accountable for on-site actions including safety protocol adherence and compliance with quality and ethical standards. Trethewy et al. (2003) emphasize that individual accountability must be supported by organizational systems that enable safe decision-making rather than punishing workers for systemic failures.

2.2.2 Organizational Accountability

Construction organizations must develop commitment to safety culture where regulatory compliance is prioritized, risks are systematically managed, and projects are completed on schedule and within budget constraints. Organizational accountability extends to workforce development, ethical business practices, and community impact management (Subramaniyan & Veerakumar, 2017; Afsar et al., 2020).

2.2.3 Project Accountability

Each construction project requires clearly defined accountability structures and reporting mechanisms. This necessitates specific role delineation, establishment of performance indicators aligned with assigned responsibilities, implementation of monitoring functions, and correction of deviations from planned outcomes. Project accountability frameworks must address the temporary and multi-organizational nature of construction projects (Michael & Sullivan, 2011; Nordin et al., 2011).

2.3 Key Domains of Accountability

2.3.1 Health and Safety

The construction industry remains among the most hazardous sectors globally. Safety accountability begins with comprehensive understanding of relevant legislation and implementation of systematic risk mitigation strategies. Proactive safety cultures prioritize preventive measures over reactive responses to incidents (Mohammadi et al., 2018; Birhane et al., 2022).

2.3.2 Quality Assurance

Meeting client requirements through adherence to project specifications is paramount. Quality accountability encompasses appropriate material selection, compliance with construction regulations, and implementation of rigorous inspection protocols throughout the building process. Quality management systems must integrate accountability at each project phase (Nyakala et al., 2021).

2.3.3 Financial Management

Construction projects require substantial financial resources. Financial accountability involves maintaining accurate and timely accounting practices, implementing rigorous expenditure controls, and eliminating wasteful spending. Transparent financial management reduces corruption risks and improves project outcomes (Sohail & Cavill, 2008).

2.3.4 Sustainability

The construction sector has significant environmental impacts. Sustainability accountability includes utilizing renewable resources, minimizing waste generation, and adhering to environmental regulations. Sustainable construction practices increasingly incorporate lifecycle assessment and circular economy principles (Kaushal & Saeed, 2024; Placino & Rugkhapan, 2024).

2.3.5 Ethical Conduct

Construction operations are vulnerable to corruption and unethical business practices. Accountability in this domain requires fair pricing strategies, commitment to transparency, and adherence to ethical decision-making principles at all organizational levels. Anti-corruption measures must address both individual and systemic factors (Sohail & Cavill, 2008; Amoah & Steyn, 2023).

Figure 2. Pros and Cons of Accountability in Construction

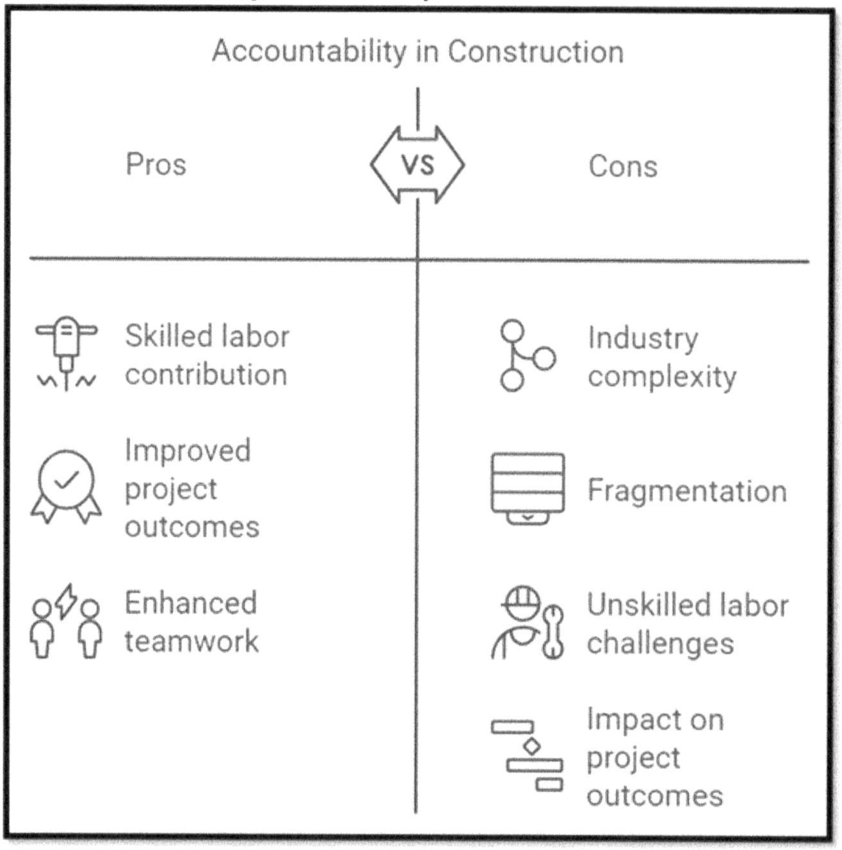

3. RECENT TRENDS IN ACCOUNTABILITY RESEARCH

3.1 Corporate Social Responsibility Integration

Recent studies examine interconnections between environmental sustainability, community engagement, accountability mechanisms, and ethical labor practices within construction contexts. These relationships carry significant societal implications for industry stakeholders and affected communities alike (Xia et al., 2018; Afsar et al., 2020).

3.2 Barriers to Ethical Conduct

Research identifies factors inhibiting accountability implementation, including transparency deficiencies, inadequate regulatory enforcement, and corruption vulnerabilities. Understanding these barriers is essential for developing effective accountability interventions (Amoah & Steyn, 2023; Nordin et al., 2011).

3.3 Educational Infrastructure Development

Scholars increasingly emphasize that construction education and training curricula must incorporate ethics and accountability components to foster responsibility culture from foundational levels. Educational institutions play crucial roles in developing professionals with strong ethical frameworks (Sands & Pearce, 2014).

3.4 Accountability Imperatives

In an industry characterized by frequent cost overruns and schedule delays, accountability ensures performance standards are maintained and consequences for non-compliance are clearly established. Systematic accountability mitigates project risks and enhances stakeholder confidence (Nyakala et al., 2020; Nyakala et al., 2021).

3.5 Digital Transformation Impacts

The rapid adoption of automation technologies and artificial intelligence solutions represents an emerging trend with significant implications. These technologies potentially enhance workforce productivity by enabling resource reallocation to higher-value tasks while introducing new accountability challenges (Su et al., 2024; Abrahams et al., 2024).

3.6 Construction Ecosystem Evolution

Researchers are examining comprehensive construction ecosystems to develop innovative frameworks addressing current inefficiencies. For established organizations, this necessitates identifying emerging threats and developing strategic responses to maintain competitive positioning (Vigren, 2024).

3.7 Environmental Sustainability Focus

Studies identify construction as a significant carbon emission source, investigating optimal resource utilization strategies and sustainable practice implementation approaches. Environmental accountability extends beyond compliance to proactive ecological stewardship (Placino & Rugkhapan, 2024; Kaushal & Saeed, 2024).

Figure 3. Recent Trends in Accountability Research

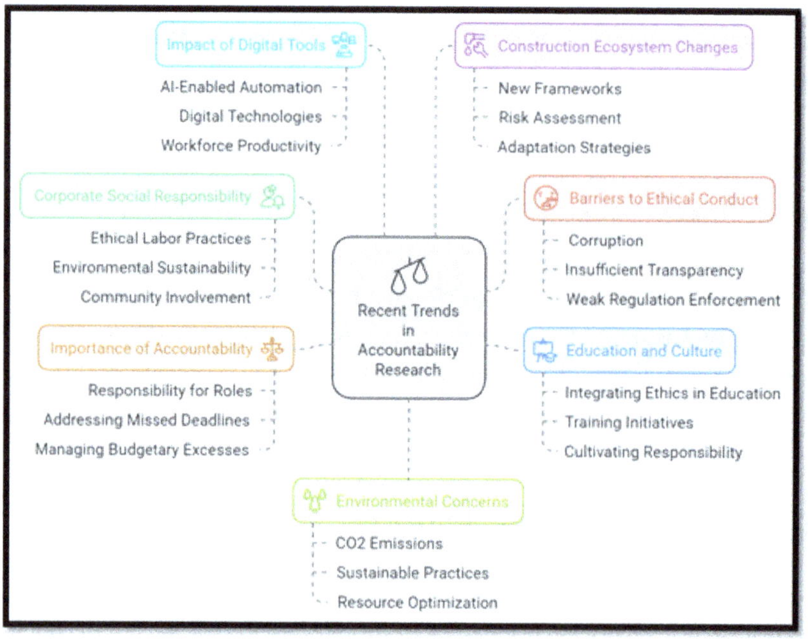

4. LITERATURE REVIEW

This review examines contemporary research regarding accountability within the construction sector, highlighting significant themes and emerging trends across multiple domains.

4.1 Evolution Beyond Traditional Risk Measurement

Historical research emphasized retrospective safety metrics such as accident rates, while current studies focus on proactive indicators and prevention strategies.

Trethewey (2003) advocates implementing measures encompassing safety culture assessment, management commitment evaluation, and employee engagement analysis to predict and prevent accidents. This trend reflects growing recognition that individual accountability represents one component within broader systemic responsibility frameworks (Birhane et al., 2022).

4.2 Understanding Unethical Behavior Foundations

Unethical practices undermine industry integrity and sustainability, prompting researchers to investigate root causes. Studies explore prevalent unethical behaviors including bid manipulation, safety standard violations, and regulatory circumvention. Amoah and Steyn (2022) examine factors constraining ethical decision-making, including schedule pressures and retaliation concerns. Research findings indicate accountability systems must promote transparency, protect whistleblowers, and cultivate organizational ethical leadership (Nordin et al., 2011; Sohail & Cavill, 2008).

4.3 Quality Management Through Accountability

Construction excellence requires integrating safety, sustainability, and customer satisfaction priorities. Contemporary academic studies position accountability alongside effective quality control mechanisms as essential success factors. Explicitly defined quality standards, clearly assigned responsibilities, and rigorous verification processes supported by multi-level accountability drive project success (Nyakala et al., 2020; Nyakala et al., 2021).

4.4 Workforce Diversity Accountability

The construction industry employs workers with diverse skill levels and cultural backgrounds. Recent academic literature emphasizes that accountability practices must address needs across workforce segments. According to Birhane et al. (2022), worker-level accountability alone proves insufficient, necessitating responsibility frameworks that address systemic challenges including language barriers, training adequacy, and cultural variations in risk perception.

4.5 Technological Integration and Responsibility

Increasing adoption of Building Information Modeling and digital project management platforms creates both opportunities and challenges for accountability implementation. While this research area remains nascent, evidence suggests technology can enhance transparency, monitor outcomes, and facilitate ethical and safety requirement fulfillment (Abrahams et al., 2024; Su et al., 2024).

5. WORKPLACE ACCOUNTABILITY

5.1 Training and Supervision Enhancement

Organizational accountability manifests through development of comprehensive training programs for all personnel, including novices. Safety components must be prominently featured in curriculum design and delivery (Trethewey, 2003). Appropriate supervision must be consistently provided during safety procedure implementation, particularly for inexperienced workers.

5.2 Role Clarity and Communication

Accountability requires clearly defined roles, responsibilities, and communication channels between stakeholders. This clarity particularly benefits unskilled workers who may lack familiarity with specific job requirements or organizational expectations (Subramaniyan & Veerakumar, 2017; Birhane et al., 2022).

5.3 Labor Practice Equity

Accountability demands that employers ensure ethical treatment for all workers regardless of skill level, providing fair compensation and safe working environments. Equitable practices build trust and enhance workforce engagement across organizational levels (Amoah & Steyn, 2023).

5.4 Vulnerable Worker Protection

Unskilled laborers face heightened exploitation vulnerability, necessitating robust regulatory frameworks, ethical oversight mechanisms, and worker advocacy initiatives. Historical examples include immigrant worker exploitation during construction booms, highlighting protection imperatives (The Boston Globe, 2016; Emanuel, 1996).

5.5 Skills Development Investment

Apprenticeship programs and comprehensive training represent sustainable long-term solutions to industry challenges. Workers acquiring industrial workplace skills reduce dependency on unskilled labor while enhancing organizational capabilities and individual career opportunities (Bah et al., 2018; Sands & Pearce, 2014).

6. RESEARCH IMPLICATIONS

The study findings underscore the critical imperative to establish comprehensive safety protocols and equitable practices throughout the construction industry. Creating environments prioritizing worker safety cultivates workplace protection and fairness while reducing accident frequency, enhancing job satisfaction, and improving productivity metrics. Future research should evaluate long-term impacts of such interventions on worker retention rates and mental health outcomes, while quantifying economic benefits derived from safer, less discriminatory workplaces. The study's broader implications indicate that policymakers and industry leaders must collaborate to develop context-appropriate safety standards and training programs addressing construction's unique operational challenges.

Cross-hierarchical employee feedback can inform strategy development, fostering safety and inclusivity cultures that promote innovation and industry growth. Organizations prioritizing safety and inclusivity simultaneously protect their workforce and enhance reputational capital, attracting premier talent and building engaged, dynamic teams (Afsar et al., 2020; Xia et al., 2018).

6.1 Safety and Fairness Valuation

Construction frequently involves high-risk environments, making rigorous safety protocol implementation essential. Industry workers face numerous hazards, with safety standard non-compliance potentially resulting in severe consequences. Safety prioritization protects employees while cultivating trust and respect cultures crucial for developing inclusive workplaces where all personnel feel valued and empowered to contribute (Mohammadi et al., 2018; Birhane et al., 2022).

6.2 Safe and Inclusive Workplace Benefits

Safety and equity-focused environments generate substantial individual and organizational benefits. Safe workplaces reduce accident probability, decreasing downtime and associated costs. When employees feel secure and equitably treated, job satisfaction increases, improving retention metrics. Enhanced satisfaction drives productivity gains as engaged personnel demonstrate greater discretionary effort (Nyakala et al., 2020; Afsar et al., 2020).

6.3 Safety Intervention Long-term Effects

Future research should examine safety intervention longitudinal impacts on retention and mental health outcomes. Understanding how safer, less discriminatory environments affect employee wellbeing is crucial for policy development. Organizations should quantify economic advantages from safety and inclusion investments, including reduced insurance premiums, decreased legal liabilities, and workforce stability benefits enhancing financial performance (Trethewy et al., 2003; Birhane et al., 2022).

6.4 Safety Standard Collaboration

Study findings highlight collaboration necessity between policymakers and industry leaders. Joint efforts can develop safety regulations and training programs addressing construction workers' specific challenges. Customizing programs to workforce needs ensures intervention effectiveness and relevance across diverse operational contexts (Sohail & Cavill, 2008; Mohammadi et al., 2018).

6.5 Employee Engagement and Cultural Transformation

Involving personnel across organizational levels in safety initiative development is essential for cultivating safety and inclusivity cultures. Employee feedback provides valuable insights regarding challenges and potential solutions. Participatory approaches enhance safety measure effectiveness while empowering employees through meaningful organizational contribution opportunities (Afsar et al., 2020; Birhane et al., 2022).

6.6 Reputational Development

Organizations prioritizing safety and diversity protect employees while building positive industry reputations. Enhanced reputations attract premium talent, as prospective employees prefer environments valuing wellbeing and promoting fairness. Diverse, motivated teams catalyze innovation and creativity, positioning organizations for sustainable success in competitive markets (Xia et al., 2018; Afsar et al., 2020).

Figure 4. Safety and Fairness in Construction

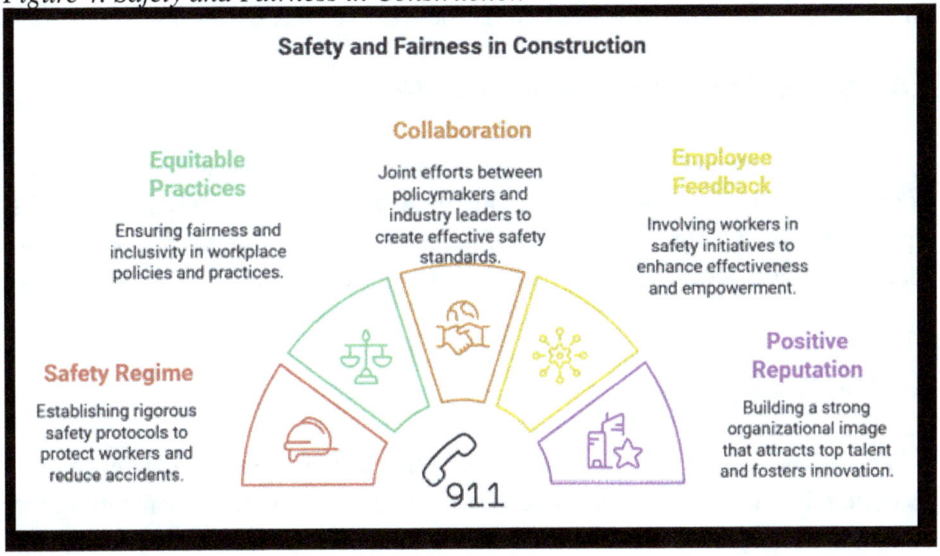

7. LIMITATIONS

7.1 Data Quality Constraints

Substantial accountability research relies on self-reported data or anecdotal evidence, introducing reliability and objectivity limitations. Robust analysis requires access to objective metrics including incident reports, audit findings, and performance indicators (Birhane et al., 2022; Mohammadi et al., 2018).

7.2 Industry Heterogeneity

The construction industry demonstrates significant heterogeneity across project types, organizational structures, and management contexts. Context-specific studies are necessary because findings may not readily transfer between different operational environments, limiting generalizability (Vigren, 2024).

7.3 Longitudinal Assessment Requirements

Evaluating long-term effects necessitates extended timeframes for intervention implementation and effectiveness monitoring. Longitudinal studies must determine impact on project outcomes, employee behavior, and organizational culture over time, requiring sustained research commitment (Xia et al., 2018; Afsar et al., 2020).

7.4 Interdisciplinary Collaboration Needs

Addressing accountability challenges requires collaboration among researchers from diverse disciplines including psychology, engineering, law, and ethics. Interdisciplinary research partnerships must be fostered to develop comprehensive solutions addressing multifaceted industry challenges (Sands & Pearce, 2014; Vigren, 2024).

8. CONCLUSIONS

This study demonstrates that the construction sector must immediately elevate accountability standards to create safe, equitable, and inclusive environments. Rather than reactive responses or blame-oriented cultures, the paper advocates systemic, accountability-centered approaches. We examine diverse accountability models spanning individual behavior, organizational policies, and regulatory oversight to highlight industry transformation potential.

The analysis reveals that robust accountability mechanisms—including formal leadership commitment, comprehensive training programs, transparent communication channels, and effective supervisory systems—are essential for promoting responsibility throughout construction organizations. These approaches empower workers, encourage safe practices, and address root causes of accidents, unethical conduct, and skill deficiencies. Prioritizing accountability over "minimizing" individual worker challenges enhances overall industry performance while emphasizing safety, development, and wellbeing for all stakeholders.

Accountability transcends compliance or risk management concerns, representing an investment in construction's future. By fostering shared responsibility cultures, transparency commitments, and sustainability practices, the construction industry can advance toward more prosperous, sustainable, and equitable outcomes benefiting all participants (Xia et al., 2018; Sohail & Cavill, 2008; Trethewey, 2003).

REFERENCES

Abrahams, T. O., Farayola, O. A., Kaggwa, S., Uwaoma, P. U., Hassan, A. O., & Dawodu, S. O. (2024). Cybersecurity awareness and education programs: A review of employee engagement and accountability. *Computer Science & IT Research Journal*, *5*(1), 100–119. DOI: 10.51594/csitrj.v5i1.708

Afsar, B., Al-Ghazali, B., & Umrani, W. (2020). Retracted: Corporate social responsibility, work meaningfulness, and employee engagement: The joint moderating effects of incremental moral belief and moral identity centrality. *Corporate Social Responsibility and Environmental Management*, *27*(3), 1264–1278. DOI: 10.1002/csr.1882

Amoah, C., & Steyn, D. (2023). Barriers to unethical and corrupt practices avoidance in the construction industry. *International Journal of Building Pathology and Adaptation*, *41*(6), 85–101. DOI: 10.1108/IJBPA-01-2022-0021

Bah, E. M., Faye, I., & Geh, Z. F. (2018). Slum upgrading and housing alternatives for the poor. In *Housing Market Dynamics in Africa* (pp. 215–253). Palgrave Macmillan. DOI: 10.1057/978-1-137-59792-2_6

Birhane, G. E., Yang, L., Geng, J., & Zhu, J. (2022). Causes of construction injuries: A review. *International Journal of Occupational Safety and Ergonomics*, *28*(1), 343–353. DOI: 10.1080/10803548.2020.1761678 PMID: 32342729

Cobbe, J., Singh, J., & Veale, M. (2023). Reviewing codes of ethics: Towards a framework for accountability in the tech sector. *Computer Law & Security Review*, *49*, 106735.

Emanuel, L. L. (1996). A professional response to demands for accountability: Practical recommendations regarding ethical aspects of patient care. *Annals of Internal Medicine*, *124*(2), 240–249. DOI: 10.7326/0003-4819-124-2-199601150-00008 PMID: 8534000

Kapri, S. S. (2023). The role of corporate governance in mitigating financial risk: An Indian experiences. *Journal of Cardiovascular Research*, *12*(6), 2114–2121.

Kaushal, V., & Saeed, E. (2024). Sustainable and Innovative Self-Healing Concrete Technologies to Mitigate Environmental Impacts in Construction. *CivilEng*, *5*(3), 549–558. DOI: 10.3390/civileng5030029

Mohammadi, A., Tavakolan, M., & Khosravi, Y. (2018). Factors influencing safety performance on construction projects: A review. *Safety Science*, *109*, 382–397. DOI: 10.1016/j.ssci.2018.06.017

Nordin, R. M., Takim, R., & Nawawi, A. H. (2011, September). Critical factors contributing to corruption in construction industry. In *2011 IEEE Symposium on Business, Engineering and Industrial Applications (ISBEIA)* (pp. 330-333). DOI: 10.1109/ISBEIA.2011.6088831

Nyakala, S., Pretorius, J., & Vermeulen, A. (2020). Construction quality process implementation as a source of competitive advantage in small and medium-sized construction projects. *Journal of Construction Business and Management, 4*(2), 46–54. DOI: 10.15641/jcbm.4.2.862

Nyakala, S., Ramoroka, D., & Ramdass, K. (2021). Factors influencing the quality of low-income housing in Polokwane Municipality South Africa. *Acta Structilia, 28*(2), 23–52. DOI: 10.18820/24150487/as28i2.2

Placino, P., & Rugkhapan, N. T. (2024). Making visible concrete's shadow places: Mixing environmental concerns and social inequalities into building materials. *Environment and Urbanization, 36*(1), 195–213. DOI: 10.1177/09562478231214140

Sands, K., & Pearce, A. (2014). Toward a framework for construction ethics education: A meta-framework of construction ethics education topics. In *Construction Research Congress 2014: Construction in a Global Network* (pp. 379-388). DOI: 10.1061/9780784413517.039

Sohail, M., & Cavill, S. (2008). Accountability to prevent corruption in construction projects. *Journal of Construction Engineering and Management, 134*(9), 729–738. DOI: 10.1061/(ASCE)0733-9364(2008)134:9(729)

Su, S., Zhong, R. Y., & Jiang, Y. (2024). Digital twin and its applications in the construction industry: A state-of-art systematic review. *Digital Twin, 2*, 15. DOI: 10.12688/digitaltwin.17664.2

Subramaniyan, V. S., & Veerakumar, K. (2017). Risk management in construction industry. *Int. J. for Risk Assesment, 2*, 1–4.

Sullivan, M., & Government Accountability Office Washington DC. (2011). *Joint strike fighter: Restructuring should improve outcomes, but progress is still lagging overall*. Government Accountability Office.

The Boston Globe. (2016). Labor trafficking in the construction industry [Special Report].

Trethewy, R. W., Atkinson, M., & Falls, B. (2003). Improved hazard identification for contractors in the construction industry. *Journal of Construction Research, 4*(01), 71–85. DOI: 10.1142/S1609945103000315

Vigren, O. (2024). Ecosystems in construction management and urban development: A comprehensive review of conceptualizations and contributions. *Construction Management and Economics*, *42*(2), 162–181. DOI: 10.1080/01446193.2023.2247496

Xia, B., Olanipekun, A., Chen, Q., Xie, L., & Liu, Y. (2018). Conceptualising the state of the art of corporate social responsibility (CSR) in the construction industry and its nexus to sustainable development. *Journal of Cleaner Production*, *195*, 340–353. DOI: 10.1016/j.jclepro.2018.05.157

Section 6
Strategic and Sustainable Futures in HRM

Chapter 13
Strategic HR Innovations for Sustainable Futures:
Integrating Scenario Planning, Resilience, and Ethical Innovation

Rishikaysh Kaakandikar
http://orcid.org/0000-0003-0349-6788
SaiBalaji International Institute of Management Sciences, India

Surekha Ningule
http://orcid.org/0009-0005-9752-3661
Siddhant Institute of Business Management, India

ABSTRACT

This Chapter explores the role of strategic human resource innovations in shaping sustainable organizational futures. It emphasizes the integration of scenario planning, resilience-building strategies, and ethical innovation within HR practices to navigate uncertainty and drive long-term value. By aligning HR strategies with sustainability goals, organizations can enhance adaptability, employee well-being, and ethical governance. The study highlights how forward-thinking HR approaches can foster resilient, agile, and ethically grounded workplaces capable of thriving in complex, evolving environments.

DOI: 10.4018/979-8-3373-4307-5.ch013

1. INTRODUCTION

1.1 Overview of Strategic HRM in the 21st Century

The way Strategic Human Resource Management operates has substantially changed during the 21st century. Administrative duties are no longer the main focus of strategic Human Resource Management, which now stands as an essential organisational success driver. These factors drive the transformation of the current scenario:

1. Technological Advancements Artificial Intelligence (AI) tools play a central role in the HR workflow by processing applications and forecasting workforce needs to provide HR staff with improved accuracy in their choices. HR departments rely on sophisticated data analytics, which drives them to base their decisions on evidence. The strategic application of data by HR professionals enables them to forecast employee retention, along with the detection of workforce deficiencies that optimise organisational talent management. HR teams dedicate themselves to strategic initiatives since the automation of payroll processing provides administrators with time to handle more vital functions. AI-based chatbots supply immediate HR answers to workers through a system which improves both employee service and workplace engagement.
2. Remote and Hybrid Work Models The sudden transition to remote work because of the COVID-19 pandemic fast-tracked hybrid work model implementations that unite office-based work with remote work. HR departments had to create remote on boarding systems rapidly through the development of virtual welcome processes and training content, and regulatory training. The Human Resources Department must create a distance-agnostic engagement program that builds workplace relationships among staff who operate from different locations. Workforce productivity monitoring demands digital solutions which allow performance tracking along with team maintenance protocols and flexible operational hours for staff members.
3. Employee Well-being Focus Organisations now prioritise work-life balance between employees' professional responsibilities and personal needs to boost satisfaction levels and retain their staff. Work parameters that adapt to individual schedules as well as distant work capabilities, serve this initiative. The Human Resources department concentrates on building workplace environments that recognise all employees by making them valued and both supported and motivated. The company has made employee assistance programs together including mental health days, accessible to its employees. The implementation of HR practices leads to burnout reduction because these practices develop balanced

work environments, which provide time for employees to rest while managing workloads effectively.

4. Diversity, Equity, and Inclusion (DEI) Organisations now pursue diversity initiatives which require them to implement hiring practices that bring together people with various genders and races, along with diverse backgrounds and abilities. DEI strategies work towards three-fold goals, setting diversity as the main focus and simultaneously promoting both fairness at all levels of compensation and advancement within the workforce. The workplace culture advances toward inclusion through HR department initiatives to establish environments in which every background feels important and honoured by their colleagues.

1.2 The Need for Sustainability in HR Practices

Organisations that want lasting success need to implement sustainability within their HR practices because it has become mandatory instead of optional. Every aspect of human resources management under sustainable practices contains environmental, social and governance elements to produce organisational worth and societal advantages. The following reasons demonstrate why sustainability is vital for HR management practices:

Organizations which implement sustainability in their HR systems achieve better employee retention together with improved employee engagement. Organizations that practice sustainable human resources management report staff engagement growth of 55% along with employee retention rates coming down by 20%.

The Deloitte survey found 77% of employees consider sustainability commitment as essential to drive them toward going beyond their roles in organizational performance. The absence of meaningful corporate social responsibility stands as a major barrier for preventing 64% of millennials from accepting employment within a given company.

Demonstrated sustainability commitment brings a better reputation, which attracts customers with matching values while attracting investors who seek sustainable businesses. The increased market share from this strategy delivers better customer loyalty for the organisation.

Future compliance regulations give organisations the chance to avoid penalties while gaining a leadership position in sustainability, because they stay ahead of environmental regulations. Organisations achieve dual environmental advantages through sustainable practice implementation while cutting down operational costs.

Strategic Human Resource Management (SHRM) has become a central pillar of organizational success in the 21st century. Unlike traditional HR roles focused on administrative tasks, modern SHRM integrates technology, sustainability, and strategy to drive business outcomes (Ulrich et al., 2012; Boxall & Purcell, 2016).

Integrating AI, automation, and data analytics has enabled HR departments to perform predictive hiring, performance analysis, and employee engagement tracking with unprecedented accuracy (SHRM, 2019; IBM, 2020). As a result, HR professionals are now expected to be strategic partners who contribute to business growth and transformation (Wright & McMahan, 2011).

1.3 Objectives and Structure of the Chapter

The chapter conducts an extensive and progressive evaluation of Strategic Human Resource Management (SHRM) development throughout the twenty-first century while emphasising sustainability practices. The introduction of sustainable practices demands HR leadership for organisations to achieve their economic and social goals as well as environmental responsibility. The chapter has the following detailed breakdown of its objectives and design:

2. OBJECTIVES OF THE CHAPTER

1. Examine the Evolution of SHRM:

This section evaluates the effects of swift technological progress on standard HR work processes. The new generation of HR processes includes AI technologies and data decision tools to increase operational efficiency and boost proactive workforce needs resolution based on data. The HR department now serves as a vital strategic force for organisational success while moving past its traditional administrative responsibilities.

A major shift within SHRM is the growing emphasis on employee well-being, ethical innovation, and sustainability. Companies like Google and Microsoft have embraced values-driven HR practices, prioritizing psychological safety and employee experience as a competitive advantage (Grant, 2013; Microsoft, 2021). Ethical innovation demands transparency in AI systems and a human-centered approach to technology adoption (European Commission, 2018; Accenture, 2020). These efforts align with broader corporate social responsibility (CSR) goals, which encourage organizations to treat sustainability not as a trend but as an essential component of long-term viability (Chatterji et al., 2009; UNGC & Accenture, 2021).

Organizations increasingly leverage scenario planning and resilience models to future-proof their workforce strategies. Scenario-based approaches, such as those implemented by Shell and IBM, help companies anticipate disruption from talent shortages, automation, or economic instability (Deloitte, 2020; Schwartz et al., 2020). These planning tools align HR strategy with external factors such as demographic shifts and legal transformations (PWC, 2021; Bersin, 2019). Building organizational resilience through agile leadership, remote work policies, and psychological safety measures has become vital in navigating uncertainty (AON Hewitt, 2018; Mayo Clinic, 2021).

The chapter evaluates the adjustments happening in the HR field which result from evolving work frameworks that blend remote and hybrid work formats. Through these changes the Human Resources department now supports the development of organizational culture and employee bond development and team collaboration between distributed workforces to ensure new methods align with organizational targets.

2.Highlight the Importance of Sustainability:

Corporate strategy now has sustainability as its fundamental strategic element. This part demonstrates how HR practice fusion with sustainability elements constructs sustainable employees who show resilience and adaptability. Incorporating sustainability through HR enables organizations to handle environmental, social and governance (ESG) impacts to achieve both long-term business success together with positive public opinion.

Through its privileged position HR can direct cultural development so employees practice responsible behaviour by making sustainability part of workplace values.

Human resources establishes itself as a fundamental driver for sustainable organization practices through implementing environmentally friendly workplaces and fair distribution networks and diversity enhancement programs.

3. Provide Actionable Insights:

The chapter incorporates a combination of practical strategy sections that provide real-world tools alongside best practices and actionable techniques which HR professionals need to enact sustainable HR initiatives. The recommendations would address both green HR policy creation and employee wellness improvement and work-life balance enhancement and hiring inclusivity development, and technology utilisation for sustainable decision-making purposes.

The chapter addresses practical sustainable workforce development through talent management methods, including recruitment techniques and performance assessment systems and employee enhancement methods to build a sustainable workforce. The guide will enable HR professionals to integrate sustainable targets within workforce planning, thus achieving sustainable worker retention and organisational growth as well as employee values that match organisational vision.

2.1 Evolution and Scope of SHRM

Evolution of SHRM

People and Organizations built Strategic Human Resource Management (SHRM) into a transformed method which started as traditional administration before evolving into a strategic business force that directly impacts organizational success. The development of SHRM can be divided into three main phases.

- 1950s–1970s: Personnel Management

Leadership in this era directed all Human Resources activities towards personnel management through fundamental administrative responsibilities like worker recruitment and legal requirements enforcement along with salary administration and benefit administration. Collectively organizations looked at HR as a support department which lacked significant power to determine strategic organizational decisions.

- 1980s: Emergence of HRM

Human Resource Management (HRM) emerged during the 1980s to replace Personnel Management and introduced three main priorities: motivated workers combined with workforce development alongside enhanced positive employee relations. Human Resource professionals started to grasp the significance of employee involvement and professional growth and better workplace environments because these elements create organizational success terms.

- 1990s and Beyond: Rise of SHRM

SHRM stood as a widely recognized concept by the 1990s. Business organizations discovered that HR capabilities surpassed administrative duties and compliance work because it directly influenced organizational achievements. The HR department evolved to perform functions involving talent management along with leadership development together with creating a positive organizational culture. SHRM dedicated its efforts to link human resource practices with executive-level business strategy through which HR became essential for sustainable business success.

Scope of SHRM

The field of SHRM exceeds typical HRM limits to create a complete system of people management. The process integrates HR policies together with organizational strategic objectives in order to generate better business results. SHRM expands its reach by means of the following activities:

- Workforce Planning Aligned with Corporate Strategy

SHRM maintains its core duty to find and retain the appropriate workforce which possesses correct aptitudes at their required time of employment. Employee planning takes on strategic value by creating personal HR approaches that directly support organizational future goals including both market expansion and innovative advancements.

- Talent Acquisition and Retention Strategies

The Society for Human Resource Management leads its activities by focusing on recruiting high-quality candidates and helping them improve their performance while keeping them within the organization. HR professionals need to accomplish tasks beyond basic hiring responsibilities since their duties extend to maintaining employee satisfaction and loyalty toward their organization. The organization must develop its employer branding initiatives as well as provide career pathway options and maintain environments dedicated to employee development and work-life equilibrium throughout personal development.

- **Leadership Development and Succession Planning**

The SHRM organization acknowledges that strong leadership exists within every organizational level. The organization's ability to grow through change periods remains strong when future leaders get developed alongside formal succession plans. The organization develops leadership development strategies to produce capable leaders who steer the company toward its strategic direction.

- Strategic Performance Management

The performance management component of strategic human resource management means more than conducting employee evaluations. The system works toward uniting personal targets with business strategic targets to establish performance expectations through feedback mechanisms and performance-driven reward systems. Every employee should make choices which steer the company based on its strategic vision.

- HR Analytics and Metrics

The increase of data-driven decision-making allows HR professionals in SHRM to use analytics tools that evaluate the success of HR practices. Employee engagement along with training ROI and turnover rates enable HR leaders to optimize decision-making and process efficiency and monitor their organizational performance outcomes.

- Change Management and Organizational Development

The operation of SHRM focuses deeply on change management because business environments experience change as an ongoing force. The organization uses SHRM to succeed through transitions like mergers and cultural changes and technological implementations. Organizational Development within HR functions provides strategic guidance during transformations so the workforce becomes adaptable and meets corporate strategic targets.

- Building a High-Performance Work Culture

SHRM exists to establish high-performance work environments through which employees reach their best performance because they are engaged and motivated and empowered. Through its environment-building efforts SHRM enables organizations to retain strategic momentum and competitive advantage together with achievement of their strategic objectives.

2.2 Linking SHRM with Organizational Sustainability

A business demonstrates organizational sustainability through its ability to sustain economic success together with fulfilling social needs and environmental performance. The focus on sustainable practices by businesses in the 21st century receives support from SHRM which works to establish sustainable principles throughout organizational cultures. The connection between SHRM and sustainability provides companies both monetary success and societal benefits as well as environmental sustainability outcomes.

How SHRM Supports Sustainability

1.Talent Sustainability

SHRM activates organizational sustainability by recruiting proficient employees in addition to sustaining their employment within the workforce. SHRM works to hire people who meet both proficiency standards and corporate sustainable goal ambitions. The organization identifies people committed to responsible social conduct as well as sustainability and ethical business principles to welcome into their workforce. Employees who actively care about sustainability tend to maintain their employment within a single organization thus developing a reliable team foundation.

SHRM holds the essential responsibility to develop sustainable values by helping employees endorse the organization's sustainable principles. SHRM enables sustainability integration within corporate cultures through their programs for employee onboarding and training together with continuous employee development initiatives. Staff members should follow and practice sustainability-driven approaches which align with organizational sustainability targets regardless of their specific contribution methods.

SHRM establishes career development programs that teach sustainable leadership and foster skills needed for sustainable long-term organizational objectives. The company enables its staff members to advance their roles while upholding its sustainable mission which maintains their commitment and drive.

2.Embedding CSR (Corporate Social Responsibility)

Corporate Social Responsibility (CSR) adopts economic social and environmental sustainability responsibilities as a fundamental commitment for companies to maintain responsible business practices in all business operations. The Society for Human Resource Management (SHRM) includes CSR elements within its standard HR operational procedures for assessment methods as well as pay structures and reward systems. Covering all CSR-based employee assessments requires measuring employee involvement with community service programs as well as their contribution to environmental sustainability initiatives and their carbon emission reduction efforts.

SHRM fulfills its essential function in organizational cultural change by running CSR-focused employee training programs about company CSR activities. The integration of sustainability-focused goals within performance evaluation strategies at SHRM enables staff partipation in social projects and environmental protection activities leading to a more dedicated workforce.

The Society for Human Resource Management promotes ethical practices by teaching staff members the significance of making ethical decisions on their tasks. Organizations implement ethical conduct measurements across performance assessments while motivating employees to make decisions regarding social and environmental outcomes of their work activities.

3.Green HRM (Green Human Resource Management)

The main objective of Green HRM is to establish environmentally sustainable practices throughout organizations. The Society for Human Resource Management promotes environmentally friendly workplace practices which include implementing paperless operations while promoting decreased energy use and maximizing resource utilization. HR professionals can launch digital on boarding platforms that decrease paper requirements and launch recycling projects among different departments.

As part of its responsibilities SHRM ensures offices maintain energy-efficient operating standards. The organization needs to adopt energy-saving regulations alongside natural light promotion and develop employee energy consumption reduction strategies. SHRM establishes directions for workers who perform their duties in remote or hybrid modes regarding how to construct energy-efficient home workplaces.

SHRM creates environmental awareness programs that train employees about sustainability concepts. The specialized training educates staff members regarding sustainability value while giving them tools to perform effective ecological footprint reduction. Staff should learn how to minimize unnecessary waste while mastering sustainable supply chain management through responsible consumption and procurement.

4.Inclusive Culture

The Society for Human Resource Management actively supports workplace inclusion as it stands as a fundamental requirement for organizational sustainability. Implementing workforce diversity and inclusion enables organizations to mirror the populations within their operating areas. The establishment of an inclusive workplace environment promotes team-based work alongside religious respect for all individuals which builds a positive brand reputation along with sustainable organizational achievement.

The Society for Human Resource Management builds respect within community relations by supporting volunteer programs through which employees participate in community outreach activities. SHRM establishes multiple channels through which employees participate in community-based social impact projects from direct humanitarian services to neighborhood organization relationships. The organization enhances its community reputation which supports its commitment to social sustainability goals.

As an organization sustains itself SHRM uses its support to foster equity between all employees. By maintaining equal employment possibilities for all personnel whomter races together with backgrounds further enhances employee connection and workplace dedication. An environment of fair treatment inspires better employee morale alongside reduced turnover and makes the organization more respected as a dedicated social employer.

5.Long-Term Planning

The sustainability role of SHRM includes workforce planning strategies that decrease employee turnover because it creates professional advancement paths and enhances company internal value. Sustainable HR practices work toward creating enduring staff relationships that prevent organizations from spending money on constant recruiting and retraining exercises leading to greater financial stability.

Through its SHRM initiative the organization promotes steady workforce development as part of its sustainability methods. Organizations that build their employees' skill sets become more flexible organizations with employees able to succeed during market changes. A commitment to long-term development enables organisations to maintain workers who remain competent in driving sustainability-related projects.

Diversity, equity, and inclusion (DEI) have emerged as ethical imperatives in HR. Companies like SAP and Tata Group demonstrate how inclusive hiring, equitable pay practices, and community-focused leadership shape global HR narratives (SAP, as cited in Unilever, 2020; Tata Group, as cited in SHRM, 2021). Promoting an inclusive culture drives innovation and reflects the evolving expectations of younger workforce generations (Grant, 2013; Wright & McMahan, 2011). National DEI standards and transparent ESG reporting are increasingly recommended by thought leaders to institutionalize these values (European Commission, 2018; World Economic Forum, 2020).

Another essential part of long-term planning in SHRM stands as Succession Planning. Succession planning through HR management enables organizations to develop internal employees who will fill leadership roles when necessary. The organization knows ongoing stability and resilience through this continual approach to support lasting growth throughout time.

2.3 Emerging Challenges and Disruptions Impacting HR

Human Resource Management through a strategic lens faces significant changes in its operational environment. Organizations operating in the contemporary 21st century must deal with numerous emerging problems which create both adaptational issues and innovative solutions for HR professionals. Different emerging difficulties extend from technological progress to demographic changes and new work strategies as well as legal complexities and economy-driven political irregularities. This article provides a comprehensive look at the recent disruptions which are impacting human resource operations.

1. Technological Disruptions

Integration of new technologies represents the most pivotal challenge which current HR professionals face. Technological advancements have transformed every step of organizational work activity including recruiting and performance evaluations which subsequently transformed human resource management systems.

- AI and Automation:

Traditional job design faces challenges because artificial intelligence (AI) and automation tools keep increasing in distribution. Artificial intelligence operates computer systems to complete tasks which humans formerly conducted including data entry together with customer support functions and scheduling activities. The HR team must reassess employee positions with new capabilities while ensemble that workforce members have proper abilities for fresh positions emerging from progress.

The automated workforce affects the entire process of workforce planning. The shift in work requirements requires Human Resource experts to predict and arrange reductions for specific job positions and develop advanced roles that involve creative human decisions and value creation.

The introduction of automation creates an essential requirement to teach both new and older skills to existing employees that will become part of their job duties. Continuous learning must be supplied by HR departments to enable employees to handle technological changes through skill development that supports organizational needs.

- HR Tech:

The latest evolution of HR platforms includes cloud-based solutions that simplify payments and beneficiary management and employee data storage functions among others. The implementation of these tools delivers efficiency to HR departments but demands regular updates about modern technology development as well as seamless system alignment.

AI-assisted screening software among other virtual recruitment tools now dominates candidate acquisition. System algorithms guide the screening of resumes for fit-based assessments and perform virtual initial interviews. HR professionals must handle the unbiased problems that exist within these systems to guarantee AI-enabled tools preserve both fairness and inclusion.

AI-based performance analysis has become a common alternative to standard performance reviews since these tools automatically track employee performance throughout the day. The utilitarian systems supply valuable information about candidates but generate concerns regarding system transparency as well as possible bias and unequal treatment of candidates.

2. Workforce Demographics and Diversity

Organizations are dealing with growing workforce diversity because workers represent different age groups and cultural backgrounds. Many challenges exist regarding diverse workforce management which HR professionals need to handle with precision.

- Multi-Generational Workforce:

Current workplaces consist of Baby Boomer workforce members as well as workers from Generation Z to Millennials. People in different age groups arrive at work with different workplace demands along with their own styles of communication and preferences. Todays work population consists of Baby Boomers who seek job stability but Millennials and Gen Z members focus on work-life purification combined with professional development and meaningful employment. Human Resources needs to construct generation-specific employee engagement approaches which target each worker's individual needs to establish synergy and high productivity within the workplace.

Businesses face staffing challenges because older workers have different motivational drivers from younger people in the workforce. The organization must adopt specific methods that will create team engagement because each staff member should feel supported through flexible benefit structures and remote options alongside personalized career development services.

- Globalization and Cultural Sensitivity:

Global expansion increases the responsibility of Human Resource departments to oversee teams which become more varied in their cultural background. The diverse workplace composition contributes significant value from different points of view yet requires organizations to apply cultural understanding along with inclusive employee approaches. The HR department needs to create training sessions to teach intercultural understanding and establish settings that support teamwork and respect among employees.

HR departments must embed diversity and equity together with inclusion concepts throughout the complete employee cycle starting from recruitment and continuing through to performance reviews and advances. Creating an organizational environment which honors diversity while providing equivalent possibilities to every staff member will drive innovation and achieve operational success.

3. Changing Work Models

The workforce has experienced profound changes because new work methods have appeared to address technological as well as social and economic changes.

- Remote and Hybrid Work:

The adoption of remote work and hybrid models became faster because of the COVID-19 pandemic thus it transformed how businesses handle HR matters. The management of remote teams requires specific strategies because remote work requires dedicated methods to keep employees involved and to track their output alongside effective collaboration in dispersed groups.

Performance monitoring alongside collaboration tasks that were previously handled by traditional HR departments prove considerably more challenging to achieve through virtual means. The implementation of remote performance monitoring tools together with teamwork connection methods along with methods to preserve organizational culture are essential because staff operates from different physical locations.

- Gig Economy:

More employees today work under short-term flexible contracts as part of the expanding flexible economy. The adjustment demands HR professionals to establish modern employee frameworks to manage temporary workers as well as maintain legal compliance and benefits programs that interest freelance labor.

Human Resources needs to establish protocols that deal with specific requirements of freelance workers along with independent contractors by providing both job security assurance and flexible working arrangements and fair payment. The proper alignment of gig workers to match both the organizational values and cultural aspects should remain a challenging task.

4. Legal and Ethical Issues

HR professionals must face substantial obstacles in their work due to permanent modifications in the legal and ethical framework.

- Compliance with Labor Laws and Data Protection:

The expansion of business operations worldwide causes international labor laws to become increasingly complicated for companies to follow. Human Resources should regularly check for legal compliance requirements across different territories because labor regulations transform quickly. The General Data Protection

Regulation (GDPR) alongside other data protection regulations established new strict requirements about how HR practitioners handle employee data collection and storage and data processing operations.

Electronic employee data demands protocols from HR departments to protect information from unauthorized access and illicit intrusions. The necessary elements for HR compliance include upholding privacy standards and maintaining data practice transparency.

- Ethical Concerns in Employee Surveillance and AI Bias:

Remote monitoring tools alongside AI technologies have prompted HR professionals to handle ethical dilemmas that result from employee surveillance activities. The enhanced productivity tools manage performance evaluation but generate doubts about personal space privacy along with employee self-governance.

When used in HR functions including recruitment and performance reviews the algorithms within AI tools frequently reproduce biases. Employee discrimination remains a concern so HR experts must create fair algorithms and regularly test them to prevent discrimination of genders and races and other protected characteristics.

5. Economic and Political Uncertainty

Strategies developed for Human Resources make up a substantial portion of their success based on how the economy along with political conditions evolve.

- Recession, Inflation, and Political Instability:

Declines in the economy as well as rising inflation together with political turbulence have negative effects on workforce stability and both recruitment and compensation systems. Section leaders need to transform their recruitment procedures according to market changes while delivering compensation benefits that match economic uncertainties while maintaining staff security during unstable conditions.

In periods of uncertainty the Human Resources function must develop resilience by providing employees with the flexibility needed for continually adapting. The organization should provide employee cross-training while implementing job rotation programs together with economic downturn contingency plans.

6. Employee Expectations

Workers currently maintain the highest set of expectations the workforce has ever seen. The workforce demands adjustments from Human Resources for delivering effective modern solutions.

- Work-Life Balance:

The workforce now demands both flexible work hours and the option to perform their duties from their home base. Employees require flexible workplace policies which should exist alongside continuing goals of performance output and productivity achievements.

- Mental Health Support:

Mental health has risen to become one of employees' main workplace concerns. The pressure on organizations to provide mental health support requires them to offer Employee Assistance Programs (EAPs) and mental health days in addition to wellness initiatives. The human resources department at the company fulfills a fundamental function by creating well-being oriented staff programs together with workplace policies.

- Purpose-Driven Work:

Numerous workers look for employment opportunities that integrate their individual beliefs. The HR department should guarantee clear mission value communication while helping employees participate in meaningful activities which benefit the society.

3. SCENARIO PLANNING IN HUMAN RESOURCE MANAGEMENT (HRM)

Scenarios represent a strategic Human Resource Management instrument that helps organizations perceive anticipated future uncertainties to create preparedness plans. Through this method HR leader develop advanced foresight regarding business environment changes so they can adapt their workforce strategies effectively. The primary difference between traditional planning and scenario planning emerges from the way scenario planning evaluates diverse likely future conditions to build adaptable HR operations.

Scenario Planning in HRM involves:

Multiple scenarios relating to changes in the economy and technology and changes in the labor market should be considered. The assessment targets how different scenarios affect workforce requirements for capabilities and organization arrangement along with employee numbers.HR strategies should remain adaptable along with being reactive to both internal and external changes.

Why is it Important in HR?

The business environment presents situations that are volatile along with uncertainty while also declaring complex and ambiguous conditions (VUCA). Scenario planning provides HR leaders with tools that help them minimize risks while getting ready for employee-workplace disruptions. An organization can link its HR strategies to extended business objectives through this approach. Facilitates data-driven, future-focused decision-making.

3.1 Conceptual Framework of Scenario Planning

The strategic tactical method of scenario planning enables organisations to create adaptable extended-term plans by determining different potential future scenarios. Through scenario planning organisations can forecast their workforce requirements given various future operating conditions in human resources management.

Conceptual Framework:

Organisations must simultaneously study external PESTEL (Political, Economic, Social, Technological, Environmental, Legal) elements and internal aspects which impact the human resources department.

The process includes recognising crucial uncertain factors which have the potential to affect personnel practices such as Artificial Intelligence system advancements and changes in labor regulations together with population movement patterns.

A set of probable future scenarios which include high automation and economic downturn and talent shortage should be developed.

The analysis evaluates personnel-related implications stemming from different scenarios regarding organisational workforce structure policy development and employee requirements assessment.

The organization must implement strategic HR responses which include designing action plans for recruitment and skill development combined with organizational structure design for all scenarios.

3.2 Tools and Techniques for HR Scenario Planning

Several tools and techniques support effective scenario planning in HR:

- **SWOT and PESTEL Analysis:** Help identify internal and external forces.

- **Scenario Matrix/Grid:** Compares two key uncertainties to develop 2x2 or 3x3 scenario matrices.
- **Trend Analysis:** Tracks labor market trends, technology adoption, and industry developments.
- **Workforce Analytics:** Uses data to forecast future skills, attrition, and demographic changes.
- **Simulation Modeling:** Creates digital models of workforce dynamics under different assumptions.
- **Delphi Technique:** Gathers expert insights to refine scenario assumptions.
- **Scenario Narratives:** Descriptive stories that illustrate possible futures to communicate and engage stakeholders.

Table 1. Tools and Techniques for HR Scenario Planning

Tool/Technique	Purpose	Application in HR Scenario Planning
SWOT & PESTEL Analysis	Identify internal strengths/ weaknesses and external opportunities/threats	Helps understand environmental and organisational factors affecting workforce planning
Scenario Matrix/ Grid	Compare key uncertainties in a matrix (2x2, 3x3)	Develops multiple future HR scenarios based on combinations of uncertainties (e.g., tech adoption vs. regulation)
Trend Analysis	Analyze historical and current data to project future trends	Tracks labour trends, skills demand, demographic shifts, etc.
Workforce Analytics	Use data for forecasting workforce needs and changes	Predicts attrition, skill gaps, and recruitment needs based on real-time data
Simulation Modelling	Create digital models of workforce behaviour	Test outcomes under different scenarios (e.g., policy changes, automation impact)
Delphi Technique	Use expert panels to refine assumptions	Gathers consensus on future HR trends and validates scenario variables
Scenario Narratives	Develop storylines for different futures	Engages stakeholders by illustrating HR impacts in plausible and relatable scenarios

3.3 Case Studies: Scenario-Based Workforce Planning in Practice

Case Study 1: Shell's Scenario Planning

Shell created the first scenario planning approach to react to both political and energy market developments.

The HR team applied various scenarios for planning workforce localisation and leadership pipelines, and reskilling for renewable energy systems.

Case Study 2: IBM

HR professionals at IBM used scenario planning to forecast alterations in international talent supplies as well as AI technological advancements.

The HR department directed its attention to building digital competencies and remote capabilities, and agile system design.

Case Study 3: NHS (UK National Health Service)

The elderly population increases, along with health policy improvements and medical breakthroughs, forming the basis of their scenarios.

The organization combines workforce planning with informed strategies to determine doctor/nurse supply together with training requirements and occupational distributions.

3.4 Benefits and Limitations of Scenario Planning in HR

Benefits:

1. The process enables HR departments to prepare beforehand instead of responding after events occur.
2. The system enables risk mitigation through disruption identification, which leads to prepared contingency plans.
3. Strategic Alignment: Aligns workforce planning with organisational strategy.
4. Agility becomes better through implementation because the process facilitates speedier adjustments to changing environmental conditions.
5. The system supports HR actions through developing training plans and staff recruitment strategies.

4. LIMITATIONS

1. Time and Resource Intensive: Requires significant data gathering and stakeholder engagement. Some unforeseen events remain possible despite scenario planning because the methods are not strictly predictive. Organisational staff face difficulties when they convert intricate situations into practice-ready human resources plans.
2. The assumptions used in the analysis may show bias due to current beliefs or leadership perspectives thus interfering with appropriate objectivity.

HR Scenario Planning Matrix

Step 1: Identify Two Critical Uncertainties

Example Uncertainties:

- Technological Adoption (Low ↔ High)
- Talent Availability (Scarce ↔ Abundant)

Table 2. Scenario Matrix

	Talent Abundant	**Talent Scarce**
High Tech Adoption	Scenario A: Digital Abundance - AI and automation integrated - Skilled talent widely available - Focus on innovation, remote work culture	Scenario B: Smart Shortage - High tech needs but talent gap persists - Need for internal reskilling, automation - Risk of burnout due to skill shortages
Low Tech Adoption	Scenario C: Stable Growth - Gradual tech changes - Sufficient workforce - Emphasis on traditional HR practices	Scenario D: Strained Legacy - Outdated systems + talent scarcity - High attrition - Urgent need for modernization and training

How to Use the Matrix?

- Develop scenario narratives for each quadrant.
- Assess HR implications: skills, hiring, training, structure.
- Design flexible strategies for each possible future.

4.1 Defining Organisational Resilience in the HR Context

Organizational Resilience is shown in an organisation when it plans ahead to cope with both gradual transformation and unforeseen interferences, thereby making it suitable for success even if there is a transformation.

The evolution of an adaptive workforce and a favourable cultural environment in HR leads to:

The workforce has to withstand normal events and unexpected ones, such as pandemics, market instabilities, and technological disturbances.

- Adapt quickly to change

The organisation has to emerge from crises without compromising its levels of productivity.

Employment learning processes make it impossible for new system flaws to arise thereon.

The strategic objectives of HR development and implementation rely on developing organisational Resilience through establishing resilience cultures, effective leadership, and workforce-oriented policies.

4.2 Agility, Flexibility, and Psychological Safety in the Workforce

Workforce Agility

Employees acquire the ability to respond appropriately if the roles, processes, or NERs change.

Teamwork is being built through the application of organisation-wide training systems and the delegation of project-oriented responsibilities down the organisation.

Workforce Flexibility

The strategy allows the staff members to decide where they would work, when, and how to deliver their work.

The employees enjoy home-based and hybrid working arrangements, flexible scheduling during the day, and job sharing through share-based programs and contractual arrangements in the workforce.

Psychological Safety

Individuals in such an environment should be secure to express their thoughts and ideas and further confess about mistakes without really fearing the consequences, which results in more innovation, team collaboration, and quick adaptation during crises.

HR Strategies to Promote These:

- Agile workforce planning
- Mental health support systems
- Flexible HR policies
- Training in empathy and adaptability in the leadership position

A trust-based atmosphere accompanied by the comprehensive mode of communication allows free inter Ä discussion among colleagues.

4.3 The Role of HR in Crisis Management and Business Continuity

Organizations rely on human resources leadership to sustain important service functions and ensure the welfare of personnel during emergencies such as epidemic outbreaks, natural calamities, and economic downturns.

Key HR Responsibilities:

Crisis Response Planning:

Formulating emergency response processes and distant work policies. The efforts to communicate with employees should uphold real-time, transparent updates and aim for absolute staff engagement.

The introduction of organisations to implement Employee Assistance Programs (EAPs) provides programs that support the welfare of employees' mental health, physical health, and financial stability.

Here, the organisation should have flexible regulations on employees' leaves and requirements and provisions regarding benefits.

Strategic Continuity Initiatives:

- Scenario-based workforce planning
- Remote onboarding and virtual learning tools.
- Succession planning for critical roles

4.4 Talent Retention and Upskilling in the Long-Term for Resilience

Talent Retention Strategies:

- Competitive compensation and benefits
- Career development pathways
- Recognition and reward systems
- Employee engagement initiatives

The management should create areas with a high sense of purpose and identification with organisational belonging.

Upskilling and Reskilling:

The organization must identify key skills for the following years: digital literacy, AI, and EI capabilities.

Healthcare providers can use digital learning platforms to obtain access to customised education streams and develop professional development aims.

There is a need for the organisation to adopt micro learning sessions with the mentorship programs and job rotation mechanisms.

Learning activities should be incorporated in performance evaluations and growth plans to achieve goals.

5. WHY IT MATTERS

Such a strategy prepares the employees for future disruptions that will impact the workplace.

Working internally with its own employees, the organization reaps two benefits: it introduces internal movement of workforce and reduces external staffing requirements.

5.1 Defining Ethical Innovation in HR

The combination of leading technologies with policies and practices for HR that don't lose ethical responsibility, develop socially inclusive solutions based on human dignity, and ensure fair and equal operations constitutes Ethical Innovation in HR.

Key Characteristics:

Purpose-driven means that the major purpose of creating better conditions for the employees and company values is declared.

Transparency in innovation implies total disclosure of the intentions, functions, and impact that innovations will have on people (such as handling data).

The approach ensures that there are no cases of exclusion or unfair disadvantages.

The ethical monitoring system has been put in place to prevent wrongful action and the imposition of harm.

Examples:

Bias prevention systems should be used in AI technologies to recruit and achieve optimal delivery.

Design of mental health tools should not invade employees' privacy during the process.

The organization must institute the guidelines to ensure reasonable access to technology for remote work platforms.

5.2 AI and Automation and the Ethics for HR Technology

Technological changes in HR management compel companies to execute their ethical obligations.

Applications:

AI-based resume evaluation and employee assistance through chatbots are contemporary forms of technology integration in human resource operations.

- Predictive analytics in performance and attrition forecasting.
- Used in payroll and attendance systems- automation

Ethical Concerns:

The algorithms are discriminatory since they carry biases from the data records in history.

AI black boxes make their decision-making process very hard to interpret. Employee monitoring systems infringe workers' privacy as they concentrate on their personal information without proper consent. Once jobs are automated, workers become jobless, causing critical issues in their survival.

Ethical Practices:

Companies should conduct bias audits of AI systems and ethically evaluate their impacts. Human supervision should always control critical decisions. The company will have to disclose information concerning its data processing practices with the explicit permission of its users. The organization should offer training programs for the employees whose work functions are automated.

5.3 Inclusive Leadership and Diversity as Moral Musts

Inclusive leadership is more than effective management; it provides an ethical code with equitable treatment and respect for human dignity because all are provided with common opportunities.

Why It Matters:

Promotes organizational justice as well as social responsibility. Various thoughts drive organizations to formulate greater innovations and make superior decisions. Builds trust and psychological safety

Diversity as an Ethical Imperative:

Removal of systemic barriers that encompass such barriers as those affecting gender and racial groups, people with disabilities, and the LGBTQ+ people demands action. Diversity targets are being integrated into practices related to recruitment, as well as systems of promotion, training, and policy formulation exercises.

HR's Role:

- Implement unbiased hiring processes
- Offer inclusive leadership training programs

HR should actively ensure that people are compensated fairly and that all employees have equal opportunities to advance. Organizations should calculate the inclusion performance and organize a response to the feedback received.

5.4 Balancing Profitability with Employee Well-being

It will not contradict the HR profit objectives from an ethical perspective because profit objectives never go against employee welfare, as they prosper together with proper management.

Challenges:

Cost-cutting measures (such as lay-offs and reduction of benefits) and the morale of the employees. Workplaces are presented with a dilemma of annual outputs against giving better life-work harmony. The adoption of surveillance technology is competing with the need to maintain staff autonomy and the exercise of trust.

Ethical Approaches:

For performance, the organizations are required to use the engagement and satisfaction metrics alongside output data. The organization should channel its efforts into developing mental health programs, flexible work arrangements, and dealing with employee burnout. Profit-sharing and incentive models need to be applied, as they promote performance delivery and teamwork on equal terms. It is more reasonable for the organization to use its resources to create employees for the long term instead of the immediate labor optimization programs.

6. COMBINED STRATEGIC MODEL OF SUSTAINABLE HRM

Sustainable HRM (Human Resource Management) refers to a long-term strategy for human resource administration that relates business strategies to the priorities of Sustainability between People and Planet and Profit. The integrated model moves scenarios forward with planning in conjunction with organizational resilience and ethical innovation, to protect the workforce from future alterations but provide strategic, ethical, and inclusive operations.

6.1 Combining Scenario Planning, Resilience, and Ethics

Table 3. Dimensions

Element	Purpose	Contribution to Sustainable HRM
Scenario Planning	Anticipate multiple futures	Prepares HR for uncertainty; helps design adaptive workforce plans
Organizational Resilience	Bounce back and grow from disruption	Builds agile, mentally strong, and change-ready teams
Ethical HR Innovation	Align technology and practices with values	Ensures fairness, inclusion, and long-term employee trust

6.2 A Framework for Implementation in Organisations

A structured framework helps translate this integrated model into an actionable strategy:

Step-by-Step Framework:

1. **Assessment & Baseline Mapping**
   - o Analyse current HR practices
   - o Identify risks, opportunities, and stakeholder needs
2. **Build Scenarios**
   - o Use tools (PESTEL, SWOT, 2x2 matrices) to map future HR contexts
   - o Create HR response plans for each scenario
3. **Embed Resilience**
   - o Design policies for agility (cross-skilling, remote work, flexi-hours)
   - o Foster psychological safety and leadership in crisis
4. **Apply Ethical Filters**
   - o Vet technologies and policies through ethical principles: transparency, consent, fairness
   - o Implement DEI (Diversity, Equity, Inclusion) frameworks
5. **Align with Strategic Goals**
   - o Ensure HR initiatives support sustainability, ESG (Environmental, Social, Governance), and long-term talent strategy
6. **Monitor, Learn & Improve**
   - o Create feedback loops to refine strategy based on real-world outcomes

6.3 Metrics and KPIs for Evaluating Sustainable HR Outcomes

To evaluate effectiveness, organizations need metrics that go beyond traditional HR performance to include sustainability, ethics, and resilience.

7. BALANCED SCORECARD INTEGRATION

These metrics can be incorporated into a **Balanced Scorecard** under the *People*, *Learning & Growth*, and *Social Responsibility* perspectives.

7.1 Policy Recommendations for Future-Ready HR Systems

Why it matters:

National and institutional policy has to shift with the rate of technological disruption, demographics, and climate-related threats to work.

Modernise Labour Legislation:

New labour laws should be established to match the modern-day working environment. This entails recasting the terms “workplace”,” working hours,” and” employment” to include remote, gig, and freelance work roles. Besides, governments ought to establish minimum standards for the digital workplace environment to guarantee protections such as the right to disconnect, a stance on ergonomics, and cybersecurity requirements for remote workers.

AI Governance in HR:

To encourage fairness and accountability, new rules should demand transparency of algorithms and regular checking of AI tools adopted in HR processes like hiring, performance evaluation, and promotions. A “human-in-the-loop” policy has to be implemented to provide a fail-safe for AI decisions, especially in HR processes where much is at risk.

National DEI Standards:

National frameworks should require payment disclosure and conduct systematic audits of pay inequalities. Public institutions will need to implement training and certification programs that are obligatory for all staff members and aim to spread DEI within different fields.

Skills & Sustainability Investments:

Policymakers should upskill and reskill ordinary people, with a greater emphasis on vulnerable sectors such as manufacturing and retail, for the benefit of all. In addition, companies that introduce eco-friendly HR processes, like the promotion of telecommuting or the use of digital HR tools, should benefit from tax concessions.

7.2 Strategic Recommendations for Business Leaders

Why it matters:

CEOs and senior leaders should lead the way in actively incorporating ethics, agility, and sustainability into their workforce strategy to future-proof their workforce.

Include HR in the Strategic Planning:

HR should jointly develop business models with the finance groups, operations, and technology departments. Using workforce analytics to gain insight into talent needs is crucial before such events as mergers, product launches, and geographic expansion.

Lead with Ethics & Empathy:

The business leaders should normalize discussions on mental health, diversity, and organisational purpose. Ethical dilemmas, such as the ones involving layoffs or pay cuts, should be resolved via open and inclusive decision-making processes.

Put Purpose & Culture Before Perks:

Corporations should establish a values-driven culture instead of spending all their money on trivial employee perks. HR policies must align with the company's core values, such as Patagonia's involvement with sustainability and Google's culture of innovation.

Implementation of ESG Reporting in HR:

Organisations should begin to release and publish HR-linked environmental, social, and governance (ESG) numbers such as employee well-being scores, training hours per employee, percentage of employees in green jobs, and the failure rate because of poor organisational culture.

7.3 The Capacity Building and HR Training Programs

Why it matters:

Old HR skills are not enough; HR agents of the current time should be tech-literate, data-savvy, ethically aware, and change leaders.

Scenario Planning and Strategic Foresight:

HR teams should be trained to construct the best-case, worst-case, and most likely workforce futures based on instruments such as PESTEL analysis, trend analysis, and driver mapping.

Organisational Resilience and Crisis Management: Training programs should include business continuity planning, psychological first aid, and strategies for dealing with return-to-work transitions after crises, pandemics, or natural disasters.

AI and HR Technology Literacy: HR teams should acquire proficiency in HR analytics through tools such as Power BI, Tableau, and simple Python. Programs should also examine responsible AI practice in recruitment and talent management and compliance with GDPR and employee data protection provisions.

DEI and Ethical Leadership: Inclusive onboarding courses and certifications, accessibility laws, and cross-cultural communication courses are essential for constructing diverse and inclusive organisations.

Sustainability and ESG: HR's Role in ESG. HR must be trained to minimize an organisation's carbon footprint through paperless onboarding, green commuting, and supporting sustainability-themed positions.

Delivery Models: These training efforts can be provided by establishing alliances with ed-tech platforms such as Coursera, edX, and SHRM. Other innovative models are gamified mobile learning for frontline HR teams, peer-to-peer learning communities, and mentoring programs.

8. CASE STUDIES AND REAL-WORLD EXAMPLES

This section draws examples of what is actually happening in practice regarding strategic, ethical, and resilient HR practices being implemented in different industries and geographies to provide insight into how they could be successfully implemented.

8.1 Cross-Industry Best Practices

In the technology world, Google (Alphabet Inc.) has led in data-driven HR, using analytics in hiring and the effective development of teams. Prestigious Projects are "Project Oxygen", which dived into identifying important managerial traits, and "Project Aristotle", which focused on psychological safety. In the manufacturing industry, Toyota has promoted Lean HR practices and continuous learning whereby employees are encouraged to stop production, believing that "what is good for the goose is also good for the gander, " and kaizen is incorporated in HR evaluations and internal movement. In the retail setting, Costco leads the league in terms of fair wages and high loyalty to staff, with wages above the industry pay rates and low turnover rates despite difficult working conditions. In health care, the Mayo Clinic has developed an environment of team-based care and resilience, and recruits for emotional intelligence. It implements programs for burnout through workload redesign and support programs.

8.2 Lessons from Global Organizations

A good example of a purpose-driven strategy toward the workforce is the Unilever company, where sustainability and well-being are grounded in performance appraisals, with flexible work pushed by its "Future of Work" program. SAP has been spearheading digital transformations by pursuing the inclusion initiative through its "Autism at Work" program and ethical AI use, in addition to the full transparency of its employees. Tata Group (India) is an example of a morally and community-oriented company regarding HR: education and housing benefits, ethics training and hotlines, and the inclusion of social impact into HR KPIS.

8.3 "Success stories" of ethical and resilient HR innovations

Microsoft has undergone a culture change under CEO Satya Nadella from a "know-it-all" to a "learn-it-all" approach, bringing in the empathetic culture, emotional intelligence, and psychological safety. Such tools as Glint help conduct real-time sentiment tracking to improve the employee experience. Patagonia distinguishes itself with values-led HR, providing paid holidays for environmental activism and family-friendly and flexible policies, which lead to great retention and loyalty. Accenture has made significant advancements in responsible AI, creating a Centre of Excellence in HR and making performance measurement transparent. The organisation also publicly monitors and declares its activities toward diversity hiring and pay equity – a demonstration of genuine accountability & inclusion.

CONCLUSION

Strategic Human Resource Management (SHRM) in the 21st century has transformed from a classical administration function to a progressive and data-focused ethical enabler of organizations. This chapter took a comprehensive look at how technological progress, changes in the demography, new work models, and the sustainability imperative were transforming HR into a strategic partner in embracing long-term corporate success. The practice of scenario planning, organizational resilience, and ethical innovation in the HR frameworks has become necessary when addressing the volatile, uncertain, complex, and ambiguous (VUCA) environment.

Lastly, aligning profitability with employee well-being is not a contradiction but a strategic advantage. Companies such as Costco and Patagonia prove that investing in fair wages, mental health, and sustainable policies results in higher retention and brand loyalty (Costco & Patagonia, as cited in Gollan et al., 2021; Jackson et al., 2011). As SHRM continues to evolve, ethical leadership, purpose-driven work, and continuous upskilling are emerging as key pillars for a sustainable and resilient future of work (Boudreau & Ramstad, 2007; Beer et al., 2015). The combined effect of these practices is a workforce that is productive, fulfilled, empowered, and aligned with long-term business and societal goals.

Compared to companies that do not align the HR practices to sustainability sensibilities – embedding diversity, equity, inclusion (DEI), green HRM, and ethical AI – organizations that adopt this integration will enjoy increased employee engagement, better retention of talent, and better social legitimacy. HR is now at the (center) stage in implementing purpose, agile and inclusive teams, and systems that put well-being, adaptability, and long-term value creation first. With the help of policy interventions, strategic leadership, capacity building, and real-world case applications, this chapter presents the actionable insights and best practices for future-ready HR systems. Finally, sustainable HRM goes beyond an operational need and is also a moral and strategic requirement in developing the future's humane, inclusive, and resilient workforce.

REFERENCES

Accenture. (2020). *Responsible AI and HR Transformation*. Accenture Insights.

Beer, M., Boselie, P., & Brewster, C. (2015). Back to the future: Implications for the field of HRM. *Human Resource Management, 54*(3), 429–446. DOI: 10.1002/hrm.21726

Bersin, J. (2019). *HR Technology Disruptions for 2019: The Rise of the Individual*. Deloitte Insights.

Boudreau, J. W., & Ramstad, P. M. (2007). *Beyond HR: The New Science of Human Capital*. Harvard Business Press.

Boxall, P., & Purcell, J. (2016). *Strategy and Human Resource Management* (4th ed.). Palgrave Macmillan. DOI: 10.1007/978-1-137-40765-8

Chatterji, A. K., Levine, D. I., & Toffel, M. W. (2009). How well do social ratings actually measure corporate social responsibility? *Journal of Economics & Management Strategy, 18*(1), 125–169. DOI: 10.1111/j.1530-9134.2009.00210.x

Deloitte. (2020). *2020 Global Human Capital Trends*. Retrieved from https://www2.deloitte.com/

European Commission. (2018). *AI Ethics Guidelines for Trustworthy AI*. Retrieved from https://ec.europa.eu/

Gollan, P. J., Kalfa, S., & Xu, Y. (2021). Strategic HRM and corporate social responsibility. *International Journal of Human Resource Management, 32*(13), 2751–2773.

Grant, A. (2013). *Give and Take: Why Helping Others Drives Our Success*. Viking.

. AON Hewitt. (2018). *Trends in Global Employee Engagement*.

IBM. (2020). *HR 3.0: Reinventing the Future of Work*. IBM Institute for Business Value.

Jackson, S. E., Renwick, D. W. S., Jabbour, C. J. C., & Muller-Camen, M. (2011). State-of-the-art and future directions for green HRM. *Zeitschrift für Personalforschung, 25*(2), 99–116.

Mayo Clinic. (2021). Team-based Care and Burnout Interventions. *Mayo Clinic Proceedings*.

Microsoft. (2021). *The Work Trend Index*. Microsoft Research.

PWC. (2021). *The Future of Work*. PricewaterhouseCoopers.

Schwartz, J.. (2020). *The social enterprise at work: Paradox as a path forward.* Deloitte.

SHRM. (2019). *AI in HR Survey*. Society for Human Resource Management.

SHRM. (2021). *Workplace Culture and Employee Engagement Report*. Society for Human Resource Management.

Ulrich, D., Brockbank, W., Johnson, D., Sandholtz, K., & Younger, J. (2012). *HR Competencies: Mastery at the Intersection of People and Business*. Society for Human Resource Management.

UNGC & Accenture. (2021). *CEO Study on Sustainability*. United Nations Global Compact.

Unilever. (2020). *Future of Work & Sustainable Living Report*. Unilever PLC.

World Economic Forum. (2020). *Jobs of Tomorrow: Mapping Opportunity in the New Economy*.

Wright, P. M., & McMahan, G. C. (2011). Exploring human capital: Putting 'human' back into strategic human resource management. *Human Resource Management Journal, 21*(2), 93–104. DOI: 10.1111/j.1748-8583.2010.00165.x

Chapter 14
Strategic Human Resource Innovations for Sustainable Organizational Futures:
Scenario Planning, Resilience Strategies, and Ethical Innovation

Natia Surmanidze
http://orcid.org/0000-0003-2116-6571
Ilia State University, Georgia

ABSTRACT

This chapter explores the strategic role of human resource innovations in shaping sustainable organizational futures within the evolving e-economy. Focusing on scenario planning, resilience strategies, and ethical innovation, the chapter examines how forward-looking HR practices can enhance organizational adaptability, long-term competitiveness, and stakeholder trust. Drawing from theories of dynamic capabilities, foresight, and ethical decision-making, the chapter provides a conceptual framework supported by case examples from digitally transformative organizations. It analyzes the integration of future-oriented planning into HR systems, the development of resilient and agile workforces, and the implementation of ethically grounded innovation in HR processes. By synthesizing academic research and practitioner insights, this chapter contributes to the discourse on sustainable and strategic human capital management in technology-driven environments.

DOI: 10.4018/979-8-3373-4307-5.ch014

INTRODUCTION

The development pace within the digital economy has significantly altered the form and function of organized businesses and the ever-changing nature of human resources within organizations. Organized businesses find themselves pressed to change HR practices to survive and sustain themselves as well as live up to their ethical responsibilities towards society (Lengnick-Hall, Beck, & Lengnick-Hall, 2011). As globalization, automation, and digitization change traditional ways of conducting businesses, change is also needed within human resources to ensure that they function strategically within organizations (Schiuma & Santarsiero, 2018).

Strategic innovations in human resources, especially scenario planning, building resilience, and ethical innovations, are now indispensable for organizations to manage uncertainty and get ready for disruptions. Scenario planning allows HR practitioners to look into possible or imagined futures to achieve pro-active rather than reactive decision-making approaches (Wright, Bradfield, & Cairns, 2013).

Conversely, the emerging technology-enabled 'smart' HR approach has raised various ethical issues pertaining to inclusivity and transparency, especially with regard to decision-support technology and AI recruitment tools, giving rise to new challenges for HR ethics (Tursunbayeva, Pagliari, & Bunduchi, 2018). Contemporary ethical practices in HR are no longer confined to ensuring statutory or reputational obligations but are instead essential for ensuring legitimacy and stakeholder confidence (Greenwood & Freeman, 2011).

To effectively address these, HRM needs to develop a more human-centered approach to its strategies. This is because while technology development is important, focus on human dignity, justice, and well-being must also get equal emphasis. As companies are integrating information technology into various human resource tasks, it has become important to pursue work relations that are not only technical but also ethical. This means that instead of only seeking to develop technology-aided strategies for better human resources, HRM needs to also seek to develop strategies for more resilient and inclusive organizations.

Worldwide inequalities in terms of digitization, labor laws, and institutional development also add to the difficulties in the execution of strategic HR innovations. For instance, companies operating within the jurisdiction of the European Union are expected to adhere to very tough data protection legislation including the provisions of GDPR, while companies operating within emerging countries tend to operate in environments where they are exposed to limited regulation, including within new market environments where they are confronted with more significant ethical issues.

The rapidly increasing pace of digitization has also emphasized the need for 'digital literacy' in organizations. As technology and advanced technology-enabled systems become more pervasive in day-to-day HR tasks, every employee in organizations must develop skills to effectively utilize technology-enabled systems. Skilling and up-skilling, once desirable interventions, are now essential for sustained business success. It is important for every employee, from front-line to leadership, to possess 'digital skills' to ensure business sustainability.

HR needs to develop cutting-edge strategies to support adaptive, inclusive, and future-oriented 'learning workspaces' to match future needs. The nature of this change also speaks to the need for inter-disciplinary cooperation. The current paradigms for strategic HR management are ever-closer to data sciences, ethics, information systems, psychology, and organizational behaviors. It has become essential for HR to align themselves with other departments within organizations, including information technology and other executive departments, to develop technically feasible and ethically valid solutions. This inter-disciplinary approach makes it possible to design intelligent HR systems, dynamic workforce strategies, and ethically informed decision-support frameworks. It also re-emphasizes HR's ability to support organizations strategically on matters pertaining to innovations and governance. This volume adds to the body of literature on SR-Ms-HR by highlighting how scenario planning, resiliency strategies, and ethical innovations are important for shaping organizations that are future-ready. This volume has provided inter-disciplinary guidance on how to develop strategies to align organizations for making them fit for the digital economy, with its emphasis on how sustainable future strategies are not only dependent on innovations and technologies but also on how work environments are to become safe and healthy for its most important asset – its human resources, working in conjunction with technology.

Objective

The aim of this chapter is to examine how strategic innovations in human resources—based on scenario planning, resilience building, and ethical innovation—can be leveraged to prepare organizations for long-term sustainability in the digital economy. This chapter aims to provide both a theoretical and pragmatic framework for human resource practitioners, scholars, and policymakers involved in the challenge of realigning human capital strategies to meet the demands of an uncertain and ethically complex business environment.

Methodology

This chapter adopts a conceptual and exploratory approach based on a thorough examination of academic literature and recent trends in strategic HRM. In addition, it will present empirical case studies from multinational corporations, technology-oriented organizations, and digital companies to illustrate the practical application of scenario planning, resilience tactics, and ethical innovation. The case studies will connect theoretical concepts with practice, providing insightful observations into success-driving factors as well as the challenges experienced by organizations at the vanguard of HR transformation.

STRATEGIC SCENARIO PLANNING IN HRM

Identifying Future Work Trends and Digital Disruption Scenarios

The modern labor market is going through profound changes, driven by the likes of advances in technology, changes in demographics, changes in climate, and changing expectations among workers. Of specific mention is the rise in remote and hybrid working patterns, driven by digital infrastructure and further accelerated by the worldwide COVID-19 pandemic. These arrangements upset traditional assumptions on productivity, performance, and motivation (Kniffin et al., 2021). In tandem with this, increases in the gig economy and platform-based work, especially among the young, are leading to new models of employment that emphasize flexibility and autonomy over job certainty. It is critical that human resource managers become aware of these changes so that they develop resilient frameworks for the workforce that are aligned with organizational goals as well as workers' values.

One important trend that is shaping organizational environments today is the application of artificial intelligence (AI) and machine learning in different functional sectors, including those in human resources. The evolution of automation is gradually taking over mundane, rule-based jobs, thus freeing up human workers to focus on decision-making efforts and creative activity (Brynjolfsson & McAfee, 2017). This transition, however, poses challenges in planning for the workforce, particularly in ensuring that important skills match with functions that might become redundant. Human resource managers need to undertake skill projection, identify weaknesses in digital capabilities, and promote the need for lifelong learning for the sake of competitiveness. Poor adjustment to such technologies can lead to a dissonance between the organizational strategic objectives and the workforce capabilities.

In concert with technological progress, changes in demographics and generational attitudes profoundly define the future shape of employment. The entry of Generation Z into the workplace brings specific values and expectations with it, which include a desire for meaningful work, values-based leadership, and advocacy for mental well-being (Francis & Hoefel, 2018). This generation is highly digital-savvy and expects instant communication and instant feedback, thus revolutionizing current performance management systems and leadership practices. In contrast, the rising age in populations in different developed countries also presents a challenge in respect to collaboration between generations and knowledge transition. Therefore, strategic scenario planning by human resources must account for such changed demographics to ensure inclusive and multigenerational workplaces that draw on a variety of diverse capabilities.

Digital disruption refers to the restructuring of organizational structures and business models that underpin employment. Conventional hierarchical structures are increasingly being replaced by networked, project-based, and interdisciplinary arrangements. The use of agile methods alongside decentralized decision-making processes has become a necessity for speedy responses to changes in the market and innovation waves (Lee, Edmondson, Thomke, & Worline, 2021). These changes call for a review of talent acquisition strategies, leadership development practices, and team dynamics. Human resource professionals are required to anticipate a variety of organizational settings—from virtual teams to flexible gig networks—and develop workforce policies designed to drive performance and cohesion in various employment arrangements. In summary, external shocks in the form of climate-related crises, geopolitical tensions, and pandemics, for example, are expected to continue shaping future workplace situations. These disruptions put the adaptability and resilience of human resource (HR) functions in ensuring business continuity, maintaining the well-being of employees, and enabling remote working arrangements to the test. Scenario planning as a process enables HR managers to develop predictive models that replicate future events and judge organizational reactions to different scenarios (Ramirez, Mukherjee, Vezzoli, & Kramer, 2015). By observing early warning signs and using systematic methods of foresight, HR can increase its capability to anticipate disruptions and embed resilience in workforce planning. Eventually, predicting and responding to emerging trends and disruption scenarios will distinguish agile organizations from those that falter in a shifting environment.

Illustrative Scenario: A mid-sized technology firm operating in Southeast Asia faced a sudden skills shortage when automation displaced 30% of administrative roles. Through scenario planning, HR leaders had already developed a contingency workforce strategy that included rapid reskilling programs, cross-trained internal talent pools, and partnerships with online learning providers. As a result, 65% of affected employees were successfully redeployed into emerging digital roles within six months, reducing turnover and maintaining operational stability.

Integrating Foresight into HR Planning Cycles

Strategic foresight applied in human resource management entails exploring plausible, likely, and desirable future states. The need for foresight has arisen as a consequence of living in a dynamic environment characterized by technological and societal change. This has created situations where classical strategic human resources planning practices are no longer sufficient. On this basis, HR practitioners can utilize foresight practices including horizon scanning, trending, and scenario-building to enhance preparedness and response to change within organizations (Habegger, 2010). In contrast to viewing workforce planning as a cyclical administrative function, foresighted HR departments take a pro-active and dynamic approach. This also means monitoring technological, economic, political, and societal trends that can potentially impact workforce availability and skills needs (Slaughter, 1997). By using foresightedness in conjunction with established HR functions related to succession, recruitment, and leadership development, organizations can effectively align their human capital strategies with evolving business needs and innovation objectives.

Cross-functional foresight teams are also a great means to integrate foresight into HR strategies. Members include HR executives, strategists, and technology experts, along with outsiders, analyzing new trends and using them to create new strategic stories for the future. This is followed by new HR interventions, including reskilling, new jobs, and flexi workforce strategies (Rohrbeck, Battistella, & Huizingh, 2015). This inclusivity adds to the usefulness and authenticity of foresight outputs. Digital technology and predictive analytics capabilities enhance foresighted workforce planning. AI and big data analytics can better track emerging patterns in human capital and provide forecasts of skills gaps in the future or estimate risks for employee turnover (Bersin, 2017). It can also provide decisions for feasible future strategies considering various circumstances, making informed workforce decisions with agility. This raises the level of HR work from support services to more strategic partnership for sustainability and innovations within organizations.

Effective foresight integration also needs relevant capabilities to be developed in HR functions. This can involve advancing skills in systems thinking, strategic analysis, or scenario-building, in addition to nurturing an environment where experimentation and learning can occur. Review sessions on foresight can assist organizations to assess their own development stage in regard to planning practices and shifts needed in this respect for improvement (Milojević & Inayatullah, 2015). It is also important to involve leadership to ensure that foresight outputs are integrated into organizations' strategy.

Tools and Practices for Long-Range Workforce Planning

The roots of strategic scenario planning trace back to military and energy forecasts in the 1960s. It has been widely applied to strategic planning within organizations later on. It plays a pivotal role in connecting uncertainty within the environment and employee readiness within HRM, helping organizations develop strategic resilience instead of relying on reactions to change (Habegger, 2010; Slaughter, 1997).

Strategic workforce planning refers to a long-term approach that integrates human capital with business strategies, technology, and future disruptions. For organizations operating within dynamic environments, HR practitioners need to focus on long-term strategies that involve more than just present workforce requirements. This approach to workforce planning entails analyzing present workforce skills, making predictions about future workforce demands, and creating strategies for future workforce gaps in skills (Cappelli, 2008). As opposed to workforce planning, strategic workforce planning is adaptable.

Competency mapping and skills analysis are basic practices adopted in long-term workforce strategies. Models derived from competency mapping and skills analysis empower organizations to evaluate core skills possessed by existing workforces and align them with new skills needed in emerging occupations. When combined with workforce analytics, competency frameworks give HR professionals foresight into occupations that are expected to change, evolve, or become redundant as a consequence of digitization and automation (Fitz-enz & Mattox, 2014). Secondly, scenario planning enhances workforce strategies to evaluate various probable future situations, which include technological disruptions, demography shifts, and geopolitical risks (Wright et al., 2013). Scenario planning enables HR professionals to develop adaptable workforce strategies to support talent pipelines in volatile environments, particularly in digitally dependent industries.

Enhancing workforce-planning efforts with DEI can improve both the resilience and sustainability efforts of organizations. Organizations can create more adaptable and innovative workforces by using data on demographics, pay equity, and inclusive hiring practices for talent acquisition, according to Hunt et al. (2018). Agility also remains important for organizations as they can quickly change direction in response to market shifts or technological change using adaptable workforce structures and up-to-date information. After analyzing how forward-thinking workforce preparation enables organizations to manage uncertainty, it is essential to address how HR systems implement workforce agility to ensure resilience through adaptive learning in the next part.

BUILDING ORGANIZATIONAL RESILIENCE THROUGH HR

Adaptive Learning Systems and Workforce Agility

In a time marked by ongoing upheaval, the value of learning and adaptability inside organizations has become a strategic imperative rather than a personal choice.

Adaptive learning systems provide holistic, technology-based systems that enable continuous skill building and re-skill for workers, addressing imminent business needs and emerging competency requirements. These systems go beyond learning management systems by involving the use of artificial intelligence, data analytics, and personalized learning tracks to enable quick and responsive learning experiences (Bersin, 2018). Embedding learning in processes, organizations enable workers to acquire relevant skills without compromising productivity levels, enhancing both individual and business agility.

Workforce agility is the capacity for organizations to rapidly mobilize, reconfigure, and redeploy people in response to both external and internal changes. Agile workers can be characterized by collaborative, cross-functional teams, flexible roles, decentralized decision-making, and a strong climate for innovation (Spreitzer, Sutcliffe, Dutton, Sonenshein, & Grant, 2005). Contrary to traditional hierarchical organizations, agile organizations switch to less hierarchical designs, with shorter planning horizons, and often utilize practices like Scrum or Kanban in order to organize work activities. In the Human Resources area, this requires the building of talent systems to enable agility—by defining flexible roles, implementing cross-training, and promoting lateral movement within the organization.

Adaptive learning systems are key enablers for workers' flexibility. By regularly updating educational material and making it appropriate for the changing business landscape, the systems allow workers to gain the knowledge and skills required to solve arising problems. For example, microlearning modules, mobile learning platforms, and AI-powered content recommendation help workers gain new skills in shorter time periods, thus increasing workers' flexibility in moving from one role or group to another (Valamis, 2020). In addition, organizations that promote the growth mindset and develop a psychologically safe environment that supports innovation are more likely to build agile learning cultures, where failures are seen as chances for learning as opposed to failure.

The role of Human Resources (HR) plays a central role in promoting organizational agility by implementing frameworks that enable adaptive capabilities. This includes competency-based educational models, career development frameworks, and dynamic performance management systems built on the principles of feedback, coaching, and dynamic goal realignment. Integrated with workforce planning, these frameworks ensure proper alignment of staff with the corresponding positions at the right times, ensuring mitigation of skill gaps and promoting operational agility (Ulrich, Younger, Brockbank, & Ulrich, 2012). In addition, HR needs to develop leadership at every tier in the organization to enable teams to make independent decisions, thereby improving responsiveness and promoting innovativeness in high-stress situations. The proper integration of workplace flexibility with learning that is adaptable requires a corporate culture that supports continuous learning, innovation, and collaboration. This cultural shift must be supported by top-level leadership and propagated through encouraging reward systems, fiscal investment in training, and open communication. Organizations with a focus on flexibility and continuous learning stand a greater chance to survive and thrive in the face of emerging technologies, market changes, and shifting customer demand. Adaptive learning systems become strategic levers for building a working population experienced in dealing with complexity and supported by long-term sustainability as a result.

Psychological Safety, Wellbeing, and Crisis Leadership

In environments that feature persistent change, great unpredictability, and digital disruption, the concepts of psychological safety and well-being among employees are seen as critical building blocks for successful human resource management. Psychological safety is defined as a shared perception within a group where members can open up with their authentic, unedited selves without fear of criticism, ostracism, or reprisal (Edmondson, 1999). This practice fosters open communication, fuels creativity, and prevents withholding essential input out of perceived risk. In today's reality of remote working, digital surveillance, and computer-assisted collaboration, maintaining psychological safety requires intentional human resource practices, leadership with emotional awareness, and inclusive communication systems that facilitate respect and trust at all levels in the organization.

Employee well-being includes not just physical but also mental, emotional, and social dimensions. The digital economy's challenges, particularly job insecurity, increased technological demands, and the blurring of professional and personal spaces, call for holistic wellbeing strategies from human resources. These might take the form of mental health interventions, flexible working arrangements, digital disconnection policies, and supervisory training for emotional support (Krekel, Ward, & De Neve, 2019). Evidence from experience shows that organizations with strong wellbeing cultures enjoy greater productivity, less absenteeism, and improved retention levels. Wellbeing is thus not a purely ethical imperative, but a strategic investment in the long-term viability of the workforce.

Crisis leadership has become a top priority for Human Resources, specifically in the wake of the COVID-19 pandemic, which brought into sharp relief the value of organizational resilience and compassionate leadership. Crisis managers who perform exceptionally well in crises demonstrate characteristics that go beyond being decisive and flexible; they are oriented towards humans first. They practice open communication, validate workers' fears, and prioritize well-being and safety even in the midst of business difficulties (Ganson, 2020). Human Resources needs to nurture and develop such managers through the inclusion of crisis management, emotional intelligence, and ethical decision-making in leadership development. This guarantees that managers not merely cope with normal problems but also navigate through tricky, high-level crises.

The role of Human Resources (HR) in promoting well-being and psychological safety includes the building of mechanisms for the detection of early signs of burnout, disengagement, and emotional exhaustion. The use of pulse surveys, digital sentiment, and check-ins enable the detection of problems before they become serious ones. Additionally, the inclusion of wellbeing metrics on performance reports and strategic dashboards emphasizes the significance in leadership conversations (Saks, 2022). HR professionals need to partner with line managers so that wellbeing is not seen as a stand-alone initiative but as part of the total experience and workplace culture. In summary, building psychological safety, encouraging employee well-being, and developing skilled crisis leadership form the building blocks for building a resilient workforce. These elements interlock: open communication as a product of psychological safety, in turn, heightens skilled crisis management and supports greater well-being. In the digital era, marked by constant change and elevated levels of anxiety, organizations that focus on the human dimensions of change stand a greater chance for maintaining performance, loyalty, and creativity in the face of challenges. Human resources' changing role is to create efficient systems as well as empathetic workplace environments in which individuals can flourish, even in conditions of uncertainty.

Designing Resilient Organizational Cultures and Structures

The notion of organizational resilience involves more than the management of crises; it is actually underpinned by strong cultural and structural qualities that support adaptability, continuity, and long-term success. An organizational culture of resilience prioritizes trust, accountability, innovation, and shared learning. These cultural factors promote the perception of confidence and psychological safety, which are vital for employees to actively problem-solve continuously, especially under high-stress conditions (Lengnick-Hall, Beck, & Lengnick-Hall, 2011). Organizations that actively support these values across different departments, leadership levels, and in remote or hybrid teams are more likely to have the ability to bounce back from disruptions and capture opportunities for growth. The Human Resources (HR) function has a central role to play in establishing and promoting such cultural norms through values-based recruitment practices, reward structures, and leadership development programs.

At the organizational level, resilient organizations move from rigid hierarchies to flexible and connected systems. Flexible organizational systems enable fast decision-making, improved cross-functional cooperation, and accelerated re-allocation of resources as situations change (Aghina, De Smet, & Weerda, 2015). Central to this model is flat organizational forms, decentralised decision-making authority, and empowered teams. These features enable frontline workers to act to change in customer demands or in addressing organizational challenges without waiting for top-level directives. Human Resources need to coordinate role definitions, performance metrics, and reward systems to enable autonomy and responsibility through all organizational levels.

Redundancy is a basic structural element of resilience. In contrast to traditional models of efficiency that aim to remove slack, resilient organizations deliberately maintain redundancies like redundant skills, redundant supply chains, or cross-trained staff to ensure business continuity in times of disruption (Vogus & Sutcliffe, 2007). Human Resources can enable this practice by developing manpower strategies that promote job rotation, competency overlap, and career successional opportunities. Redundancy can appear unproductive in the short run, but in times of crisis, the rapid redeployment of skills and resources is vital for survival.

Channels of communication become paramount in building both cultural and structural resilience. Clearly defined, open, and two-way channels provide employees with accurate and timely information in times of uncertainty. It is also vital that the channels enable two-way communication through which leadership can make well-informed decision-making based on input from frontline workers (Duchek, 2020). The Human Resources section can facilitate this program by putting in place tools like virtual town hall meetings, encouraging listening, and building social networks in the workplace that promote open communications. A communication culture that is inclusive not only promotes trust, but also increases the cohesiveness and agility of the organization in times of change.

In summary, building a strong organizational structure and culture is a strategic effort that requires deliberate design and continuous refinement. The Human Resources division has a dual role to function as both the designer and custodian for this shift—incorporating resilience practices in organizational systems, policies, and daily activities. This includes developing leadership habits that embody resilience and empathy, building organizational traditions that emphasize resilience, and utilizing facts to measure cultural vibrancy. Organizations that embed resilience both in cultural and structural systems are best positioned to navigate disruptions, recover from crises, and create persistent value in the digital age.

Balancing Automation and Human Dignity

The increasing reliance on automation and artificial intelligence (AI) in organizational functions poses a tremendous challenge to human resource management, especially in upholding the dignity of man in the face of technological advancement. As much as automation certainly has improvements in efficiency and cost savings in business undertakings, it also raises essential questions relating to displacement, skill degradation, and reduced personal interaction in the workplace (Acemoglu & Restrepo, 2019). It is the responsibility of human resource practitioners to master this challenge by making use of automation in a manner that complements, as opposed to replaces, human capabilities. The focus must be on restructuring job tasks to facilitate distinctly human traits—such as empathy, creativity, and sound reasoning—thereby putting individuals at the center of organizational success.

The preservation of dignity in this age of rising automation requires going beyond job preservation; it requires the acknowledgment of the intrinsic value of every individual employee as well as a workplace that encourages contribution, autonomy, and inclusion. It is critical to bring in ethical aspects in developing and using artificial intelligence systems, especially in human resource activities like recruitment, performance evaluation, and monitoring workers. The use of unfair algorithms or opaque decision-making processes may lead to discriminatory practice and loss of trust (Binns, 2018). In order to counter such problems, organizations should prioritize transparency, auditability, and oversight by humans in AI-powered tools, thus setting up ethical governance as a central part of its digital human resource architecture.

Reconfiguration of job roles is a key approach towards achieving a balance between automation and maintaining human dignity. Rather than viewing automation as a simple replacement for human labor, organizations can use it to free up employees from repetitive, low-value tasks, and thus prioritize tasks requiring greater levels of involvement and with greater impact. For instance, chatbots can handle simple employee queries, and therefore enable HR professionals to concentrate on more challenging and demanding talent development issues. Likewise, predictive analytics can help in workforce planning while still leaving decision-making with humans. Such approaches create a symbiotic partnership between humans and machines where technology plays the role of an assistant and not a substitute (Davenport & Ronanki, 2018).

The Human Resource function here involves strategic as well as ethical dimensions. Leaders need to anticipate the possible impacts that automation can make on workers' morale, career growth, and the organization's overall culture. Clear communication about objectives and goals of automation efforts helps reduce workers' fear and resistance. Training and upskilling efforts are also a must, as they enable workers to move to new positions and achieve professional advancement in the organization. This pre-emptive investment in workers represents a commitment to dignity, fairness, and shared prosperity, leading to loyalty and trust among employees as well as ensuring psychological safety (Schwab & Zahidi, 2020). Ultimately, the balance between automation and human dignity requires a values-driven approach that aligns technological innovation with goals of human well-being. Human resource practitioners play a critical role in advancing responsible innovation that protects individual rights, promotes equity, and strengthens the social fabric in the workplace. As businesses increasingly rely on intelligent systems to drive performance, their long-term success will depend on their ability to preserve the dignity of their workforce. The organizations that are most resilient and most highly regarded will be those that place ethical considerations at the heart of their digital transformation programs, thereby ensuring that technology is used to augment and not compromise the human experience.

Applied Scenario: A European logistics company introduced AI-based scheduling software. Initial implementation reduced human decision-making and increased employee dissatisfaction. After an ethics-led HR intervention, the company redesigned the system to include human review checkpoints and employee input, improving trust and restoring engagement.

Diversity, equity, and Inclusion in Tech-Driven HR Systems

In the modern digital environment, organizations are increasingly reliant on technological solutions to optimize human resource operations, such as recruitment, performance evaluation, talent development, and workforce analytics. While such systems bring improved efficiency and scalability, they also create new challenges, as well as opportunities, for advancing diversity, equity, and inclusion (DEI). If not carefully designed, technology-enabled HR systems can perpetuate current biases and systemic inequalities, especially when algorithms are trained on biased data or unclear decision-making criteria (Raghavan, Barocas, Kleinberg, & Levy, 2020). It is therefore essential that contemporary HR leadership assumes the critical role of ensuring technology is aligned with DEI goals.

Automated hiring technologies also have the capacity to perpetuate systemic bias, especially if those systems are built with historical hiring data that can include biases. Technologies like facial recognition software, resume screening software, and personality tests can inherently be biased if they're not properly tested and audited for fairness (Ajunwa, 2020). To counteract such risks, organizations need to implement inclusive data practices, perform algorithmic audits, and involve a diverse group of stakeholders in the development and implementation stages of such systems. In addition, it is important to incorporate ethical AI frameworks and principles for responsible design in the procurement stage and at the point of implementation, so diversity and equity become part of system design instead of policy goals.

At the same time, technology has the power to profoundly support diversity, equity, and inclusion (DEI) when deployed with intentional consideration. Human resources analytics can identify trends involving underrepresentation or differences in compensation by department, job function, or geography, allowing companies to make targeted interventions based on the evidence (Huang, Krivkovich, & Starikova,

2019). Inclusion metrics-tracking systems, for example, such as membership participation rates from diverse backgrounds, promotion, and turnover rates, support evidence-based decision-making. In addition, gamification software and virtual reality (VR) continue to be used to teach unconscious bias, inclusive leadership, and cross-cultural communications in a scalable and interactive format.

The integration of DEI into tech-driven HR systems also depends on organizational culture and leadership commitment. Technology should not be seen as a substitute for human judgment or accountability. Instead, it should complement inclusive leadership practices by providing better data, fostering transparency, and amplifying underrepresented voices. For instance, anonymous employee feedback tools can empower marginalized groups to speak up safely, while internal mobility platforms can democratize access to career opportunities. HR's role is to ensure that these tools are not only accessible but also aligned with a clear DEI strategy and measurable goals.

Ultimately, embedding DEI into tech-driven HR systems requires a systems-thinking approach that addresses not just technology but also policies, culture, and leadership behavior. Organizations must continuously monitor and adapt their HR technologies to ensure that they serve equity and inclusion objectives, rather than unintentionally undermining them. As digital transformation accelerates, the organizations that will lead in performance and reputation are those that use technology not only to optimize efficiency but to elevate fairness, opportunity, and dignity for all employees.

To increase accountability within technology-enabled initiatives related to diversity, equity, and inclusion (DEI), organizations should have governance structures in place that are dedicated to overseeing and guiding inclusive technology practices. These can include AI ethics boards, DEI task forces, and data equity review boards, made up of interdisciplinary members from human resources, legal counsel, information technology, and employee resource groups. Their charge is to review technology proposals, conduct equity impact assessments, and assure that tools used are consistent with organizational values and regulatory requirements. In addition, regular reporting on DEI results—nested within sustainability or environmental, social, and governance (ESG) reporting—further entrenches transparency and signals to internal and external stakeholders that DEI is not a superficial effort, but a measurable and ongoing commitment (Binns, 2018).

The implementation of equitable human resource technologies in international operations presents additional challenges. Diversity, equity, and inclusion (DEI) priorities and legal mandates show considerable divergence in various regions, and organizations must therefore adapt their technological solutions to meet local cultural and legal conditions. For instance, demographic data collection may be encouraged in some jurisdictions as a way to measure equity, while in others it may be limited or be considered sensitive due to privacy reasons or historical circumstances. Accordingly, multinational organizations must strike a balance between global consistency and local relevance by developing DEI strategies in collaboration with regional teams and ensuring that inclusive technologies reflect both broad global principles and specific local conditions (O'neil, 2017). Looking ahead, the future of DEI in HR technology will be shaped by innovations that integrate emotional intelligence, real-time bias detection, and personalized inclusivity pathways. Emerging tools that use natural language processing to identify exclusionary language in job descriptions or communication platforms are already enhancing inclusive hiring and team dynamics. Similarly, adaptive learning platforms can now tailor DEI training to individual employee experiences, improving engagement and retention of underrepresented groups. As AI continues to evolve, so too will its capacity to support nuanced, empathetic, and data-informed DEI efforts—provided that organizations remain committed to ethical oversight and human-centered design.

Ethical Frameworks for AI and Algorithmic Decision-Making in HR

As algorithmic frameworks and artificial intelligence become ever more central to the practice of managing people, they need to be guided by ethical principles in the design, rollout, and oversight. These frameworks, which include candidate screening, performance monitoring, and labor analytics, power critical decisions with the capacity to significantly impact individuals' careers and well-being. Ethical frameworks act as necessary safeguarding devices to guarantee that algorithmic decision-making in HR practice is fair, transparent, and aligned with principles for the respect for human rights (Jobin, Ienca, & Vayena, 2019). Without them, organizations inadvertently risk reinforcing bias, eroding trust, and facing possible exposure to legal or reputational risk. Therefore, integrating ethics into algorithmic systems goes beyond compliance; it is a vital strategic imperative.

The underlying principles for the ethical use of artificial intelligence in human resources include fairness, transparency, accountability, privacy, and human oversight. Fairness is critical in preventing algorithms from discriminating against individuals based on gender, ethnicity, age, or other protected characteristics. Transparency refers to the understandability of algorithmic decision-making processes—both employees and candidates should have the capacity to understand how decisions are obtained. Accountability involves ascertaining who is responsible when negative results occur, while privacy relates to the sensitive nature of employee data. Finally, human oversight asserts that important decisions are not controlled by machines alone, but involve human judgment (Floridi et al., 2018). Together, these principles form the foundation of trustworthy artificial intelligence in human resource environments.

The application of such ethical values requires instituting working practices and regulatory frameworks. For instance, organizations can create AI ethics boards that include human resources practitioners, data experts, legal experts, and employee representatives. These boards can examine algorithmic instruments before they can be deployed, monitor their impacts, and verify compliance with ethical standards and labor laws. Periodic auditing of algorithms and doing impact assessments can be essential in detecting biases, assessing unintended consequences, and modifying systems as necessary (Binns, 2018). In addition, the application of ethical checklists, fairness toolkits, and avenues for employee input can enable ethical innovation at every stage of AI.

Global standards and frameworks are being established in order to help organizations with this undertaking. The OECD AI Principles, the European Union's Ethics Guidelines for Trustworthy AI, and UNESCO's Recommendation on the Ethics of Artificial Intelligence provide comprehensive guidance applicable to human resource practices (OECD, 2019; European Commission, 2019; UNESCO, 2021). They highlight the need for participatory governance, stakeholder engagement, and respect for cultural and contextual diversity. Adoption of such frameworks in human resource practices ensures that technology respects the dignity and autonomy of workers and supports efficiency and alignment with strategic goals. Ethical use of AI in human resources does not call for the total absence of automation, but instead highlights the need for inclusive and responsible regulation.

Ultimately, ethical guidelines act as a steering framework to tackle the complexity surrounding algorithmic decision-making in human resources. They help organizations balance innovation and responsibility, ensuring that technology is used to help heighten, not diminish, the humanity in employment. As the speed in digitalization accelerates, the ethically applied use of AI will increasingly define the credibility and legitimacy of HR processes. Organizations that make a proactive attempt at implementing such guidelines not only minimize potential pitfalls but also create more inclusive, open, and fair working environments—assets that exemplify long-term success in the electronic economy.

In order to properly apply ethical frameworks in Human Resources (HR), organizations need to first gauge internal readiness. This requires auditing current HR technologies, examining data governance guidelines, and determining digital competency levels among HR personnel and higher leadership levels. Integrating ethical Artificial Intelligence (AI) is far from a simple matter of technological application; instead, it presents a capacity-building challenge that requires ongoing education, investment in resources, and cultural alignment. HR professionals need to be instructed not just in the use of AI systems, but in the careful evaluation of those outputs for possible ethical transgressions. Organizations that focus on ethical literacy in every managerial level are better situated to anticipate risks and adjust governance models in a dynamic environment based on emerging technologies (Morley et al., 2021). In addition, ethical leadership plays a fundamental role in shaping how algorithmic tools are used, expressed, and governed in human resource systems. Leaders set the tone for whether artificial intelligence is considered a threat, a neutral tool, or an augmentation that embodies the values of the organization in HR practice. Ethical leadership is more than compliance with legal requirements; it is about showing transparency, ensuring fairness, and building employee trust in technology-infused systems. Leaders who engage workers in discussions about AI adoption, solicit their feedback, and make public commitments to equity-oriented results help create a context in which innovation is grounded in shared ethical values and human-centered principles.

CASE STUDIES AND COMPARATIVE INSIGHTS

Case Examples from Leading Digital Firms

Forward-thinking digital companies are taking the lead in adopting strategic human resource innovations that enable the building of sustainable, flexible, and ethically-minded organizations. These companies often become labs for innovating in scenario-based planning methods, flexible talent management practices, and technologically-facilitated human resource practices. A study of these practices reveals valuable insights into the alignment between the strategy for the workforce and the fast-changing and volatile climate of the digital economy. High-tech companies like Microsoft, Salesforce, and Spotify show that creativity, flexibility, and inclusive innovation aren't just concepts; they are vital operating principles that guide their human resource models and workplace cultures (Dery, Sebastian, & van der Meulen, 2017).

Microsoft has received significant attention for its transformation in human resource practices under CEO Satya Nadella's leadership. The company has moved from a culture of performance to one focused on a growth mindset philosophy, which emphasizes learning, collaboration, and agility (Dweck, 2016). Microsoft has incorporated scenario planning into its talent management by forecasting future skill needs, especially in artificial intelligence and cybersecurity, and launched initiatives like the global skilling initiative to train 25 million people worldwide. Additionally, the company's HR analytics capabilities enable leaders to make data-driven decisions in real-time on workforce trends, levels of engagement, and inclusion gaps, thus demonstrating how digital tools can enable strategic, people-centered human resource management.

Salesforce, a leader in customer relationship management (CRM) software, has emerged as a trailblazer in the application of ethical business practices and employee well-being in its human resource management system. The firm has codified its Ohana culture, with values built upon trust, customer success, and equality. In addition, it uses artificial intelligence and predictive analytics to identify opportunities for internal talent mobility and to help remove biases in hiring and promotion processes (Bersin, 2018). The firm also releases yearly data on equality, linking diversity performance with executive pay—such practice is a demonstration of commitment to responsibility and openness in building a diverse workforce.

Spotify is a prime example of agility in the area of human resources. The organization has adopted the "Spotify model," a unique structural setup involving squads, tribes, chapters, and guilds that enable autonomy, cross-functional collaboration, and distributed decision-making (Kniberg & Ivarsson, 2012). The human resources division, termed as the "People Team," supports this setup by promoting continuous learning and testing through strong feedback channels, digital learning platforms, and personalized career tracks. Thus, Spotify can reconfigure teams in a matter of minutes in sync with changing requirements, exemplifying the utility of workforce agility and flexibility in real-world environments.

These organizations show a high potential to promote psychological safety and encourage the freedom to express by employees. For instance, Microsoft and Salesforce both regularly conduct employees' surveys, following up with targeted approaches to increase inclusivity and extend mental health supports. In the wake of the COVID-19 pandemic, they introduced mental health days, changed remote working practices, and advocated for open communication from the top down. These efforts demonstrate that resilience in organizations is not built solely through structural systems but through cultural values and leadership practices (Kniffin et al., 2021). By taking proactive steps to prevent disruption, such organizations demonstrate a combination of foresight, ethical awareness, and people-focused innovation in the field of human resources.

Experience from digital innovators suggests that strategic application of human resource innovation—in the form of forward-looking planning, versatile organizational forms, digital skills development strategies, and moral artificial intelligence—extends beyond pilot projects or abstract models. These practices become woven into the essential business plan and continually refined through guiding principles based on real-time feedback and input from the labor force. Incorporating forward-thinking readiness and flexibility into their human resource processes, companies like Microsoft, salesforce, and Spotify serve as models for how human resources can enable long-term success in a constantly shifting digital marketplace.

A notable example is Google (Alphabet Inc.), which has been at the forefront of innovative applications in the field of people analytics and data-driven human resource decision-making. The so-called "Project Oxygen" and "Project Aristotle" efforts are widely cited for their findings on the qualities of successful managers and high-performing teams, emphasizing the importance of psychological safety, empathy, and inclusive leadership (Garvin, 2013). In addition, the company uses predictive modeling methods to assess talent risks as well as to personalize learning experiences for employees in different departments. Google's open experimentation culture, combined with rigorous feedback mechanisms, promotes continuous workforce innovation, thus allowing the company to attract and retain top talent while adapting to changing business needs.

IBM has taken a leading position in the field of ethical artificial intelligence in human resources. The company has developed internal guidelines for the management of AI in order to ensure transparency and fairness in its talent management processes. The firm's "Watson Career Coach" utilizes artificial intelligence to provide personalized career development coaching, with transparency in the explanation of its suggestions (Boudreau & Rice, 2015). In addition, IBM has incorporated bias detection features into its hiring algorithms and is actively involved in offering training to human resources professionals in the ethical application of AI. By incorporating ethical considerations into its model for HR technology, IBM demonstrates how digital businesses can leverage innovation with integrity.

Unilever, a consumer goods company with a presence worldwide, has significantly changed its graduate hiring strategy through digitalization efforts. The company has embraced digital video interviewing enabled by AI, as well as online tests aimed at measuring cognitive, social, and emotional abilities, thus improving scalability and evidence-based characteristics in the hiring process. Unilever also includes human oversight to ensure fairness and prevent bias by algorithms (Kantrowitz, 2019). In addition, its digital HR strategy is part of greater sustainability and equity goals, reflecting a value-based approach in contrast to one that is purely efficiency-oriented in managing talents. Adobe is a prime example of how workplace innovation can promote the empowerment of employees and encourage a performance-oriented culture. The organization moved away from its traditional performance-review system to a continuous feedback system known as "Check-Ins" that promotes regular, casual conversations between managers and employees on objectives, professional development, and overall well-being (Marr, 2016). Adobe also leverages real-time analytics to measure workplace engagement and has invested a lot in diversity and inclusion metrics. Pay equity public audits and employee-initiated councils on inclusion by the firm represent the successful embedding of data, open communication, and distributed decision-making, thus inculcating organizational culture and trust.

Lessons from Startups and E-Platform-Based Organizations

Startups and digital ecosystem enterprises operate within intensely volatile and competitive environments, thus standing as natural catalysts for innovations in HR and resilience. Unlike traditional companies, startups often operate without pre-existing legacy systems and hierarchical constraints, allowing them to experiment with flexible HR models, apply fast-paced learning cycles, and make data-informed choices from the inception. These organizations typically integrate HR approaches into business approaches right from the inception, prioritizing cultural alignment, scalable talent models, and lean processes. The experiences derived from them offer valuable insights into how flexibility, anticipatory perception, and a digital focus can be leveraged to nurture workplace environments that balance agility with a focus on human values (Blank, 2013).

One valuable lesson from startup businesses is that organizational culture plays a vital role in success. In environments without established processes, culture becomes the glue that brings decision making and actions together. Organizations like Buffer and Basecamp almost deliberately developed a culture based on transparency, autonomy, and a serene balance between work and personal lives. For example, Buffer publicly posts its pay structure, equity deals, and in-house goals for performance onto the internet, building a climate of trust and justice (Gascoigne, 2020). This strategy not only draws in those who believe in such a setup, but also inculcates psychological safety and organizational resilience in environments that scale fast.

Startups clearly demonstrate the substantial benefits that flexible organizational structures can bring in both increasing agility and resilience. Rather than being bound by pre-specified job descriptions, many startups use project-based job roles or skill matrices to distribute tasks based on current priorities and the capabilities of the workforce. This enables the rapid re-allocation of teams in reaction to marketplace changes. E-commerce businesses like Shopify, for instance, grew by utilizing remote working practices, streamlining the onboarding, and investing in interdisciplinary digital learning environments (Lunden, 2020). These strategies demonstrate the power of flexible human resource systems that evolve synchronically with the organization without compromising staff experience and performance levels.

E-platform organizations like Airbnb, Uber, and Deliveroo offer extra insight, specifically with regard to labor adaptability and algorithmic rulemaking. These platforms, while subject to critique over the rights accorded to gig workers and the precarious nature of their work, also show the potential to leverage data for real-time coordination between labor supply and demand. Human resource practices implications are that the models need not be replicated without scrutiny; rather, the aim is to explore how platform technologies can promote transparency, fairness, and flexibility in established employment systems. For instance, in-house talent marketplaces can enable employees to be matched with projects, mentors, or sideways roles on the basis of skills and aspirations—thus representing platform principles in a more stable employment system (Boudreau & Lakhani, 2016). Finally, entrepreneurial spirit values constant testing and continuous feedback. Organizations like GitLab, which is a purely remote organization, maintain open feedback through transparent OKRs (Objectives and Key Results), asynchronous channels, and shared HR guidelines (GitLab Handbook, 2023). Such openness promotes shared responsibility for the organization's evolution and increases the firm's responsiveness to arising threats and opportunities. By adopting lean, repeated approaches in human resources—like piloting wellbeing projects or applying A/B testing to educational content—startups demonstrate how responsiveness and staff input can be integral to the firm, even in fluid environments.

Policy and Compliance Practices in Different E-Economy Regions

As digital transformation reshapes labor markets worldwide, there is a significant divergence in policy and compliance practices relating to human resource management between regions. These divergences reflect not just differing legal traditions but also different cultural norms, economic incentives, and levels of digital development. In developed economies, such as those of the European Union, regulatory regimes increasingly focus on the ethical use of technology, data protection, and the protection of employee rights in platform-based working arrangements. A case in point is the General Data Protection Regulation (GDPR), which places strict obligations on how organizations handle the collection, storage, and use of employee data—requiring human resource systems to embed core principles of transparency, accountability, and consent (Voigt & Von dem Bussche, 2017).

Conversely, North America, in the form of the United States, implements a largely market-based system that emphasizes innovation and corporate autonomy. While U.S. businesses, in comparison, face relatively fewer restrictions in the use of algorithms and data, the rise in advocacy organizations and state-level bills (e.g., the California Consumer Privacy Act) reveals a trend toward greater protections for workers in the modern digital age (Cate & Mayer-Schönberger, 2013). Compliance in such a situation generally requires a sensitive balance between legal flexibility and reputation risk management, especially as stakeholders put pressure on progressively more technology-intensive employers to assume greater ethical duties.

In summary, successful innovation in the area of human resources in the digital age requires organizations to skillfully negotiate with both responsiveness and caution the regional policy differences. Multinational organizations need to align international human resource strategies with local regulators' expectations, making sure digital solutions, AI frameworks, and workforce analytics software serve not only functional needs but also comply with legal and ethical requirements in different territories. This includes tailoring employees' consent processes, adapting performance management systems in line with labor laws, and implementing compliance assessments. By proactively adapting to evolving regulations, organizations can avert possible risks, increase stakeholders' trust, and facilitate long-term digital transformation in a variety of geographical environments.

CONCLUSION

The digital economy is redefining the future employment landscape, organization form, and people management at a pace that is unmatched in historical precedent. As companies move away from the factory-based systems towards knowledge-based, technology-oriented paradigms, HR practitioners face the challenge of being able to sense disruptions, create robust organizations, and drive ethical innovation. In this chapter, we have elucidated the critical role that strategic human resource practices—based on scenario planning, self-learning methods, responsive workers, and ethical values—can take in building resilient futures for organizations.

In addition, robust organizational systems and cultures do not occur by chance. They take a deliberate effort in the form of methods that promote autonomy, inclusiveness, and collaborative learning. An organization's ability to display structural flexibility is directly related to that organization's competence in empowering and aligning individuals with changing goals, from the eradication of hierarchical levels to the development of environments that center on feedback. Cultural resilience, supported by open communication and shared responsibility, ensures that organizations sustain their inherent essence and unity despite adversities.

The chapter also brought to the fore the ethical dimensions surrounding innovations in human resources, specifically in the area of automation and AI. As digital technologies hold a lot of promise in maximizing HR effectiveness and enhancing decision-making, it is critical that they be governed by strong ethical standards to protect human dignity, prevent bias, and promote equity. This is especially so in areas like recruitment, performance management, and staff monitoring, where algorithm-based decisions directly affect workers' careers and well-being. Human-centered design principles, algorithm explainability, and inclusive data practices should be seen as essential building blocks for every technology-based HR system.

Empirical studies by leading digital businesses like Microsoft, Salesforce, and Spotify, as well as observations from early startups and platform businesses, have shown that strategic anticipation, organizational responsiveness, and value-based leadership become real practices instead of theoretical concepts. These companies have shown that innovation in human resources can be a vital business competency, thus suggesting that it is possible to achieve business growth without compromising the ethos of trust, integrity, and resilience. These case experiences offer actionable frameworks that organizations in different industries and geographies can utilize.

Ultimately, the worldwide difference in policy and compliance environments requires a dual strategy by human resources executives that is simultaneously globally consistent and locally responsive. The varying sets of regulations in different regions—e.g., Europe's GDPR and AI ethical guidelines, Asia's national governments, and Latin America's incipient data protection laws—show that successful HR innovation would need to be both situationally sensitive as well as rooted in essential principles. By navigating this complex environment with strategic vision and unshakeable ethical dedication, organizations can maximize performance in the digital marketplace in transition. In summary, the future course for human resource management rests on the capacity for balancing foresight and flexibility, innovation and morals, and technology growth with values that respect the dignity of individuals. This chapter discusses the strategic innovations in HR that go beyond functional effectiveness; instead, they become necessary for building organizational sustainability, well-being in the workplace, and long-term value creation. Human resource managers who recognize and act upon this urgent need will not only protect organizations from the looming challenges but also help to create a more sustainable and just workplace. Ultimately, the sustainability of future organizations will depend not only on technological capability, but on the ethical, resilient, and human-centered design of their human resource systems. This chapter positions HR innovation as a strategic cornerstone of long-term organizational survival and societal value creation.

REFERENCES

Acemoglu, D., & Restrepo, P. (2019). Artificial intelligence, automation, and work. In Agrawal, A., Gans, J., & Goldfarb, A. (Eds.), *The Economics of Artificial Intelligence: An Agenda* (pp. 197–236). University of Chicago Press. DOI: 10.7208/chicago/9780226613475.003.0008

Aghina, W., De Smet, A., & Weerda, K. (2015). Agility: It rhymes with stability. McKinsey Quarterly. https://www.mckinsey.com/business-functions/organization/our-insights/agility-it-rhymes-with-stability

Ajunwa, I. (2020). The paradox of automation as anti-bias intervention. *Cardozo Law Review, 41*(4), 1671–1704. https://cardozolawreview.com/the-paradox-of-automation-as-anti-bias-intervention/

Bersin, J. (2017). HR technology disruptions for 2018: Productivity, design, and intelligence reign. Deloitte Insights. https://www2.deloitte.com

Bersin, J. (2018). A new paradigm for corporate training: Learning in the flow of work. Deloitte Insights. https://www2.deloitte.com

Bersin, J. (2018). AI comes to HR: How artificial intelligence is changing the way people are managed. *Deloitte Review*, *22*, 114–123.

Binns, R. (2018). Algorithmic accountability and public reason. *Philosophy & Technology*, *31*(4), 543–556. DOI: 10.1007/s13347-017-0263-5 PMID: 30873342

Binns, R. (2018). Fairness in machine learning: Lessons from political philosophy. *Proceedings of the 2018 Conference on Fairness, Accountability and Transparency*, 149–159. DOI: 10.1145/3287560.3287596

Blank, S. (2013). *The startup owner's manual: The step-by-step guide for building a great company*. K&S Ranch Press.

Boudreau, J. W., & Rice, S. (2015). IBM's approach to human capital analytics. People + Strategy, 38(3), 56–63.

Boudreau, K. J., & Lakhani, K. R. (2016). Innovation experiments: Researching technical advance, knowledge production, and the design of supporting institutions. *Innovation Policy and the Economy*, *16*(1), 135–167. DOI: 10.1086/684988

Brynjolfsson, E., & McAfee, A. (2017). *Machine, platform, crowd: Harnessing our digital future*. W. W. Norton & Company.

Cappelli, P. (2008). *Talent on demand: Managing talent in an age of uncertainty*. Harvard Business Press.

Cate, F. H., & Mayer-Schönberger, V. (2013). Notice and consent in a world of Big Data. *International Data Privacy Law*, *3*(2), 67–73. DOI: 10.1093/idpl/ipt005

Davenport, T. H., & Ronanki, R. (2018). Artificial intelligence for the real world. *Harvard Business Review*, *96*(1), 108–116.

Dery, K., Sebastian, I. M., & van der Meulen, N. (2017). The digital workplace is key to digital innovation. *MIS Quarterly Executive*, *16*(2), 135–152.

Duchek, S. (2020). Organizational resilience: A capability-based conceptualization. *Business Research*, *13*(1), 215–246. DOI: 10.1007/s40685-019-0085-7

Dweck, C. S. (2016). *Mindset: The new psychology of success*. Random House.

Edmondson, A. (1999). Psychological safety and learning behavior in work teams. *Administrative Science Quarterly*, *44*(2), 350–383. DOI: 10.2307/2666999

European Commission. (2019). Ethics guidelines for trustworthy AI. https://ec.europa.eu/futurium/en/ai-alliance-consultation

Fitz-enz, J., & Mattox, J. R. (2014). *Predictive analytics for human resources*. Wiley. DOI: 10.1002/9781118915042

Floridi, L., Cowls, J., Beltrametti, M., Chatila, R., Chazerand, P., Dignum, V., Luetge, C., Madelin, R., Pagallo, U., Rossi, F., Schafer, B., Valcke, P., & Vayena, E. (2018). AI4People—An ethical framework for a good AI society: Opportunities, risks, principles, and recommendations. *Minds and Machines*, *28*(4), 689–707. DOI: 10.1007/s11023-018-9482-5 PMID: 30930541

Francis, T., & Hoefel, F. (2018). 'True Gen': Generation Z and its implications for companies. McKinsey & Company. https://www.mckinsey.com/industries/consumer-packaged-goods/our-insights/true-gen-generation-z-and-its-implications-for-companies

Ganson, B. (2020). *Leadership in complex crises: An institutional perspective*. Stockholm Environment Institute.

Garvin, D. A. (2013). How Google sold its engineers on management. Harvard Business Review. https://hbr.org/2013/12/how-google-sold-its-engineers-on-management

Gascoigne, J. (2020). The transparency code: Building trust through openness at Buffer. Buffer Open Blog. https://buffer.com/resources/transparency/

GitLab Handbook. (2023). The remote playbook: How GitLab operates a fully remote company. https://about.gitlab.com/handbook/

Greenwood, M., & Freeman, R. E. (2011). Ethics and HRM: The contribution of stakeholder theory. *Business & Professional Ethics Journal, 30*(3/4), 269–292. DOI: 10.5840/bpej2011303/413

Habegger, B. (2010). Strategic foresight in public policy: Reviewing the experiences of the OECD, Singapore, and Finland. *Futures, 42*(1), 49–58. DOI: 10.1016/j.futures.2009.08.002

Huang, J., Krivkovich, A., & Starikova, I. (2019). Women in the workplace 2019. McKinsey & Company. https://www.mckinsey.com/featured-insights/diversity-and-inclusion/women-in-the-workplace

Jobin, A., Ienca, M., & Vayena, E. (2019). The global landscape of AI ethics guidelines. *Nature Machine Intelligence, 1*(9), 389–399. DOI: 10.1038/s42256-019-0088-2

Kantrowitz, A. (2019). Unilever's hiring AI: Less biased or more? BuzzFeed News. https://www.buzzfeednews.com/article/alexkantrowitz/unilever-hiring-ai-artificial-intelligence-recruiting

Kniberg, H., & Ivarsson, A. (2012). Scaling agile at Spotify. Spotify Labs Whitepaper. https://blog.crisp.se/wp-content/uploads/2012/11/SpotifyScaling.pdf

Kniffin, K. M., Narayanan, J., Anseel, F., Antonakis, J., Ashford, S. P., Bakker, A. B., Bamberger, P., Bapuji, H., Bhave, D. P., Choi, V. K., Creary, S. J., Demerouti, E., Flynn, F. J., Gelfand, M. J., Greer, L. L., Johns, G., Kesebir, S., Klein, P. G., Lee, S. Y., & Vugt, M. V. (2021). COVID-19 and the workplace: Implications, issues, and insights for future research and action. *The American Psychologist, 76*(1), 63–77. DOI: 10.1037/amp0000716 PMID: 32772537

Krekel, C., Ward, G., & De Neve, J. E. (2019). Employee wellbeing, productivity, and firm performance. Saïd Business School Working Paper. DOI: 10.2139/ssrn.3356581

Lee, M. Y., Edmondson, A. C., Thomke, S., & Worline, M. C. (2021). Building agile organizations: The role of emotional intelligence and psychological safety. *Harvard Business Review, 99*(3), 78–87.

Lengnick-Hall, C. A., Beck, T. E., & Lengnick-Hall, M. L. (2011). Developing a capacity for organizational resilience through strategic human resource management. *Human Resource Management Review, 21*(3), 243–255. DOI: 10.1016/j.hrmr.2010.07.001

Lunden, I. (2020). Shopify launches new app and business tools to help merchants adapt to COVID-19 realities. TechCrunch. https://techcrunch.com/2020/04/28/shopify-covid19-updates/

Marr, B. (2016). Why Adobe abolished performance reviews and how they did it. Forbes. https://www.forbes.com/sites/bernardmarr/2016/02/16/why-adobe-abolished-performance-reviews-and-how-they-did-it/

Milojević, I., & Inayatullah, S. (2015). Narrative foresight. *Futures*, *73*, 151–162. DOI: 10.1016/j.futures.2015.08.007

Morley, J., Floridi, L., Kinsey, L., & Elhalal, A. (2021). From what to how: An initial review of publicly available AI ethics tools, methods and research to translate principles into practices. *Science and Engineering Ethics*, *27*(4), 1–31. DOI: 10.1007/s11948-021-00300-3 PMID: 31828533

O'neil, C. (2017). *Weapons of math destruction: How big data increases inequality and threatens democracy*. Crown.

OECD. (2019). OECD principles on artificial intelligence. https://www.oecd.org/going-digital/ai/principles/

Raghavan, M., Barocas, S., Kleinberg, J., & Levy, K. (2020). Mitigating bias in algorithmic hiring: Evaluating claims and practices. *Proceedings of the 2020 Conference on Fairness, Accountability, and Transparency (FAT)*, 469–481. DOI: 10.1145/3351095.3372828

Ramirez, R., Mukherjee, M., Vezzoli, S., & Kramer, A. M. (2015). Scenarios as a scholarly methodology to produce 'interesting research'. *Futures*, *71*, 70–87. DOI: 10.1016/j.futures.2015.06.006

Rohrbeck, R., Battistella, C., & Huizingh, E. (2015). Corporate foresight: An emerging field with a rich tradition. *Technological Forecasting and Social Change*, *101*, 1–9. DOI: 10.1016/j.techfore.2015.11.002

Saks, A. M. (2022). Integrating employee engagement, wellbeing, and job satisfaction: A dynamic and strategic HR approach. *Human Resource Management Review*, *32*(3), 100833. DOI: 10.1016/j.hrmr.2021.100833

Schiuma, G., & Santarsiero, F. (2018). Human resource management practices and organizational resilience: Evidence from the manufacturing sector. *Measuring Business Excellence*, *22*(2), 26–37. DOI: 10.1108/MBE-11-2017-0071

Schwab, K., & Zahidi, S. (2020). The future of jobs report 2020. World Economic Forum. https://www.weforum.org/reports/the-future-of-jobs-report-2020

Slaughter, R. A. (1997). Developing and applying strategic foresight. *ABN Report*, *5*(10), 13–27.

Spreitzer, G., Sutcliffe, K., Dutton, J., Sonenshein, S., & Grant, A. M. (2005). A socially embedded model of thriving at work. *Organization Science*, *16*(5), 537–549. DOI: 10.1287/orsc.1050.0153

Tursunbayeva, A., Pagliari, C., & Bunduchi, R. (2018). Ethics of health-related IT use in the workplace: A review of the literature. *Health Policy and Technology*, *7*(2), 135–151. DOI: 10.1016/j.hlpt.2018.03.004

Ulrich, D., Younger, J., Brockbank, W., & Ulrich, M. (2012). *HR from the outside in: Six competencies for the future of human resources*. McGraw-Hill.

UNESCO. (2021). Recommendation on the ethics of artificial intelligence. https://unesdoc.unesco.org/ark:/48223/pf0000381137

Valamis. (2020). The future of corporate learning. Valamis Whitepaper. https://www.valamis.com/resources/future-of-corporate-learning

Vogus, T. J., & Sutcliffe, K. M. (2007). Organizational resilience: Towards a theory and research agenda. *2007 IEEE International Conference on Systems, Man and Cybernetics*, 3418–3422. DOI: 10.1109/ICSMC.2007.4414160

Voigt, P., & Von dem Bussche, A. (2017). *The EU General Data Protection Regulation (GDPR): A practical guide*. Springer International Publishing. DOI: 10.1007/978-3-319-57959-7

Wright, G., Bradfield, R., & Cairns, G. (2013). *Scenario planning: A field guide to the future*. Wiley.

Chapter 15
Strategic Human Resource Innovations for Sustainable Organizational Futures

S. Ida Evangeline
http://orcid.org/0000-0003-2997-7897
Government College of Engineering, Tirunelveli, India

ABSTRACT

This chapter explores the transformative role of strategic human resource (HR) innovation in enabling sustainable and ethically grounded organizational futures in the context of the e-economy. As digital disruption, labor market volatility, and rising stakeholder expectations redefine the nature of work, HR must evolve from a transactional function to a strategic partner in foresight, adaptability, and moral leadership. The chapter presents an integrated framework built on three interdependent pillars: scenario planning, resilience-building, and ethical innovation. Scenario planning provides the HR with the tools to predict disruptions in its workforce and then create flexible talent planning. Resilience-building bolsters organizational and human capability to respond to change using nimble structures and collective leadership and well-being cultures. Ethical innovation safeguards the new HR technologies and practices, matching them to the ideas of fairness, transparency, and accountability to the stakeholders.

DOI: 10.4018/979-8-3373-4307-5.ch015

1. INTRODUCTION

In an era marked by relentless technological advancement, evolving work paradigms, and mounting ecological and societal pressures, organizations are increasingly compelled to rethink their internal structures, capabilities, and strategic orientations. Human resource (HR) may prove to be the most important lever in this transformation as it is a field traditionally considered as support, and one which is on its way to becoming a strategic warrior of resilient and ethically attuned future. With the never-ending evolution and turmoil of the digital economy, the ability of the HR department to foresee change, instill flexibility, and instill considerations of ethical futurism is more critical than ever (Budhwar et al. 2023).

The emergence of the e-economy has radically transformed the basis of why, where and how people work. Powered by the technologies including artificial intelligence (AI) and machine learning, blockchain and online platforms, modern organizations encounters a high rate of shifting talent requirements and business model. The working environment has shifted to the virtual, hybrid and globalized workspace; employment relationships are now becoming more transactional and fluid and the very parameters of productivity, engagement and well-being are increasingly being debated and re-written. Such changes present an unprecedented challenge as well as opportunities to the HR department (Madanchian et al. 2023).

Within this environment, a conservative HR approach based fundamentally on compliance, cost-cutting and hoarding talent is inadequate to respond to the multifaceted needs of future-ready organizations. Instead, what is needed is a move towards strategic HR innovation: a form of people management that is more active, integrated and values driven that aligns people management with long-term organizational response and societal roles. A strategy like this should go beyond reactive policy work and aspire to engineer organizational cultures and systems that can succeed in the environment of uncertainty, ambiguity and quick changes (Votto et al. 2021).

This chapter discusses this transformative agenda through consideration of three convergent pillars namely: scenario planning, building resilience, and ethical innovation. Such dimensions are not the technical proficiencies only, but fundamental orientations which can allow HR to transform its operational excellence to strategic eye sights and ethical stewardship. Scenario planning also provides the HR with the capabilities to plot various futures, determine new emerging skillset and develop adaptive talent strategies. Resilience-building is one of the key solutions to organizational resilience as well as human thriving through psychological safety, flexibility, and responsiveness to systems. And, lastly, ethical innovation points to the significance of the trust, justice, and accountability of stakeholders in HR practices as digital tools become more and more primary mediators of the process of applying, assessment, engagement, etc.

Collectively, these strategic orientations can create a strong, coherent structure of sustainable HR innovation and it should not only be informed by technology, but also by what is human and ethically grounded. Through this triad, the chapter considers that HR can and should step up to the role of leadership in forming organizational futures that shape both business imperative and societal good.

We will formulate this argument in detail in the rest of the chapter. It starts by putting the ongoing process of work redesign in the context of the e-economy, in terms of its larger parameters. Then it discusses the three key pillars of strategic approaches, namely scenario planning, resilience and ethical innovation, and it refers to new emerging practices and referring to cases to demonstrate how it can be done. Lastly, it covers some of the major preventable impediments in implementation and suggests an integrated model of strategic HR innovation as a roadmap that organizations can follow to future-proof themselves in an ethically sustainable and socially responsive way.

This chapter addresses the HR professionals, organisational leaders and scholars to reconsider HR, no more as a service department, but rather as a critical custodian of sustainable futures. HR can play a more pivotal role in creating businesses that are not merely digitally competent, but also socially relative and with a permanently robust bottom. HR can achieve this, by taking it strategic yet innovative approach of innovating around foresight, resilience and ethics.

2. HR IN THE AGE OF THE E-ECONOMY

The emergence of the e-economy—an economy increasingly driven by electronic platforms, digital data flows, and algorithmic coordination—has upended traditional paradigms of work, employment, and organizational design. In such a digital mediation world, organizations cannot be defined any more in terms of geography, time zone or a hierarchy. Rather they are turning fluid, networked and more knowledge based on knowledge workers, digital infrastructure and on-the-fly capability. This change has not only immediate and significant effect on human resource management in its operating levels, but also on its strategic intent (Tomé, 2025).

The main problem behind this change is an alteration of work itself. Remote work, hybrid work, gig and platform employment, and augmented intelligence jobs are going mainstream. The more standard employment contracts are also being replaced by more relaxed, contingent and of projects nature of contract. At the same time, employees are placing strong emphasis on trust, purposeful work, and identity with organizational values especially to matters that involve environmental sustainability, social justice, and ethical consideration of technology. These anticipations are not marginal happenings, in the digital economy, they are the center protocols in attracting and maintaining talent (Pinheiro et al. 2023).

Further, companies are becoming data-rich and insight-poor. Although digital HR systems today generate huge amounts of employee data including productivity and wellness indicators, the issue is how to find ways to turn them into actionable insights in an ethically sound way, one that is ethically harvested, analytically used, and strategically aligned. The emergence of people analytics, AI-based recruiting applications, and algorithm-based performance evaluation also brings new capabilities but with them new and thorny ethical and governance issues. Digital literacy, algorithmic accountability and stakeholder transparency are to be added to the scope of HR in this respect.

It has to be seen against this backdrop that the conventional lines of HR as a supporting unit are fading. Administrative HR-related to payroll, compliance, and enforcement of policies- is needed but not enough. What is desperately required is a transformed HR service that serves as a form planner of organizational foresight, change and resilience. This entails the development of prospective abilities that include system thinking, scenario development, ethics foresight and change management, which do not dwell in the transactional activities of the organization, but rather continue to speak to the longevity of the organization in a business environment that is complex and uncertain (Pantea et al. 2025).

In a number of organizations this change is already in progress. CHROs are also being repositioned as strategic partners of the C-suite, providing input on decisions around business continuity, digital transformation, ESG (environmental, social and governance) strategy and engaging with stakeholders. The iteration of RIS is in recognizing RISs not only as managers of people, but also as the designers of work ecosystems creating cultures, technologies, and capabilities that may work dynamically to respond to external shocks, as well as internal disruptions. The COVID-19 pandemic gave us a glimpse of this broader mandate as HR functions were swiftly able to implement remote work policies, mental health initiatives and new talent strategies to sustain business operations and keep employees safe.

However this reorientation is therefore not smooth. HR departments in most cases are hobbled by legacy systems, silos and short-term metrics of performance which prevent out-of-the-box thinking and systemic thinking. There is still a wide discrepancy between the discourse related to strategic HR and its application in everyday life, especially in small and medium enterprises or spheres where the process of digitalization is in its initial stages. To overcome this disjuncture, it is necessary to consciously reinvent the purpose of HR, re-skill its professionals and restructure its success measures (Barsegyan et al. 2021).

In this chapter, rather than framing HR innovation as add-on or value-added, the author rather makes the case that it is necessity that companies transform themselves through re-figuration addressable only through HR innovation to recover its position in survival and ethical legitimacy within the e-economy. The following sections will describe the utility of scenario planning, resilience-building, and ethical innovation as some of the guiding tools in this change. Each provides a prism that HR can use to expect disruption, integrate sustainability and develop a culture of workforce flexibility and responsibility.

3. SCENARIO PLANNING FOR WORKFORCE FUTURES

In the volatile, uncertain, complex, and ambiguous (VUCA) environment of the digital economy, the ability to anticipate and adapt to change has become a defining organizational capability. Scenario planning, a structured method for exploring and preparing for multiple plausible futures, offers a powerful strategic tool for human resource professionals seeking to future-proof their workforce strategies. In contrast to conventional forecasting, where a linear extrapolation of historical trends is commonly involved, scenario planning is not based on certainty, viewing the continuation of a linear trend as only one of many paths possible and subject to random shocks, new technology and even shifts in social values. Including scenario planning as part of HR strategy allows an organization to develop an adaptive capacity, to co-align talent development with future requirements, as well as a culture of learning and innovation (Fadeev et al. 2021).

At its simplest, a scenario structure consists in building narratives of what the future may look like when different drivers--technological, economic, political, environmental, and social drive conditions--are combined in different ways. Examples of some of these drivers in the HR context could be the emergence of generative AI in knowledge work, population aging or entry of Gen Z into the workforce, changing employee requirements related to flexibility and purpose fulfilment, and geopolitical events that impact talent migration or supply chain. Systematically scoping out areas of key uncertainty and understanding how they may combine with each other, HR leaders can use such an approach to build a portfolio of plausible scenarios to break any assumptions and reveal underlying risks and opportunities.

An example is where an HR team may look at four scenarios of items in the future workforce that occur with two key uncertainties in mind: the degree of AI incorporation in the workplace (low or high) and the regulation established around digital work (open regulation or tightly regulated). It could be one world that is highly AI but is loosely regulated and the productivity is very high with ethics being a major debate or it could be a world that is low AI but highly regulated with human-related work and social securities. In both instances the workforce planning consequences, i.e., skills development, organization design, recruiting practices and culture values, would differ considerably (Anguelov, 2021).

The proactive mode assists HR with the shift towards being proactive as opposed to crisis management. As an example, a scenario planning may help to identify emerging skillsets that are not yet required, but can be mission-critical in five to ten years. It can inform learning and development investment pathways to accommodate many futures rather than a single possible path. It can also lay bare structural weaknesses e.g. overreliance on a particular type of work, poor digital literacy among senior managers or weak remote working capabilities that must be overcome no matter what happens in the future.

Moreover, participatory strategy development can be done under the scenario planning. Incorporating varying stakeholders in scenario workshops, including but not confined to cross-functional, geographic and seniority level of business can promote strategic orientation, cognitive blind spots identification, and organizational buy-in. It also heralds a culture of inclusion and openness to change as it is not about HR purely deploying policy but creating futures with the workforce (Bustamante Izquierdo et al. 2023).

Scenario planning is already becoming part and parcel of the HR practice of some progressive organizations. Long-run labor market scenarios have enabled multinational firms to reengineer their models of acquiring talents in the global market. Scenario-based approaches have been adopted by the government agencies in Blueprinting the workforce gaps in the critical government services as well as the future competencies in leadership. Think tanks and universities are generating open-access foresight toolkits to enable HR practitioners to plug in scenario logics into their daily decision-making.

Nevertheless, difficulties are experiences. Scenario planning involves time, facilitating skills and toleration of ambiguity and these are not characteristic of operational-oriented HR teams. It is also likely to encounter opposition in top-down cultures where the long-term perspective is not highly valued or where the prevailing attitude favours efficiency above adventuring. Conquering these impediments is based on the mastery of scene planning not really as a speculative exercise, however, as a basis of strategic flexibility and invention directly by HR leaders (Huang et al. 2023).

To conclude, scenario planning is a crucial innovation available to HR in the era of digitalization. It promotes flexibility, insight and preparedness by training organisations in thinking in prospective in a context that allows a series of possible futures to be considered. It makes HR forward-sensing organ of the organization, and not a backward-looking one--able to steer workforce strategies through the fog of uncertainty and into sustainable, values-aligned futures.

4. BUILDING ORGANIZATIONAL RESILIENCE THROUGH HR

As organizations operate within increasingly turbulent environments—marked by global crises, disruptive technologies, workforce fragmentation, and rising social expectations—the concept of resilience has emerged as a strategic imperative. The challenge of organizational resilience is no longer about surviving and recovering when a shock occurs but rather about learning through them by coming out as better, more internally consistent and more able to manage the continuingly complex world around us. HR functions are in a particularly good place to spearhead this transformation. Introducing individual, team, and systems level resilience through HR can support development of the adaptive muscle needed to achieve sustainability in the long term.

Resilience here is not just a psychological process but is structural also. On an individual level, it is the provision of emotional, cognitive and social tools that will assist employees to deal with stress, uncertainty and perpetual change. At the organization level, it entails laying out mechanisms, cultures and leadership paradigm that promotes quick recovery, continuous learning as well as proactive adaptation. Nurturing the two aspects through HR is critical since it influences hiring policies, learning trajectories and leadership and culture in the workplace (Yu et al. 2022).

Ambiance of psychological safety is one of the key defining aspects of resilience-building in HR, which is the perception held by a group of people that they can engage in interpersonal risk-taking without any fear of being humiliated or punished. Teams that feel free to raise their concerns, admit their failure, or propose unusual solutions will be more willing to innovate and collaborate and react to external shocks in a timely way. Psychological safety can be institutionalized by providing inclusive leaders training, open feedback systems and value-based performance reviews. As an example, the changeover of a traditional measurement of performance to team or developmental performance can indicate a change in punitive surveillance to developmental support.

The other pillar of resilience is work structure. Empowered decisions by cross-functional digital collaboration teams Agile teams are a flexible alternative to traditional hierarchies. They reconstitute themselves depending on the emerging needs, ability to learn fast due to negative feedback and cross boundary operations. In this case, HR should structure roles and processes in a way that promotes flexibility, develops inter-disciplinary approach and forms rewards on the team-oriented behaviors, as opposed to siloed behaviors. This can be accompanied with experimentation with flexible job architectures, internal mobility programs, and rotational assignments so that workers may be exposed to more diversity enlarging the extent and capability of resilience (Liang & Cao, 2021).

The other key element in organizational resilience is employee well-being. Exacerbated by remote work and digital overload, stress burnout, mental fatigue, work/life imbalance are effective ways to undermine the adaptive capacity. Innovative HR policies are now combining well-being in a central operating-priority rather than a fringe-benefit. This entails support of mental health, flexible routines, digital healthy policies, and a focus on rest, recovery and boundaries in knowledge work. As an example, firms that partner with resilience through focus weeks with no meetings or provide sabbaticals as a career development process are institutionalizing resilience instead of it being a personal act.

Resilience is also dependent upon the development of leadership. Leaders have to act not merely in a skillful and goal-oriented way, but in a way that is emphatic, humble, and that how to lead through uncertainty in volatile contexts. HR has to, therefore, reconsider leadership pipelines, not just selecting performance but also developing emotions, systems-based awareness and crisis preparedness. It is possible to develop resilient cultures of leadership by using coaching, mentoring, peer networks and experiential ways of learning (Ngoc Su et al. 2021).

There are numerous examples of case. Concrete examples of the COVID-19 pandemic saw certain companies across the globe switch to a top-down to structured leadership model to a distributed leadership approach in which the local teams were empowered to address the specific issues facing the local community. Some built in resilience variables into their HR scorecards, monitoring not just turnover and participation, but the ability to change, the reconnection time, the team unity aspect. These enterprises realized that resilience is not an abstract construct--it is a quantifiable skill that can be enhanced in the human systems that HR can assist in shaping and sustaining.

Still, the construction of resilience cannot happen without challenges. Adaptive capacity can be crippled by organizational inertia, culture that is too rigid, and an overdependence on efficiency measures. Resilience can be used incorrectly meaning endurance in some companies-which pressures workers to recover without even considering the underlying systematic factors that lead to breakdowns in the first place. HR should protect against such a pitfall by spreading the resilience as a human-and-systems-informed approach (Alipour et al. 2022).

To sum it up, organizational resilience is an agile, teachable characteristic- and HR is the primary architect of it. Agile work structures, physically and psychologically safe working environments, well-being ecosystems or models along with emotionally intelligent leadership paradigm can help the HR incorporate resilience into the organization. Not only increasing the level of crisis readiness, it also creates a culture of ongoing development, consistency, and sustainability all of which is needed to escape the uncertainties of the digital era.

5. ETHICAL INNOVATION IN HR PRACTICES

As organizations embrace digital transformation and data-driven decision-making, the ethical dimensions of human resource (HR) innovation have come to the forefront. Given the growing perception of fairness, transparency, accountability and human dignity both in terms of hiring procedures that are being increasingly replaced by algorithmic hiring in the e-economy, ever-more frequent remote surveillance and automated performance evaluation, concerns with legality cannot be put aside. Ethical innovation, in the meaning used here, i.e., a conscious effort to incorporate moral considerations into HR technologies, practices and cultures, is not an issue of compliance. It is a tactical requirement in creating trust, credibility and sustainable organizational existence.

Human Resources Ethics of innovating human resources starts with the essential question, how can organizations engage emerging technologies, as well as the redesign of systems of work in a manner that contributes to, rather than detracts from, human flourishing? More than mitigation of risk or policy checklists are involved. It also requires active, ethically oriented innovation- an initiative that focuses on stakeholder welfare, predicts unintended outcomes, and imbues justice as an organizational value (Wen et al. 2021).

The first is the application of artificial intelligence (AI) and machine learning of HR analytics. These instruments have great potential, i.e. the possibility forecasting employee turnover as well as having the potential to optimize hiring decisions, yet they entail what can be considered dire consequences. Training data biases, unexplainable algorithm decision making and excessive dependence on automated systems may create a discriminatory result or degrade individual agency. Ethical HR innovation demands the responsible utilization of such tools, well-proven governance schemes, continuous auditing and openness towards the affected employees. HR leadership needs to be sure that AI, when used, is there as an aide, and not a replacement to human judgment, with the power to have recourse and feedback remaining important to the candidates as well as the employees.

The other ethical frontier is in recruitment and promotions. Organizations are also more and more using digital profiles, psychometric testing, and gamified assessments to help organization generate talent in a digital economy. Although these instruments have the potential to enhance efficiency, at the same time, they can solidify discrimination habitats unless evaluated critically through cultural, socioeconomic, or neurodiverse lenses of bias. Ethical innovation in this case implies developing inclusive assessment models, diversifying talent pipelines and building alternative pathways in the case of candidates with non-traditional backgrounds. It also means going beyond superficial measurements of diversity to consider equity and inclusion at more fundamental structural levels; including pay transparency, access to mentors and representation on decision-making committees (Ye et al. 2023).

The diversity, equity and inclusion (DEI) initiatives are by themselves an important component of ethical HR innovation. Diversity, equity and inclusion is a side project in many organizations, devoid of main strategy. However, in an imaginative HR model, DEI is incorporated into all other parts of workforce planning, leadership design, and cultural design. These aspects are developing data-driven analyses of systemic barriers, including the voices of the marginalized in the policy-making, and integrating inclusive norms into daily routines, i.e., the formatting of meetings and giving feedback. DEI is a moral and also a business-essential practice as diverse teams are more creative, resilient, and have a high-quality decision-making process.

Ethical innovation also covers the way organizations determine and conduct work itself. Gig workers, freelancers, and remote contributors cannot feel the security of usual HR safeguards in the platform economy. This provokes the essence of whether they should regard as a worker, what rights they deserve and what is the approach that organisations should take between adaptability and fairness. Some forward thinking HR models are currently testing the waters of portable benefits, platform cooperatives, and forms of hybrid employment that provide more stability without losing independent workers? autonomy. Ethical innovation in this area will necessitate HR to champion the adoption of inclusive labor models that inform the conditions of digital working and at the same time dictate standards of basic dignity and security (Shah & Soomro, 2023).

A potential last and yet most potent lever toward ethical HR innovation is the organizational culture. Values and behaviors support policies and tools which make them only as effective as they are and not otherwise. One of the major ways through which HR can play the central role is creation of clear codes of conduct, open discussion, and rewarding ethical leadership at all levels. Ethical storytelling, rituals and concrete symbolic action, such as the ways ethical violations are addressed and ways impact is celebrated, can all support an ethical identity that governs under-pressure decision-making. An established ethical culture, in particular in times of crisis or uncertainty, can service as an internal guide toward right decision-making into difficult choices with integrity and confidence by organizations.

Notably, ethical innovation is not a rigid outcome but part of an on-going process of reflection, learning, and co-creation. HR has to involve the employees as active participants of the process and not mere recipients of policy. Cose is organizations have ethical tensions that can surface early using ethical listening tools, participatory design workshops, and are more likely to be owned by the workers when their solutions are led by employees in employee-led advisory groups (Awwad Al-Shammari et al. 2022).

Altogether, ethical innovation is not the opposite of technological advancement, rather, it is the facilitator of the latter. Organizational success over time depends on the presence of trust, diversity, and accountability; however, the application of ethical considerations within the design and practice of HR procedures allows organizations to realize the potential of the available digital tools, and maintain a sustainable business model. HR, the steward of organizational values and people systems lies in a better position to drive this change and ensure innovation happens in the service of humanity and not the other way around.

6. BARRIERS AND ENABLERS OF STRATEGIC HR INNOVATION

While the promise of strategic HR innovation is compelling—particularly in aligning scenario planning, resilience, and ethical imperatives—realizing this vision is far from straightforward. There are certain barriers which are mostly considered major hindrances to the adoption, scalability and institutionalization of transformative HR practices in organizations. We also know that there are key mobilisers, when they are turned on, they can jumpstart significant change. To drive a conceptual ambition to one based on sustained implementation, understanding both sides of such dynamic is imperative to the HR leader or policymaker.

Short-termism Short-termism is one of the most enduring obstacles. Short-termism refers to the inclination to focus on short-term production, profitability goals, economic costs, etc at the cost of long- term capabilities building. HR programs, which emphasize resilience training, nurturing ethical cultures, or scenario planning, have tended to flounder in places with a strong financial orientation and short time frames measuring return on investment. There is such pressure to do more with less, particularly within small HR departments, that there is little room to experiment, engage in foresighting activities, or think with any type of system awareness. That leads to reactive, compliance oriented and under-utilised as a strategic lever HR (Pandey et al. 2025).

HR innovation is held back by legacy systems as well as strict hierarchies. The persistence of old fashioned HR information systems (HRIS), data systems which are siloed and bureaucratic frameworks of authorization which impede the arrival of flexibilities, data-driven and collaborative measures still prevail in many organizations. Innovation can only occur when systems, insights and stakeholder inputs are integrated yet the HR usually exist in silos, independent of the strategic planning, IT infrastructure and change management tasks. Such a gap throttles the flexibility and effectiveness of HR-led changes.

Digital inequity and capability gaps are another significant challenge, whether it is in the HR teams or the workforce in general. It is necessary, not only to establish the technical framework of supporting AI-based tools of HR or predictive analytics, but also to introduce the fluency of HR professionals with the digital environment. Many practitioners lack the literacy in data or the training of ethics to address a responsible governance of these tools and are therefore prone to the dependency, or bad implementations, on the vendor. Meanwhile, those employees who lack digital tools and training opportunities can be left out of new workforce models, fueling inequalities to the detriment of the ethical underpinnings of innovation (Correia et al. 2024).

Cultural resistance is a key role as well. Strategic HR innovation is inhospitable to organizations that value control rather than trust, conformity instead of diversity, or tradition as compared to experimentation. Within these climates, more "soft" HR efforts, e.g. strategies like psychological safety, well-being, or inclusive leadership, can easily get ignored or remain underfunded. Further, there is the threat of losing face or failure, which can give rise to risk-averse policies not taking unconventional routes thinking about roles and values or revisiting policies.

One can however counter these barriers with powerful enablers. The most influential is leaders commitment. When top executives promote HR as more than a support profession, but a strategic unit, they establish an openness where new ideas can be brought to fruition. This involves committing to future-oriented HR initiatives, seeing HR leaders as part of enterprise planning and publicly supporting strategies that encourage resilient cultures and ethical cultures.

The other key enabler is cross-functional collaboration. HR innovation is not a standalone process- it is best when augmented with relationships in key areas, such as IT (to aid in the digital transformation), finance (to aid in alignment of the resources), legal (to aid in compliance and ethics), and operations (to aid in the execution). Innovation teams or HR innovation practices can be made up of interdisciplinary groups that act as experiment labs to test new ideas so that solutions can be innovative not just visionary, but practical and contextualized (Le, 2024).

Besides, external standards and institutional rules are starting to encourage the ethical and sustainable HR practices. As an example, international standards such as, ISO 30414 (Human Capital Reporting) and ESG reporting initiatives are helping organizations to pay closer attention to the disclosure of people strategies, and the monitoring to a more transparent way. Such mechanisms may motivate organizations to be more conscious and values-oriented in innovating their HR.

Lastly, the power of the staff link and shared production is also coming into force. When employees are encouraged to be a part of forming HR policies, testing digital equipment or outlining ethical guidelines, they are your allies as opposed to being mere recipients. Such a participatory culture helps not only augment the relevance and legitimacy of HR innovations, but also helps build a practice of ownership and flexibility, which is key to enabling long-term change.

As a means to negotiate the conflicting nature of barriers and enablers, HR leaders need to develop a systems-thinking mindset. It includes interdependency-mapping, search of leverage points, and interventions that are context-sensitive as well as evolutionarily adaptive. Instead of going perfectly, it should be an iterative learning approach: Pilot "small-scale disruptive innovation", measure its effects, scale the models that work with the knowledge that new, unintended outcomes may occur (Lin et al. 2024).

To conclude, HR strategic innovation appears to be a non-linear process rather than a straightforward one; it is a complicated change process influenced by organizational context, leadership posture, technological capacity and cultural readiness. In foreseeing those barriers and taking proactive steps to cultivating enablers, HR can move beyond gradual change to transformational change; redefining itself and its purpose as a co-architect of sustainable, ethical and future-ready organizations.

7. INTEGRATED FRAMEWORK: STRATEGIC HR FOR SUSTAINABLE FUTURES

Having explored scenario planning, resilience-building, and ethical innovation as distinct but interrelated pillars of strategic HR transformation, this section synthesizes these elements into an integrated framework. The idea is to equip the HR leaders with a conceptual and practical model capable of interconnecting workforce strategy to the requirements of e-economy and the values of sustainable organic organization development. In this context HR does not act as service provider but a systems designer, active to drive the future of organisations based on their insight, foresight and ethics (Vong et al. 2025).

At the heart of this integrated approach is a **triadic model** composed of three mutually reinforcing domains:

1. **Foresight and Anticipation (Scenario Planning)**

This domain represents the cognitive and strategic capacity of HR to explore multiple possible futures and prepare the organization accordingly. It includes horizon scanning, labor market modeling, technological trend analysis, and the use of structured scenario-building methods to inform decision-making. The goal is not to predict the future, but to broaden the organization's field of vision, reduce strategic blind spots, and foster a mindset of preparedness across all HR functions.

2. **Adaptive Capacity and Human Resilience (Resilience Strategies)**

This domain focuses on enabling both individuals and systems to absorb disruption, learn from adversity, and regenerate stronger than before. HR contributes by embedding psychological safety, agile structures, and well-being mechanisms into the workplace. It also cultivates leadership traits like emotional intelligence, improvisational skill, and distributed authority—ensuring that the organization is not brittle but responsive and human-centered in times of change.

3. **Values Alignment and Accountability (Ethical Innovation)**

The third domain anchors HR innovation in ethical principles, stakeholder legitimacy, and social responsibility. It governs how digital tools are implemented, how fairness is ensured in hiring and promotions, how DEI is mainstreamed, and how cultural norms are codified. Ethical innovation ensures that organizational transformation is not only effective, but just and inclusive—preserving trust and moral coherence amid rapid technological shifts.

These three areas are not linear phases or independent functions- they engage with each other. As an example, scenario planning would expose ethical tensions within workforce models in years to come (e.g. more gigification with no protections), and action should be taken to address this through ethical policy design in advance. Just as well, foresight scenarios (e.g. through the preparation of future pandemics or digital burnout) can inform resilience tactics and ethical considerations can define acceptable limits to adaptation (i.e. no productivity surveillance that demeans dignity).

The integrated framework thus encourages HR to operate in **nested time horizons**:

- **Short-term**: Address immediate disruptions and employee needs through agile response systems and well-being supports.
- **Medium-term**: Align learning and talent strategies with plausible future scenarios and emerging skill demands.
- **Long-term**: Embed ethical and ecological principles into the organization's DNA, shaping culture and governance systems for lasting sustainability.

This temporal layering helps HR balance operational demands with strategic vision, and efficiency with integrity.

To implement this integrated model, organizations may consider the following practical enablers:

- Establishing **HR foresight teams** or embedding futurists within HR departments.
- Creating **resilience metrics and dashboards** that track psychological health, adaptability, and team coherence.
- Institutionalizing **ethical review boards** for HR technologies, with cross-functional participation.
- Designing **inclusive innovation labs** where employees co-develop future scenarios, test new work models, and assess cultural impacts.

The renewed system of measurement of success is additionally demanded by the integrated framework. Conventional HR KPIs focused on issues like the rate of turnover, time-to-hire or training completion- are not adequate to reflect the richness of systematic evolution. New measures could be foresight maturity, resilience index scores, ethical alignment scores, or scenario-informed strategic responsiveness. These indicators can assist in monitoring how well HR is indeed having a positive impact on sustainable futures as opposed to simply optimising existing operations (Ekuma, 2024).

Last, the framework should be dynamic and situation-specific. There is no one blue print that will work in every organization. The ensuing factors that will determine this model such as cultural values, regulatory environment, industry dynamics, and resource limitations will determine how this model will be adopted as well as adapted. The point is not fanatical obedience, but continuous education, the involvement of people in the process of designing and bold leadership that understands HR as a strategic renewal and the preservation of human dignity in the digital era, rather than as a cost center.

8. CONCLUSION

As the e-economy redefines the contours of work, employment, and organizational purpose, human resource (HR) functions are being called to rise far beyond their traditional boundaries. This chapter has argued that strategic HR innovation—anchored in scenario planning, resilience-building, and ethical practice—is not merely a response to change, but a proactive method of shaping more sustainable, adaptive, and values-driven organizational futures.

Scenario planning provides the HR professional with the vision and ability to consider multi-faceted workforce trends and offer approaches that support future readiness over acting in response. Meanwhile, resilience-building is about human and systemic ability to resist and adapt to change; by putting employee well-being, agile leadership and inclusive culture at the center of organisational design. Ethical innovation to make sure that HR practices are carried out with justice, honor, and responsibility in the digital, analytical, and algorithmic world, as well as in the fluid employment systems.

All these pillars create a unified and doable structure to redesign the strategic contribution of HR in a digital world. They refute our thinking that HR is an administrative or reactive construct and in fact prove that it stands at the centre of automating future-readiness, social legitimacy and institutional sustainability.

Moving into the future, there are a number of directions that strategic HR innovation will assume. On the one hand, there will be a rationale of more pronounced human-AI co-management with the necessity of the HR to establish a hybrid system of governance that unites efficiency with the ethicality of algorithmic decision-making. Second, there will be a need to rethink HR approaches to planetary thinking, which integrates ecological sustainability into workforce strategies as labor markets and organizational legitimacy become broadly dependent on climate risk, and environmental justice. Third, the participatory patterns of governance will make it more prominent, and work futures are driven more through participation, co-creation and shared responsibility of employees, communities and others that have a vested interest.

Because these futures will require a new way of thinking, a new mindset HR leaders would have to develop would be that of a strategic visionary with emphasized responsibility and ethos combined with systems-thinking and human understanding and fluency of technology and morality. This evolution does not only involve novelty in either tools or policies. It is a more fundamental transformation of purpose: out of the control of people as resources to the enabling of people as co-creators of resilient, ethical and purposeful futures organisations.

REFERENCES

Alipour, N., Nazari-Shirkouhi, S., Sangari, M. S., & Vandchali, H. R. (2022). Lean, agile, resilient, and green human resource management: The impact on organizational innovation and organizational performance. *Environmental Science and Pollution Research International, 29*(55), 82812–82826. DOI: 10.1007/s11356-022-21576-1 PMID: 35761135

Anguelov, K. (2021, May). Applications of artificial intelligence for optimization of business processes in enterprise resource planning systems. In *2021 12th national conference with international participation (ELECTRONICA)* (pp. 1-4). IEEE. DOI: 10.1109/ELECTRONICA52725.2021.9513677

Awwad Al-Shammari, A. S., Alshammrei, S., Nawaz, N., & Tayyab, M. (2022). Green human resource management and sustainable performance with the mediating role of green innovation: A perspective of new technological era. *Frontiers in Environmental Science, 10*, 901235. DOI: 10.3389/fenvs.2022.901235

Barsegyan, N. V., Vodolazhskaya, E. L., & Chekanova, E. V. (2021, April). Optimization of the petrochemical enterprise control system focused on resource conservation. [). IOP Publishing.]. *Journal of Physics: Conference Series, 1889*(4), 042060. DOI: 10.1088/1742-6596/1889/4/042060

Budhwar, P., Chowdhury, S., Wood, G., Aguinis, H., Bamber, G. J., Beltran, J. R., Boselie, P., Lee Cooke, F., Decker, S., DeNisi, A., Dey, P. K., Guest, D., Knoblich, A. J., Malik, A., Paauwe, J., Papagiannidis, S., Patel, C., Pereira, V., Ren, S., & Varma, A. (2023). Human resource management in the age of generative artificial intelligence: Perspectives and research directions on ChatGPT. *Human Resource Management Journal, 33*(3), 606–659. DOI: 10.1111/1748-8583.12524

Bustamante Izquierdo, J. P., Puertas, E. B., Hernández Hernández, D., & Sepúlveda, H. (2023). COVID-19 and human resources for health: Analysis of planning, policy responses and actions in Latin American and Caribbean countries. *Human Resources for Health, 21*(1), 21. DOI: 10.1186/s12960-023-00795-8 PMID: 36918895

Correia, A. B., Farrukh Shahzad, M., Moleiro Martins, J., & Baheer, R. (2024). Impact of green human resource management towards sustainable performance in the healthcare sector: Role of green innovation and risk management. *Cogent Business & Management, 11*(1), 2374625. DOI: 10.1080/23311975.2024.2374625

Ekuma, K. (2024). Artificial intelligence and automation in human resource development: A systematic review. *Human Resource Development Review, 23*(2), 199–229. DOI: 10.1177/15344843231224009

Fadeev, A., Komendantova, N., Cherepovitsyn, A., Tsvetkova, A., & Paramonov, I. (2021). Methods and priorities for human resource planning in oil and gas projects in Russia and OPEC. *OPEC Energy Review*, *45*(3), 365–389. DOI: 10.1111/opec.12213

Huang, X., Yang, F., Zheng, J., Feng, C., & Zhang, L. (2023). Personalized human resource management via HR analytics and artificial intelligence: Theory and implications. *Asia Pacific Management Review*, *28*(4), 598–610. DOI: 10.1016/j.apmrv.2023.04.004

Le, P. B. (2024). Applying knowledge-based human resource management to drive innovation: The roles of knowledge sharing and competitive intensity. *Management Research Review*, *47*(4), 602–621. DOI: 10.1108/MRR-02-2023-0154

Liang, F., & Cao, L. (2021). Linking employee resilience with organizational resilience: The roles of coping mechanism and managerial resilience. *Psychology Research and Behavior Management*, *14*, 1063–1075. DOI: 10.2147/PRBM.S318632 PMID: 34321935

Lin, Z., Gu, H., Gillani, K. Z., & Fahlevi, M. (2024). Impact of green work–life balance and green human resource management practices on corporate sustainability performance and employee retention: Mediation of green innovation and organisational culture. *Sustainability (Basel)*, *16*(15), 6621. DOI: 10.3390/su16156621

Madanchian, M., Taherdoost, H., & Mohamed, N. (2023). AI-based human resource management tools and techniques; a systematic literature review. *Procedia Computer Science*, *229*, 367–377. DOI: 10.1016/j.procs.2023.12.039

Ngoc Su, D., Luc Tra, D., Thi Huynh, H. M., Nguyen, H. H. T., & O'Mahony, B. (2021). Enhancing resilience in the Covid-19 crisis: Lessons from human resource management practices in Vietnam. *Current Issues in Tourism*, *24*(22), 3189–3205. DOI: 10.1080/13683500.2020.1863930

Pandey, S. C., Modi, P., Pereira, V., & Fosso Wamba, S. (2025). Empowering small farmers for sustainable agriculture: A human resource approach to SDG-driven training and innovation. *International Journal of Manpower*, *46*(4), 652–675. DOI: 10.1108/IJM-11-2023-0655

Pantea, M., Roberts, K., & Dabija, D. (2025). *Higher education and work in the knowledge economy*. Palgrave Macmillan. DOI: 10.1007/978-3-031-80618-6

Pinheiro, W., da Silva, E. P., & de Freitas, F. A. (2023). Circular Economy and the Development of Sustainable Products Through the Application of E-waste. *Electronic Waste Management: Policies, Processes, Technologies, and Impact*, 124-133.

Shah, N., & Soomro, B. A. (2023). Effects of green human resource management practices on green innovation and behavior. *Management Decision*, *61*(1), 290–312. DOI: 10.1108/MD-07-2021-0869

Tomé, E. L. S. (2025). *Intangibles in the Knowledge Economy*. Springer. DOI: 10.1007/978-3-031-86660-9

Vong, K. C., Udomvitid, K., Ueki, Y., Intalar, N., Pongsathornwiwat, A., Pannakkong, W., Komolavanij, S., & Jeenanunta, C. (2025). Strategic Human Resource Development for Industry 4.0 Readiness: A Sustainable Transformation Framework for Emerging Economies. *Sustainability (Basel)*, *17*(15), 6988. DOI: 10.3390/su17156988

Votto, A. M., Valecha, R., Najafirad, P., & Rao, H. R. (2021). Artificial intelligence in tactical human resource management: A systematic literature review. *International Journal of Information Management Data Insights*, *1*(2), 100047. DOI: 10.1016/j.jjimei.2021.100047

Wen, Q., Wu, Y., & Long, J. (2021). Influence of ethical leadership on employees' innovative behavior: The role of organization-based self-esteem and flexible human resource management. *Sustainability (Basel)*, *13*(3), 1359. DOI: 10.3390/su13031359

Ye, P., Liu, L., & Tan, J. (2023). The influence of organisational justice and ethical leadership on employees' innovation behaviour. *European Journal of Innovation Management*, *26*(4), 1129–1149. DOI: 10.1108/EJIM-08-2021-0421

Yu, J., Yuan, L., Han, G., Li, H., & Li, P. (2022). A study of the impact of strategic human resource management on organizational resilience. *Behavioral Sciences (Basel, Switzerland)*, *12*(12), 508. DOI: 10.3390/bs12120508 PMID: 36546991

KEY TERMS AND DEFINITIONS

Adaptive Organizations: Organizational structures that learn, change and adapt quickly and constantly to both internal and external changes through being flexible, decentralized and staffed with empowered teams.

Diversity, Equity and Inclusion (DEI): A collection of beliefs and actions that can establish equal treatment, access and representation of people of diverse backgrounds in an organization.

E-Economy: The digital-driven economic model making work platforms-based and involving automation, AI, the work at a distance, and data-focused business models.

Ethical Innovation (in HR): The intentional integration of ethical principles—such as fairness, transparency, and inclusivity—into HR policies, technologies, and decision-making processes.

Foresight in HR: The use of future-oriented tools and thinking (e.g., horizon scanning, trend analysis) by HR professionals to anticipate talent needs and design future-ready workforce strategies.

HR Ethical AI: Application of artificial intelligence to HR operations (e.g. hiring or performance evaluation) regulated by ethics to guarantee accountability, explanation, and fairness.

HR Innovation: The design and implementation of novel HR strategies, technologies, or processes that improve workforce outcomes, organizational adaptability, or ethical alignment.

Organizational Resilience: The ability of the corporation to withstand shocks, cope with changes and develop due to principled learning, dynamism and strong support systems.

Psychological Safety: A collective team conviction that interpersonal risks (e.g. speaking around or making mistakes) can be undertaken without the imminent risk of adverse outcomes.

Scenario Planning: A systematic process to identify and develop a series of plausible futures in order to influence decision-making and make organizations ready to face uncertainty.

Strategic Human Resource Management (SHRM): An approach to managing people that aligns HR practices with long-term organizational goals, emphasizing proactive planning, agility, and value creation.

Chapter 16
Strategic Human Resource Transformation in the E-Economy and Navigating the Nexus of Technology and Society

S. Pushpalatha
http://orcid.org/0009-0003-8730-0670
Saveetha School of Management, SIMATS, Saveetha University, Chennai, India

R. Duraipandian
http://orcid.org/0000-0003-2932-0270
Saveetha School of Management, SIMATS, Saveetha University, Chennai, India

ABSTRACT

In this chapter, the transformative function of strategic human resource management (SHRM) within the evolving e-economy is examined, with a focus on the intersection of technology and society to redefine HR practices. HR must transform into a strategic driver of inclusivity, innovation, and agility as organizations navigate digital disruption and societal shifts. This chapter addresses SHRM strategies, ethical challenges, accessibility, emerging trends, and practical recommendations by incorporating conceptual and theoretical frameworks. It proposes models for sustainable, ethical, and technologically aligned HR transformation while laying the groundwork for future research through a focus on human-centric adaptation and data-informed decisions.

DOI: 10.4018/979-8-3373-4307-5.ch016

INTRODUCTION

The E-Economy a digital economic environment based on e-commerce, automation, AI, and data-centric ecosystems is transforming the global business landscape due to rapid technological advancements and societal evolution. In this new paradigm, Strategic Human Resource Management (SHRM) must go beyond administrative and transactional responsibilities to build organizational agility, creativity, and resilience (Ulrich, 2016). The digital economy requires advanced technical skills and an adaptive, inclusive, and strategically oriented workforce (Schwab, 2017). Technology and human-centric transformation are at the heart of strategic HRM today. Strategic HR transformation in the e-economy requires rethinking policies, procedures, systems, and people strategies to match human resources with digital capabilities. In this new environment, employees co-create digital value rather than just perform duties. Cloud computing, machine learning, virtual collaboration platforms, and remote work have transformed corporate operations and HR assistance for workforce planning, performance management, talent development, and organisational culture (Bersin, 2021). While societal demands for justice, sustainability, and purpose rise, HR drives Environmental, Social, and Governance (ESG) goals (CIPD, 2022). The Fourth Industrial Revolution and AI, block chain, IoT, and augmented reality are changing industrial methods and work (World Economic Forum, 2023). These advances generate new prospects for wealth generation and innovation, but they also raise ethical issues, digital inequalities, surveillance concerns, and automation-related job losses (Susskind & Susskind, 2015). Indeed, HR directors must rethink existing talent paradigms and create technologically native, ethical, and socially responsible methods. HR must use technological foresight and human empathy to navigate this technology-society intersection. Organisations must balance efficiency with upskilling, mental well-being assistance, diversity and inclusion (D&I) programs, and purpose-driven leadership (Boudreau & Jesuthasan, 2018). Thus, strategic HR transformation involves creating a flexible, inclusive, and ethical organization that integrates data and choices while putting people first. In the e-economy, work is redefined not only where and how but also why. Millennials and Gen Z expect purpose, flexibility, equity, and progress in the workplace (Gallup, 2021). These expectations are changing employee value offerings and requiring firms to rethink workforce acquisition, engagement, and retention. The pandemic exposed worldwide digital preparedness weaknesses in workforce resilience, leadership communication, and digital infrastructure (Carnevale & Hatak, 2020). Strategic HR is now essential for recovery, innovation, and transformation. Additionally, data-driven HR provides predictive insights for workforce analytics, performance optimization, and employee experience design. People Analytics helps organisations pinpoint engagement, burnout, inclusiveness gaps, and learning needs (Davenport, Harris & Shapiro, 2010). However, data privacy, algorithmic bias, and ethical governance create concerns, emphasizing the need for a balanced, regulatory-compliant strategy (Tursunbayeva et al., 2018). To manage this complex landscape, HR professionals need digital and ethical literacy. The e-economy breaks down cultural barriers. Agile HR systems that facilitate cross-time zone and cross-cultural communication are needed for virtual teams, global gig workers, and hybrid models (Kniffin et al. HR must prioritize psychological safety, digital health, and adaptable leadership to connect scattered teams. HR professionals must also learn design thinking, digital ethics, systems thinking, and strategic foresight (Cascio & Montealegre, 2016). Strategic Human Resource Transformation is now essential for future-ready enterprises. Redesigning HR operating paradigms, embracing cross-functional cooperation, and using technology to match people strategies with business goals are required. However, societal issues including equity, privacy, skill gaps, and inclusive cultures must remain strategic priorities. This chapter critically examines how HR leaders and practitioners may strategically integrate technology and societal agendas to revolutionize the e-economy. It will examine strategic HR transformation's conceptual and theoretical foundations, practical frameworks and visual models, and real-world ramifications, including best practices, ethical issues, and future research. Managing technology disruption, workforce inclusiveness, accessibility, and HR transformation for organizational agility are key issues.

Importance and Purpose of the Chapter

Strategic Human Resource Transformation is important to organizational renewal in the 21st-century e-economy due to the rapid convergence of digital technologies and changing social expectations. This change is about redefining HR's role in determining the future of work, business culture, and societal values, not automating HR activities or adopting new tools. This chapter discusses how human resource management (HRM) must adapt to technological innovation and social responsibility and why it is important for organizations, employees, and society. This transformation can build human-centric, agile, and digitally intelligent enterprises. As digital disruption intensifies, organizations are realizing that long-term competitiveness depends on adopting new technologies and having the necessary people, skills, and cultures to use them (Bughin et al., 2018). People strategies are key to expanding digital transformation, according to McKinsey (2022). So strategic HR must be more predictive, individualized, inclusive, and ethical. HR faces expanding social expectations, including diversity and inclusion, sustainability, and worker rights in a digital-first world (EY, 2023). Social justice, mental health, environmental sustainability, and digital ethics now overlap in the workplace. HR must now balance these complex and frequently conflicting demands with business strategy and the greater good. This chapter purposefully integrates HR transformation's technological and sociological aspects. Digital HR conversations frequently focus on tools like AI-powered recruitment, learning management systems, and robotic process automation without considering their human, ethical, and systemic impacts (Meijerink et al., 2021). Many societal critiques of HR ignore commercial technology use. This chapter offers a balanced, strategic perspective based on commercial outcomes and social accountability to overcome this gap. This chapter provides a framework for scholars and practitioners studying or implementing strategic HR change. The chapter shows how HR can promote digital change by combining theoretical ideas, conceptual frameworks, and empirical facts. It also fills the knowledge vacuum on how strategic HRM may boost the digital economy while respecting human dignity, justice, and sustainability (Bondarouk & Brewster, 2016). Furthermore, the chapter acknowledges contextual adaptation. Strategic HR change cannot be standardized. What works for a multinational IT corporation may not for a government agency or start up? Therefore, this chapter emphasizes strategic agility and local responsiveness, suggesting customized techniques that account for organisational culture, worker demography, and industry dynamics (Snell, Morris, & Bohlander, 2015 It also promotes evidence-based HR, where data and analytics inform decisions without overshadowing intuition and empathy. This chapter is current and futuristic. The pandemic has forever changed work, showing HR systems' strengths and weaknesses (Kniffin et al., 2021). HR leaders face remote work, hybrid models, mental health problems, and digital weariness. AI, block chain, and immersive technologies like the metaverse indicate that we are just beginning a deeper shift (Deloitte, 2023). This chapter assesses existing conditions and predicts future scenarios, suggesting research opportunities. Strategic HR transformation's social impact emphasizes its importance. HR can tackle inequality, gender and racial gaps, worker mental health, and sustainability goals when done effectively (ILO, 2021). Ignored or badly performed, it can increase marginalization, surveillance, and employment insecurity. This discourse matters because the stakes are great. This chapter concludes by promoting a new view of HR as a strategic partner in creating ethical, adaptive, and high-performing organizations. These new competencies, leadership paradigms, and cultural narratives must match people strategies with technical change and societal good. Humanizing the digital economy through HR is the goal, not just digitizing HR.

BACKGROUND

Strategic human resource transformation in the e-economy is driven by three macro trends: business process digitization, changing employee expectations, and the growing requirement for firms to meet their social duties. These pressures are forcing organisations to transition from administrative HR to a strategic, future-facing department that combines digital fluency with ethical foresight. E-commerce, real-time data exchange, and algorithm-driven decision-making have transformed how firms generate, deliver, and collect value. Business paradigms are changing as AI, blockchain, and cloud computing transform operations (Brynjolfsson & McAfee, 2014). HRM can construct resilient, flexible, and innovation-ready workforces during this change. The pace of the Fourth Industrial Revolution, which combines physical, digital, and biological technology, has changed work structures and required ongoing upskilling and reskilling (Schwab, 2017). HR was traditionally a support function that handled payroll, compliance, hiring, and administrative records. This evolved into Human Capital Management (HCM), stressing personnel and labor capabilities as strategic assets for competitive advantage (Becker & Huselid, 2006). These changes have led to Strategic Human Resource Management (SHRM), which integrates HR strategy with company strategy to drive performance, innovation, and transformation in the digital age (Wright & McMahan, 2011). External drivers accelerated this change. The 2008 global financial crisis drove firms to rethink operational efficiency and personnel adaptability. The COVID-19 pandemic disrupted labor markets, accelerated digital adoption, and changed employee-employer interactions (Carnevale & Hatak, 2020). Strategic HR firms adopted remote work infrastructure and protected employee well-being faster than others. Internal organizational dynamics change. Flatter, cross-functional, and autonomous work arrangements are replacing hierarchical, command-and-control management as work becomes more knowledge-intensive and innovation-driven (Gratton, 2021). Careers are shifting from fixed positions to skill-based models and lifetime employment to fluid gig ecosystems because employees want customization, flexibility, and meaning (Deloitte, 2023). These changes force HR to rethink how they empower and manage people. The increased demand for CSR, ESG, and inclusive practices complicates this scenario. Companies are under pressure from employees, consumers, investors, and authorities to be transparent, sustainable, and equitable (Kiron et al., 2015). Equity recruiting, inclusive culture, ESG-aligned goal-setting, and psychological safety are HR's key to implementing these ideals (CIPD, 2022). HR technology has shaped transformation. Digital solutions like AI-powered recruitment platforms and cloud-based HRIS have automated regular HR tasks and given HR real-time data and predictive analytics (Marler & Boudreau, 2017). For instance, workforce analytics can accurately predict attrition risks, optimize learning pathways, and analyze engagement levels. These advances pose data privacy, algorithmic bias, and decision-making dehumanization concerns (Tursunbayeva et al., 2018). HR faces new difficulties and opportunities from hybrid work settings and global virtual teams. Collaboration, digital communication, performance tracking, and employee wellbeing must change for a remote workforce (Kniffin et al., 2021). An environment without physical presence requires HR to foster cohesion, productivity, and trust. The workforce demographic shift is another important background aspect. Millennials and Gen Z, who are increasingly the global workforce, want flexible, meaningful, and socially responsible work (Gallup, 2021). Digital natives and social activists shape company expectations and cultures. HR must create inclusive policies, L&D initiatives, and leadership development programmes that reflect these new generational ideals (Bersin, 2020). Finally, global labor market inequalities like the digital divide, gender pay discrepancies, and geographic disadvantages shape HR change. Technology can worsen inequalities without purposeful action (ILO, 2021). HR professionals can ensure the digital economy is efficient and fair as gatekeepers of opportunity and advocates of equity. Digitization, demographic trends, globalization, and changing social norms affect strategic HR transformation in the e-economy. Organizations must embrace technology while protecting human values, promoting inclusion, and anticipating workforce demands. This chapter explores how HR can lead transformation at the intersection of technology and society from a structured and holistic approach.

Structure of the Chapter

The chapter is structured in the following manner in order to produce a narrative that is both coherent and insightful:

- **Conceptual Framework:** Defines important constructs and the interrelationships.
- **Theoretical Framework:** Providing academic underpinnings for analysis.
- **Strategic Human Resource Management in the E-Economy:** Analyzes digital disruptions and HR's adaptive tactics.
- **Navigating Tech-Society Nexus:** A discussion on the ethical, cultural, and inclusion imperatives.
- **Solutions and Recommendations:** In addition to providing best practices and tactics that can be implemented.
- **Future Research Directions:** Identifying gaps in knowledge and prospective academic contributions.
- **Conclusion:** Recapitulates the most important takeaways and encourages readers to take action.

CONCEPTUAL FRAMEWORK

Definition of Key Concepts

Strategic Human Resource Management (SHRM)

The foundation of this concept is Strategic Human Resource Management (SHRM), which denotes the long-term alignment of HR practices with an organization's strategic objectives to enhance business performance and cultivate a flexible workforce (Wright & McMahan, 2011). SHRM transitions the HR department from administrative assistance to a strategic partner that connects personnel, culture, and technology to address competitive demands.

E-Economy

The e-economy is characterized as an economic environment propelled by digital technology, marked by connection, data-centric activities, and digitally mediated transactions (Tapscott, 1996). In this economy, business models depend on digital platforms, cloud computing, artificial intelligence, and real-time analytics. Human resource functions must adapt in this context to maintain relevance and efficacy.

Digital Transformation

Digital Transformation denotes the thorough implementation and assimilation of digital technology to fundamentally alter organizational operations, value delivery, and stakeholder engagement (Westerman et al., 2014). This entails the integration of AI in recruitment, the utilization of analytics for performance management, and the implementation of digital platforms for learning and development inside HR.

Technology-Society Nexus

The Technology-Society Nexus encapsulates the intersection of swift technology progress with changing cultural values, encompassing ethics, justice, diversity, and sustainability (Zuboff, 2019). Human Resources must recognize the ethical ramifications of technology utilization, especially regarding its impact on human autonomy, privacy, inclusiveness, or well-being.

Interconnection of Concepts

Strategic HR transformation in the e-economy depends on these concepts' relationship. SHRM links digital transformation technologies to organizational purpose and employee-centric values. HR ensures ethical and inclusive AI and automation use in enterprises. Using AI in hiring involves technological implementation and frameworks to avoid algorithmic bias and protect candidate privacy. The e-economy requires ongoing innovation, adaptability, and reactivity. Thus, SHRM must promote agile workforce development through upskilling, reskilling, and cross-functional training. People analytics helps HR make data-driven decisions by revealing performance patterns, engagement levels, and workforce hazards. This creates privacy, consent, and data ethics considerations, which relates to the technology-society nexus. Growing emphasis on inclusive work culture and employee experience incorporates social expectations into company strategy. HR practices must promote trust and flexibility in the post-pandemic, hybrid workplace. For burnout prevention, wellness programs now offer digital mental health assistance, ergonomic home offices, and asynchronous communication. These ideas reinforce each other. Technological advances provide tools and platforms, strategic HR practices define how to use them, and societal values provide the ethical compass to maintain human dignity, fairness, and inclusiveness.

Visual Representation

This chapter, presents the conceptual framework as a three-tiered structure:

- The foundational layer comprises the technology infrastructure, including AI, big data analytics, cloud systems, and collaboration platforms. These technologies delineate the operational framework of the e-economy and present substantial opportunities for HR reform. Nevertheless, they also provide concerns including employment displacement, surveillance, and digital inequality.
- The Strategic HRM Layer, positioned above, functions as the operational core that interprets and employs these technologies. In this context, HR functions as a strategic facilitator, utilizing digital tools to enhance processes including as recruiting, performance evaluations, and employee engagement, while concurrently addressing concerns such algorithmic bias and technology-induced stress. This layer is where policies, learning systems, compensation models, and cultural practices are formulated and synchronized with company objectives.

- The uppermost layer comprises societal imperatives, which denote the macro-level factors that drive HR strategy. This encompasses demands for ethical artificial intelligence, prioritizing of mental health, integration of sustainability, and mandates for diversity and inclusion.

Human Resources serves as the conduit between society and technology, guaranteeing that digital transformation is both effective and ethically inclusive. This stratified model demonstrates the fluid exchange of influence: technical advancements compel HR to modify its systems; HR, therefore, must execute these modifications in alignment with overarching societal norms. The layers are interrelated; each cannot operate optimally in isolation from the others. Implementing AI without social control might result in exclusion, while advocating for inclusion without sufficient technology may constrain scalability and efficiency. This illustrative depiction underscores the chapter's primary argument: that HR transformation in the digital economy transcends mere digitization, necessitating the establishment of systems where technology and human values mutually evolve for enduring organizational impact.

THEORETICAL FRAMEWORK

This chapter uses theories from human resource management, organizational behavior, sociology, and technology studies. This concept helps explain Strategic Human Resource Transformation in the E-Economy, especially how digital disruption and changing social dynamics affect HR practices. The chapter provides a solid framework for studying technology and society in HR by basing the investigation in classical and contemporary theories.

Resource-Based View (RBV)

The Resource-Based View (RBV) of the firm holds that firms gain persistent competitive advantage by managing valuable, rare, inimitable, and non-substitutable (VRIN) resources (Barney, 1991). One of the most important resources is human capital. The RBV stresses the strategic relevance of establishing a digitally literate, flexible, and innovation-oriented workforce that can use technology to create value in the e-economy. HR transformation is necessary to optimize talent strategies to use digital tools while preserving cultural and social assets.

Human Capital Theory

Human Capital Theory, which complements the RBV, regards skills, knowledge, and abilities as capital that can be developed to boost production and organizational performance (Becker, 1964). This approach supports HR's digital-age focus on continual learning, reskilling, and employee development. It also supports digital inclusiveness and talent management equality. To stay competitive and socially responsible, firms must strategically invest in human capital as technology disrupts routine work.

Socio-Technical Systems (STS) Theory

The framework also uses Socio-Technical Systems (STS) Theory, which highlights the interconnection of social (people, culture, relationships) and technical (technology, infrastructure) systems in an organization (Trist & Bamforth, 1951). STS theory illuminates how technological change affects human roles, decision-making, and organisational culture. STS advises HR practitioners to combine technological upgrades with cultural adaptability, employee involvement, and systemic thinking for successful digital transformation.

Institutional Theory

Institutional Theory examines how conventions, regulations, societal expectations, and regulatory frameworks affect organisational behaviour (DiMaggio & Powell, 1983). This theory helps explain why HR reform must match with internal and external demands including ESG obligations, diversity mandates, and ethical governance. In an e-economy with real-time reputation risk and more public scrutiny, HR must guarantee that digital strategies are fair, inclusive, and accountable.

Technology Acceptance Model (TAM)

This methodology also uses the Technology Acceptance Model (TAM) to study workplace technology adoption (Davis, 1989). TAM found that perceived utility and ease of use strongly impact employee technology adoption. TAM emphasizes the need of simple, user-friendly HR technology, training, and change management in HR digital transformation. It advocates involve users in technology selection and implementation to reduce employee resistance.

Lewin's Change Management Model

Lewin's Change Management Model unfreeze, change, refreeze explains HR departments' digital transformation from a behavioral perspective (Lewin, 1947). This model shows how HR can support cultural transformations, skill reconfiguration, and new workflows. HR methods must include empathy, communication, and resilience due to change's emotional and psychological effects.

Stakeholder Theory

Stakeholder Theory emphasizes the need of meeting the requirements of all stakeholders, not just shareholders (Freeman, 1984), strengthening the theoretical framework. In the e-economy, HR must address employee satisfaction and performance as well as HR technology's effects on customers, suppliers, communities, and regulators. To satisfy a wide spectrum of stakeholders concerned with justice and accountability, AI in HR decisions must be open and auditable.

Critical Management Studies (CMS)

Critical Management Studies (CMS) examine power dynamics, inequities, and unintended implications of management methods (Alvesson & Willmott, 1992). CMS is crucial in the digital age, when monitoring, algorithmic decision-making, and gig employment threaten job stability, privacy, and worker rights. HR transformation must thoroughly evaluate the social impacts of adopting technologies that may reinforce systemic prejudices or reduce employee autonomy.

This theoretical framework helps HR professionals and researchers comprehend change as a complex process involving technology capability, human potential, ethical duty, and institutional legitimacy. It guides the creation of efficient, flexible, humanistic, and future-ready HR systems.

RESEARCH METHODOLOGY

This chapter studies complex emergent phenomena like strategic HR transformation in the dynamic e-economy using qualitative exploratory methods. The chapter conceptualizes how digital and societal developments are altering HRM using secondary data from academic literature, policy reports, white papers, and recent case studies. This strategy works for conceptual book chapters seeking theoretical and practical understanding rather than hypothesis testing. Interpretive reasoning helps academics uncover patterns, correlations, and conceptual relationships between

AI, HRM, organisational agility, digital inclusion, and ethics in non-linear, multi-disciplinary scenarios (Creswell, 2014). Data was collected from Scopus, Web of Science, Google Scholar, and institutional databases from the World Economic Forum (2023), Deloitte Insights (2022), McKinsey & Company (2021), and CIPD (2022). Industry reports and peer-reviewed publications on 2014–2024 HRM, digital transformation, organizational development, and ethical AI governance were preferred. To ensure theoretical saturation, the literature was studied until common themes, frameworks, and conceptual gaps arose. North American, European, and Asian studies illustrate global e-economy and HR revolution. Triangulating literature with real-world activities and policy directives boosted credibility. Thomas & Harden (2008) used thematic synthesis to identify important themes and patterns in a large literary collection. HR automation, ethics, strategic agility, employee well-being, and digital inclusiveness emerged from reading, note-taking, and coding. The chapter's cross-disciplinary approach draws from sociology, information systems, ethics, organizational psychology, and strategic management. The digital transformation of HR influences technical, social, psychological, and cultural elements, hence methodological heterogeneity is intentional. The complicated interaction between technology and society is better grasped with this method. Qualitative and interpretive methods are used, while quantitative data from reports (e.g., employee attitude surveys, digital readiness indices, AI adoption rates) supports claims. These data sources contextualize arguments and highlight global HR trends, not statistics. The chapter ethically addresses technology's effects on marginalized groups and labor equity. The evaluation examined AI adoption ethics, data protection, algorithmic transparency, and worker autonomy (Zuboff, 2019; Eubanks, 2018). HR technology research on prejudice, discrimination, and surveillance weighed innovation and efficiency equally. Balance ensures digital HR's strengths and downsides are covered. Concept maps showed how chapter structure affects human capital, technology, and social responsibility. Early sections like the conceptual and theoretical framework narratively organized conceptual linkages for methodological coherence. Qualitative synthesis reports limited generalizability of concept research without primary data. The technique is strong due to its depth, diversity, and ability to solve complex, multidimensional problems. E-economy HR managers receive practical guidance, best practices, and strategic suggestions based on significant empirical research and rigorous synthesis. The study approach supports the chapter's academic and practical goals. It critiques literature ethically and derives conclusions utilizing theories and concepts. Full, evidence-based story helps organizations manage strategic HR change and satisfy digital social standards.

STRATEGIC HUMAN RESOURCE TRANSFORMATION IN THE E-ECONOMY

Strategic Human Resource Transformation in the e-economy rethinks digital organization human capital management, empowerment, and connectivity. Unlike administrative operations and compliance, e-economy HR shapes innovation, agility, and organizational resilience. It strategically advances technology, worker skills, and social impact (Ulrich, 1997; Wright et al., 2001). The e-economy requires HR agility, foresight, and digital fluency due to digitization, data-centric operations, and platform-based ecosystems. Rapid market changes, remote and hybrid work patterns, global competition for digital skills, and AI's extensive impact have caused firms to reassess their people strategy (Deloitte, 2022). Strategic HR transformation aligns organizations, processes, and talents to use technology humanely. AI-driven recruitment, predictive workforce planning, and cloud-based people management underpin this move. Solutions that decrease prejudice, eliminate tedious chores, and enable data-driven decision-making increase HR's strategic competencies (Marler & Boudreau, 2017). HR professionals can focus on organizational development and cultural transformation by deploying AI-powered chat bots for onboarding and requests. HR transformation involves leadership, culture, and attitudes, not just technology. To encourage creativity and risk-taking, HR directors must support learning agility and psychological safety. Culture is firms' invisible glue, thus Schein (2010) thinks any transformation attempt that ignores it will fail. Thus, HR must protect culture in the digital age from technology change that outpaces human flexibility and inclusivity. HR strategy must align with corporate strategy for transformation. Business forecasting should include workforce planning, performance management should include digital KPIs, and people analytics should predict attrition, skills gaps, and leadership pipeline vulnerabilities (Bersin, 2020). To adapt faster to market changes and engage employees, top IT organizations co-create business and talent strategies. Strategic workforce development is an HR priority since skills are the new money in the e-economy. HR must lead the move from role-based to skills-based talent management as jobs disappear and new positions emerge swiftly. Monitoring skill taxonomies, designing learning paths, and working with schools enable upskilling and reskilling (World Economic Forum, 2023). Coursera and Degreed are connected into enterprise learning ecosystems for real-time, customized learning. Digital disruption impacts stress, mental health, and work-life balance, thus HR reform must address them. Covid-19 showed old work paradigms' fragility and boosted HR priority to well-being (Kniffin et al., 2021). Modern HR strategies use technology, communication, empathy, and wellness to manage employee experience (EX). Microsoft's workplace strategies include mental health days, AI-enabled well-being assessments, and digital detox. E-commerce necessitates smart HR initiatives like DEIB. Digital technology's transparency and interconnection have made discrimination more evident and unethical. Thus, strategic HR must ensure that all digital tools—from hiring algorithms to promotion analytics—are bias-free and support equality (Eubanks, 2018). This requires comprehensive audits, inclusive design thinking, and HR, IT, and legal team coordination. Transactional to employee experience-focused HR shows how workplace personalization and voice are developing. Current employees need intuitive UI, mobile accessibility, and AI-driven customization. To listen and respond dynamically, HR needs pulse surveys, sentiment analysis, and feedback analytics. The change increases engagement, decreases turnover, and aligns personnel with company values (Bersin, 2020). Leadership development has changed. Adaptation, empathy, and digital skills define digital leadership, not authority. Strategic HR must restructure leadership pipelines to generate "digital leaders" who can manage complex, ambiguous, and fast-changing teams. AI-based assessments and real-time feedback provide in-depth learning, coaching, and scenario preparation (McKinsey & Company, 2021). Remote employment, global mobility, and digital labor require HR policy changes. Update data privacy policies, meet global labor laws, and protect IP in hybrid workplaces. Strategic HR must promote ethical AI use to prevent surveillance, algorithmic prejudice, and data exploitation (Zuboff, 2019). Strategic HR transformation flattens hierarchies and allows cross-functional agile teams. HR business partner models, centers of excellence, and shared services platforms optimize and scale organizations. These strategies allow HR to handle regional discrepancies while adopting enterprise-wide personnel strategy (Ulrich, 2016). Finally, strategic HR transformation demands digital HR capabilities. HR workers should understand data science, design thinking, change management, and digital ethics. To boost employee value and company performance, HR directors must work with CIOs, data officers, and product owners (Deloitte, 2022). Finally, e-economy strategic HR transformation requires technology and human-centered design. Digital-first HR boosts agility, resilience, and diversity. Strategic HR advises companies on people management and workplace change.

NAVIGATING THE NEXUS OF TECHNOLOGY AND SOCIETY

Current HR transformation necessitates tech-society integration. Value creation, employee-peer interactions, and corporate operations depend on this intersection. AI, automation, the IoT, block chain, and big data have altered business and the social contract between employers, employees, consumers, producers, institutions, and individuals. Social and technological, digital society's e-economy. Organizations may no longer consider technology adoption technical. Every digital invention impacts ethics, psychology, society, and politics. These interdependencies necessitate HR changes. To promote justice, privacy, sustainability, and human dignity in digital transition, strategic HR departments must speak social impact language (Zuboff, 2019). Technology-based socialization promotes this nexus. Face recognition, productivity monitors, algorithms, and remote surveillance affect hiring, performance evaluations, and privacy. Technology reflects society's values and biases (Eubanks, 2018). HR must choose and audit such technologies for fairness, openness, and accountability. Skewed data may extend discrimination as AI becomes more important in talent acquisition (Binns et al., 2018). HR closes digital units. Rapid technological advancement may exclude non-digital people. Separation creates socioeconomic inequalities for marginalized groups (UNESCO, 2022). Mobile-first HR apps, accessible user interfaces, digital literacy, and disability assistive technologies should be supported by strategic HR. This ensures digital transformation doesn't exclude. Junction needs moral leadership. Leaders must use technology ethically and encourage staff to discuss social issues related to digital projects. Ethics or HR committees can create and employ AI. HR ethical assessments boost trust, reputational risk, and employee engagement (Floridi et al., 2018). Social trends like work-life blurring are caused by technology. Digital platforms, remote work, and connectivity cause weariness and availability. The "always-on" world of digital devices produces fatigue, anxiety, and mental illness. Strategic HR must establish boundaries, humanize digital workflows, and promote well-being. A sustainable digital workplace requires the right to disengage, virtual wellness, and compassionate leadership training (Kniffin et al., 2021). Employee voice and behavior change via technology. Employees organize, protest, and promote environmental and social causes on social media and internal channels. External stakeholders and employees hold firms accountable. Strategic HR must address these processes through institutional input, debate, and joint decision-making. Companies should represent their beliefs and support society in a society that promotes employee citizenship (Grant, 2013). Technology altered jobs. The gig economy, platform work, and algorithmic labor have altered employer-employee relationships. Flexible strategies lack job security, benefits, and promotion. Organisations need strategic HR to manage non-traditional work. Freelancers, contractors, and digital nomads need respect, salary, and benefits (De Stefano, 2016). Data governance involves tech and society. Employers acquire massive biometric and productivity data. Data enhances personalization and performance but decreases privacy and autonomy. Strategic HR data ethics requires transparency, informed permission, and explicit data access, use, and preservation. Earn trust and accountability by following the GDPR and India's Digital Personal Data Protection Act (2023). Digital HR may impact society's ESG. Digital monitoring technologies control diversity and supply chain ethics ESG, while remote labor reduces carbon footprints. Digital HR activities linked to sustainability goals assist organisations achieve legal and regulatory obligations and benefit society (Eccles & Klimenko,

2019). HR strategy must prepare people for digital disruption. Technology, digital citizenship, ethics, culture, and systems thinking are taught. Workers can safely navigate the e-economy with these skills (Ferrari & Punie, 2013). Learning and development strengthens organizations and society. Society-technology interplay demands collaborative governance. HR, IT, legal, compliance, communications, and external stakeholders must collaborate on fair, efficient, inclusive digital projects. Cross-functional teams, cooperative seminars, and scenario-based planning align business strategy with societal norms. Technology-society connection is strategic, not hard. HR experts who master this will construct digital, socially responsible, future-ready firms. Socially responsible digital HR practices boost e-economy trust, reputation, and success.

SOLUTIONS AND RECOMMENDATIONS

The proactive e-economy strategic HR transformation mixes digital efficiency and social responsibility. Cloud platforms, AI, and automation should improve agility, scalability, and employee engagement in a digital-first HR strategy. These tools simplify hiring, onboarding, performance management, and training (Marler & Parry, 2016). AI-driven candidate tracking minimizes hiring prejudices, while cloud-based learning systems improve careers (Deloitte, 2023). Data-driven HR value chain decisions require strategic people analytics. A good people analytics unit should use predictive models to identify workforce trends, talent shortages, and retention issues for prompt, evidence-based action (Davenport et al., 2010; Boudreau & Cascio, 2017). Teaching agility and continuous learning is another option. HR must LinkedIn-reskill and upskill workers. Learning or graduating as technology advances. World Economic Forum (2023): E-economy workers need growth mindset and self-directed learning. Every HR tech needs ethics. Human resources IT implementation must be ethical to encourage fairness, transparency, and accountability (Floridi et al., 2018). Data-driven and AI-driven decision-making are growing. The Indian GDPR (2023) requires bias-checked recruitment algorithms and employee data privacy. Digital transformation must be inclusive. Digitalization should not increase organizational or social inequality. Thus, HR should make digital platforms accessible to all employees, regardless of handicap, socioeconomic background, or computer literacy. Multilingual support, mobile accessibility, and assistive technologies increase workplace equity (UNESCO, 2022; CIPD, 2021). Humanize digital employee experiences to prevent burnout. Empathetic leadership, personalized well-being therapies, and belonging-fostering digital platforms must sustain human interactions while automating productivity (Kniffin et al., 2021). Virtual coaching, sentiment analysis dashboards, and AI-powered wellness apps foster workplace compassion. To implement these changes, HR needs agile operating models, cross-functional cooperation, and iterative design. Agile HR teams can quickly prototype hybrid work and digital inclusion solutions (Gifford & Young, 2021). Development of leadership requires change. Modern leaders must be moral, tech-savvy, and emotionally intelligent. HR should create digital, real-world complexity-based leadership programs. Leadership labs, peer-to-peer learning, and virtual simulations address business, technology, and society (McKinsey, 2021). Digital transformation requires organizational change skills to succeed and stay. HR practitioners must communicate, involve stakeholders, and activate change agents to manage change (Hiatt, 2006). Continuous improvement and cross-level feedback loops enable flexibility. To serve society, HR should include ESG and net-zero in its workforce strategy. Digital HR systems can monitor workforce diversity for ESG reporting, carbon footprints, and emission-reducing remote labor (Eccles & Klimenko, 2019). Last, HR should update strategy with schools, civic groups, and IT enterprises. Public-private partnerships boost digital literacy, job readiness, and community engagement. HR collaboration boosts organisational resilience and social impact (OECD, 2021). These responses and suggestions show HR must link tech innovation and social good. People-centered, ethical, and inclusive change may benefit all e-economy stakeholders.

Best Practices

E-economy strategic HR transformation requires proven, adaptive best practices. Integration of technology, ethics, and inclusivity. Top HR transformation firms stress efficiency, employee empowerment, trust, fairness, and innovation. Integrating HR transformation with the company's digital strategy is wise. HR should transform, not preserve, enterprises. HR leaders must participate in executive decisions, use people data to drive digital investments, and link personnel planning with innovation goals (Ulrich & Dulebohn, 2015). Workforce analytics helps IBM and Google navigate strategic decisions (Bersin, 2022). HR tech and activities should be employee-centered. HR departments may increase adoption and delight by co-creating solutions with employees using empathy. By engaging employees, onboarding and wellness apps reduce change resistance (Brown, 2009; IDEO, 2020). Change HR requires constant listening and feedback. Pulse surveys, sentiment analysis, and AI-enabled voice-of-the-employee technology help top companies change labor policy (Gartner, 2021). These methods boost participation and identify burnout and exclusion. Microsoft detects collaboration and work-life balance concerns early via live dashboards and AI (Microsoft, 2021). Digital HR solutions that boost DEI are recommended. To reduce bias, transformative HR needs inclusive tools and spaces. Top companies disclose DEI data, evaluate their algorithms, and make them accessible across demographics for accountability (Kaplan & Donovan, 2021). In their HR digital ecosystem, Accenture's "Inclusion Starts with I" campaign emphasizes fairness and belonging through inclusive AI. Agile HR is a digital economy best practice. Scrum and Kanban help HR teams deliver value quickly. Agile HR models promote departmental collaboration, initiative launch, and business alignment (Denning, 2018). Spotify's "squad" model, where cross-functional teams work independently and flexibly to fulfill HR goals, works effectively. Digital skills and inclusive leadership are HR reform priorities. The digital workplace leader must support transformation, ethical technology use, and psychological safety. Salesforce and Unilever develop well-rounded, future-ready CEOs through digital simulations, ethical AI laboratories, and mentoring (McKinsey, 2021). Mental resilience and wellness are becoming best behaviors, not benefits. Blurred work-life lines stress and burnout in the digital-first workplace. Virtual therapy, mindfulness apps, and flexible work design boost productivity, loyalty, and innovation (Kniffin et al., 2021). SAP's AI-powered emotional wellbeing tracking helped managers aid workers. Ethical AI, digital product management, data science, HR teams, behavioral design. HR professionals need digital economy cross-disciplinary capabilities. Analytics, AI ethics, and agile project management skills increase HR's strategic credibility (CIPD, 2022). Finally, HR digital strategy ethics and governance are needed for trust and compliance. GDPR and data protection compliance, responsible AI usage policies, and transparent employee data use communication channels are provided (Floridi et al., 2018). Digital trust leaders support ethical technology use. Best HR practices encourage human-centered, agile, ethical, and inclusive departments. Using these tactics consistently helps e-economy enterprises succeed, retain competitive staff, and change society.

Addressing Ethical Challenges

Strategic HR transformation in the e-economy needs ethical behavior to maintain employee trust, dignity, and sustainability. From AI-based recruitment and performance monitoring to algorithmic decision-making and biometric tracking, HR digitization raises ethical challenges. These issues could hinder change and affect the company's brand, legal position, and personnel (Floridi et al., 2018; Mittelstadt, 2016). Fairness and algorithmic bias are ethical issues. Many companies use AI to screen candidates, estimate turnover, and set salaries. These fast and scalable technologies may prolong social inequality. Previous recruitment data may increase gender or racial bias in AI systems (O'Neil, 2016). Regular algorithm audits, diversified stakeholder AI governance, and fairness-aware machine learning models alter HR ethically (Raji & Buolamwini, 2019). Employees should be notified and given remedies if AI makes unfair choices. Ethical issues include employee privacy and spying. Remote and hybrid work is increasing, thus firms are evaluating productivity, keystrokes, email tone, and employment duration. Performance- and responsibility-based surveillance can violate privacy and psychological safety (Ball, 2021). Ethical HR transformation needs efficiency and autonomy. Informed consent, data collection boundaries, anonymization, and employee opt-out of invasive monitoring are best practices (Zuboff, 2019). Privacy-by-design should govern digital HR technology selection and development. Data openness and informed consent are ethical. Many employees don't understand survey, sensor, or wearable data use, sharing, or storage. Human resources ethics require data utilization transparency, especially for sensitive mental health, physiological, and behavioral metrics. Personal data processing and the right to access, alter, or delete information must be explained in plain language to employees (EU, 2016; India's DPDP Act, 2023). HR automation may dehumanize decision-making. AI makes hiring, promotion, and termination decisions without human oversight, quantifying complex human experiences. The probability of critical thinking errors and reduced empathy and contextual judgment rise (Binns et al., 2018). Companies could lessen this with a "human-in-the-loop" approach where algorithms supplement human judgment. This makes life-changing decisions contextual and accountable. Digital inequality and marginalization raise ethical issues. For HR services, not all employees have digital tools, high-speed internet, or digital literacy. These restrictions may alienate emerging-region elderly and low-income workers (UNESCO, 2022). Alternative access, digital literacy, and inclusive design are needed for ethical HR transformation. Hyper-connected digital workplaces impair mental and emotional health. Therapy trigger technology, performance management, and emotion monitoring require sensitivity and agreement. Monitoring or influencing workers may induce anxiety or distrust (Kniffin et al., 2021). Ethics requires HR professionals to emphasize mental health, accept digital well-being norms, and use technology to improve employee wellness. Finally, HR professionals' ethical inadequacy hinders responsible change. Leaders often lack AI, data science, and digital labor ethics knowledge. Thus, ethical capacity-building training, certifications, advisory boards are crucial. For proper HR technology use, organizations need ethics committees or digital ethics officers. Finally, strategic HR change requires ethics. Policy, thought, and stakeholder participation are needed. Integrate justice, accountability, transparency, and human dignity into every phase of digital HR transformation to protect human values. Ethical transformation fosters trust, legitimacy, and a just, inclusive, sustainable digital future.

Enhancing Accessibility

HR must change to increase digital diversity, equity, and involvement. Companies adapting to the e-economy must make all digital tools, platforms, and communication systems accessible to all employees, regardless of physical ability, neurodiversity, socioeconomic status, geography, or technological proficiency. HR recruitment, onboarding, development, engagement, and retention require accessibility (Burgstahler, 2015). Digital exclusion limits major company access. Remote workers may struggle with virtual training, meetings, and performance reviews without internet or equipment (UNESCO, 2022). Screen reader-incompatible, text-to-speech, or poorly designed platforms might challenge impaired workers. Design HR tech internationally. HR software should be offline, mobile, WCAG-compliant, and voice/text-enabled (W3C, 2018). To improve accessibility, digital HR technology design and deployment must incorporate inclusive user testing. Piloted by diverse staff, accessible solutions are practical, successful, and relevant. MS and SAP HR IT have accessibility engineers and inclusive designers (Microsoft, 2021). These companies provide neuro diverse and multilingual staff with AI-powered virtual meeting captioning, language translation, and real-time mood tracking. Also important is language accessibility. Bilingual and multicultural workers need HR support. Performance systems, learning platforms, and multilingual employee portals. Our global workforce receives HR messages in multiple languages and dialects (Google Diversity Report, 2022). Beyond technology, cognitive and emotional accessibility matter. On digital platforms, ADHD, autism, and dyslexia employees may need different interaction patterns, more visual signals, or less cognitive burden. Better graphics, navigation, and task customization make environments cognitively accessible (Austin & Pisano, 2017). IBM's cognitive-friendly HR and neurodiversity hiring foster neurodiversity. Accessibility tips include HR and manager training. Lack of empathy, not technology, limits access. To establish policies and engage staff, HR managers must understand digital accessibility, disability inclusion, and culturally sensitive communication. Accessible and inclusion training boosts disability employee satisfaction and retention, per SHRM (2023). Flexible work schedules and environments increase accessibility. Remote work, flexible hours, asynchronous collaboration tools, and decreased travel allow employees with health, caregiving, or transportation issues to work. Ergonomics, virtual collaborative training, and wellness stipends improve workplace accessibility (Deloitte, 2023). For accessibility monitoring and enhancement, firms need feedback channels. Anonymous questionnaires, employee feedback loops, and digital accessibility testing prioritize adjustments. Businesses that are inclusive promote accessibility. HR system analytics can close real-time utilization gaps (Gartner, 2021). Develop HR strategy, evaluation, and reporting. ESG and diversity reporting should include disability adoption, assistive tool use, and inclusive platform use. Assessments improve digital equity and accountability (Eccles & Klimenko, 2019). Civic society, disability groups, and IT companies promote HR accessibility. NGO-government collaboration aids accessibility certifications, inclusive design, and scaled assistive technologies (OECD, 2021). Ability

Net and Enable India give regional enterprises access. Strategy Transforming HR must improve e-economy equity through accessibility. Worker empowerment, social justice, and inclusivity are its goals. HR solutions help firms maximize employee potential, innovate via diversity, and be ethical and forward-thinking.

FUTURE RESEARCH DIRECTIONS

Firms and HR experts must conduct extensive academic and practical research to navigate the complex e-economy. AI, data analytics, remote work platforms, and digital ecosystems are altering HRM, requiring stronger theoretical models, empirical validations, and cross-disciplinary insights. Future research should prioritize ethics, diversity, human progress, and efficiency (Bondarouk & Brewster, 2016). AI's long-term impact on employee engagement and behavior is crucial. AI has improved recruitment, performance prediction, and workforce planning, but its psychological, emotional, and social effects are unknown. Future study should examine how long algorithmic system interactions affect leadership trust, job happiness, motivation, and perceived justice, especially among underrepresented staff (Tambe, Cappelli, & Yakubovich, 2019). Study AI in organizational human interactions. Brain diversity and HR digital convergence matter. HR system optimization is uncertain, yet businesses recognize neurodiversity's benefits. Explore adaptable interfaces, cognitive load-reducing technologies, and AI-driven hiring and training (Austin & Pisano, 2017). Learning how neuro diverse people utilize technology would improve workplace equity and performance. HR digital transformation and cross-cultural dynamics research is promising. Due to legislation, cultural traditions, and economic constraints, emerging countries digitize HR faster than Western study. Asian, African, and Latin American research suggest digital HR must change (Farndale et al., 2017). Research could examine how regional internet access, digital skills, and legal protections affect HR digitization. HR ethical AI governance research needed. Responsible HR AI frameworks are lacking. Fairness, accountability, and transparency in HR tech implementation can be achieved through research. HRM, law, philosophy, and computer science are needed to balance algorithmic efficiency and human oversight in sensitive processes including layoffs, promotions, and health monitoring (Binns et al., 2018; Floridi, 2018). HR digital transformation and organizational resilience are priorities. Companies must prepare HR systems for pandemics, natural disasters, and recessions. Cloud-based HRIS, AI-enabled scenario planning, and virtual leadership development may affect shock resilience (Ulrich & Dulebohn, 2015; Deloitte, 2021). Compare digital tools, employee empowerment, and agility. Gig, freelance, and hybrid workers are understudied. Platform-based labor requires HR tools to manage, assist, and include non-traditional workers. Examine contingent labor HR tech's effects on rights, benefits, learning, and performance (Kässi & Lehdonvirta, 2018). On-demand remote labor risks business culture and loyalty. Study tech-stress and digital health. Brain fatigue, burnout, and distraction result from digitization. Future research should evaluate how HR systems can identify and prevent digital overload, tailor workloads, and encourage healthy work cycles. Study the long-term mental health effects of 24/7 connectivity and algorithmic nudges (Kniffin et al., 2021). Green HRM and digital sustainability are promising research topics. For net-zero and ESG compliance, virtual hiring, e-learning, paperless administration, and remote working promote sustainability. Digital HR may reduce carbon emissions and boost workplace sustainability (Renwick et al., 2016). Curriculum will emphasize HR professional digital knowledge and capacity. Analytics, AI ethics, behavioral science, and system design may be excluded from advanced HR training. CIPD (2022) will explore HR professional transdisciplinary training—micro-credentials, simulations, peer networks. In digital transformation, assess employee agency. Top-down digital HR systems engage employees passively. Employee-made digital rules and tools reduce opposition and boost ownership (Grote & Guest, 2017). Staff affect technology, algorithmic decision-making, and data governance. E-economic plan HR transformation requires ethics, diversity, resilience, equity, and creativity. Future research will help practitioners build compassionate, inclusive, and sustainable HR systems that improve technology and society.

Emerging Trends

E-economy HR management is changing rapidly due to labor, workplace, and workforce developments. Hyper-personalization from analytics, machine learning, and AI is changing employee experience. Personalising learning routes, performance feedback, and wellness programmes can boost engagement and retention (Deloitte, 2021). HR becomes increasingly tailored to employee goals and situations. HR relies on AI-powered hiring and management. AI-automated HR operations include resume screening, video interview analysis, attrition prediction, and chatbot-driven candidate interaction. However, algorithmic recruiting and promotion ethics remain problematic (Upadhyay & Khandelwal, 2018). A skills-based workforce architecture transition is occurring. As jobs become more flexible and projects cross-functional, companies are rethinking HR strategies around dynamic skills rather than job titles. Gloat and Eightfold AI skills taxonomies deploy talent and tailor development to make workforces more adaptable and inclusive (World Economic Forum, 2023). Evidence-based decision-making requires HR analytics. Real-time data lets HR executives predict attrition, monitor diversity, and optimize team performance using predictive modeling and prescriptive analytics (Minbaeva, 2018). These insights inform more objective and purposeful HR initiatives that support organizational goals.

Transformational trends include digital well-being and mental health integration. Remote workers experience digital tiredness, loneliness, and burnout when work and life merge. Companies are adding mental health apps, AI-based mood monitoring, and resilience training to HR ecosystems (Kniffin et al., 2021). Workplace productivity increasingly includes well-being. The workplace has transformed with hybrid and borderless workers. HR must create inclusive and fair asynchronous communication, virtual team-building, and culturally sensitive management for global and time-zoned personnel (Morgeson et al., 2021). Digital-first HR emphasizes trust, openness, and flexibility. Another HR trend is ESG goals. HR defends sustainability, diversity, and ethics as stakeholders' demand accountability. DEI tracking, remote carbon-reduction cooperation, and green employment are becoming industry practices (Eccles & Klimenko, 2019). HR uses blockchain for decentralized credential authentication, performance records, and payroll. Blockchain, though new, will boost trust and transparency in global and gig economies (Lacity, 2018). Ethical and inclusive HR tech is growing. Fairness and user-centered design are growing in HR tech as digital platforms alter employment. Binns et al. (2018) and Raji (2020) use bias identification, algorithmic audits, and participatory development to achieve employee equality. Reskilling and lifelong learning are strategic. As skill half-lives diminish, corporations use micro-learning, AI-curated learning routes, and gamified training. Coursera, LinkedIn Learning, and Degreed are used in HR systems to train personnel (Bersin, 2021). Interconnected changes have transformed HR from operational efficiency to strategic foresight and ethical leadership. HR leaders who build flexible, inclusive, and resilient firms employing these trends will succeed in the e-economy. Society and technology are converging, challenging HR norms and enabling research, policy innovation, and human-centric organizational design.

CONCLUSION

Human resource management must link technical innovation and values owing to the e-economy. Formerly administrative, HR now emphasizes agility, digital resilience, and social responsibility. HR professionals must reconcile ethics, diversity, and sustainability with AI, automation, and analytics. AI, machine learning, block chain, and HR data change hiring, engagement, and retention. These technologies provide hyper-personalized employee experiences, evidence-based decision-making, and real-time workforce analytics. HR must rethink its strategic role in a digital economy that emphasizes speed, innovation, and stakeholder alignment (Ulrich et al., 2017; Minbaeva, 2018). Transactional management must be replaced with proactive, trend-predicting, fast-adapting leadership for strategic HR transformation. HR must now support diversity, sustainability, ESG, environmental and ethical outcomes, and inclusive workplaces (Eccles & Klimenko, 2019). HR strategies are being assessed for social impact and efficiency. To improve fairness, openness, and accountability in hiring and performance management, use technology ethically (Binns et al., 2018; Raji, 2020). Tech-enabled leadership integrity boosts HR's strategic credibility. The chapter also illustrated how digital workplaces require new HR and employee capabilities. Skills over jobs, remote and hybrid work, and gig economy necessitate adaptive, lifelong learning ecosystems. To make work a learning environment, HR must promote curiosity, adaptability, and digital literacy (Bersin, 2021). Update learning systems, work procedures, awards, and performance indicators for career mobility and workforce flexibility. Digital humanization matters. Companies must avoid depersonalization, bias, and exclusion as AI and automation take over HR. Technology should improve human skills, not replace empathy. AI-based mental health help, inclusive performance dashboards, and block chain-powered decentralized HR systems show how ethical and inclusive technology may improve well-being, trust, and fairness. Technological affordances, human values, institutional norms, and contextual awareness are needed for sociotechnical digital HR transformation (Orlikowski, 1992; Lepak et al., 2006. E-economy strategic HR reforms require a robust conceptual framework, the chapter noted. Transformation matrix principles include ethical AI, digital fluency, employee empowerment, and strategic agility. They demonstrate current HR management, skill, culture, and technology. HR directors use visuals and theoretical models to traverse this complexity and match procedures with company and social goals. Integrative and transdisciplinary HR reform is studied in this chapter. Future research should merge information systems, behavioral science, and ethics to establish digital HR frameworks. Research on algorithmic justice, virtual culture, digital well-being, and gig worker inclusion shows HR professionals' expanding challenges and promise. To be responsive, accountable, and resilient, organizations must fill knowledge gaps. Finally, effective human resource transformation in the e-economy requires synchronization between people, technology, purpose, performance, company success, and social advancement. Digitizing processes and humanizing the digital enterprise can help HR professionals lead this shift. Technology-society nexus is best negotiated by HR policies that respect people above platforms. This may help enterprises maintain digital economy competitiveness and establish an ethical, inclusive, and sustainable future.

REFERENCES

Alvesson, M., & Willmott, H. (1992). On the idea of emancipation in management and organization studies. *Academy of Management Review, 17*(3), 432–464. DOI: 10.2307/258718

Austin, R. D., & Pisano, G. P. (2017). Neurodiversity as a competitive advantage. *Harvard Business Review, 95*(3), 96–103.

Ball, K. (2021). *Workplace surveillance: An overview.* International Labour Organization.

Barney, J. (1991). Firm resources and sustained competitive advantage. *Journal of Management, 17*(1), 99–120. DOI: 10.1177/014920639101700108

Becker, B. E., & Huselid, M. A. (2006). Strategic human resources management: Where do we go from here? *Journal of Management, 32*(6), 898–925. DOI: 10.1177/0149206306293668

Becker, G. S. (1964). *Human capital.* National Bureau of Economic Research.

Bersin, J. (2021). *HR technology market 2021: Disruption ahead.* Josh Bersin Company.

Binns, R., Veale, M., Van Kleek, M., & Shadbolt, N. (2018). 'It's reducing a human being to a percentage': Perceptions of justice in algorithmic decisions. *CHI Conference on Human Factors in Computing Systems*, 1–14. DOI: 10.1145/3173574.3173951

Bondarouk, T., & Brewster, C. (2016). Conceptualising the future of HRM and technology research. *International Journal of Human Resource Management, 27*(21), 2652–2671. DOI: 10.1080/09585192.2016.1232296

Boudreau, J., & Cascio, W. (2017). Human capital analytics: Why are we not there? *Journal of Organizational Effectiveness: People and Performance, 4*(2), 119–126. DOI: 10.1108/JOEPP-03-2017-0021

Brynjolfsson, E., & McAfee, A. (2014). *The second machine age: Work, progress, and prosperity in a time of brilliant technologies.* W. W. Norton & Company.

Bughin, J., Catlin, T., Hirt, M., & Willmott, P. (2018). Why digital strategies fail. *The McKinsey Quarterly, 1*(1), 14–25.

Burgstahler, S. (2015). Opening doors or slamming them shut? Online learning practices and students with disabilities. *Social Inclusion (Lisboa), 3*(6), 69–79. DOI: 10.17645/si.v3i6.420

Carnevale, J. B., & Hatak, I. (2020). Employee adjustment and well-being in the era of COVID-19: Implications for human resource management. *Journal of Business Research, 116*, 183–187. DOI: 10.1016/j.jbusres.2020.05.037 PMID: 32501303

Cascio, W. F., & Montealegre, R. (2016). How technology is changing work and organizations. *Annual Review of Organizational Psychology and Organizational Behavior, 3*(1), 349–375. DOI: 10.1146/annurev-orgpsych-041015-062352

Chartered Institute of Personnel and Development (CIPD). (2022). Environmental, social and governance (ESG): An introduction. CIPD. https://www.cipd.org/

Creswell, J. W. (2014). *Research design: Qualitative, quantitative, and mixed methods approaches* (4th ed.). Sage Publications.

Davenport, T. H., Harris, J., & Shapiro, J. (2010). Competing on talent analytics. *Harvard Business Review, 88*(10), 52–58. PMID: 20929194

Davenport, T. H., Harris, J. G., & Morison, R. (2010). *Analytics at work: Smarter decisions, better results*. Harvard Business Press.

Davis, F. D. (1989). Technology acceptance model: TAM. *Information Seeking Behavior and Technology Adoption, 205*(219), 5.

De Stefano, V. (2016). Introduction: Crowdsourcing, the gig-economy and the law. *Comparative Labor Law & Policy Journal, 37*(3).

Deloitte. (2021). 2021 Global Human Capital Trends: The social enterprise in a world disrupted. https://www2.deloitte.com

Deloitte. (2023). *Global human capital trends 2023*. Deloitte Insights.

DiMaggio, P. J., & Powell, W. W. (1983). The iron cage revisited: Institutional isomorphism and collective rationality in organizational fields. *American Sociological Review, 48*(2), 147–160. DOI: 10.2307/2095101

Eccles, R. G., & Klimenko, S. (2019). The investor revolution. *Harvard Business Review, 97*(3), 106–116.

Eubanks, V. (2018). Automating inequality: How high-tech tools profile, police, and punish the poor. Macmillan+ ORM.

Farndale, E., Brewster, C., Ligthart, P., & Poutsma, E. (2017). The effects of market economy type and foreign MNE subsidiaries on the convergence and divergence of HRM. *Journal of International Business Studies, 48*(9), 1065–1086. DOI: 10.1057/s41267-017-0094-8

Ferrari, A., & Punie, Y. (2013). DIGCOMP: A framework for developing and understanding digital competence in Europe.

Floridi, L., Cowls, J., Beltrametti, M., Chatila, R., Chazerand, P., Dignum, V., Luetge, C., Madelin, R., Pagallo, U., Rossi, F., Schafer, B., Valcke, P., & Vayena, E. (2018). AI4People—An ethical framework for a good AI society: Opportunities, risks, principles, and recommendations. *Minds and Machines*, *28*(4), 689–707. DOI: 10.1007/s11023-018-9482-5 PMID: 30930541

Freeman, R. E. (1984). *Strategic management: A stakeholder approach.* Pitman.

Gallup. (2021). How millennials want to work and live. Gallup, Inc. https://www.gallup.com/

Grant, A. (2013). In the company of givers and takers. *Harvard Business Review*, *91*(4), 90–97. PMID: 23593770

Gratton, L. (2021). Four principles to ensure hybrid work is productive work. *MIT Sloan Management Review*, *62*(2), 11A–16A.

Guest, D. E. (2017). Human resource management and employee well-being: Towards a new analytic framework. *Human Resource Management Journal*, *27*(1), 22–38. DOI: 10.1111/1748-8583.12139

International Labour Organization. (2021). *World employment and social outlook: Trends 2021*. ILO.

Jesuthasan, R., & Boudreau, J. (2018). *Reinventing jobs: A 4-step approach for applying automation to work.* Harvard Business Press.

Kaplan, M., & Donovan, M. (2021). *The inclusion dividend: Why investing in diversity and inclusion pays off* (2nd ed.). DG Press.

Kässi, O., & Lehdonvirta, V. (2018). Online labour index: Measuring the online gig economy for policy and research. *Technological Forecasting and Social Change*, *137*, 241–248. DOI: 10.1016/j.techfore.2018.07.056

Kiron, D., Kruschwitz, N., Reeves, M., & Goh, E. (2015). The benefits of sustainability-driven innovation. *MIT Sloan Management Review*, *56*(2), 69–73.

Kniffin, K. M., Narayanan, J., Anseel, F., Antonakis, J., Ashford, S. P., Bakker, A. B., Bamberger, P., Bapuji, H., Bhave, D. P., Choi, V. K., Creary, S. J., Demerouti, E., Flynn, F. J., Gelfand, M. J., Greer, L. L., Johns, G., Kesebir, S., Klein, P. G., Lee, S. Y., & Vugt, M. (2021). COVID-19 and the workplace: Implications, issues, and insights for future research and action. *The American Psychologist*, *76*(1), 63–77. DOI: 10.1037/amp0000716 PMID: 32772537

Lacity, M. C. (2018). Addressing key challenges to making enterprise block chain applications a reality. *MIS Quarterly Executive*, *17*(3), 201–222.

Lepak, D. P., Smith, K. G., & Taylor, M. S. (2006). Value creation and value capture in strategic human resource management. *Academy of Management Review*, *29*(1), 180–194. DOI: 10.5465/amr.2007.23464011

Lewin, K. (1947). Group decision and social change. *Readings in Social Psychology*, *3*(1), 197–211.

Marler, J. H., & Boudreau, J. W. (2017). An evidence-based review of HR Analytics. *International Journal of Human Resource Management*, *28*(1), 3–26. DOI: 10.1080/09585192.2016.1244699

Marler, J. H., & Parry, E. (2016). Human resource management, strategic involvement and e-HRM technology. *International Journal of Human Resource Management*, *27*(19), 2233–2253. DOI: 10.1080/09585192.2015.1091980

Meijerink, J., Boons, M., Keegan, A., & Marler, J. (2021). Algorithmic human resource management: Synthesizing developments and cross-disciplinary insights on digital HRM. *International Journal of Human Resource Management*, *32*(12), 2545–2562. DOI: 10.1080/09585192.2021.1925326

Minbaeva, D. (2018). Building credible human capital analytics for organizational competitive advantage. *Human Resource Management*, *57*(3), 701–713. DOI: 10.1002/hrm.21848

Mittelstadt, B. (2016). Automation, algorithms, and politicsl auditing for transparency in content personalization systems. *International Journal of Communication*, *10*, 12.

Morgeson, F. P., Brannick, M. T., & Levine, E. L. (2021). *Job and work analysis: Methods, research, and applications for human resource management*. SAGE Publications.

Orlikowski, W. J. (1992). The duality of technology: Rethinking the concept of technology in organizations. *Organization Science*, *3*(3), 398–427. DOI: 10.1287/orsc.3.3.398

Raji, I. D., & Buolamwini, J. (2019). Actionable auditing: Investigating the impact of publicly naming biased performance results of commercial ai products. Proceedings of the 2019 AAAI/ACM Conference on AI, Ethics, and Society, 429–435.

Raji, I. D., Smart, A., & White, R.. (2020). Closing the AI accountability gap: Defining an end-to-end framework for internal algorithmic auditing. *ACM Conference on Fairness, Accountability, and Transparency (FAccT)*. DOI: 10.1145/3351095.3372873

Renwick, D. W., Redman, T., & Maguire, S. (2016). Green human resource management: A review and research agenda. *International Journal of Management Reviews, 18*(1), 1–14. DOI: 10.1111/j.1468-2370.2011.00328.x

SHRM. (2021). *The state of the workplace: 2021 report.* Society for Human Resource Management.

Snell, S. A., Morris, S. S., & Bohlander, G. (2015). *Managing human resources.* Cengage Learning.

Susskind, R., & Susskind, D. (2015). *The future of the professions: How technology will transform the work of human experts.* Oxford University Press. DOI: 10.1093/oso/9780198713395.001.0001

Tambe, P., Cappelli, P., & Yakubovich, V. (2019). Artificial intelligence in human resources management: Challenges and a path forward. *California Management Review, 61*(4), 15–42. DOI: 10.1177/0008125619867910

Trist, E. L., & Bamforth, K. W. (1951). Some social and psychological consequences of the longwall method of coal-getting. *Human Relations, 4*(1), 3–38. DOI: 10.1177/001872675100400101

Tursunbayeva, A., Di Lauro, S., & Pagliari, C. (2018). People analytics—A scoping review of conceptual boundaries and value propositions. *International Journal of Information Management, 43*, 224–247. DOI: 10.1016/j.ijinfomgt.2018.08.002

Ulrich, D. (1997). Measuring human resources: An overview of practice and a prescription for results. *Human Resource Management, 36*(3), 303–320. DOI: 10.1002/(SICI)1099-050X(199723)36:3<303::AID-HRM3>3.0.CO;2-#

Ulrich, D. (2016). HR at a crossroads. *Asia Pacific Journal of Human Resources, 54*(2), 148–164. DOI: 10.1111/1744-7941.12104

Ulrich, D., Brockbank, W., Johnson, D., Sandholtz, K., & Younger, J. (2017). *HR competencies: Mastery at the intersection of people and business.* Society for Human Resource Management.

Ulrich, D., & Dulebohn, J. H. (2015). Are we there yet? What's next for HR? *Human Resource Management Review, 25*(2), 188–204. DOI: 10.1016/j.hrmr.2015.01.004

Upadhyay, A. K., & Khandelwal, K. (2018). Applying artificial intelligence: Implications for recruitment. *Strategic HR Review, 17*(5), 255–258. DOI: 10.1108/SHR-07-2018-0051

Westerman, G., Bonnet, D., & McAfee, A. (2014). *Leading digital: Turning technology into business transformation.* Harvard Business Press.

World Economic Forum. (2023). Future of Jobs Report 2023. https://www.weforum.org/reports

Wright, P. M., Dunford, B. B., & Snell, S. A. (2001). Human resources and the resource based view of the firm. *Journal of Management*, *27*(6), 701–721. DOI: 10.1177/014920630102700607

Wright, P. M., & McMahan, G. C. (2011). Exploring human capital: Putting 'human' back into strategic human resource management. *Human Resource Management Journal*, *21*(2), 93–104. DOI: 10.1111/j.1748-8583.2010.00165.x

Zlate, S. (2014). Leadership and organizational culture in the context of innovation. *Procedia: Social and Behavioral Sciences*, *124*, 345–354.

Zuboff, S. (2019). *The age of surveillance capitalism: The fight for a human future at the new frontier of power*. PublicAffairs.

KEY TERMS AND DEFINITIONS

Agile HR: A flexible, iterative methodology in human resources that prioritizes responsiveness, collaboration, and continual enhancement to accommodate evolving business requirements.

Artificial Intelligence (AI): The emulation of human cognitive functions in robots designed to think, learn, and adapt independently.

Block chain in HR: A decentralized digital ledger utilized in human resources for the safe and transparent verification of employee credentials, contracts, and payroll.

Digital Literacy: The capacity to utilize digital tools, platforms, and data responsibly and efficiently, particularly in professional and educational contexts.

Digital Transformation: The thorough integration of digital technologies by a business to optimize processes, elevate customer value, and stimulate creativity.

Digital Well-being: The condition of an individual's mental, physical, and emotional health in relation to their engagement with digital technologies and professional settings.

E-Economy: A digitally facilitated economy defined by the utilization of internet technology, data-informed decision-making, and platform-centric business models across several sectors.

Employee Empowerment: A managerial strategy that grants employees autonomy, accountability, and authority in decision-making pertaining to their responsibilities.

Employee Experience (EX): The cumulative encounters and perspectives employees encounter during their tenure inside a firm, including culture, tools, processes, and leadership.

Ethical AI: The creation and application of artificial intelligence systems that are transparent, equitable, and consistent with human rights and ethical standards.

Gig Economy: A labor market defined by the dominance of short-term contracts, freelancing, and independent work enabled by digital networks.

Green HRM: Human resource practices that foster environmental sustainability and enhance employee involvement in attaining eco-friendly objectives.

HR Analytics: The utilization of statistical and data analysis methodologies on HR data to enhance decision-making about talent, performance, and organizational processes.

Human-Centric Approach: A design and management philosophy that emphasizes employee well-being, values, experiences, and empowerment within technology-driven systems and organizational frameworks.

Inclusive Workplace: A setting in where various persons are esteemed, respected, and empowered to contribute to their maximum potential without discrimination.

Organizational Resilience: The capacity of an organization to foresee, prepare for, react to, and adjust to gradual changes and abrupt disruptions in order to endure and thrive.

Remote and Hybrid Work Models: Flexible employment structures wherein individuals operate exclusively from remote locations or oscillate between home and office environments, frequently facilitated by digital technologies.

Socio-Technical Processes Theory: A theoretical framework highlighting the interaction between social processes and technology within employment environments.

Strategic Human Resource Management (SHRM): The anticipatory administration of personnel matched with enduring corporate objectives, merging HR strategies with business strategies to enhance performance and adaptability.

Workforce Agility: The capacity of individuals and the company to swiftly adjust to evolving situations, technologies, and business requirements.

Chapter 17
Sustainable Human Resource Management and Development Through Innovative Approaches and Practices

Valentin Vasilev
http://orcid.org/0000-0002-0074-9578
Higher School of Security and Economics, Bulgaria

Ivan Petre Efremovski
International Slavic University - Sveti Nikole, North Macedonia

Zaza Gigauri
http://orcid.org/0009-0008-6488-7639
Caucasus International University, Georgia

ABSTRACT

In the last decade, the role of human resource management (HRM) in organizational effectiveness has significantly evolved and reached a new level, becoming a key driver of development and sustainability in all its dimensions. This chapter presents key ideas and scenarios that illustrate innovative approaches and models defining the new role of HRM. The focus is placed on innovative practices aimed at sustainable human resource development, including well-being policies and well-being indicators as components of a strategic organizational approach. An additional emphasis is placed on the concept of sustainable HRM through the presentation of relevant practical examples.

DOI: 10.4018/979-8-3373-4307-5.ch017

1. INTRODUCTION

"To be human is not about perfection. It is the effort to be good, even when the world is not."
"A Man Called Ove" – Fredrik Backman

We are living in interesting times. The dynamics of the labor market and rapid technological changes are creating new challenges for human resource management, with a growing focus on a different category – "talent". One of the main challenges is the shortage of qualified personnel in certain sectors. Many organizations struggle to find employees with the necessary skills, forcing them to invest more heavily in training and reskilling.

On the other hand, hybrid and remote work models are also setting new requirements (Gigauri, 2021). Talent management now extends far beyond physical presence in the office. It requires the use of digital tools for engaging, assessing, and developing employees, regardless of their location, thus shifting the entire paradigm of working with people.

Generational differences are another important factor. Younger employees (e.g., Generation Z) have different expectations from the workplace; they value flexibility, meaningful work, and opportunities for self-expression (Taibah & Ho, 2023). Organizations must adapt in order to attract, retain, and motivate this generation.

Additionally, mental health and well-being are gaining significance. Organizations that create an environment that supports personal growth and work–life balance tend to be more successful in the long term.

This brief palette of challenges forms a foundation upon which effective human resource management policies can be built, gradually shaping HR into a sustainable and talent-centered function within organizations.

This chapter discusses challenges in HR managements while searching sustainable solutions. It reviews previous studies in talent management and sustainable human resource management (HRM). The chapter explores tools, models, and indicators of sustainable HRM and provides examples from various organizations. Finally, it suggests innovative solutions, approaches, and practices in human capital management and development.

2. CHALLENGES IN HUMAN RESOURCE MANAGEMENT – IN SEARCH OF SUSTAINABLE SOLUTIONS

Human resource management and development is becoming an increasingly complex process with distinct practical importance and undoubtedly deserves in-depth study. It has long been examined in two aspects: as a process and as a characteristic.

According to Marc Brackett: *"Our emotional life is a rollercoaster, soaring high one moment and plummeting the next... our emotional state is one of the most important aspects of our lives. It drives everything else and its influence is all-encompassing."*

With advancements in psychology and management sciences, the study of the human factor has evolved to examine HRM both as a process and as a characteristic. This has led to the emergence of three directions:

(1) As a characteristic. HRM is a set of specific qualities that can be successfully applied when well understood;
(2) As a process. HRM is a direct, non-coercive influence and coordination of group actions toward achieving a common goal;
(3) As both a process and a characteristic. HRM is a direct, non-coercive influence by individuals possessing the relevant traits to achieve specific goals, with growing attention to sustainability practices.

These theoretical frameworks provide a foundational basis for understanding HRM development, which will be elaborated further below.

Furthermore, sustainable human resource management (SHRM) strives to demonstrate how organizations integrate sustainability into their policies and practices. Examples of SHRM are becoming increasingly common and applied.

SAP, for instance, has introduced sustainability-oriented training programs, including modules on environmental protection, circular economy, and energy efficiency. Benefits include: stronger employee engagement in sustainability, development of environmentally responsible corporate culture, enhanced external brand image. Moreover, Google applies "green hiring criteria," prioritizing candidates with experience in sustainable or socially responsible projects (Yıldırım & Vasilev, 2024). The long-term benefits are: build a sustainable HR profile, from the recruitment stage, reduce the "ecological footprint" of human capital, support ESG strategies (Environmental, Social, Governance). In addition, IKEA promotes mental health and sustainable productivity through flexible and hybrid work models, allowing reduced stress and better well-being, lower office costs, improved employee retention and motivation.

However, employees often lack understanding of what data workplace systems collect and how decisions are made, leading to a "black box" scenario only accessible to system developers (Karaboğa, 2023). The concept of well-being policies is becoming integral in management discourse. These are defined as: "A set of targeted actions, programs, and measures developed and implemented by institutions, organizations, or governments to improve overall quality of life and satisfaction—both personally and professionally."

Cross-sector collaboration (business, public, non-profit, and government) can generate long-term value and innovation. Digital technologies allow entrepreneurs to involve the public in their sustainability missions. Awareness-building strengthens the ecosystem for sustainable entrepreneurship (Gigauri et al., 2025).

Well-being policies focus on physical, mental, and social health, covering areas such as healthcare and prevention, education and workplace conditions, social protection and housing, cultural access and work–life balance.

Humanity's relationship with the environment has transformed due to industrialization, technological advancement, and global interconnectedness (Sharma & Biloria, 2024).

As a result, well-being indicators such as subjective happiness, security, emotional stability, social connectedness, are becoming core components of modern HR strategies (Serafimova et al., 2025). Examples of such policies in organizations include flexible schedules, mental health support, physical activity programs, development opportunities, inclusive and value-driven work culture (Nayak et al., 2024).

The table below outlines key areas and example opportunities for well-being and sustainable HR development programs and policies.

Table 1. Key areas and examples of sustainable HR development programs

Key Area	Example Programs and Policies
Mental Health and Emotional Well-being	Psychological support programs, free counseling services, campaigns to reduce mental health stigma.
Public Space and Urban Environment	Creation of parks, pedestrian zones, accessible and clean urban areas – encouraging active living and social connectedness.
Social Inclusion and Connectedness	Community support centers, intergenerational programs, initiatives to include marginalized groups.
Access to Healthy Food and Active Living	Urban gardens, school kitchens, promotion of sports and physical activity through municipal programs.
Transport and Mobility	Accessible, safe, and convenient public transportation enabling participation in social and economic life.

continued on following page

Table 1. Continued

Key Area	Example Programs and Policies
Education and Personal Development	Educational and cultural programs for all ages, developing skills, and fostering a sense of purpose and progress.
Civic Voice and Participation in Decision-making	Public consultations, participatory budgeting, feedback platforms – enhancing sense of belonging and control.

Source: Authors' own work

In relation to the presented conceptual vision regarding the use of such policies for targeted impact on Human Resource Management (HRM), it is important to also draw attention to the most common Well-being Indicators, which are increasingly the subject of research interest and are being applied in both the public and business sectors. These indicators are presented in Table 2.

Table 2. Well-being indicators and measures

Indicator	What it Measures
Subjective well-being	Levels of happiness, life satisfaction, emotional states (positive/negative experiences).
Mental and physical health	Self-rated health, access to healthcare services, life expectancy.
Education and skills	Level of education, access to training, literacy, participation in lifelong learning.
Housing and environment	Housing security, access to clean air/water, green spaces, pollution levels.
Social connection and community	Sense of belonging, social support, trust in people and institutions.
Work and life balance	Employment, job satisfaction, time for personal life and recreation.
Material well-being	Income, financial security, ability to meet basic needs.
Civil rights and participation	Participation in elections, sense of democratic legitimacy and influence in public decision-making.
Personal safety and security	Crime rates, sense of safety at home and in the community.
Sustainability and future	Environmental care, sustainable practices, intergenerational balance, long-term outlook.

Source: Authors' own work

The importance of utilizing, analyzing, and applying information based on these and other indicators is fundamental for strategic decision-making and the formulation of policies in the field of Human Resource Management (HRM). It gradually transforms HRM into a highly focused activity aimed at sustainable solutions.

On the other hand, transformational leaders assist by helping them transcend their self-interests and self-centered values (Afsharbakeshlo et al., 2024). Therefore, it helps the HR to receive support from leaders which further builds vision for the future (Abdallah & Ismail, 2024).

Among the organizations that stand out through their work and results in the area of such indicators, we highlight several whose research that has provided us with clarity and direction regarding their practical applicability in HRM strategies. Table 3 presents some well-established organizations whose activities and analyses have been used as a foundation for the present work.

Table 3. Key Indexes related to sustainable HRM

Key Examples of Indicators	Measurement	Source
OECD Better Life Index	Uses 11 dimensions, including health, work–life balance, income, environment, and more. An interactive platform for comparing life well-being across OECD countries.	https://www.oecd.org/en/data/tools/oecd-better-life-index.html
UNDP Human Development Index (HDI)	Measures health, education, and income. The official page for the Human Development Index and related Data Center of the United Nations Development Programme.	https://hdr.undp.org/data-center/human-development-index
Gallup World Poll	Focuses on life experiences and emotional well-being. The most comprehensive global survey measuring public opinion and well-being around the world.	https://www.gallup.com/analytics/318875/global-research.aspx
Social Progress Index & Gross National Happiness Index (Bhutan)	Offer alternative approaches to measuring quality of life. Bhutan's Gross National Happiness Index is a constitutionally embedded model based on nine domains of well-being	https://www.socialprogress.org/social-progress-index ; https://worldpopulationreview.com/country-rankings/happiest-countries-in-the-world

Source: Authors' own work

The role of these studies and indicators is essential in sustainable human resource management for several key reasons. First, they measure quality of life beyond GDP. These indices go beyond traditional economic metrics (such as Gross Domestic Product) and incorporate social, cultural, psychological, and environmental dimensions to provide a more comprehensive view of human well-being. Second, they provide a global and comparable perspective. Using standardized methodologies, these indicators enable international comparisons between countries and regions, highlighting best practices, inequalities, and specific developmental needs (Kaur et al., 2022). Third, they guide policy and resource allocation. Data from these indices are often used by governments, international organizations, and NGOs to formulate public policies, prioritize reforms, assess the impact of interventions, and more (Fallah Shayan et al., 2022). Furthermore, they raise awareness and civic engagement. The publication and discussion of such indices motivate citizens, media, and academic communities to demand accountability, transparency, and better governance from institutions. Additionally, they stimulate innovation in social development. Indices such as the Gross National Happiness Index (GNH) and the Social Progress Index introduce alternative paradigms for measuring success and progress – centered around happiness, sustainability, social capital, and empathy, rather than just economic growth.

Thus, these indicators can serve as a valuable barometer for identifying key areas upon which HR policies can be built, leading to focused and sustainable solutions.

3. INNOVATIVE SOLUTIONS, KEY APPROACHES, AND PRACTICES IN HUMAN CAPITAL MANAGEMENT AND DEVELOPMENT

Innovative practices and solutions in the pursuit of sustainable development in human resources can be presented in various ways and from different managerial perspectives. For the purposes of this paper, we focus on several tools suitable for adaptation and implementation in real-world settings, accompanied by the key characteristics that make them particularly significant from a practical standpoint:

- **Talent attraction and retention programs**. These are critical due to the intense competition for qualified professionals, especially in sectors such as IT, healthcare, and engineering (Orlandi et al., 2024). Younger generations, in particular, seek meaningful work, flexibility, and a healthy work–life balance, which organizations must address to remain competitive and attractive.
- **Digitalization and automation**. The integration of advanced technologies necessitates reskilling and upskilling of employees. In this context, HR systems are becoming data-driven, often integrating AI and People Analytics to optimize processes and enhance decision-making (Blanco González Tejero et al., 2024).
- **Hybrid and remote work models**. Especially after the COVID-19 pandemic, organizations are increasingly adopting new forms of work (Gigauri, 2020). This requires fresh approaches to leadership, motivation, and performance tracking. It also brings new challenges related to employee engagement, trust-building, and team culture.

- **Mental health and emotional intelligence**. Rising levels of stress, burnout, and anxiety necessitate HR strategies focused on emotional well-being and the creation of a supportive work environment (Morris et al., 2025). Organizations must invest in policies and practices that promote psychological safety and resilience.
- **Diversity, inclusion, and ethics**. Diversity in gender, age, culture, and experience is increasingly seen as a core driver of innovation. However, it requires careful management of differences, alongside ethical policies and anti-discrimination practices, to foster inclusion and ensure fair treatment across the organization (Buengeler et al., 2018).

3.1. Talent Management as a Model for Sustainable Human Resource Management

Talent management is a system of activities aimed at identifying, developing, and retaining key employees within an organization. It is a strategic process that links human resources to the long-term goals of the organization. Importantly, talent is not limited to top-level management positions; it can be found at any level, as long as there is potential and motivation for development.

A good talent management strategy creates an environment where employees have the opportunity to grow and give their best. Trust, autonomy, and care for employees are at the heart of effective talent management. The process involves several stages from identifying potential talent, to developing individual development plans, and providing a motivational environment that supports growth. For this reason, leaders must aim to create more leaders –not just followers, which is one of the key objectives of talent management.

A well-developed talent management strategy brings numerous benefits. It improves team performance, reduces employee turnover, and increases employee engagement. In a world where innovation and rapid change are the norm, the need for adaptive and motivated people is greater than ever (Stefanova et al., 2025).

Organizational culture and employee motivation are directly influenced by the way talent is managed (Chatterjee et al., 2023). When employees see opportunities for growth and feel appreciated, they are more likely to stay with the company and give their best effort.

Therefore, main emphasis of talent management should be placed on identifying individuals with high potential, developing their skills through training and mentorship, providing opportunities for career advancement, and creating a work environment that retains and motivates them.

3.2. Talent Management Tools

Talent management does not happen "by instinct", rather it relies on specific tools and methods that help organizations identify, develop, and retain key employees. Using the right tools enables more objective decision-making and the building of a consistent people-management strategy. In this regard, talent management tools and programmes, highlighted below, include performance appraisal, assessment centers, individual development plans, talent management software, 360-degree feedback, motivational and engagement strategies.

Performance Appraisal. One of the most commonly used tools to track how well an employee performs their assigned tasks. It can include both quantitative and qualitative indicators. Regular performance evaluations help identify high-potential employees and areas for development (Alimansyah & Takahashi, 2023).

Assessment Centers. A structured form of evaluation that uses a combination of simulations, interviews, and competency tests. These are typically used to assess leadership potential, decision-making abilities, teamwork, and more. Commonly applied in managerial selection or for internal promotions (Donald et al., 2023).

Individual Development Plans (IDPs). These are personalized programs developed jointly between an employee and their manager (Lejeune et al., 2021). They include professional development goals, training needs, and growth opportunities. This tool not only motivates employees but also shows that the company is investing in their future.

Talent Management Software. Modern technology enables comprehensive human capital management through specialized platforms. These typically include modules for recruitment, evaluation, training, development, feedback, and more. Such systems provide centralized data and facilitate analysis and decision-making (Faqihi & Miah, 2023).

360-Degree Feedback. A method in which an employee receives feedback not only from their supervisor, but also from colleagues, subordinates, and even clients. This offers a more complete picture of their behavior and impact. It is especially useful for developing self-awareness and leadership skills (Souki et al., 2025).

Motivational and Engagement Programs. In addition to assessment and development, motivation plays a critical role. The model "Motivation 4.0" (Vasilev et al., 2024) is one of the new management tools that adds significant value to organizational processes. It focuses on: Emotional Intelligence, Corporate Social Responsibility (CSR), Green HRM and Benchmarking / Storytelling. Naturally, the model also allows for tools such as recognition systems, bonuses, flexible working hours, and work–life balance. These tools help increase engagement and retain top talent over the long term.

Succession Planning. A strategic tool to ensure continuity in key organizational roles (Mehreen & Ali, 2022). Potential successors are identified, and stages for their development and preparation are planned, so that transitions happen smoothly when needed.

3.3. Examples from Real Organizations

Talent management in practice is often illustrated through successful examples of real-world companies that have built effective systems for attracting, developing, and retaining key employees. These organizations typically invest significant resources in creating a culture that promotes innovation and staff development.

Google is one of the most well-known examples of a company that implements comprehensive talent management strategies. Its approach includes flexible working conditions, encouragement of creativity, and continuous learning. Google uses both traditional and modern methods for recruitment and development, offering employees opportunities to engage in various projects and programs for personal and professional growth.

Another example is IBM, which places special emphasis on succession planning and leadership development. IBM invests in mentorship programs and digital learning platforms, combining traditional approaches with new technologies for managing talent.

Microsoft also promotes a culture based on learning and adaptability. The company encourages employees to develop a growth mindset and regularly organizes training sessions and courses to improve competencies.

4. CONCLUSION

Modern human capital management requires the creation of added value, which can be achieved through three main strategic HR policies: Flexibility in approach, data-driven decision-making (data-driven HR), and a human-centered attitude grounded in emotional intelligence.

Talent management, as a core element of sustainable development, is a critical success factor for every modern organization. In a dynamic business environment and amid increasing competition for skilled professionals, effective talent management enables companies to build sustainable competitive advantage. By systematically identifying, developing, and retaining key talent, organizations create conditions for growth and innovation.

Contemporary approaches and best practices in talent management emphasize an individualized approach to employees, focusing on their motivation and professional development. The challenges related to attracting and retaining talent require strategic and flexible solutions tailored to the specific context of each organization.

In this regard, future directions in both research and practice call for a rethinking of many of the traditional paradigms in human resource management within the context of digital transformation. This includes integrating socio-technical systems theory, institutional theory, and critical perspectives, and clearly confirms that strategic HR innovations are essential for a sustainable organizational future.

Investing in talent management is an investment in the organization's future, not only improving the work climate, but also enhancing overall performance and long-term resilience by supporting high levels of individual and organizational development.

Let us conclude with the words of Stephen King: *"True wisdom comes when you stop listening to yourself and start hearing others."*

Finding sustainable solutions in human resource management depends on the key role of building and maintaining a community of like-minded individuals who share common values and goals, and pursue them in new and collaborative ways. Such a process can only be effective through deep, meaningful communication.

REFERENCES

Abdallah, R. K., & Ismail, O. A. (2024). Modern leaders, revolutionary results: Steering transformation in today's world. In Abdallah, A., Alkaabi, A., & Al-Riyami, R. (Eds.), *Cutting-edge innovations in teaching, leadership, technology, and assessment* (pp. 134–147). IGI Global Scientific Publishing., DOI: 10.4018/979-8-3693-0880-6.ch010

Afsharbakeshlo, Z., Omidvar, M., & Gigauri, I. (2024). Green Transformational Leadership: A Systematic Literature Review and Future Research Suggestion. *Marketing and Resource Management for Green Transitions in Economies*, 47-74.

Alimansyah, M., & Takahashi, Y. (2023). Talent management practices for non-high potentials in the public sector: effect of appraisal methods on work outcomes. In *Evidence-based HRM: a Global Forum for Empirical Scholarship*, 11(4), 659-674. Emerald Publishing Limited.

Blanco González Tejero, C., Ulrich, K., & Ribeiro-Navarrete, S. (2024). Personal factors and innovative training as influential elements in the intrapreneurial trend. *Management Decision*, *62*(10), 2969–2985.

Buengeler, C., Leroy, H., & De Stobbeleir, K. (2018). How leaders shape the impact of HR's diversity practices on employee inclusion. *Human Resource Management Review*, *28*(3), 289–303. DOI: 10.1016/j.hrmr.2018.02.005

Chatterjee, S., Chaudhuri, R., Vrontis, D., Mahto, R. V., & Kraus, S. (2023). Global talent management by multinational enterprises post-COVID-19: The role of enterprise social networking and senior leadership. *Thunderbird International Business Review*, *65*(1), 77–88. DOI: 10.1002/tie.22248

Donald, W. E., Baruch, Y., & Ashleigh, M. J. (2023). Technological transformation and human resource development of early career talent: Insights from accounting, banking, and finance. *Human Resource Development Quarterly*, *34*(3), 329–348. DOI: 10.1002/hrdq.21491

Fallah Shayan, N., Mohabbati-Kalejahi, N., Alavi, S., & Zahed, M. A. (2022). Sustainable Development Goals (SDGs) as a framework for corporate social responsibility (CSR). *Sustainability (Basel)*, *14*(3), 1222. DOI: 10.3390/su14031222

Faqihi, A., & Miah, S. J. (2023). Artificial Intelligence-Driven Talent Management System: Exploring the Risks and Options for Constructing a Theoretical Foundation. *Journal of Risk and Financial Management*, *16*(1), 31. DOI: 10.3390/jrfm16010031

Gigauri, I. (2020). Remote working concerns during the covid-19 pandemic. *International Journal of Social Science and Economic Research*, *5*(10), 2803–2818. DOI: 10.46609/IJSSER.2020.v05i10.005

Gigauri, I. (2021). Organizational support to HRM in times of the COVID-19 pandemic crisis. *European Journal of Marketing and Economics*, *4*(1), 16–30. DOI: 10.26417/492dnl43d

Gigauri, I., Vasilev, V., & Sidova, D. (2025). The role of leadership and corporate social responsibility for sustainable entrepreneurship: Good practices from Georgia and Bulgaria. In Gigauri, I. (Ed.), *Sustainable entrepreneurship and family business for women's empowerment* (pp. 165–176). IGI Global Scientific Publishing., DOI: 10.4018/979-8-3693-8694-1.ch008

Karaboğa, T. (2023). The impact of Industry 4.0 on talent management practices: A systematic review. In Ince, F. (Ed.), *Leadership perspectives on effective intergenerational communication and management* (pp. 1–19). IGI Global Scientific Publishing., DOI: 10.4018/978-1-6684-6140-2.ch004

Kaur, B., Gangwar, V. P., & Dash, G. (2022). Green marketing strategies, environmental attitude, and green buying intention: A multi-group analysis in an emerging economy context. *Sustainability (Basel)*, *14*(10), 6107. DOI: 10.3390/su14106107

Lejeune, C., Beausaert, S., & Raemdonck, I. (2021). The impact on employees' job performance of exercising self-directed learning within personal development plan practice. *International Journal of Human Resource Management*, *32*(5), 1086–1112. DOI: 10.1080/09585192.2018.1510848

Mehreen, A., & Ali, Z. (2022). The interplay between employee development factors and succession planning in predicting employee performance: Evidence from retail banks. *Industrial and Commercial Training*, *54*(3), 528–543. DOI: 10.1108/ICT-10-2021-0072

Morris, E. A., Siddiq, F., & Blumenberg, E. (2025). Worse commute, better life? The journey to work, job characteristics, and well-being. *Transportation Research Interdisciplinary Perspectives*, *32*, 101508. DOI: 10.1016/j.trip.2025.101508

Nayak, A., Satpathy, I., & Poddar, S. (2024). The radical transformation: Leveraging green marketing's potential for a sustainable future. In Yıldırım, S., Yıldırım, D., Demirtaş, I., & Kandpal, V. (Eds.), *Green transition impacts on the economy, society, and environment* (pp. 166–181). IGI Global Scientific Publishing., DOI: 10.4018/979-8-3693-3985-5.ch010

Orlandi, L. B., Pocek, J., Kraus, S., Zardini, A., & Rossignoli, C. (2024). Digital workers' stress: The role of digital creativity in the future jobs. *Journal of Innovation & Knowledge*, *9*(2), 100492. DOI: 10.1016/j.jik.2024.100492

Serafimova, V., Dissanayake, H., Iddagoda, A., & Vasilev, V. (2025). Inclusive leadership and corporate social responsibility for women's empowerment: From good ideas to sustainable solution. In Gigauri, I. (Ed.), *Sustainable entrepreneurship and family business for women's empowerment* (pp. 177–202). IGI Global Scientific Publishing., DOI: 10.4018/979-8-3693-8694-1.ch009

Sharma, A., & Biloria, D. (2024). Changing societies adjusting to environmental initiatives. In Yıldırım, S., Yıldırım, D., Demirtaş, I., & Kandpal, V. (Eds.), *Green transition impacts on the economy, society, and environment* (pp. 324–339). IGI Global Scientific Publishing., DOI: 10.4018/979-8-3693-3985-5.ch018

Souki, K., Aad, S. S., & Karkoulian, S. (2025). The impact of 360-degree feedback on innovative behavior within the organization: The mediating role of organizational justice. *The International Journal of Organizational Analysis*, *33*(3), 584–602. DOI: 10.1108/IJOA-12-2023-4146

Stefanova, D., Bacheva, K., & Vasilev, V. (2025). Conceptual convergence: Disinformation, fake news, and information influence as a triad of security threats in the context of Society 5.0. [ETR]. *Engineering for Rural Development*, *5*, 291–296. DOI: 10.17770/etr2025vol5.8470

Taibah, D., & Ho, T. C. (2023). The moderating effect of flexible work option on structural empowerment and generation Z contextual performance. *Behavioral Sciences (Basel, Switzerland)*, *13*(3), 266. DOI: 10.3390/bs13030266 PMID: 36975291

Vasilev, V., Stefanova, D., & Icheva, M. (2024). Green human resource management as a component of sustainable organizational development in environmental and natural economics. [ETR]. *Engineering for Rural Development*, *1*, 402–407. DOI: 10.17770/etr2024vol1.7966

Yıldırım, S., & Vasilev, V. (2024). The future of green collar workers: Green transition in employment. In Yıldırım, S., Yıldırım, D., Demirtaş, I., & Kandpal, V. (Eds.), *Green transition impacts on the economy, society, and environment* (pp. 1–16). IGI Global Scientific Publishing., DOI: 10.4018/979-8-3693-3985-5.ch001

Chapter 18

The Gig Economy and Digital Payments: A Pathway Out of Poverty

Zokir Mamadiyarov
Termez University of Economics and Service, Termez, Uzbekistan

Artiqova O'g'iljon
Mamun University, Uzbekistan

Shokhjakhon Akhmedov
Urgench State University, Uzbekistan

Aboubaker Khoualed
http://orcid.org/0000-0003-4096-7497
Badji Mokhtar University, Algeria

Munir Ahmad
http://orcid.org/0000-0003-4836-6151
Survey of Pakistan, Pakistan

ABSTRACT

This chapter examines the transformative potential of the gig economy, supported by digital payment systems, as a pathway out of poverty for marginalized and low-income populations. It explores how flexible, short-term work opportunities, combined with secure and traceable digital payments, can enhance income generation, financial inclusion, and skill development. The chapter critically analyzes structural, technological, and social challenges, including income instability, platform dependency, and digital literacy gaps, and emphasizes the complementary roles of governments,

DOI: 10.4018/979-8-3373-4307-5.ch018

platforms, and NGOs in fostering inclusive and sustainable gig work ecosystems. Emerging trends, research gaps, and policy implications are also discussed to guide future strategies for equitable economic empowerment.

INTRODUCTION

Poverty in low-income and marginalized communities remains urgent across the world, and is frequently affected by structural inequalities that suppress access to safe work, formal financial services, and means of social protection (Bhadra, 2021; De Schutter et al., 2023; Lee, 2023; Pollard & Booth, 2019). In most areas, traditional labor markets do not meet the special conditions of such groups in terms of geographical location, human capabilities, and time. Therefore, people often have to depend on informal employment that is usually inconsistent, underpaid, and lacks the necessary provision of healthcare, retirement savings, or legal insurance (Chen et al., 2002; Ugargol & Parvathy, 2023). This economic precariousness not only restricts short-term economic stability but also impairs the subsequent chance at social mobility and accretion of wealth.

To address these issues, the gig economy has been identified as revolutionary, where there is a form of work delivery in a short-term and flexible manner, which is mediated via digital platforms (Lin & Zhang, 2023; Novitz, 2021; Stopforth, 2023). The platforms also match the workers with the tasks that can include ride-sharing and delivery jobs, as well as freelance digital work, and may not necessarily need any formal qualification or front-end investment. The gig economy offers a different avenue through which individuals do not have access to structured work through a system capable of producing immediate returns. Nonetheless, although the gig work model has been attractive to many because of its flexibility and accessibility, the model is not devoid of difficulties such as income insecurity, severe lack of labor protection, and source of dependence on digital literacy and use of platforms.

Along with such a change in the labor force is the sudden acceleration of digital payment options, which are transforming the way gig economy workers handle their incomes. Use of digital payments facilitates safe, real-time, auditable income transfers and lessens dependency on cash and informal financial sources (Putrevu & Mertzanis, 2024a). What is more, these systems give access to expanded financial services such as microloans, savings schemes, and insurance, which expand financial inclusion and provide mechanisms that may contribute to long-run economic resilience. When used together with gig work, digital payments can solve some of the systemic challenges that excluded marginalized groups in the past, to work toward a better financial position.

This combination of labor commodification and the inclusive nature of financial technologies poses serious questions of how technology is applied in poverty reduction. Does engagement in the gig economy, buttressed, in this case, with a trustworthy infrastructure of digital payment, offer a way out of poverty that is not self-defeating? This chapter addresses this question by critically looking into the possibilities and limitations of gig work, studying the effect that digital financial tools have, and looking at applications in the field in a variety of different contexts. The chapter seeks to illuminate the potential and constraints of this emerging economic system by providing a data-informed yet refined perspective in order to serve as a source of opportunity on how the digital innovations could be utilized as the means to further enable livelihoods characterized by greater equity and resilience.

GIG ECONOMY LANDSCAPE

The gig economy is one of the radical transformations of the global labor market that can be defined as short-term, flexible, and task-oriented employment with the mediation of digital platforms (Putrevu & Mertzanis, 2024b). In contrast to standard full-time work, gig work is normally characterized by service or pay-per-unit or job-by-job remuneration and frequently in the absence of the extended contractual requirements. Such a structure means that workers have a lot of control over when, where, and how to work, which allows them to either group-gig or take up individual gigs and continue with personal responsibility or pursue other sources of income. Although such flexibility is desirable and may be a type of trade-off, there is a lack of social protection, unreliable income, and a lack of access to other benefits, which can be health insurance, retirement plans, or paid leave. To highlight the structural differences between conventional employment and gig work, Figure 1 illustrates a comparative view of their defining characteristics.

Figure 1. Comparative Structure of Traditional Employment vs. Gig Economy

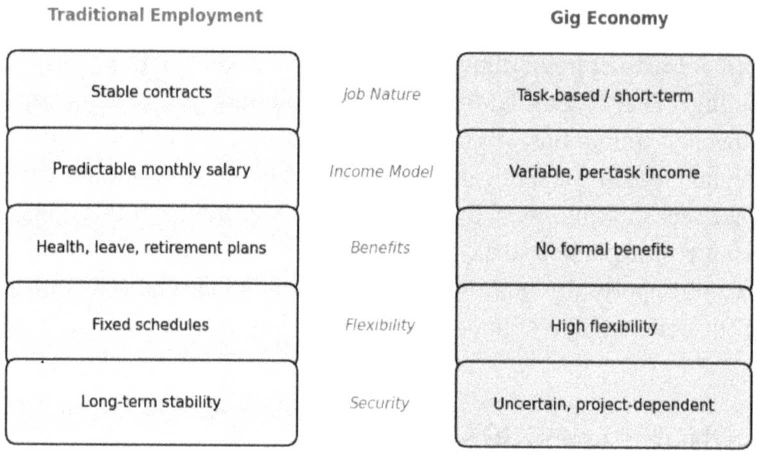

Digital platforms became the most important mediators of gig work to close the gap between supply and demand in various fields (Au-Yeung & Qiu, 2022; Li et al., 2021). Delivery and ride-hailing, which in the case of Uber, Bolt, and Foodpanda, constitute the urban markets of mobility and logistics, offer consumers fast and on-demand services using their platforms, besides generating revenue streams for workers. Examples of freelance labor markets include Upwork, Fiverr, and Toptal, which allow skilled workers such as graphic designers, software developers, content creators, and consultants to produce their specialized skills on a global level (Batmunkh et al., 2022; Chaudhary & Niroula, 2024; Gussek & Wiesche, 2023). Microtasks Crowdsourced microtask sites, such as Amazon Mechanical Turk, outsource small and repetitive tasks, like data labeling or article moderation, to a decentralized workforce (Sun et al., 2022; Zulfiqar et al., 2022). In parallel, there is the emergence of dedicated platforms that cover on-demand professional services (legal consulting, tutoring, and healthcare assistance) and typically combine rating mechanisms and algorithms to match with quality and efficiency. Table 1 categorizes the major types of gig platforms, illustrating their focus, examples, and challenges faced by workers.

Table 1. Types of Digital Platforms in the Gig Economy

Platform Type	Examples	Core Services	Worker Profile	Challenges
Ride-hailing & Delivery	Uber, Bolt, Foodpanda	Urban mobility, logistics	Drivers, riders	High fees, safety risks
Freelance Marketplaces	Upwork, Fiverr, Toptal	Creative & professional services	Skilled freelancers	High competition
Microtasking Platforms	Amazon MTurk	Data labeling, content moderation	Global distributed workforce	Low pay per task
Specialized Services	LegalZoom, Telehealth apps	Legal, tutoring, healthcare	Professionals	Regulatory complexity

In recent years, an industry has grown around the gig economy, fueled by the ability to innovate with technology, the ubiquity of smartphones, and the availability of on-demand services in this growing market segment. This development differs in different locations: in the highly developed economies, digital freelancing and knowledge-based gigs have been adopted with huge success due to the availability of strong internet connectivity, a legal regulatory environment, and a highly skilled workforce. By contrast, the rates of adoption of app-mediated service delivery and informal gig work are accelerating in emerging economies and are locally mediated by the specific demands of local labor markets, patterns of urbanization, availability of transport, and socio-economic limitations. Within such environments, gig platforms are very frequently able to act as vital income sources to populations lacking access to the formal job market and, at the same time, can be subject to the systematic vulnerability of unstable or unreliable pay, fees charged by the companies, and a limited range of labor benefits.

Taken together, the gig economy represents what has been characterized as a two-sided story of promise and threat: it promises more jobs, more income, the growth of entrepreneurship, and a willingness to adapt to the changing nature of the labor market; yet it also highlights issues related to employment rights, social equity and the sustainability of platform-mediated employment platforms in the long term. Such dynamics demand a multi-dimensional view which takes into account technological enablers, conducive economic incentives, regulatory environments, and socio-cultural factors that determine not only the participation in work, but also the change of platform in itself.

Engagement

The practice of gig work is especially high among marginalized and low-income groups, blocked by structural factors from pursuing formal employment (Cappelli & Eldor, 2021; Janadari & Preena, 2020; Van Belle et al., 2023). To numerous people, particularly women, rural dwellers, the young, and those working in the informal sector, the gig economy provides an important platform to supplement their household financial earnings, become financially self-sufficient, and even test entrepreneurial activities that they would be unable to do. This type of employment may offer flexible avenues to manage home matters, their tuition, or the weather at labs, which is especially appealing to people who were locked outside of the regular employment sector.

But engagement in the gig economy is predetermined by various interacting backgrounds such as legal literacy, access to stable internet and devices, surrounding regulations, and cultural or social norms. In other areas, women might be limited in mobility or feel unsafe, or they may have societal pressure and be unable to pursue specific kinds of gig work, e.g., a ride-hailing or parcel delivery. Younger demographics or the people with high aptitudes in digital literacy, on the other hand, can more easily find their option in an online virtual work system, by taking advantage of global economic needs of specialized services like design, programming, or content production. Other factors, like limitations of infrastructure, such as poor internet or prohibitive cost of smartphones, also determine who takes part and what kind of gigs can be done in a particular context.

Becoming aware of these trends is key to determining the level of inclusivity and the potential to reduce poverty in the gig economy. Although gig platforms may generate economic opportunities due to unequal access, they may also contribute to socio-economic inequality. Development practitioners, platform designers, and policymakers must, therefore, consider strategies that would respond to the digital divides, avenues of more targeted training, and the provisions of safe and equitable participation, thus maximizing the potential of the gig economy, which might provide a means of sustainable and inclusive livelihoods. Table 2 summarizes the intersecting factors—technological, social, and regulatory—that shape how different groups engage with gig work.

Table 2. Factors Shaping Engagement in the Gig Economy

Factor	Influence on Participation	Example
Digital literacy	Enables/limits online freelancing	Skilled youth are more likely to access Fiverr
Infrastructure	Internet & device access affect participation	Rural areas face connectivity issues
Social norms	Gender roles influence platform use	Women less present in ride-hailing
Age & skills	Younger, tech-savvy workers dominate online gigs	Youth in coding, design
Regulation	Shapes worker rights & protections	Formal vs. informal settings

Economic and Social Potential

There are important economic and social possibilities offered by gig work to marginalized communities beyond the direct income-generating possibilities. Economically, engagement in platform-mediated work can allow the household to access immediate income with ease, thus helping to satisfy their short-term monetary necessities in addition to promoting income diversification (Loganathan, 2022; Malik et al., 2021; Okunkova et al., 2023). This is associated with the workers being able to mix several gig activities or while working gig jobs by blending them with conventional jobs, which is likely to iron out fluctuation in income and make workers less susceptible to economic downturns. Also, gig work tends to foster the acquisition of skills, including digital and communication skills, as well as skills specific to an industry, increasing long-term employability in both the digital and the traditional labor markets. Figure 2 outlines the dual economic and social pathways through which gig work can foster empowerment, while highlighting opportunities for both immediate and long-term benefits.

Figure 2. Economic and Social Pathways of Gig Work

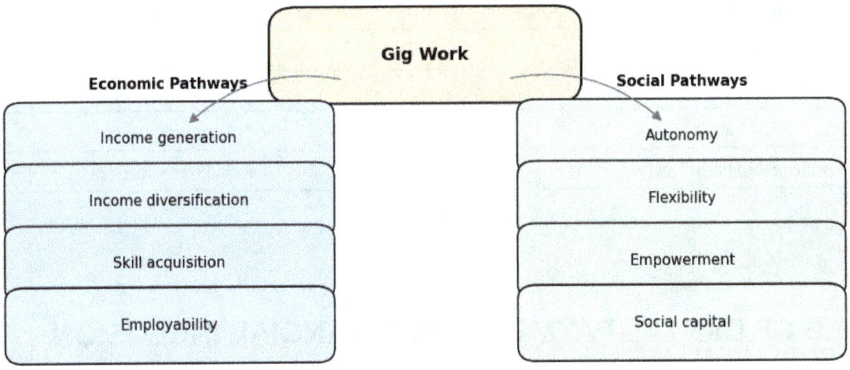

Socially, gig work has the potential to lead to more autonomy and self-determination, with the ability of individuals to organize work around household or caregiving duties. Being exposed to different work, projects, and people, as well as working alongside various professionals, can expand the scope of careers, widen social capital, and provide learning experiences that otherwise would not have been possible, especially for women, the youth, and in rural areas. The gig economy can be used to empower economically disadvantaged individuals by reducing the barriers of entry and providing flexible work opportunities because it acts as a complement to other initiatives, such as financial inclusion programs, skills training, and mentorship, that would support and add to its underlying work opportunities and other favorable policy and regulatory environments.

Nevertheless, to realize this potential, the challenges that still exist would need to be overcome. Gig work may be made more precarious by income volatility, reliance on the platform, and poor access to social protections, and these workers may be primarily affected by inequality of access to digital skills and infrastructure, which can multiply existing social and economic inequalities. In order to leverage the full developmental potential of gig work, the stakeholders can be required to implement context-sensitive interventions, which can be a blend of technology access, regulatory protection, and capacity-strengthening initiatives. It is only in such ways that the gig platforms can make a positive contribution to sustainable livelihoods, inclusive economic growth, and equitable access to the emerging labour market. Table 3 presents the gig economy's dual narrative, balancing its promises of flexibility and opportunity against the persistent challenges of precarity and inequality.

Table 3. Dual Narrative of the Gig Economy

Opportunities	Challenges
Flexibility in work schedules	Income volatility
Access to global labor markets	Lack of social protections
Skill acquisition & digital literacy	Platform dependency
Income diversification	Unequal digital access
Entrepreneurship pathways	Regulatory uncertainty

ROLE OF DIGITAL PAYMENTS IN FINANCIAL INCLUSION

The application of the digital payment system has moved to be the pillar in financial inclusion, especially for gig workers and marginalized groups who previously experienced hurdles when trying to access formal banking services. These systems provide an opportunity to make online transfer of income safely and in real-time, which is traceable and eliminates most of the risks of losing money incurred when they are delivered in traditional cash-based models, including the loss of money, late payments, and lack of records that are immutable. The process of receiving payment by gig workers is made more convenient by using mobile money, e-wallet, and digital banking system applications, thus receiving payment directly from platforms or clients in real time, which makes it reliable and timely.

Accountability brings with it accountability and trust, which has been instilled by the transparency of the digital payment systems. Transaction histories can display verifiable data about the work done and money paid, which can decrease the number of disagreements between the workers and platforms and increase the level of trust among workers in the digital labor practices. Over and above instantaneous compensation, online payment systems also enable financial planning, savings, and access to credit or microloans that create economic resilience avenues in the long term. In addition, the integration with other digital financial tools, e.g., automated tax reporting, budgeting applications, or savings platforms, can lead to workers being able to manage their various income sources and plan their future investments in a better way. Table 4 summarizes the major mechanisms by which digital payments advance financial inclusion and their corresponding implications for gig workers and marginalized populations.

Table 4. Mechanisms through which Digital Payments Foster Financial Inclusion

Mechanism	Description	Implications for Gig Workers
Secure, real-time payments	Reduces theft, delays, and disputes	Timely and reliable compensation
Transaction transparency	Creates verifiable income records	Builds trust, reduces disputes
Financial footprint	Provides income history	Access to credit, loans, insurance
Integrated tools	Automated savings, tax, and budgeting apps	Encourages disciplined financial habits
Economic participation	Extends access beyond formal jobs	Supports inclusion and resilience

To marginal and low-income groups, these systems offer economic opportunities to people otherwise attached to irregular work and economic instability by extending the economic participation patterns beyond traditional labor markets. Therefore, these systems allow gig employment to be more than a quick cash arrangement but a gateway into wider financial security and integration. Digital payments are a multiplier of socio-economic opportunities provided by the gig economy since accessibility plus security, plus traceability come together in keeping workers able to use technology to attain more economic self-sufficiency and sustainability.

Implications for Financial Behaviors and Economic Empowerment

In addition to being the means of easing the transaction process, digital payment systems are found to have deep consequences on financial behaviors and, more generally, economic empowerment. These systems can help gig workers and disadvantaged groups to save and plan their finances systematically by opening transparent, safe, and structured financial avenues. Most of the apps have automated deposits, goal-oriented savings plans, and the option to use micro-investment current financial budgeting, which teaches people to spend wisely and enables them to save over a period (Aashish et al., 2025; Allon et al., 2023; Mohd Daud et al., 2024).

Moreover, the auditable payment history of the organisations that digital payment systems produce presents formal financial traces of workers, who were formerly outside or met the banking system. Such forms of documentation may be acceptable forms of evidence of income and financial stability to open up microloans, personal financing, and insurance products to the informal or platform-based worker, who has lacked access so far. With the possibility of using such financial services, one can have greater autonomy in being ready to deal with emergencies, investing in education or skill training, or becoming an entrepreneur.

All of these mechanisms can together turn gig work into a path to long-term stability and resiliency in earnings. Digital payment systems use alternative sources of earning to eliminate the risk by having a backup plan, enhancing earning security in the short-term, as well as allowing marginal workers to accumulate their assets, plan strategically, and engage more in the formal economy in the long term. By doing so, digital finance integration into the ecosystem of work on a gig-by-gig basis turns into a lever of inclusive growth and economic empowerment.

Robust Infrastructure and Targeted Capacity-Building Initiatives

Nonetheless, the effective deployment of the digital payment systems depends on the availability of sound technological infrastructure and specific capacity-building efforts. Access to high-quality internet connectivity, use of smartphones, and secure and interoperable digital ecosystems are core preconditions to effective engagement in the digital economy. Such conditions tend to be distributed unequally, more so in rural or underserved areas, which may operate as a barrier to inclusion (Mieruch & McFarlane, 2023; Qiu et al., 2021; Ray et al., 2024).

Digital literacy is also rather important as it provides a user with the ability to use a financial application or service safely, to realize how the transaction mechanism works, and how to manage personal accounts and keep oneself safe regarding cyber-attacks or scammers. Even digitally designed payment systems can fail to reach their full potential without proper training and support for all the populations involved, thereby exposing those who are most vulnerable to risks or being left behind. Table 5 summarizes the key barriers and their implications for inclusion.

Table 5. Barriers to Effective Digital Payment Integration

Barrier	Challenge	Implication
Infrastructure gaps	Poor internet/smartphone access	Exclusion of rural/underserved workers
Digital literacy	Lack of user skills and awareness	Risk of fraud or misuse
Platform design	Complexity and lack of interoperability	Limits accessibility
Regulation gaps	Weak data privacy or consumer protection	Erodes trust in systems

It is necessary to combat these problems by coordinating the efforts of policy-makers, financial institutions, technology players, and gig platforms. Joint efforts would guarantee the creation of efficient user-friendly systems with high accessibility and security, which is to be supported through education programs and the acquisition of financial and digital literacy. Trust and credibility in the ecosystem are also augmented through regulatory control that may include handling data privacy, transaction security, and consumer protection standards. Figure 3 presents the ecosystem enablers required to maximize financial inclusion.

Figure 3. Enablers of Inclusive Digital Payment Ecosystems

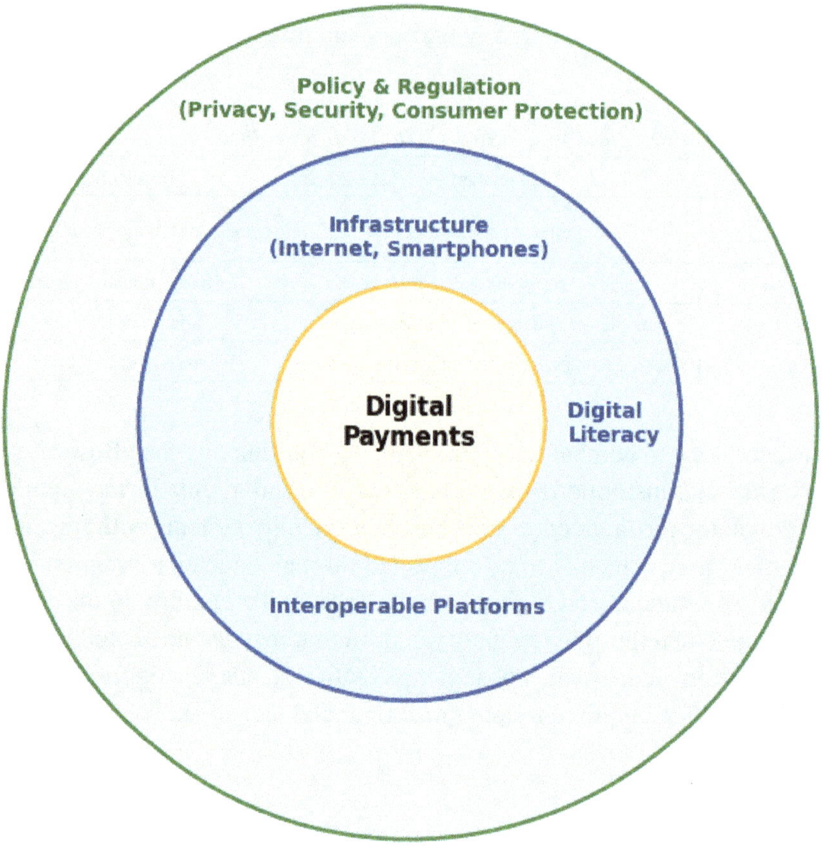

Against this backdrop, digital payment systems become more than just payment tools; this is because they can be used as strategic tools that can multiply the potential of the gig economy in terms of bringing economic empowerment, financial resilience, and an inclusive growth experience. Technology accessibility, user education, and policy support can facilitate gig work to become a dependable means of income generation instead of an insecure source of income to support long-term economic inclusion.

OPPORTUNITIES AND CHALLENGES FOR POVERTY ALLEVIATION

Advantages

Digital payment systems and the gig economy provide innovative possibilities in alleviating poverty, especially among the low-income and marginalized groups. It has one of its most noticeable benefits, which is flexibility: gig work allows people to organize their involvement in labor and activities according to personal timetables and family tasks, as well as geographical constraints. Such flexibility enables employees to generate revenue without being tied down by fixed schedules and work places, which is particularly useful for women, caregivers, the population in the countryside, and others who cannot work full-time due to mobility or capacity constraints in conventional work environments.

In addition to flexibility, jobbing is a main source of income. Through participation in various short-term assignments/projects, the workers can complement their household incomes and ownership of multiple revenue sources, cushioning uncertainties of the local or seasonal level economic activity. This flexibility in terms of income-earning sources increases financial resilience and offers a way to financial stability to households in cases where they might not otherwise be able to rely on regular or formal income. Engagement in gig labor also helps to acquire abilities and develop professionally. Digital technologies have exposed workers to new technologies, client handling, and specialized job requirements, and, therefore, have developed skills that can be transferred, namely digital literacy, communications skills, project management, and problem-solving. These not only boost the performance in the gig economy but also increase the chances of workers being employed and working in other labor markets with more chances of security or even better remuneration.

With the ability to be flexible, diversify income, and delegate some skills, the gig economy can be seen as a multilateral empowerment of the economy, in which one can prosper by relying on accessible digital payment systems. It enables people to participate in work that is sensitive to personal conditions, expands financial independence, and offers viable avenues to secure upward mobility to set up the foundation for sustainable contribution to digital economic activity. Table 6 summarizes the main opportunities that the gig economy, powered by digital payments, offers for poverty alleviation.

Table 6. Opportunities of the Gig Economy for Poverty Alleviation

Opportunity	Description	Key Beneficiaries
Flexibility	Work structured around personal schedules and locations	Women, caregivers, rural workers
Income Diversification	Multiple short-term tasks buffer against seasonal or local economic fluctuations	Low-income and informal households
Skill Acquisition	Exposure to digital tools, client interaction, and project management enhances employability	Youth, emerging professionals
Economic Empowerment	Greater financial autonomy and resilience via accessible digital payment systems	All marginalized populations

Substantial Risks

Although there a benefits of the gig economy, it has major risks and structural weaknesses. One of the problems that is very urgent is income instability. The income of gig workers is explicitly dependent on the availability of work, demand on platforms, and their competition with each other, making the form of income highly variable and unforeseeable. This volatility may compromise the financial security of low-income households or those who do not have savings, making it hard to plan their budget and increasing the risk of facing economic shocks. The lack of formal social protections is the other important issue. In comparison to the old employment, the gig jobs do not usually offer such benefits as health insurance, paid leave, retirement payoffs, or unemployment aid. The absence of such a safety net puts workers at a direct risk, e.g., medical emergency or loss of income, as well as a long-term risk, e.g., a lack of retirement savings and/or financial stability with age.

These risks are also made worse by platform dependency. The profitability of workers is directly reliant on the operational stance of the platforms individually, as well as the algorithmic policies and fee structures. Uneven notice of change in task allocation, commission rates, or access rules of income can be a major change to income, often without consultation and appeal to the worker. Such dependency limits bargaining power, decreases autonomy, and introduces natural domination between the workers and the platforms, showing the structural precarity in the gig economy. Collectively, these obstacles serve as a reminder that although the gig economy can present economic benefits in terms of flexibility, it also needs accompanying measures, including regulatory safeguards, social safety nets, and digital literacy and skills training to manage risk and provide those engaging in the gig economy with the means to pursue gains in the best interest of long-term sustainable, equitable economic progress.

There are structural impediments that also curtail the potential of gig work in providing poverty alleviation on a long-term basis. The regulatory deficiency in labor law and internet business in general usually does not have formal recognition of the employees in the gig economy, resulting in uncertainty regarding their hiring status, taxes, and workplace protections. Such legal ambiguities undermine the safeguards and limit fair treatment. Concurrently, digital divides existing due to sparse access to smartphones, low-cost internet, and digital literacy leave out a significant number of potential participants, especially within rural or underserved settings, which only serves to further drive the pre-existing socioeconomic inequality. The presence of policy deficits, i.e., weak financial inclusion programs and a lack of established social safety nets, increases the gap between gig work and digital payment systems and the ultimate creation of economic power. The obstacles that need to be overcome can require the efforts of civil society, platform operators, and governments. Central interventions can involve regulatory change to protect the rights of workers, specific digital and vocational training programs, investment in inclusive infrastructure, and augmentation of the network of social protection. With the ability to both foster opportunity and mitigate risk, the gig economy can become an effective means out of poverty, so long as the supportive and equitable ecosystems are constructed in a deliberate and systematic way. Table 7 outlines the structural barriers that limit the gig economy's capacity to achieve sustained poverty alleviation, emphasizing the systemic gaps in regulation, access, and policy support.

Table 7. Structural Barriers to Sustainable Poverty Alleviation

Structural Barrier	**Impact**	**Mitigation Strategy**
Regulatory Gaps	Ambiguity in worker classification, taxation, and labor rights weakens protections	Labor law reform, platform regulation
Digital Divide	Limited access to smartphones, the internet, and literacy excludes rural/underserved groups	Investment in infrastructure, targeted digital training
Policy Shortcomings	Weak financial inclusion and social safety nets reduce resilience	Expanded social protection and inclusion initiatives

DATA-DRIVEN INSIGHTS

In order to determine the effective contribution of the gig economy and digital payment systems on curbing poverty in the real world, it is imperative that empirical evidence from different countries and socio-economic backgrounds is analysed to evaluate their beneficial role in poverty alleviation. In Kenya, mobile payment systems (e.g., M-Pesa) have played a revolutionary role in income management by informal and gig workers (e.g., ride-hailers, deliverers, and other small-scale businesses). Studies have shown that the users of M-Pesa are now having increased access to microcredit, better financial security, as well as developing savings ability and better access to other financial products, which they can use to invest in small businesses or even education, among others. Likewise, in India, online platforms, like Swiggy, Zomato, and UrbanClap (now Urban Company), have enabled flexible work opportunities to low-income youth and urban informal workers who gain supplementary cash income and access several skills in digital service delivery and customer relations, and logistics management. When surveyed about their experience in these gig worker platforms, it is clear that despite the overall median income being rather modest, the employments of instant and easily accountable digital payment methods in the form of mobile wallets exponentially improve the reliability of income, decrease the usage of unformalized cash-based transactions, and make the overall financial resilience much higher on average. The cases shown together demonstrate that with available digital payment infrastructure, gig work has the potential to make realistic contributions to economic stability and gradual poverty alleviation, especially among people who have traditionally never been able to access regular workplaces.

The quantitative and qualitative approaches are relatively specific in terms of the results of gig work in various socio-economic settings. Latin America Research exemplifies freelance platforms and app-based service delivery in nations including Brazil and Mexico, and professional success in this area has proved to have significant increases in household earnings, labor market integration, and economic independence among the people previously marginalized. Digital trail of transactions enables employees to better balance their irregular costs and obtain small-scale credit to ease their gradual financial lifting. There are, however, downsides tempering these gains, and these downsides include income volatility, the ability to have little or no social protection, as well as harsh competition in the digital sphere, which threatens to make consistent earnings unsustainable. Qualitative interviews also show the psychosocial aspects of the work in the gig economy: employees often find increased self-efficacy, a sense of empowerment, and more freedom of choice on work schedules, and report stress surrounding uncertainty, platform dependency, and the unstable nature of task-based work. Together, such findings highlight that although the gig economy has economic and social potential to deliver, the latter can be achieved only with the addition of other support systems, institutional, regulatory, and financial, to limit structural flaws.

The contextual factors that are crucial in the determination of the effectiveness of the gig economy and digital payment in the alleviation of poverty are identified through comparative analyses across countries. The effects are most favorable in such areas where a strong digital infrastructure, easy access to financial services, and a favorable regulatory regime, vis-à-vis a high platform availability, allow workers to convert temporary earnings to more permanent and viable economic returns. Conversely, the constraints imposed by the vulnerability of certain areas with a low level of internet connectivity, digital literacy, and social protection would be even more heightened in these regions because gig work may have a positive external effect by supporting the precarious livelihood instead of functioning as a safe approach to poverty exit. All these case studies reinforce the argument that although gig work and the digital payment system have a large potential to empower economically, their economic implications are neither universal nor automatic. To realize meaningful, inclusive benefits can depend on integrated interventions to make technologies more friendly to all in terms of accessibility, the inclusion of the underbanked, labor protection, and regulatory support, all reflective of the socio-economic realities of the localities in which they operate. Table 8 summarizes key country-level examples, highlighting observed benefits, challenges, and contextual factors influencing the impact of gig work and digital payments on poverty alleviation. Figure 4 illustrates this duality using a balanced scale metaphor, symbolizing the equilibrium needed between opportunity and risk.

Figure 4. Dual Nature of the Gig Economy

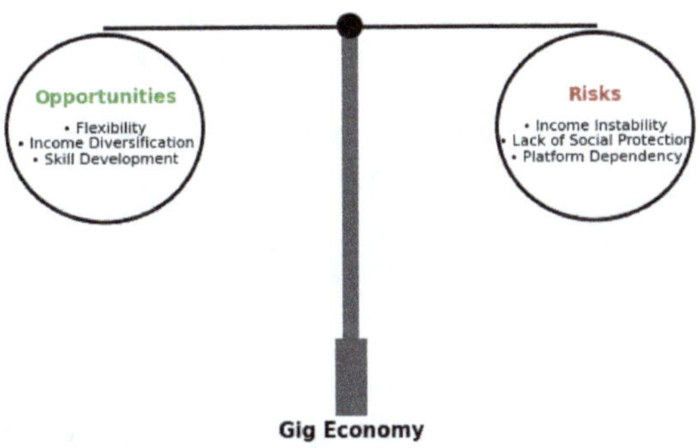

Table 8. Summary of the Country-Level Insights on Gig Work

Country / Region	Key Platforms & Sectors	Observed Benefits	Challenges / Limitations	Contextual Factors
Kenya	M-Pesa (mobile money), ride-hailing, and delivery services	Increased financial security, higher savings, improved access to credit, investments in small businesses, and education	Limited platform options in rural areas; reliance on mobile network coverage	Strong mobile money infrastructure; widespread adoption of mobile payments
India	Swiggy, Zomato, UrbanClap; urban gig services	Flexible income opportunities, supplemental earnings, digital skill acquisition, instant, traceable payments	Modest median earnings; dependence on platform algorithms; urban-rural disparities	Growing digital economy, urban concentration of gig platforms, and expanding smartphone penetration
Brazil & Mexico (Latin America)	Freelance platforms, app-based service delivery	Household income improvements, labor market participation, autonomy, access to microcredit, and better expense management	Earnings volatility, limited social protections, high platform competition, and stress from uncertainty	Variable internet connectivity; digital literacy gaps; nascent social protection frameworks
Comparative Insights	–	Potential for economic empowerment and financial inclusion	Impact is highly context-dependent; technological, social, and policy barriers influence outcomes	Integrated support ecosystem (infrastructure + financial services + regulation) enhances success; weak ecosystems limit benefits

CONCLUSION

The discussion of the digital payment systems and gig economy shows how it can become a way of escaping poverty, and the discussion identifies the structural, technological, and social barriers that have to be overcome to achieve this potential. Multi-layered frameworks can help in improving inclusivity and stability of work in gigs. On the policy level, governments can also introduce policies and regulations of labor that acknowledge the right of gig workers, offering protection schemes and minimum income levels, as well as offering social safety nets and protection through providing access to health care insurance and retirement plans. At the same time, financial inclusion efforts and those supporting mobile wallets, microloans, and savings programs can enhance the economic impact of gig payments to turn temporary earnings into financial stability. Capacity building through digital literacy interventions and programs is also very important to make sure the marginalized groups can safely and efficiently operate within the sphere of the digital ecosystem.

The functions of the different stakeholders-government, platforms, and non-governmental organizations (NGOs) are complementary and support each other. Enabling regulatory environments and private investment in infrastructure to support digital payments and platform accessibility can be designed by governments. Work platforms also have a responsibility of ensuring the presence of a fair remuneration package, policies that are clearly understandable, and grievance redressal mechanisms for the workers. It means that NGOs and community organizations can fill local gaps, such as training, advocacy support, and access to the sources of financial literacy information, which neither government nor platforms can fill independently. The involvement of these actors in a collaborative manner is necessary to promote the ecosystem where the potential of gig work to reduce poverty is at its highest.

In the future, new trends show that by integrating such technologies as artificial intelligence, algorithm-based task assignment, and blockchain-based payment processing, efficiency, transparency, and human autonomy in the field of the gig economy can go even further. Nevertheless, there are still research gaps, especially in the long-term socio-economic effects of gig work on marginalized communities and the relation of digital labor to social protection, as well as ways to reduce platform dependency and income instability. The longitudinal, comparative research in various regions, and evidence-based research on various vulnerabilities at the intersections are areas those future studies need to be employed. By tackling the issues associated with the gig economy head-on, the latter can become a productive instrument of economic inclusion and leave the sidelined communities with a set of real opportunities to achieve stability in terms of finances, skills, and self-identification.

REFERENCES

Aashish, D., Pallavi, T., Mukund, T., & Arpit, W. (2025). *The Gig Economy Revolution: Rethinking Talent Management*. Chyren Publication.

Allon, G., Cohen, M. C., & Sinchaisri, W. P. (2023). The Impact of Behavioral and Economic Drivers on Gig Economy Workers. *Manufacturing & Service Operations Management*, *25*(4), 1376–1393. Advance online publication. DOI: 10.1287/msom.2023.1191

Au-Yeung, T. C., & Qiu, J. (2022). Institutions, Occupations and Connectivity: The Embeddedness of Gig Work and Platform-Mediated Labour Market in Hong Kong. *Critical Sociology*, *48*(7–8), 1169–1187. Advance online publication. DOI: 10.1177/08969205221090581

Batmunkh, A., Fekete-Farkas, M., & Lakner, Z. (2022). Bibliometric Analysis of Gig Economy. *Administrative Sciences*, *12*(2), 51. Advance online publication. DOI: 10.3390/admsci12020051

Bhadra, S. (2021). Vulnerabilities of the Rural Poor in India during pandemic COVID-19: Social Work perspective for designing sustainable emergency response. *Asian Social Work and Policy Review*, *15*(3), 221–233. Advance online publication. DOI: 10.1111/aswp.12236 PMID: 35655795

Cappelli, P., & Eldor, L. (2021). Contracting, engagement, and the "gig" economy. In *A Research Agenda for Employee Engagement in a Changing World of Work*. DOI: 10.4337/9781789907858.00015

Chaudhary, P., & Niroula, P. K. (2024). Connecting the Dots in Digital Labor Marketplace: A Bibliometric Review of Global Gig Dynamics. *International Journal of Entrepreneurship. Business and Creative Economy*, *4*(1), 160–181. Advance online publication. DOI: 10.31098/ijebce.v4i1.2076

Chen, M., Jhabvala, R., & Lund, F. (2002). Supporting workers in the informal economy: a policy framework. *ILO Working Paper on the Informal Economy, Employment Sector, November*.

De Schutter, O., Frazer, H., Guio, A. C., & Marlier, E. (2023). The Escape from Poverty: Breaking the Vicious Cycles Perpetuating Disadvantage. In *The Escape from Poverty: Breaking the Vicious Cycles Perpetuating Disadvantage*.

Gussek, L., & Wiesche, M. (2023). IT Professionals in the Gig Economy: The Success of IT Freelancers on Digital Labor Platforms. *Business & Information Systems Engineering, 65*(5), 555–575. Advance online publication. DOI: 10.1007/s12599-023-00812-z

Janadari, N., & Preena, R. (2020). The Gig Economy and Workforce. *Contemporary Developments in Human Resource Management, 1*(February).

Lee, J. Y. (2023). Economic Inequality, Social Determinants of Health, and the Right to Social Security. *Health and Human Rights, 25*(2). PMID: 38145137

Li, Z., Hong, Y., & Zhang, Z. (2021). The Empowering and Competition Effects of the Platform-Based Sharing Economy on the Supply and Demand Sides of the Labor Market. *Journal of Management Information Systems, 38*(1), 140–165. Advance online publication. DOI: 10.1080/07421222.2021.1870387

Lin, Y., & Zhang, J. (2023). The Fight Against Platform Capitalism: An Inquiry into the Global Struggles of the Gig Economy. *Chinese Journal of Communication, 16*(3), 347–349. Advance online publication. DOI: 10.1080/17544750.2023.2243390

Loganathan, M. (2022). Assessing Social Sustainability in the Gig Economy. *The Indian Journal of Labour Economics : the Quarterly Journal of the Indian Society of Labour Economics, 65*(3), 831–843. Advance online publication. DOI: 10.1007/s41027-022-00399-1

Malik, R., Visvizi, A., & Skrzek-lubasińska, M. (2021). The gig economy: Current issues, the debate, and the new avenues of research. *Sustainability (Basel), 13*(9), 5023. Advance online publication. DOI: 10.3390/su13095023

Mieruch, Y., & McFarlane, D. (2023). Gig Economy Riders on Social Media in Thailand: Contested Identities and Emergent Civil Society Organisations. *Voluntas, 34*(6), 1232–1242. Advance online publication. DOI: 10.1007/s11266-022-00547-7 PMID: 36471890

Mohd Daud, S. N., Osman, Z., Samsudin, S., & Phang, I. G. (2024). Adapting to the gig economy: Determinants of financial resilience among "Giggers.". *Economic Analysis and Policy, 81*, 756–771. Advance online publication. DOI: 10.1016/j.eap.2024.01.002

Novitz, T. (2021). Gig work as a manifestation of short- termism: Crafting a sustainable regulatory agenda. *Industrial Law Journal, 50*(4), 636–661. Advance online publication. DOI: 10.1093/indlaw/dwab027

Okunkova, E. A., Kosorukova, I. V., Lazareva, T. G., Korolyuk, E. V., & Bogomolova, A. V. (2023). Global gig economy: Prospects and key growth threats for developing countries. *International Journal of Work Innovation*, *3*(4), 403. Advance online publication. DOI: 10.1504/IJWI.2023.128862

Pollard, C. M., & Booth, S. (2019). Food insecurity and hunger in rich countries—it is time for action against inequality. In *International Journal of Environmental Research and Public Health* (Vol. 16, Issue 10). DOI: 10.3390/ijerph16101804

Putrevu, J., & Mertzanis, C. (2024a). The adoption of digital payments in emerging economies: Challenges and policy responses. *Digital Policy. Regulation & Governance*, *26*(5), 476–500. Advance online publication. DOI: 10.1108/DPRG-06-2023-0077

Putrevu, J., & Mertzanis, C. (2024b). The adoption of digital payments in emerging economies: Challenges and policy responses. *Digital Policy. Regulation & Governance*, *26*(5), 476–500. DOI: 10.1108/DPRG-06-2023-0077

Qiu, S., Xu, Z., & Bhatt, B. (2021). The Sharing Economy Platforms in Rural China: Bridging Institutional Voids Through Institutional Entrepreneurship. In *Sharing Economy at the Base of the Pyramid: Opportunities and Challenges*. DOI: 10.1007/978-981-16-2414-8_4

Ray, B., Sengupta, A., & Varma, A. (2024). The gig verse: building a sustainable future. In *International Journal of Organizational Analysis* (Vol. 32, Issue 10). DOI: 10.1108/IJOA-08-2023-3946

Stopforth, G. (2023). Decent work for on-demand workers in the modern-day GIG economy. In *University of the free state bloemfontein*. Issue March.

Sun, Y., Ma, X., Ye, K., & He, L. (2022). Investigating Crowdworkers' Identify, Perception and Practices in Micro-Task Crowdsourcing. *Proceedings of the ACM on Human-Computer Interaction, 6*(GROUP). DOI: 10.1145/3492854

Ugargol, A. P., & Parvathy, L. (2023). Precarity of Informal Work, Absence of Social Security, and Ageism: The Persistence of Social Inequalities and Challenges for Older Adults' Labor Force Participation in India. In *Handbook of Aging*. Health and Public Policy., DOI: 10.1007/978-981-16-1914-4_173-2

Van Belle, J. P., Howson, K., Graham, M., Heeks, R., Bezuidenhout, L., Tsibolane, P., du Toit, D., Fredman, S., & Mungai, P. (2023). Fair work in South Africa's gig economy: A journey of engaged scholarship. *Digital Geography and Society*, *5*, 100064. Advance online publication. DOI: 10.1016/j.diggeo.2023.100064

Zulfiqar, M., Malik, M. N., & Khan, H. H. (2022). Microtasking Activities in Crowdsourced Software Development: A Systematic Literature Review. In *IEEE Access* (Vol. 10). DOI: 10.1109/ACCESS.2022.3148400

About the Contributors

Agnieszka Wójcik-Czerniawska, Ass. Prof. at SGH- Warsaw School of Economics; Department of Management and Finance. The PhD of Economics field- Management based on the thesis" Development strategies of enterprises in the biofuel sector"; MBA in Spanish- ICEX-CECO- Madrid, DBA (Doctor of Business Administration,), LL.D (Doctor of Laws), DPH (Doctor of Public Health). Visiting Professor at many foreign Universities in Europe (Italy, Spain, France) and World (Peru, Kenya, Turkey, Georgia). The area of research are connected with: modern finance, finance technology, digital currency, financial isolation, silver generation, circular economy, innovative marketing, society in digitalization world. The participant in many international conferences in all around the world. The keynote speak in world conferences in: Milan, Turkey, Republic of South Africa, Ireland, Bahrain, London . The polyglot with more than twelve languages.

***

Rahmath Nisha is a dedicated professional with comprehensive, hands-on experience in Human Resource Management (HRM), having successfully managed the entire employee life cycle—from recruitment and onboarding to performance management and employee engagement. She holds an MBA in Human Resource Management, where she was recognized as a Gold Medalist and awarded the title of Best Outgoing Student. Her academic journey began with a Bachelor's degree in Electronics and Communication Engineering, showcasing her diverse educational foundation. Currently serving as an Assistant Professor, she combines industry expertise with academic insight to mentor and inspire the next generation of HR professionals.

A.K. Subramani is a distinguished academic with a PhD in Business Administration from Manonmaniam Sundaranar University, Tirunelveli, India. With

18 years of teaching experience, he has made significant contributions to the field of human resource management and organisational behaviour. He has an impressive publication record with 80 articles in international journals, including two papers in the ABDC-A category, eight in the ABDC-B category, three in the ABDC-C category, 30 in Scopus-indexed journals, and eight in Web of Science journals. He has served as a resource person for various training workshops on SPSS and AMOS software packages

Gayathri A.R. holds an undergraduate degree in Optometry (B.Optom) and is currently pursuing her MBA with a specialization in Hospital and Human Resource Management. With a strong foundation in eye care and clinical practice, combined with managerial training, she brings a well-rounded and interdisciplinary perspective to the healthcare sector. Gayathri is deeply interested in enhancing patient care systems through efficient hospital administration. Her core strengths lie in healthcare analytics, communication, and team coordination. She is passionate about bridging clinical expertise with management practices to deliver impactful solutions that improve healthcare delivery and organizational performance.

Munir Ahmad is a seasoned professional in the realm of Spatial Data Infrastructure (SDI), Geo-Information Productions, Information Systems, and Information Governance, boasting over 25 years of dedicated experience in the field. With a PhD in Computer Science, Dr. Ahmad's expertise spans Spatial Data Production, Management, Processing, Analysis, Visualization, and Quality Control. Throughout his career, Dr. Ahmad has been deeply involved in the development and deployment of SDI systems specially in the context of Pakistan, leveraging his proficiency in Spatial Database Design, Web, Mobile & Desktop GIS, and Geo Web Services Architecture. His contributions to Volunteered Geographic Information (VGI) and Open Source Geoportal & Metadata Portal have significantly enriched the geospatial community. As a trainer and researcher, Dr. Ahmad has authored over 50 publications, advancing the industry's knowledge base and fostering innovation in Geo-Tech, Data Governance, and Information Infrastructure, and Emerging Technologies. His commitment to Research and Development (R&D) is evident in his role as a dedicated educator and mentor in the field.

Seethalakshmi B is a dedicated academic and Research Scholar at SRM Institute of Science and Technology, Kattankulathur, specializing in Human Resource Management with a focus on team roles, organizational effectiveness, and AI-driven HR practices. With over 12 years of experience in teaching, research, and administration, she has held key positions including Executive Assistant to the Pro Vice-Chancellor at Hindustan Institute of Technology and Science and Administrative

Coordinator at Kalai's Vidhyamandhir School. Her research and publications explore the intersection of digital transformation, emotional intelligence, and workforce analytics, contributing to Scopus-indexed journals and edited volumes. Recipient of the IEP Research Scholar Award (Global Young Achiever Awards 2024), she continues to advance scholarly work in strategic HR intelligence and digital maturity, aiming to build resilient and future-ready organizations.

Ivan Efremovski, Specialist in the field of human resources management and public administration. Lead author in the field of administrative process and effective public management. With publications in the field of organizational culture, motivation and management.

Wissal Errayem is a digital marketing professional and recent Master's graduate in Management – Digital Marketing from WSB Merito University, Warsaw, Poland. With a Bachelor's in Finance & Accounting and experience at Accenture and Société Générale, she specializes in digital campaign optimization, data analysis, and strategic consulting. Fluent in Arabic, French, and English, Wissal is passionate about applying analytical insights to understand consumer behavior and drive effective marketing strategies across global contexts.

Zaza Gigauri is a PhD student of the Doctoral Program in Business Administration, Faculty of Business and Technology, Caucasus International University (Georgia). He holds Master's degree in Psychology from Saint Andrew the First-Called Georgian University (Georgia), with Honors. He has worked as a journalist for many years and has business experience. His research interests include Sustainable Marketing, Responsible Marketing, Fashion Marketing, Fashion Psychology and Consumer Behavior. He is actively engaged in his Blog "Samosze" about the Psychology and Marketing of Fashion.

Gopika D is currently pursuing a Master of Business Administration (MBA) at St. Joseph's College of Engineering, India. She holds a Bachelor's degree in Business Administration (BBA). Her academic background is rooted in business and management studies. She is interested in exploring Reinventing Human Resource Management in and the future of work. She aims to build a professional career in the field of business administration, contributing to both industry practices and academic research.

Zbigniew Grzymała, PhD, DSc, Associate Professor, Institute of Finance, Department of Enterprise. Number of years of work in the current company: at the Warsaw School of Economics – 33 years. For 12 years he was the head of the Department of Economics and Finance of Local Government. Key qualifications:

ratio analysis of the company (balance sheet, income statement, employment and wages, fixed assets, etc.); strategic analysis of the organization (creating strategies for the development of organizations, especially local government units), analysis of the commune budget (income, expenses); analysis and evaluation of the effectiveness of capital expenditures in infrastructure, including logistics infrastructure, cost-benefit analysis, business plan and feasibility studies of investment projects, life cycle of products in municipal industries, economics of the public sector, economic policy, spatial policy, spatial management, restructuring of the municipal sector, ecologist – Circular Economy, including energy transformation of municipal economy, management property. Participation in many research projects on urban economy and the SME sector. Author of numerous publications on the issues of local government, municipal management, including the waste management industry. The classes with the students will be about " Circular economy models in the enterprises".

S. Ida Evangeline, presently working as an Assistant Professor in the Department of Electrical and Electronics Engineering at the Government College of Engineering, Tirunelveli, Tamilnadu, India. She obtained her Bachelor's in Electrical and Electronics Engineering from Manonmaniam Sundaranar University in 2003, and Master's in Power Systems Engineering from Anna University, Chennai, Tamilnadu, India in 2005. She completed her PhD degree in 2023 at Anna University, Chennai, Tamilnadu, India. She has published six research papers in international journals. Her current research interests include optimal power flow, renewable energy, soft computing, machine learning, and deep learning.

M. Jayaseely is an Assistant Professor at the School of Management Studies, Sathyabama Institute of Science and Technology, Chennai. She holds a Doctorate in Commerce from Holy Cross College (Autonomous), affiliated with Bharathidasan University, Tiruchirappalli. She has further pursued an M.Phil. in Commerce from Bharath Institute of Higher Education and Research, an M.Com in Banking and Insurance, an M.A. in English from Annamalai University, along with B.Ed. and M.Ed. degrees from Sathyabama University. She has over 18 years of teaching experience, specializing in Banking, Insurance, and Human Resource Management. She has authored more than thirty research papers published in reputed journals, including Scopus, UGC CARE-listed, Web of Science, and other peer-reviewed journals. She has actively participated in and presented papers at various national and international conferences. In addition, she has served as a resource person for several institutions, delivering training sessions on soft skills and personality development. Dr. Jayaseely also excels in the domains of education, guidance and counselling, personality development, communication, and soft skills enhancement.

D. Joel Jebadurai is working as a Associate professor in Department of MBA, St.Joseph's college of Engineering OMR Chennai Tamilnadu India. He has published more than 50 research articles in various peer reviewed journals. He has undertaken the funded projects and written two books also.

Rishikaysh Kaakandikar boasts an exceptional academic journey, spanning over 12 years of dedicated teaching and a year of valuable industrial experience, and currently holds the esteemed position of Associate Professor at SaiBalaji Education Society's SaiBalaji International Institute of Management Sciences in Pune. His scholarly contributions shine brightly, encompassing a remarkable portfolio of over 40 research papers in prestigious journals. A sought-after intellectual resource, He has contributed substantially to academia through guest lectures, seminars, workshops, and conferences at esteemed institutions across India. His insights have enriched the academic community and stimulated engaging discussions on various facets of his field. He is a prominent finance columnist for leading newspapers in Maharashtra, including Sakal, Lokmat, Punyannagari, and Prabhat.

Aboubaker Khoualed is a Senior Lecturer in Banking and Financial Economics. He earned his PhD in Economics from Badji Mokhtar University, Annaba, Algeria. His research spans a wide range of areas, including banking and financial economics, banking marketing, banking regulation, Islamic banking, and the knowledge economy. Dr. Khoualed has contributed extensively to the academic community through publications in specialized journals and presentations at international conferences.

Pawan Kumar, PhD, is a prominent academic and researcher with over 20 years of expertise in business studies. A professor at Graphic Era Deemed to be University, Dehradun, India, he has supervised six PhD scholars and published over 60 research papers, including 40 in SCOPUS/ Web of Science, and 14 books, including eight indexed in Scopus. His works, featured by prominent publishers like Emerald, IGI Global, Nova Science, and Cambridge Scholars, have gained recognition. Dr. Kumar earned his PhD in Commerce from Kurukshetra University in 2007 and holds an M.Phil. and M.Com. Degrees. Specializing in finance, banking, and securities markets, he has authored books on green finance, AI, and fintech. His innovative research includes five patents and has served as a guest editor for Scopus-indexed journals. In 2022, he received the prestigious Researcher Award from Chandigarh University. Dr. Kumar's impactful work on sustainable finance, blockchain, and fintech is globally recognized. His active participation in high-impact conferences and faculty development programs reflects his commitment to advancing research, teaching, and innovation in commerce and management.

N. Madhu is an Assistant Professor in the Department of Management Studies. He holds a doctorate from Andhra University and has been actively contributing to the field of management research. He has published several research papers in reputed journals, including UGC Care-listed and Scopus-indexed publications. With his academic expertise and research orientation, Dr. Madhu continues to contribute to knowledge creation and dissemination in the area of management studies.

Zokir Mamadiyarov is working in the Department of Finance and Tourism at Termez University of Economics and Service, Termez, Uzbekistan.

Vinodh N is currently pursuing his PhD as a Research Scholar at Saveetha School of Management, SIMATS, Saveetha University, Chennai. Currently, he serves as an Assistant Professor in the MBA Department at St. Joseph College of Engineering, Chennai, Tamil Nadu, India. He earned his Master of Philosophy (M.Phil) degree from Sri Venkateshwara University, Tirupati, and holds an MBA from Madras University, Chennai. With over fifteen years of teaching experience across various esteemed educational institutions in Chennai, Mr. He exemplifies a strong commitment to academia and scholarly research. His contributions to the field are underscored by his publications in SCOPUS indexed journals.

Surekha Suresh Ningule is a distinguished academician and researcher with expertise in Human Resource Management (HRM), organizational leadership, and digital transformation. She currently serves as Assistant Professor and Head of the Department at Siddhant Institute of Business Management, Pune, India. Bringing over 15 years of experience across academia, research, and industry, Dr. Ningule holds a Ph.D. in HRM, along with postgraduate degrees in MBA, M.Sc., and a B.Ed. Her research interests include Industry 4.0, data-driven decision-making, talent acquisition, women's leadership, and digital HR practices. She has contributed significantly to academic literature and actively engages in scholarly dialogue through platforms such as ResearchGate. Dr. Ningule is widely acknowledged for her dedication to nurturing research-oriented environments within management education. She mentors students and professionals in academic writing and thesis development, striving to bridge the gap between theoretical insights and practical implementation. Her work is instrumental in promoting organizational resilience, ethical innovation, and sustainable leadership in today's dynamic business world.

O'g'iljon Artiqova is currently working as a lecturer at the Faculty of Economics of Ma'mun University. She obtained her Bachelor's degree in Economics (by sectors and industries) from Urgench State University during 2019–2023, and successfully completed her Master's degree in Economics at Urgench State University in 2023–2025. She began her academic career in 2024 at Urgench State

University, working as a lecturer at the Department of Economics. At present, she continues her professional activity at Ma'mun University within the Department of Accounting. Throughout her academic career, she has authored more than 10 scientific publications, including articles published in internationally recognized journals indexed in Scopus and Web of Science. Her current research interests include environmental economics, regional economics, and applied econometrics. She has C1-level proficiency in English.

P. Arokiya Prasad is an Associate Professor in the Department of Electrical and Electronics Engineering at St. Joseph's College of Engineering. He is dedicated to teaching, research, and guiding students toward academic and professional excellence. With strong expertise in electrical systems and innovative technologies, he contributes significantly to the department's growth. Dr. Prasad actively mentors students in technical projects and skill development activities. He continues to inspire young engineers through his commitment to quality education and innovation.

Pranaya currently working as an Assistant Professor at Aditya Institute of Technology & Management, Tekkali, India. She is interested in HRM, performance management and people management research. She has published many articles and book chapters.

R. Durai Pandian is a Professor of Finance & Accounting at Saveetha School of Management, Saveetha University, Chennai. With 26 years of teaching and research experience, he has previously held leadership roles at Garden City University, Bangalore, and PES University. Beginning his career in academia in 2000, following over seven years in the hotel industry, Dr. Pandian has since contributed significantly to research, mentoring, and academic development. He holds a Ph.D. from Alagappa Institute of Management, an MBA from Manipal University, and has completed an FDPM at IIM Ahmedabad. A UGC Junior Research Fellowship awardee, he has authored over 55 research papers and holds multiple awards, patents, and copyrights. His interests also include historical research and sustainable organic farming.

R. Duraipandian is a Principal in the Department of management at Saveetha University.

Purushothaman R, is a dedicated researcher and academician, currently serving as a Research Assistant at the Srinivasa Ramanujan Center, SASTRA University, Kumbakonam. His research interests span across multiple disciplines, including circular economy, supply chain management, operations management, general management, and human resource management. With a passion for advancing knowledge in these fields, he actively contributes to academia through research and scholarly pursuits.

R. Alamelu is working as a Senior Assistant Professor in the Department of Commerce and Management Studies, Srinivasa Ramanujan Centre, SASTRA Deemed University, Kumbakonam, Thanjavur, Tamil Nadu, India. She is a passionate management enabler with a blend of research and academic experience and competency in developing and delivering learner-centric pedagogy with a teaching experience of 25 years. She contributed articles and research papers at different conferences at national and international levels, and written case studies, and published 83 papers in SCOPUS--indexed international journals. She pursued her doctoral degree in Quality Management and coordinated several seminars, conferences and conducted Quality improvement programmes for over a decade. She has authored a book titled 'Management Information System' and is actively involved as a consultant for selected tiny industries in Tamil Nadu. Currently, she supervises two part-time research scholars, and her research areas are Supply Chain Management, Human Resource Analytics, and Circular economy.

N. Santosh Ranganath, currently working as an Assistant Professor in the Department Commerce and Management Studies, Dr. B.R. Ambedkar University, Srikakulam, Andhra Pradesh, India. He did his MBA, M.Phil. and Ph.D. also qualified in UGC - NET and AP - SET. He specialized in teaching Operations Research Techniques, Quantitative Techniques, Operations Management, Research Methodology and Statistical Analysis. He is having experience of over 19 years in teaching and research for post graduate students of M.Com. and M.B.A. He published 7 books and above 100 research articles in reputed national and international journals. He presented more than 150 papers in different areas of management at various National and International Conferences. He is the Life Member for the Indian Commerce Association (ICA), New Delhi, Indian Society of Mathematics and Mathematical Sciences, International Association of Academicians and Researchers and Forum for Intellectual Academicians and Researchers.

Rismawati is a distinguished academic and consultant with a robust focus on sustainability reporting. She currently holds the position of lecturer and Head of the Quality Assurance Institute at Universitas Muhammadiyah Palopo, where she has been pivotal in ensuring the quality of university processes and outputs since February 2020. Additionally, she serves as an Assurer for Sustainability Reporting at the National Center for Sustainability Reporting in Jakarta, specializing in the evaluation of sustainability reports for mining companies across Indonesia. Her academic qualifications are extensive, comprising a Bachelor's degree in Economics and Accounting, a Master's degree in Accounting Science, and a Doctorate in Accounting from Universitas Brawijaya, Malang. Rismawati is also a certified specialist in sustainability reporting, risk management, and tax planning, holding several prestigious certifications including Certified Sustainability Reporting Specialist (CSRS), Certified Risk Management Practitioner (CRMP), Certified Management Accountant (CMA) and Certified Enterprise Risk Analysis (CERA). In her professional capacity, she has provided consultancy services in financial management and tax compliance for companies such as PT. Reski Barito Timur and PT. Helay Raya. Furthermore, she has authored multiple publications on Social Accounting, Sustainability Accounting, Management Accounting and CSR, contributing significantly to the academic community. Her interests in reading, writing, and travel reflect her commitment to lifelong learning and professional growth in her field.

Pushpalatha S is a Research scholar in the Department of Management at Saveetha University. Research focuses on Human Resource Management.

Salju, S.E., M.M., is a senior academic and professor of management at Universitas Muhammadiyah Palopo. He completed his undergraduate studies in economics at STIE Muhammadiyah Palopo and earned both his Master's and Doctoral degrees in Management from Universitas Muslim Indonesia (UMI) Makassar. His academic career spans decades of service as a lecturer, researcher, and institutional leader. He previously served as the Chair of STIE Muhammadiyah Palopo and later as the Rector of Universitas Muhammadiyah Palopo. Throughout his leadership, he emphasized institutional transformation, academic quality improvement, and research capacity building. His involvement in various training programs—ranging from academic writing and test construction to research methodology—demonstrates his commitment to continuous academic development. Prof. Salju has presented papers at numerous national and international conferences, and his scholarly works have been published in various academic journals. His book, "Manajemen Sumber Daya Manusia: Konsep Dasar, Tantangan dan Strategi Menghadapi Era Society 5.0", reflects his expertise in human resource management in the context of technological disruption. He is also active in academic and professional associations, contributing to discourse and policy development in higher education. With a passion for scholarship, he continues to write, publish, and inspire the next generation of academics and professionals.

K. Santhana Lakshmi is an accomplished academician and Associate Professor & Chairperson (MBA) at the Faculty of Management, SRM Institute of Science and Technology, Kattankulathur, with over 18 years of teaching and 8 years of industry experience. She holds a Ph.D. in Human Resource Management and multiple postgraduate qualifications in Labour Management, Public Administration, and Business Administration. A recognized HR leader and researcher, she has guided several Ph.D. scholars and authored numerous Scopus and ABDC-indexed publications on work-life balance, leadership, digital transformation, and organizational behavior. Dr. Lakshmi has successfully secured multiple funded projects worth over 10 million, contributed to innovation in management education through gamification and experiential learning, and received prestigious honors including the HR Excellence Award 2025 and Outstanding Mentor Award 2024. Her research and leadership continue to drive excellence in human resource development and academic innovation.

Asadullah Shah is Professor at Department of computer science, Kulliyyah of information and communication technology, IIUM. Dr. Shah has a total of 26 years teaching and research experience. He has more than 100 research publications in International and national journals and conference proceedings. Additionally, he authored one book and currently editing another book. Dr. Shah has done his undergraduate degree in Electronics, Master's degree in Computer Technology from the University of Sindh, and PhD in Multimedia Communication, from the University Of Surrey, England, UK. His areas of interest are multimedia compression techniques, research methodologies, speech packetization and statistical multiplexing. He has been teaching courses in the fields of electronics, computers, telecommunications and management sciences.

Amrik Singh is working as Professor in the School of Hotel Management and Tourism at Lovely Professional University, Punjab, India. He obtained his Ph.D. degree in Hotel Management from Kurukshetra University, Kurukshetra. He started his academic career at Lovely Professional University, Punjab, India in the year 2007. He has published more than 40 research papers in UGC and peer-reviewed and Scopus/Web of Science) journals. He has published 12 patents and 01 patent has been granted in the inter-disciplinary domain. Dr. Amrik Singh participated and acted as a resource person in various national and international conferences, seminars, research workshops, and industry talks. His area of research interest is accommodation management, ergonomics, green practices, human resource management in hospitality, waste management, AR VR in hospitality, etc. He is currently guiding 8Ph.D. scholars and 2 Ph.D. scholars have been awarded Ph.D.

A.K. Subramani has completed a PhD in Business Administration at Manonmaniam Sundaranar University, India. He has around 16 years of teaching experience. He has published more than 60 articles which includes ABDC A,B,C and also including International Journal of Work Organisation and Emotion . He is expert in methodologies including Topic Modelling. He has received the 'Teaching and Research Excellence Award', Distinguished Teacher Award Management, and 'Best Educationist Award'. He is a member of the review committee of Emerald publishers, Inderscience Publishers, and the Serbian Journal of Management.

Natia Surmanidze has significant experience in research and teaching and is actively involved in the development of academic programs and quality assurance processes. Her papers have been published in numerous high-ranking journals, including those indexed in Scopus and Web of Science. She is engaged in academic networks across Europe and the Caucasus. Her professional roles include serving as an accreditation expert, peer reviewer, and member of the editorial boards of international journals. She is also a member of the Sectoral Benchmarking Council of Business Administration at the National Center for Educational Quality Enhancement (NCEQE) of Georgia. She actively participates in international scientific research and regularly presents papers at global conferences. Additionally, she has extensive mentoring experience across all levels of higher education. She teaches courses in finance, business communication, and research methods at both undergraduate and graduate levels, in Georgian and international programs.

Valentin Vasilev is a Adjunct Lecturer at New Bulgarian University /NBU/ from 2013. He was a "professor" of "National Security" ("Crisis Situations and Human Resource Management") at the Higher School of Security and Economics /HSSE/, city of Plovdiv and head of the "Center for Leadership and Public Policies" at the same educational institution /2021-2025/. In the period from 2000 to 2021, he was part of the South-West University "Neofit Rilski", Blagoevgrad, being the deputy dean of the Faculty of Law and History from 2010 to 2019. He is the author of more than a hundred publications in scientific publications in Bulgaria and abroad, as well as seven monographic publications in the field of human resources management, crisis situations; the team form of work; motivation and organizational behavior; public management and public policies and others.Professor Vasilev has extensive practical experience in the public sector, such as: Deputy Mayor of Blagoevgrad Municipality /2007-2010/; Public Mediator /Ombudsman/ of the Municipality of Blagoevgrad.

D Velumoni has Master's degree in Management and Doctoral degree in the field of "Rational and Irrational factors influencing Equity Investors and its impact on Investment Satisfaction". She is qualified with NET and SET in Management during the year 2012 conducted by UGC. She is currently working as Associate Professor in the Department of Management Studies, Sathyabama Institute of Science and

Technology, Chennai. She has presented and published more than 15 research papers in International Journals & Conferences, 5 Scopus Indexed Journals and 14 UGC listed Journals. Her research interests include Investment Analysis, Behavioral Finance, Financial Literacy and Personal Finance. She has also published books such as Security Analysis and Portfolio Management and Financial Management. She has organized many events and acted as resource person for many workshops and competitions. Her services have been well acknowledged and appreciated for her contribution to industry, teaching and research for more than 24 years.

Koppala Venugopal, a professor in Management Studies at Aditya Institute of Technology and Management at Srikakulam, A.P. has had an adroit experience of academic, Research and community service. He has contributed 5 Projects, 2 patents, 10 books, 70 publications, 48 paper presentations, 56 resource talks and 12 memberships. He is guiding 4 scholars from various universities. His exceptional interest industry interface has made his efforts dexterous.

Yamuna. D, possess 15 years of teaching experience in the field of management studies, currently serving as an Assistant Professor at Sathyabama Institute of Science and Technology, OMR, Chennai for the past two years. She is a practicing academician with a dual post graduate degree in MBA with UGCNET (Mgmt)., M.Com and Ph.D in Finance. She has been involved in the postgraduate Teaching, Financial services Research, training & sharing knowledge of corporate finance. As Professor, she handled many subjects like Accounting, Financial Management, Security Analysis, Banking Finance and Insurance etc to undergraduate and post graduate students of Management studies. Her passion for research enabled to publish many research articles with high impact journals and reputed book publication.

Index

A

B

C

D

E

F

G

H

I

M

O

P

R

S

T

U

W

www.ingramcontent.com/pod-product-compliance
Lightning Source LLC
LaVergne TN
LVHW061529290926
849162LV00004B/723